P9-BYE-912

IDENTITY

AND

ANXIETY

IDENTITY AND ANXIETY

SURVIVAL OF THE PERSON IN MASS SOCIETY

EDITED BY

Maurice R. Stein, Arthur J. Vidich AND *David Manning White*

THE FREE PRESS OF GLENCOE, ILLINOIS

To PAUL RADIN

For allowing us to share his critical vision

Printed in the United States of America

Library of Congress Catalog Number 60-7091

DESIGNED BY SIDNEY SOLOMON

Preface and Acknowledgments

We wish to thank the contributors to this volume for permission to publish their essays and to reaffirm our conviction that their works have made a central contribution to understanding the important problems confronting men in the twentieth century. Special thanks are due a number of our colleagues who have allowed us to print their essays for the first time. It is clear that the merit of the volume rests upon the work of our contributors.

Friends and students have generously helped us to complete our joint work as editors. Professor Stein's social psychiatry classes at Brandeis University, over the past four years, have played the important part of reacting to the essays in a lively and searching way. The opinions and responses of his students, particularly the critical essays written by those in the class of Spring, 1959, have helped us to judge the coherence of the volume as a whole. We are deeply indebted to Victor Walter, Irving Howe, Max Lerner, Franz von Lichtenberg, Gail Anglada, Joseph Freeman, Warren Paley, Jack Grant, Elizabeth Merrylees, and Richard G. White for encouraging and assisting us at various stages during our work on the project. Stanley Diamond, who was instrumental in initiating the project in its early stages, was unable to continue as an editor due to an extended research trip to Africa. We especially wish to thank Professor Diamond for the insight he contributed to the idea of the book and for his willingness to have the project continue in his absence.

Our collaboration on this project was linked in part to projects each of us had worked on independently. Further treatment of some of the themes developed in this volume will be found in *The Eclipse of Community* (Princeton, 1960), *Small Town in Mass Society* (Princeton, 1958), and *Mass Culture* (Free Press, 1957).

Finally, we wish to thank our wives, Bernice Stein, Virginia Wicks Vidich, and Catherine White, who have helped in all phases of our work.

M.S.
A.V.
D.W.

Contents

Preface and Acknowledgments 7

Contributors 13

Identity and History: An Overview, *by Maurice R. Stein and Arthur J. Vidich* 17

I. *Central Perspectives*

A. IDENTITY

The Problem of Ego Identity, *by Erik H. Erikson* 37

Culture Change and Character Structure, *by Margaret Mead* 88

The Stranger, *by Alfred Schuetz* 98

On Reason and Freedom, *by C. Wright Mills* 110

B. ANXIETY

Centrality of the Problems of Anxiety in Our Day, *by Rollo May* 120

Psychiatric Aspects of Anxiety, *by Frieda Fromm-Reichmann* 129

The Social Psychology of Fear, *by Kurt Riezler* 144

Repression, Anxiety, and the Self, *by Leo Schneiderman* 157

Anxiety and Psychotherapy, *by Carl Whitaker and Thomas P. Malone* 166

II. *Sources of Identity and Anxiety in Mass Life*

A. THE TERROR AND THERAPY OF WORK

The Meaning of Work in Bureaucratic Society, *by Joseph Bensman and Bernard Rosenberg* 181

The Myth of the Happy Worker, *by Harvey Swados* 198

Careers, Personality, and Adult Socialization, *by Howard S. Becker and Anselm L. Strauss* 205

The Commercial Artist, *by Mason Griff* 219
Some Unsolved Problems of the Scientific Career, *by Lawrence S. Kubie* 241

B. THE POLITICAL ESTRANGEMENT

Anxiety and Politics, *by Franz Neumann* 269
The Politics of Decivilization, *by E. V. Walter* 291
Politics and the English Language, *by George Orwell* 308
The Orgamerican Fantasy, *by Harold Rosenberg* 319

C. THE ENCIRCLED MIND

What Teaching Does to Teachers, *by Willard Waller* 329
The Freedom to Be Academic, *by Paul Goodman* 351
Notes on the Death of Culture, *by William Earle* 367
The Future of the Humanities in General Education, *by I. A. Richards* 383

D. SECONDARY SOURCES OF IDENTITY IN MASS SOCIETY: RELIGION, RACE, SEX, AND THE FAMILY

Thoughts on the Future of the Family, *by Barrington Moore* 391
The Pornography of Death, *by Geoffrey Gorer* 402
The Semi-Adequate Male, *by David Manning White* 407
Slick-Paper Christianity, *by Dan Wakefield* 410
Decisions for Christ: Billy Graham in New York, *by Kurt and Gladys E. Lang* 415
Identity, Anxiety, and the Jew, *by Aaron Antonovsky*
Cats, Kicks, and Color, *by Harold Finestone* 435

E. THE DISSOLUTION OF IDENTITIES

Characteristics of Total Institutions, *by Erving Goffman* 449
Methods of Forceful Indoctrination, *by Robert J. Lifton* 480
The Dissolved Identity in Military Life, *by Arthur J. Vidich and Maurice R. Stein* 493
Brainwashing and Menticide, *by Joost A. M. Meerloo* 506

III. *The Evolution of Personal Styles in Mass Society*

A. PERSONAL STYLES AND THE ARTS

Poetry and Tradition, *by C. M. Bowra* 523
Another Way of Looking at the Blackbird, *by Irving Howe* 532

B. PERSONAL STYLES AND HUMAN PSYCHOLOGY

Individuality of Thought, *by John Cohen* 540

The Ego and Mystic Selflessness, *by Herbert Fingarette* 552

C. PERSONAL STYLES AND THE STUDY OF HISTORY

History and Our Times, *by Eric Dardel* 584

The Axial Age of Human History, *by Karl Jaspers* 597

The Literature of Primitive Peoples, *by Paul Radin* 606

D. PRODUCTIVITY AND EXISTENCE

Productivity and Existence, *by Martin Buber* 628

NOTES 633

Contributors

AARON ANTONOVSKY is a sociologist who has specialized in studies of minority groups and is now on a post-doctorate fellowship in Iraq.

HOWARD BECKER, JR. is a sociologist who has written widely on the sociology of occupations and is now affiliated with Community Studies, Inc., Kansas City, Missouri.

JOSEPH BENSMAN, co-author of *Small Town in Mass Society*, is a sociologist and a student of contemporary society.

C. M. BOWRA, whose most recent work is *The Greek Experience*, is a classicist and warden of Wadham College, Oxford.

MARTIN BUBER, philosopher, author of *Pointing the Way*, and other works, is professor of philosophy at Hebrew University in Jerusalem.

JOHN COHEN is author of *Humanistic Psychology* and professor of psychology at the University of Edinburgh.

ERIC DARDEL, noted French historian, is author of *L'homme et la terre*.

WILLIAM EARLE is professor of philosophy at Northwestern University and author of the book, *Objectivity*.

ERIK ERIKSON, author of *Young Man Luther*, is a psychoanalyst at the Austin Riggs Center for Psychoanalysis.

HAROLD FINESTONE is a sociologist specializing in criminology at the Institute for Social Research in Chicago.

HERBERT FINGARETTE is a philosopher at the University of California in Goleta, California.

FRIEDA FROMM-REICHMANN* is the author of *Principles of Intensive Psychotherapy* and was a psychoanalyst at the William Alanson White Institute.

ERVING GOFFMAN is the author of *The Presentation of Self in Everyday Life* and is a sociologist at the University of California, Berkeley.

PAUL GOODMAN is a psychoanalyst and has recently published the novel, *The Empire City*.

GEOFFREY GORER is an English anthropologist and author of *The American People*.

---

* Deceased.

MASON GRIFF is a sociologist at Montana State University and has a forthcoming book on Commercial Artists.

IRVING HOWE, author of *Politics and the Novel,* is professor of English at Brandeis University.

KARL JASPERS is professor of philosophy at the University of Basel in Switzerland. He is the author of *Man in the Modern Age.*

LAWRENCE KUBIE, author of *Neurotic Distortion of the Creative Process,* is a psychoanalyst at Yale University.

GLADYS LANG is a sociologist at Brooklyn College and has specialized in studies of mass behavior.

KURT LANG is a sociologist at Queens College and has specialized in the study of mass behavior.

ROBERT LIFTON is a psychoanalyst who has studied Chinese thought-reform programs.

THOMAS MALONE is co-author of *The Roots of Psychotherapy,* and teaches at Emory University in Georgia.

ROLLO MAY is co-editor of *Existence* and a psychologist at Columbia University.

MARGARET MEAD, the author of *Male and Female,* is an anthropologist at Columbia University.

JOOST MEERLOO is a psychoanalyst and author of *The Rape of the Mind.*

C. WRIGHT MILLS, whose latest book is *The Sociological Imagination,* is professor of sociology at Columbia College.

BARRINGTON MOORE is author of *Political Power and Social Theory,* and is professor of political sociology at Harvard University.

FRANZ NEUMANN,* political scientist, is author of *Behemoth.*

GEORGE ORWELL,* social critic and essayist, is best known for his book, *Nineteen Eighty-Four.*

PAUL RADIN* is the author of *Primitive Man as Philosopher* and was professor of Anthropology at Brandeis University.

I. A. RICHARDS, the co-author of *The Meaning of Meaning,* philosopher and literary critic, is now teaching at Harvard.

KURT RIEZLER* is author of *Man: Mutable and Immutable* and formerly professor of philosophy at the New School for Social Research in New York.

BERNARD ROSENBERG is the author of *The Values of Veblen,* and professor of sociology at New York City College.

HAROLD ROSENBERG is a social critic and essayist who has recently published *The Tradition of the New.*

---

* Deceased.

LEO SCHNEIDERMAN is professor of social psychology at Willimantic State Teachers College, Connecticut.

ALFRED SCHUETZ* was a philosopher. He is author of the phenomenological study, *Multiple Realities.*

ANSELM STRAUSS is a social psychologist at the University of California and has recently published *Mirrors and Masks.*

HARVEY SWADOS has written the novel, *On the Line,* and teaches at Sarah Lawrence.

DAN WAKEFIELD, a journalist who specializes in commentaries on American society, has recently written *Island in the City.*

WILLARD WALLER,* author of *The Sociology of Teaching,* was for many years a professor at Columbia University.

E. V. WALTER is professor of political science at Brandeis University and author of a forthcoming study on Freud, Simmel, Weber, and Durkheim.

CARL WHITAKER is co-author of *The Roots of Psychotherapy,* and a faculty member of Emory University in Georgia.

---

* Deceased.

MAURICE R. STEIN AND ARTHUR J. VIDICH

Identity and History:* An Overview

SHAKESPEARE'S PLAYS, taken as a whole, embrace the central issues and problems dealt with in this book. Central to Hamlet's character is the search for personal reality in a society where collective reality can no longer be taken for granted. His search becomes a quest for his own identity, but he discovers that he can find this only by scrutinizing the relations he has with the real and assumed personae of those around him. It is this that launches Hamlet into his epical reality-testing program, in which he balances at all times the passionate character of various persons, the roles they are supposed to play in relation to him, the feelings he is supposed to have towards them in his reciprocal role, the feelings he actually has, and finally, the feelings and actions he ought to display according to his scheme of higher values and identities. Hamlet discovers that men and women assume the most glorified poses and roles—particularly those that will confirm and protect their preferred self-images.

In *Othello*, Shakespeare shows how some men's passions can lead them to assume "false" self-images and roles that destroy their lives. Thus, Othello is misled by Iago who presents himself as an advisor and friend, while he is, in reality, dominated by evil motives. Responding to Iago's pretense of friendship and yielding to his own suppressed impulses, Othello assumes the identity of a murderer and destroys both Desdemona and himself. Shakespeare carefully makes clear, however, that Othello is more than a murderer—that he is also dignified and noble. What is emphasized is the precariousness of the nobility, the ever-present two-sidedness of his character which continues to the end without internal resolution or harmony.

A Shakespearean character is almost always multisided. The front

* The authors want to thank David Manning White for help in preparing this essay and to mention that he is in substantial accord with the viewpoints expressed in it.

he presents in one setting is not the one he presents in another. His identity depends on the particular situation, and yet, in the course of the drama, he responds to his experience and exhibits an underlying consistency in the development of his character. As Shakespeare fashions the drama, it is always possible for his characters to change, depending upon their capacity to know themselves and others. The gaining of such knowledge presents the character with true possibilities for choice. An instance of this is the great confrontation scene in *Troilus and Cressida* where Troilus and Ulysses come upon Diomedes seducing and being seduced by Cressida. All four are watched by Thersites, whose ranting "locates" the scene in the least honorable context. Each of the five "characters" modifies the meaning of the "seduction" according to his own perspective. Shakespeare and his "ideal" audience resonate to these multiple, mutually qualifying levels of meaning, giving primacy to none and a place to all. Troilus, the frustrated Romeo, has at least two "Cressidas" (Diomedes' and his), so that his world becomes "bifold," and his sanity is sustained.

We, too, hold on to our sanity by learning to appreciate "multiple realities." Like Troilus, we learn that "This is and is not Cressida." Ironic awareness of the manifold contexts, interpretations, and motives that qualify human character and action has become an indispensable item in our equipment for living. Perhaps our greatest danger lies in becoming attached to any exclusive interpretation of reality, but the second greatest remains the abandonment of the search for reality. Hamlet's energy can no longer be taken for granted and, were he a twentieth-century hero, he would undoubtedly have talked himself out of his madness on the analytical couch long before his fatal stab at Polonius. Shakespeare's plays as a whole can be seen as a magnificent repertory of personal styles revealed in their innermost psychic being. There is a tremendous awareness of these psychic states and a daring willingness to push the psyche to its extreme limits. What emerges is the conviction that men can grow, that choices matter, that man is both determined and self-determining.

Like our time, Elizabethan England was a period of rapid transition; however, this catch phrase "rapid transition," applied to the two periods, conceals profound likenesses and differences between them. Sorting these out is a project for a different kind of book, but the point may be made that the place for exploring the more dramatic aspects of life may have shifted from the theatre to the analyst's couch. Freud has made us aware of the great repressed human dramas that underlie the "psychopathology of everyday life." Shakespeare moved in realms beyond these private dramas to delineate the public dramas that arise when nobility and depravity are stretched to their outermost limits. Most of us live our lives in an intermediate realm, where the dramatic intensities of the couch and the theatre remain latent. Our collection of essays aims at providing concepts for interpreting this intermediate realm, although it occasionally strays to the noble anxieties and noble identities that claim the attention of men who have shaken off the shackles of mass society.

Erik Erikson, in the first contribution to our volume, introduces an important distinction between two pathological aspects of identity —identity-diffusion and identity-foreclosure. These are not character types, although there are people who typically employ one or the other as a way of responding to experience. We are all familiar with people who have a definition of themselves and the world that excludes novelty or change. This is certainly an element of the "authoritarian" syndrome and the bureaucratic personality. We also know people who absorb all experience without assimilating it on its own terms. Dilettantes and perhaps Riesman's "other-directed" men live at this superficial plane. Needless to say, there are tremendous pressures in everyday life forcing us to "foreclose" our conceptions of ourselves and of our world. One source of such pressure is the many diffuse stimuli that force themselves onto our attention. The formless variety of modern life and the onslaught of external events evoke an inner formlessness and passivity; the diffuse identity becomes a technique of adjustment allowing one to cope with an incoherent, formless reality.

Neither diffusion nor foreclosure can ever be total, and even the most constricted person, living in the most constricting social setting, retains some capacity for introspective play. Erikson argues that society must provide institutionalized "moratoria," in which its adolescents can "play" at adult roles, to see how they feel before they make their crucial life choices. Temporary foreclosures must be permitted, and it is the adult's responsibility to guarantee that the youngster does not get irrevocably "typed." Totalitarian societies type their youngsters as quickly as they can and confine the range of permissible identities within a narrow sphere. Mass democracies broaden the range of permissible identities, but fail to provide the time or facilities for serious experimentation with any of them. In either case, genuine "playfulness" is no longer part of the human experience. Only a few exceptional individuals are able to create their own "moratoria," and it is interesting that the three major figures about whom Erikson has said the most—Freud, Luther, and Shaw—all had to carve out their own. Unfortunately, there are no "quiet places" like Luther's monastery available to most people. Today's schools, their closest equivalent, mirror the dilemmas and anxieties of the larger society far more effectively than they provide shelter from them.

Awareness of the threat to personal identity is not confined to a small circle of intellectuals. Anxieties about susceptibility to "hidden persuaders" manifest themselves at all levels of the population, and, despite Riesman's efforts to allay this, everybody is worried about being overly other-directed. One of the fundamental operating assumptions of our society is the view that human beings are pliable and can be molded into any shape required by those who command the identity-molding agencies. This, of course, is the explicit working assumption of the advertising industry, political propagandists, military leaders, public relations counselors, mass entertainers, and even some educators. Too much attention has been paid to the substance of advertising appeals and too little to the assumptions of identity-plasticity upon which the industry rests. To take the most blatant example, advertising appeals regularly to anxieties about bodily characteristics and their social acceptability. The formula, boy meets girl, boy smells girl, girl smells bad, boy rejects girl, girl uses sponsor's product, boy smells girl, girl smells good, boy loves girl, is clearly an important archetype in the modern collective unconscious. A simple word like "halitosis" transforms an inevitable bodily characteristic into a deadly social disease and earns a fortune in the process.

However, advertising is simply the most obvious aspect of the systematic manipulation of anxieties in our society. It is more easily laughed at than many of the others, because it involves manipulation in comparatively minor areas of life. Perhaps this is why it has become one of the major sources of modern humor. You can get a laugh from most audiences just by repeating a current slogan in an ironic tone. Moving from advertising to the more somber aspects of human vulnerability arouses deeper anxieties: jokes about the dehumanizing effects of work are less common, and, until Jules Pfeiffer, no one seemed to want to make horrible fun of the atom bomb.

We have avoided concentrating on the mass media because we feel that this group has been satisfactorily covered by the volume titled *Mass Culture*. The problem is no longer one of calling attention to the dangers of mass culture; rather, it is one of spelling out a program for doing something about them. In the same context, paradoxical though it may seem, we feel that there is no longer any need for programmatic exhortations about the dangers of mass society. Plaints about the sorry state of our society and our culture have become commonplace and have, therefore, become part of the defensive cliché system which wards off real fears aroused by concrete dangers.

The search for vocabularies capable of expressing the character of present-day threats to identity carried us into an exploration of many disciplines. Several psychoanalysts besides Erikson have found their way to this range of problems. It has clearly been a central concern of existentialist thinkers, although their language sometimes obscures this. Social scientists, especially those who have been influenced by Freud, provided another source of important concepts and observations. Humanist critics, dedicated to preserving and extending the classical tradition, proved exceptionally useful. As a glance at the table of contents will show, we have drawn from a broad variety of sources; we hope that the resulting multiplicity of vocabularies will not distort the underlying messages beyond recognition.

This multiplicity of vocabularies must be confronted realistically and honestly, or it will lead to exactly the kind of confusion that we aim to avoid. No reader of this volume is likely to be equally well versed in all of the languages employed by all of the contributors. However, we would argue that an imaginative and intelligent reader can find his way into the separate thought worlds of each if he is willing to devote sufficient time and effort. In some instances, this might involve following up footnoted references or perhaps reading other books by the author in question. Indeed, one strategy for resisting the fragmentation and ritualization of thought in mass society is to develop a "sixth" sense for the command that an author has over his material and a "seventh" sense for the relevance of his presentation to one's own growing intellectual apparatus. Not many of us are able to judge Karl Jaspers' great hypothesis about the role of the Axial Age in history, a highly abbreviated version of which is presented in the article included in this reader. To understand its full significance, one must explore Jaspers' detailed exposition in *The Origin and Goal of History*, as well as its relation to the main body of his philosophic and sociological writings. Even more importantly, one must use the hypothesis in one's own reading of the literature of the Oriental and Occidental classical period to test its illuminating powers. The ramifications of this single short article lead in many directions. Our "sixth" and "seventh" senses allow us to anticipate the "weight" that it must be given in determining our future. Few serious readers will be in a position to dismiss Jaspers lightly, but each must determine for himself how influential he is to become.

We are trembling on the verge of one of the great dilemmas of modern life. So much has been made physically "available" to us by modern technology, yet there has been no accompanying development of intellectual or aesthetic sensibilities. Consequently, we stand in the position of being deluged, not so much by the material poured forth by the media, as by our collection of paperback classics.

Putting the issue more concretely, it is clear that our earlier reference to Shakespeare's *Troilus and Cressida* must have meant something different to a man who has seen this play produced, read it several times, and placed it within the larger contexts of Shakespeare's writing and the history of European drama, than it did to the man who but vaguely remembers Shakespeare and this play from college. Most readers, like the authors of this introduction, will fall somewhere between these extremes. We are repeatedly told that knowing Shakespeare involves "knowing" his period, his fellow dramatists, his critics through the centuries, his relation to antiquity and to the medieval world, etc. Yet few of us are brought directly into contact with the "world" of Shakespeare in our daily lives. The pressure to respond to daily exigencies—leaving Shakespeare to the specialists—is immense. It is a pressure that must be deeply and honestly felt before it can be effectively resisted.

There is a sense in which Shakespeare cannot be left to the specialists, any more than can Homer, Plato, Montaigne, or the other great figures of the Western tradition. The specialists cannot be left to assume our responsibility which is, at the same time, our privilege; namely, living in the historical plane of the civilization of which we are part. This task is made easier by the availability of the classics but made harder by our commitments to "specialties," by narrowed experiences, and by sensibilities which render us more susceptible to the mass media than to the classics. The Western tradition is available but not accessible. To transform availability into accessibility requires an enormous effort of will. It is essential that the real magnitude of this effort should not be allowed to generate such tremendous anxieties that a retreat into "specialisms" appears as the only feasible alternative.

In its broadest dimensions, the problem of how to recapture our historical heritage is the central one of this reader. We have attempted to transcend the ordinary "educationist" discussion of these issues, since we feel that this is no longer relevant to the problem as it confronts us. Liberal arts slogans deteriorate into clichés as rapidly as do most other liberal doctrines in the face of mass society. We wish to pin down the sources of these mass pressures in their institutional and psychological manifestations, so that the issues can be raised in a new and more useful fashion. This may occasionally take us through extremely depressing territory, especially in those sections where the processes of identity dissolution are explored, but this territory cannot be avoided if higher ground is to be gained.

Each of our contributors confronts an aspect of this problem in his own way, although all of them are not necessarily aware of its total dimensions. The humanists and existentialists seem more concerned with the larger issues, but less capable of concrete interpretations; while the social scientists and the psychoanalysts contribute useful specific analyses, without necessarily fitting them back into the larger context. By bringing the two traditions together within the same volume, we hope that they will reflect on one another and so help in the formation of new relationships. In selecting our contributors, we were forced to subordinate our own technical vocabularies to the problem that we elected to consider. Underlying this whole enterprise is the assumption that it is still possible to assume a serious "generalist" identity while remaining immersed in "specialized" bodies of knowledge. We have tried not to let our own preferences for certain vocabularies blind us to the advantages of those which we find less congenial or familiar. The sensitive reader must be willing to do the same.

The body of our reader contains many articles that exhibit the difficulties involved in doing this. We all become identified with "specialist" vocabularies and have a vested interest in asserting their superiority over alternative vocabularies. This is especially true where we cannot quite understand the alternative vocabularies and feel threatened by them. We have taken a "playful" attitude towards these competing vocabularies in an effort to transform the anxiety provoked by their strangeness into pleasure in using them to expand our vision of reality. This may require patience and will undoubtedly be painful, but we are convinced that it is worthwhile. When we find someone whose angle of vision and range of sympathy is broader or deeper than our own, we must be ready to accept him as a teacher. To put it another way, we must guard against reacting to strangeness by foreclosing our identity. At the same time, however, we must be careful not to become collectors of diffuse impressions. True identity-play involves the use of "sixth" and "seventh" senses, and these presuppose a time perspective which enables us to envisage returning to the same teacher, or perhaps the same essay, when our capacity to be enlightened more closely approximates the author's capacity to enlighten.

A book of readings can all too easily contribute to the loss of discrimination that characterizes the passive audience in mass society. To counter this, we have arranged the essays so as to provoke differentiated responses. We juxtapose quite divergent intellectual styles to show how the same issues can be illuminated from various standpoints. In doing this, we wish also to call attention to the overtones, the implied qualities and qualifications which convey something of the background and experience of the writer. Our contributors come from many different "worlds," and their interpretations of "reality" differ, but something can be learned from each by paying attention to the particular qualities conveyed by his work. Despite their many languages, styles, and world views, we feel that our contributors would be able to understand each other, simply because they are concerned with the same problems.

The book is designed to highlight this unity around problems. Part I, "Central Perspectives," introduces the central concepts employed throughout the volume: identity and anxiety are defined and examined in their several dimensions. The purpose of Part I is to bring forth the working distinctions that must be available in order to proceed with interpretation. Erikson's concepts of identity-diffusion, identity-foreclosure, identity-play, and the psychosocial moratorium are among the most important. It is helpful to keep his distinctions in mind when reading the later essays, but it is also useful to remember that Erikson focuses on psychotherapy, as distinct from social analysis. The other essays in the section on identity supply sociological and social-psychological concepts necessary for bringing the identity issues peculiar to mass society into focus. There are many themes in the section on anxiety which deserve special attention. The distinction between fear and anxiety, the relationship between anxiety and death, and the double-edged character of anxiety are explored.

These central perspectives consist of theories about identity and anxiety that allow us to undercut conventional interpretations of many important social issues. They have the added advantage of being phrased in terms that strike familiar chords. A few years ago, for example, there was widespread concern among American intellectuals about the decline of "nonconformity." These essays shift the concern from nonconformity to identity. As the criteria of conformity become less clear in all areas of life, and as it becomes evident that "nonconformity" can become equally stereotyped and meaningless, attention must shift to the broader plane of the search for identity. This search may become popularized also, leaving it open to simplification as it becomes absorbed by mass culture. However, it is a useful and broadened focus of attention. This search forms the core of many modern novels and plays, and it is possible to interpret recent literary history in these terms. The writings of Franz Kafka, James Joyce, Samuel Beckett, Jean-Paul Sartre, and many others, lend themselves readily to this interpretation, because they underscore the anxieties and dilemmas that arise in modern man's quest for identity. We are in accord with the literary men who see the fragmentation of reality and experience as decisive events for the modern personality.

Part II traces the threats to stable identity imposed by the great political and social upheavals of our time. These have become so pervasive that it almost appears as if the anxiety they arouse can only be managed by defensive apathy. Public challenges, like the threat of atomic war and depression, are matched by direct private challenges expressed statistically in a rising divorce rate and a rising rate of mental illness. The latter cannot be avoided through apathy, and their effects on identity-formation can hardly be underestimated. Small wonder that the "cool cat" has become the ideal of the younger generation; there is little point in getting "steamed up" over issues of this magnitude. And there are no political ideologies from the left to the right that even begin to provide satisfactory explanations for the conditions besetting us, not to mention the programs put forth to ameliorate them.

The various sections in Part II point to the need for carefully distinguishing the several phases of social identifications. Thus, in a period like the present, political identities have for the most part become meaningless, but work identities have been invested with profound meaning—at least by the middle class. The job becomes the main basis for self-justification. Occupational ideology is almost compulsively affirmed, despite the existence of threatening evidence of its inadequacy. Career failure becomes the major disaster to those who commit their total selves to a job. Ideological differences within occupations are made the basis for bitter struggles for self-affirmation, especially among intellectuals. The bitterness displayed by advocates of different methods in social science provides a sublime instance of this. Calling attention to the role of the career, to occupational ideologies, and to occupational struggles in general terms is not sufficient to equip any insider for exploring his own commitments and their limitations. We have carefully selected studies which explore occupational "facework" in detailed terms, taking into account and interpreting the anxieties any such exploration arouses. A major problem in modern mass societies is the possibility that widespread economic dislocations will activate work anxieties, to the point of leaving the persons affected vulnerable to "totalitarian" solutions. Our political essays point to this range of problems and so provide a link to the essays on work.

Since our approach to identity involves heavy stress on the availability of institutionalized moratoria provided by the society, a section on education seemed essential. Here we examine the effects of teaching on teachers and students. Our contributors cut through the argument between "progressive" and "traditional" educators, by raising questions about the circumstances promoting and retarding creative identity-experimentation in school settings. When teachers themselves foreclose their "identities" by adopting narrowly technical styles, they can hardly provide students with suitable models, nor can they tolerate the anxieties that genuine experimentation by their students would arouse. Even the classical subjects, including philosophy, can be studied or taught in a technical fashion, and we need only point out that the career-driven college professor does not differ in essentials from his industrial and business counterparts.

Other identity-forming agencies in modern life are taken up under the general heading of secondary sources, because we feel they do not provide firm anchorages in the contemporary world. The problems of familial identity are legion. So are discussions of them. We have included only a few articles on this topic and on the equally well-covered matter of ethnic and religious identities. As mentioned earlier, we leave the realm of recreational identities untouched. The requirement that leisure should be genuinely "recreative," rather than blandly recuperative, is not taken seriously by many groups in mass society, and those that do often become so desperate in their serious play that the pursuit becomes an end in itself. We feel that current efforts at "reviving" religious, ethnic, familial, and leisure identities, that ignore the devitalizing effects of modern work and politics, are doomed to failure. They become elements in the dissolution of authentic identity, because the magnitude of the realities that must be denied in order to sustain such enterprises saps already waning energies and promotes negative anxiety. Sexual-identity issues are a special problem handled most effectively by the psychoanalysts, and, rather than placing the articles dealing with them in a separated section, these discussions have been dispersed throughout the book. The theme of systematic identity-dismantling and reconstruction is illustrated by essays on brainwashing, military training, and total institutions; however, we wish to emphasize the continuity between these dramatic cases and the pervasive manipulation of identity that suffuses mass society.

After these exhaustive portrayals of the pitfalls awaiting the person who would develop a personal style in mass society, the last section, Part III, should come as a welcome change of pace. The reader of Part II, however, may notice that some of the essays address themselves to diagnosing identity issues in mass society with an eye toward suggesting plausible alternative solutions. In light of the diffuseness and oversimplification characterizing conventional discussions of these same topics, it is likely that our essays will arouse considerable anxiety; indeed, something has gone wrong if they do not. Just as Freud had to employ harsh words to penetrate the anxieties and defenses that covered sexual problems, so must the analyst of identity use sharp, and possibly painful, language. The sharpness and realism of our rather pessimistic analyses must be confronted squarely.

We do not presume to offer any short-cut solutions. Most of our essays, in fact, insist on taking the long way around; they all demand that the reader expand his world by including within it cultural forms ordinarily excluded. The theme of Part III is that personal styles must rest upon the development of historical, interpersonal, and aesthetic sensibilities of a kind hardly encouraged, if not actively discouraged, by most of the settings in which we live. However, the very existence of the essays demonstrates that it is still possible to live on complex levels of differentiated realities. Our contributors are all working and living within contemporary times, but their products show that they have access to vital qualities emerging in world history and, perhaps more important, that they are able to incorporate these qualities into their intellectual efforts. By disclosing the fruits of their own civilization, they demonstrate that it is still possible to civilize oneself.

All of the contributors to Part III could properly be called "generalists." Although they hold official positions of one kind or another, the names of these positions—professor of this, that, or another subject—hardly circumscribe the scope of their interests or talents. Many of the essays could easily have been placed in all three of our subcategories; all deal with psychology, the arts, and history in a unitary fashion. They do not provide formulae for finding a personal style; rather, they are examples of successful accomplishment of this most hazardous task, providing a basis for hope that personal identity is possible. The exemplary quality of these essays renders any attempt at summarizing them both presumptuous and futile.

We can learn much by examining the kinds of intellectual identities that these contributors disclose. Most of them are competent in both the humanities and the social sciences. The combination of philosophy and psychiatry appears to be a common one. All show a lively concern with the classics of literature. Highly developed historical consciousness is apparent in most of the essays. These men tend to live in many "historical" worlds: several have established deep contact with Oriental civilization, and one at least, Paul Radin, breaks through an even more difficult barrier, to find common ground with non-westernized Africans and Eskimos. The range of their concerns is enormous, and most readers, including the editors, will have to rely upon their "sixth" and "seventh" senses in assessing these works. Consistent with their personal styles, these authors suggest directions for future intellectual adventures, rather than charting territory most of us have already covered.

Evolving a personal style within a mass society can only be seen as a challenge. It is the kind of challenge which permits us to take little for granted, including our own motives. One must find his way into historical, interpersonal, and aesthetic worlds ordinarily inaccessible within the conventional limits of our sensibilities. To do this, we must be prepared to loosen the boundaries of our identities and to confront the anxiety that this exposure inevitably evokes without immediately foreclosing. This involves arranging life circumstances so that exposure to new materials and experiences becomes part of ongoing work and leisure routines. Regulating the circumstances of exposure to expand the boundaries of identity, without at the same time allowing them to become diffuse, is a most delicate task.

At the level of interpersonal relations, achieving a personal style involves a high degree of self-insight, especially into the limiting effects of one's habitual responses. Autonomy, with respect to the influence of the standards and opinions of intimates, must be maintained without sacrificing the capacity to establish close relationships. This means being able to choose close friends without being dominated by unconscious needs and identifications. A repertory of interpersonal patterns which embraces and encourages expressions of individuality, in others as well as in oneself, is eagerly sought, but rarely achieved. Personal styles disclosed by others, which appear to embody alien qualities and values, will evoke anxiety, and much depends on how we respond to this. It can provide a stimulus for broadening our range of experience and empathy, or it can force us to retreat to narrow and rigid identities.

Appreciating great art rests upon a similar imaginative faculty. One must be ready to suspend one's conventional ordering principles while entering into the world-order of the art object. Since the "ordering" principles of great art are deeper and different from conventional reality-orders, sufficient time must be allowed for appreciation to mature. We often suspect that a poet or a painter has a great deal to say to us, despite the fact that we cannot immediately respond to his work. Secondary sources on the period, critical essays, and exposure to related works by other artists can be very helpful, but one must always be prepared to wait patiently, allowing appreciation to grow at its own pace. Artificial "appreciation," generated by a desire to display one's "sensitivity" or to be fashionable, only clutters the way. The fact that our "spontaneous" sensibilities are often only sufficient to establish immediate contact with contemporary popular art forms need not interfere, so long as it is recognized. Sensibility can be cultivated by confronting the inevitable disparity between what our experience at any point enables us to enjoy, and what our "anticipatory" senses suggest we might someday be able to appreciate.

It is still possible to listen to the words of Homer and Shakespeare, but only if we are also able to listen to the words spoken by the poets and novelists of our own time. The latter may require as much patience and discrimination as the former, since our spontaneous sensibilities need not be any better suited for grasping the deeper meanings of Yeats and Eliot than they are for capturing the sonorous complexities of Elizabethan drama. The great artists of any period establish special worlds which can stand in quite distant relationships to the everyday worlds of the period. Modern artists often push, and find themselves pushed, far beyond everyday worlds and the perceptions of Everyman. One feature of modern art that helps account for its difficulty is the fact that many modern artists, unlike most modern men, live in the world of history. Much of the difficulty of T. S. Eliot's "Wasteland" lies in its allusions to the several worlds of Western history, the East, and primitive societies, which the poet juxtaposes, as part of the human heritage, to the emptiness of modern life. Unless one "knows" the heritage, or can at least sense its character on some level, the point of the juxtaposition is lost.

In our time, the development of historical consciousness has become even more difficult than the cultivation of aesthetic sensibility or the achievement of interpersonal awareness. There are several reasons for this. Contemporary society changes so rapidly in its external features that the relevance of the recent past hardly has time to sink in before the physical evidence for its existence disappears. So much energy is devoted to keeping up with changing fashions that little is left for establishing or savoring continuities in the various spheres of life. This focus on novelty and recency is buttressed by the immense difficulties that confront the person whose curiosity extends beyond the recent past. There are enough books pouring forth every year on important aspects of American history, European history, and world history to overwhelm the most diligent reader. Sorting the wheat from the chaff requires specialized knowledge, and it is hard to discover which "sorters" or critics to trust. These objective difficulties combine with and encourage the decline in historical empathy, i.e., the capacity to imaginatively enter into and appreciate earlier historical periods on their own terms.

There is a close relationship between the imaginative sensitivity required in interpersonal, aesthetic, and historical awareness. They all rest upon the capacity to broaden individual identity, by exposing it to alternative life programs without destroying their qualities or losing one's own. The central temptation to be avoided is that of "simplification," and the faculty to be cultivated is that of identity-play. Perhaps the most important insight yielded by an analysis of mass society is the recognition that a society of this kind tends to reduce human existence to a flat plane of defensive functioning, by foreshortening time perspectives and ignoring multiple levels of reality. Indeed, one source of Freud's significance lies in his emphasis on the restoration of memory and genuine feeling in human affairs, as well as his development of a set of therapeutic strategies for achieving this. Psychoanalysis holds revolutionary implications just because it cuts through impersonal postures to touch the dormant human core.

We advance a conception of modern mass society that embodies a dialectical synthesis of two extreme views. Modern social life is clearly laden with savage destructive possibilities at the individual, the organizational, the national, and the international levels. The mushroom cloud is a good symbol for the worst extreme, but neither can we ignore the incredible inhumanity involved in the Nazi concentration camps. The threats of world destruction and the disappearance of genuine individuals hang over our age. Totalitarianism, we may add, is always a political possibility in the mass democracies. However, within these same democracies, at the institutional and personal planes, new opportunities continuously appear. The almost infinite productive capacity of modern technology and its potential for relieving the human suffering stemming from economic shortages is an emergent phenomenon which no serious social analyst can ignore. Furthermore, there are intellectual movements—existentialism and psychoanalysis among them—which evidence the emergence of a higher level of consciousness. The very extremities that our contributors explore and analyze, the proliferation of immense bodies of unintegrated knowledge and experience, and the recognition of the problems involved in making the available knowledge and experience accessible, contain the seeds of new possibilities. Our lack of distinctive styles and deep loyalties can lead us to submerge our individuality in mass life, or it can help us throw off parochial loyalties and stylistic blinders and prepare us to acquaint ourselves with the broadest range of human possibilities. The seeds are there, but whether they bear flowers or weeds depends on the care they receive.

In the body of this book, we have tried to present material that explores the threats to authentic identity as far as they can presently be traced, and as specifically as they can presently be identified. We have also included material that reveals the possibilities of raising the level of human consciousness as high as it can be raised in our time. We are well aware that few can attain the synthetic plane displayed in Part III. This book tries to sharpen insight into the most crushing problems and the most amazing possibilities in the contemporary situation. It is hard for a single author to embrace both poles, and that is exactly the justification for putting together a collection on these themes. A few of our authors—especially Richards, Jaspers, Radin, and Buber—impress us as having achieved a full vision, but it is not accidental that they are men in their seventies and eighties. We cannot hope to match their achievement, but we can try to learn from it.

Significantly, a perspective akin to ours can be found in several recent volumes not represented in this reader. We feel closely identified with the viewpoints set forth by such writers as Eric Kahler in

The Tower and the Abyss, William H. Whyte, Jr., in *The Organization Man,* David Riesman in *Individualism Reconsidered,* Erich Fromm in *The Sane Society,* and Helen Lynd in *On Shame and the Search for Identity;* by Hannah Arendt in *The Human Condition,* Norman O. Brown in *Life against Death,* Paul Tillich in *The Courage To Be,* Herbert Marcuse in *Eros and Civilization,* Benjamin Nelson in *The Idea of Usury,* and by Allen Wheelis in *The Quest for Identity.* We did not include sections from these authors because they express their arguments in such an organic fashion that wrenching parts of them out of the total work would distort the meaning rather than enhance it. Then too, they are all readily available.

There are two other kinds of material that we would like to have included within the covers of this book. First, and most obvious, are the classic statements about the problems of interpreting modern society, contained in the works of Sigmund Freud, Karl Marx, Emil Durkheim, Max Weber, Georg Simmel, Thorstein Veblen, George Herbert Mead, and Karl Mannheim. An early outline included selections from their work, but it became obvious that they would swallow the entire volume, since theorists of this stature cannot be presented in fragments. Their books form the permanent background upon which we, and many of our contributors, depend. The second omission, also necessitated by lack of space, is the absence of any literary or poetic representations of our themes. This deficiency is partly met by quotations in the articles included, but we would like to have had selections by W. H. Auden, T. S. Eliot, W. B. Yeats, D. H. Lawrence, Franz Kafka, and others. Let us suggest two other readers for someone to consider: the first could present the classic analyses and diagnoses of mass society, and the second could collect artistic and literary portrayals of the modern condition.

Finding one's way through the morass of contemporary life is, indeed, no easy task. Learning to live on a plane of complex historical reality, without losing one's grip on the requirements of everyday life, is especially precarious. One must keep a watchful eye on one's stock responses, and the best that can be hoped for is cultivated spontaneity. Buber ties together most of the issues when he closes our book with the admonition not to confuse existence and productivity. Learning to ask the right questions and to get satisfaction from continuous experimentation in seeking answers is more than half the battle. One must at least consider the possibility that the way in which we respond to Shakespeare is no less important for us than the way in which we organize our careers. Or, to put it another way:

> To know men is to be wise:
> To know one's self is to be illumined.
> To conquer men is to have strength:
> To conquer one's self is to be stronger still,
> And to know when you have enough is to be rich.
> For vigorous action may bring a man what he is determined to have,
> But to keep one's place (in the order of the universe) is to endure;
> And to die and not be lost, this is the real blessing of long life.*

---

* Lao-tzu, "Tao Te Ching," chap. xxxiii, in E. R. Hughes (ed.), *Chinese Philosophy in Classical Times* (*Everyman*, No. 973).

I

CENTRAL PERSPECTIVES

a. IDENTITY

ERIK HOMBURGER ERIKSON[1]*

The Problem of Ego Identity

Introduction

IN A NUMBER OF WRITINGS (8, 9, 10, 11) I have been using the term *ego identity* to denote certain comprehensive gains which the individual, at the end of adolescence, must have derived from all of his preadult experience in order to be ready for the tasks of adulthood. My use of this term reflected the dilemma of a psychoanalyst who was led to a new concept not by theoretical preoccupation but rather through the expansion of his clinical awareness to other fields (social anthropology and comparative education) and through the expectation that such expansion would, in turn, profit clinical work. Recent clinical observations have, I feel, begun to bear out this expectation. I have, therefore, gratefully accepted two opportunities[2] offered me to restate and review the problem of identity. The present paper combines both of these presentations. The question before us is whether the concept of identity is essentially a psychosocial one, or deserves to be considered as a legitimate part of the psychoanalytic theory of the ego.

First a word about the term identity. As far as I know Freud used it only once in a more than incidental way, and then with a psychosocial connotation. It was when he tried to formulate his link to Judaism, that he spoke of an "inner identity"[3] which was not based on race or religion, but on a common readiness to live in opposition, and on a common freedom from prejudices which narrow the use of the intellect. Here, the term

---

Reprinted from the *Journal of the American Psychoanalytic Association*, IV, No. 1 (1956), 58-121, by permission of the author and the publisher. (Copyright 1956, by *Journal of the American Psychoanalytic Association.*)

* *Ed. Note.*—All numbered footnotes will be found at the end of the book. All numbered references will be found at the end of the article.

identity points to an individual's link with the unique values, fostered by a unique history of his people. Yet, it also relates to the cornerstone of this individual's unique development: for the importance of the theme of "incorruptible observation at the price of professional isolation" played a central role in Freud's life (12). It is this identity of something in the individual's core, with an essential aspect of a group's inner coherence, which is under consideration here: for the young individual must learn to be most himself where he means most to others—those others, to be sure, who have come to mean most to him. The term identity expresses such a mutual relation in that it connotes both a persistent sameness within oneself (self-sameness) and a persistent sharing of some kind of essential character with others.

I can attempt to make the subject matter of identity more explicit only by approaching it from a variety of angles—biographic, pathographic, and theoretical—and by letting the term identity speak for itself in a number of connotations. At one time, then, it will appear to refer to a conscious *sense of individual identity;* at another, to an unconscious striving for a *continuity of personal character;* at a third, as a criterion for the silent doings of *ego synthesis;* and, finally, as a maintenance of an inner *solidarity* with a group's ideals and identity. In some respects the term will appear to be colloquial and naïve; in another, vaguely related to existing concepts in psychoanalysis and sociology. If, after an attempt at clarifying this relation, the term itself will retain some ambiguity it will, so I hope, nevertheless have helped to delineate a significant problem, and a necessary point of view.

I begin with one extreme aspect of the problem as exemplified in the biography of an outstanding individual—an individual who labored as hard on the creation of a world-wide *public identity* for himself, as he worked on his literary masterpieces.

Biographic: G.B.S. (70) on George Bernard Shaw (20)

When George Bernard Shaw was a famous man of seventy, he was called upon to review and to preface the unsuccessful work of his early twenties, namely, the two volumes of fiction which had never been published. As one would expect, Shaw proceeded to make light of the production of his young adulthood, but not without imposing on the reader a detailed analysis of young Shaw. Were Shaw not so deceptively witty in what he says about his younger years, his observations probably would have been recognized as a major psychological achievement. Yet, it is

Shaw's mark of identity that he eases and teases his reader along a path of apparent superficialities and sudden depths. I dare to excerpt him here for my purposes, only in the hope that I will make the reader curious enough to follow him on every step of his exposition (41).

G.B.S. (for this is the public identity which was one of his masterpieces) describes young Shaw as an "extremely disagreeable and undesirable" young man, "not at all reticent of diabolical opinion," while inwardly "suffering . . . from simple cowardice . . . and horribly ashamed of it." "The truth is," he concludes, "that all men are in a false position in society until they have realized their possibilities and imposed them on their neighbors. They are tormented by a continual shortcoming in themselves; yet they irritate others by a continual overweening. This discord can be resolved by acknowledged success or failure only: everyone is ill at ease until he has found his natural place, whether it be above or below his birthplace." But Shaw must always exempt himself from any universal law which he inadvertently pronounces; so he adds: "This finding of one's place may be made very puzzling by the fact that there is no place in ordinary society for extraordinary individuals."

Shaw proceeds to describe a crisis (of the kind which we will refer to as an *identity crisis*) at the age of twenty. It is to be noted that this crisis was not caused by lack of success or the absence of a defined role but by too much of both: "I made good in spite of myself, and found, to my dismay, that Business, instead of expelling me as the worthless imposter I was, was fastening upon me with no intention of letting me go. Behold me, therefore, in my twentieth year, with a business training, in an occupation which I detested as cordially as any sane person lets himself detest anything he cannot escape from. In March 1876 I broke loose." Breaking loose meant to leave family and friends, business and Ireland, and to avoid the danger of success without identity, of a success unequal to "the enormity of my unconscious ambition." He granted himself a prolongation of the interval between youth and adulthood, which we will call a *psychosocial moratorium*. He writes: ". . . when I left my native city I left this phase behind me, and associated no more with men of my age until, after about eight years of solitude in this respect, I was drawn into the Socialist revival of the early eighties, among Englishmen intensely serious and burning with indignation at very real and very fundamental evils that affected all the world." In the meantime, he seemed to avoid opportunities, sensing that "Behind the conviction that they could lead to nothing that I wanted, lay the unspoken fear that they might lead to something I did not want." This *occupational* part of the moratorium was reinforced by an *intellectual* one: "I cannot learn anything that does not interest me. My memory is not indiscriminate; it rejects and selects; and its selections are not academic. . . . I congratulate myself on this; for I am firmly persuaded that every unnatural activity of the brain is as mischievous as any unnatural activity of the body. . . . Civilization is always wrecked by giving the governing classes what is called secondary education. . . ."

Shaw settled down to study and to write as he pleased, and it was then that the extraordinary workings of an extraordinary personality came to the fore. He managed to abandon the *kind* of work he had been doing without relinquishing the work *habit*: "My office training had left me with a habit of doing something regularly every day as a fundamental condition of industry as distinguished from idleness. I knew I was making no headway unless I was doing this, and that I should never produce a book in any other fashion. I bought supplies of white paper, demy size, by sixpence-worths at a time; folded it in quarto; and condemned myself to fill five pages of it a day, rain or shine, dull or inspired. I had so much of the schoolboy and the clerk still in me that if my five pages ended in the middle of a sentence I did not finish it until the next day. On the other hand, if I missed a day, I made up for it by doing a double task on the morrow. On this plan I produced five novels in five years. It was my professional apprenticeship. . . ." We may add that these five novels were not published for over fifty years; but Shaw had learned to write as he worked, and to wait, as he wrote. How important such initial *ritualization of his worklife* was for the young man's inner defenses may be seen from one of those casual (in fact, parenthetical) remarks with which the great wit almost coyly admits his psychological insight: "I have risen by sheer gravitation, too industrious by acquired habit to stop working (*I work as my father drank*.)"[4] He thus points to that combination of *addictiveness* and *compulsivity* which we see as the basis of much pathology in late adolescence and of some accomplishment in young adulthood.

His father's "drink neurosis" Shaw describes in detail, finding in it one of the sources of his biting humor: "It had to be either a family tragedy or family joke." For his father was not "convivial, nor quarrelsome, nor boastful, but miserable, racked with shame and remorse." However, the father had a "humorous sense of anticlimax which I inherited from him and used with much effect when I became a writer of comedy. His anticlimaxes depended for their effect on our sense of the sacredness (of the subject matter). . . . It seems providential that I was driven to the essentials of religion by the reduction of every factitious or fictitious element in it to the most irreverent absurdity."

A more unconscious level of Shaw's Oedipal tragedy is represented—with dreamlike symbolism—in what looks like a screen memory conveying his father's impotence: "A boy who has seen 'the governor' with an *imperfectly wrapped-up goose under one arm* and *a ham in the same condition under the other* (both purchased under heaven knows what delusion of festivity) *butting* at the garden wall in the belief that he was *pushing open the gate,* and *transforming his tall hat to a concertina* in the process, and who, instead of being overwhelmed with shame and anxiety at the spectacle, has been so *disabled by merriment* (uproariously shared by the maternal uncle) that he has hardly been able to rush to the rescue of the hat and pilot its wearer to safety, is clearly not a boy who will make tragedies of trifles instead of *making trifles of tragedies.* If you cannot get rid of the family skeleton, you may as well make it dance." It is obvious that the analysis of the psychosexual elements in Shaw's identity could find a solid anchor point in this memory.

Shaw explains his father's downfall with a brilliant analysis of the socioeconomic circumstances of his day. For the father was "second cousin to a baronet, and my mother the daughter of a country gentleman whose rule was, when in difficulties, mortgage. That was my sort of poverty." His father was "the youngest son of a younger son of a younger son," and he was "a downstart and the son of a downstart." Yet, he concludes: "To say that my father could not afford to give me a university education is like saying that he could not afford to drink, or that I could not afford to become an author. Both statements are true; but he drank and I became an author all the same."

His mother he remembers for the "one or two rare and delightful occasions when she buttered my bread for me. She buttered it thickly instead of merely wiping a knife on it." Most of the time, however, he says significantly, she merely "accepted me as a natural and customary phenomenon and took it for granted that I should go on occurring in that way." There must have been something reassuring in this kind of impersonality, for "technically speaking, I should say she was the worst mother conceivable, always, however, within the limits of the fact that she was incapable of unkindness to any child, animal, or flower, or indeed to any person or thing whatsoever. . . ." If this could not be considered either a mother's love or an education, Shaw explains: "I was badly brought up because my mother was so well brought up. . . . In her righteous reaction against . . . the constraints and tyrannies, the scoldings and browbeatings and punishments she had suffered in her childhood . . . she reached a negative attitude in which having no substitute to propose, she carried domestic anarchy as far as in the nature of things it can be carried." All in all, Shaw's mother was "a thoroughly disgusted and disillusioned woman . . . suffering from a hopelessly disappointing husband and three uninteresting children grown too old to be petted like the animals and the birds she was so fond of, to say nothing of the humiliating inadequacy of my father's income."

Shaw had really three parents, the third being a man named Lee ("meteoric," "impetuous," magnetic"), who gave Shaw's mother lessons in singing, not without revamping the whole Shaw household as well as Bernard's ideals: "Although he supplanted my father as the dominant factor in the household, and appropriated all the activity and interest of my mother, he was so completely absorbed in his musical affairs that there was no friction and hardly any intimate personal contacts between the two men: certainly no unpleasantness. At first his ideas astonished us. He said that people should sleep with their windows open. The daring of this appealed to me; and I have done so ever since. He ate brown bread instead of white: a startling eccentricity."

Of the many elements of identity formations which ensued from such a perplexing picture, let me single out only three, selected, simplified and named for this occasion by me.

1. The Snob.—"As compared with similar English families, we had a power of derisive dramatization that made the bones of the Shavian skeletons rattle more loudly." Shaw recognizes this as "family snobbery mitigated by the family sense of humor." On the other hand, "though my mother was not consciously a snob, the divinity which hedged an Irish lady of her period was not acceptable to the British suburban parents, all snobs, who were within her reach (as customers for private music lessons)." Shaw had "an enormous contempt for family snobbery," until he found that one of his ancestors was an Earl of Fife: "It was as good as being descended from Shakespeare, whom I had been unconsciously resolved to reincarnate from my cradle."

2. The Noisemaker.—All through his childhood, Shaw seems to have been exposed to an oceanic assault of music making: the family played trombones and ophicleides, violincellos, harps, and tambourines—and, most of all (or is it worst of all) they sang. Finally, however, he taught himself the piano, and this with dramatic noisiness. "When I look back on all the banging, whistling, roaring, and growling inflicted on nervous neighbors during this process of education, I am consumed with useless remorse. . . . I used to drive (my mother) nearly crazy by my favorite selections from Wagner's Ring, which to her was 'all recitative,' and horribly discordant at that. She never complained at the time, but confessed it after we separated, and said that she had sometimes gone away to cry. If I had committed a murder I do not think it would trouble my conscience very much; but this I cannot bear to think of." That, in fact, he may have learned to get even with his musical tormentors, he does not profess to realize. Instead, he compromised by becoming—a music *critic*, i.e., one who *writes about* the noise made by others. As a critic, he chose the *nom de plume* Corno di Bassetto—actually the name of an instrument which nobody knew and which is so meek in tone that "not even the devil could make it sparkle." Yet Bassetto became a sparkling critic, and more:

"I cannot deny that Bassetto was occasionally vulgar; but that does not matter if he makes you laugh. Vulgarity is a necessary part of a complete author's equipment; and the clown is sometimes the best part of the circus."

3. The Diabolical One.—How the undoubtedly lonely little boy (whose mother listened only to the musical noisemakers) came to use his imagination to converse with a great imaginary companion, is described thus: "In my childhood I exercised my literary genius by composing my own prayers . . . they were a literary performance for the entertainment and propitiation of the Almighty." In line with his family's irreverence in matters of religion, Shaw's piety had to find and to rely on the rockbottom of religiosity which, in him, early became a mixture of "intellectual integrity . . . synchronized with the dawning of moral passion." At the same time it seems that Shaw was (in some unspecified way) a little devil of a child. At any rate, he did not feel identical with himself when he was good: "Even when I was a good boy, I was so only theatrically, because, as actors say, I saw myself in the character." And indeed, at the completion of his identity struggle, i.e., "when Nature completed my countenance in 1880 or thereabouts (I had only the tenderest sprouting of hair on my face until I was 24), I found myself equipped with the upgrowing moustaches and eyebrows, and the sarcastic nostrils of the operatic fiend whose airs (by Gounod) I had sung as a child, and whose attitudes I had affected in my boyhood. Later on, as the generations moved past me, I . . . began to perceive that imaginative fiction is to life what the sketch is to the picture or the conception to the statue."

Thus G. B. S., more or less explicitly, traces his own roots. Yet, it is well worth noting that what he finally *became*, seems to him to have been as *innate*, as the intended reincarnation of Shakespeare referred to above. His teacher, he says, "puzzled me with her attempts to teach me to read; for I can remember no time at which a page of print was not intelligible to me, and can only suppose that I was born literate." However, he thought of a number of professional choices: "As an alternative to being a Michelangelo I had dreams of being a Badeali (note, by the way, that of literature I had no dreams at all, any more than a duck has of swimming)."

He also calls himself "a born Communist" (which, we hasten to say, means a Fabian Socialist), and he explains the peace that comes with the *acceptance of what one seems to be made to be;* the "born Communist . . . knows where he is, and where this society which has so intimidated him is. He is cured of his MAUVAISE HONTE. . . ." Thus "the complete outsider" gradually became his kind of complete insider: "I was," he said, "outside society, outside politics, outside sport, outside the Church" —but this "only within the limits of British barbarism. . . . The moment music, painting, literature, or science came into question the positions were reversed: it was I who was the Insider."

As he traces all of these traits back into childhood, Shaw becomes aware of the fact that only a *tour de force* could have integrated them all: ". . . if I am to be entirely communicative on this subject, I must add that the mere rawness which so soon rubs off was complicated by a deeper strangeness which has made me all my life a sojourner on this planet rather than a native of it. Whether it be that I was born mad or a little too sane, my kingdom was not of this world: I was at home only in the realm of my imagination, and at my ease only with the mighty dead. Therefore, I had to become an actor, and create for myself a fantastic personality fit and apt for dealing with men, and adaptable to the various parts I had to play as author, journalist, orator, politician, committee man, man of the world, and so forth. In this," so Shaw concludes significantly, "I succeeded later on only too well." This statement is singularly illustrative of that faint disgust with which older men at times review the inextricable identity which they had come by in their youth—a disgust which in the lives of some can become mortal despair and inexplicable psychosomatic involvement.

The end of his crisis of younger years, Shaw sums up in these words: "I had the intellectual habit; and my natural combination of critical faculty with literary resource needed only a clear comprehension of life in the light of an intelligible theory: in short, a religion, to set it in triumphant operation." Here the old Cynic has circumscribed in one sentence what the identity formation of any human being must add up to. To translate this into terms more conducive to discussion in ego-psychological and psychosocial terms: Man, to take his place in society must acquire a "conflict-free," habitual use of a dominant *faculty*, to be elaborated in an *occupation;* a limitless *resource,* a feedback, as it were, from the immediate *exercise* of this occupation, from the *companionship* it provides, and from its *tradition;* and finally, an intelligible *theory* of the processes of life which the old atheist, eager to shock to the last, calls a religion. The Fabian Socialism to which he, in fact, turned is rather an *ideology*, to which general term we shall adhere, for reasons which permit elucidation only at the end of this paper.

Genetic: Identification and Identity

1.—The autobiographies of extraordinary (and extraordinarily self-perceptive) individuals are a suggestive source of insight into the development of identity. In order to find an anchor point for the discussion of the universal genetics of identity, however, it would be well to trace its development through the life histories or through significant life episodes of "ordinary" individuals—individuals whose lives have neither become professional autobiographies (as did Shaw's) nor case histories, such as will be discussed in the next chapter. I will not be able to present such material here; I must, instead, rely on impressions from daily life, from participation in one of the rare "longitudinal" studies of the personality development of children,[5] and from guidance work with mildly disturbed young people.

Adolescence is the last and the concluding stage of childhood. The adolescent process, however, is conclusively complete only when the individual has subordinated his childhood identifications to a new kind of identification, achieved in absorbing sociability and in competitive apprenticeship with and among his age-mates. These new identifications are no longer characterized by the playfulness of childhood and the experimental zest of youth: with dire urgency they force the young individual into choices and decisions which will, with increasing immediacy, lead to a more final self-definition, to irreversible role pattern, and thus to commitments "for life." The task to be performed here by the young person and by his society is formidable; it necessitates, in different individuals and in different societies, great variations in the duration, in the intensity, and in the ritualization of adolescence. Societies offer, as individuals require, more or less sanctioned intermediary periods between childhood and adulthood, institutionalized *psychosocial moratoria*, during which a lasting pattern of "inner identity" is scheduled for relative completion.

In postulating a "latency period" which precedes puberty, psychoanalysis has given recognition to some kind of *psychosexual moratorium* in human development—a period of delay which permits the future mate and parent first to "go to school" (i.e., to undergo whatever schooling is provided for in his technology) and to learn the technical and social rudiments of a work situation. It is not within the confines of the libido theory, however, to give adequate account of a second period of delay, namely, adolescence. Here the sexually matured individual is more or less retarded in his psychosexual capacity for intimacy and in the psychosocial readiness for parenthood. This period can be viewed as a *psychosocial moratorium* during which the individual, through free role experimentation, may find a niche in some section of his society, a niche which is firmly defined and yet seems to be uniquely made for him. In finding it, the young adult gains an assured sense of inner continuity and social sameness which will bridge what he *was* as a child and what he is *about to become*, and will reconcile his *conception of himself* and his *community's recognition* of him.

If, in the following, we speak of the community's response to the young individual's need to be "recognized" by those around him, we mean something beyond a mere recognition of achievement; for it is of great relevance to the young individual's identity formation that he be responded to, and be given function and status as a person whose gradual growth and transformation make sense to those who begin to make sense to him. It has not been sufficiently recognized in psychoanalysis that such recognition provides an entirely indispensable support to the ego in the specific tasks of adolescence, which are: to maintain the most important ego defenses against the vastly growing intensity of impulses (now invested in a matured genital apparatus and a powerful muscle system); to learn to consolidate the most important "conflict-free" achievements in line with work opportunities; and to resynthesize all childhood identifications in some unique way, and yet in concordance with the roles offered by some wider section of society—be that section the neighborhood block, an anticipated occupational field, and association of kindred minds, or, perhaps (as in Shaw's case) the "mighty dead."

2.—Linguistically as well as psychologically, identity and identification have common roots. Is identity, then, the mere sum of earlier identifications, or is it merely an additional set of identifications?

The limited usefulness of the *mechanism of identification* becomes at once obvious if we consider the fact that none of the identifications of childhood (which in our patients stand out in such morbid elaboration and mutual contradiction) could, if merely added up, result in a functioning personality. True, we usually believe that the task of psychotherapy is the replacement of morbid and excessive identifications by more desirable ones. But as every cure attests, "more desirable" identifications, at the same time, tend to be quietly subordinated to a new, a unique Gestalt which is more than the sum of its parts. The fact is that identification as a mechanism is of limited usefulness. Children, at different stages of their development identify with those *part aspects* of people by which they themselves are most immediately affected, whether in reality or fantasy. Their identifications with parents, for example, center in certain overvalued and ill-understood body parts, capacities, and role appearances. These part aspects, furthermore, are favored not because of their social acceptability (they often are everything but the parents' most adjusted attributes) but by the nature of infantile fantasy which only gradually gives way to a more realistic anticipation of social reality. The final identity, then, as fixed at the end of adolescence is superordinated to any single identification with individuals of the past: it includes all significant identifications, but it also alters them in order to make a unique and a reasonably coherent whole of them.

If we, roughly speaking, consider introjection-projection, identification, and identity formation to be the steps by which the ego grows in ever more mature interplay with the identities of the child's models, the following psychosocial schedule suggests itself:

The mechanisms of *introjection and projection* which prepare the basis for later identifications, depend for their relative integration on the satisfactory mutuality (9) between the *mothering adult(s) and the mothered child*. Only the experience of such mutuality provides a safe pole of self-feeling from which the child can reach out for the other pole: his first love "objects."

The fate of *childhood identification*, in turn, depends on the child's satisfactory interaction with a trustworthy and meaningful hierarchy of roles as provided by the generations living together in some form of *family*.

Identity formation, finally, begins where the usefulness of identification ends. It arises from the selective repudiation and mutual assimilation of childhood identifications, and their absorption in a new configuration, which, in turn, is dependent on the process by which a *society* (often through subsocieties) *identifies the young individual*, recognizing him as somebody who had to become the way he is, and who, being the way he is, is taken for granted. The community, often not without some initial mistrust, gives such recognition with a (more or less institutionalized) display of surprise and pleasure in making the acquaintance of a newly emerging individual. For the community, in turn, feels "recognized" by the individual who cares to ask for recognition; it can, by the same token, feel deeply—and vengefully—rejected by the individual who does not seem to care.

3.—While the end of adolescence thus is the stage of an overt identity *crisis*, identity *formation* neither begins nor ends with adolescence: it is a lifelong development largely unconscious to the individual and to his society. Its roots go back all the way to the first self-recognition: in the baby's earliest exchange of smiles there is something of a *self-realization coupled with a mutual recognition*.

All through childhood tentative crystallizations take place which make the individual feel and believe (to begin with the most conscious aspect of the matter) as if he approximately knew who he was—only to find that such self-certainty ever again falls prey to the *discontinuities of psychosocial development* (3). An example would be the discontinuity between the demands made in a given milieu on a little boy and those made on a "big boy" who, in turn, may well wonder why he was first made to believe that to be little is admirable, only to be forced to exchange this effortless status for the special obligations of one who is "big now." Such discontinuities can amount to a crisis and demand a decisive and strategic repatterning of action, and with it, to *compromises* which can be compensated for only by a consistently accruing sense of the social value of such increasing commitment. The cute or ferocious, or good small boy, who becomes a studious, or gentlemanly, or tough big boy must be able—and must be enabled—to combine both sets of values in a recognized identity which permits him, in work and play, and in official and in intimate behavior to be (and to let others be) a big boy *and* a little boy.

The community supports such development to the extent to which it permits the child, at each step, to orient himself toward a complete "*life plan*" with a hierarchical order of roles, as represented by individuals of different age grades. Family, neighborhood, and school provide contact and experimental identification with younger and older children and with young and old adults. A child, in the multiplicity of successive and tentative identifications, thus begins early to build up expectations of what it will be like to be older and what it will feel like to have been younger—expectations which become part of an identity as they are, step by step, verified in decisive experiences of psychosocial "fittedness."

4.—The *critical phases* of life have been described in psychoanalysis primarily in terms of instincts and defenses, i.e., as "typical danger situations" (23). Psychoanalysis has concerned itself more with the encroachment of psychosexual crises on psychosocial (and other) functions than with the specific crisis created by the maturation of each function. Take, for example, a child who is learning to speak: he is acquiring one of the prime functions supporting a sense of individual autonomy and one of the prime techniques for expanding the radius of give-and-take. The mere indication of an ability to give intentional sound-signs immediately obligates the child to "*say* what he wants." It may force him to *achieve* by proper verbalization the attention which was afforded him previously in response to mere gestures of needfulness. Speech not only commits him to the kind of voice he has and to the mode of speech he develops; it also *defines him* as one responded to by those around him with changed diction and attention. They, in turn, expect henceforth to be understood by him with fewer explanations or gestures. Furthermore, a spoken word is a *pact:* there is an irrevocably committing aspect to an utterance remembered by others, although the child may have to learn early that certain commitments (adult ones to a child) are subject to change without notice, while others (his) are not. This intrinsic relationship of speech, not only to the world of communicable facts, but also to the social value of verbal commitment and uttered truth, is strategic among the experiences which support (or fail to support) a sound ego development. It is this psychosocial aspect of the matter which we must learn to relate to the by now better known *psychosexual* aspects represented, for example, in the autoerotic enjoyment of speech; the use of speech as an erotic "contact"; or in such organ-mode emphases as eliminative or intrusive sounds or uses of speech. Thus the child may come to develop, in the use of voice and word, a particular combination of whining or singing, judging or arguing, as part of a new element of the future identity, namely, the element "one who speaks and is spoken to in such-and-such-a-way." This element, in turn, will be related to other elements of the child's developing identity (he is clever and/or goodlooking and/or tough) and will be compared with other people, alive or dead, judged ideal or evil.

It is the ego's function to integrate the psychosexual and psychosocial aspects on a given level of development, and, at the same time, to integrate the relation of newly added identity elements with those already in existence. For earlier crystallizations of identity can become subject to renewed conflict, when changes in the quality and quantity of drive, expansions in mental equipment, and new and often conflicting social demands all make previous adjustments appear insufficient, and, in fact, make previous opportunities and rewards suspect. Yet, such developmental and normative crises differ from imposed, traumatic, and neurotic crises, in that the process of growth provides new energy as society offers new and specific opportunities (according to its dominant conception and institutionalization of the phases of life). From a genetic point of view, then, the process of identity formation emerges as an *evolving configuration*—a configuration which is gradually established by successive ego syntheses and resyntheses throughout childhood; it is a configuration gradually integrating *constitutional givens, idiosyncratic libidinal needs, favored capacities, significant identifications, effective defenses, successful sublimations, and consistent roles.*

5.—The final assembly of all the converging identity elements at the end of childhood (and the abandonment of the divergent ones)[6] appears to be a formidable task: how can a stage as "abnormal" as adolescence be trusted to accomplish it? Here it is not unnecessary to call to mind again that, in spite of the similarity of adolescent "symptoms" and episodes to neurotic and psychotic symptoms and episodes, adolescence is not an affliction, but a *normative crisis,* i.e., a normal phase of increased conflict characterized by a seeming fluctuation in ego strength, and yet also by a high growth potential. Neurotic and psychotic crises are defined by a certain self-perpetuating propensity, by an increasing waste of defensive energy, and by a deepened psychosocial isolation; while normative crises are relatively more reversible, or, better, traversable, and are characterized by an abundance of available energy which, to be sure, revives dormant anxiety and arouses new conflict, but also supports new and expanded ego functions in the searching and playful engagement of new opportunities and associations. What, under prejudiced scrutiny, may appear to be the onset of a neurosis, often is but an aggravated crisis which might prove to be self-liquidating and, in fact, contributive to the process of identity formation.

It is true, of course, that the adolescent, during the final stage of his identity formation, is apt to suffer more deeply than he ever did before (or ever will again) from a diffusion of roles; it is also true that such diffusion renders many an adolescent defenseless against the sudden impact of previously latent malignant disturbances. In the meantime, it is important to emphasize that the diffused and vulnerable, aloof and uncommitted, and yet demanding and opinionated personality of the not-too-neurotic adolescent contains many necessary elements of a semideliberrate role experimentation of the "I dare you" and "I dare myself" variety. Much of this apparent diffusion thus must be considered *social play* and thus the true genetic successor of childhood play. Similarly, the adolescent's ego development demands and permits playful, if daring, experimentation in fantasy and *introspection*. We are apt to be alarmed by the "closeness to consciousness" in the adolescent's perception of dangerous id contents (such as the Oedipus complex), and this primarily because of the obvious hazards created in psychotherapy, if and when we, in zealous pursuit of our task of "making conscious," push somebody over the precipice of the unconscious who is already leaning out a little too far. The adolescent's leaning out over any number of precipices is normally an experimentation with experiences which are thus becoming more amenable to ego control, provided they can be somehow communicated to other adolescents in one of those strange codes established for just such experiences—and provided they are not prematurely responded to with fatal seriousness by overeager or neurotic adults. The same must be said of the adolescent's "fluidity of defenses," which so often causes raised eyebrows on the part of the worried clinician. Much of this fluidity is anything but pathological; for adolescence is a crisis in which only fluid defense can overcome a sense of victimization by inner and outer demands, and in which only trial and error can lead to the most felicitous avenues of action and self-expression.

In general, one may say that, in regard to the social play of adolescents, prejudices similar to those which once concerned the nature of childhood play are not easily overcome. We alternately consider such behavior irrelevant, unnecessary, or irrational, and ascribe to it purely regressive and neurotic meanings. As in the past the study of children's spontaneous games was neglected in favor of that of solitary play,[7] so now the mutual "joinedness" of adolescent clique behavior fails to be properly assessed in our concern for the individual adolescent. Children and adolescents in their presocieties provide for one another a sanctioned moratorium and joint support for free experimentation with inner and outer dangers (including those emanating from the adult world). Whether or not a given adolescent's newly acquired capacities are drawn back into infantile conflict depends to a significant extent on the quality of the opportunities and rewards available to him in his peer clique, as well as on the more formal ways in which society at large invites a transition from social play to work experimentation, and from rituals of transit to final commitments:

all of which must be based on an implicit mutual contract between the individual and society.

6.—Is the sense of identity conscious? At times, of course, it seems only too conscious. For between the double prongs of vital inner need and inexorable outer demand, the as yet experimenting individual may become the victim of a transitory extreme *identity consciousness* which is the common core of the many forms of "self-consciousness" typical for youth. Where the processes of identity formation are prolonged (a factor which can bring creative gain) such preoccupation with the "self-image" also prevails. We are thus most aware of our identity when we are just about to gain it and when we (with what motion pictures call "a double take") are somewhat surprised to make its acquaintance; or, again, when we are just about to enter a crisis and feel the encroachment of identity diffusion —a syndrome to be described presently.

An increasing sense of identity, on the other hand, is experienced preconsciously as a sense of psychosocial well-being. Its most obvious concomitants are a feeling of being at home in one's body, a sense of "knowing where one is going," and an inner assuredness of anticipated recognition from those who count. Such a sense of identity, however, is never gained nor maintained once and for all. Like a "good conscience," it is constantly lost and regained, although more lasting and more economical methods of maintenance and restoration are evolved and fortified in late adolescence.

Like any aspect of well-being or for that matter, of ego synthesis, a sense of identity has a preconscious aspect which is available to awareness; it expresses itself in behavior which is observable with the naked eye, and it has unconscious concomitants which can be fathomed only by psychological tests and by the psychoanalytic procedure. I regret that, at this point, I can bring forward only a general claim which awaits detailed demonstration. The claim advanced here concerns a whole series of criteria of psychosocial health which find their specific elaboration and relative completion in stages of development preceding and following the identity crisis. This is condensed in Figure I.

Identity appears as only one concept within a wider conception of the human life cycle which envisages childhood as a *gradual unfolding of the personality through phase-specific psychosocial crises:* I have, on other occasions (9, 10), expressed this *epigenetic principle* by taking recourse to a diagram which, with its many empty boxes, at intervals may serve as a check on our attempts at detailing psychosocial development. (Such a diagram, however, can be recommended to the serious attention only of those who can take it *and* leave it.) The diagram (Figure I), at first, contained only the double-lined boxes along the descending diagonal (I,1 – II,2 – III,3 – IV,4 – V,5 – VI,6 – VII,7 – VIII,8) and, for the sake of initial orientation, the reader is requested to ignore all other entries for the moment. The *diagonal* shows the sequence of psychosocial crises. Each of these boxes is shared by a criterion of relative psychosocial health and the corresponding criterion of relative psychosocial ill-health: in "normal" development, the first must persistently outweigh (although it will never completely do away with) the second. The sequence of stages thus represents a successive development of the component parts of the psychosocial personality. Each part exists in some form (verticals) before the time when it becomes "phase-specific," i.e., when "its" psychosocial crisis is precipitated both by the individual's readiness and by society's pressure. But each component comes to ascendance and finds its more or less lasting solution at the conclusion of "its" stage. It is thus *systematically related* to all the others, and all depend on the proper development at the proper *time* of each; although individual make-up and the nature of society determine the rate of development of each of them, and thus the *ratio* of all of them. It is at the end of adolescence, then, that identity becomes phase-specific (V,5), i.e., must find a certain integration as a relatively conflict-free psychosocial arrangement—or remain defective or conflict-laden.

With this chart as a blueprint before us, let me state first which aspects of this complex matter will *not* be treated in this paper: for one, we will not be able to make more definitive the now very tentative designation (in *vertical* 5) of the precursors of identity in the infantile ego. Rather, we approach childhood in an untraditional manner, namely, from young adulthood backward—and this with the conviction that early development cannot be understood on its own terms alone, and that the earliest stages of childhood can not be accounted for without a unified theory of the whole span of pre-adulthood. For the infant (while he is not spared the chaos of needful rage) does not and cannot build anew and out of himself the course of human life, as the reconstruction of his earliest experience ever again seems to suggest. The smallest child lives in a community of life cycles which depend on him as he depends on them, and which guide his drives as well as his sublimations with consistent feedbacks. This verity necessitates a discussion of the psychoanalytic approach to "environment" to which we shall return toward the end of this paper.

A second systematic omission concerns the psychosexual stages. Those readers who have undertaken to study the diagrams of psychosexual development in *Childhood and Society* (9) know that I am attempting to lay the ground for a detailed account of the dovetailing of psychosexual and psychosocial epigenesis, i.e., the two schedules according to which component parts, present throughout development, come to fruition in successive stages. The essential inseparability of these two schedules is implied throughout this paper, although only the psychosocial schedule, and in fact only one stage of it, is brought into focus.

	1.	2.	3.	4.	5.	6.	7.	8.
I. INFANCY	Trust vs. Mistrust				Unipolarity vs. Premature Self-Differentiation			
II. EARY CHILDHOOD		Autonomy vs. Shame, Doubt			Bipolarity vs. Autism			
III. PLAY AGE			Initiative vs. Guilt		Play Identification vs. (Oedipal) Fantasy Identities			
IV. SCHOOL AGE				Industry vs. Inferiority	Work Identification vs. Identity Foreclosure			
V. ADOLESCENCE	Time Perspective vs. Time Diffusion	Self-Certainty vs. Identity Consciousness	Role Experimentation vs. Negative Identity	Anticipation of Achievement vs. Work Paralysis	Identity vs. Identity Diffusion	Sexual Identity vs. Bisexual Diffusion	Leadership Polarization vs. Authority Diffusion	Ideological Polarization vs. Diffusion of Ideals
VI. YOUNG ADULT					Solidarity vs. Social Isolation	Intimacy vs. Isolation		
VII. ADULTHOOD							Generativity vs. Self-Absorption	
VIII. MATURE AGE								Integrity vs. Disgust, Despair

FIGURE 1

What traditional source of psychoanalytic insight, then, *will* we concern ourselves with? It is: first pathography; in this case the clinical description of *identity diffusion.* Hoping thus to clarify the matter of identity from a more familiar angle, we will then return to the over-all aim of beginning to "extract," as Freud put it, "from psychopathology what may be of benefit to normal psychology."

Pathographic: The Clinical Picture of Identity Diffusion

Pathography remains the traditional source of psychoanalytic insight. In the following, I shall sketch a syndrome of disturbances in young people who can neither make use of the institutionalized moratorium provided in their society, nor create and maintain for themselves (as Shaw did) a unique moratorium all of their own. They come, instead, to psychiatrists, priests, judges, and (we must add) recruitment officers in order to be given an authorized if ever so uncomfortable place in which to wait things out.

The sources at my disposal are the case histories of a number of young patients who sought treatment following an acutely disturbed period between the ages of sixteen and twenty-four. A few were seen, and fewer treated, by me personally; a larger number were reported in supervisory interviews or seminars at the Austen Riggs Center in Stockbridge and at the Western Psychiatric Institute in Pittsburgh; the largest number are former patients now on record in the files of the Austen Riggs Center. My *composite sketch* of these case histories will remind the reader immediately of the diagnostic and technical problems encountered in adolescents in general (5) and especially in any number of those young borderline cases (28) who are customarily diagnosed as preschizophrenias, or severe character disorders with paranoid, depressive, psychopathic, or other trends. Such well-established diagnostic signposts will not be questioned here. An attempt will be made, however, to concentrate on certain common features representative of the common life crisis shared by this whole group of patients as a result of a (temporary or final) inability of their egos to establish an identity: for they all suffer from *acute identity diffusion.* Obviously, only quite detailed case presentations could convey the full necessity or advisability of such a "phase-specific" approach which emphasizes the life task shared by a group of patients as much as the diagnostic criteria which differentiate them. In the meantime, I hope that my composite sketch will convey at least a kind of impressionistic plausibility. The fact that the cases known to me were seen in a private institution in the Berkshires, and at a public clinic in industrial Pittsburgh, suggests that at least the two extremes of socioeconomic status in the United States (and thus two extreme forms of identity problems) are represented here. This could mean that the families in question, because of their extreme locations on the scale of class mobility and of Americanization, may have conveyed to these particular children a certain hopelessness regarding their chances of participating in (or of successfully defying) the dominant American manners and symbols of success.[8] Whether, and in what way disturbances such as are outlined here also characterize those more comfortably placed somewhere near the middle of the socioeconomic ladder, remains, at this time, an open question.

1. *Time of Breakdown.*—A state of acute identity diffusion usually becomes manifest at a time when the young individual finds himself exposed to a combination of experiences which demand his simultaneous commitment to *physical intimacy* (not by any means always overtly sexual), to decisive *occupational choice*, to energetic *competition*, and to *psychosocial self-definition.* A young college girl, previously overprotected by a conservative mother who is trying to live down a not-so-conservative past, may, on entering college, meet young people of radically different backgrounds, among whom she must choose her friends and her enemies; radically different mores especially in the relationship of the sexes which she must play along with or repudiate; and a commitment to make decisions and choices which will necessitate irreversible competitive involvement or even leadership. Often, she finds among very "different" young people, a comfortable display of values, manners, and symbols for which one or the other of her parents or grandparents is covertly nostalgic, while overtly despising them. Decisions and choices and, most of all, successes in any direction bring to the fore conflicting identifications and immediately threaten to narrow down the inventory of further tentative choices; and, at the very moment when time is of the essence, every move may establish a binding precedent in psychosocial self-definition, i.e., in the "type" one comes to represent in the types of the age-mates (who seem so terribly eager to type). On the other hand, any marked *avoidance of choices* (i.e., a moratorium by default) leads to a sense of outer *isolation* and to an *inner vacuum* which is wide open for old libidinal objects and with this for bewilderingly conscious incestuous feelings; for more primitive forms of identification; and (in some) for a renewed struggle with archaic introjects. This regressive pull often receives the greatest attention from workers in our field, partially because we are on more familiar ground wherever we can discern signs of regression to infantile psychosexuality. Yet, the disturbances under discussion here cannot be comprehended without some insight into the specific nature of transitory adolescent regression as an attempt to postpone and to avoid,

as it were, a psychosocial foreclosure. A state of paralysis may ensue, the mechanisms of which appear to be devised to maintain a state of minimal actual choice and commitment with a maximum inner conviction of still being the chooser. Of the complicated presenting pathology only a few aspects can be discussed here.

2. *The Problem of Intimacy.*—The chart which accompanied the preceding chapter shows "Intimacy vs. Isolation" as the core conflict which follows that of "Identity vs. Identity Diffusion." That many of our patients break down at an age which is properly considered more preadult than postadolescent, is explained by the fact that often only an attempt to engage in intimate fellowship and competition or in sexual intimacy fully reveals the latent weakness of identity.

True "engagement" with others is the result and the test of firm self-delineation. As the young individual seeks at least tentative forms of playful intimacy in friendship and competition, in sex play and love, in argument and gossip, he is apt to experience a peculiar strain, as if such tentative engagement might turn into an interpersonal fusion amounting to a loss of identity, and requiring, therefore, a tense inner reservation, a caution in commitment. Where a youth does not resolve such strain he may isolate himself and enter, at best, only stereotyped and formalized interpersonal relations; or he may, in repeated hectic attempts and repeated dismal failures, seek intimacy with the most improbable partners. For where an assured sense of identity is missing even friendships and affairs become desperate attempts at delineating the fuzzy outlines of identity by mutual narcissistic mirroring: to fall in love then often means to fall into one's mirror image, hurting oneself and damaging the mirror. During lovemaking or in sexual fantasies, a loosening of *sexual identity* threatens: it even becomes unclear whether sexual excitement is experienced by the individual or by his partner, and this in either heterosexual or homosexual encounters. The ego thus loses its flexible capacity for abandoning itself to sexual and affectual sensations, in a fusion with another individual who is both partner to the sensation and guarantor of one's continuing identity: fusion with another becomes identity loss. A sudden collapse of all capacity for mutuality threatens, and a desperate wish ensues to start all over again, with a (quasi-deliberate) regression to a stage of basic bewilderment and rage such as only the very small child knew.

It must be remembered that the counterpart of intimacy is *distantiation*, i.e., the readiness to repudiate, to ignore, or to destroy those forces and people whose essence seems dangerous to one's own. Intimacy with one set of people and ideas would not be really intimate without an efficient repudiation of another set. Thus, weakness or excess in repudiation is an intrinsic aspect of the inability to gain intimacy because of an incomplete identity: whoever is not sure of his "point of view" cannot repudiate judiciously.

Young persons often indicate in rather pathetic ways a feeling that only a merging with a "leader" could save them—an adult who is able and willing to offer himself as a safe object for experimental surrender and as a guide in the relearning of the very first steps toward an intimate mutuality, and a legitimate repudiation. To such a person the late adolescent wants to be an apprentice or a disciple, a follower, sex mate, or patient. Where this fails, as it often must from its very intensity and absoluteness, the young individual recoils to a position of strenuous introspection and self-testing which, given particularly aggravating circumstances or a history of relatively strong autistic trends, can lead him into a paralyzing borderline state. Symptomatically, this state consists of a painfully heightened sense of isolation; a disintegration of the sense of inner continuity and sameness; a sense of over-all ashamedness; an inability to derive a sense of accomplishment from any kind of activity; a feeling that life is happening to the individual rather than being lived by his initiative; a radically shortened time perspective; and finally, a basic mistrust, which leaves it to the world, to society, and indeed, psychiatry to prove that the patient does exist in a psychosocial sense, i.e., can count on an invitation to become himself.

3. *Diffusion of Time Perspective.*—In extreme instances of delayed and prolonged adolescence an extreme form of a disturbance in the *experience of time* appears which, in its milder forms, belongs to the psychopathology of everyday adolescence. It consists of a sense of great urgency and yet also of a loss of consideration for time as a dimension of living. The young person may feel simultaneously very young, and in fact baby-like, and old beyond rejuvenation. Protests of missed greatness and of a premature and fatal loss of useful potentials are common among our patients as they are among adolescents in cultures which consider such protestations romantic; the implied malignancy, however, consists of a decided disbelief in the possibility that time may bring change, and yet also of a violent fear that it might. This contradiction often is expressed in a general slowing up which makes the patient behave, within the routine of activities (and also of therapy) as if he were moving in molasses. It is hard for him to go to bed and to face the transition into a state of sleep, and it is equally hard for him to get up and face the necessary restitution of wakefulness; it is hard to come to the hour, and hard to leave it. Such complaints as, "I don't know," "I give up," "I quit," are by no means mere habitual statements reflecting a mild depression: they are often expressions of the kind of despair which has been recently discussed by Edward Bibring (4) as a wish on the part of the ego "to let itself die." The assump-

tion that life could actually be made to end with the end of adolescence (or at tentatively planned later "dates of expiration") is by no means entirely unwelcome, and, in fact, can become the only pillar of hope on which a new beginning can be based. Some of our patients even require the feeling that the therapist does not intend to commit them to a continuation of life if (successful) treatment should fail to prove it really worth while; without such a conviction the moratorium would not be a real one. In the meantime, the "wish to die" is only in those rare cases a really suicidal wish, where "to be a suicide" becomes an inescapable identity choice in itself. I am thinking here of a pretty young girl, the oldest of a number of daughters of a mill worker. Her mother had repeatedly expressed the thought that she would rather see her daughters dead than become prostitutes; at the same time she suspected "prostitution" in the daughter's every move toward companionship with boys. The daughters were finally forced into a kind of conspiratorial sorority of their own, obviously designed to elude the mother, to experiment with ambiguous situations and yet probably also to give one another protection from men. They were finally caught in compromising circumstances. The authorities, too, took it for granted that they intended to prostitute themselves, and they were sent to a variety of institutions where they were forcefully impressed with the kind of "recognition" society had in store for them. No appeal was possible to a mother who, they felt, had left them no choice; and much good will and understanding of social workers was sabotaged by circumstances. At least for the oldest girl (and this, because of a number of reasons) no other future was available except that of another chance in another world. She killed herself by hanging after having dressed herself up nicely, and having written a note which ended with the cryptic words "Why I achieve honor only to discard it. . . ."

Less spectacular but not less malignant forms and origins of such "negative identities" will be taken up later.

4. *Diffusion of Industry*.—Cases of severe identity diffusion regularly also suffer from an acute upset in the sense of workmanship, and this either in the form of an inability to concentrate on required or suggested tasks, or in a self-destructive preoccupation with some one-sided activities, i.e., excessive reading. The way in which such patients sometimes, under treatment, find the one activity in which they can re-employ their once lost sense of workmanship, is a chapter in itself. Here, it is well to keep in mind the stage of development which precedes puberty and adolescence, namely, the elementary school age, when the child is taught the prerequisites for participation in the particular technology of his culture and is given the opportunity and the life task of developing a sense of workmanship and work participation. The school age significantly follows the Oedipal stage: the accomplishment of real (and not only playful) steps

toward a place in the economic structure of society permits the child to reidentify with parents as workers and tradition bearers rather than as sexual and familial beings, thus nurturing at least one concrete and more "neutral" possibility of becoming like them. The tangible goals of elementary practice are shared by and with age-mates in places of instruction (sweathouse, prayer house, fishing hole, workshop, kitchen, schoolhouse) most of which, in turn, are graphically separated from the home, from the mother, and from infantile memories: here, however, wide differences in the treatment of the sexes exist. Work goals, then, by no means only support or exploit the suppression of infantile instinctual aims; they also enhance the functioning of the ego, in that they offer a constructive activity with actual tools and materials in a communal reality. The ego's tendency to turn passivity into activity here thus acquires a new field of manifestation, in many ways superior to the mere turning of passive into active in infantile fantasy and play; for now the inner need for activity, practice, and work completion is ready to meet the corresponding demands and opportunities in social reality (25, 20).

Because of the immediate Oedipal antecedents of the beginnings of a work identity, the diffusion of identity in our young patients reverses their gears toward Oedipal competitiveness and sibling rivalry. Thus identity diffusion is accompanied not only by an inability to concentrate, but also by an excessive awareness as well as an abhorrence of competitiveness. Although the patients in question usually are intelligent and able and often have shown themselves successful in office work, in scholastic studies and in sports, they now lose the capacity for work, exercise, and sociability and thus the most important vehicle of social play, and the most significant refuge from formless fantasy and vague anxiety. Instead infantile goals and fantasies are dangerously endowed with the energy emanating from matured sexual equipment and of vicious aggressive power. One parent, again, becomes the goal, the other, again, the hindrance. Yet, this revived Oedipal struggle is not and must not be interpreted as exclusively or even primarily a sexual one: it is a turn toward the earliest origins, an attempt to resolve a diffusion of early introjects and to rebuild shaky childhood identifications—in other words, a wish to be born again, to learn once more the very first steps toward reality and mutuality, and to acquire the renewed permission to develop again the functions of contact, activity, and competition.

A young patient, who had found himself blocked in college, during the initial phase of his treatment in a private hospital nearly read himself blind, apparently in a destructive overidentification with father and therapist both of whom were professors. Guided by a resourceful "painter in residence" he came upon the fact that he had an original and forceful talent to paint, an activity which we prevented by advancing treatment from becoming self-destructive overactivity. As painting proved a help in the patient's gradual acquisition of a sense of identity of his own, he dreamed one night a different version of a dream which previously had always ended in panicky awakening. Now he fled, from fire and persecution, into a forest which he had sketched himself; and as he fled into it, the charcoal drawing turned into live woods, with an infinite perspective.

5. *The Choice of the Negative Identity.*—The loss of a sense of identity often is expressed in a scornful and snobbish hostility toward the roles offered as proper and desirable in one's family or immediate community. Any part aspect of the required role, or all parts, be it masculinity or femininity, nationality or class membership, can become the main focus of the young person's acid disdain. Such excessive contempt for their backgrounds occurs among the oldest Anglo-Saxon and the newest Latin or Jewish families; it easily becomes a general dislike for everything American, and an irrational overestimation of everything foreign. Life and strength seem to exist only where one is not, while decay and danger threaten wherever one happens to be. This typical case fragment illustrates the superego's triumph of depreciation over a young man's faltering identity: "A voice within him which was disparaging him began to increase at about this time. It went to the point of intruding into everything he did. He said, 'if I smoke a cigarette, if I tell a girl I like her, if I make a gesture, if I listen to music, if I try to read a book—this third voice is at me all the time—"You're doing this for effect; you're a phony."' This disparaging voice in the last year has been rather relentless. The other day on the way from home to college, getting into New York on the train, he went through some of the New Jersey swamplands and the poorer sections of the cities, and he felt that he was more congenial with people who lived there than he was with people on the campus or at home. He felt that life really existed in those places and that the campus was a sheltered, effeminate place."

In this example it is important to recognize not only an overweening superego, overclearly perceived as an inner voice, but also the acute identity diffusion, as projected on segments of society. An analogous case is that of a French-American girl from a rather prosperous mining town, who felt panicky to the point of paralysis when alone with a boy. It appeared that numerous superego injunctions and identity conflicts had, as it were, short-circuited in the obsessive idea that every boy had a right to expect from her a yielding to sexual practices, popularly designated as "French."

Such estrangement from national and ethnic origins rarely leads to a complete denial of *personal identity* (34), although the angry insistence on being called by a particular given name or nickname is not uncommon among young people who try to find a refuge from diffusion in a new name label. Yet confabulatory reconstructions of one's origin do occur: a high-school girl of Middle-European descent secretly kept company with Scottish immigrants, carefully studying and easily assimilating their dialect and their social habits. With the help of history books and travel guides she reconstructed for herself a childhood in a given milieu in an actual township in Scotland, apparently convincing enough to some descendants of that country. Prevailed upon to discuss her future with me, she spoke of her (American-born) parents as "the people who brought me over here," and told me of her childhood "over there" in impressive detail. I went along with the story, implying that it had more inner truth than reality to it. The bit of reality was, as I surmised, the girl's attachment, in early childhood, to a woman neighbor who had come from the British Isles; the force behind the near-delusional "truth" was the paranoid form of a powerful death wish (latent in all severe identity crises) against her parents. The semideliberateness of the delusion was indicated when I finally asked the girl how she had managed to marshal all the details of life in Scotland. "Bless you, sir," she said in pleading Scottish brogue, "I needed a past."

On the whole, however, our patients' conflicts find expression in a more subtle way than the abrogation of personal identity: they rather choose a *negative identity*, i.e., an identity perversely based on all those identifications and roles which, at critical stages of development, had been presented to the individual as most undesirable or dangerous, and yet, also as most real. For example, a mother whose first-born son died and who (because of complicated guilt-feelings) has never been able to attach to her later surviving children the same amount of religious devotion that she bestows on the memory of her dead child may well arouse in one of her sons the conviction that to be sick or dead is a better assurance of being "recognized" than to be healthy and about. A mother who is filled with unconscious ambivalence toward a brother who disintegrated into alcoholism may again and again respond selectively only to those traits in her son which seem to point to a repetition of her brother's fate, in which case this "negative" identity may take on more reality for the son than all his natural attempts at being good: he may work hard on becoming a drunkard and, lacking the necessary ingredients, may end up in a state of stubborn paralysis of choice. In other cases the negative identity is dictated by the necessity of finding and defending a niche of one's own against the excessive ideals either demanded by morbidly ambitious parents or seemingly already realized by actually superior ones: in both cases the parents' weaknesses and unexpressed wishes are recognized by the child with catastrophic clarity. The daughter of a man of brilliant showmanship ran away from college and was arrested as a prostitute in the Negro quarter of a Southern city; while the daughter of an influential Southern Negro preacher was found among narcotic addicts in Chicago. In such cases it is of utmost importance to recognize the mockery and the vindictive pretense in such role playing; for the white girl had not really prostituted herself, and the colored girl had not really become an addict—yet. Needless to say, however, each of them had put herself into a marginal social area, leaving it to law enforcement officers and to psychiatric agencies to decide what stamp to put on such behavior. A corresponding case is that of a boy presented to a psychiatric clinic as "the village homosexual" of a small town. On investigation, it appeared that the boy had succeeded in assuming this fame without any actual acts of homosexuality except one, much earlier in his life, when he had been raped by some older boys.

Such vindictive choices of a negative identity represent, of course, a desperate attempt at regaining some mastery in a situation in which the available positive identity elements cancel each other out. The history of such a choice reveals a set of conditions in which it is easier to derive a sense of identity out of a *total* identification with that which one is *least* supposed to be than to struggle for a feeling of reality in acceptable roles which are unattainable with the patient's inner means. The statement of a young man, "I would rather be quite insecure than a little secure," and that of a young woman, "At least in the gutter I'm a genius," circumscribe the relief following the total choice of a negative identity. Such relief is, of course, often sought collectively in cliques and gangs of young homosexuals, addicts, and social cynics.

A relevant job ahead of us is the analysis of snobbism which, in its upper-class form, permits some people to deny their identity diffusion through a recourse to something they did not earn themselves, namely, their parents' wealth, background, or fame. But there is a "lower lower" snobbism too, which is based on the pride of having achieved a semblance of nothingness. At any rate, many a late adolescent, if faced with continuing diffusion, would rather *be nobody or somebody bad, or indeed, dead—and this totally, and by free choice—than be not-quite-somebody*. The word "total" is not accidental in this connection, for I have endeavored to describe in another connection (13) a human proclivity to a "totalistic" reorientation when, at critical stages of development, reintegration into a relative "wholeness" seems impossible. We will return to this problem in the last chapter.

6. *Transference and Resistance.*—What I can say here about the therapeutic problems encountered with the patients described must be restricted to an attempt at relating to the concepts of identity and diffusion such matters of therapeutic technique as have been elaborated by workers in the field of borderline cases.[9]

On facing therapy, some of the patients under discussion here undergo a phase of particular malignancy. While the depth of regression and the danger of acting out must, of course, guide our diagnostic decisions, it is important to recognize, from the start, a mechanism present in such turn for the worse: I would call it the "rock-bottom attitude." This consists of a quasi-deliberate giving in on the part of the patient to the pull of regression, a radical search for the rock-bottom—i.e., both the ultimate limit of regression and the only firm foundation for a renewed progression.[10] The assumption of such a deliberate search for the "baseline" means to carry Ernst Kris's "regression in the service of the ego" to an extreme: the fact that the recovery of our patients sometimes coincides with the discovery of previously hidden artistic gifts, suggests further study of this point (29).

The element of deliberateness added here to "true" regression is often expressed in an all-pervasive mockery which characterizes the initial therapeutic contact with these patients; and by that strange air of sadomasochistic satisfaction, which makes it often hard to see and harder to believe, that their self-depreciation and their willingness to "let the ego die" harbors a devastating sincerity. As one patient said: "That people do not know how to succeed is bad enough. But the worst is that they do not know how to fail. I have decided to fail well." This almost "deadly" sincerity is to be found in the patients' very determination to *trust nothing but mistrust*, and yet to watch from a dark corner of their mind (and indeed, often from the corner of an eye) for new experiences simple and forthright enough to permit a renewal of the most basic experiments in trustful mutuality. The therapist, manifestly faced with a mocking and defiant young adult, actually must take over the task of a mother who introduces a baby to life's trustworthiness. In the center of the treatment is the patient's need to redelineate himself, and thus to rebuild the foundations of his identity. At the beginning these delineations shift abruptly, even as violent shifts in the patient's experience of his ego boundary take place before our eyes: the patient's mobility may suddenly undergo a "catatonic" slowdown; his attentiveness may turn into overwhelming sleepiness; his vasomotor system may overreact to the point of producing sensations of fainting; his sense of reality may yield to feelings of depersonalization; or the remnants of his self-assurance may disappear in a miasmic loss of a sense of physical presence. Cautious but firm inquiry will reveal the probability that a number of contradictory impulses preceded the "attack." There is first a sudden intense impulse to completely destroy the therapist, and this, it seems with an underlying "cannibalistic" wish to devour his essence and his identity. At the same time, or in alternation, there occurs a fear and a wish to be devoured, to gain an identity by being absorbed in the therapist's essence. Both tendencies, of course, are often dissimilated or somatized for long periods, during which they find a manifestation (often kept secret) only after the therapeutic hour. This manifestation may be an impulsive flight into sexual promiscuity acted out without sexual satisfaction or any sense of participation; enormously absorbing rituals of masturbation or food intake; excessive drinking or wild driving; or self-destructive marathons of reading or listening to music, without food or sleep.

We see here the most extreme form of what may be called *identity resistance* which, incidentally, far from being restricted to the patients described here, is a universal form of resistance regularly experienced but often unrecognized in the course of some analyses. Identity resistance is, in its milder and more usual forms, the patient's fear that the analyst, because of his particular personality, background, or philosophy, may carelessly or deliberately destroy the weak core of the patient's identity and impose instead his own. I would not hesitate to say that some of the much discussed unsolved transference neuroses in patients, as well as in candidates in training, is the direct result of the fact that the identity resistance often is, at best, analyzed only quite unsystematically. In such cases the analysand may throughout the analysis resist any possible inroad by the analyst's identity while surrendering on all other points; or he may absorb more of the analyst's identity than is manageable within the patient's own means; or he may leave the analysis with a lifelong sense of not having been provided with some essence owed to him by the analyst.

In cases of acute identity diffusion this identity resistance becomes the core problem of the therapeutic encounter. Variations of psychoanalytic technique have in common that the dominant resistance must be accepted as the main guide to technique and that interpretation must be fitted to the patient's ability to utilize it. Here the patient sabotages communication until he has settled some basic—if contradictory—issues. The patient insists that the therapist accept his negative identity as real and necessary (which it is and was) without concluding that this negative identity is "all there is to him." If the therapist is able to fulfill both of these demands, he must prove patiently through many severe crises that he can maintain understanding and affection for the patient without either devouring him or offering himself for a totem meal. Only then can better known forms of transference, if ever so reluctantly, emerge.

These are nothing more than a few hints regarding the phenomenology of identity diffusion as reflected in the most outstanding and immediate transferences and resistances. Individual treatment, however, is only one facet of therapy in the cases under discussion. The transferences of these patients remain diffused, while their acting out remains a constant danger. Some, therefore, need to undergo treatment in a hospital environment in which their stepping out of the therapeutic relationship can be observed and limited; and in which first steps *beyond* the newly won bipolar relationship to the therapist meet with the immediate support of receptive nurses, co-operative fellow patients, and helpful instructors in a sufficiently wide choice of activities.

7. *Specific Factors in Family and Childhood.*—In the discussion of patients who have a relevant pathogenic trend in common, we are apt to ask what their parents have in common. I think that one may say that a number of the mothers in our case histories have in common three outstanding traits. First, a pronounced status awareness, of the climbing and pretentious, or of the "hold-on" variety. They would at almost any time be willing to overrule matters of honest feeling and of intelligent judgment for the sake of a façade of wealth, propriety, and "happiness": they, in fact, try to coerce their sensitive children into a pretense of a "natural" and "glad-to-be-proper" sociability. Secondly, they have the special quality of a penetrating omnipresence; their very voices and their softest sobs are sharp, plaintive, or fretful, and cannot be escaped within a considerable radius. One patient, all through childhood had a repetitive dream of a pair of flapping scissors flying around a room: the scissors proved to symbolize his mother's voice, cutting, and cutting off.[11] These mothers love, but they love fearfully, plaintively, intrusively; they are themselves so hungry for approval and for recognition that they burden their young children with complicated complaints, especially about the fathers, and they plead with the children to justify by their existence their mother's existence. They are highly jealous and highly sensitive to the jealousy of others; in our context it is especially important that the mother is intensely jealous of any sign that the child may identify primarily with the father, or, worse, base his very identity on that of the father. It must be added that whatever these mothers are, they are more so toward the patient; the conclusion is inescapable that these patients, in turn, have, from the beginning, deeply hurt their mothers by shying away from them, and this because of an utter intolerance of extreme temperamental differences. These differences, however, are only extreme expressions of an essential affinity: by which I mean to imply that the patient's excessive tendency to withdraw (or to act impulsively) and the mother's excessive social intrusiveness have in common a high degree of social vulnerability. Behind the mother's persistent complaints, then, that the father failed to make a woman out of her, is the complaint, deeply perceived by both mother and child, that the patient failed to make a mother out of her.

The fathers, while usually successful, and often outstanding in their particular fields, do not stand up against their wives at home because of an excessive mother dependence on them, in consequence of which the fathers also are deeply jealous of their children. What initiative and integrity they have either surrenders to the wife's intrusiveness or tries guiltily to elude her: in consequence of which the mother becomes only the more needy, plaintive, and "sacrificial" in her demands upon all or some of her children.

Of the relationship of our patients to their brothers and sisters I can only say that it seems to be more symbiotic than most sibling relationships are. Because of an early identity hunger, our patients are apt to attach themselves to one brother or sister in a way resembling the behavior of twins (7): except that here we have one twin, as it were, trying to treat a non-twin as a twin. They seem apt to surrender to a total identification with at least one sibling in ways which go far beyond the "altruism by identification" described by Anna Freud (15). It is as if our patients surrendered their own identity to that of a brother or sister in the hope of regaining a bigger and better one by some sort of merging. For periods they succeed; the letdown which must follow the breakup of the artificial twinship is only the more traumatic. Rage and paralysis follow the sudden insight that there is enough identity only for one, and that the other seems to have made off with it.

The early childhood histories of our patients are, on the whole, remarkably bland. Some infantile autism is often observed early but usually rationalized by the parents. Yet one has the general impression that the degree of malignancy of the acute identity diffusion in late adolescence depends on the extent of this early autism, which will determine the depth of regression and the intensity of the encounter between new identity fragments and old introjects. As to particular traumata in childhood or youth, one item seems frequent, namely, a severe physical trauma either in the Oedipal period or in early puberty—and this in connection with a separation from home. This trauma may consist of an operation or a belatedly diagnosed physical defect; it may be an accident or a severe sexual traumatization. Otherwise the early pathology conforms with that expected as typical for the dominant psychiatric diagnosis given.

8. *The Therapeutic Design.*—I promised a composite sketch, and a sketch I have presented. Again, only the detailed presentation of a few cases could elucidate the relation of ego weakness to congenital proclivities, on the one hand, and to the educative deficiency of families and classes, on the other. In the meantime, the most immediate clarification of the ego's relationship to its "environment" ensues from the study of the young patient's recovery in a hospital setting, i.e., the study of his determined "oneliness" (as a young woman patient put it); of his tendency to exploit and provoke the hospital environment; of his growing ability to utilize it; and finally, of his capacity to leave this kind of institutionalized moratorium and to return to his old or new place in society. The hospital community offers the clinical researcher the possibility of being a participant observer not only in the individual patient's personal treatment, but

also in the "therapeutic design" which is to meet the legitimate demands of patients who share a life problem—here identity diffusion. It stands to reason that such a common problem receives elucidation, as the hospital community plans on meeting the specific requirements of those who failed in it: in this case the hospital becomes a planfully institutionalized world-between-worlds, which offers the young individual support in the rebuilding of those most vital ego functions, which—as far as he ever built them—he has relinquished. The relationship to the individual therapist is the cornerstone for the establishment of a new and honest mutuality of function which must set the patient's face toward an ever so dimly perceived and ever so strenuously refuted future. Yet, it is the hospital community in which the patient's first steps of renewed social experimentation take place. The privileges and obligations of such a community immediately demand his subjection to and his initiation in a communal design which will also strive to meet his and his fellow patients' needs—and incidentally, also, those of the staff: for it stands to reason that a communal setting such as a hospital is characterized not only by the identity needs of those who happen to be the patients, but also of those who choose to become their brothers' (and sisters') keepers. The discussion of the ways in which professional hierarchy distributes the functions, the rewards, and the status of such keepership (and thus opens the door for a variety of counter-transferences and "crosstransferences" which, indeed, make the hospital a facsimile of a home) is entering the literature on the subject of hospital morale (i.e., 2, 40). From the point of view of this paper, such studies prepare for discussion also the danger of the patient's choosing the very role of a patient as the basis of his crystallizing identity: for this role may well prove more meaningful than any potential identity experienced before.

9. *Once More: The Diagram.*—Diagrams have a quiet coerciveness all their own. Especially a diagram which has neither been completed nor discarded becomes a conceptual Harvey: one converses with it unawares. In therapeutic work, one tries to ignore the embarrassing fact that now and again the diagram looks over one's shoulder, as it were, and makes a suggestion; nor do the patients appreciate such atmospheric interferences. Only as I concluded this impressionistic survey of some of the main features of identity diffusion, did it occur to me to "locate" them on the chart: and it cannot be denied that they clarify previously vague parts of the diagram and suggest specific expansions of theory. Insisting, then, that in principle Harveys should remain expendable, we will briefly outline what this one can teach us.

The original chart showed only the diagonal, i.e., the successive achievement (or failure) of the main components of relative psychosocial health. However, it bore the legend: "Above the diagonal there is space for a future elaboration of the precursors of each of these solutions, all of which begin with the beginning; below the diagonal there is space for the designation of the derivatives of these solutions in the maturing personality."

Because all the *verticals* "begin with the beginning," one hesitates to enter even tentative terms into the top boxes. Yet, work with borderline cases (adolescent, juvenile, and infantile) suggests that the infantile frontier, to which they have all regressed, is that of a basic mistrust in their *self-delineation* and of a basic doubt in the possibility of any relationship of *mutuality*. The chart, tentatively, assumes that a successful struggle on the earliest psychosocial frontier of infancy (i.e., the trust-mistrust frontier), if well guided by a favorable maternal environment, leads to a dominant sense of *Unipolarity* (I, 5) by which is meant something like a dominant sense of the goodness of individual existence. This, I believe, deserves to be differentiated from the narcissistic omnipotence ascribed to this age. While as yet vulnerably dependent on direct, continuous, and consistent maternal support, an actual sense of the reality of "good" powers, outside and within oneself, must be assumed to arise. Its negative counterpart is a diffusion of contradictory introjects and a predominance of fantasies which pretend to coerce hostile reality with omnipotent vengeance. Once gained, however, the psychosocial foundation of unipolarity subsequently permits *Bipolarization* (II, 5) or what, in id terms, has been called the cathexis of objects. This permits an outgoing experimentation with powerful but loving individuals who retain consistent reality, even though they may go before they come, deny before they give, seem indifferent before they, again, become attentive. In transitory or lasting forms of autism, the child can be seen to shy away from or to despair of such bipolarization, always in search of an illusory good "oneliness."

Subsequent *Play and Work Identifications* (III, 5–IV, 5) with powerful adults and with older and younger age-mates need no further discussion here; the literature on the preschool and school stage amply illustrates the gains and the defeats of these more obviously psychosocial periods.

It is the horizontal (V) which contains the *derivatives of earlier relative achievements which now become part and parcel of the struggle for identity*. It is necessary to emphasize (and possible to illustrate briefly) the principle, according to which early relative achievements (diagonal) when considered at a later stage (any horizontal below the diagonal) must be reviewed and renamed in terms of that later stage. Basic Trust, for example, is a good and a most fundamental thing to have, but its psychosocial quality becomes more differentiated as the ego comes into the possession of a more extensive apparatus, even as society challenges and guides such extension.

To begin, then, with the pathology just described: *Time Diffusion*

(V, 1) or a loss of the ego's function of maintaining perspective and expectancy is related to the *earliest crises in life* (I, 1), and this because of the fact that the experience of temporal cycles and of time qualities are inherent in and develop from the initial problems of mounting need tension, of delay of satisfaction, and final unification with the satisfying "object." As tension increases, future fulfillment is anticipated in "hallucinatory" images; as fulfillment is delayed, moments of impotent rage occur in which anticipation (and with it, future) is obliterated; the perception of an approaching potential satisfaction, again, gives time a highly condensed quality of intense hope and feared disappointment. All of this contributes temporal elements to the formation of basic trust, i.e., the inner conviction that—after all—sufficient satisfaction is sufficiently predictable to make waiting and "working" worth while. Whatever the original inventory of time qualities are, our most malignantly regressed young people are clearly possessed by general attitudes which represent something of a mistrust of time as such: every delay appears to be a deceit, every wait an experience of impotence, every hope a danger, every plan a catastrophe, every potential provider a traitor. Therefore, time must be made to stand still, if necessary by the magic means of catatonic immobility—or by death. These are the extremes which are manifest in few, and latent in many cases of identity diffusion; yet, every adolescent, I would believe, knows at least fleeting moments of being at odds with time itself. In its normal and transitory form, this new kind of mistrust quickly or gradually yields to outlooks permitting and demanding an intense investment in a future, or in a number of possible futures. If these, to us, seem often quite "utopian" (i.e., based on expectations which would call for a change in the laws of historical change as we know them), we must, for the moment, postpone any judgment of value. The adolescent —or some adolescents—may need, at all costs, an outlook with a perspective worth an investment of energy. The actual realizability of such an outlook may be a matter of later learning and adjusting, and often a matter of historical luck.

In the following, I shall let each step on the chart lead to a few suggestive *social considerations* which were only briefly touched on in the foregoing. To envisage a future, the young adult may also need that something which Shaw called "a religion" and "a clear comprehension of life in the light of an intelligible theory." I indicated at the beginning that we would call this something-between-a-theory-and-a-religion, an *ideology*, a term highly conducive to misunderstanding. At this point let me stress only the *temporal* element in world views which might be called ideological: they are grouped around *a utopian simplification of historical perspective* (salvation, conquest, reform, happiness, rationality, technological mastery) in accordance with newly developing identity potentials. Whatever else ideology is (30, 39), and whatever transitory or lasting social forms it takes, we will tentatively view it here and discuss it later—*as a necessity for the growing ego* which is involved in the succession of generations, and in adolescence is committed to some new synthesis of past and future: a synthesis which must include but transcend the past, even as identity does.

We proceed to *Identity Consciousness* (V, 2) the ancestors of which are *Doubt* and *Shame* (II, 2). They counteract and complicate the sense of autonomy, i.e., the acceptance of the psychosocial fact of being, once and for all, a separate individual, who actually and figuratively must stand on his own feet. Here, I beg to quote myself (8): "Shame is an emotion insufficiently studied,[12] because in our civilization it is so early and easily absorbed by guilt. Shame supposes that one is completely exposed and conscious of being looked at: in one word, self-conscious. One is visible and not ready to be visible; which is why we dream of shame as a situation in which we are stared at in a condition of incomplete dress. Shame is early expressed in an impulse to bury one's face, or to sink, right then and there, into the ground. But this, I think, is essentially rage turned against the self. He who is ashamed would like to force the world not to look at him, not to notice his exposure. He would like to destroy the eyes of the world. Instead he must wish for his own invisibility. . . . Doubt is the brother of shame. Where shame is dependent on the consciousness of being upright and exposed, doubt, so clinical observation leads me to believe, has much to do with a consciousness of having a front and a back—and especially a 'behind.' . . . This basic sense of doubt in whatever one has left behind forms a substratum for later and more verbal forms of compulsive doubting; which finds its adult expression in paranoiac fears concerning hidden persecutors and secret persecutions threatening from behind and from within the behind." Identity Consciousness then is a new edition of that original *doubt*, which concerned the trustworthiness of the training adults and the trustworthiness of the child himself—only that in adolescence, such self-conscious doubt concerns the reliability and reconcilability of the whole span of childhood which is now to be left behind. The obligation now to achieve an identity, not only distinct but also distinctive, is apt to arouse a painful over-all *ashamedness*, somehow comparable to the original shame (and rage) over being visible all around to all-knowing adults—only that such potential shame now adheres to one's identity as a being with a *public history*, exposed to *age-mates* and *leaders*. All of this, in the normal course of events, is outbalanced by that *Self-Certainty*, which comes from the accrued sense of an ever increased identity at the conclusion of each previous crisis, a certainty now characterized by an increasing sense of independence from the family as the matrix of childhood identifications.

Among the societal phenomena corresponding to this second conflict there is a universal trend toward some form of *uniformity* (and sometimes to special uniforms or distinctive clothing) through which incomplete self-certainty, for a time, can hide in a group certainty, such as is provided by the badges as well as the sacrifices of investitures, confirmations and initiations. Even those who care to differ radically must evolve a certain uniformity of differing (Snobs, Zoot-suiters). These and less obvious uniformities are supported by the institution of comprehensive *shaming* among peers, a judgmental give-and-take and free banding together which leaves only a few "holding the bag" in painful (if sometimes creative) isolation.

The matter of the choice of a *Negative Identity* (V, 3) as against *free Role Experimentation* has been discussed. The position of these terms on the chart signifies their obvious connection with the earlier conflict (III, 3) between free *Initiative* (in reality, fantasy, and play) and Oedipal guilt. Where the identity crisis breaks through to the Oedipal crisis and beyond it, to a crisis of trust, the choice of a negative identity remains the only form of initiative, complete denial of guilt or complete denial of ambition the only possible ways of managing guilt. On the other hand, the normal expression of relatively guilt-free initiative at this stage is a kind of disciplined role experimentation which follows the unwritten codes of adolescent subsocieties.

Of the social institutions which undertake to channel as they encourage such initiative, and to provide atonement as they appease guilt, we may point here, again, to *initiations* and *confirmations*: they strive, within an atmosphere of mythical timelessness, to combine some form of sacrifice or submission with an energetic guidance toward sanctioned and circumscribed ways of action—a combination which assures the development in the novice of an optimum of compliance with a maximum sense of fellowship and free choice. This ego aspect of the matter (namely, the achievement of a sense of a choice as a result of ritual regimentation) as yet awaits study and integration with the better explored sexual aspects of initiation rites and related rituals, official or spontaneous. Armies, of course, utilize this potentiality.

As we approach the middle region of the chart, we find that a more detailed discussion of the terms used has already been offered. Extreme *Work Paralysis* (V, 4) is the logical sequence of a deep sense of inadequacy (regressed to a sense of basic mistrust) of one's general equipment. Such a sense of inadequacy, of course, does not usually reflect a true lack of potential: it may, rather, convey the unrealistic demands made by an ego ideal willing to settle only for omnipotence or omniscience; it may express the fact that the immediate social environment does not have a niche for the individual's true gifts; or it may reflect the paradoxical fact that an individual in early school life was seduced into a specialized precocity which early outdistanced his identity development. All of these reasons, then, may exclude the individual from that experimental competition in play and work through which he learns to find and to insist on *his* kind of achievement and work identity.

Social institutions support the strength and the distinctiveness of work identity by offering those who are still learning and experimenting a certain *status-of-the-moratorium,* an apprenticeship or discipleship characterized by defined duties, sanctioned competitions, and special freedoms, and yet potentially integrated with the hierarchies of expectable jobs and careers, castes and classes, guilds and unions.

In Box V, 5 we again meet the diagonal, and the over-all focus of this paper; crossing it we enter the area of psychosocial elements which are not derivatives but precursors of future psychosocial crises. The first such element (V, 6) is *Sexual Identity* vs. *Bisexual Diffusion,* the most immediate precursor of *Intimacy* vs. *Isolation.* Here the sexual mores of cultures and classes make for immense differences in the psychosocial differentiation of masculine and feminine (32), and in the age, kind, and ubiquity of genital activity. These differences can obscure the common fact discussed above, namely, that the development of psychosocial intimacy is not possible without a firm sense of identity. Bisexual diffusion can lead young adults toward two deceptive developments. Induced by special mores, or otherwise seduced, they may foreclose their identity development by concentrating on early genital activity without intimacy; or, on the contrary, they may concentrate on social or intellectual status values which underplay the genital element, with a resulting permanent weakness or genital polarization with the other sex. Different mores (27) demand from some the ability to postpone genital activity, and from others, the early ability to make it a "natural" part of life: in either case, special problems ensue which may well impair true heterosexual intimacy in young adulthood.

Social institutions here offer ideological rationales for a *prolongation of the psychosexual moratorium* in the form of complete sexual abstinence, in the form of genital activity without social commitment, or in the form of sexual play without genital engagement (petting). What a group's or an individual's "libido economy" will stand for, depends to some extent on the identity gain which accrues from such preferred sexual behavior.

The study of horizontal V of the chart, then, reveals certain systematic consistencies in the described elements of identity diffusion, and in those of identity formation. As pointed out parenthetically, these consistencies correspond to certain social institutions, which (in ways still to be elucidated) support the ego needs and ego functions subsumed under the term identity. In fact, the two remaining boxes of horizontal V (which at any rate are marginal to this clinical section) cannot be approached at all without a discussion of social institutions. The prime institution which awaits clarification here is that system of ideals which societies present to the young individual in the explicit or implicit form of an *ideology*. To ideology we may, in tentative summary, ascribe the function of offering youth (1) an overly clear perspective of the future, encompassing all foreseeable time, and thus counteracting individual "time diffusion"; (2) an opportunity for the exhibition of some uniformity of appearance and action counteracting individual identity consciousness; (3) inducement to collective role and work experimentation which can counteract a sense of inhibition and personal guilt; (4) submission to leaders who as "big brothers" escape the ambivalence of the parent-child relation; (5) introduction into the ethos of the prevailing technology, and thus into sanctioned and regulated competition; and (6) a seeming correspondence between the internal world of ideals and evils, on the one hand, and, on the other, of the outer world with its organized goals and dangers in real space and time: a geographic-historical framework for the young individual's budding identity.

I am aware of having, in the conclusion of a pathographic sketch, "sketched in" some references to phenomena which are the domain of social science. I can justify this only with the assumption that clinical work, in cutting through the immense diversity of individual pathology in order to arrive at some workable generalities, may well come upon an aspect of matters institutional which the historical and the economic approach has necessarily neglected. Here, however, we must first attempt to bring some order into the terminological household of our own field, and this especially where it overlaps with areas of social science.

Societal: Ego and Environment

1.—It has not escaped the reader that the term identity covers much of what has been called the self by a variety of workers, be it in the form of a self-concept (George H. Mead, 31), a self-system (Harry S. Sullivan, 42), or in that of fluctuating self-experiences described by Schilder (38), Federn (14), and others.[13] Within psychoanalytic ego psychology, Hartmann, above all, has circumscribed this general area more clearly when in discussing the so-called *libidinal cathexis of the ego in narcissism*, he comes to the conclusion that it is rather a self which is thus being cathected. He advocates a term "*self-representation*," as differentiated from "object representation" (22). This self-representation was, less systematically, anticipated by Freud in his occasional references to the ego's "attitudes toward the self" and to fluctuating cathexes bestowed upon this self in labile states of "self-esteem" (19). In this paper, we are concerned with the *genetic continuity* of such a self-representation—a continuity which must lastly be ascribed to the work of the ego. No other inner agency could accomplish the selective accentuation of significant identifications throughout childhood; and the gradual integration of self-images in anticipation of an identity. It is for this reason that I have called identity, at first, ego identity. But in brashly choosing a name analogous to "ego ideal," I have opened myself to the query as to what the relationship of these two concepts is.

Freud assigned the *internalized perpetuation* of cultural influences to the functions of the "superego or ego ideal" which was to represent the commands and the prohibitions emanating from the environment and its traditions. Let us compare two statements of Freud's which are relevant here. "The super-ego of the child is not really built up on the model of the parents, but on that of the parents' super-ego; it takes over the same content, it becomes the vehicle of tradition and of all the age-long values which have been handed down in this way from generation to generation. You may easily guess what great help is afforded by the recognition of the super-ego in understanding the social behavior of man, in grasping the problem of delinquency, for example, and perhaps, too, in providing us with some practical hints upon education. . . . Mankind never lives completely in the present. The *ideologies of the super-ego*[14] perpetuate the past, the traditions of the race and the people, which yield but slowly to the influence of the present and to new developments, and, so long as they work through the super-ego, play an important part in man's life" (18). Freud, it is to be noted here, speaks of the "ideologies of the super-ego," thus giving the superego ideational content; yet he also refers to it as a "vehicle," i.e., as a part of the psychic system through which ideas work. It would seem that by ideologies of the superego Freud means the superego's specific contributions to the archaic, to the magic in the inner coerciveness of ideologies.

In a second statement Freud acknowledges the social side of the ego ideal. "The ego-ideal is of great importance for the understanding of group psychology. Besides its individual side, this ideal has a social side; it is also the common ideal of a family, a class, or a nation" (19).

It would seem that the terms superego and ego ideal have come to be distinguished by their different relation to phylogenetic and to ontogenetic history. The superego is conceived as a more archaic and thoroughly internalized representative of the evolutionary principle of morality, of man's *congenital proclivity* toward the development of a primitive, categorical conscience. Allied with (ontogenetically) early introjects, the superego remains a rigidly vindictive and punitive inner agency of "blind" morality. The ego ideal, however, seems to be more flexibly bound to the ideals of the particular *historical period* and thus is closer to the ego function of reality testing.

Ego identity (if we were to hold on to this term and to this level of discourse) would in comparison be even closer to *social reality* in that as a subsystem of the ego it would test, select, and integrate the self-representations derived from the psychosocial crises of childhood. It could be said to be characterized by the more or less *actually attained but forever to-be-revised* sense of the reality of the self within social reality; while the imagery of the ego ideal could be said to represent a set of *to-be-strived-for but forever not-quite-attainable ideal* goals for the self.

However, in using the word self in the sense of Hartmann's self-representation, one opens the whole controversy to a radical consideration. One could argue that it may be wise in matters of the ego's perceptive and regulative dealings with its self to reserve the designation "ego" for the subject, and to give the designation "self" to the object. The ego, then, as a central organizing agency, is during the course of life faced with a changing self which, in turn, demands to be synthesized with abandoned and anticipated selves. This suggestion would be applicable to the *body ego*, which could be said to be the part of the self provided by the attributes of the organism, and, therefore, might more appropriately be called the body self. It concerns the ego ideal as the representative of the ideas, images, and configurations, which serve the persistent comparison with an *ideal self*. It, finally, would apply to what I have called *ego identity*. What could consequently be called the *self-identity* emerges from all those experiences in which a sense of temporary self-diffusion was successfully contained by a renewed and ever more realistic self-definition and social recognition. *Identity formation thus can be said to have a self-aspect, and an ego aspect.* It is part of the ego in the sense that it represents the ego's synthesizing function in meeting one of its frontiers, namely, the actual social structure of the environment and the image of reality as transmitted to the child during successive childhood crises. (The other frontiers would be the id, and the demands made on the ego by our biological history and structure; the superego and the demands of our more primitively moralistic proclivities; and the ego ideal with its idealized parent images.) Identity, in this connection, has a claim to recognition as the adolescent ego's most important support, in the task of containing the post-pubertal id, and in balancing the then newly invoked superego as well as the again overly demanding ego ideal.

Until the matter of ego vs. self is sufficiently defined to permit a terminological decision, I shall use the bare term identity in order to suggest a social function of the ego which results, in adolescence, in a relative psychosocial equilibrium essential to the tasks of young adulthood.

2.—The word "psychosocial" so far has had to serve as an emergency bridge between the so-called "biological" formulations of psychoanalysis and newer ones which take the cultural environment into more systematic consideration.

The so-called basic *biological* orientation of psychoanalysis has gradually become a habitual kind of *pseudo biology*, and this especially in the conceptualization (or lack thereof) of man's "environment." In psychoanalytic writings the terms "outer world" or "environment" are often used to designate an uncharted area which is said to be outside merely because it fails to be inside—inside the individual's somatic skin, or inside his psychic systems, or inside his self in the widest sense. Such a vague and yet omnipresent "outerness" by necessity assumes a number of ideological connotations, and, in fact, assumes the character of a number of world images: sometimes "the outer world" is conceived of as reality's conspiracy against the infantile wish world; sometimes as the (indifferent or annoying) fact of the existence of other people; and then again as the (at least partially benevolent) presence of maternal care. But even in the recent admission of the significance of the "mother-child relationship," a stubborn tendency persists to treat the mother-child unit as a "biological" entity more or less isolated from its cultural surroundings which then, again, becomes an "environment" of vague supports or of blind pressures and mere "conventions." Thus, step for step, we are encumbered by the remnants of juxtapositions which were once necessary and fruitful enough: for it was important to establish the fact that moralistic and hypocritical social demands are apt to crush the adult and to exploit the child. It was important to conceptualize certain intrinsic antagonisms between the individual's and society's energy households. However, the implicit conclusion that an individual ego could exist against or without a specifically human "environment," i.e., social organization, is senseless; and as for its "biological" orientation, such an implicit assumption threatens to isolate psychoanalytic theory from the rich ecological insights of modern biology.

It is, again, Hartmann (23) who opens the way to new considerations. His statement that the human infant is born preadapted to an "average expectable environment" implies a more truly biological as well as an inescapably societal formulation. For not even the very best of mother-child relationships could, by themselves, account for that subtle and complex "milieu" which permits a human baby not only to survive but also to develop his potentialities for growth and uniqueness. Man's ecology includes among its dimensions constant natural, historical, and technological readjustment; which makes it at once obvious that only a perpetual social metabolism and a constant (if ever so imperceptible) restructuring of tradition can safeguard for each new generation of infants anything approaching an "average expectability" of environment. Today, when rapid technological changes have taken the lead, the matter of establishing by scientific means and of preserving in flexible forms an "average expectable" continuity in child rearing and education has, in fact, become a matter of human survival.

The specific kind of preadaptedness of the human infant (namely, the readiness to grow by predetermined steps through institutionalized psychosocial crises) calls not only for one basic environment, but for a whole chain of such successive environments. As the child "adapts" in spurts and stages, he has a claim, at any given stage reached, to the next "average expectable environment." In other words, the human environment must permit and safeguard a series of more or less discontinuous and yet culturally and psychologically consistent steps, each extending further along the radius of expanding life tasks. All of this makes man's so-called biological adaptation a matter of life cycles developing within their community's changing history. Consequently, a psychoanalytic sociology faces the task of conceptualizing man's environment as the persistent endeavor of the older and more adult egos to join in the organizational effort of providing an integrated series of average expectable environments for the young egos.

3.—In a recent paper which thoughtfully, yet somewhat sweepingly reviews efforts at approaching the relation of culture and personality, Hartmann, Kris, and Loewenstein state: "Cultural conditions could and should be viewed also with the question in mind which and what kind of opportunities for ego functions in a sphere free from conflict they invite or inhibit" (24). In regard to the possibility of studying the reflection of such "cultural conditions" in the psychoanalysis of individuals, the writers seem less encouraging. They state: "Analysts too are aware of differences of behavior caused by cultural conditions; they are not devoid of that common sense which has always stressed these differences, but their impact on the analytic observer tends to decrease as work progresses and as available data move from the periphery to the center, that is from manifest behavior to data, part of which is accessible only to an analytic investigation." The present paper ventures to suggest that rather central problems of ego development, which are, indeed, "accessible only to an analytic investigation," demand that the psychoanalyst's awareness of cultural differences go well beyond that "common sense" which the three authors (being themselves outstanding cosmopolitans) seem to find sufficient in this particular area of observation, while they would assuredly urge a more "analyzed" common sense in other areas.

In order to approach this whole matter psychoanalytically, it may well be necessary for the individual psychoanalyst to ask himself what particular configuration of drives, defenses, capabilities, and opportunities led him into the choice of this ever-expanding field. Some search in this area may clarify the fact that some of the most heated and stubborn answers to the question of what psychoanalysis *is* or *is not* originate in another question of great urgency, namely: what psychoanalysis *must be* (or *must remain or become*) to a particular worker because a particular psychoanalytic "identity" has become a cornerstone of his existence as a man, a professional, and a citizen. I am not denying here the necessity, in a suddenly expanding and unexpectedly popular field, to define the original sources of its inspiration and the fundamentals of its specific propriety. Yet, psychoanalysis, in its young history, has offered rich opportunities for a variety of identities: it gave new function and scope to such divergent endeavors as natural philosophy and Talmudic argument; medical tradition and missionary teaching; literary demonstration and the building of theory; social reform and the making of money. Psychoanalysis as a movement has harbored a variety of world images and utopias which originated in the various states of its history in a variety of countries, and this as a result of the simple fact that man, in order to be able to interact efficiently with other human beings, must, at intervals, make a *total orientation out of a given stage of partial knowledge*. Individual students of Freud thus found their identity best suited to certain early theses of his which promised a particular sense of psychoanalytic identity, and with it, an inspiring ideology. Similarly, overstated antitheses to some of Freud's tentative and transient theses have served as bases for professional and scientific identities of other workers in the field. Such identities easily find elaboration in ideological schools and in irreversible systematizations which do not permit of argument or change.

In speaking of scientific proof and scientific progress in a field which deals directly with the immediate needs of men, it is necessary to account not only for methodological, practical, and ethical factors, but also for the necessity of a professional identity backed by an ideological quasi synthesis of the available orientations. Sooner or later, then, training analyses must encompass the varieties of professional identity formation in candidates-for-training while theoretical teaching must throw light also on the ideological background of principal differences in what is felt to be most practical, most true, and most right at various stages of this developing field.

4.—The discussion of "professional identities" has necessarily led us beyond identity formation proper, to its derivatives in later, truly adult stages. I will make one more step into adulthood, before returning in conclusion, to the problem of ideological polarization as an aspect of the societal processes which meets a necessity of adolescent ego development.

I have already implied a hypothesis which goes beyond that of Hartmann, Kris, and Loewenstein, who state that "cultural conditions could and should be viewed *also*[15] with the question in mind which and what kind of opportunities for ego functions in a sphere free from conflict they invite or inhibit." It may well be that the relationship between the organized values and institutional efforts of societies, on the one hand, and the mechanisms of ego synthesis, on the other, is more systematic; and that, at any rate, from a psychosocial point of view, basic social and cultural processes can *only* be viewed as the joint endeavor of adult egos to develop and maintain, through joint organization, a maximum of conflict-free energy in a mutually supportive psychosocial equilibrium. Only such organization is likely to give consistent support to the young egos at every step of their development.

I have characterized the psychosocial gains of adult ego development with the terms Intimacy, Generativity, and Integrity (VI,6–VII,7–VIII,8 on the chart). They denote a postadolescent development of libidinal cathexes in *intimate engagements;* in parenthood or other *forms of "generating"*;[16] and, finally, in the most *integrative experiences* and values accrued from a lifetime. All of these developments have ego aspects and social aspects; in fact, their very alternatives (Isolation, VI,6–Self-Absorption, VII,7–and Despair, VIII,8) can be held in check only by the individual's fitting participation in social endeavors which "invite opportunities for ego functions in spheres free from conflict." The older generation thus needs the younger one as much as the younger one depends on the older; and it would seem that it is in the sphere of this mutuality of drives and interest throughout the development of the older as well as the younger generations that certain basic and universal values such as love, faith, truth, justice, order, work, etc., in all of their compensatory power and defensive strength, become and remain important joint achievements of individual ego development and of the social process. In fact, as our clinical histories begin to reveal, these values provide indispensable support for the ego development of the growing generations, in that they give some specific superindividual consistency to parental conduct (although *kinds* of consistency–including consistent kinds of being inconsistent–vary with value systems and personality types).

The intrinsic complication and the peculiar social pathology adhering to the *verbal conventions* and *formal institutions* which communicate and perpetuate social values periodically call for special societal processes which will recreate the "average expectability" of the environments either through ceremonial rededication, or through systematic reformulation. In both cases, selected leaders and elites feel called upon to demonstrate a convincing, a "charismatic" kind of generalized generativity, i.e., a superpersonal interest in the maintenance and the rejuvenation of institutions. In recorded history, some such leaders are registered as "great"; they, it seems, are able, out of the deepest personal conflicts to derive the energy which meets their period's specific needfulness for a resynthesis of the prevalent world image. At any rate, only through constant rededication will institutions gain the active and inspired investment of new energy from their young members. More theoretically stated: only by maintaining, in its institutionalized values, meaningful correspondences to the main crises of ego development, does a society manage to have at the disposal of its particular group identity a maximum of the conflict-free energy accrued from the childhood crises of a majority of its young members.[17]

Before briefly applying this general assumption to ideology, I must ask the reader to take one more look at the chart. In boxes V,6–V,7–and V,8 he will find whatever indication I can give of the precursors in adolescence of what later on is Intimacy, Generativity, and Integrity. The struggle for *Sexual Identity*, V,6, while, at first, consumed with the question as to what kind of a male or female one is, through the selective search for *Intimacy*, VI,6, approaches the problem of a choice of a future co-parent. The clarification, through a firmer identity formation, of one's status as a *follower* (of some) and a *leader* (of others) V,7, permits the early development of a responsibility toward younger age-mates which, although an important social phenomenon in its own right, is a precursor of the sense of responsibility for the next generation *(Generativity)* VII,7. Finally, some form of *Ideological Polarization*, V,8, some breakdown of the multiplicity of values into a few which coerce commitment, must be part and parcel of this gradual reversal of roles, through which the "identified" individual becomes a figure of identification for the young. Such polarization, however, cannot fail eventually to become a critical part of the problem of *Integrity*, VIII,8: a matter which we saw reflected in Shaw's statement (41): that he "succeeded only too well" in living the public identity "G.B.S.," i.e., in the polarization of his propensities for acting like an actor on the stage of life, and for acting as a reformer in social reality.

5.–Shaw, of course, was a studiedly spectacular man. But, to extend a Shavianism quoted above: a clown is often not only the best but also the most sincere part of the Great Show. It is, therefore, worth while at this point to review the words chosen by Shaw to characterize the story of his "conversion": "I was *drawn into* the Socialist *revival* of the early eighties, among Englishmen *intensely serious* and *burning with indignation* at very *real* and very *fundamental evils* that affected *all the world*." The words here italicized convey to me the following implications. "Drawn into": an ideology has a compelling power. "Revival": it consists of a traditional force in the state of rejuvenation. "Intensely serious": it permits even the cynical to make an investment of sincerity. "Burning with indignation": it gives to the need for repudiation the sanction of righteousness. "Real": it projects a vague inner evil on a circumscribed horror in reality. "Fundamental": it promises participation in an effort at basic reconstruction of society. "All the world": it gives structure to a totally defined world image. Here, then, are the elements by which a group identity harnesses in the service of its ideology the young individual's aggressive and discriminative energies, and encompasses, as it completes it, the individual's identity. Thus, identity and ideology are two aspects of the same process. Both provide the necessary condition for further individual maturation and, with it, for the next higher form of identification, namely, the *solidarity linking common identities.* For the need to bind irrational self-hate and irrational repudiation makes young people, on occasion, mortally compulsive and conservative even where and when they seem most anarchic and radical; the same need makes them potentially "ideological," i.e., more or less explicitly in search of a world image held together by what Shaw called "a clear comprehension of life in the light of an intelligible theory."

As far as Fabian Socialists are concerned, Shaw seems fully justified in using terms characterizing an ideology of marked intellectual brilliance. More generally, an ideological system is a coherent body of shared images, ideas, and ideals which (whether based on a formulated dogma, an implicit *Weltanschauung,* a highly structured world image, a political creed, or a "way of life") provides for the participants a coherent, if systematically simplified, over-all orientation in space and time, in means and ends.

The word "ideology" itself has somewhat of a bad name. By their very nature ideologies contradict other ideologies as "inconsistent" and hypocritical; and an over-all critique of ideology characterizes its persuasive simplifications as a systematic form of collective hypocrisy (30). For it is true that the average adult, and, in fact, the average community, if not acutely engaged in some ideological polarization, are apt to consign ideology to a well-circumscribed compartment in their lives, where it remains handy for periodical rituals and rationalizations, but will do no undue harm to other business at hand. Yet, the fact that ideologies are simplified conceptions of what is to come (and thus later can serve as rationalizations for what has come about) does not preclude the possibility that at certain stages of individual development and at certain periods in history, ideological polarization, conflict, and commitment correspond to an inescapable inner need. Youth needs to base its rejections and acceptances on ideological alternatives vitally related to the existing range of alternatives for identity formation.

Ideologies seem to provide meaningful combinations of the oldest and the newest in a group's ideals. They thus channel the forceful earnestness, the sincere asceticism, and the eager indignation of youth toward that social frontier where the struggle between conservatism and radicalism is most alive. On that frontier, fanatic ideologists do their busy work and psychopathic leaders their dirty work; but there, also, true leaders create significant solidarities. All ideologies ask for, as the prize for the promised possession of a future, uncompromising commitment to some absolute hierarchy of values and some rigid principle of conduct: be that principle total obedience to tradition, if the future is the eternalization of ancestry; total resignation, if the future is to be of another world; total martial discipline, if the future is to be reserved for some brand of armed superman; total inner reform, if the future is perceived as an advance edition of heaven on earth; or (to mention only one of the ideological ingredients of our time) complete pragmatic abandon to the processes of production and to human teamwork, if unceasing production seems to be the thread which holds present and future together. It is in the totalism and exclusiveness of some ideologies that the superego is apt to regain its territory from identity: for when established identities become outworn or unfinished ones threaten to remain incomplete, special crises compel men to wage holy wars, by the cruelest means, against those who seem to question or threaten their unsafe ideological bases.

We may well pause to ponder briefly the over-all fact that the technological and economic developments of our day encroach upon all traditional group identities and solidarities such as may have developed in agrarian, feudal, patrician, or mercantile ideologies. As has been shown by many writers, such over-all development seems to result in a loss of a sense of cosmic wholeness, of providential planfulness, and of heavenly sanction for the means of production (and destruction). In large parts of the world, this seems to result in a ready fascination with totalistic world views, views predicting milleniums and cataclysms, and advocating self-appointed mortal gods. Technological centralization today can give small groups of such fanatic ideologists the concrete power of totalitarian state machines (13).

Psychoanalysis has made some contributions to the understanding of these developments especially in so far as they reflect the universal anxieties, inner dependencies and vulnerabilities adhering to the common fact of human childhood. Psychoanalysis can also help to understand the fact that even in civilized beings the superego's paternalistic-primitive simplicity may call for an irrational trust in superpolice chiefs on earth, now that the heavenly discipline which encompassed earlier world images seems to have lost its convincing firmness. However, the application of the psychoanalytic instrument to the questions as to how man changes in his depth as he changes the expanses of his environment, and as to who is affected (and how, and how deeply), by technological and ideological changes (13)—these questions must await better formulations of the ego's relationship to work techniques, to the technological "environment," and to the prevalent division of labor.

6.—In a recent seminar in Jerusalem[18] I had an opportunity to discuss with Israeli scholars and clinicians the question of what the identity of an "Israeli" is, and thus to envisage one extreme of contemporary ideological orientations. Israel fascinates both her friends and her enemies. A great number of ideological fragments from European history have found their way into the consciousness of this small state; and many of the identity problems which have occupied a century and a half of American history are being faced in Israel within a few years. A new nation is established on a distant coast (which does not seem to "belong" to anybody) out of oppressed minorities from many lands, a new identity based on imported ideals which are libertarian, puritanic, and messianic. Any discussion of Israel's manifold and most immediate problems sooner or later leads to the extraordinary accomplishments and the extraordinary ideological problems posed by the pioneer Zionist settlers (now a small minority) who make up what is known as the Kibbutz movement. These European ideologists, given—as it were—a *historical moratorium* created by the peculiar international and national status of Palestine first in the Ottoman Empire and then in the British mandate, were able to establish and to fortify a significant *utopian bridgehead* for Zionist ideology. In his "homeland," and tilling his very home soil, the "ingathered" Jew was to overcome such evil identities as result from eternal wandering, merchandising, and intellectualizing (9) and was to become *whole* again in body and mind, as well as in nationality. That the Kibbutz movement has created a hardy, responsible, and inspired type of individual, nobody could deny, although certain details of its educational system (such as the raising of children, from the very beginning, in Children's Houses, and the rooming together of boys and girls through the high school years) are under critical scrutiny, both in Israel and abroad. The fact is, however, that in Israel a utopia was established on a frontier exposed all around, under conditions reminiscent of those faced by the Mormons. This historical fact is the only possible framework for judging the rationale and the rationalizations of the style of life which ensued. For no doubt, these pioneers (comparable to this country's settlers, who, in turn, utilized the historical moratorium offered by the discovery of an empty continent, for the establishment of a new "way of life") provided a new nation, sprung up overnight, with a historical ideal. A legitimate question, however, and one not too foreign to this country's historians, concerns the relationships of a revolutionary elite to those who subsequently crowd into and thrive on the lands occupied and on the gains made.[19] In Israel, the by now somewhat exclusive elite of Kibbutzniks faces that incomparably larger part of the population which represents an ideologically all but indigestible mixture: the masses of African and Oriental immigrants, powerful organized labor, the big city dwellers, the religious orthodoxy, the new state bureaucracy—and then, of course, the "good old" mercantile class of middlemen. Furthermore, the more uncompromising part of the Kibbutz movement has not failed to place itself between the two worlds to both of which Zionism maintains strong historical bonds: American and British Jewry (which bought much of the Kibbutz land from Arab absentee landlords) and Soviet Communism, to which the (shall we say) communalistic Kibbutz movement[20] felt ideologically close—only to be repudiated by Moscow as another form of deviationism.

The Kibbutz movement thus is one example of a modern ideological utopia which freed unknown energies in youths who considered themselves as of one "people," and created a (more or less explicit) group ideal of pervading significance—if of quite unpredictable historical fate in an industrial world. However, Israel is, undoubtedly, one of the most ideology-conscious countries that ever existed; no "peasants" nor workmen ever argued more about the far-reaching meanings of daily decisions. The subtler meanings of ideology for identity formation can probably be fathomed best by comparing highly verbal ideologies with those transitory systems of conversion and aversion which exist in any society, in that no-man's land between childhood and adulthood more or less derisively called adolescence—exist as the most meaningful part of a young person's or a young group's life, often without the knowledge, or indeed, curiosity, of the adults around them. It must be assumed that much of the spontaneous polarization of tastes, opinions and slogans which occupy the arguments of youths, and much of the sudden impulse to join in destructive behavior, are loose ends of identity formation waiting to be tied together by some ideology.

7.—In the pathographic section of this paper I have pointed to the *total choice* of a negative identity in individuals who could achieve such escape on the basis of autistic and regressive proclivities.

The escape of many gifted if unstable young individuals into a private utopia or, as another patient put it, a "majority of one," might not be necessary were it not for a general development to which they feel unable to submit, i.e., the increasing demand for standardization, uniformity and conformity which characterizes the present stage of this our individualistic civilization. In this country, the demand for large-scale conformity has not developed into explicit totalitarian ideologies; it has associated itself with the total dogmas of churches and with the stereotypes of businesslike behavior, but, on the whole, shuns political ideology. We appreciate as we study the capacity of our youth to manage the identity diffusion of an industrial democracy with simple trustfulness, with playful dissonance, with technical virtuosity, with "other-minded" solidarity (37)—and with a distaste for ideological explicitness. What exactly the implicit ideology of American youth (this most technological youth in the world) is—that is a fateful question, not to be lightly approached in a paper of this kind. Nor would one dare to assess in passing the changes which may be taking place in this ideology and in its implicitness, as a result of a world struggle which makes a military identity a necessary part of young adulthood in this country.

It is easier to delineate that malignant turn toward a *negative group identity* which prevails in some of the youth especially of our large cities, where conditions of economic, ethnic, and religious marginality provide poor bases for positive identities: here negative group identities are sought in spontaneous clique formations ranging all the way from neighborhood gangs and jazz mobs, to dope rings, homosexual circles, and criminal gangs. Clinical experience can be expected to make significant contributions to this problem. Yet, we may well warn ourselves against an uncritical transfer of clinical terms, attitudes, and methods to such public problems. Rather, we may come back to a point made earlier: teachers, judges, and psychiatrists, who deal with youth, come to be significant representatives of that strategic act of "recognition" (the act through which society "identifies" its young members and thus contributes to their developing identity) which was described at the beginning of this paper. If, for simplicity's sake, or in order to accommodate ingrown habits of law or psychiatry, they diagnose and treat as a criminal, as a constitutional misfit, as a derelict doomed by his upbringing, or–indeed–as a deranged patient, a young person who, for reasons of personal or social marginality, is close to choosing a negative identity, that young person may well put his energy into becoming exactly what the careless and fearful community expects him to be–and make a total job of it.

It is hoped that the theory of identity, in the long run, can contribute more to this problem than to sound a warning.

Summary.–In my attempt to circumscribe the problem of identity I have been "all over the map." I do not propose to leave the matter in this condition: as far as is possible, studies taking into account the specific dynamic nature of selected media (life history, case history, dream life, ideology) will follow. In the meantime, and in summary: identity, in outbalancing at the conclusion of childhood the potentially malignant dominance of the infantile superego, permits the individual to forego excessive self-repudiation and the diffused repudiation of otherness. Such freedom provides a necessary condition for the ego's power to integrate matured sexuality, ripened capacities, and adult commitments. The histories of our young patients illustrate the ways in which aggravated identity crises may result from special genetic causes and from specific dynamic conditions. Such studies, in turn, throw new light on those more or less institutionalized rites and rituals, associations, and movements through which societies and subsocieties grant youth a world between childhood and adulthood: a psychosocial moratorium during which extremes of *subjective experience*, alternatives of *ideological choice*, and potentialities of *realistic commitment* can become the subject of social play and of joint mastery.

References

1. Ackerman, N. W. "Social Role and Total Personality," *American Journal of Orthopsychiatry*, XXI (1951), 1-17.

2. Bateman, J. F., and Dunham, H. W. "The State Mental Hospital as a Specialized Community Experience," *American Journal of Psychiatry*, CV (1948), 445-49.

3. Benedict, R. "Continuities and Discontinuities in Cultural Conditioning," *Psychiatry*, I (1938), 161-67.

4. Bibring, E. "The Mechanism of Depression." P. Greenacre (ed.), in *Affective Disorders*. New York: International Universities Press, 1953.

5. Blos, P. "The Contribution of Psychoanalysis to the Treatment of Adolescents," in M. Heiman (ed.), *Psychoanalysis and Social Work*. New York: International Universities Press, 1953.

6. Brenman, M. "On Teasing and Being Teased: And the Problem of 'Moral Masochism,'" *The Psychoanalytic Study of the Child*, VII. New York: International Universities Press, 1952. Pp. 264-85.

7. Burlingham, D. *Twins*. New York: International Universities Press, 1952.

8. Erikson, E. H. "Ego Development and Historical Change," *The Psychoanalytic Study of the Child*, II. New York: International Universities Press, 1946. Pp. 359-96.

9. Erikson, E. H. *Childhood and Society*. New York: W. W. Norton, 1950. London: Imago Publishing Co., 1951.

10. Erikson, E. H. "Growth and Crises of the 'Healthy Personality,'" in M. J. E. Senn (ed.), *Symposium on the Healthy Personality*, Supplement II to the transactions of the fourth conference on *Problems of Infancy and Childhood*. New York: Josiah Macy, Jr. Foundation, 1950.

11. Erikson, E. H. "On the Sense of Inner Identity," in *Health and Human Relations*. New York: The Blakiston Company, 1953.

12. Erikson, E. H. "The Dream Specimen of Psychoanalysis." *Journal of the American Psychoanalytic Association*, II (1954), 5-56.

13. Erikson, E. H. "Wholeness and Totality," in C. J. Friedrich (ed.), *Totalitarianism*, Proceedings of a conference held at the American Academy of Arts and Sciences, March 1953. Cambridge: Harvard University Press, 1954.

14. Federn, P. *Ego Psychology and the Psychoses*. New York: Basic Books, 1952.

15. Freud, A. *The Ego and the Mechanisms of Defense*. New York: International Universities Press, 1946.

16. Freud, A. in collaboration with Dann, S. "An Experiment in Group Upbringing," in *The Psychoanalytic Study of the Child*, VI. New York: International Universities Press, 1951. Pp. 127-68.

17. Freud, S. (1926) "Ansprache an die Mitglieder des Vereins B'nai B'rith," in *Gesammelte Werke*, XVII. London: Imago Publishing Co., 1941. Pp. 49-53.

18. Freud, S. (1932) *New Introductory Lectures on Psychoanalysis*. Lecture 31: The Anatomy of the Mental Personality. New York: W. W. Norton, 1933.

19. Freud, S. (1914) "On Narcissism: An Introduction," *Collected Papers*, IV. London: Hogarth Press, 1948.

20. Ginsburg, S. W. "The Role of Work," *Samiksa*, VIII (1954).

21. Hartmann, H., Kris, E., and Loewenstein, R. M. "Notes on the Theory of

Aggression," in *The Psychoanalytic Study of the Child*, III and IV. New York: International Universities Press, 1949. Pp. 9-36.

22. Hartmann, H. "Comments on the Psychoanalytic Theory of the Ego," in *The Psychoanalytic Study of the Child*, V. New York: International Universities Press, 1951. Pp. 74-96.

23. Hartmann, H. "Ego Psychology and the Problem of Adaptation," in D. Rapaport (ed.), *Organization and Pathology of Thought*. New York: Columbia University Press, 1951.

24. Hartmann, H., Kris, E., and Loewenstein, R. M. "Some Psychoanalytic Comments on 'Culture and Personality,'" in G. B. Wilbur and W. Muensterberger (eds.), *Psychoanalysis and Culture*. New York: International Universities Press, 1951.

25. Hendrick, I. "Work and the Pleasure Principle," *Psychoanalytic Quarterly*, XII (1943), 311-29.

26. James, W. "The Will to Believe," *New World*, V (1896).

27. Kinsey, A. C., Pomeroy, W. B., and Martin, C. E. *Sexual Behavior in the Human Male*. Philadelphia: W. B. Saunders Co., 1948.

28. Knight, R. P. "Management and Psychotherapy of the Borderline Schizophrenic Patient," *Bulletin Menninger Clinic*, XVII (1953), 139-50.

29. Kris, E. "On Preconscious Mental Processes," in *Psychoanalytic Explorations in Art*. New York: International Universities Press, 1952.

30. Mannheim, K. *Utopia and Ideology*. New York: Harcourt, Brace, 1949.

31. Mead, G. H. *Mind, Self and Society*. Chicago: University of Chicago Press, 1934.

32. Mead, M. *Male and Female*. New York: William Morrow, 1949.

33. Newcomb, T. M., *et al.* (eds.). *Readings in Social Psychology*. New York: Henry Holt and Co., 1953.

34. Piers, G. and Singer, M. B. *Shame and Guilt*. Springfield, Ill.: Charles C. Thomas, 1953.

35. Rapaport, D. *Emotions and Memory*. 2d ed. New York: International Universities Press, 1950.

36. Rapaport, D. "Some Metapsychological Considerations Concerning Activity and Passivity." Unpublished.

37. Riesman, D. *The Lonely Crowd*. New Haven: Yale University Press, 1950.

38. Schilder, P. *The Image and Appearance of the Human Body*. New York: International Universities Press, 1951.

39. Schilder, P. *Psychoanalysis, Man and Society*. New York: W. W. Norton, 1951.

40. Schwartz, M. S., and Will, G. T. "Low Morale and Mutual Withdrawal on a Mental Hospital Ward," *Psychiatry*, XVI (1953), 337-53.

41. Shaw, G. B. *Selected Prose*. New York: Dodd, Mead and Co., 1952.

42. Sullivan, H. S. *The Interpersonal Theory of Psychiatry*. New York: W. W. Norton, 1953.

MARGARET MEAD

Culture Change and Character Structure

As ANTHROPOLOGISTS, we deal with two levels of analysis—on the one hand, the study of the structure and functioning of social groups, in which, although detailed observations may be made on individual behavior, the psychology of the individual is not examined; and, on the other, the study of the relationships between the psychology of the individual, the culture within which he lives, and the structure and functioning of the social groups of which he is a member. Radcliffe-Brown has repeatedly argued that it is possible to give a self-contained account of a society, without recourse to any examination of the psychological structure of its individual members, and without invoking in any way the individual differences among them, except in so far as these differences are formally patterned. Thus, the study of culture as an abstraction based on observed traditional behavior of the members of a given group at a given period of time has proved a workable approach to a synchronic statement about many primitive societies.[1]

However, as soon as any diachronic questions are raised, the whole position is altered. If we are to avoid statements of action at a temporal distance, such as "the slowness of the industrial revolution in Germany was a major cause of World War I," or "the open frontier was responsible for the fluidity of the American class system," and substitute for them scientifically valid descriptions of social process—descriptions of how, in fact, an antecedent condition of society is converted into some subsequent condition—it seems necessary to include in our investigations a study of the individuals who are concerned in the change. We need to consider such individuals both as representatives of cultural regularities which are themselves undergoing change, and as specified persons who have been able to act in given ways because of the peculiarities of their own life histories. Many of the changes which are recorded in the long-time spans of conventional history (such as "the decay of the monarchy" or "the rise of popular government") occur sporadically in the behavior of individuals,

Reprinted from *Social Structure* (1949), pp. 18-34, by permission of the author and the publisher. (Copyright 1949, by Oxford University Press.) See also the author's "The Implications of Culture Change for Personality Development," *American Journal of Orthopsychiatry*, XXVII (1947), 633-46.

and only gradually become consolidated into identifiable pattern changes. While such changes are going on, innumerable moments of choice occur, and the explanation of the choices taken may often lie in idiosyncratic factors in the lives of key individuals. It seems probable, therefore, that, as we approach a study of diachronics, making contemporary studies of social change as it occurs, rather than relying upon reconstructions from haphazardly preserved and fragmentary materials, it will be necessary to develop methods of dealing with the relevant aspects of the individual psychology of the participants. Any systematic attempt to include the psychological structure of individuals must rely, of course, not only upon an adequate psychological theory, but also upon adequate cultural theories regarding the process of cultural standardization of behavior, the nature of character-formation, and the way in which idiosyncratic behavior is to be referred systematically to a cultural and societal base. Such an adequate theory will be dependent upon theoretical advances in a number of different fields.[2] This paper will attempt to introduce a preliminary degree of order into one aspect of this problem. It will deal with the sorts of regularities which can be discriminated in the character-structures of individuals in societies which are changing at different rates and with different degrees of culture-contact.

The Problem in a Homogeneous Society

The problems of describing the correspondences between the structure of a homogeneous, slowly changing society and the character-structure of the individuals who embody the culture of that society are beginning to be defined.[3] We have blocked out conceptually a large number of such areas as: the relationship between the representations of family structure and political structure in the psychology of the individual, or the relationship of both family and political structure to the conception of the supernational; the pattern of sequences of initiative and response characteristic of parent-child or child-child relationships as they appear also in the interaction between master and servant, leader and follower; and the correspondences between the types of sanction used in a society and the types of conscience-structure found in the individuals. We have already a considerable amount of observational work on, and analysis of, these problems, and, while the subject has in no sense been fully explored, some of the outlines at least may be said to have been sketched in.

In this preliminary attempt to introduce one degree of order into the data on cultural change, the unique features of each society and the special insights to be derived from a study of its particular institutions will no longer be emphasized. Instead, attention will be focused on those regularities of character-formation which are functions of cultural homogeneity. Here we shall be dealing with well-described societies, about which formal statements can be made with considerable confidence. On the other hand, all statements of regularities postulated for changing culture-contact societies will necessarily be tentative and, to a degree, suggesive rather than systematic.

The terms "homogeneous" and "slow-changing" will be used as synonyms, provided the rate of change of items of culture is less than the rate at which adults can assimilate the new items.[4] Cultures to which these terms apply will be contrasted with those which are changing rapidly. No rapidly changing culture has real homogeneity, since rapid change results in differences between generations comparable to differences in culture, in that there are groups of individuals, belonging to different generations, who embody different discriminable attitudes.

As relevant characteristics of personality development in homogeneous and slowly changing societies, we may identify: the *sequential consistency* between the experience of a growing child at one period and at another; the *summation* or total expression of the gamut of cultural experience in the behavior of the adult members of the society; the *prefiguring* of future experience as the child sees others go through sequences through which he will later go; the *consolidation* of past experience as the growing individual sees younger individuals go through sequences culturally identical with those through which he has passed; and the increasing *automaticity* of behavior and the consequent increasing *sureness* which accompany maturation.

These characteristics of growing up in a homogeneous society need little elaboration for anthropologists, who will recognize at once that an indulgent childhood and a harsh initiation—or an exacting childhood and indulged adolescence—may coexist within the learning pattern of a given culture, and that experience of such contrasts may have consistent implications for character-structure. They will often have documented the extent to which a single act—the presentation of a gift, the avoidance of an affinal relative, the arrangement of an offering—contains within its ritual idiom the major presuppositions of a culture. Whether we describe the resulting personality types in words implying ethical judgement,[5] or, in time, develop some neutral terms for the purpose is not relevant here. The products of homogeneity are a vanishing type at this period in history, but, as they constitute the group participating in the primary phase of culture-contact, an accurate appraisal of the regularities in their character formation is essential.

The Problem in Different Stages of Contact

By "primary culture-contact" I shall mean those situations in which an individual reared in one cultural setting has to adjust, either as an immigrant or as a native into whose group others immigrate, to another set of cultural values, both sets of values coming from homogeneous, slowly changing cultures. Whenever one part of this contact relationship is no longer to be referred to a homogeneous culture, but rather to some later stage of culture-contact, certain complexities are added to the picture. If, for example, a regiment of soldiers, all from the same remote rural region of the occident, come into face-to-face relations with a non-occidental people, the situation may have primary culture-contact character. If, on the other hand, the regiment is composed of men drawn from the mixed population of a metropolitan city, the contact may contain secondary as well as primary culture-contact features. A full "secondary culture-contact" condition occurs when both sets of individuals under discussion have been reared in groups already affected by primary or secondary culture-contacts, and in which representatives of homogeneous cultures are relatively rare, even aberrant. Because there may be any number of varieties of such culture-contact, no rigid distinction can be made between primary and secondary culture-contact. Even a very loose distinction, however, seems to be useful, although, of course, actual situations will not, in most cases, be as clear-cut as any systematic discussion makes them seem.

In primary culture-contact, the impact on character formation will differ systematically as between the effects of the new environment on the personalities of the immigrants, and the effects of such immigration of members of other cultures on the personalities of the native members of the community. Among the immigrants, we find a variety of adjustments, all derived from the fact that the immigrant brings to the new environment a personality shaped in a previous and different environment. He may, while living and working in the new culture, continue to refer all of his behavior to the values of his original culture, adjusting only to the concrete realities of his new situation—learning proper names, bus routes, how to give change—but continuing to interpret these activities in the old terms. He may enter the new culture so determined to become a part of it that he actually succeeds in putting large sections of his former life and values out of his consciousness, and even his use of his mother tongue may become stumbling or disappear altogether. He may pattern his relationship to the new culture in terms of work alone, continuing to live in a cultural enclave in all other respects. He may work among immigrants from his original culture but marry a wife from the new culture and channel his culture-contact relationships through a changing home pattern. He may continue to preserve only single items from the old culture—continue to take a newspaper from his former country, maintain membership in a national organization, or insist on the familiar old rituals at holiday time or for *rites de passage*, etc.

We may next consider the native population into whose society immigrants come. The content is of another order here, whether the immigrants enter in superordinate relationships as governors, and teachers, in coordinate relationships as traders or travelers, or in subordinate relationships as slaves, unskilled workers, or performers of socially devalued tasks. The study of this sort of contact situation may increase our understanding of the differences between culture contact and generation break. The native remains among his own people, surrounded by an environment to each detail of which he has learned to respond in a culturally coherent manner. Into this environment intrude individuals who either take the place of familiar figures or introduce into his life new types of events towards which he has no traditional behavior. His habitual responses are interrupted and distorted, even as he himself attempts to pursue an even course in a familiar world. As he makes one ineffective attempt after another to evoke intelligible responses from the immigrant—who stands in a familiar place and is often clothed like the native himself, but whose posture and gestures are all keyed to a different emphasis—the result is not a feeling that he must review his own character, but a feeling that his world has been fragmented. "In the beginning God gave to every people a cup of clay from which they drank their lives—our cup is broken," said the California Indians; "We have lost our road," said the Plains Indians, as the figures and forms of an immigrant and alien culture crowded into their lives.

The position of members of the older generation faced by drastic alteration in the behavior of their sons' generation is somewhat analogous to that of the native whose orientation is disturbed by the invasion of his familiar world by individuals with different sets of habits. The members of the older generation still see the cultural scene as theirs, and the behavior of the next generation as inappropriate and disruptive. In occasional instances, of course, the culture of the next generation may be accepted by the older generation as more valid than their own, and in that case they may invade it. Their disorientation is then more like that of the immigrant, while the younger generation is subjected to a disorientation more like that of the native.

Secondary culture-contact, even in its very simplest forms—as in the case of children of a group of Sicilian immigrants to a rural American community, or American Indian children whose parents have just been placed on a reservation—is a great deal more complicated than primary culture-contact. The growing child receives simultaneously impacts reflecting the original cultural values of his parents and impacts from the contemporary culture in which he is growing up. If his parents migrated from a rural economy to a large industrial center, he experiences a disciplinary pattern shaped on the farm combined with a wage-earning pattern fitted to the city. If his parents have come from another country, the language spoken at home may come to be a symbol of one part of life, that spoken at school of quite a different part. If his parents belong to a native group whose way of life has been disrupted by immigrants, he will experience no such sequence, but instead will be presented with both the native ways of his parents and the new ways of the immigrants as parts of one world in which he is being reared. Perhaps a useful analogy here is the matter-of-factness with which the child of parents who have seen the invention of the automobile or the airplane accepts automobiles, airplanes, and horses as all equally intelligible parts of transportation, without any realization of the sequence of invention. Events which have been sequential in the lives of his forebears become contemporaneous in his own life, and his responses will differ accordingly.

Individuals reared in a secondary culture-contact situation which has become stabilized may show a considerable degree of regularity in their character structure. In the United States, certain expectations may reasonably be entertained of the children of immigrant parents. Parental values will decrease in importance, and children and adolescents will turn more to their contemporaries for approval and disapproval. Sanctions, such as shame and pride, appropriate to such a horizontal organization will appear. If such a second generation group forms either a very large majority or a very small minority in a given society, the process of stabilization will be easier than if the group which has experienced secondary culture-contact and the group that has not are more evenly matched in size.

The patterns of behavior developed by the second generation are likely to be thin, but sufficiently reliable and internally consistent to permit of viable relationships both with other second generation persons[6] and with native members of the country in which they live. However sharp the contrast—whether it be between a nomadic North American Indian tribe and New England-bred farmers, between South American Indians and Italian immigrants, between Lapps and Russians, or Eskimos and Danes—the individual who is reared in the culture-contact situation still learns that there are systematic patterns of behavior. There will be conflicts, especially in the relationship between parents and children, but, if no new changes take place, the second generation may be expected to develop a type of character structure upon which a different but integrated culture can be built.

If, however, the growing child experiences not one simple contrast in the behavior of those about him, but a great variety of degrees of contrast, we have a still more complicated situation. This condition is becoming increasingly characteristic of the modern world, in which individuals and groups migrate from one country to another, live, not in enclaves, but intermingled with members of groups in different culture-contact phases, move easily from one type of industrial pursuit to another, oscillate between rural and urban economies, and make great shifts in class alinement in a very few years. Children grow up in homes in which each parent represents a different form of secondary culture-contact; all four grandparents may have different backgrounds. Teacher, physician, nurse, social worker, policeman, grocer—each in turn represents some different form of culture-conflict or generation-conflict. The child who is reared in a homogeneous culture undergoes a large number of experiences which are all part of one whole, however great the apparent discontinuities among them. The child whose parents have undergone primary culture-contact experiences in confused and often unsystematic fashion, two sets of internally coherent patterns. But for the modern child in a modern city, virtually all coherence disappears. Each act which the child encounters as he is fed, bathed, dressed, hushed to sleep, and wakened again may stem from some different background, and there may be no consistency between any two of them. Gentleness of touch and ferocity of corrective methods alternate without meaning, and rewards and punishments follow no recognizable sequence. Clothes are unadapted to activities, furniture unadapted to ways of sleeping and sitting, cutlery and crockery unsuited to the ways in which the child it taught to eat and drink. The arrangement of every room is unpredictable; the electric switch is seldom in the same place. A hand held out for help may meet instead a slap, a pinch, a lollipop.

Out of a social structure which permits modern man such mobility, both horizontal and vertical, which places hardly any restraint on the cultural gap he may attempt to bridge by marriage, which provides an economy no longer requiring high skill and long habituation, there has developed a learning situation which is producing a special type of character-formation. This new type of character-structure is bound to become more characteristic of ever wider areas of the world, unless the changes now in progress are arrested by totalitarian regimes of enforced homogeneity. We do not yet know whether it is a type of character-structure which will be capable of building up new social forms after the "residue of an age of faith" is exhausted.

The Situational Approach to Life

It is possible, however, to advance some preliminary hypotheses about the order of regularities which will be found in the character-structures of those reared under continually shifting conditions of secondary culture-contact, where rapid technological changes, sharp generation conflicts, and frequent new migrations prevent any stable second generation pattern from developing. The illustrations will be taken from the American scene, with an assumption that comparable features would be found elsewhere.

First, the growing child develops an approach to life which I, stressing the habit of taking each situation as a single unit and adapting rapidly and fully to it, have called *situational*,[7] and Erikson, stressing the type of commitment which occurs when every situation in life must be so regarded, has called *tentative*.[8] Thus we have the extreme surface openness of the American character, with its capacity for rapid intimacy and rapid acceptance of group membership, and also the lack of expectation of the coherence or permanency characteristic of homogeneous cultures.

Second, there is a tendency to reduce all values to simple scales of dollars, school grades, or some other simple quantitative measure, whereby the extreme incommensurables of many different sets of cultural values can be easily, though superficially, reconciled and placed in a hierarchical order. Such a reduction of incommensurable values appears to be a usual phenomenon in societies which have recently undergone marked changes involving culture-contact. The fairly recent cultures of the American Plains Indians, in which groups with different traditions all adjusted to the buffalo-hunting horse culture which developed after the discovery of America, show a curious resemblance to the present American culture, where money income or the size of one's name in neon lights are analogous to "counting coup" as a measure of success. The rapidity of the spread of institutions like the Ghost Dance may also be referred to the way in which a new, simple value scale simplifies intolerable conflicts resulting from contrasts in culture.

It is in these latter phases of secondary culture-contact, in which the child's learning experiences are among individuals representing a great variety of forms of primary and secondary culture-contacts, generation change and intra-societal shift, that we find expressions of the immigrant's sense of personality distortion and the native's sense of a shattered outer world. The perception of the outer world becomes atomized, as the growing child is no longer presented with a coherent set of culturally interrelated experiences to guide his perception. Relationships disappear and experience is broken down into small, discrete bits which may be given temporary meaning in any one of a thousand patterns but lack coherent relationship to any one pattern. It is as if a child were taught to perceive a human skeleton not as a single system of functionally relevant, articulated, noninterchangeable units, but instead as composed of two hundred-odd irregular and comparably meaningless bits—as if, in fact, a picture of a skeleton had been reduced to a jig-saw puzzle, each bit of which might also fit into a hundred other designs.[9]

Atomization of the External World

This atomization of the external world has a variety of manifestations. Instead of a wide modulation of affective tone, in which very different tones of voice and quality of attention are given to the disparate and incommensurable elements in a complex pattern, all orders of experience come to be treated in the same tone. The master of ceremonies in a radio program has no difficulty in maintaining an even-tenor voice as he deals *seriatim* with soft drinks, the batting average of a baseball player, a recent great president, and the atom bomb. Knowledge becomes a matter of facts as such, rather than of their organization and interpretation, and skill becomes a large number of small, precise aptitudes, rather than a way of life. In the school, science is taught in separate segments—chemistry one year, physics another—without cross-reference. Instead of a single international policy, or a co-ordinated domestic policy, there are many distinct programs advocated by groups or parties who show very little recognition of the inconsistencies among and within the programs they advocate. Human beings are perceived within a set of categories which permit ready interchangeability.[10] Courtship and marriage come to be almost as impersonal as the choice involved in marrying one of three cross-cousins in a small primitive tribe; there is a difference in time relations but a common impersonality. In a system in which kinship regulates marriage, the limitation on personal factors in choice is set by past situations which define the range of choice for living individuals. In modern America, relationships are defined, and thus the range of choice limited, by present situations, work in the same office, attendance at the same college, membership in the same club. In a primitive society of the type mentioned, individuals are required to accept a relationship because of a marriage two generations earlier. In modern America individuals accept friends and marriage partners from among those who are presented to them through the fortuitous circumstances of their contemporary work and residence arrangements.

I have stressed the way in which American companionship, partnership, and marriage arrangements, which are dependent upon ephemeral situations, resemble kinship-patterned primitive societies in order to emphasize the fact that patterning, though of a highly simplified type, develops even in a very disturbed and confused culture-contact society. The apparent complexity of American culture, with its enormous number of publications, radio programs, amusements, makes of automobiles, changing styles, etc., hides a basic simplification.[11] All of these superficially diverse patterns are atomized in a way which makes the likenesses among them more easily perceived than the differences. It is the interchangeability of a film, a radio program, and an evening of bowling which is stressed, rather than their incomparability. As an accompaniment of this strenuous effort at simplification, ethical attitudes tend to be expressed in very black and white terms, or to be so qualified in situational terms as to seem very cynical.[12]

Thus the personality type which develops where most of the rearing adults have experienced secondary culture-contact reflects, on the one hand, the native's sense of a shattered outer world, which comes from the rapid impingement of immigration, technological change and urbanization, and, on the other, the sense of internal disorientation of the immigrant. The outer world appears atomized into meaningless units; the inner world also loses its structure and becomes fragmented and chaotic, in that the structure which usually results from the process of growing up in a human culture is often not only not strong enough to resist strain, but also not coherent enough to retain some semblance of form when the breakdown occurs. The increase of schizophrenia, in which all relationship with organized cultural reality is relinquished, is probably one symptom of this condition.

A recent intensive American study, in which individuals who showed either a very high degree of hatred of socially disadvantaged groups, as measured on an elaborate questionnaire, or a very high degree of friendly sympathy toward such groups, has yielded some very suggestive results.[13] The group characterized by an unusual amount of hatred showed a type of character-formation with a high amount of outer conformity, but a lack of inner order against which the outward conformity might be seen as a defense. This group contained a large number of culturally "normal" individuals and also individuals with some marked psychotic trends. The contrast group of those who were sympathetic with the disadvantaged contained many neurotic personalities, individuals with sufficient strength to maintain a difficult relationship to the world without breaking down. They had accepted the contradictions and discrepancies inherent in American culture, and, instead of handling these contradictions by denying them, they had internalized the conflict.

It may be suggested that in extreme culture-contact conditions, such as now exist in the United States and will probably become more widespread over the world, these are some of the types of adjustment which may be expected to develop. We may find an extreme oversimplification, a re-categorizing of cultural experience into such characteristic American forms as fraternities, clubs, etc. Such solutions, among which gambling and betting in the United States, parts of Latin America, and Australia may also be mentioned, provide superficially coherent contexts in which the personality can act without making an attempt at any basic reorientation. Religious and political movements which base their appeal upon the existence of the disorientation and offer a single formula under which all the fragmented aspects of life can be brought together again are another characteristic form in such cultures.

A third attempt at solution comes from efforts to increase the complexity of the broken and oversimplified culture, not by any single solution or any surface multiplication of organizational forms, but by a change in the level of organization, both in the personality-structure and in the social forms. One example of such a change is the increase in awareness of social process which is often, even in primitive societies, a concomitant of culture-contact or migration. It is probably not without significance that the therapy which is offered to the psychotic individual, whose oversimplifications have broken down, tends to involve a *decrease* in complexity or organization, as in treatment by electric shock, insulin shock, or frontal lobotomy. The typical therapies for the neurotic, on the other hand, are the various laborious, exacting forms of psychoanalysis, in which the personality is reorganized on a *higher* level of complexity and awareness.

We are entering an era in history when an understanding of cultural change is essential. Synchronic studies have provided us with descriptions of cultural systems of varying complexity and varying types of character structure. For an understanding of the changes from one system to another we need material on the way in which individuals exposed to various forms of secondary culture contact, either directly or through the mediation of previously exposed adults, take their personality structure from the conditions of cultural instability, and become the sources of new forms of cultural order.

ALFRED SCHUETZ

The Stranger: An Essay in Social Psychology

THE PRESENT PAPER intends to study, in terms of a general theory of interpretation, the typical situation in which a stranger finds himself in his attempt to interpret the cultural pattern of a social group which he approaches and to orient himself

Reprinted from *The American Journal of Sociology*, XLIX (1944), 499-507, by permission of the author and the University of Chicago Press. (Copyright 1944, by the University of Chicago Press.)

within it. For our present purposes, the term "stranger" shall mean an adult individual of our times and civilization who tries to be permanently accepted or at least tolerated by the group which he approaches. The outstanding example for the social situation under scrutiny is that of the immigrant, and the following analyses are, as a matter of convenience, worked out with this instance in view. But by no means is their validity restricted to this special case. The applicant for membership in a closed club, the prospective bridegroom who wants to be admitted to the girl's family, the farmer's son who enters college, the city-dweller who settles in a rural environment, the "selectee" who joins the Army, the family of the war worker who moves into a boom town—all are strangers according to the definition just given, although in these cases the typical "crisis" that the immigrant undergoes may assume milder forms or even be entirely absent. Intentionally excluded, however, from the present investigation, are certain cases the inclusion of which would require some qualifications in our statements: (a) the visitor or guest who intends to establish a merely transitory contact with the group; (b) children or primitives; and (c) relationships between individuals and groups of different levels of civilization, as in the case of the Huron brought to Europe—a pattern dear to some moralists of the eighteenth century. Furthermore, it is not the purpose of this paper to deal with the processes of social assimilation and social adjustment which are treated in an abundant and, for the most part, excellent literature,[1] but rather with the situation of approaching which precedes every possible social adjustment and which includes its prerequisites.

As a convenient starting-point we shall investigate how the cultural pattern of group life presents itself to the common sense of a man who lives his everyday life within the group among his fellow-men. Following the customary terminology, we use the term "cultural pattern of group life" for designating all the peculiar valuations, institutions, and systems of orientation and guidance (such as the folkways, mores, laws, habits, customs, etiquette, fashions) which, in the common opinion of sociologists of our time, characterize—if not constitute—any social group at a given moment in its history. This cultural pattern, like any phenomenon of the social world, has a different aspect for the sociologist and for the man who acts and thinks within it.[2] The sociologist (as sociologist, not as a man among fellow-men which he remains in his private life) is the disinterested scientific onlooker of the social world. He is disinterested in that he intentionally refrains from participating in the network of plans, means-and-ends relations, motives and chances, hopes and fears, which the actor within the social world uses for interpreting his experiences of it; as a scientist he tries to observe, describe, and classify the social world as clearly as possible in well-ordered terms in accordance with the scientific ideals of coherence, consistency, and analytical consequence. The actor within the social world, however, experiences it primarily as a field of his actual and possible acts and only secondarily as an object of his thinking. In so far as he is interested in knowledge of his social world, he organizes this knowledge not in terms of a scientific system but in terms of relevance to his actions. He groups the world around himself (as the center) as a field of domination and is therefore especially interested in that segment which is within his actual or potential reach. He singles out those of its elements which may serve as means or ends for his "use and enjoyment,"[3] for furthering his purposes, and for overcoming obstacles. His interest in these elements is of different degrees, and for this reason he does not aspire to become acquainted with all of them with equal thoroughness. What he wants is *graduated knowledge* of relevant elements, the degree of desired knowledge being correlated with their relevance. Put otherwise, the world seems to him at any given moment as stratified in different layers of relevance, each of them requiring a different degree of knowledge. To illustrate these strata of relevance we may—borrowing the term from cartography—speak of "isohypses" or "hypsographical contour lines of relevance," trying to suggest by this metaphor that we could show the distribution of the interests of an individual at a given moment with respect both to their intensity and to their scope by connecting elements of equal relevance to his acts, just as the cartographer connects points of equal height by contour lines in order to reproduce adequately the shape of a mountain. The graphical representation of these "contour lines of relevance" would not show them as a single closed field but rather as numerous areas scattered over the map, each of different size and shape. Distinguishing with William James[4] two kinds of knowledge, namely, "*knowledge of acquaintance*" and "*knowledge about*," we may say that, within the field covered by the contour lines of relevance, there are centers of explicit knowledge *of* what is aimed at; they are surrounded by a halo knowledge *about* what seems to be sufficient; next comes a region in which it will do merely "to put one's trust"; the adjoining foothills are the home of unwarranted hopes and assumptions; between these areas, however, lie zones of complete ignorance.

We do not want to overcharge this image. Its chief purpose has been to illustrate that the knowledge of the man who acts and thinks within the world of his daily life is not homogeneous; it is (1) incoherent, (2) only partially clear, and (3) not at all free from contradictions.

1) It is incoherent because the individual's interests which determine the relevance of the objects selected for further inquiry are themselves not integrated into a coherent system. They are only partially organized under plans of any kind, such as plans of life, plans of work and leisure, plans for every social role assumed. But the hierarchy of these plans

changes with the situation and with the growth of the personality; interests are shifted continually and entail an uninterrupted transformation of the shape and density of the relevance lines. Not only the selection of the objects of curiosity but also the degree of knowledge aimed at changes.

2) Man in his daily life is only partially—and we dare say exceptionally—interested in the clarity of his knowledge, i.e., in full insight into the relations between the elements of his world and the general principles ruling those relations. He is satisfied that a well-functioning telephone service is available to him and, normally, does not ask how the apparatus functions in detail and what laws of physics make this functioning possible. He buys merchandise in the store, not knowing how it is produced, and pays with money, although he has only a vague idea what money really is. He takes it for granted that his fellow-man will understand his thought if expressed in plain language and will answer accordingly, without wondering how this miraculous performance may be explained. Furthermore, he does not search for the truth and does not quest for certainty. All he wants is information on likelihood and insight into the chances or risks which the situation at hand entails for the outcome of his actions. That the subway will run tomorrow as usual is for him almost of the same order of likelihood as that the sun will rise. If, by reason of a special interest, he needs more explicit knowledge on a topic, a benign modern civilization holds ready for him a chain of information desks and reference libraries.

3) His knowledge, finally, is not a consistent one. At the same time he may consider statements as equally valid which in fact are incompatible with one another. As a father, a citizen, an employee, and a member of his church, he may have the most different and the least congruent opinions on moral, political, or economic matters. This inconsistency does not necessarily originate in a logical fallacy. Men's thought is just spread over subject matters located within different and differently relevant levels, and they are not aware of the modifications they would have to make in passing from one level to another. This and similar problems would have to be explored by a logic of everyday thinking, postulated but not attained by all the great logicians from Leibnitz to Husserl and Dewey. Up to now the science of logic has primarily dealt with the logic of science.

The system of knowledge thus acquired—incoherent, inconsistent, and only partially clear, as it is—takes on for the members of the in-group the appearance of a *sufficient* coherence, clarity, and consistency to give anybody a reasonable chance of understanding and of being understood. Any member born or reared within the group accepts the ready-made standardized scheme of the cultural pattern handed down to him by ancestors, teachers, and authorities as an unquestioned and unquestionable guide in all the situations which normally occur within the social world. The knowledge correlated to the cultural pattern carries its evidence in itself—or, rather, it is taken for granted in the absence of evidence to the contrary. It is a knowledge of trustworthy *recipes* for interpreting the social world and for handling things and men in order to obtain the best results in every situation with a minimum of effort by avoiding undesirable consequences. The recipe works, on the one hand, as a precept for actions and thus serves as a scheme of expression: whoever wants to obtain a certain result has to proceed as indicated by the recipe provided for this purpose. On the other hand, the recipe serves as a scheme of interpretation: whoever proceeds as indicated by a specific recipe is supposed to intend the correlated result. Thus it is the function of the cultural pattern to eliminate troublesome inquiries by offering ready-made directions for use, to replace truth hard to attain by comfortable truisms, and to substitute the self-explanatory for the questionable.

This "thinking-as-usual," as we may call it, corresponds to Max Scheler's idea of the "relatively natural conception of the world" (*relativ natürliche Weltanschauung*);[5] it includes the "of-course" assumptions relevant to a particular social group which Robert S. Lynd describes in such a masterly way—together with their inherent contradictions and ambivalence—as the "Middletown-spirit."[6] Thinking-as-usual may be maintained as long as some basic assumptions hold true, namely: (1) that life and especially social life will continue to be the same as it has been so far, that is to say, that the same problems requiring the same solutions will recur and that, therefore, our former experiences will suffice for mastering future situations; (2) that we may rely on the knowledge handed down to us by parents, teachers, governments, traditions, habits, etc., even if we do not understand their origin and their real meaning; (3) that in the ordinary course of affairs it is sufficient to know something *about* the general type or style of events we may encounter in our life-world in order to manage or control them; and (4) that neither the systems of recipes as schemes of interpretation and expression nor the underlying basic assumptions just mentioned are our private affair, but that they are likewise accepted and applied by our fellow-men.

If only one of these assumptions ceases to stand the test, thinking-as-usual becomes unworkable. Then a "crisis" arises which, according to W. I. Thomas' famous definition, "interrupts the flow of habit and gives rise to changed conditions of consciousness and practice"; or, as we may say, it overthrows precipitously the actual system of relevances. The cultural pattern no longer functions as a system of tested recipes at hand; it reveals that its applicability is restricted to a specific historical situation.

Yet the stranger, by reason of his personal crisis, does not share the above-mentioned basic assumptions. He becomes essentially the man who has to place in question nearly everything that seems to be unquestionable to the members of the approached group.

To him the cultural pattern of the approached group does not have the authority of a tested system of recipes, and this, if for no other reason, because he does not partake in the vivid historical tradition by which it has been formed. To be sure, from the stranger's point of view, too, the culture of the approached group has its peculiar history, and this history is even accessible to him. But it has never become an integral part of his biography, as did the history of his home group. Only the ways in which his fathers and grandfathers lived become for everyone elements of his own way of life. Graves and reminiscences can neither be transferred nor conquered. The stranger, therefore, approaches the other group as a newcomer in the true meaning of the term. At best he may be willing and able to share the present and the future with the approached group in vivid and immediate experience; under all circumstances, however, he remains excluded from such experiences of its past. Seen from the point of view of the approached group, he is a man without a history.

To the stranger, the cultural pattern of his home group continues to be the outcome of an unbroken historical development and an element of his personal biography which for this very reason has been and still is the unquestioned scheme of reference for his "relatively natural conception of the world." As a matter of course, therefore, the stranger starts to interpret his new social environment in terms of his thinking-as-usual. Within the scheme of reference brought from his home group, however, he finds a ready-made idea of the pattern supposedly valid within the approached group—an idea which necessarily will soon prove inadequate.[7]

First, the idea of the cultural pattern of the approached group which the stranger finds within the interpretive scheme of his home group has originated in the attitude of a disinterested observer. The approaching stranger, however, is about to transform himself from an unconcerned onlooker into a would-be member of the approached group. The cultural pattern of the approached group, then, is no longer a subject matter of his thought but a segment of the world which has to be dominated by actions. Consequently, its position within the stranger's system of relevance changes decisively, and this means, as we have seen, that another type of knowledge is required for its interpretation. Jumping from the stalls to the stage, so to speak, the former onlooker becomes a member of the cast, enters as a partner into social relations with his co-actors, and participates henceforth in the action in progress.

Second, the new cultural pattern acquires an environmental character. Its remoteness changes into proximity; its vacant frames become occupied by vivid experiences; its anonymous contents turn into definite social situations; its ready-made typologies disintegrate. In other words, the level of environmental experience of social objects is incongruous with the level of mere beliefs about unapproached objects; by passing from the latter to the former, any concept originating in the level of departure becomes necessarily inadequate if applied to the new level without having been restated in its terms.

Third, the ready-made picture of the foreign group subsisting within the stranger's home-group proves its inadequacy for the approaching stranger, for the mere reason that it has not been formed with the aim of provoking a response from, or a reaction of, the members of the foreign group. The knowledge which it offers serves merely as a handy scheme for interpreting the foreign group and not as a guide for interaction between the two groups. Its validity is primarily based on the consensus of those members of the home group who do not intend to establish a direct social relationship with members of the foreign group. (Those who intend to do so are in a situation analogous to that of the approaching stranger.) Consequently, the scheme of interpretation refers to the members of the foreign group merely as objects of this interpretation, but not beyond it, as addressees of possible acts emanating from the outcome of the interpretive procedure and not as subjects of anticipated reactions toward those acts. Hence, this kind of knowledge is, so to speak, insulated; it can be neither verified nor falsified by responses of the members of the foreign group. The latter, therefore, consider this knowledge—by a kind of "looking-glass" effect[8]—as both irresponsive and irresponsible and complain of its prejudices, bias, and misunderstandings. The approaching stranger, however, becomes aware of the fact that an important element of his "thinking-as-usual," namely, his ideas of the foreign group, its cultural pattern, and its way of life, do not stand the test of vivid experience and social interaction.

The discovery that things in his new surroundings look quite different from what he expected them to be at home is frequently the first shock to the stranger's confidence in the validity of his habitual "thinking-as-usual." Not only the picture which the stranger has brought along of the cultural pattern of the approached group but the whole hitherto unquestioned scheme of interpretation current within the home group becomes invalidated. It cannot be used as a scheme of orientation within the new social surroundings. For the members of the approached group *their* cultural patterns fulfills the functions of such a scheme. But the approaching stranger can neither use it simply as it is nor establish a general formula of transformation between both cultural patterns permitting him, so to speak, to convert all the co-ordinates within one scheme of orientation into those valid within the other—and this for the following reasons.

First, any scheme of orientation presupposes that everyone who uses it looks at the surrounding world as grouped around himself who stands at its center. He who wants to use a map successfully has first of all to know his standpoint in two respects: its location on the ground and its representation on the map. Applied to the social world, this means that only members of the in-group, having a definite status in its hierarchy and also being aware of it, can use its cultural pattern as a natural and trustworthy scheme of orientation. The stranger, however, has to face the fact that he lacks any status as a member of the social group he is about to join and is therefore unable to get a starting-point to take his bearings. He finds himself a border case outside the territory covered by the scheme of orientation current within the group. He is, therefore, no longer permitted to consider himself as the center of his social environment, and this fact causes again a dislocation of his contour lines of relevance.

Second, the cultural pattern and its recipes represent only for the members of the in-group a unit of coinciding schemes of interpretation as well as of expression. For the outsider, however, this seeming unity falls to pieces. The approaching stranger has to "translate" its terms into terms of the cultural pattern of his home group, provided that, within the latter, interpretive equivalents exist at all. If they exist, the translated terms may be understood and remembered; they can be recognized by recurrence; they are at hand but not in hand. Yet, even then, it is obvious that the stranger cannot assume that his interpretation of the new cultural pattern coincides with that current with the members of the in-group. On the contrary, he has to reckon with fundamental discrepancies in seeing things and handling situations.

Only after having thus collected a certain knowledge of the interpretive function of the new cultural pattern may the stranger start to adopt it as the scheme of his own expression. The difference between the two stages of knowledge is familiar to any student of a foreign language and has received the full attention of psychologists dealing with the theory of learning. It is the difference between the passive understanding of a language and its active mastering as a means for realizing one's own acts and thoughts. As a matter of convenience, we want to keep to this example in order to make clear some of the limits set to the stranger's attempt at conquering the foreign pattern as a scheme of expression, bearing in mind, however, that the following remarks could easily be adapted with appropriate modifications to other categories of the cultural pattern such as mores, laws, folkways, fashions, etc.

Language as a scheme of interpretation and expression does not merely consist of the linguistic symbols catalogued in the dictionary and of the syntactical rules enumerated in an ideal grammar. The former are translatable into other languages; the latter are understandable by referring them to corresponding or deviating rules of the unquestioned mother-tongue.[9] However, several other factors supervene.

1) Every word and every sentence is, to borrow again a term of William James, surrounded by "fringes" connecting them, on the one hand, with past and future elements of the universe of discourse to which they pertain and surrounding them, on the other hand, with a halo of emotional values and irrational implications which themselves remain ineffable. The fringes are the stuff poetry is made of; they are capable of being set to music but they are not translatable.

2) There are in any language terms with several connotations. They, too, are noted in the dictionary. But, besides these standardized connotations, every element of the speech acquires its special secondary meaning derived from the context or the social environment within which it is used and, in addition, gets a special tinge from the actual occasion in which it is employed.

3) Idioms, technical terms, jargons, and dialects, whose use remains restricted to specific social groups, exist in every language, and their significance can be learned by an outsider too. But, in addition, every social group, be it ever so small (if not every individual), has its own private code, understandable only by those who have participated in the common past experiences in which it took rise or in the tradition connected with them.

4) As Vossler has shown, the whole history of the linguistic group is mirrored in its way of saying things.[10] All the other elements of group life enter into it—above all, its literature. The erudite stranger, for example, approaching an English-speaking country is heavily handicapped if he has not read the Bible and Shakespeare in the English language, even if he grew up with translations of those books in his mother-tongue.

All the above-mentioned features are accessible only to the members of the in-group. They all pertain to the scheme of expression. They are not teachable and cannot be learned in the same way as, for example, the vocabulary. In order to command a language freely as a scheme of expression, one must have written love letters in it; one has to know how to pray and curse in it and how to say things with every shade appropriate to the addressee and to the situation. Only members of the in-group have the scheme of expression as a genuine one in hand and command it freely within their thinking-as-usual.

Applying the result to the total of the cultural pattern of group life, we may say that the member of the in-group looks in one single glance through the normal social situations occurring to him and that he catches immediately the ready-made recipe appropriate to its solution. In those situations his acting shows all the marks of habituality, automatism, and half-consciousness. This is possible because the cultural pattern provides by its recipes typical solutions for typical problems available for typical actors. In other words, the chance of obtaining the desired result by applying a standardized recipe is an objective one; that is open to everyone who conducts himself like the anonymous type required by the recipe. Therefore, the actor who follows a recipe does not have to check whether this objective chance coincides with a subjective chance, that is, a chance open to him, the individual, by reason of his personal circumstances and faculties, which subsists independently of the question whether other people in similar situations could or could not act in the same way with the same likelihood. Even more, it can be stated that the objective chances for the efficiency of a recipe are the greater, the fewer deviations from the anonymous typified behavior occur, and this holds especially for recipes designed for social interaction. This kind of recipe, if it is to work, presupposes that any partner expects the other to act or to react typically, provided that the actor himself acts typically. He who wants to travel by railroad has to behave in that typical conduct of the type "passenger," and vice versa. Neither party examines the subjective chances involved. The scheme, being designed for everyone's use, need not be tested for its fitness for the peculiar individual who employs it.

For those who have grown up within the cultural pattern, not only the recipes and their efficiency chance but also the typical and anonymous attitudes required by them are an unquestioned "matter of course" which gives them both security and assurance. In other words, these attitudes by their very anonymity and typicality are placed not within the actor's stratum of relevance which requires explicit knowledge *of* but in the region of mere acquaintance in which it will do to put one's trust. This interrelation between objective chance, typicality, anonymity, and relevance seems to be rather important.[11]

For the approaching stranger, however, the pattern of the approached group does not guarantee an objective chance for success but rather a pure subjective likelihood which has to be checked step by step, that is, he has to make sure that the solutions suggested by the new scheme will also produce the desired effect for him in his special position as outsider and newcomer who has not brought within his grasp the whole system of the cultural pattern but who is rather puzzled by its consistency, incoherence, and lack of clarity. He has, first of all, to use the term of W. I. Thomas, to *define* the situation. Therefore, he cannot stop at an approximate acquaintance with the new pattern, trusting in his vague knowledge *about* its general style and structure but needs an explicit knowledge *of* its elements, inquiring not only into their *that* but into their *why*. Consequently, the shape of his contour lines of relevance by necessity differs radically from those of a member of the in-group as to situations, recipes, means, ends, social partners, etc. Keeping in mind the above-mentioned interrelationship between relevance, on the one hand, and typicality and anonymity, on the other, it follows that he uses another yardstick for anonymity and typicality of social acts than the members of the in-group. For, to the stranger, the observed actors within the approached group are not—as for their co-actors—of a certain pre-supposed anonymity, namely, mere performers of typical functions, but individuals. On the other hand, he is inclined to take mere individual traits as typical ones. Thus, he constructs a social world of pseudo-anonymity, pseudo-intimacy, and pseudo-typicality. Therefore, he cannot integrate the personal types constructed by him into a coherent picture of the approached group and cannot rely on his expectation of their response. And even less can the stranger himself adopt those typical and anonymous attitudes which a member of the in-group is entitled to expect from a partner in a typical situation. Hence the stranger's lack of feeling for distance, his oscillating between remoteness and intimacy, his hesitation and uncertainty, and his distrust in every matter which seems to be so simple and uncomplicated to those who rely on the efficiency of unquestioned recipes which have just to be followed but not understood.

In other words, the cultural pattern of the approached group is to the stranger not a shelter but a field of adventure, not a matter of course but a questionable topic of investigation, not an instrument for disentangling problematic situations but a problematic situation itself and one hard to master.

These facts explain two basic traits of the stranger's attitude toward the group which nearly all sociological writers dealing with this topic have rendered special attention, namely (1) the stranger's objectivity and (2) his doubtful loyalty.

1) The stranger's objectivity cannot be sufficiently explained by his critical attitude. To be sure, he is not bound to worship the "idols of the tribe" and has a vivid feeling for the incoherence and inconsistency of the approached cultural pattern. But this attitude originates far less in his propensity to judge the newly approached group by the standards brought from home than in his need to acquire full knowledge *of* the elements of the approached cultural pattern and to examine for this purpose with care and precision what seems self-explanatory to the in-group. The deeper reason for his objectivity, however, lies in his own bitter experience of the limits of the "thinking-as-usual," which has taught him that a man may lose his status, his rules of guidance, and even his history, and that the normal way of life is always far less guaranteed than it seems. Therefore, the stranger discerns, frequently with a grievous clear-sightedness, the rising of a crisis which may menace the whole foundation of the "relatively natural conception of the world," while all those symp-

toms pass unnoticed by the members of the in-group, who rely on the continuance of their customary way of life.

2) The doubtful loyalty of the stranger is unfortunately very frequently more than a prejudice on the part of the approached group. This is especially true in cases in which the stranger proves unwilling or unable to substitute the new cultural pattern entirely for that of the home group. Then the stranger remains what Park and Stonequist have aptly called a "marginal man," a cultural hybrid on the verge of two different patterns of group life, not knowing to which of them he belongs. But very frequently the reproach of doubtful loyalty originates in the astonishment of the members of the in-group that the stranger does not accept the total of its cultural pattern as the natural and appropriate way of life and as the best of all possible solutions of any problem. The stranger is called ungrateful, since he refuses to acknowledge that the cultural pattern offered to him grants him shelter and protection. But these people do not understand that the stranger in the state of transition does not consider this pattern as a protecting shelter at all but as a labyrinth in which he has lost all sense of his bearings.

As stated before, we have intentionally restricted our topic to the specific attitude of the approaching stranger which precedes any social adjustment and refrained from investigating the process of social assimilation itself. One single remark concerning the latter may be permitted. Strangeness and familiarity are not limited to the social field but are general categories of our interpretation of the world. If we encounter in our experience something previously unknown and which therefore stands out of the ordinary order of our knowledge, we begin a process of inquiry. We first define the new fact; we try to catch its meaning; we then transform step by step our general scheme of interpretation of the world in such a way that the strange fact and its meaning becomes compatible and consistent with all the other facts of our experience and their meaning. If we succeed in this endeavor, then that which formerly was a strange fact and a puzzling problem to our mind is transformed into an additional element of our warranted knowledge. We have enlarged and adjusted our stock of experiences.

What is commonly called the process of social adjustment which the newcomer has to undergo is but a special case of this general principle. The adaptation of the newcomer to the in-group which at first seemed to be strange and unfamiliar to him is a continuous process of inquiry into the cultural pattern of the approached group. If this process of inquiry succeeds, then this pattern and its elements will become to the newcomer a matter of course, an unquestionable way of life, a shelter, and a protection. But then the stranger is no stranger any more, and his specific problems have been solved.

C. WRIGHT MILLS

On Reason and Freedom

THE CLIMAX OF THE SOCIAL SCIENTIST'S concern with history is the idea he comes to hold of the epoch in which he lives. The climax of his concern with biography is the idea he comes to hold of man's basic nature, and of the limits it may set to the transformation of man by the course of history.

All classic social scientists have been concerned with the salient characteristics of their time—and the problem of how history is being made within it; with "the nature of human nature"—and the variety of individuals that come to prevail within their periods. Marx and Sombart and Weber, Comte and Spencer, Durkheim and Veblen, Mannheim, Schumpeter, and Michels—each in his own way has confronted these problems. In our immediate times, however, many social scientists have not. Yet it is precisely now, in the second half of the twentieth century, that these concerns become urgent as issues, persistent as troubles, and vital for the cultural orientation of our human studies.

I

Nowadays men everywhere seek to know where they stand, where they may be going, and what—if anything—they can do about the present as history and the future as responsibility. Such questions as these no one can answer once and for all. Every period provides its own answers. But just now, for us, there is a difficulty. We are now at the ending of an epoch, and we have got to work out our own answers.

We are at the ending of what is called The Modern Age. Just as Antiquity was followed by several centuries of Oriental ascendancy, which Westerners provincially call The Dark Ages, so now The Modern Age is being succeeded by a post-modern period. Perhaps we may call it: The Fourth Epoch.

From *The Sociological Imagination* by C. Wright Mills (pp. 165-76). (Copyright 1959, by Oxford University Press, Inc.) Reprinted by permission of the author and publisher.

The ending of one epoch and the beginning of another is, to be sure, a matter of definition. But definitions, like everything social, are historically specific. And now our basic definitions of society and of self are being overtaken by new realities. I do not mean merely that never before within the limits of a single generation have men been so fully exposed at so fast a rate to such earthquakes of change. I do not mean merely that we feel we are in an epochal kind of transition, and that we struggle to grasp the outline of the new epoch we suppose ourselves to be entering. I mean that when we try to orient ourselves—if we do try—we find that too many of our old expectations and images are, after all, tied down historically: that too many of our standard categories of thought and of feeling as often disorient us as help to explain what is happening around us; that too many of our explanations are derived from from the great historical transition from the Medieval to the Modern Age; and that when they are generalized for use today, they become unwieldy, irrelevant, not convincing. I also mean that our major orientations—liberalism and socialism—have virtually collapsed as adequate explanations of the world and of ourselves.

These two ideologies came out of the Enlightenment, and they have had in common many assumptions and values. In both, increased rationality is held to be the prime condition of increased freedom. The liberating notion of progress by reason, the faith in science as an unmixed good, the demand for popular education and the faith in its political meaning for democracy—all these ideals of the Enlightenment have rested upon the happy assumption of the inherent relation of reason and freedom. Those thinkers who have done the most to shape our ways of thinking have proceeded under this assumption. It lies under every movement and nuance of the work of Freud: To be free, the individual must become more rationally aware; therapy is an aid to giving reason its chance to work freely in the course of an individual's life. The same assumption underpins the main line of Marxist work: Men, caught in the irrational anarchy of production, must become rationally aware of their position in society; they must become "class conscious"—the Marxian meaning of which is as rationalistic as any term set forth by Bentham.

Liberalism has been concerned with freedom and reason as supreme facts about the individual; Marxism, as supreme facts about man's role in the political making of history. The liberals and the radicals of The Modern Period have generally been men who believed in the rational making of history and of his own biography by the free individual.

But what has been happening in the world makes evident, I believe, why the ideas of freedom and of reason now so often seem so ambiguous in both the new capitalist and the Communist societies of our time: why

Marxism has so often become a dreary rhetoric of bureaucratic defense and abuse; and liberalism, a trivial and irrelevant way of masking social reality. The major developments of our time, I believe, can be correctly understood neither in terms of the liberal nor the Marxian interpretation of politics and culture. These ways of thought arose as guide-lines to reflection about types of society which do not now exist. John Stuart Mill never examined the kinds of political economy now arising in the capitalist world. Karl Marx never analyzed the kinds of society now arising in the Communist bloc. And neither of them ever thought through the problems of the so-called underdeveloped countries in which seven out of ten men are trying to exist today. Now we confront new kinds of social structure which, in terms of "modern" ideals, resist analysis in the liberal and in the socialist terms we have inherited.

The ideological mark of The Fourth Epoch—that which sets it off from The Modern Age—is that the ideas of freedom and of reason have become moot; that increased rationality may not be assumed to make for increased freedom.

II

The role of reason in human affairs and the idea of the free individual as the seat of reason are the most important themes inherited by the twentieth-century scientists from the philosophers of the Enlightenment. If they are to remain the key values in terms of which troubles are specified and issues focused, then the ideals of reason and of freedom must now be restated as problems in more precise and solvable ways than have been available to earlier thinkers and investigators. For in our time these two values, reason and freedom, are in obvious yet subtle peril.

The underlying trends are well known. Great and rational organizations—in brief, bureaucracies—have indeed increased, but the substantive reason of the individual at large has not. Caught in the limited milieux of their everyday lives, ordinary men often cannot reason about the great structures—rational and irrational—of which their milieux are subordinate parts. Accordingly, they often carry out series of apparently rational actions without any ideas of the ends they serve, and there is the increasing suspicion that those at the top as well—like Tolstoy's generals—only pretend they know. The growth of such organizations, within an increasing division of labor, sets up more and more spheres of life, work, and leisure, in which reasoning is difficult or impossible. The soldier, for example, "carries out an entire series of functionally rational actions accurately without having any idea as to the ultimate end of this action" or the function of each act within the whole. (Cf. Mannheim, *Man and Society* [New York: Harcourt, Brace, 1940], p. 54.) Even men of technically supreme intelligence may efficiently perform their assigned work and yet not know that it is to result in the first atom bomb.

Science, it turns out, is not a technological Second Coming. That its techniques and its rationality are given a central place in a society does not mean that men live reasonably and wthout myth, fraud, and superstition. Universal education may lead to technological idiocy and nationalist provinciality—rather than to the informed and independent intelligence. The mass distribution of historic culture may not lift the level of cultural sensibility, but rather, merely banalize it—and compete mightily with the chance for creative innovation. A high level of bureaucratic rationality and of technology does not mean a high level of either individual or social intelligence. From the first you cannot infer the second. For social, technological, or bureaucratic rationality is not merely a grand summation of the individual will and capacity to reason. The very chance to acquire that will and that capacity seems in fact often to be decreased by it. Rationally organized social arrangements are not necessarily a means of increased freedom—for the individual or for the society. In fact, often they are a means of tyranny and manipulation, a means of expropriating the very chance to reason, the very capacity to act as a free man.

Only from a few commanding positions or—as the case may be—merely vantage points in the rationalized structure, is it readily possible to understand the structural forces at work in the whole which thus affect each limited part of which ordinary men are aware.

The forces that shape these milieux do not originate within them, nor are they controllable by those sunk in them. Moreover, these milieux are themselves increasingly rationalized. Families as well as factories, leisure as well as work, neighborhoods as well as states—they, too, tend to become parts of a functionally rational totality—or they are subject to uncontrolled and irrational forces.

The increasing rationalization of society, the contradiction between such rationality and reason, the collapse of the assumed coincidence of reason and freedom—these developments lie back of the rise into view of the man who is "with" rationality but without reason, who is increasingly self-rationalized and also increasingly uneasy. It is in terms of this type of man that the contemporary problem of freedom is best stated. Yet such trends and suspicions are often not formulated as problems, and they are certainly not widely acknowledged as issues or felt as a set of troubles. Indeed, it is the fact of its unrecognized character, its lack of formulation, that is the most important feature of the contemporary problem of freedom and reason.

III

From the individual's standpoint, much that happens seems the result of manipulation, of management, of blind drift; authority is often not explicit; those with power often feel no need to make it explicit and to justify it. That is one reason why ordinary men, when they are in trouble or when they sense that they are up against issues, cannot get clear targets for thought and for action; they cannot determine what it is that imperils the values they vaguely discern as theirs.

Given these effects of the ascendant trend of rationalization, the individual "does the best he can." He gears his aspirations and his work to the situation he is in, and from which he can find no way out. In due course, he does not seek a way out: he adapts. That part of his life which is left over from work, he uses to play, to consume, "to have fun." Yet this sphere of consumption is also being rationalized. Alienated from production, from work, he is also alienated from consumption, from genuine leisure. This adaptation of the individual and its effects upon his milieux and self results not only in the loss of his chance, and in due course, of his capacity and will to reason; it also affects his chances and his capacity to act as a free man. Indeed, neither the value of freedom nor of reason, it would seem, are known to him.

Such adapted men are not necessarily unintelligent, even after they have lived and worked and played in such circumstances for quite some time. Karl Mannheim has made the point in a clear way by speaking of "self-rationalization," which refers to the way in which an individual, caught in the limited segments of great rational organizations, comes systematically to regulate his impulses and his aspirations, his manner of life and his ways of thought, in rather strict accordance with "the rules and regulations of the organization." The rational organization is thus an alienating organization: the guiding principles of conduct and reflection, and in due course of emotion as well, are not seated in the individual conscience of the Reformation man, or in the independent reason of the Cartesian man. The guiding principles, in fact, are alien to and in contradiction with all that has been historically understood as individuality. It is not too much to say that in the extreme development the chance to reason of most men is destroyed, as rationality increases and its locus, its control, is moved from the individual to the big-scale organization. There is then rationality without reason. Such rationality is not commensurate with freedom but the destroyer of it.

It is no wonder that the ideal of individuality has become moot: in our time, what is at issue is the very nature of man, the image we have of his limits and possibilities as man. History is not yet done with its exploration of the limits and meanings of "human nature." We do not know how profound man's psychological transformation from the Modern Age to the contemporary epoch may be. But we must now raise the question in an ultimate form: Among contemporary men will there come to prevail, or even to flourish, what may be called The Cheerful Robot?

We know of course that man can be turned into a robot, by chemical and psychiatric means, by steady coercion and by controlled environment; but also by random pressures and unplanned sequences of circumstances. But can he be made to want to become a cheerful and willing robot? Can he be happy in this condition, and what are the qualities and the meanings of such happiness? It will no longer do merely to assume, as a metaphysic of human nature, that down deep in man-as-man there is an urge for freedom and a will to reason. Now we must ask: What in man's nature, what in the human condition today, what in each of the varieties of social structure makes for the ascendancy of the cheerful robot? And what stands against it?

The advent of the alienated man and all the themes which lie behind his advent now affect the whole of our serious intellectual life and cause our immediate intellectual malaise. It is a major theme of the human condition in the contemporary epoch and of all studies worthy of the name. I know of no idea, no theme, no problem, that is so deep in the classic tradition—and so much involved in the possible default of contemporary social science.

It is what Karl Marx so brilliantly discerned in his earlier essays on "alienation"; it is the chief concern of Georg Simmel in his justly famous essay on "The Metropolis"; Graham Wallas was aware of it in his work on The Great Society. It lies behind Fromm's conception of the "automation." The fear that such a type of man will become ascendant underlies many of the more recent uses of such classic sociological conceptions as "status and contract," "community and society." It is the hard meaning of such notions as Riesman's "other-directed" and Whyte's "social ethic." And of course, most popularly, the triumph—if it may be called that—of such a man is the key meaning of George Orwell's *1984*.

On the positive side—a rather wistful side nowadays—the larger meanings of Freud's "id," Marx's "Freiheit," George Mead's "I," Karen Horney's "spontaneity," lie in the use of such conceptions against the triumph of the alienated man. They are trying to find some center in man-as-man which would enable them to believe that in the end he cannot be made into, that he cannot finally become, such an alien creature—alien to nature, to society, to self. The cry for "community" is an attempt, a mistaken one I believe, to assert the conditions that would eliminate the probability of such a man, and it is because many humanist thinkers have come to believe that many psychiatrists by their practice produce such alienated and self-rationalized men that they reject these adaptive endeavors. Back of all this—and much more of traditional and current worrying and thinking among serious and sensible students of man—there lies the simple and decisive fact that the alienated man is the antithesis of the Western image of the free man. The society in which this man, this cheerful robot, flourishes is the antithesis of the free society—or in the literal and plain meaning of the word, of a democratic society. The advent of this man points to freedom as trouble, as issue, and—let us hope—as problem for social scientists. Put as a trouble of the individual—of the terms and values of which he is uneasily unaware—it is the trouble called "alienation." As an issue for publics—to the terms and values of which they are mainly indifferent—it is no less than the issue of democratic society, as fact and as aspiration.

It is just because this issue and this trouble are not now widely recognized, and so do not in fact exist as explicit troubles and issues, that the uneasiness and the indifference that betoken them are so deep and so wide in meaning and in effect. That is a major part of the problem of freedom today, seen in its political context, and it is a major part of the intellectual challenge which the formulation of the problem of freedom offers to contemporary social scientists.

It is not merely paradoxical to say that the values of freedom and reason are back of the absence of troubles, back of the uneasy feeling of malaise and alienation. In a similar manner, the issue to which modern threats to freedom and reason most typically lead is, above all, the absence of explicit issues—to apathy rather than to issues explicitly defined as such.

The issues and troubles have not been clarified because the chief capacities and qualities of man required to clarify them are the very freedom and reason that are threatened and dwindling. Neither the troubles nor the issues have been seriously formulated as the problems of the kinds of social science I have been criticizing in my work. The promise of classic social science, in considerable part, is that they will be.

IV

The troubles and issues raised up by the crises of reason and freedom cannot of course be formulated as one grand problem, but neither can they be confronted, much less solved, by handling each of them microscopically as a series of small-scale issues, or of troubles confined to a scatter of milieux. They are structural problems, and to state them requires that we work in the classic terms of human biography and of epochal history. Only in such terms can the connections of structure and milieux that effect these values today be traced and causal analysis be conducted. The crisis of individuality and the crisis of history-making; the role of reason in the free individual life and in the making of history—in the restatement and clarification of these problems lies the promise of the social sciences.

The moral and the intellectual promise of social science is that freedom and reason will remain cherished values, that they will be used seriously and consistently and imaginatively in the formulation of problems. But this is also the political promise of what is loosely called Western culture. Within the social sciences, political crises and intellectual crises of our time coincide: serious work in either sphere is also work in the other. The political traditions of classic liberalism and of classic socialism together exhaust our major political traditions. The collapse of these traditions as ideologies has had to do with the decline of free individuality and the decline of reason in human affairs. Any contemporary political restatement of liberal and socialist goals must include as central the idea of a society in which all men would become men of substantive reason, whose independent reasoning would have structural consequences for their society, its history, and thus for their own life fates.

The interest of the social scientist in social structure is not due to any view that the future is structurally determined. We study the structural limits of human decision in an attempt to find points of effective intervention, in order to know what can and what must be structurally changed if the role of explicit decision in history-making is to be enlarged. Our interest in history is not owing to any view that the future is inevitable, that the future is bounded by the past. That men have lived in certain kinds of society in the past does not set exact or absolute limits to the kinds of society they may create in the future. We study history to discern the alternatives within which human reason and human freedom can now make history. We study historical social structures, in brief, in order to find within them the ways in which they are and can be controlled. For only in this way can we come to know the limits and the meaning of human freedom.

Freedom is not merely the chance to do as one pleases; neither is it merely the opportunity to choose between set alternatives. Freedom is, first of all, the chance to formulate the available choices, to argue over them—and then, the opportunity to choose. That is why freedom cannot exist without an enlarged role of human reason in human affairs. Within an individual's biography and within a society's history, the social task of reason is to formulate choices, to enlarge the scope of human decisions in the making of history. The future of human affairs is not merely some set of variables to be predicted. The future is what is to be decided—within the limits, to be sure, of historical possibility. But this possibility is not fixed; in our time the limits seem very broad indeed.

Beyond this, the problem of freedom is the problem of how decisions about the future of human affairs are to be made and who is to make them. Organizationally, it is the problem of a just machinery of decision. Morally, it is the problem of political responsibility. Intellectually, it is the problem of what are now the possible futures of human affairs. But the larger aspects of the problem of freedom today concern not only the nature of history and the structural chance for explicit decisions to make a difference in its course; they concern also the nature of man and the fact that the value of freedom cannot be based upon "man's basic nature." The ultimate problem of freedom is the problem of the cheerful robot, and it arises in this form today because today it has become evident to us that *all* men do *not* naturally *want* to be free; that all men are not willing or not able, as the case may be, to exert themselves to acquire the reason that freedom requires.

Under what conditions do men come to *want* to be free and capable of acting freely? Under what conditions are they willing and able to bear the burdens freedom does impose and to see these less as burdens than as gladly undertaken self-transformations? And on the negative side: Can men be made to want to become *cheerful* robots?

In our time, must we not face the possibility that the human mind as a social fact might be deteriorating in quality and cultural level, and yet not many would notice it because of the overwhelming accumulation of technological gadgets? Is not that one meaning of rationality without reason? Of human alienation? Of the absence of any free role for reason in human affairs? The accumulation of gadgets hides these meanings: Those who use these devices do not understand them; those who invent them do not understand much else. That is why we may *not*, without great ambiguity, use technological abundance as the index of human quality and cultural progress.

To formulate any problem requires that we state the values involved and the threat to those values. For it is the felt threat to cherished values—such as those of freedom and reason—that is the necessary moral substance of all significant problems of social inquiry, and as well of all public issues and private troubles.

The values involved in the cultural problem of individuality are conveniently embodied in all that is suggested by the ideal of The Renaissance Man. The threat to that ideal is the ascendancy among us of The Cheerful Robot.

The values involved in the political problem of history-making are embodied in the Promethean ideal of its human-making. The threat to that ideal is twofold: On the one hand, history-making may well go by default, men may continue to abdicate its willful making, and so merely drift. On the other hand, history may indeed be made—but by narrow elite circles without effective responsibility to those who must try to survive the consequences of their decisions and of their defaults.

I do not know the answer to the question of political irresponsibility in our time or to the cultural and political question of The Cheerful Robot. But is it not clear that no answers will be found unless these problems are at least confronted? Is it not obvious, that the ones to confront them, above all others, are the social scientists of the rich societies? That many of them do not now do so is surely the greatest human default being committed by privileged men in our times.

b.
ANXIETY

ROLLO MAY

Centrality of the Problem of Anxiety in Our Day

> Now there are times when a whole generation is caught . . . between two ages, two modes of life, with the consequence that it loses all power to understand itself and has no standards, no security, no simple acquiescence.
>
> —Herman Hesse, *Steppenwolf*.

EVERY ALERT CITIZEN of our society realizes, on the basis of his own experience as well as his observation of his fellow-men, that anxiety is a pervasive and profound phenomenon in the middle of the twentieth century. The alert citizen, we may assume, would be aware not only of the more obvious anxiety-creating situations in our day, such as the threats of war, of the uncontrolled atom bomb, and of radical political and economic upheaval; but also of the less obvious, deeper, and more personal sources of anxiety in himself as well as in his fellow-men—namely, the inner confusion, psychological disorientation, and uncertainty with respect to values and acceptable standards of conflict. Hence to endeavor to "prove" the pervasiveness of anxiety in our day is as unnecessary as the proverbial carrying of coals to Newcastle.

Since the implicit sources of anxiety in our society are generally recognized, our task in this introductory chapter is somewhat more specific. We shall point out how anxiety has emerged, and has to some slight extent been defined, as an *explicit* problem in many different areas in our culture.

Reprinted from *The Meaning of Anxiety* (1950), pp. 3-15, by permission of the author and the publisher. (Copyright 1950, by the Ronald Press Company.)

It is as though in the present decade the explorations and investigations in such diverse fields as poetry and science, or religion and politics, were converging on this central problem, anxiety. Whereas the period of two decades ago might have been termed the "age of covert anxiety"—as we hope to demonstrate later in this chapter—the present phase of our century may well be called, as Auden and Camus call it, the "age of overt anxiety." This emergence of anxiety from an implicit to an explicit problem in our society, this change from anxiety as a matter of "mood" to a recognition that it is an urgent issue which we must at all costs try to define and clarify, are, in the judgment of the present writer, the significant phenomena at the moment. Not only in the understanding and treatment of emotional disturbances and behavioral disorders has anxiety become recognized as the "nodal problem," in Freud's words; but it is now seen likewise to be nodal in such different areas as literature, sociology, political and economic thought, education, religion, and philosophy. We shall cite examples of testimony from these fields, beginning with the more general and proceeding to the more specific concern with anxiety as a scientific problem.

In Literature

If one were to inquire into anxiety as exhibited in the American literature, say, of 1920 or 1930, one would be forced in all probability to occupy oneself with symptoms of anxiety rather than overt anxiety itself. But though signs of open, manifest anxiety were not plentiful in that period, certainly the student could find plenty of symptomatic indications of underlying anxiety. *Vide,* for example, the pronounced sense of loneliness, the quality of persistent searching—frantically and compulsively pursued but always frustrated—in the writings of a novelist like Thomas Wolfe.[1]

In 1950, however, our inquiry is simpler because anxiety has now emerged into overt statement in contemporaneous literature. W. H. Auden has entitled his latest poem with the phrase which he believes most accurately characterizes our period, namely, *The Age of Anxiety.*[2] Though Auden's profound interpretation of the inner experience of the four persons in this poem is set in the time of war—when "necessity is associated with horror and freedom with boredom"[3]—he makes it very clear that the underlying causes of the anxiety of his characters, as well as of others of this age, must be sought on deeper levels than merely the occasion of war. The four characters in the poem, though different in temperament and in background, have in common certain characteristics of our times: loneliness, the feeling of not being of value as persons, and the experience of not being able to love and be loved, despite the common need, the common effort, and the common but temporary respite provided by alcohol. The sources of the anxiety are to be found in certain basic trends in our culture, one of which, for Auden, is the pressure toward conformity which occurs in a world where commercial and mechanical values are apotheosized:

> We move on
> As the wheel wills; one revolution
> Registers all things, the rise and fall
> In pay and prices. . . .[4]
>
> . . . this stupid world where
> Gadgets are gods and we go on talking,
> Many about much, but remain alone,
> Alive but alone, belonging—where?—
> Unattached as tumbleweed.[5]

And the possibility facing these persons is that they too may be drawn into the mechanical routine of meaninglessness:

> . . . The fears we know
> Are of not knowing. Will nightfall bring us
> Some awful order—Keep a hardware store
> In a small town. . . . Teach science for life to
> Progressive girls—? It is getting late.
> Shall we ever be asked for? Are we simply
> Not wanted at all?[6]

What has been lost is the capacity to experience and have faith in one's self as a worthy and unique being, and at the same time the capacity for faith in, and meaningful communication with, other selves, namely one's fellow-men.[7]

The French author, Albert Camus, in a phrase parallel to Auden's, designates this age as "the century of fear," in comparison with the seventeenth century as the age of mathematics, the eighteenth as the age of the physical sciences, and the nineteenth as that of biology. Camus realizes that these characterizations are not logically parallel, that fear is not a science, but "science must be somewhat involved, since its latest theoretical advances have brought it to the point of negating itself while its perfected technology threatens the globe itself with destruction. Moreover, although fear itself cannot be considered a science, it is certainly a technique."[8]

Another writer who graphically expresses the anxiety and anxiety-like states of people in our period is Franz Kafka. The remarkable surge of interest in the 1940's in the writings of Kafka is important for our purposes here because of what it shows in the changing temper of our time; the fact that increasing numbers of people are finding that Kafka speaks significantly to them must indicate that he is expressing some profund aspects of the prevailing experience of many members of our society. In Kafka's novel *The Castle*,[9] the chief character devotes his life to a frantic and desperate endeavor to communicate with the authorities in the castle who control all aspects of the life of the village, and who have the power to tell him his *vocation* and give some meaning to his life. *Kafka's hero is driven "by a need for the most primitive requisites of life, the need to be rooted in a home and a calling, and to become a member of a community."*[10] But the authorities in the castle remain inscrutable and inaccessible, and Kafka's character is as a result without direction and unity in his own life and remains isolated from his fellows. What the castle specifically symbolizes could be debated at length, but since the authorities in the castle are represented as the epitome of a bureaucratic efficiency which exercises such power that it quenches both individual autonomy and meaningful interpersonal relations, it may confidently be assumed that Kafka is in general writing of those aspects of his bourgeois culture of the late nineteenth and early twentieth centuries which so elevated technical efficiency that personal values were largely destroyed.

Herman Hesse, writing less in literary symbols than Kafka, is more explicit about the sources of modern man's anxiety. He presents the story of Haller, his chief character in the novel *Steppenwolf*, as a parable of our period.[11] Hesse holds that Haller's—and his contemporaries'—isolation and anxiety arise from the fact that the bourgeois culture in the late nineteenth and early twentieth centuries emphasized mechanical, rationalistic "balance" at the price of the suppression of the dynamic, irrational elements in experience. Haller tries to overcome his isolation and loneliness by giving free rein to his previously suppressed sensuous and irrational urges (the "wolf"), but this reactive method yields only a temporary relief. Indeed, Hesse presents no thoroughgoing solution to the problem of the anxiety of contemporaneous Western man, for he believes the present period to be one of those "times when a whole generation is caught . . . between two ages." That is to say, bourgeois standards and controls have broken down, but there are as yet no social standards to take their place. Hesse sees Haller's record "as a document of the times, for Haller's sickness of the soul, as I now know, is not the eccentricity of a single individual, but the sickness of the times themselves, the neurosis of that generation to which Haller belongs . . . a sickness which attacks . . . precisely those who are strongest in spirit and richest in gifts."[12]

In Sociological Studies

The emergence of awareness of anxiety as an overt sociological problem in an American community during the third and fourth decades of our century is seen when we compare the Lynds' two studies of Middletown.[13] In the first study, made in the 1920's, anxiety is not an overt problem to the people of Middletown, and the topic does not appear in the Lynds' volume in any of its explicit forms. But anyone reading this study from a psychological viewpoint would suspect that much of the behavior of the citizens of Middletown was symptomatic of *covert anxiety*—for example, the compulsive work ("businessmen and workingmen seem to be running for dear life" in the endeavor to make money[14]), the pervasive struggle to conform, the compulsive gregariousness (*vide* the great emphasis on "joining" clubs), and the frantic endeavors of the people in the community to keep their leisure time crammed with activity (such as "motoring"), however purposeless this activity might be in itself.[15] But only one citizen—whom the Lynds describe as a "perspicacious" observer—looked below these symptoms and sensed the presence of covert apprehension: of his fellow townsmen he observed, "These people are all afraid of something; what is it?"[16]

But the later study of the same community made in the 1930's presents a very different picture: *overt anxiety is now present*. "One thing everybody in Middletown has in common," the Lynds observe, "is insecurity in the face of a complicated world."[17] To be sure, the immediate, outward occasion of anxiety was the economic depression; but it would be an error to conclude that the inclusive *cause* of the emerging anxiety was economic insecurity. The Lynds accurately relate this insecurity in Middletown to the *confusion of role* which the individual was then experiencing; the citizen of Middletown, they write, "is caught in a chaos of conflicting patterns, none of them wholly condemned, but no one of them clearly approved and free from confusion; or, where the group sanctions are clear in demanding a certain role of a man or woman, the individual encounters cultural requirements with no immediate means of meeting them."[18] This "chaos of conflicting patterns" in Middletown is one expression of the pervasive social changes occurring in our culture, which are intimately connected with the widespread anxiety of our times. The Lynds observe that, since "most people are incapable of tolerating change and uncertainty in all sectors of life at once,"[19] the tendency in Middletown was toward a retrenchment into more rigid and conservative economic and social ideologies. This ominous development as a symptom of, and defense against, anxiety points toward the discussion of the relation between anxiety and political authoritarianism in the next section.

In the Political Scene

Turning to the political scene, we again find pronounced anxiety evidenced both in symptomatic and in overt forms. Without going into the complex determinants of fascism, we wish to note that it is born and gains its power in periods of widespread anxiety. Tillich describes the situation in Europe in the 1930's out of which German fascism developed:

> First of all a feeling of *fear* or, more exactly, of indefinite anxiety was prevailing. Not only the economic and political, but also the cultural and religious, security seemed to be lost. There was nothing on which one could build; everything was without foundation. A catastrophic breakdown was expected every moment. Consequently, a longing for security was growing in everybody. A freedom that leads to fear and anxiety has lost its value; better authority with security than freedom with fear![20]

In such periods, people grasp at political authoritarianism in the desperate need to be relieved of anxiety. *Totalitarianism in this sense may be viewed as serving a purpose on a cultural scale parallel to that in which a neurotic symptom protects an individual from a situation of unbearable anxiety.*[21] With some very significant differences, communistic totalitarianism fulfills a similar function.[22] As we shall endeavor to indicate later in this study, fascism and communism are not only economic phenomena, but are also the product of the spiritual, ethical, and psychological vacuum which characterized the breakdown of the bourgeois tradition in Western Europe.[23] As Martin Ebon phrases it, communism is a product of "the desperate wish to find a purpose in what seems confusion and emptiness."[24] In this confusion and emptiness one thing did exist, namely anxiety; and we are submitting that totalitarianism gains its foothold to a considerable extent because, like a symptom, it "binds" and provides some relief from the anxiety.[25]

In addition to anxiety in the above symptomatic forms, *unsystematized* anxiety has been increasingly evident in the sociopolitical scene in the past decade. The frequent references to Roosevelt's sentence in his first inaugural, "The only thing we have to fear is fear itself," testify to the fact that large numbers of people have become increasingly aware of "fear of fear," or more accurately, anxiety, in the face of the radical sociopolitical changes in our day. The emergence of the atom bomb brought the previously inchoate and "free-floating" anxiety of many people into sharp focus. The stark possibilities of modern man's situation are stated in an impassioned expression of the crystallization of anxiety at that moment by Norman Cousins:

> The beginning of the Atomic Age has brought less hope than fear. It is a primitive fear, the fear of the unknown, the fear of forces man can neither channel nor comprehend. This fear is not new; in its classical form it is the fear of irrational death. But overnight it has become intensified, magnified. It has burst out of the subconscious into the conscious, filling the mind with primordial apprehensions. . . . Where man can find no answer, he will find fear.[26]

Even if we should escape being confronted with actual death in a shooting and atomic war, the anxiety inhering in our portentous world situation would still be with us. The historian Arnold Toynbee has stated his belief that overt warfare on a world scale is not probable in our lifetime, but that we shall remain in a "cold" war for a generation, which will mean a perpetual condition of tension and worry. To live in a state of anxiety for a generation is, indeed, a horrendous prospect! But the picture is not inevitably black: Toynbee holds that the tension in the persistent cold war can be used constructively as our motivation for bettering our own socioeconomic standards in the West. The present writer agrees with Toynbee that our political and social survival depends both on our capacity for tolerating the anxiety inherent in the threatening world situation (and thus not irrationally precipitating war as a way out of the painful uncertainty) and also on our capacity for turning this anxiety to constructive uses.[27]

In Philosophy and Religion

The fact that anxiety has emerged as a central problem in contemporaneous philosophy and religion is not only a general, but also a specific indication of the prevalence of anxiety in our culture. It is a specific indication in the respect that anxiety has become most prominent in the thought of those theologians, like R. Niebuhr, who are most intimately concerned with the economic and political issues of our day; and in those philosophers, like Tillich and M. Heidegger, who have experienced in their own lives the cultural crises and upheavals of Western society in the past three decades.[28]

Tillich describes anxiety as man's reaction to the threat of *nonbeing.* Man is the creature who has self-conscious awareness of his being, but he is also aware that at any moment he might cease to exist.[29] Thus in philosophical terms anxiety arises as the individual is aware of being as over against the ever present possibility of nonbeing.[30] "Nonbeing" does not mean simply the threat of physical death—though probably death is the most common form and symbol of this anxiety. The threat of nonbeing lies in the psychological and spiritual realms as well, namely the threat of *meaninglessness* in one's existence.[31] Generally the threat of meaninglessness is experienced negatively as a threat to the existence of the self (the experience of the "dissolution of the self" in Goldstein's term). But when this form of anxiety is confronted affirmatively—when the individual both realizes the threat of meaninglessness and takes a stand against the threat—the result is a strengthening of the individual's feeling of being a self, a strengthening of his perception of himself as distinct from the world of nonbeing, of objects.

Niebuhr makes anxiety the central concept of his theological doctrine of man. To Niebuhr every act of man, creative or destructive. involves some element of anxiety. Anxiety has its source in the fact that man is on one hand finite, involved like the animals in the contingencies and necessities of nature; but on the other hand has freedom. Unlike "the animals he sees this situation [of contingency] and anticipates its perils," and to this extent man transcends his finiteness. "In short, man, being both bound and free, both limited and limitless, is anxious. Anxiety is the inevitable concomitant of the paradox of freedom and finiteness in which man is involved."[32] Much will be said later in the present study about anxiety as the precondition of neurosis; it is significant that Niebuhr, in parallel theological terms, makes anxiety "the internal precondition of sin. . . . Anxiety is the internal description of the state of temptation."[33]

In Psychology

"Anxiety is the most prominent mental characteristic of Occidental civilization," R. R. Willoughby asserts. He then presents statistical evidence for this assertion in the form of the rising incidences in three fields of social pathology which he believes may reasonably be understood as reactions to anxiety, namely *suicide*, the *functional forms of mental disorder*, and *divorce*.[34] Suicide rates for the last 75 to 100 years show a steady increase in the majority of the countries of continental Europe. With regard to the functional forms of mental illness, Willoughby holds, "it seems probable . . . that there is a real rise in incidence of mental disease even when the greatest reasonable allowance is made for increasing facilities for hospitalization and insight in diagnosis."[35] The divorce rates for every country except Japan have shown a steady upward trend in the twentieth century. Willoughby believes the incidence of divorce is a measure of the inability of the members of the culture to tolerate the additional stress of the critical marital adjustment, and the higher incidence must presuppose a considerable load of anxiety in the culture.[36]

We would not question Willoughby's purpose in introducing these statistics, namely, to substantiate the "commonsense proposition that there is in our civilization a large and increasing incidence of anxiety." But there might rightly be considerable question as to whether the relation between these statistical evidences and anxiety is as direct as he holds. Suicide can be due to other motivations than anxiety—revenge is one example. And the rising incidence of divorce would seem to be due to changing social attitudes toward divorce as well as to the prevalence of anxiety. But certainly the three groups of statistics Willoughby presents indicate radical social upheavals in our society which involve psychological and emotional trauma. To the present writer it seems more logical to regard rising divorce, suicide, and mental disease rates as symptoms and products of the traumatically changing state of our culture, and to regard anxiety also as a symptom and product of that cultural state. And certainly a culture described by these statistics would be a culture which generates much anxiety.

Anxiety has gradually come to be seen as a central problem in learning theory, in dynamic psychology, and specifically in psychoanalysis and other forms of psychotherapy. While it long has been recognized that apprehensions and fears, particularly those related to approval or punishment from parents and teachers, exerted much power over the child in school, not until recently have there been scientific recognitions of the innumerable subtle expressions and influences of anxiety permeating the child's educational and classroom experience. For this appreciation of anxiety as a focal problem in learning theory, and the scientific formulation thereof, we are indebted to such learning psychologists as Mowrer, Miller, and Dollard.

More than three decades ago, Freud singled out anxiety as the crucial problem of emotional and behavioral disorders. Further development of psychoanalysis has only substantiated his proposition, until it is now recognized on all sides that anxiety is the "fundamental phenomenon of neurosis," or in Horney's term, the "dynamic center of neuroses." But not only in psychopathology; in the actions of "normal" people as well as "abnormal," it is now recognized that anxiety is much more prevalent than was suspected several decades ago. From the viewpoint of dynamic psychology, Symonds accurately notes that "it would surprise most persons to realize how much of their behavior is motivated by a desire to escape anxiety by either reducing it or disguising it in one way or another."[38] Whether we are concerned with "normal" or pathological behavior, Freud was correct in saying that the solution to the "riddle" of anxiety "must cast a flood of light upon our whole mental life."[39]

FRIEDA FROMM-REICHMANN

Psychiatric Aspects of Anxiety

The most unpleasant and at the same time the most universal experience, except loneliness, is anxiety. We observe both healthy and mentally disturbed people doing everything possible to ward off anxiety or to keep it from awareness.

Mentally disturbed people try to dispel anxiety by developing mental symptoms. In fact as first stated by Freud, mental symptoms are at the same time both the expression of unbearable anxiety and the means of warding it off (9). In other words mental symptoms and mental illness can be understood simultaneously as the outcome of anxiety and as a defense against it. Mental illness can be understood as a person's response to unbearable anxiety. Therefore, anxiety constitutes an essential problem in psychotherapy.

This holds true even though we consider anxiety to be an experience by no means limited to the mentally disturbed. As initially stated, we realize that anxiety in its milder forms is a universal human phenomenon. Philosophers and psychologists have known and advanced this knowledge for a long time. In their eagerness to be great helpers and healers, psychiatrists have been and are still partly inclined to overlook the difference between what may be called the normal anxieties of the emotionally healthy and the neurotic or psychotic excess anxiety which should be subject to psychotherapy. For a long time, psychiatrists and psychotherapists have also overlooked the fact that anxiety not only has negative, disintegrative facets but also some positive, constructive ones. As we set out to clarify the philosophy of psychotherapy regarding neurotic and psychotic anxieties, we must keep these two aspects of anxiety clearly in mind.

Anxiety, as we know, shows in a great variety of ways. Subjectively it may be experienced as a most unpleasant interference with thinking processes and concentration, as a diffuse, vague and frequently objectless feeling of apprehension or as a discomforting feeling of uncertainty and helplessness. As it arises in its milder forms, it may show objectively by a shift in tone of voice, and/or tempo of speech, by a change of posture,

Reprinted from *An Outline of Psychoanalysis* (1955), pp. 113-36, by permission of the author's estate and the publisher.

gesture and motion, also by the anxious person's intellectual or emotional preoccupation or blocking of communication. In people who are even more anxious, anxiety manifests itself psychologically in more or less marked degrees of paralysis of thought and action. The well-known physical manifestations that may be caused by anxiety are symptoms of a hyperactive sympathetic system such as change of turgor, perspiration, tremor, sensation of a lump in the throat, sinking abdominal sensations, diarrhea, vomiting, changes in pupillar reactions, in heart beat, pulse rate, and respiration. If anxiety-states become so severe that the anxiety-stricken person cannot handle them, mental symptoms and mental illness are the final outcome.

In the rare cases when anxiety is so severe that all these expressions of it and all defenses against it fail to bring relief, panic or terror may be the outcome. Panic, as defined by H. S. Sullivan, is an extreme concentration of attention and the direction of all available energy toward only one goal—escape, swift flight from internal dangers which are poorly envisaged, and in the case of failure to escape, by a temporary disintegration of personality with random destructive tendencies against oneself and others. Also according to Sullivan, terror is anxiety of a cosmic quality in the face of a primitively conceived threat of danger. The terror-stricken person feels himself to be alone among deadly menaces, more or less blindly fighting for his survival against dreadful odds (29, 30). Fortunately, terror and panic are short-lived. The organism produces quick defenses against the devastating influence which panic or terror of prolonged duration would exert. John Vassos' empathic pictorial work on Phobia (which, incidentally, is dedicated to H. S. Sullivan) should be mentioned here as an impressive contribution to the understanding of terror and panic (34).

In contrast to these various forms of anxiety, fear is a useful, rational kind of fright elicited by realistic external dangers. To be described presently, and in contrast to fear, are the dangers from within, which elicit anxiety.

What is anxiety in terms of its conceptions in dynamic psychiatry? Freud says in "The Problems of Anxiety," that anxiety is felt by a person at the realization of formerly repressed inacceptable drives and wishes; his anxiety is with regard to loss of love and punishment, i.e., along the lines of Freud's libidinal concepts, castration-fear (9).

We need not go into the discussion of Freud's older explanation of anxiety as the result of repressed sexual desires (5), because he rejected it himself in "The Problems of Anxiety."

Sullivan shares with Freud the concept of the anxiety-arousing power of inacceptable thoughts, feelings, drives, wishes, and actions. But in the framework of his interpersonal conceptions he sees these forbidden inner experiences as interpersonal ones, not as instinctual drives per se; also the expected punishment is not seen as castration-fear. Rather, it is experienced by the anxious person as the anticipated disapproval, i.e., loss of love, from the significant people of his early life, from whom he has originally learned to discriminate between acceptable and inacceptable drives, attitudes, and actions. Later on this fear of disapproval may be transferred from the original significant people who trained and educated the anxious person to their emotional successors. Guilt feelings, separately described by other authors, are obviously inherent in Sullivan's conception of anxiety (29, 30, 31, 32).

This disapproval by the significant people of one's early life, to which both Freud and Sullivan refer, is vital enough to account for severe anxieties, because the infant and the young child are dependent upon the early important people for fulfillment of their basic needs. The infant's survival depends upon the loving care he is given by the mothering ones of his infancy.

Nearly all psychological concepts of anxiety have, in common with Freud and Sullivan, this one basic conception: that anxiety is tied up with the inner danger of inacceptable thoughts, feelings, wishes, or drives which elicit the expectation of loss of love and approval or of punishment. No matter how much these conceptions may differ in their explanatory details and regardless of whether or not this aspect of anxiety is explicitly mentioned in these conceptions, it is a viewpoint now commonly shared.

Let me quote a few outstanding representatives of various psychiatric schools of thinking. Rank speaks of separation anxiety which people first experience at birth and subsequently throughout their lives, present at all phases of personality-development and individuation, from weaning, i.e., separation from mother's breast, to separation from one's fellow men, by death (26).

Adler uses his concept of inferiority feelings where other authors speak of anxiety. He asserts that these inferiority feelings can be overcome by people only in affirmation and strengthening of their social bonds with society, by enforcing the sense of belonging to a social group (1).

Horney emphasizes the central significance of the interrelatedness between anxiety and hostility—anticipated in others and sensed in the anxious person himself; here again anxiety is seen as being tied up with the fear of disruption of one's interpersonal relationships (19).

Poulson, Berdyaev, Halmos, Kardiner, Riesman and other social psychologists find the source of man's anxiety in his psychological isolation, his alienation from his own self and from his fellow men. They consider this the common fate of man in modern society, irrespective of his state of emotional health (3, 10, 18, 22, 27). A poetic version of this viewpoint may be found in Auden's "Age of Anxiety" (2).

Goldstein's conception of anxiety as being the subjective experience of a danger to existence in the face of failure may also imply anxiety regarding loss of love and recognition by those who recognize the anxious person's failure (15, 16).

The same holds true for Rollo May's definition of anxiety as "the apprehension set off by a threat to some value which the individual holds essential to his existence as a personality"[1] (23). Again this concept implies the fear of losing interpersonal recognition or acceptance since this could be tied up with the loss of essential values in the life of the individual. I will return later to the discussion of some other aspects of the conceptions of these authors. At this point I am primarily interested in demonstrating the ubiquitously implied acceptance of the concept that anxiety is connected with anticipated fear of punishment and disapproval, withdrawal of love, disruption of interpersonal relationships, isolation, or separation.

This conception of anxiety as the expression of the anticipated loss of love and approval, or separation, social isolation, or disruption of one's interpersonal relationships implies its close psychological affinity to loneliness. In fact, I believe that many of the emotional states to which psychiatrists refer as anxiety actually are states of loneliness or fear of loneliness.[2]

Now I wish to return to the discussion of the psychodynamics of anxiety. According to Sullivan, the infant and child's need for love and approval and the anxiety connected with rejection and disapproval are utilized by the significant adults in handling the necessary early processes which are designed to train the infant and child for his interpersonal adjustment, his socialization and acculturalization. Out of this educative process evolves the part of human personality which Sullivan has called "self-system." This self-system operates in the service of people to obtain satisfaction without incurring too much anxiety. In the process of establishing the self-system certain infantile trends must be barred from awareness, dissociated. If they break into awareness, anxiety will reappear because the structure of the self-system, the nature of which tends toward rigid maintenance of its protective status quo, is threatened with change. The defensiveness against change makes for the danger of personal rigidity, which in turn increases the potentialities for further anxiety (29, 30). This anxiety connected with change is eternally in conflict with man's general innate tendencies toward growth, toward the change which is implied and particularly with the innate motivation of mental patients toward health. One of the great responsibilities of the psychotherapist is to help patients face and overcome this conflict constructively (12).

I would like to offer an additional explanatory concept about the factors which make people expect punishment, disapproval and loss of love and which has helped me to understand better than I did previously the psychological significance of the anxieties of people in general and of mental patients in particular. Let us ask again: what do people disapprove of most gravely in themselves, i.e., which trends in themselves do they expect will bring the most severe disapproval on the part of the significant people in their lives? Are there other significant causes for the anxiety-arousing anticipation of disapproval and isolation in addition to those we have quoted? Let me offer the following hypothetical answer.

It is a well-known psychological fact that a person will misvalue the significant people of his childhood to the extent to which his early interpersonal tie-ups remain unresolved. If these early interpersonal patterns stand uncorrected, people will distort the image of various people whom they meet in the course of their lives. They may or may not dimly sense that they do so, but they will not recognize the interpersonal misconceptions of their early childhood as the root of the distortions of their interpersonal relationships.

An adult person who finds himself compulsively appraising other people inadequately, incorrectly evaluating their reactions, acting upon and responding to them in line with these misconceptions in terms of early patterns of living, may many times become semi-aware of his erroneous judgment and behavior. However, he may feel inadequate and helpless in his dim wish or attempt to change and correct his judgment and his emotional reactions because he is unaware of their unconscious roots, the unmodified fixations to the patterns of interpersonal relationships which he acquired in his early years. This helplessness in the face of the need to change anachronistic, distorted patterns of interpersonal relationships meets with self-disapproval and discontent; it interferes with the innate tendency to self-realization; it produces deep insecurity in people and meets with the anticipated disapproval of others; thus, it is the expression of anxiety and it produces further anxiety. Goldstein could demonstrate this type of anxiety in his brain-injured patients. When they were faced with a simple task which they could not accomplish for reasons unknown to them, stemming from their neurological brain injury, they became the prey of an abject feeling of helplessness, of nothingness, or a "catastrophic reaction," as Goldstein has called it (15, 16).

The hypothesis is offered that mentally disturbed people frequently develop a "catastrophic reaction," anxiety, in response to their compulsively determined inability to change their distorted, immature patterns of interpersonal relationships. This task may be set by the demands of their own conscience or by the actual or assumed demands of their elders or friends. This helplessness in the presence of the need to envision and to relate oneself adequately to other people, i.e., in accordance with one's chronological age and with one's psychological reality without full awareness of its causes, is most frightening, for more than one reason. It elicits a general feeling of helplessness and paralysis. It means that the person concerned is living in an unreal psychological world and that he feels he is in danger of pulling the people of his environment actually or in fantasy into the same threatening abyss of unreality. Being unable to successfully avail himself of the possibility of using new means of evaluating people and of relating himself meaningfully to them amounts to being blocked in the utilization of learning processes which serve growth and change. This absence of growth and change is tantamount to psychological stagnation and emotional sterility, i.e., psychological death (14). In other words, the repetition-compulsion to follow early patterns of interpersonal evaluation and relatedness and the inability to learn to replace them by new patterns, deprives a person of the freedom to live and move about in the world of psychological reality which should be his, deprives him of the freedom for self-realization and conveys feelings of stagnation and sterility, hence the fear of psychological death, of Tillich's "not being," or Goldstein's "nothingness" (15, 16, 33).

By "self-realization" I mean (to repeat a definition I have previously given [12]) a person's use of his talents, skills and powers to his satisfaction within the realm of his own freely established realistic set of values. Furthermore, I mean the uninhibited ability of patients to reach out for and to find fulfillment of their needs for satisfaction and security, as far as it can be obtained, without interfering with the laws and customs which protect the needs of their fellow-men. Goldstein's "self-actualization," Fromm's "productive character," Whitehorn's "mature personality" and the "self-affirmation" of the existentialists are formulations of the same concept (10, 15, 35). In the classical psychoanalytic literature insufficient attention has been given so far to the concept of self-realization as a great source, if not the greatest source, of human fulfillment. Freud has referred to it in his teachings on secondary narcissism and ego-ideal formation, but he has dealt more with the investigation of the origin of the phenomenon than with the elaboration on the psychological significance of the end-product, mature self-realization (7, 8).

The lack of freedom for self-realization and the feeling of stagnation and "nothingness" that goes with it, this sense of psychological death, seems to me to be at the root of many people's anxiety. To repeat, they cling to infantile interpersonal patterns, and as a result feel helpless without really knowing why. They are unable to grow emotionally, to develop or change. They are not able to think, feel, and act according to their chronological age. They live anachronously in a deadening emotional rut where they compulsively continue to distort their interpersonal images of new people whom they meet, and to misvalue the interpersonal reactions and behavior of these people along the line of the conceptions gained in their unresolved interpersonal childhood contacts.

Example: A young woman, Anna, went to see her older friend and confidant, Mr. N., whom she trusted unequivocally. Anna asked him to contact certain significant people in her family and explain to them some facts about her life which she felt would be of immeasurable value for them and for her in the general family picture. Mr. N. assured Anna of his complete willingness to do this and when Anna left him she was confident that Mr. N. would take care of the situation with understanding and skill. For valid rational reasons, which are beside the point of our discussion, Mr. N. decided later not to meet the members of the family and have a talk with them along the lines suggested by Anna. He did not have an opportunity to discuss this with her. When Anna found out about it a few days later, she felt deep resentment against Mr. N. and developed a spell of severe anxiety. Why? She felt that her friend had not accepted her appraisal of the total situation nor given it serious consideration. She also felt he had treated her the same way her parents had always done; to judge everything the little girl suggested or offered for consideration as not being worthy of serious thought on their part, "little girls are too emotional." Anna realized though, that her resentment against Mr. N., whom she felt had betrayed her and had not taken her suggestion seriously was, somehow, unfounded and sensed dimly that he might well have fallen down on their agreement for valid, rational reasons. However, she felt completely incapable of overcoming her resentment and her severe spell of anxiety lasted for hours. The semi-awareness she had about the irrationality of her anxiety and resentment did not help any until, by psychoanalytic investigation, she finally discovered the reasons, of which she had been unaware. Then she recognized that her resentment was due to a distortion of the present situation between her and Mr. N., in the light of the unresolved interpersonal pattern of living with the parents of her childhood ("little girl"—"too emotional"—judgment and suggestions deserve no consideration).

Jurgen Ruesch's interesting new concept of anxiety which he gained from observation and investigation of people under stress, fits into this context. He says that anxiety arises as a result of overstimulation which cannot be discharged by action (28). The anxious people who have been described are barred from discharging tension by action, from converting anxiety into euphoria because they live in a state of "not-being," or "nothingness."

The anxiety producing aspects of people's unresolved early tie-ups and involvements, of which they are only partially aware, receive additional reinforcement because so many of these anxiety producing aspects are experienced as forbidden and elicit anxiety connected guilt feelings. Love for the parent of the opposite sex and competitive hatred of the parent of the same sex should be mentioned here as the most outstanding example of such anxiety and guilt-evoking psychological constellations.

The resolution of such early tie-ups with the parents of one's childhood, which I have implicitly recommended as a preventive against anxiety, should not be confused with manifestations of a child's outwardly breaking away from his parents. Children who succeed in breaking away from their parents early may experience increased anxiety, since this emerging independence of a child meets with a sense of loss on the part of the parents, hence frequently with their disapproval of the child.

The psychology of masturbation is illustrative of our last statement. There has been much discussion about the following question: Why are there so many children who never have been exposed to any warning against masturbation and many adults who intellectually do not consider masturbation forbidden or dangerous and yet there are practically no people who masturbate without feeling guilty and anxious about it? How can we explain this fact? I believe that guilt eliciting masturbatory fantasies are only partly, if at all, responsible. Many cases of masturbatory feelings of guilt and anxiety seem to be connected with the fact that masturbation represents a child's first act of independence from his parents or others who have raised and mothered him. He needs his elders for the fulfillment of all his basic needs; getting food and fresh air and for being kept clean and getting fresh clothes and bedding. Masturbation is the only pleasure he can obtain without their help. As such, it constitutes an act of breaking away from one's parents, for which the child feels guilty and anxious regardless of the permissive or non-permissive attitude of the elders towards the act of masturbation per se.

It has been stated that practically no one in this culture gets ideally rid of his early interpersonal tie-ups and the resulting interpersonal problems. In other words, almost no one is entirely prepared to face the anxiety-provoking dangers of his present life, fully undistorted by interpersonal entanglements with the "ghosts of his past" and with full command of his adult emotional equipment. As Grinker puts it, in his research on "Anxiety and Psychosomatic Transactions": "The stimulus" (which arouses anxiety) "must be perceived in the light of inner expectation originating at an early and particularly helpless time in the organism's history, to be dangerous to its protective attachments and hence to his existence," i.e., to have the power to produce anxiety (17).

People's fear of nothingness, of helplessness in the face of "psychological death," as it has been postulated here as being a central cause of human anxiety, has a factual correlate in the practically universal experience of anxiety with regard to actual death as a general phenomenon. The fact that life ends with death remains to most people an inconceivable experience of ultimate psychobiological separation. To others, the fact that time and cause of death are unpredictable conveys a painful sense of ultimate powerlessness. This fear and anxiety of death gains reinforcement from the fact that it does not stand only for itself but is also an expression and a symbol of other unknown and unpredictable forces which govern human existence. "It is this fact of our being in a finite and limited time, the awareness of (our) mortality and uncertainty of the future," which renders us helpless and anxious, as Podolsky puts it (25). That is, people seem to feel the same helplessness and anxiety in the face of the phenomenon of actual death as they do in the face of the above defined personal experience of "psychological death."

There are various ways in which people may try to counteract the anxiety and the narcissistic hurt inflicted on them when they are faced with the necessity of accepting the reality of death. The powerfulness of these defenses is a measuring rod for the intenseness of the anxiety which people try to fight off with them.

The religious concept of the Hereafter is the greatest attempt to counteract the inconceivable separation experience which is death.

The well known phenomenon of people's guilt feelings after the death of a close person is, in my judgment, caused not only by the ambivalence toward the deceased, but also and more so by people's anxiety about the uncertainty and unpredictability which go with the very nature of life and death. Feeling guilty about someone's death means assuming part of the responsibility. If we are partly responsible, the inconceivable, unpredictable character of death is mitigated; it is put into some more acceptable context with that which man can influence—or fails to influence—by virtue of his own skills and powers.

A more pathological way of counteracting the anxiety connected with death is used by certain emotionally disturbed people to whom its uncertainty is so anxiety provoking and unbearable that they evade its acceptance, or at least find satisfaction in fantasying that they can evade it, by committing suicide. To these people, suicide means doing away with the unpredictability of the end of their lives. As if, by their own determination, they take the power of decision out of the hands of the Lord, of fate or of nature, as their conceptions may be (36, 37).

These examples show that the defenses people feel the need to erect against the anxieties connected with actual death are just as powerful as the symptoms with which mental patients try to protect themselves against the anxiety connected with "psychological death."

Some psychoanalysts may ask at this point, how this concept of anxiety in the face of psychological and factual death ties up with the classical psychoanalytic concept of the death instinct? Freud postulated, in his metapsychological treatise. "Beyond the Pleasure Principle," that man is born with aggressive and destructive impulses against himself and others (6). Man's death instinct, according to Freud, operates throughout his life as the expression of these self-destructive tendencies against himself.

Other psychoanalysts in writing about this topic have tried to prove the existence of the death-instinct in terms of what, in their judgment, are self-destructive operations which we can observe in most people, such as their neglect in seeking medical help for obviously harmful pathological processes (24). I believe this seemingly self-destructive behavior can be better understood as the outcome of man's fear of death than as the response to his death-instinct. He does not consult the doctor lest he be faced with a fatal prognosis of his ailment which might increase his fear of death.

I find myself in agreement with Sullivan, Fromm, and several other dynamic psychiatrists and psychoanalysts who do not find any evidence of primary in-born hostile and destructive tendencies in the human mind, but who deduct from their psychiatric experience that the rise of hostile and destructive tendencies is the outcome of and the response to the adversities of people's interpersonal experiences throughout their lives. Consequently, these authors do not see any evidence of the original existence of self-destructive tendencies of a death instinct, as a given ubiquitous phenomenon (11, 29).

Irrespective of the controversial issue of Freud's concept of the death instinct, we agree with his conceptions that man must have some kind of an inner awareness, or sense some kind of reflection of the changes of the organism which take place daily and hourly in the direction of its final dissolution and death. I believe that man's inner awareness of these changes of the organism on its gradual way from birth to death contribute to his fear of death and to his anxiety of the unknown which is connected with the facts of death, rather than their being an expression of his death instinct.

So much about the anxiety connected with what I have called "psychological death" and about the anxiety connected with the psychological facts of actual death as a general human phenomenon. Our data corroborates our introductory statement about there being almost no one permanently free from anxiety. Yet, healthy people learn to handle their anxieties without converting them into symptoms. They may even be able to turn them into assets, a topic on which I have elaborated elsewhere (13).

In the same context, let me also quote Horney who states that both types of anxiety, that of the mentally healthy and of mentally disturbed people, render them helpless and this helplessness in turn produces more anxiety, "secondary" anxiety. However, Horney says that anxiety in the face of actual death and of the other powers of nature must be accepted and does not call for the development of the defense mechanism and of the hostility and destructiveness which people develop in response to other —neurotic or psychotic—forms of helplessness and anxiety. The contrary may even be true (19). Grinker corroborates this viewpoint when he states: "If anxiety is mild, it is stimulating and facilitates increased and efficient action or thought" (16).

As Fromm pointed out, anxiety in the face of the overwhelming and unpredictable powers of nature, which is the common fate of all of us, may be used as a motivation for increasing the common bonds between human beings.

Freud, and also Adler, have emphasized the viewpoint that human efforts to allay anxiety have led to the development of civilization. Jung and Adler also emphasize the positive powers of constructive defense which may be aroused in people for the sake of counteracting their anxiety (1, 6, 21).

The existentialists, including one of the outstanding psychiatrists among them, Binswanger, stress the constructive aspects of anxiety even more. They consider it the equivalent of the tension aroused in a person who is able to face the universe and the task which is set to men, to conquer the emanations of the universe by action (4, 35).

States of anxiety which are severe enough to call for expression and defense by mental symptoms, i.e., the states of excess anxiety of which neurotic and psychotic patients suffer, are, of course, not constructive except for the times when they are reduced to milder degrees.

It should not be overlooked though, that the anxiety of mental patients under treatment can be psychotherapeutically utilized as a signpost indicating underlying conflicts and as a challenge to solve them. This holds true for neurotic patients as well as for psychotics. In fact, it may be generally stated that mild degrees of anxiety, discomforting as they may be, can be useful danger signals to mentally healthy and to mentally disturbed people (9, 35).

Some readers may be surprised that I suggest psychotherapeutic intervention not only with excess anxiety in neurotic patients but also in psychotics. Clinical experience during the last 25 or 30 years has taught dynamic psychiatrists that both neurotic and psychotic excess anxieties can be successfully treated with psychoanalysis or psychoanalytically oriented dynamic psychotherapy. Time and space permitting, I could corroborate this statement with many examples from my own experience and that of many other psychiatrists who work with both types of patients. We cannot enter into a discussion of the psychotherapeutic techniques which dynamic psychiatrists use in the treatment of anxiety. If our initial statement is correct, that anxiety is at the root of every mental disturbance, then it is also true that any discussion of psychotherapeutic methods in the treatment of neurotic and psychotic anxieties would amount to writing a paper on psychotherapy at large.

I will restrict myself, therefore, to the following brief comments: We have seen that people who suffer from anxiety are at best only semi-aware of its causes. Therefore, the focal point of all psychotherapeutic guidance or treatment of anxiety states is to help the anxious person uncover and understand the unconscious reasons for his helplessness and anxiety. Beyond that it follows from our distinction between mild degrees of anxiety and their predominantly constructive aspects and severe degrees of anxiety with their predominantly disjunctive aspects, that the specific psychotherapeutic usefulness of dynamic psychiatrists in helping anxious patients, encompasses three central therapeutic tasks. One therapeutic goal should be to guide people in understanding and then accepting and learning to live with and to utilize mild degrees of anxiety. In the case of more intensive states of anxiety, the psychotherapeutic goal should be to help people (patients), for preventive reasons, uncover, resolve and integrate the causes of these anxieties, lest they lead up to an expression by mental symptoms which simultaneously are used as defenses against the awareness of these anxiety states. In cases where a person's anxiety is severe enough to express itself in mental symptomatology and mental illness, the psychotherapeutic goal should be to help the mental patient with the methods of intensive psychoanalytically oriented dynamic psychotherapy to gain insight into the emotional roots of his anxiety and of his symptomatology, to understand the psychodynamic linkage between anxiety and symptomatology and to face, work through, and eventually vanquish his excess anxiety. Caution is indicated regarding the timing and the dosage of therapeutic intervention and enlightenment, lest a patient be made to face more dynamic insight into his anxiety and greater amounts of open anxiety than he can accept at a given time.

The discussion of the psychotherapeutic aspects of anxiety would be more than incomplete if its focus were not extended to the problem of anxiety in psychotherapists. If it is true that there is practically no one who is permanently free from anxiety, and/or none in whom anxiety cannot be temporarily aroused by all kinds of adverse experiences, then this fact, of course, holds true for psychotherapists as well. In their case, we are especially interested in the feelings of anxiety which may, sometimes, be brought forth in them by their patients.

A psychotherapist who does not know and integrate this fact, who dreams about his non-vulnerability to anxiety, be it aroused in his exchange with patients or other persons, a psychotherapist who dreams about "complete emotional security" as an unreal goal for his own inner life, cannot guide his mental patients to wholesome, constructive testing and evaluation of their anxieties and to a constructive adjustment to the facts and data of their internal and external reality. Awareness of his anxiety, not freedom from or denial of it and sufficient emotional security to accept and handle it is the philosophical attitude toward anxiety to be expected of a competent, mature psychiatrist. Incidentally, there was a time when it was my belief that a well-analyzed psychotherapist should be altogether free from anxiety and emotional insecurity. As a matter of fact, my printed elaborations on such utopianism can still be read in my book "Principles of Intensive Psychotherapy" (12). To repeat, I now believe, or better still, I know that a state of mind permanently free of anxiety is utopianism for the psychotherapist by the same token that it is for anyone else.

There are many pitfalls in the psychiatrist's interaction with patients and for that matter, in the interaction of other people engaged in responsible interpersonal guidance of their fellow men, if they are not willing and able to accept the awareness of a certain amount of anxiety and emotional insecurity within themselves. Conversely, there is a great and constructive source of help for psychotherapeutic effectiveness in the psychiatrist's awareness and creative acceptance of his own anxieties whenever they are elicited. The therapist's anxiety is frequently indicative of emotional experiences in patients which arouse anxiety in him. Thus the psychiatrists' anxiety becomes an important divining rod for the discovery of many emotional experiences of patients, which might otherwise remain undiscovered and hidden for a long time, as in the case of a psychiatrist who would not feel free to use his own anxiety as a guide to anxiety-provoking emotional experiences in patients.

A therapist's denial of his own anxieties may cause him to overlook the possibility of his contaminating patients with them, a danger which in extreme cases may only be eliminated or corrected by its free discussion between patient and doctor, or for that matter between any other two participants in such an experience. Furthermore, in a therapist, denial of anxiety may arouse all kinds of defenses in him which will interfere with his therapeutic usefulness. That is, he may feel he must reassure himself against the onslaught of anxiety aroused in him by a patient by giving the patient uncalled for reassurance. Or, he may try to propitiate his patient by assuming, for his own defense, all types of roles in the therapeutic process (e.g., the "better" parent, the "great" doctor), instead of operating for the benefit of the patient. A psychotherapist (like any other person participating in an interpersonal exchange) is only able to listen with unimpaired alertness, perceptiveness and creative responsiveness, i.e., he is only able to operate effectively, to the extent to which there is no interference from defense against his own recognized anxiety.

At present, I am engaged along with several colleagues at Chestnut Lodge, in a research project on the intuitive elements in the doctor's therapeutic approach to schizophrenics. There, we have ample opportunity to observe clearly the marked interference with free utilization of intuitive abilities stemming from our anxiety, with regard to our patients, as well as with regard to our colleagues in the research group, as long as this anxiety operates unrecognized.

There is one more important psychotherapeutic issue which is in danger of being obscured in cases of psychiatrists' unrecognized anxiety. A therapist who fails to recognize and to accept his own anxieties will also fail to differentiate correctly between the type and the degree of pathological excess anxiety in mental patients, which is subject to treatment, and the general human experience of non-pathological anxieties which everyone may suffer and utilize as part of the business of living. To put the same thought differently: psychotherapists are not Gods who can change man's fate, which includes everyone, at times, being submitted to states of anxiety. In their role as individual psychiatrists, they cannot alter, except very slowly and imperceptively, the structure of a culture and a society which may elicit anxiety in its members. However, psychiatrists can and should be useful in man's fight against his individual, irrational excess anxieties, and in encouraging people to accept and integrate constructively and without psychotherapeutic help the milder degrees of anxiety which we may loosely call "normal" anxiety.

Summary

Anxiety is seen as a universal emotional experience. The reader's attention is directed toward the realization that milder degrees of anxiety have both disintegrative and constructive aspects.

Severe degrees of anxiety are described as leading up to the development of mental illness, mental symptoms being simultaneously an expression of severe anxiety and a defense against it.

The existing genetic theories on anxiety are briefly reviewed, and the fear of anticipated disapproval, withdrawal of love, and separation from significant environmental figures is discussed as a factor, about the genetic significance of which most authors agree.

The hypothesis is offered that the genesis of anxiety may also be understood as a result of unresolved early emotional tie-ups with significant persons of one's early environment. People are stuck with these early interpersonal patterns and with their early interpersonal evaluation which remain uncorrected. These fixations, of which people are only partially aware, if at all, render them psychologically helpless, interfere with their ability to change, with their growth, maturation and self-realization, and with their correct evaluation of their own and other peoples' interpersonal interactions. The result is "psychological death," which elicits anxiety. This anxiety is compared to the anxiety which is called forth in most people by factual death and similar phenomena which are beyond human control and, therefore, arouse helplessness and anxiety.

A distinction is proposed between psychotherapeutic guidance in cases of milder forms of anxiety and psychotherapeutic intervention in cases of severe forms of anxiety, which lead to neurotic or psychotic symptom-formation and mental illness.

Finally, the anxieties which may be elicited in psychotherapists during the treatment situation are discussed in their constructive and in their disintegrative aspects.

References

1. Adler, Alfred. *The Neurotic Constitution.* Translated by Bernard Glueck. New York: Moffat, Yard & Co., 1917.
2. Auden, W. H. *The Age of Anxiety.* New York: Random House, 1946.
3. Berdyaev, Nicholas. *Solitude and Society.* London: 1938.
4. Binswanger, Ludwig. *Grundformen und Erkenntnis Menschlichen Daseins.* Zurich: Max Niehans Verlag, 1942.
5. Freud, Sigmund. *A General Introduction to Psychoanalysis.* New York: Liveright, 1935; Garden City Publ. Co., 1943. (Chapter on Anxiety)
6. Freud, Sigmund. *Beyond the Pleasure Principle.* London: Hogarth Press, 1942.
7. Freud, Sigmund. "On Narcissism: An Introduction," in *Collected Papers,* IV. London: Hogarth Press, 1946. Pp. 30-59.
8. Freud, Sigmund. *The Ego and the Id.* London: Hogarth Press, 1935.
9. Freud, Sigmund. *Problems of Anxiety.* New York: Norton, 1936.
10. Fromm, Erich. *Man for Himself.* New York: Rinehart, 1947.
11. Fromm, Erich. "Selfishness and Self-love," *Psychiatry,* II (1939), 507-23.
12. Fromm-Reichmann, Frieda. *Principles of Intensive Psychotherapy.* Chicago: University of Chicago Press, 1950.
13. Fromm-Reichmann, Frieda. "Remarks on the Philosophy of Mental Disorders," *Psychiatry,* IX (1946), 293-308.
14. Fromm-Reichmann, Frieda. "Psychoanalysis and Dynamic Psychotherapy. Similarities and Differences," *Journal of the American Psychoanalytic Association,* II (1954), 711-21.
15. Goldstein, Kurt. *Human Nature in the Light of Psychopathology.* Cambridge: Harvard University Press, 1940.
16. Goldstein, Kurt. *The Organism.* New York: American Book Co., 1939.
17. Grinker, Roy R. *Psychosomatic Research.* New York: Norton, 1953.
18. Halmos, Paul. *Solitude and Privacy.* New York: Philosophical Library, 1953.
19. Horney, Karen. *New Ways in Psychoanalysis.* New York: Norton, 1939.
20. Horney, Karen. *The Neurotic Personality of Our Time.* New York: Norton, 1937.
21. Jung, C. G. *Collected Papers on Analytical Psychology.* Translated by C. E. Long. London: Baillere, Tindall & Cox, 1920.
22. Kardiner, Abram. *The Psychological Frontiers of Society.* New York: Columbia University Press, 1945.
23. May, Rollo. *The Meaning of Anxiety.* New York: Ronald Press, 1951.
24. Menninger, Karl. *Man against Himself.* New York: Harcourt, Brace, 1938.

25. Podolsky. "The Meaning of Anxiety," *Diseases of the Nervous System*, XIV (1953), 4.

26. Rank, Otto. *Will Therapy and Truth and Reality*. New York: Knopf, 1945.

27. Riesman, David. *The Lonely Crowd*. New Haven, Yale University Press, 1950.

28. Ruesch, Jurgen. "The Interpersonal Communication of Anxiety." *Symposium of Stress* (Wash., D.C.: Walter Reed Army Medical Center, 1953), 154-64.

29. Sullivan, H. S. *Conceptions of Modern Psychiatry*. Wash., D.C.: The Wm. Alanson White Found., 1947. New Edition, New York: Norton, 1953.

30. Sullivan, H. S. *The Interpersonal Theory of Psychiatry*. New York: Norton, 1953.

31. Sullivan, H. S. "The Meaning of Anxiety in Psychiatry and in Life," *Psychiatry*, XI (1948), 1-13.

32. Sullivan, H. S. "The Theory of Anxiety and the Nature of Psychotherapy," *Psychiatry*, XII (1949), 3-12.

33. Tillich, Paul. *The Courage To Be*. New Haven: Yale University Press, 1952.

34. Vassos, John. *Phobia*. New York: Covici-Friede, 1931.

35. Weigert, Edith. "Existentialism and Its Relation to Psychotherapy," *Psychiatry*, XII (1949), 399-412.

36. Zilboorg, Gregory. "Considerations on Suicide with Particular Reference to that of the Young," *American Journal of Orthopsychiatry* (1937).

37. Zilboorg, Gregory. "Suicide Among Civilized and Primitive Races," *American Journal of Psychiatry*, XCII (1936), 1347-69.

KURT RIEZLER

The Social Psychology of Fear

I

MAN'S FEAR is fear *of* something or *for* something: *of* illness, loss of money, dishonor; *for* his health, family, social status. The relation of the first something to the second something and their respective relevances determine the particular kind and intensity of our fear.

Reprinted from the *American Journal of Sociology*, XLIX, No. 2 (1944), by permission of the University of Chicago Press. (Copyright, 1944, by the University of Chicago Press.)

The one and the other something have a definite nature. We know what they are like. We may not know which of several knowable possibilities will occur. The particular relation of our knowledge to our ignorance gives a particular color to our fear.

In the concrete case fear is never alone. We always hope, if only that the thing we are afraid of will not happen. Man faces great danger without fear, if a strong desire, emotion, passion sways his heart. Men and animals in rage are blind to danger. Hope can conquer fear. Man, a gambler by nature, hopes against hope.

Man, as a striving being, finite, in a world that is never entirely of his own making, is forever in between some kind of fear and some kind of hope, some kind of knowledge and some kind of ignorance. Fear and hope are at odds: hope wants fear removed; it demands action. Fear lets hope dread its end. Fear, mingling in our hope, hope mingling in our fear—each pleads for knowledge against the other's weakness for ignorance.

Both fear and knowledge have a social dimension. We cannot start from "Man" written with a capital and with a turn of our hand substitute for the universal man the isolated individual. No man is Man—everyone is this or that man among men. An "I" takes into account what things are to a "You" and a "We"—or, to use an expression of Mead, human beings "take one another's roles." Not knowing, I rely on your knowledge: you are not afraid. Or you are afraid but you do not know; I know—lean on me. The child looks at its mother; the mother reassures the child. Every society that deserves the name is a "universe of discourse." A man's fear does not depend merely on his individual knowledge and ignorance. Within the universe of discourse the knowledge of the others reassures my ignorance; the ignorance of the others shakes my confidence in my knowledge. We need not resort to "contagion," "suggestion," "imitation."

Fear of something for something seems to be partial fear. This something has a definite character which if not known is knowable. There is, however, total fear. First, the fear of death. We are afraid of death for our life; our life includes everything.

We know death—it has a definite character. We may not know how much suffering our dying will impose or the kind of life after death, if there is any. Our fear of death blends with our fear of our suffering in dying, with our fear of, or hope for, a life beyond. Our knowledge, doubt, or ignorance gives to our fear of death a particular tint. Though we know at any moment that we must die, we do not fear death all the time, except in some remote or dark corner of our mind. We cannot escape death; we can only try to postpone it. We shove back the idea. We observe death around us, but we ourselves do not die—as yet. It is the other fellow who dies. Life refuses to think of death. This is the way of the living to protect life against the power of death.

Death seems to be eminently individual. Everybody must die his own death for himself. Dying isolates the individual. Yet death has a social dimension, too. Death is final only for the individual. Though death ends our hoping, it does not end the content of our hopes. Everyone is entitled to slight the difference, yet no one can deny it. Isaac, dying, blesses Jacob. He lives in and hopes for his children. They will carry on—though Isaac has no hope of sharing Jacob's rise. Isaac's death ends Isaac for Isaac; it does not end the world in which he lived, loved, and cared. Another man dies and sees his world, task, family, country, reputation, or whatever he cared for tottering to their fall. Both fear death—their fear has a different quality. The death of the soldier in victory and defeat is not entirely the same. The one cannot partake in the joy of a winning cause; the other need not partake in the misery of a lost cause. The content of hope and care survives in the first case, perishes in the second. Though the difference may disappear in the extreme loneliness of the very last hour, it is still real in the last but one.

Social psychology cannot deal with any phenomenon of social life on the basis of the conceptual scheme of an individual psychology that, putting Ego in the center, refers the world as behavioral environment or phenomenal field to the individual by a one-way arrow. No sane man really thinks of himself merely as the center of his world. Nobody conceives of the world in which he lives as merely his phenomenal field or behavioral environment. This field points and refers to something beyond itself: the world in which we and our fellow men live, everybody's potential environment, interpreted not merely by ourselves but by the "universe of discourse" in which we live. The theory of knowledge may refer the world to a transcendental subject. If the psychologist refers the phenomenal field to the psychological subject, he should not forget that the concrete individual returns the reference: everybody, however egocentric, refers himself and his phenomenal field to an objective world which is the world of the others, in one way or the other, be it in love or hate, in care, work, or a task. In this world the Ego is not the center. If the environment is what it is relatively to the individual, the individual cannot help being to himself what he is relatively to the world in which he lives. There are two arrows, both pointing both ways and interacting in a give and take. Social psychology cannot follow an individual psychology that forgets the other arrow.

II

These introductory remarks hurry through difficult terrain and jump many a hurdle. They are intended to articulate our ordinary fear in a preliminary way.

There is a kind of fear that is not fear of something definite for something definite. It can be described as fear of everything for everything or of nothing for nothing. In extreme cases this indefinite fear can be more "total" and worse than the fear of death. Men may commit suicide to escape its extreme misery.

Under the name of "anxiety" or basic anxiety" this fear has come to be of particular interest since Kierkegaard handed to the German "existential" philosophy of the twentieth century the distinction between *Furcht* and *Angst*, and psychopathologists discovered an "anxiety neurosis."

The German *Angst*, the French *angoisse*, the English *anguish*, and the Latin *angustiae* all stem from a root which connotes "pressure," "narrowness." The corresponding word in Greek, used with some emphasis by the Christian fathers, is *stenochoria*, "the narrow space." Man's chest feels constricted. Anxiety closes walls in on man.

I may assume that this anxiety is not entirely alien to anyone. It is vague—but it may be more powerful for its vagueness. As there is no definite threat or danger upon which we could act, it paralyzes action. As the shapeless daughter of the shapeless night, it calls in the dark on the child or the lonely man. It seems to be an eminently individual experience. The presence of companions keeps it away. So it seems.

The relation of this indefinite fear to our knowledge and ignorance is dubious. Traditional psychology offers but little help. Kierkegaard and his followers answer: We fear *das Nichts*—nothingness. This is, however, hardly the result of a psychological analysis. It is a philosophical device peculiar to a situation in which a man who has lost both his god and his world is thrown back on himself and faces *das Nichts*. At least this *nihil metaphysicum* must be specified. There are too many logically different *nihils*. It seems to be a *nihil privativum*. But the privation is again a specific privation.

Common sense may suggest that this anxiety is merely a presentment of an evil that might befall us. We simply do not know which of the many known and knowable evils it will be. This may suffice in some light cases in which our anxiety still borders on ordinary fear. It does not suffice in other cases.

What do we mean by knowledge and ignorance? We know this and that—Mr. Brown or Chicago. There are other things we do not know—Mr. Smith or Kansas City. If our knowledge were merely of this kind—a knowledge of some items out of an aggregate of unknown items—paralyzed by fear, we could not move or act. Fortunately we know more. We know what Mr. Smith can be or is likely to be. He will not suddenly turn into an elephant and trample us down. He will keep within the limits of a definite order. We know, or assume we know, this order. Though we do not know what will happen, we know what can happen—either this or that. Every possible change or event, even our own death, will keep within the scheme of a certain order. This order we trust; it is the order of the world in which we live. On this basis and by means of this scheme we identify, classify, characterize things. We give them a place in this order. If there are things we do not know, we merely mean that we do not yet know their place. But they have a place. The order is all-comprehensive. Thus a preformed scheme limits and specifies our fear and guides our action—whether we are primitive or civilized, animal or man.

We arrive at the railway station of a town we do not know. The town is not simply "an unstructured area in the cognitive structure of the psychological field." We know what it is like: a maze of streets, houses standing on firm ground, people walking and knowing their way. The cognitive structure of our environment is not merely the present phenomenal field. It includes the rules to which any change of the present phenomenal field will submit. We know that the phenomenal field is only our present aspect of the field of all the others. It is pre-structured and knowable. We merely fill out a preformed scheme. Moreover, we rely on the others: their actual knowledge is our own potential knowledge. Our fear is limited to meeting gangsters, creditors, relatives, a former love. Our reaction to a totally unstructured area, if there were any, would be an anxiety neurosis.

Our hope likes to go beyond this order into the realm of the impossible. We know, however, that this hope is vain. We draw a line between the possible and impossible. Hope transgresses, fear never transgresses, this line. The impossible does not frighten us. If, however, under the shock of an experience that shatters our scheme of order, we doubt or no longer trust this scheme, the dividing line fades and indefinite fear invades the bewildered soul.

Now it might be possible to specify the *nihil* in Kierkegaard's concept of anxiety. Nobody can be prevented from interpreting fear of death as fear of an absolute nothing. Anxiety, however, is not simply fear of death. In anxiety we do not fear nothingness. We fear something; we do not know it and feel unable to know what it is. This nothing is still something, though it is deprived of any definite character. It fits no scheme; it is beyond our reach. It deprives us of our trust in any order. It is not absolute nothingness but absolute "otherness." It would not be frightening if it were "nothing." It is frightening because it is still "something"—though not to be known, not to be acted upon. This anxiety may blend with the fear of death; the difference is still a psychological reality and accounts at least for a particular color in our fear of death.

III

I turn to the interpretation of different cases of anxiety. Though each case has a long story to tell, rapid glances will suffice.

a) A human being is alone in a wood at night. Dead leaves rustling cause, as Luther says, deadly fright. I cannot compel anybody to go beyond saying simply that this man is afraid for his life or his wallet, of a gangster behind a tree. In most cases we might discover another note, however faint: a feeling as if something extraordinary, hardly possible, could happen—ghosts, voices of the dead. Darkness deprives us of the definite shape of the things that in daylight testify to the order on this well-rounded earth. Moreover, we are alone; there are no others on whom we can rely. Two children in the same situation are afraid, each for himself. The younger relies on the older—he will know. The older, knowing he is relied upon, hides his fear.

b) In modern experiments animals are treated to an anxiety neurosis.[1] The behavioristic approach seems to demand, first, that the mental system of cats be disorganized by a highly artificial conditioning of their responses. Then they are frightened by a series of unexpected and inexplicable events produced by the devilish contrivances of the modern scientist: electric currents, wind blowing out of dishes of food, walls of their cages closing in upon them. The desired result occurs: the cats go mad. However short the cat memory, they do not eat for days. Friendly petting speeds recovery. The experimenter cannot get the same results with dogs. The dog, closer than the cat to human beings, relies on the observer. He may bark furiously, but he does not get a neurosis—unless the observer, too, takes the pains to lose his mind. We may assume that even the cat world which we do not know has a cognitive structure and some scheme of order that such experiments upset.

If the experimenter could do to human beings what he does to cats, confronting an isolated human being with events as inexplicable as these events are to the cat, everybody could be treated to an anxiety neurosis.

c) After World War I psychologists and neurologists in Germany made a careful study of incurable cases of soldiers wounded in the brain.[2] Diverse faculties of these men, necessary for ordinary living, have been impaired. They succeed, within certain limits, in developing substitute techniques by which they are able to carry on in the minutely and rigidly ordered environment of their hospitals. Everything must always be in its usual place. They are fettered to the particular order of an environment of extreme rigidity and narrowness, unable to detach themselves from, or to move beyond, this order. Any change, disturbance, or new task threatens the whole of this order and leads to a "catastrophic reaction," in which their neurosis recurs. As this order is the basis of any action they are capable of, any change finds them helpless and throws them into a kind of fear which, in the extreme case, may well be worse and more total than the fear of death to a healthy mind. It swallows up their world. Their scheme of order remains precarious even when not challenged by any event. It is an individual scheme, lacking any social support. There is no universe of discourse to confirm it as a matter of course. As they sense its precariousness and suspect an impending change, they fear an attack of their fear, half-consciously aware of a constant threat.

d) I oppose to this case of extreme rigidity an example of a scheme of extreme flexibility: the world of the growing child. The child has not yet an established scheme of order, a system of permanences embracing the world. Yet the child does not live in a constant state of indefinite fear. Though we might say that he explores his world in between anxiety and curiosity, his curiosity usually gets the better of his anxiety.

His system of order is in the making. Though any actual knowledge is still narrow, his mind is open to a wide range of what is possible. As he explores the world, the real and the imaginary blend—he does not yet draw our dividing-line. His play is half-serious, his seriousness half-play. Slowly he enlarges his still narrow world, reorganizing its assumed order with every new experience. All his permanences are still *ad hoc*: assumptions to be made, revised, and abandoned. Thus he stumbles along the edge of an abyss, blindly, yet carefully, a little anxious, yet more curious, shrinking back at every touch of anxiety and trying again, ignoring demands he cannot meet, shunning the unknowable. Ignorance of danger protects the play of a tentative knowledge.

We cannot isolate the child. The process in which he forms his preliminary world could not proceed if the child were not aware of living in the world of his elders. His first assumption is his mother and her knowledge. Here, again, individual psychology easily leads astray. The mother is not simply one of many items in a phenomenal field. The entire phenomenal field is referred to the mother. The assumption of her knowledge underlies and accompanies every hypothesis the child makes concerning the nature of things. As the child builds up his own world, he "learns" the world of his elders. Objectification mixes giving names and learning the names. The child himself has a name; he is Jack or simply "he" long before he discovers the Ego. The reference to his mother and her knowledge protects the play of curiosity against anxiety. Frightened, the child hides behind his mother's apron.

e) It is amazing how much danger and fright a soldier in battle can stand: (i) when in action; (ii) if there is still hope, however slight, of survival; (iii) when he knows and can identify the danger; (iv) when relying on someone who shows no fear. The more flexible his cognitive faculties, the less exposed is the soldier to neurotic shocks. The nervous intellectual is safer than many a robust and healthy peasant. The most courageous soldier, able to face any direct threat of death, may tremble in an indefinite situation of unknown and unidentifiable dangers. French-African soldiers, fearless warriors, do not understand the situation in modern warfare. They trust, however, the knowledge of their white officers. Only in the case of tanks did the white officer find himself without power over their fear, until he succeeded in demonstrating some similarity between tanks and elephants, in behavior and treatment. After this war, interesting studies may become possible concerning the interrelation between particular kinds of fear and the peculiarities of modern weapons which differ widely in the amount of knowledge and awareness they permit.

IV

In these examples, the distinction between our ordinary fear of and for a definite thing and our indefinite anxiety corresponds to the distinction between our knowledge and ignorance of this or that item and our knowledge and ignorance of the scheme of order to which all possible items will submit.

This scheme of order of the possible is a system of rules, principles, and assumptions which are taken for granted. Its structure is complex. Such systems can be very different with respect not only to the content of the rules but also to their structural properties. They are never merely aggregates of habits, inherited or acquired, concerning certain rules for this, and other rules for that, case. They are systems; if they are inconsistent, they pretend to be consistent. They claim to cover every possible case. They order our worlds—the worlds in which we think of ourselves as living, acting, moving.

I disregard all controversies of the theory of knowledge concerning the origin and growth of this system. They have no bearing on the psychology of fear. Likewise, I disregard the thorny problems posed by the nature, complexity, and possible variations of these systems. They would lead beyond the scope of this study. The axioms of such a system may be known a priori or a posteriori; they may be "true" or erroneous, mere assumptions, hypotheses, conventions; they may be rational or magical. In the case of the primitive man it may mean the rules of magic, the norms of a society of men, animals, spirits, demons, gods. In many a concrete case of an ordinary citizen in this rational age of ours, it may encompass rational principles as well as all kinds of empirical rules, from the geometry of space, the categories in which we think, the law of causality, to such dubious assumptions as that there is "progress" or that the big banks will never suddenly close their windows. His is a world in which a great many things cannot happen. In both cases it means a universal system of permanences which, rightly or wrongly, we take for granted and on the basis of which we give to any new experience an orderly place in our world.

This system is the basis of our action. If we do not know the nature of a danger, we make an assumption. Without such an assumption, we cannot act. Without such a scheme, we cannot even make such an assumption. We have moral principles, individual or social norms of decent behavior. We cannot, however, translate these principles or norms into concrete behavior except on the basis of such a scheme of order. Usually we are not even asked to do any such translating, as these principles and norms are already formulated in terms of our scheme of order. Hence, we might understand that a serious threat to the scheme of order of the possible can deprive human beings not only of their capacity for action but also of any standards of decent behavior they might have. In this case man knows neither what he could nor what he should do. Even hope, losing its guide, loses its force.

These systems, though systems of permanences, undergo change. They are in a continuous, though usually slow, process of growth and decay, integration and disintegration, organization, revision, reorganization, disorganization. At any phase, however, the people who live in and conceive of the world in terms of such a system assume that its rules are permanent. We can call such a scheme of order the "geometry" of our mental space. There is a great variety of possible geometries. We might best think of such a geometry as being a stratified system of axioms, upper strata being based on lower strata. On the ground of basic axioms, other axioms, meaning an additional order, can undergo change without upsetting the system as a whole. No individual or group can stand a sudden and radical overturn of the entire system of permanences which supports the consistency of any meanings, principles of action, norms of behavior, expectations or memories. Such a *bouleversement* spells madness.

A new experience may fit into our preconceived scheme. It gets its place in our world. Another experience may not fit. We make it fit as far as possible or we reject it. We all have our own way of interpreting away whatever cannot be made to fit—even scientists have a way.

Some basic assumptions, of both the rational and the religious man, can be upheld under all circumstances. A hypothesis must work if it provides a possible explanation for every instance in which it does not seem to work. Then the hypothesis becomes an "axiom." We do not doubt that everything has a natural cause just because in a particular instance we do not know the cause. The religious man need not doubt the wisdom and justice of the Almighty because he does not understand His inscrutable will. We refer to our ignorance and uphold the axiom.

A new experience may force us to revise something in our system of permanences. Individuals, societies, mental ages, periods of a civilization, differ widely in their capacity for such revision. Sometimes it seems as if the particular permanence that cannot be maintained is ingrained in or intergrown with other more basic permanences that cannot be changed without upsetting the entire system. In this case the system is rigid. The rigidity or flexibility of our system determines our capacity for restructuring or reorganizing our present psychological field. The rigid mind is more, the flexible mind less, exposed to an attack of indefinite fear.

The system of things that is taken for granted is socially established, daily confirmed by the testimony of the society in which we live. It orders the universe of discourse. Whatever happens is interpreted in its terms. It has an enormous power. The ordinary individual deviates only within the range of the alternatives it offers or at least tolerates.

The universe of discourse guards the individual against indefinite fear. The individual easily succumbs either when cut off from the universe of discourse or when this universe fails to provide any support. "Man, like the generous vine, supported lives."

In every phase of the history of a society, small or large, we find a stratified system of things that are taken for granted. Different systems differ widely as to the staying-power they convey to a society, their resistance to shocks, their guiding force. The analysis of the structural qualities of such a system at a given moment is the most important, though the most difficult, part of the task of a social psychologist who in times of stress might be called upon to diagnose the danger of "collective insecurity."

V

As the analysis of even one concrete case of collective insecurity would go beyond the scope and space of this study, I restrict myself to a few tentative and fragmentary remarks about the structure and role of the universe of discourse in a religious and a rational age, in a democratic and a totalitarian society.

Collective insecurity may be interpreted as an agglomeration of many definite reasons for definite fear threatening the multiplicity of individuals in a society: the civilian population in modern war—husbands, sons, and fathers are killed in battle, air raids destroy houses at night, the Gestapo calls in the morning. These are enough reasons for fear. Yet everybody knows what it is like. I distinguish from this possible meaning of collective insecurity another meaning in which an indefinite fear invades a community and deprives even the reasons for definite fear of a distinctness on which to act. Nobody knows what to fear or what to do. In this case the behavior of a society is different.

The Christian Fathers find the heathen in constant anxiety. In the third century the universe of discourse throughout the universal empire is an impenetrable jungle of competing superstitions. The divine principle behind the countless gods of the Roman pantheon is a mere word without power except for a few remnants of a dying upper class. Hundreds of gods, great and small, competing with, but forced to tolerate, one another, and innumerable hordes of priests, magicians, prophets, sorcerers, soothsayers, conjurers, and astrologers outscream one another in selling hopes and fears. The individual, entangled in an inescapable maze, is hardly able to take a single step without elaborate rites to expel real or imaginary evils. The universe of discourse gives no lead—the practices contradict one another, and no god or demon should be offended. The individual, squeezed between opposite pressures, moves helplessly in an uncontrollable world. Shifting and precarious communities offer no support for any individual choice. Only the strong cling to Isis or Mythras, or are satisfied to wear a little golden serpent around their necks and to ignore the others and their gods. In this situation the Christian God defeats all his competitors. Only one survives: the Jewish god. He, however, no less tolerant than the Christian god but almost contented with his chosen people, hardly competed in the world at large.

The reasons for the Christian victory are diverse. Only some of them bear on the problem of fear. Gods owe their birth and power to other human needs and passions beyond mere fear. *Timor non fecit deos,* though *sacerdotes fecerunt timores.* Yet fear had a share in the Christian victory. Not the fear of the Christian God but the fear of their multiple fears drove the heathen into the worship of the only God. Threefold was the protection they found: (1) Intolerance and exclusive fervor simplified and systematized their scheme of the world: a jungle was turned into an orderly country with a simple system of roads and ways. (2) An exclusive community as a closed universe of discourse upheld and confirmed this system. (3) The Christian God, whether the God of Abraham and Jacob or Christ, is a personal God—a God of love and care and hope, the father to whose knees the trembling flock of his children flee in distress—stronger than any fear, definite or indefinite, to those who confide, endure, and pray. Thus the one humble God of the Christians defeated the glamorous many and freed the chest of the heathen pressed in anguish, by mixing awe into their fear, hope into their awe, love into their hope—in a unique way never equaled by any other god.

To the rational man of the industrial age everything has a "natural" cause; no demons interfere. Yet, in times of crisis, he too can be gripped by indefinite fear. I outline briefly the causes of his potential weakness.

We should start by realizing that the rational man is the heir of a long period of relative security in which he accumulated a great many matters-of-course to be taken for granted. This dubious training may be partly responsible for his vulnerability. His scheme of order is rational only in theory. It is not enough to posit a natural cause. We must know it. The causes of an economic or social crisis in our time are of infinite complexity. From the mere law of causality nobody can derive any guidance for action. The system of things the average man takes for granted consists mainly of vague general rules, simplified experience, ingrained as habits. They supply the modern man with a set of substitute causes. They guide his judgment and action. After a period of peaceful prosperity the relative order of economic life becomes the absolute order of the world. Man may accept the fact that there are, and apparently must be, business cycles, though he fails to understand their causes. A little more of a slump, and many things happen for which no place is provided in his orderly world. He no longer knows what can or is likely to happen. A halo of indefinite fear strangely blurs his distinct reasons for definite fear. He resorts to others, to the universe of discourse. But the shattered scheme of order is not merely his individual system: it is the system of assumptions that underlie the universe of discourse itself.

Something has happened to the universe of discourse. We sense it, though we find it difficult to say what it is. We may realize it only in the acute crisis, though it may have happened long ago and at no particular time. It seems suddenly as if nobody really believes in what he still takes for granted. Capitalists are no longer entirely and naïvely sure of their capitalism, socialists are strangely unsure of their socialism. An artificial note suggests a convulsive effort; voices are strained. Suddenly great old words have a hollow sound. Freedom? The average man knows in his heart what it means. His conscious concept, however, is tied up with and formulated in terms of these or those material conditions. They have been taken for granted—and now they are threatened. He cannot recognize freedom, and so all meaning goes overboard and leaves a vacuum. What does "freedom of speech," "pursuit of happiness," or "democracy" mean, unless I know how to earn a decent living by doing decent work? The scaffold of thinking that guides discourse begins to totter—confidence deserts, indefinite fear invades the bewildered mind, impairs our faculty of orientation and thus of action.

The universe of discourse splits wide apart. Different splits cross one another. Simplified substitute causes stand up against one another. Who or what is responsible? Different sides shout in different languages, each for itself, past the others' ears. There is no longer "discourse." There is no response—no reasoning, no exchange of arguments. Hostile groups, rallying around different "causes," have no basis on which to argue. Humor, wit, jokes, disappear. They presuppose detachment; anxiety does not joke. In elections these try to explain complex causes and mutter without conviction impotent reasons of expediency for caution—the others, grimly determined, cry for change at any price. If democratic leaders do not succeed in restoring the frame of reference and restructuring the mental space, even the ordinary citizen of average decency is in danger of falling victim to the great simplifier, the emotional leader, the scourge of modern society.

Whenever we analyze such a situation, our emphasis is on economic insecurity caused by mass unemployment. When everybody has a job, there is no mental insecurity at large. Granted; yet societies in different periods, different strata and different groups within a society, differ in their psychological capacity to stand economic insecurity. Moreover, "having a job" by no means plays only an economic role. The universe of discourse in industrial society is not merely a universe of talk. It is an enormous combination of interrelated activities in a process of production, distribution, and consumption. Our job is part of the way we participate in the universe of discourse, as a little wheel here or there. Without a job we should be cut off from this process and might feel insecure, even if we got our full wages by means of unemployment insurance. Modern man without a job is strangely alone. He is badly equipped to be alone. "Entertainment" is but escape.

The universe of discourse breaks asunder; the democratic procedure is stalled. "Causes" are hopelessly entangled. The voice of wavering governments no longer reaches the average citizen. Collective insecurity shakes the precarious security of an unsupported individual. This is the psychological hour of the totalitarian leader. He masters the indefinite fear.

How does he proceed? There is a market place crowded with worried people, listening to a megaphone. The raucous voice of *der Führer* shouts in a tone of utmost determination: "German men and women, the first thing is the primary thing! The second thing is secondary!" The social psychologist should not laugh at this momentous proposition. Truisms carry weight in the rational age. Obviously, the man is right. First things come first. He knows what comes first, what second—it is a considerable time since anybody knew that. He has a way, a line—he acts.

He gives a simple frame of reference, simple causes; whoever joins him gets rid of confusion. Many join for no other reason, in a convulsive effort at voluntary blindness. First things come first—no efficient action without obedience. The citizen obeys. The leader eliminates the universe of discourse, which anyway was merely the vehicle of insecurity. Discourse is manipulated. He gets the monopoly of manipulation. Voluntary groups are broken up, prohibited, or "coordinated." Everybody gets his place in the machine—a job—and is told what to do and to think. Spontaneous discourse still plays a role within the ruling gang until disposed of by purges. Indefinite fear is replaced by the definite fear of the Gestapo —compliance or death being the only alternatives.

It is a simple system. The transition from the democratic to the totalitarian system is easy when indefinite fear paves the way. The way back is likely to be difficult—it needs more than the removal of this or that ruler or gang. A common scheme of order must be restored to support a universe of spontaneous discourse, without which no democracy is a democracy. Only definite reasons for hope can conquer the power of indefinite fear. Despair cannot be expected to produce a democracy of respectable people.

LEO SCHNEIDERMAN

Repression, Anxiety, and the Self

Introduction

ONE CANNOT SEPARATE the awareness of self—above all, the self as a distillation of past experience—from the process by which the self-image was constructed, namely, observation, learning, and forgetting. Not only does the self emerge out of the remembrance and transvaluation of events, including subjective events, but it is diminished, as well, when self-related thoughts and feelings are forgotten. This much is reasonable. But what if a person fails to adequately perceive what is going on around him, and overlooks even those details which are, or should be, of the greatest consequence to him? Or—a more serious possibility—what if he fails to make note of his own reactions? The latter oversight may cause him to remember events merely in their external aspect; that which the self should have learned about itself will remain unlearned, because unperceived. Insofar as prior perceptions

Published for the first time in this volume.

and the inferences related to them are part of the self, the person's failure on the perceptual plane may have fateful consequences for the clarity of the self, and may affect actions based on the purposes of the self.

It is the purpose of this paper to discuss the role of anxiety, as a factor in the constriction of the perceptual field, and to suggest what may happen to the self in the face of diverse demands stemming from various situations. We will make special reference to the concept of *situational morality*, as an interpretation of how the self comes to terms with the external world.

Self and Not-Self

To the extent that a person responds selectively to various aspects of a situation involving himself, one may surmise that he observes and remembers whatever has adaptive significance for him. If he learns something about *himself*, it is only because he has focused his attention upon a sector of his perceptual field that bears on his definition of self. In a sense, one learns about the nature of his being by ignoring that which is understood to partake of the not-self.

Under ordinary conditions of living, a person is free to pay attention to, or to ignore, aspects of a situation that are relevant to the self. He may be mistaken, however, concerning the true significance of those events which he regards as relevant to the self and its adaptive strivings. Furthermore, he may not understand if the self has been enhanced or diminished, as a result of an encounter with another person. Again, it may not be possible to determine whether some tangible expression of himself, perhaps some saliency hitherto unnoticed, has evoked a particular reaction in another person. What is worse, it may be impossible to trace the chain of events that has culminated in a given effect upon *himself*. In considering the complexity of social situations, it is obvious that the position of the self, in relation to the pressures emanating from others, is ambiguous indeed. What is self, and what is not-self in a social context? What events, what spoken words, what gestures, what intentions are to be remembered, ultimately becoming accretions to the self? What momentary transactions are to be forgotten? What has gone unnoticed, perchance to turn up again at some untoward moment, claiming to be a part of the self? We must also remember that although an ego-alien event might have escaped complete perceptual inclusion, it may have achieved unconscious access to the self.

Repression.—In clinical usage, repression is often distinguished from mere forgetting, by the implication that forgotten contents sometimes have a way of making themselves known through a substitution process. When something is said to be repressed, it implies that it persists in some unrecognized form. It is as if an illogical stimulus-generalization has occurred. Such generalizations, at least in humans, involve forming equivalent responses to phenomena known to be disparate. It is this situation that provides a basis for symbolic substitution in repression. It is as if a learned, equivalent response ceases to be a synthesis of merely *disparate* events: the conceptualized events now include aspects of the original perceptual situation that are completely *irrelevant*, from the standpoint of the self, as well as disparate. The fluidity of the initial perceptual experience is reinstated, and stimuli become substitutes for each other. The rules of substitution are not those of logical synthesis, however, but, rather, of accidental redintegration.

In keeping with the psychoanalytic view of forgetting, anxiety may be identified as the inhibiting agent in repression. There is nothing new about this way of looking at repression. What is important, perhaps, is that the repressed contents reappear, not only in disguised form, but in a form denoting that some kind of generalization has occurred. Those aspects of the stimulus situation, that the perceiver initially did not relate to each other in a generic sense, may reappear under a new generic designation. The process of repression is here interpreted as taking on the character of a gate keeper for concept-formation. It determines whether the perceiver will form concepts that are appropriate to the stimuli that they subsume, or concepts that combine loosely associated, and adaptively insignificant, stimulus properties. In this connection, Reed has illustrated experimentally that subjects may develop inconsistent, as well as consistent, concepts. He cites findings consistent with the expectation ". . . that the amount of retention increases directly with the degree of meaningfulness or integration in the material."[1]

Obviously, not all concepts that are learned by the individual are of equal importance in influencing his behavior. Also, not all of one's concepts help in crystallizing broad segments of one's experience into explicit attitudes and beliefs. Moreover, there may occur syntheses of experience that include inappropriate elements. If repression is regarded as related to incomplete and distorted perception of punishing experiences, it is reasonable to predict that concept-formation will resemble less and less a process of logical induction, the closer one approaches concepts built up out of unpleasant experiences.

Self-Concept

It is not surprising if the above line of reasoning should bring to mind a number of related questions concerning integrative aspects of personality. One may ask, for example, what conditions promote the formation of conceptual attitudes toward one's self, toward other people, toward objects and situations, and toward the progress of one's life. For the present purpose, we may single out the self-concept and briefly discuss its relation to repression.

Hazlitt has maintained that the child's conception of the physical world differs from that of adults insofar as it is based on less experience, rather than on qualitative defects,[2] i.e., animism, artificialism, etc., such as Piaget has described. Piaget's assertion, then, that in the beginning the child cannot discriminate self and world,[3] can be reinterpreted to mean that the distinction between self and not-self is built up slowly and continually, and possibly never is perfect. The very act of conceptualizing the self as a distinct entity must be the result of many different varieties of experience. Probably, such experience consists of learning to distinguish between events that originate in the self, or affect the self, on the one hand, and events that are not connected with the self, on the other. Together with this kind of learning, one might hypothesize that the individual comes to recognize events that produce in him *intense* emotional reactions, as different from events that are "mild," though self-related, too. The individual's ability to focus on emotion-arousing events would seem to have some bearing on the completeness of his developing self-concept. From this standpoint, it is possible to predict that incomplete perception of anxiety-arousing events may prevent their generalization into explicit self-attitudes. In particular, it may be supposed that accurate generalization of *painful* events will be inhibited, or if learning does take place, explicit attitudes will not emerge, but, rather, automatic response tendencies that find no integrated representation in the self-concept.

Since it is the inaccurate and unintegrated way in which he recalls emotion-arousing events that distinguishes the repressive person, it may be argued that one cannot be repressive, and at the same time have a subjectively well-defined conception of self—of one's own needs and preferred roles. The repressive person, who does not relate painful events to his private universe of self-related concepts, cannot relate aspects of his present experience to the whole of his abstracted past experience. Repression and conceptualization would seem to denote antagonistic processes, with regard to the formation of a clear awareness of self. Behaviorally, one might expect to find that when the repressive person goes through what should be a subjectively painful experience, i.e., humiliation, he may respond immediately in an intensely emotional way, yet afterward be unable to acknowledge to himself the intense impact of the experience. It is as if, in abstracting from the concrete aspects of the situation, he fails to base his generalizations on those stimulus properties which were most painful, and which elicited from him the most intense response, initially.

His self-concept, built up out of many such incompletely generalized situations, will consist eventually of many "Pollyanna" attitudes. A serious implication of this situation is that the behavior of the repressive person will not be integrated with his past experience. He forever will be responding to unpleasant situations as if he expected them to be congruent with his unrealistic, bland self-concept, and will become upset when his expectations are thwarted. With this assumption in mind, the behavior of the repressive person might be described as consisting of cycles of momentary excitation, followed by partial extinction. The excitations are too intense to be perceived in a discriminating way, and too quickly forgotten to be worked into a consistent conceptual framework. To the extent that unpleasant experiences are remembered and conceptualized, they may receive inappropriate symbolic expression. Such expression is bound to be ego-alien, insofar as it is based on perception in which self-related aspects of situations are directly interchangeable with other stimulus properties. The self-concept of the repressive person, therefore, will contain many irreconcilable elements, and, as a result, his behavior may be expected to be variable, reflecting his underlying anxiety.

The foregoing discussion may help to illuminate one of the differences between the repressive person and the paranoid. Possibly the former does not impose enough of a coherent structure on events, especially events that affect him personally. The latter seems to impose on his experience an overly explicit, and too well-integrated set of generalizations. The paranoid person is so keenly aware of events that may be interpreted as self-related, that his generalizations, perforce, must be based on many painful experiences, as well as pleasurable ones. It is perhaps in reaction to such unbearable memories, generalized into systematic attitudes, that the paranoid must evolve his defense of projection. The position of the "normal" person may be at some point midway between the non-conceptualizing, repressive person, and the one who is prone to over-generalize from events that he perceives to be self-related. As a consequence, the "normal" person's conception of self will be neither vague and unrealistic, nor very precise, either.

Anxiety

How does the "normal" person maintain his somewhat indeterminate conception of self from situation to situation? What is the effect of anxiety, induced by situations, on the clarity and the ethical character of the self? We suggest, in the following outline, the conditions under which anxiety is transformed into a type of useful, highly-adaptive social response, which leaves the self protected from the impact of its own emotions and its own imperatives while it promotes the highest vigilance, albeit uncritical, toward the behavior of others.

This perspective leads us to make two observations about anxiety. First, we shall try to demonstrate the social usefulness of anxiety for the self, in those situations where there is an absence of an immutable moral standard, a not too infrequent condition for action. Second, the occurrence of a moral failure cannot be viewed as a basis for the emergence of anxiety. We are prepared to argue that both moral *and* "immoral" actions occur in response to direct social pressures, and are productive of anxiety only when they violate the prescribed definition of the context in which they occur. That is, anxiety may occur as readily in a person who behaves morally in an "immoral" social climate, as in one who acts unjustly in an atmosphere of general good will. With this possibility in mind, we shall propose, later, a definition of neurosis in which the super-ego, conceived as the carrier of fixed moral imperatives, has no place.

But what of those countless persons who suffer from neurotic anxiety because of a conflict between opposing wishes? Are we not dealing here with the effects of a strong and inflexible conscience? It may be maintained, with as much reason, perhaps, that the sufferer is possessed with a fear of direct retaliation or disapproval by others, rather than an obsessive dread of moral commandments that he has been taught in the past. It is not anxiety in the sense of a vague fear of something unknown, or a reaction that has been detached from its proper object, that is experienced by the sufferer; it is the realization that he is in danger from his fellow men. In a community where it is permissible to commit murder, let us say, in the name of self-defense, or "honor," or for some other reason, it may be supposed that anxiety will not be experienced by the murderer.

Freud, in his essay, *Thoughts for the Times on War and Death,* has expressed this idea with great clarity, but has left the impression that only in critical times is there likely to occur a suspension of moral imperatives. A less sanguine view might be that in times of peace, as well as war, society provides a mandate for aggressive actions. It is not enough to say, in this regard, that "dangerous" impulses are so defined precisely because they are antisocial. We must proceed, instead, to a closer examination of what society encourages and what it enjoins. We may discover that society does not speak out in a clear, commanding voice concerning the lawfulness of expressing impulses that are directly derivative of hostile wishes. We refer here to such unambivalent forms of behavior as verbal aggression, snobbishness, indifference to the feelings of others, pursuit of power, and many similar behavioral forms that not only are widely sanctioned, but actually are considered the *only* appropriate response in many circumstances. The fate of "benign" behavioral forms such as support, permissiveness, empathy, conciliation, etc., that might be thought to stand in an antithetical relation to those above mentioned, is not hard to imagine. The former may take on the character of taboos, and *their* expression may become dangerous. The view that neurotic anxiety develops because we are forced to repress our hostile wishes is incomplete, insofar as it does not comprehend the indifferent, and even *facilitative,* attitude of society toward various forms of aggression.

We may now ask if neurotic anxiety indeed develops as a consequence of not being permitted to act as one might wish. We should regard it as a reasonable hypothesis that the very opposite is true: that most men are not anxious in a neurotic sense, precisely because society permits them to act aggressively in a multitude of directly satisfying ways. It may be opposed to this claim that it makes light of the facts of neurosis. Rather than seeking to abolish the fact of neurotic anxiety, with which we are all familiar, we are concerned with reversing the traditional balance (in the clinician's mind) between neurosis and character disorder. The latter designation no longer need be applied only to psychopaths. It may be expanded to include vast numbers of "respectable" people who are at peace with their own bad intentions, and feel free to act upon them. Similarly, the incidence of true neurotic disturbance needs to be minimized. Possibly, the relation of the neurotic person to the disordered character is that of an exception to the general rule. To be neurotic, one must have an appreciation of unpracticed—including benign—behavioral forms and motivations, and at the same time be in conflict over one's inability to act as one might wish, i.e., contrary to social usage. It might be said that the person who is anxious in a neurotic sense has not repressed his impulses at all, but instead has been impelled to act in keeping with them, at the same time that he is aware of their antitheses. Like the respectable disordered character, the neurotic generally acts the way he is expected to act by his associates, but unlike the former, he is not happy about his actions.

The question of neurotic depression presents a somewhat different problem than that of anxiety. If, as we have suggested, the incorporation of a set of consistent and exclusive moral values is a rare occurrence, why do people become depressed and filled with guilt? Under such circumstances, is it not proper to infer a fear of punishment, since the depressed person himself reminds us of his unworthiness, and begs to be punished?

We often may observe still another component, in addition to the supposedly ambivalent character of neurotic depression, and this is nothing more than self-pity. It is possible to think of the melancholic as a person who feels that despite his essential goodness, something valued has been taken away from him unjustly, or some deserved object has been withheld arbitrarily. It is as if he has carried out a set of previously reinforced actions, only to find at last that the expected reward was to be denied. The source of distress is to be found not in the individual's feeling that he has been unworthy of his proper standards, but in his sensitivity to the implied rejection of him by his fellow-men (or by a personified fate), even though he has been deserving of something better.

Neurotic anxiety and depression both may now be seen as the direct result of an interpersonal process, in which the sufferer feels that he has lost the good will of his fellows in some way. This formulation implies that neurotic conflicts are not entirely intrapsychic, but involve as well the individual's relation to the presumed reality of his social setting. The person who does not experience neurotic anxiety or depression, and who is also free of other neurotic symptoms, we may suppose to be no less sensitive to other persons and their attitudes toward him. In his case, however, he has no reason to feel estranged from others. The development of such freedom from conflict with the social environment becomes comprehensible if we take a second look at moral "reality" as it exists for the growing child.

As we know, moral percepts are communicated to the child by both word and example. The assumption often has been made, by those who think in terms of an internalized conscience, that the reality of the word corresponds to the reality of the example. For example, if a child is taught verbally to treat all persons as equals, it is expected that eventually he will learn this lesson, and come to act upon it. The fact that his parents, and the people around him, act in quite a different way is ignored as a likely source of confusion for the young learner. If we acknowledge at this point what already is well known—that in most societies there is, and probably always has been a great discrepancy between principle and practice—we cannot help but see that verbal rules frequently are not reinforced by behavioral facts. It is well to ask, then, how learning can be thought to take place in the absence of realistic incentives. Returning to our example above, it is obvious that the child who is so unobserving of his parental behavior as to actually respond to people as if there were no differences between them, soon will be reminded by his parents of numerous qualifications and points of expediency that constitute *their* social "reality," and upon which they base their actions. As a consequence, we may expect that children will be unable to learn to act upon a symbolic "reality" of moral rules that has no counterpart in social "reality."

The moral "reality" of the child, then, is anchored in social expectations. It may be predicted, therefore, that no set of expectations, no matter how consistent or how compelling in an abstract ethical sense, will long be able to guide an individual's conscience, without frequent reinforcements in his day to day experience. If we may speak of a conscience at all, it is as a *process* that must be renewed throughout the lifetime of the individual by means of his social sensitivity, adaptability, and situational flexibility. The view that anxiety is the consequence of a moral failure must be reinterpreted as referring to a *social* failure. Our proposal does not seek to reduce all morality to a vulgar expediency, but is aimed at calling attention to the "reality" of the immediate social scene, in contrast to that ambiguous and temporally remote "reality" which the superego has been thought to represent. We might conclude that the person who overcomes his ability to react sensitively to the realities of his self- and social world, and succeeds in acting upon moral imperatives that are "real" for him, will be responding autistically. However, that such behavior may be "realistic," i.e., receive reinforcement in the form of favorable consequences for the individual in certain situations, is not denied.

In summary, only those values which were derived from behavior initially rewarded in a social context will become a part of the self. Since rewards in a specialized and fragmented society will tend to be erratic and situationally determined, the self is apt to possess these same qualities. Where moral imperatives having currency within a pluralistic value system cannot become part of a permanent and autonomous conscience, they will exist mainly as unrewarded ideals detached from the significant self. Anxiety, then, results from the assessment of the self as a failure in the context of highly particularized, unrelated situations.

CARL A. WHITAKER AND THOMAS P. MALONE

Anxiety and Psychotherapy

I saw and heard, and knew at last
The How and Why of all things, past,
And present, and forevermore.
The Universe, cleft to the core,
Lay open to my probing sense,
That sickening, I would fain pluck thence
But could not,—Nay? but needs much suck
At the great wound, and could not pluck
My lips away till I had drawn
All venom out. —MILLAY*

Bilaterality of Affect in Psychotherapy

PSYCHOTHERAPY in its most elemental form represents an interchange of affect between two people. A traditional concept that the affect resides solely in the patient and that the therapist simply perceives and evaluates this affect objectively does not cover the full range of this interpersonal relationship. Nor does the therapist simply reflect or resonate to the affective state of the patient in order to enable the patient to better accept his own feelings. The actual experience of the working therapist is neither objective nor impersonal. Beyond his professional involvement, the therapist also participates personally in this relationship with all the affect and personal feeling that he would ordinarily have in a comparable interpersonal relationship of a nonprofessional character. Therapy cannot be understood if psychiatry persists in placing primary emphasis upon the patient and his feelings. In contrast, when the element of bilaterality is visible, many of the problems of therapy become clear. The very process of therapy has its foundations in the duality of the affective participation of both individuals. Without the affective participation of the therapist, therapy is not possible. This participation goes beyond simple empathy with the patient's feelings, goes

Reprinted by permission of the authors and the publisher, from *The Roots of Psychotherapy*, by Whitaker and Malone (pp. 119-34). Copyright 1953. McGraw-Hill Book Company, Inc.

* Lines from "Renascence," in *Renascence and Other Poems* (New York: Harper & Brothers). Copyright, 1912, 1940, by Edna St. Vincent Millay.

beyond a vicarious experience of feeling in response to the patient's feelings and, when analyzed, appears as a rapid alternation in feeling in both participants, each responding to the other with different feelings, the totality of which moves the process of therapy along toward its conclusion.

Therapy as defined by the authors occurs only if the therapist becomes so personally involved that he pushes his own growing edge and inherits a little more of his own potential energy. Whatever the specific expression of affect in therapy, the orienting concept presents therapy as a bilateral interchange of affect. The affect in either participant relates both quantitatively and qualitatively to the affect of the other participant. In any particular instance, the feelings in both may be identical or they may be more or less related; but often they are diametrically opposed. In all instances, the depth of feeling in either participant varies directly with the depth of feeling in the other. Were it possible to plot the changing intensity of feeling in both, one would find that intensity in each grows, throughout the process of therapy, with the intensity of feeling in the other.

Anxiety in Psychotherapy

The problem of psychotherapy, in many ways, centers around the dynamics of anxiety. Other affective states present themselves, but have therapeutic import primarily in their relationship to anxiety. Understanding of the role of anxiety in the process of psychotherapy should then clarify many of the problems of affective interpersonal dynamics. The reader's awareness of the role of anxiety in psychopathology is assumed, and the following discussion deals exclusively with its place in psychotherapy.

Anxiety as used in this chapter differs in some ways from the term as used currently in psychiatric literature. Anxiety, to the authors, represents the most primitive form which affect, or feeling, can take in the human being. As such, anxiety represents unorganized affect. This affect has both subjective and expressive components. It differs from other affects, however, in that both subjectively, and in its motor and biochemical expressions, the quality of disorganization predominates. In this sense, it represents the basic, or most primitive, affect seen in the infant. Out of the matrix of the anxiety experienced by the child soon after birth, other affects or feeling tones differentiate, i.e., become organized. Thus ego development in the child correlates directly with an increasing organization of affective states out of unorganized energy or affect, i.e., out of anxiety. The structuring of personality occurs around the organization of affect (anxiety). This organization occurs, of course, in the multiple, ever-expanding interpersonal relationships of the child. The final organization of affect, for example, the sentiment of love and the capacity to love, is intrapersonal, but as initially experienced it occurs in the parent-child relationship. The intrapersonal affective organization is preceded by, and reflects, an interpersonal experience emerging from the organization of complex feelings derived from anxiety.

The implications of this for psychotherapy can be clarified. In the infant, anxiety arises whenever the supporting interpersonal relationship fails, since there is as yet no firm intrapersonal organization of affect. In the adult, anxiety as defined above arises whenever the organization of affect in the individual breaks down, i.e., whenever his ego breaks down. Likewise the adult, like a child, may organize his affect, not intrapersonally, but around interpersonal relationships. An adult whose relationship to another adult supports his infantile need will respond with anxiety whenever that interpersonal relationship collapses. This peculiarly intimate and dynamic relationship between interpersonal and intrapersonal organization of affect finds its clearest expression in psychotherapy. The process of psychotherapy represents an effort to better structure the personality through the organization of affect intrapersonally in the patient as a result of the adequacy of the interpersonal organization of affect between patient and therapist.

Whenever the intrapersonal organization of affect breaks down (disintegration of the ego), or where an inadequate, infantile adult loses security in an interpersonal relationship, the result is anxiety. Here, the anxiety has a *negative* quality. It is associated with inadequacy and, as such, is a direct expression of the pathology of the patient. Such negative anxiety provides much of the motivation of the patient seeking psychotherapy. It pervades the initial phases of the process of psychotherapy, and the outcome depends largely on the capacity of the therapist to convert this to more constructive drives.

In this chapter, reference will also be made to *positive* anxiety. This differs from negative anxiety in its dynamic origins. In contrast to negative anxiety, which arises out of psychopathology, positive anxiety occurs in an individual who finds himself in an interpersonal relationship within the matrix of which he perceives the possibility of better organizing his affect (growing). In these instances, new and unorganized affect becomes mobilized for growth. Thus, the mobilization of potential for growth also takes the form of anxiety in therapeutic relationships. Because anxiety promotes growth in these instances, it is termed positive anxiety. Whether the anxiety stems from pathology in the intrapersonal organization of affect, or from the mobilization of affect for growth, in either instance it antecedes the development of capacity to utilize feeling in interpersonal relationships. Looked at from this perspective, anxiety assumes central importance in the whole therapeutic process. The therapist deals with anxiety both in the disorganization and in the reorganization of the personality within his interpersonal relationship to the patient. Anxiety accompanies the most fundamental biological processes of growth, integration, and differentiation, as these occur in psychotherapy. With regression or differentiation, the anxiety expressed is usually of a *negative* quality. When the process involves integration, the anxiety expressed has a more positive aim and function.*

Negative and positive anxiety not only differ in origin and function, but also are subjectively distinguished by the patient. Where the anxiety centers around increasing integration, tenseness and expectancy predominate over panic and apprehensiveness. Where the anxiety stems from a breakdown of defensive mechanisms, panic and apprehensiveness assume threatening proportions. Patient and therapist each experience these differences in the process of psychotherapy.

In this sense, then, anxiety accompanies all movement in therapy. Whenever they are present, one can be sure that the interpersonal relationship is moving, or changing in some respect. The anxiety may be in either patient or therapist, as each separately perceives the possibility of more adequate integration in response to the feeling potential in the other person. On the other hand, it may represent a breakdown in a previously rigid and pathological organization of affect in either the patient or the therapist. The movement or change has value in either instance. Negative anxiety associated with a breakdown of the patient's or therapist's defenses usually antecedes positive anxiety associated with the onset of a more healthy organization of affect within the matrix of this relationship. In many cases, however, the opposite is true, and the anxiety first experienced has positive qualities. This is particularly true where the patient seeking help has a great deal of maturity and adequacy, with minimal psychopathology. Such a patient seeks further development of his own potential. The anxiety of the mature therapist likewise has positive aims. Having worked through most of his gross psychopathology, he seeks better integration and organization of his own affect intrapersonally through his relationship with each patient. He has anxiety commensurate with his intuition of the potential depth of the interpersonal relationship with a particular patient. This presages growth for him. The growing pains are the anxiety. The resolution of the anxiety, whether negative or positive, reflects successful growth and better integration in either or both participants.

A great deal could be said of the relationship of anxiety to various psychiatric diseases dealt with in therapy. Such a consideration, however, would take us far afield into the implications of a therapeutic approach to the whole problem of psychopathology. It has been the experience of the

* Sören Kierkegaard talks about the despair of not being a person and the despair of being a person (since one can never be all the person one yearns to be).

authors that psychotic patients present a problem because of the inability of the therapist to empathize with their unorganized affective responses. This makes the development of a therapeutic relationship with the psychotic a more difficult task. Nonetheless, the therapist who attempts therapy with psychotics may rapidly develop a certain amount of positive anxiety because of the primitive quality of the psychotic's personal demands. On this basis, the therapist can develop the relationship, provided he can tolerate his own anxiety.

In contrast, therapy with a neurotic initially demands very little of the therapist since the anxiety in the neurotic is largely organized around a pathological symptom or syndrome. The therapist aims at breaking through this syndrome, creating negative anxiety so that the therapeutic process can continue. Therapy with the neurotic proceeds after the defensive patterns are breached, releasing negative anxiety. Therapy with the psychotic proceeds after enough of the patient's positive anxiety becomes organized to serve as a motivation force for deeper emotional participation. In either case, anxiety becomes the psychological drive which serves as the basis for growth in the patient. In much the same way that growth in other areas depends on stress, so emotional growth originates in stress, one aspect of which is anxiety.

Anxiety in psychotherapy has a specific relationship to the process of symbolization. Symbolization ordinarily binds anxiety, and in the therapeutic process, the patient symbolizes the therapist as a specific method of binding the emerging anxiety within the interpersonal relationship between him and the therapist. This enables the patient to tolerate an increasing amount of affect and to release energy previously bound in neurotic mechanisms. Anxiety also arises in the symbolized therapist, although this ordinarily has a positive quality in direct proportion to the intensity of the negative anxiety in the patient.

Not only does anxiety motivate the important process of symbolization in therapy, but it provides the necessary energy for the other dynamics of therapy. Thus, the transferences of the patient arise out of the anxiety he feels in his relationship with the therapist. Transference does not arise in the beginning phases of therapy where the patient has minimal anxiety in the interpersonal relationship. After the patient develops a symbolic relationship with the therapist, the transference phenomenon occurs primarily as a way of containing the increasing negative anxiety which the patient feels. In the same manner, counter-transference in the therapist arises when the patient's relationship to him provokes infantilism or threatens his defensive mechanisms. His counter-transference contains the resultant negative anxiety. In contrast, where his feelings, including anxiety, are positive in character, the dynamics which these engender in him make up his therapist vector, or what has been referred to earlier as his "mature counter-transference." All of the psychodynamics which obtain in therapy arise out of, and are motivated by, anxiety in some measure. Introjection, fantasy, projection, etc., arise out of the same matrix. Whether the dynamic is expressed interpersonally or is therapeutically functional depends in each instance on whether it arises out of negative anxiety or positive anxiety. When it arises out of the former, the psychodynamic expressed is that of a patient; when it arises out of the latter, the psychodynamic expressed interpersonally is that of a therapist. This is so whether the therapist-vector or patient-vector be present in either participant at any given time. When the anxiety felt in any relationship is positive in both participants, the relationship can be said to be mature in character. This also defines a mature constructive social interpersonal relationship.

Anxiety Alterations in the Process of Psychotherapy

The isolation necessary in psychotherapy augments the development of anxiety in the patient in the beginning phases of therapy by removing some of the supports which obtain in the real world. With the isolation comes an increasing awareness by the patient of the possibility for direct satisfaction of his unconscious needs. With the removal of these cultural controls, anxiety, as defined earlier in this chapter, increases in intensity. This makes more sense when one looks upon cultural patterns as acceptable ways of organizing interpersonal affect. The break through out of these interpersonal patterns leaves the affect in the patient relatively disorganized, assuming, of course, no well-integrated intrapersonal organization of affect. Faced with the loss of predetermined patterns of behavior, the patient has little to which to retreat, being insufficiently integrated to organize and express his affect maturely.

As the relationship develops, however, anxiety gradually diminishes in intensity, by becoming organized around the therapist in this relatively acultural but more symbolic relationship. In this matrix, unconscious need and primitive affect slowly organize to express the needs of the patient. Free of many parentally imposed and culturally reinforced patterns of relating, underlying needs are expressed directly. Toward the end of therapy, as the patient turns more and more affectively to the cultural situations, anxiety seems to increase as he once again makes the transition from the relative safety of the therapeutic interpersonal organization of affect to the stress of living in the real community. Anxiety in the ending phase, however, does not have the threatening quality, nor the intensity, of the anxiety which developed as the patient entered the symbolic relationship with the therapist. At that point when the therapeutic process moved into the area of regression, the anxiety of the patient developed in direct proportion to the increasing capacity of the therapist to see the potential in the patient. The therapist's capacity to assay this potential correlates directly with his own positive anxiety, i.e., the gradual recognition of the possibility of his finding new capacities in himself. Thus, at every point, the therapist's increasing positive anxiety buffers the patient's negative anxiety.

The deeper the regression associated with the more primitive transferences the greater is the affective on the part of each participant. The therapist tends to push farther into the therapeutic relationship than does the patient. This precipitates more anxiety in the patient. In the latter part of the regressive phase, and as the therapeutic process approaches the core phase, the patient's negative anxiety amounts to veritable panic. He says, "I feel as though I am going crazy. I'm afraid I'll never come back again." The therapist at this point must assume the responsibility for overwhelming the defensive dynamics of the patient so that the homeostatic state between them becomes bilaterally supportive. The negative anxiety of the patient and the positive anxiety of the therapist are summated then to make an interpersonal homeostasis which enables the patient to go on into the core phase of therapy.

Anxiety and Communication

The relationship of anxiety to the important problem of communication in psychotherapy presents interesting facets. Like any other form of behavior, communication is based on need, i.e., it is motivated. The deeper the level of communication the more profound the motivation needed for such communication. The needs which motivate such communication may be, first, the need to transmit affect to another and/or the need to understand affect which is perceived only partially. In this sense, communication on an affective, usually nonverbal level almost always follows anxiety in one or both participants. The actual communication represents an interpersonal resolution of shared anxiety. It represents an interpersonal organization of primitive affect into a more economical, less threatening form. Although communication is anteceded by anxiety, the experience of communicating itself is startlingly free of anxiety, and accompanied ordinarily by other more gratifying affective or feeling tones. There comes a sudden increase in anxiety whenever the patient and therapist fail to communicate, i.e., whenever their interpersonal organization of affect has broken down. If the failure to communicate is profound enough, the resulting anxiety may assume almost catastrophic proportions or intensities. The anxiety indicates the breakdown in communication. The above refers essentially to nonverbal affective communication. Anxiety also interferes with verbal ideational communication, but this does not present a problem of any moment in psychotherapy.

Apparently, anxiety also serves as a measure of the quality of the therapeutic process. Actually, the authors believe that the degree of the patient's anxiety in the regressive phase of therapy can be taken as a direct measure of the amount of energy brought to the therapeutic process. Thus the degree of positive anxiety in the therapist, based upon his hope of inducing certain body-image changes in himself, is the limiting factor in the degree of negative anxiety possible for the patient. In the ending phase of therapy, the therapist becomes concerned with integrating the changes brought about in him by this therapeutic experience. The patient's withdrawal thus occasions some anxiety. This places the patient in the role of a therapist. The therapist then becomes, for a moment, the patient to his own patient. This dynamic also enables the patient to see his own potential, and helps effect the termination of the professional-therapeutic relationship.

Functions of Anxiety for the Therapist

The above analysis suggests that the adequate therapist could use his anxiety as an important asset to the psychotherapeutic process. He gauges the movement of the relationship in terms of his perception of the intensity and quality of the patient's anxiety together with the subjective experience of his own anxiety. When the process lags, movement is augmented by those techniques which serve to increase his own positive anxiety or the patient's negative anxiety. Stimulation of anxiety then becomes an over-all procedure for pushing the process of psychotherapy along toward termination. This does not imply, of course, the indiscriminate and insensitive provocation of anxiety in the patient whenever the process has reached an impasse or whenever the therapist feels inadequate. It only implies such provocation as the therapist professionally and personally feels his relationship can adequately organize. On occasion, the therapist, though unsure of the adequacy of his relationship with the patient, may provoke anxiety with the hope of breaking through an enduring impasse. Such calculated risk-taking becomes necessary at times, even though he remains uncertain that the primitive affect so released will take acceptable form.

Anxiety functions for the therapist in a number of specific ways. (1) It antecedes meaningful communication, indicating to the therapist areas of need in the patient and, more significantly, his own areas of emotional blindness. To facilitate this communication, partial regressions in him may serve to establish some resonance with the psychotic segment of the patient. These partial regressions are ordinarily accompanied by anxiety—the anxiety of a temporary disorganization. (2) Apart from communication, development of negative anxiety in the therapist always presages his assumption of patient status. (3) Anxiety also arises whenever the therapist's residual pathology is touched. This provides a basic element in the motivation for pushing his own growing edge and achieving greater personal capacity in his own experiences with patients. The negative anxiety which accompanies any highlighting of his residual pathology usually has another aspect. Growth beyond this point stimulates, in the therapist, a great deal of positive anxiety which he then makes available to the patient. Without such positive anxiety he would be unable to carry the patient through certain critical transitions in the over-all process of treatment. As long as the therapist remains comfortable with his anxiety experiences, and still senses their potential usefulness, he can share these experiences with the patient. When such is not the case, anxiety in the therapist becomes a serious detriment to the process of therapy and sets up a counter-transference impasse.

Repression of affect in either the therapist or the patient has a characteristic action on the therapeutic process as such. Repression in the patient at the onset of treatment produces the recurrent problems faced by every therapist. The release of this repression is brought about by the amount of communicated affect from the therapist. Repression by the therapist, on the other hand, presents quite a different problem. This originates from his response to the patient and involves anxiety aroused by the specific area into which the patient is pushing with his transference. Confronted with repression in the therapist, the patient retreats only to offer to the therapist another facet of his pathology in the effort to establish a therapeutic relationship. Repression in the therapist may take many forms, e.g., a flight into consciousness (interpretation). At times, nonetheless, the therapist's tolerance of the repressions of the patient reassures the patient of the therapist's respect for his individuality and integrity. The limitations of time and the realities of their personal and professional lives effectively govern the repression necessary in the subtle balance of reality and transference. Thus, each one knowing the time limit of the interview can push the limits of his tolerance for anxiety with the sureness of their reality-bound separation at the end of the interview.

Tolerance for anxiety increases as the participants communicate more adequately, in addition to being proportional to the wellness of each. It decreases when the reality limitations of the relationship become uncertain, as well as when the pathology of the therapist dovetails with that of the patient. When either participant's tolerance for anxiety is exceeded, repression occurs. This may reveal itself as increased resistance, symptom formation, anxiety-binding techniques, and flight into consciousness. In any event, the manner in which anxiety arises, is tolerated, or is compromised reflects not only disturbance in the patient, but more significantly the adequacy or inadequacy of his relationship to the therapist.

Repression has a very clear-cut relationship to the communication of affect in therapy. The patient, wanting to know the quality of affect in the therapist, represses a certain amount of affect in himself and assays the anxiety developed in the therapist. The therapist, with affective feeling tones about the patient or anxiety about his own participation, unconsciously perceives the patient's response to his repressions. His own participation varies with these unconscious perceptions. When repression in one produces anxiety in the other, the therapeutic process moves along, with assurance in each of the bilateral emotional involvement. To recapitulate, we can define several generalizations. (1) The therapist's denial of the patient's negative anxiety elicits repression in the patient. This is equally true whichever participant expresses patient vectors. (2) Whenever affect in one of the participants induces repressed affect in the other, then the repression spills over to the process itself, with a resultant therapeutic impasse. (3) Repression in the therapist results in a feeling of rejection or feelings of separation in the patient. This separation produces anxiety.

There are technical cues to the presence of repression. Exhaustion of the therapist after an interview indicates his repression during the interview itself. The fatigue arises out of the repression of affect. Along the same line, elation or depression in the therapist ordinarily indicates approaching ending in the relationship. A feeling of urgency or expectancy and of being stimulated ordinarily indicates progress into the core phase of therapy. Intellectualization and theoretical reminiscing about the interview, or expressions of tolerance by the therapist with what has occurred during the interview, are strong evidence of an impasse.

The relationship of anxiety to the impasse can be stated very briefly. An impasse exists whenever one of two situations obtains: (1) where there is an absence of affect in one or both participants over a period of time; (2) where there is a single affect which characterizes the relationship over a period of time. In this latter case, the irreversibility of the persistent feeling is ordinarily based in an impasse. In a more fundamental sense, an impasse exists when both participants are simultaneously patients, both having persistent negative anxiety with no positive anxiety. In such cases, resolution of the impasse almost always produces a rapid increase in the amount of anxiety which then pervades the relationship. This usually originates in an increase in the intensity of the negative anxiety bilaterally which, in turn, gives rise to some positive anxiety in one of the two participants. This provides the necessary motivation for movement out of the impasse into a successive phase of the therapeutic process.

Anxiety and Aggression

The specific patterns of interpersonal exchange of feeling which emerge out of anxiety in one of the participants are infinite. These depend on the personality of both participants—their needs, defensive mechanisms, and maturity. Fundamentally, however, anxiety usually eventuates in either repression or aggression. If, because of the quality of the relationship, the anxiety cannot be interpersonally channeled, intrapersonal organization of the anxiety results, i.e., repression, and/or the resultant defense mechanisms associated with repression. In contrast, when the interpersonal relationship has a therapeutic quality so that the anxiety in one of the participants can be organized within it, then the most primitive interpersonal organization of anxiety takes the form of aggression.

Aggression then becomes an important affect channel in the organization of the patient's anxiety into more security-providing behavior. Such a concept of aggression as a necessary affect in psychotherapy needs further clarification. Expression of hostility in the therapeutic relationship is fraught with danger. Because of this, therapists ordinarily hesitate to express any aggressive feelings toward the patient. They even limit the amount of aggression the patient can express. When the primary emphasis centers on the negative qualities of aggression, then these precautions are probably warranted. If the aggression expressed aims at the destruction of the object against which it is directed, then such aggression does serious damage in psychotherapy. Reconsideration, however, of the origin of aggression in the infant provides a clear rationale for its use in psychotherapy. Here, the emphasis lies more on its positive qualities. Anxiety in the infant gives rise first to diffuse motor responses which, when organized and directed against an object in the environment, are called aggressive. Such aggression in infants aims initially not at the destruction of the object, but at securing a relationship with that object necessary for the satisfaction of a need in the infant, usually hunger. Only in the later development of the child when the problem of ambivalence arises does aggression take on a specifically hostile quality. The same sequence holds true in psychotherapy. Anxiety, as primitive unorganized affect in one participant, finds expression within the relationship as an effort to obtain from the other participant the responses necessary to the satisfaction of his needs and the alleviation of his anxiety. This primitive outgoing effort at need satisfaction provides the core of healthy aggression.

Whether or not aggression has a positive aim depends directly on the quality of the anxiety which motivates it. When positive anxiety arises out of the therapist's awareness of the difference between what the patient could be and what the patient is, the resultant aggression has a positive, therapeutic aim. When the therapist introjects the patient and develops a fantasy relationship within himself to the introject, the difference between this relationship and the actual relationship may give rise to severe positive anxiety about their interpersonal relationship. This positive anxiety again gives rise to therapeutic aggression.

When, in contrast, the aggression arises out of negative anxiety in either participant because of a threat to their defense mechanisms, the aggression has a more destructive aim. This has no place in psychotherapy except to precipitate the therapist into doing something about himself.

From positive aggression other more complex affects emerge. These include the varied expressions of love, e.g., parental feelings, sexual response, respect, tenderness, sympathy, and other more complex sentiments. The interpersonal experience of organizing positive aggression and then love out of the same matrix, resolves for the patient, experientially, the core problem of ambivalence. This provides the patient with a behavioral basis for expanding his interpersonal relationship into one compatible with the cultural pattern.

Therapeutic aggression as defined above, when directed against repression in the patient, leads to an increase in the patient's negative anxiety. In contrast, when therapeutic aggression is directed against an area in the patient which had been worked through previously, the aggression elicits a mature response, leading to an increase in positive anxiety. In either instance, in addition to the development of more mature interpersonal affects, aggression in therapy invariably leads to some increase in positive anxiety. After the core phase has been reached, and an adequate relationship between patient and therapist has been established, aggression on the part of the therapist may be inappropriate, and usually signifies the therapist's premonition of ending. Even so, it is usually motivated by positive anxiety and has a positive aim. More complex feelings, with repressive origins like guilt and shame, in the therapist, may mask aggression which has a negative aim.

II

SOURCES OF IDENTITY AND ANXIETY IN MASS LIFE

a. THE TERROR AND THERAPY OF WORK

JOSEPH BENSMAN AND BERNARD ROSENBERG

The Meaning of Work in Bureaucratic Society

Conflicts between Bureaucratic Roles and the Personal Needs of the Official

BUREAUCRACY is designed only as a technical system of administration. In practice it is much more than that. This difficulty constitutes an inherent cause of organizational problems, such as those that are bound to plague bureaucrats everywhere. To the official himself, the bureaucracy is a whole way of life, no less exacting than other ways of life. It makes sharp demands, it imposes rigid codes and stringent standards, and it places a special kind of stress upon him as a *total* individual.

To play his role as a bureaucrat at all adequately is to pay a heavy social and psychological price. The official has to repress certain prebureaucratic sentiments that may have been instilled in him as a youth, and he will invariably be forced to reject or neglect nonoccupational roles that are more continuous with his self than with his profession. When those sentiments and roles having no connection with his job are very meaningful to him, the official becomes less of a bureaucrat; on the other hand, if his bureaucratic role has been deeply internalized, he will be anxious and unhappy about subordinating it to other things. He can attempt to

Published for the first time in this volume.

stabilize the conflicting values and roles within himself, or deliberately pick and choose among them. When this occurs, bureaucracy may be said to have changed the personality of its officials, and when a large number of officials are affected, it also modifies the dominant character-structure of the society.

We will discuss briefly some conflicts generated by the fulfillment of bureaucratic roles, as well as their impact upon the bureaucrat and bureaucracy.

Compulsive Sociability in Bureaucracy

A large number of bureaucrats (scientists, accountants, and other pure technicians) are pure "pencil pushers," men more oriented to abstract symbols than to colleagues or clients. However, by far the majority of bureaucrats are "people-pushing" white collar employees, for whom association with others is a constant requirement. The ordinary bureaucrat is situated in a fixed and highly structured relationship to the public and to other officials, whether they are superiors or subordinates. Satisfactory performance of his tasks is grounded in his ability to secure their co-operation, good will, and support. Furthermore, his chances for advancement depend as much upon whether higher officials like him, trust him, and feel at ease with him, as they do upon his objective qualifications and his technical efficiency.

With respect to subordinates, the bureaucrat's success will hinge, to a great extent, on getting them to "produce" for him. Likewise, he must take care not to let other sides of his personality, especially those revealing his real preferences, his personal likes and dislikes, intrude upon any negotiation with either his equals or with outsiders. Up and down the line, large-scale organization puts a high premium on muted discord and surface harmony, as it does on everyone's being likeable and pleasant.

This emphasis is a recurrent, not a constant, one. To a degree, it matches behavior prescribed for the courtier in handbooks like Castiglione's *The Courtier* and Lord Chesterfield's *Letters to His Son.* Surly behavior was appropriate in aristocratic societies among noblemen close to princes and kings. The courtier had, however, only to please those above him. Bureaucracy, which is so much a matter of "teamwork" and "co-operation," constrains the individual to please all his associates: those equal to and below him, as well as those above him. The English yeoman, the independent farmer, and the frontiersman achieved historical fame for their possession of traits directly opposite to those that shape contemporary officials. The sense that poverty or prosperity depended mostly upon their own efforts gave them a feeling of independence, confidence, and even cockiness. It allowed them to be unpleasant without running any great risk of economic loss. Niceness had not yet become compulsory—or compulsive.

Self-Rationalization in Bureaucracy

In an employee society, "personality" becomes a market commodity, one that has measurable cash value in terms of present and future income to its possessor. Once the alert bureaucrat recognizes this, he sets out to acquire his magic key to success. That quest Karl Mannheim has brilliantly analyzed as a "self-rationalization." In Mannheim's words:

> By self-rationalization we understand the individual's systematic control of his impulses—a control which is always the first step to be taken if an individual wants to plan his life so that every action is guided by principle and is directed towards the goal he has in mind. . . . Modern society attains perhaps its highest stage of functional rationalization in its administrative staff, in which the individuals who take part not only have their specific actions prescribed . . . but in addition have their life-plan to a large extent imposed in the form of a "career," in which the individual stages are specified in advance. Concern with a career requires a maximum of self-mastery since it involves not only the actual processes of work but also the prescriptive regulation both of ideas and feelings that one is permitted to have and of one's leisure time.

Self-rationalization appears when the official begins to view himself as a merchandisable product which he must market and package like any other merchandisable product. First an inventory is necessary. He must ask: what are my assets and liabilities in the personality market? What defects must be banished before I can sell myself? Do I have the right background? If not, how can I acquire it? With such questions, the inventory is converted into a market-research project. The answers give him findings with which to remodel his personality. The bureaucratic personality is molded out of available raw materials, shaped to meet fluctuating demands of the market.

Old habits are discarded and new habits are nurtured. The would-be success learns when to simulate enthusiasm, compassion, interest, concern, modesty, confidence, and mastery; when to smile, with whom to laugh, and how intimate or friendly he can be with other people. He selects his home and its residential area with care; he buys his clothes and chooses styles with an eye to their probable reception in his office. He reads or pretends to have read the right books, the right magazines, and the right newspapers. All this will be reflected in "the right line of conversation" which he adopts as his own, thereafter sustaining it with proper inflections. His tone is by turns disdainful, respectful, reverential, and choleric, but always well attuned to others. He joins the right party and espouses the political ideology of his fellows. If he starts early and has vision, he marries the right girl, or if he has been guilty of an indiscretion, he may disembarrass himself of the wrong girl. Every one of these procedures is a marketing operation—with its own imponderable hazards. If the operation succeeds, our official will have fabricated a personality totally in harmony with his environment; in a great many ways it will resemble the personality of his co-workers. The drive for self-rationalization implies nothing less than adult socialization, or, in the majority of cases, radical re-socialization.

The Organization Man

The pressure in bureaucratic organizations which forces an individual to make himself amiable, sweet-tempered, and bland, results in conspicuous conformity, but the standards of conformity vary from organization to organization. Standards for a military officer, an academician, a businessman, a journalist, a medical technician, and a civil servant are obviously not the same. Yet, for all their differences, they have in common a deeply assimilated inclination to search for *external* standards, by which their interests, activities, and thoughts can be consciously directed. Each man takes on the special tincture of his organizational environment. Each tends to focus his projected self on those qualities which will be most pleasing to others. Since the others are similarly occupied, everyone's personality is fractionated. Part of it can be seen; the rest is subdued and hidden. Bureaucratic organizations sweeten and soften the visible personality.

The sweetening process, however, requires denying other portions of the self. Officials strive to develop those aspects of their personality which fit the bureaucratic milieu. This makes it difficult for them to develop aspects that are "out-of-phase." Hypertrophy in one direction spells atrophy in another. One consequence of self-rationalization as a technique to control personality is that, after some time has passed, the poseur may find that he is a different person. With much practice, "control" becomes unnecessary; the bureaucratic mask becomes the normal face, and refractory impulses get buried beyond reactivation. Functionaries are then, in the fullest sense, Organization Men.

Special Bureaucratic Stresses

The bureaucratic atmosphere may seem to be warm and friendly; officials are encouraged to call each other by their first names, and except in the armed forces, "pulling rank" clumsily tends to be offensive. There is an outward show of civility, politeness and decency. Conspicuous harassment of subordinates is condemned by every efficiency expert and human engineer in America, usually on the ground that it reduces efficiency. Yet tensions are aroused even in the smoothest bureaucracy, and there they cannot be publicly aired. This may make them harder to contain. These stresses can cause officials to violate the norms of their organization and nullify its purposes. The stresses we have in mind are related to impersonality, isolation, and powerlessness.

Let us recall that the principle of uniform administration is based upon specific rules, carried out by those whose duties are rigorously prescribed. Bureaucratic officials are placed in relationship to each other by the rules, and deal with each other—as they do with the outside world—according to fixed regulations. They are not supposed to be influenced by personal preference, affinity, taste, or choice. They deal with and see each other because the situation obliges them to do so. Office contacts of a particular kind are required, and each party to them knows that they are required. Every intraoffice relationship is covered by formal specifications, which, because of their official nature, cannot easily be executed or accepted with spontaneity, or empathy, or a sense of personal identification. But without some degree of warmth no durable human interaction has ever been observed to take place. If dehumanization is the objective, it is never wholly attainable. On the other hand, human spontaneity knows no bounds; it cannot be safely restrained by offices and rules, and is therefore likely to cause trouble. A common compromise occurs in the form of controlled warmth or planned spontaneity; synthetic emotion is meant to pass for real warmth and spontaneity, but it does not actually commit officials beyond the point of involvement formally demanded of them. They act out their parts, performing or discarding them as necessity and convenience require. Such roles are never really internalized.

In the bureaucratic milieu, which is a vortex of togetherness, other-directedness, teamwork, and co-operation, the individual finds it exceedingly difficult to relate or commit himself to his associates. He learns that they respond as shallowly or as deceptively as he does to them. This awareness makes him wary of the apparent camaraderie others offer in their official capacity. Thus, in the midst of endless interaction with clients and other officials, the individual feels isolated, unbreakably tied to, and hopelessly cut off from, those others he will see every working day of his life. Ironically, the greatest measure of social and psychological isolation may be traced to two very different, if not opposite, structures: the city with its extremely loose organization, and the bureaucracy with its extremely tight organization.

The Quest for Identification in Informal Groups

Bureaucratic impersonality bemuses the official at precisely that point where he feels a deep personal need to identify with and relate to people as people. Like almost every other human being, the official has acquired his basic orientation to social life in the family and in other primary groups, where deeper, more intimate, and unpremeditated responses are provided. His formative environment generates expectations that formal bureaucratic organization is not capable of satisfying. Consequently, the bureaucrat improvises patterns of response, calculated to satisfy extra-occupational needs by means that go beyond—and outside of—the prescriptions of his official role.

The quest for personal identification often leads one official to seek out others. In defiance of all the proprieties and all the rules, he may make attachments that have no organizational sanction. As this process spreads, the office comes to be reorganized into informal and unofficial friendship-groups, cliques whose existence is unrecognized in the table of organization. Such cliques form as the result of physical propinquity, or they sprout from common interests, common ambition, common resentment, or common ethnic origin. Each clique evolves a common core of standards from the initial consensus of its members, and again, they may clash with those of the organization. Such separate standards include the restriction of output and systematic violation of office procedure (so that the clique punishes what the highest officials reward). Clique control is perhaps most serious when it is informally responsible for promoting policies which lack official authority to back them up. The clique is hospitable to personnel, from different departments and at different levels of authority, who establish their own channels of communication. They have little regard for preconceived blueprints, reaching each other and selected segments of the public without "clearance" from above. In this way, gossip circulates, secrets are revealed, information is leaked—and official policy has been unofficially nullified.

The informal group has its informal leaders. These leaders are men who, through their network of personal friendship and influence, bring other persons into continuous unofficial interaction. A clique leader is not necessarily an official of the highest rank. The situation which then presents itself—in extreme cases—is such that the nominal bosses exert less influence than those without title to authority. There is no other way to gain intimate knowledge of cliques than by joining them—which those on top and those outside are often precluded from doing. When men vested with official authority try to get things done by using the formal administrative machinery, they may find that machinery inadequate and obsolescent. At the same time, those who manipulate the informal network of clique communications do get things done—by breaking all the rules.

The many cliques in a large office are often at odds with each other. Individual bureaucrats compete for raises, promotions, niches, and prestige symbols. To that competition they bring not only their own rivalries, but also such support as can be mustered from friends, partisans, and cliques. Not just separate individuals, but whole cliques choose sides, lining up on a host of issues that pertain to office politics. They reward their friends on the basis of personal loyalty rather than performance, and they hinder or penalize even those enemies who completely fulfill legitimate functions.

In these circumstances, the bureaucratic regime is turned upside down. Despite its outward quiescence, the office becomes a battleground in which "politics" is a potent weapon, and one in which mines and traps are common dangers. An official may unsuspectingly befriend one of his colleagues who belongs to the wrong camp, and thereby consign himself to oblivion. Or he may hitch his wagon to a floundering team; he may be identified with an unstable clique on its way down—and suffer personally for all the failures of that clique.

In sum: the formation of cliques tends to alter operational bureaucracy to something quite different from its ideal type. The uniformity, predictability, and precision built into it are processed out of it by intervening social and emotional factors. For this reason alone, bureaucracy can never be perfectly smooth or absolutely efficient.

Disidentification with the Bureaucracy

The search for personal identity in social relationships that are not wholly purposive and functional is one of several tendencies. Some bureaucrats, overwhelmed by the impersonality of their work, give up the idea that it is meaningful or that it is a suitable medium for self-realization. They turn to, and enlarge upon, other aspects of life, while doing as little work as possible in offices that are distasteful to them. The major locus of meaning lies in the family, a hobby, a satisfying style of consumption, contact with people from other spheres, in philandering, in romantic dalliance, in suburban and exurban affairs, in the affectations of "Upper Bohemia," or in any of several idiosyncratic activities.

By denying the meaningfulness of their work, they become less devoted and less efficient. They minimize their duties and perform them in a routinely competent way, giving no more thought to the office than is irreducibly necessary. They systematically avoid decisions, pass the buck, and take no action whenever possible. In his analysis of the United States Navy Officers Corps, Arthur K. Davis found "avoiding responsibility: the philosophy of do-the-least," or "shunting responsibility upward" both common and complex; it was surrounded by social, personal, and technical conditions, and it could be disastrous. At the lower and middle levels of bureaucracy, officials are strongly tempted "to slide (problems) into their superior's lap by asking advice, requesting instructions, securing approval in advance." But, Davis says, "For the man at the top there is no such escape from the strains of decision except by a do-nothing policy." Timid or indifferent bureaucrats who pass the buck and who, when on top, avoid decisions are the bureaucrats whose public imagery has fixed itself upon the popular imagination. Here the man corresponds to the prototype. He has abandoned his initial hope of upward mobility, and looks elsewhere for satisfaction.

To achieve positive action and speedy disposition of business, a bureaucracy needs *esprit de corps,* high morale and enthusiastic dedication. If an organization is staffed with apathetic bureaucrats, its purposes are less and less likely to be achieved.

Over-identification

The very same sense of isolation that leads one bureaucrat out of the organization to seek his "self" will lead another to "over-identify" with the organization. In this case the organization as a whole is substituted for other identifications and for various social relationships. A clear and familiar case (not without pathos) occurs when the lowly clerk employed by a large, powerful, and well-known agency, reaches for the halo of his organization to cover his anonymity and powerlessness in it. He speaks knowingly of policies and practices which circulate through the office grapevine, but are many times removed from himself. He implies by use of the pronouns "we" and "our" that the organization's policies and practices are his policies and practices, that he somehow had a hand in making them. Since he must conceal his actual position in order to exploit it among strangers, his life is sharply divided between office and home. With a fictitious title and some histrionic ability, an elevator man employed by one of the large communications companies, who is domiciled in a fashionable suburb, and who looks, dresses and talks like a Madison Avenue hot-shot can effectively exploit his connection. This is what the Captain from Koepnig did in Kaiser Wilhelm's Germany, when he pretended to be an officer and was accepted as such. The assumption of a false identity is increasingly possible in societies that give higher prestige to the organization than they do to the innumerable individuals who must make it work.

Identification with "The Rules"

Another kind of over-identification manifests itself in inordinate and inflexible adherence to rules. To the outsider such rigidity looks like senseless obstructionism, and he finds it maddening enough to have changed the word "bureaucracy" from a label into an epithet. To the functionary whose personal identity has been swallowed up by the organization, rules that are precise, orderly, fixed, and certain, may represent a source of psychological security not otherwise available to him.

In the grip of his passion for legalism, a bureaucratic virtuoso follows the letter of every rule, never deviating, never counting the consequences or considering what possible harm he does to others. Javert, the police official of Victor Hugo's *Les Miserables*, is a perfect example of the legalist. Far beyond the call of duty, Javert remorselessly pursues a man of whose excellent character and good deeds he is fully aware, putting aside his own knowledge and disregarding the sympathy that wells up in him. When confronted with the ineluctable choice between rampant legalism and personal conviction, he takes his life.

Nazi documents, captured after World War II, indicate that on the day Adolf Hitler committed suicide and Russian troops were marching through the streets of Berlin, officials of the Reichschancellery were too busy to look out of their windows. They were engaged in estimating and ordering paper clips for the next fiscal year!

Legalism, which Davis has called the psychology of affirm-and-conform, and for which he lays down a golden rule, "Follow the book or pass the buck," is perhaps the most dangerous and pathological outgrowth of bureaucratic organization. Davis deals with the seriousness of overemphasis upon instrumental devices, among naval officers in time of war. He cites two striking examples:

> In one large air unit, even the most trivial correspondence was routed up to the Chief of Staff and often to the Admiral, then down to the appropriate department for action. Here the reply was drafted, typed, routed back to the top for approval and signature (often refused, pending minor changes) and finally routed down to the despatching office. Mail which a clerk should have handled in and out in 24 hours was thus sent to the top and back two or three times, drawing attention from 8 to 12 persons over a ten-day period.
>
> We cite next the behavior of certain heavy-bomber crews on anti-submarine patrols. Because of their short tour of duty, the infrequency of submarine sightings, and the complexity of anti-submarine tactics, these air crews usually made several errors in the course of an attack. For this they would be sharply criticized by their superiors. Hence arose a serious morale problem. At least three flight crews in one flight squadron began going out for "quiet patrols" by their own admission. Observing the letter of their

instructions legalistically, they flew their patrols exactly as charted. If a suspicious object appeared a few miles abeam, their course lay straight ahead.

The use of forms and of standard procedures, the transmutation of mechanics into a Sacred Cow, and the reduction of a task to many phases in which only a few persons (or no one at all) can understand the whole flow of a single operation: these are among the factors that contribute most heavily to legalism. And legalism is widely, subtly, and grossly converted into a means of self-identification.

Inversion of Identification

Consider another kind of over-identification, one that occurs at higher levels of administration. In contrast to the individual who submerges his own identity in the organization, there is the top official who conceives of the organization, or the department he heads, as an extension of his own ego. The administrative apparatus—human and material—is seen by him chiefly as a means for his personal action, a machine he can use to execute his will. Thus a standard army phrase for reporting the number of troops under one's command used to be, "I have (so many units) in my hand."

Such an approach is taken up by some men who have successfully worked their way up the hierarchy, and who have developed a healthy respect for their own ability. To the extent that this respect is unwarranted, it may result in a gross neglect of the "mechanical" side of organization, a tendency to ignore educated advice from specialists of lower rank, and the manipulation of an organizational apparatus for personal rather than corporate ends. To regard the organization as an extension of one's own ego is flagrantly to violate that cardinal principle of bureaucracy which separates official existence from personal life.

Powerlessness

The feeling of powerlessness often experienced by modern administrators is fundamentally related to the structure of bureaucracy. That structure is notable for its strict hierarchy and the marked differences—in authority, rank, income, and prerogatives—between men at various levels. Such differences exist in any form of social organization, but they are greatly sharpened in a bureaucracy where each job is as systematically defined as all duties and privileges are clearly delineated.

Structurally, every bureaucrat knows where he stands, who is above him and who is below him. He knows this by direct perception or by informed guesswork. It is possible for him to compare his salary, his benefits, and his chances of promotion with those of others, to notice how others get along with each other and whether they are on the "outs" with key figures. It does not take an unusually perceptive actor to realize that he may be one of those functionaries who actually has little power and no real leverage in the organization.

A second form of structurally determined powerlessness issues from the bureaucracy's segmented and specialized nature. As individuals and departments divide and subdivide the performance of a single operation, there are times when no one person can envisage the total task. More often, it seems chaotic to everyone except the co-ordinator and those few persons taken into his confidence. The first atomic bomb was produced at Los Alamos in just such an atmosphere; most of those engaged in the Manhattan Project had no knowledge of its real purpose. The everyday conduct of bureaucratic affairs which do not involve top secrets may be quite as mystifying to those who are responsible for them. In the case of almost every bureaucrat, his assignments originate in another department, they are passed on to him, and finally completed in still other departments. He works only on one phase of a job, in accordance with directives from above, which, from his worm's eye view, may not make sense. To a detailed specialist, facets of the job other than his own are seldom clear, and he may do no more than conjecture uncertainly about them. He sees what look to him like avoidable mistakes made by bosses who do not have his special competence, and who are therefore viewed with some disdain. This is stylized into the wry and half-serious belief that the men in charge got there by making mistakes so repeatedly that they had to be kicked upstairs. More serious is the belief that luck, marriage, apple-polishing, and boot-licking make for success.

In almost every bureaucracy there is a myth of incompetence which lower officials cherish about higher officials. It is assumed that somehow incompetence mixed with smooth talking and aided by "connections" is what it takes to come out on top. The existence of this myth is a rough gauge of the resentment that powerless people feel for their ostensibly powerful superiors. Resentment—that peculiar emotion which begins with striving and is heightened by impotence—is most especially evoked among lower- and middle-ranking officials who cannot realistically expect to attain power. It leads to disidentification from the bureaucracy.

White-collar Sabotage

This disidentification is concretely expressed by the bureaucrat who gossips, complains, and searches for errors. In a more advanced stage, it includes passive resistance and subtle sabotage. One's duty is performed in ways that are procedurally correct and yet make the task impossible to accomplish. With no show of malice whatsoever, one's superiors may be deliberately exposed to the probability of error and ridicule. The claim that messages are unclear, that directives are ambiguous, and that therefore misunderstanding cannot be avoided, is a technique instantly familiar to modern readers as Schweikism—after *The Good Soldier Schweik*, by Jaroslav Hasek. Schweik is an obedient Yes Man and an effective saboteur in the Austro-Hungarian army; he does at once everything the officers tell him to do and nothing they tell him to do. Schweik is prototypic. His methods are still widely employed by enlisted men in armies everywhere. Government bureaus are still subject to Schweikism, as they are to the disloyalty of men who reveal office secrets, leak embarrassing data to the press, or otherwise put higher-ups "on the spot." Private business zealously guards its secrets; for a functionary to betray them would be unpardonable; this is true even when everybody in the industry knows what everybody else knows. According to Raymond Loewy there is no more significant difference among American automobiles than there is among cake mixes. Loewy, an industrial engineer who designed the postwar Studebaker, explains that this sameness has come about because every company produces "imitative, over-decorated chariots, with something for everyone laid over a basic formula design that is a copy of someone else's formula design." With that, Loewy divorces himself from the automotive industry and, hence, never identified with it, is free to report that:

> Detroit spends an annual fortune to insure its lack of originality. . . . To protect its styling studios, Ford has a force of 20 security guards commanded by an ex-FBI agent. Different-colored passes admit different people to specific different rooms and to those rooms only. Unused sketches and clay models are destroyed. Ford's studio locks can be changed within an hour if somebody loses a key. To pierce such a wall of secrecy, each company employs spies and counter-spies, rumorists and counter-rumorists. Rival helicopters flutter over high-walled test tracks. Ford guards peer at an adjacent water tower with a 60-power telescope to make sure no long-range camera is mounted on it by a rival concern. One automotive company installed a microphone in a blond's brassiere and sent her off to seduce a secret. . . . All secrets are discovered! The shape of a Ford hubcap! The number of square inches of chromium on the new Buick! The final result is that all the companies know all the secrets of all the other companies, and everyone brings out the same car.

To reveal known or unknown secrets is a form of *lesé majesté* practiced only by the disaffected and the dis-identified. Frontline officials in this condition do not remain unidentified. They re-identify—usually with clients, taking their side, waiving rules, and forgetting standard forms. Into this category fall the relief investigator who grants an applicant's claim without carefully checking it; the insurance adjuster who okays the obviously excessive claim of a policy-holder; the foreman who sides with workers in his plant rather than with management; and the supervisor who, instead of correcting his subordinates' mistakes, covers them up. In all such cases, the official who feels powerless in relation to his superiors, stretches, bends, or breaks the regulations so that he can give a better break to persons still less powerful than himself. And in all such cases, personal interaction is substituted for impersonal procedure. Powerlessness and impersonality are negated—at the organization's expense. Such behavior frequently elicits sympathy; it is viewed as human-all-too-human kindness.

Authoritarianism

The public has much less patience with another response to powerlessness, which motivates the bureaucrat who is hedged in on one side to break out in search of power on another side. A lowly clerk, squelched by his superiors, may redirect the resentment that comes over him. He can do this by abusing his clients. So can the case worker who uses legal and extralegal methods to humiliate or otherwise punish those in need of his help. To them, he represents the awful power of a large agency. The official who has no other source of power, who regards himself as an insignificant part of the organization, is very powerful indeed when he faces outsiders who are dependent upon him. Similarly, a middle-level boss may exult in tyrannizing without mercy over his subordinates precisely because he has so little over-all discretion. He may be compulsive and petty about minor matters for the reason that his area of jurisdiction is petty and unimportant. James Jones's novel, *From Here to Eternity*, is an extended illustration of the fact that such abuse can be torture to its victim.

Every office holder knows that the petty tyrant who overpowers his underlings is simultaneously capable of meekness and sycophancy to those who out-rank him. Such conduct is all of a piece. It may properly be called authoritarian, for it is based upon the premise that authority as such, any and every kind of authority, must be respected. The relation of that authority to wisdom or purpose—or even sanity—goes unquestioned, as Herman Wouk argues in his postwar best seller, *The Caine Mutiny*. That novel placed the onus of scorn on a naval officer who disobeyed his deranged captain, thereby evincing illegitimate disrespect for authority, even insane authority.

In the presence of a superior, the authoritarian bureaucrat is eager to please, musters all the charm in his possession, snaps to attention, fawns, and generally acts with extravagant deference. No matter how much he privately resents his debasement, he gives his all to it. Away from his superiors, despite the humiliation rankling within him, he finds it necessary to humiliate others. He demonstrates his own authority, if only to prove to himself that he is not a rabbit after all.

This pattern of behavior, familiar to psychologists as dominance and submission, is especially common in any bureaucracy. It is no doubt embedded in the individual personality as a trait that makes bureaucratic employment attractive in the first place, but that employment in its objective form accentuates the trait. It produces individual suffering, and, when widespread, it can produce a fundamental weakening of the organization.

Authoritarian Misinformation

As a communications system, bureaucracy transmits information up the line in a stream of data, messages, and reports, and down the line in a stream of orders, instructions, and morale-making propaganda. In its lateral flow, the system conveys gossip and stimulates interdepartmental negotiation. Insofar as it effects the movement of upward communications, submissive behavior has certain negative consequences. A subordinate is, among other things, supposed to function as "the eyes and ears" of his superior. He is supposed to keep his superior informed, to protect him from making errors based on misinformation or ignorance of the facts. He is even required, if necessary, to disagree with his superior and to explain his reasons for disagreeing. Otherwise he is a poor watchdog. Now, the submissive official is afraid to disagree. On the contrary, he seeks out his superior's opinions and assembles data which will support them. By selective inattention to data that might ruffle established thinking, he isolates his superior, validates mistaken notions, and gives them an expert aura of infallibility. Without accurate information from below, the policy maker is helpless. He is stripped of independent knowledge of the social or political or economic reality in which he operates, and about which he is expected to make intelligent decisions.

The judicious and secure bureaucrat avoids sycophantic subordinates, because he knows that they are likely to isolate him from reality. At some levels, he will invite advance criticism of his decisions, even encouraging a systematic statement of objections. Just as an attorney sometimes prepares his opponent's case, the better to refute it, so the efficient administrator faces all weaknesses in his own position, its possible loopholes, contingencies, and repercussions. He can proceed only after many arguments have been presented, by taking them into account and then making his decision with some sense of its manysidedness. Lately, bureaucracies have institutionalized internal criticism by setting up special departments for that purpose. They may use an "Inspector General's Office," the self-survey, independent commissions, and managerial consultants.

The authoritarian administrator shies away from independent criticism of his work. He demands subservience of lower bureaucrats who feel that it is risky to provide him with unpleasant information. Critical and independent views, like inconvenient facts, are interpreted as personal criticism and as symptoms of disrespect or of impudence. This attitude conditions subordinates to feed him a steady diet of cheerful good news, automatic assent, and insincere agreement. The result is that he increasingly makes his decisions in a vacuum. Such a situation has been known to demoralize the foreign service of more than one country. When diplomats, ambassadors, consuls, and attachés on the spot are too fearful to report what they see, preferring to report what others think they see from a great distance, serious miscalculations are bound to occur. To clog the channels of communication within a foreign ministry or a department of state with intimidated personnel, is to invite needless and possibly mortal peril.

Power-seeking and Office Politics

Still another response to the feeling of powerlessness among those below is for those above to urge upon them the desirability of pursuing power. The logic they try to instill dictates that, since a man lacks power by reason of his low rank, he can overcome his lack only by gaining higher rank. Those who accept this logic, the young, the ambitious, the undefeated, are not really daunted by an objective and—presumably temporary—lack of power, which is parallel to that of children who will one day supplant their powerful elders.

Thus, one bureaucratic segment, particularly in the middle and upper layers, is made up of extremely ambitious individuals strongly motivated to the acquisition of power. From this group come the office politicians, the apple-polishers, the toadies, and favor-seekers, ever ready to betray their equals and their superiors. These are the Machiavellians who organize and lead factions capable of tearing an office apart. When successful they may purge an organization of unsuccessful rivals—and then regroup, creating new lines of antagonistic co-operation, until they are once more convulsed by the same tactics. Friends are imported and allies enlisted in the battle to strengthen their hard-won position. Past political debts are paid. Bureaucrats become warriors who, if they are not "fur us," are "agin us" in the battle of all against all. It is possible to overstimulate the appetite for power. If, after much deprivation, men are spurred on primarily by this hunger, the organization's functional objectives exist merely as a setting, wherein the power-starved ravenously wage their battle.

What happens in this setting to the non-political, personally unambitious, and professionally zealous official? At first he may find the execution of his tasks more difficult, for it is impeded by other officials who are more concerned with jockeying for position than with their occupational roles. Finding that the "politics" his associates practice makes it hard for him to do his job, he concludes that the only way to get it done is to line up "political" support for his "nonpolitical" goals. Regardless of his own inclinations, he is forced to become a politician and to do things he dislikes. Doing them, he sometimes discovers that he is a good politician who can now accomplish things previously impossible. However, he is now less likely to want to accomplish those things. If this transformation takes place, our man may well be destined for a high executive role in which politics will dominate his life. Thenceforth, he must balance and co-ordinate the divergent factional and political activities within his organization.

The Powerlessness of the Intellectual

Another kind of anxiety is aroused in the bureaucrat who has strong academic and intellectual interests. These interests prompt him to view everyday problems with a broad and total sweep. He experiences the narrowness of jurisdictional limitations only as a bureaucrat. His self-image is that of a thinker employed, far below his capacity, as a technician and a hack by poorly educated ignoramuses. Frequently his disenchantment with the organization is a sudden one. Ultimately he either adopts some of the aforementioned responses—or resigns. There is much turnover of intellectuals in bureaucracies. Some repair to less bureaucratic pastures; others move from job to job, restlessly seeking a bureaucracy in which their talents can be given fuller scope. If, in the process of experiencing these limitations, they capitulate and accept a greatly circumscribed role, intellectuals can become quite valuable specialists and eventually move into top administrative positions. They have been socialized to the bureaucracy.

A cautionary word must be added. All of our descriptions distort the appearance of bureaucracy as it visibly operates. These conditions exist, but within a context of overwhelmingly routine work, often neither pleasant nor unpleasant. Moreover, there is nothing so psychically burdensome or intolerably harsh about bureaucracy that it cannot be softened by ordinary social activities or sweetened by "seeing the better side of things." If there are economists (in this case, Kenneth Boulding) who warn that

"Beyond a certain point increase in the scale of organization results in a breakdown of communication, in a lack of flexibility, in bureaucratic stagnation and insensitivity," who liken the bureaucratic monster to a dinosaur leaving free men breathing space only in the interstices of its path, there are cheerful academicians (in this case, Harlan Cleveland, Dean of the Maxwell Graduate School of Citizenship and Public Affairs at Syracuse University) to offer consolation.

> My impression is that "large-scale" organization generally implies loose organization. Precisely because big organizations make most of the vital decisions affecting our destiny, more people are participating in those decisions than ever before. . . .
>
> In a household managed by people who can walk and talk, a baby begins to experience a sense of personal freedom when it masters the techniques of walking and talking. Just so, in a world dominated by large-scaleness, it is those individuals who learn to work with and in large-scale organizations who have a rational basis for feeling free. There are, of course, plenty of free men who work—for giant corporations or government agencies—but they aren't those who are so afraid of them that they scurry into the "interstices" of smallness. I have no doubt that a large number of middle-grade bureaucrats in the Soviet Union have so mastered the system that they are, in a sense, experiencing within its limits a significant measure of personal freedom. The reason is that the Soviet is not, as Mr. Boulding protests, a "one-firm state," but a myriad collection of manageable size bound together by leadership and a sense of destiny in ways not so fundamentally different from other nations as they (and we) like to assume.

Real bureaucracy is neither as efficient as its ideal type suggests, nor as cruel and inefficient as our treatment of its pathologies suggests. Not all people are frustrated by bureaucracy—towards which they may have gravitated by predisposition. No bureaucracy is exclusively staffed with pathological types. The negative tendencies we have sketched are, however, as much a reality as the positive ones. These tendencies pose typical problems and present typical difficulties which most white-collar workers encounter at one time or another in the course of their careers.

To a certain extent they are inescapable, simply because bureaucracy is here to stay. As society is more and more dominated by largeness, bureaucracy's share of our total life cannot but grow with it. The future, if there is to be one, points to ever greater degrees of hugeness. Beyond that, Boulding is correct in saying, "The electric calculator, the punched card, operations research and decision theory all point to a still further revolution in the making . . ." toward still more bureaucracy.

HARVEY SWADOS

The Myth of the Happy Worker

"From where we sit in the company," says one of the best personnel men in the country, "we have to look at only the aspects of work that cut across all sorts of jobs—administration and human relations. Now these are aspects of work, abstractions, but it's easy for personnel people to get so hipped on their importance that they look on the specific tasks of making things and selling them as secondary. . . ."

—*The Organization Man*,
by William H. Whyte, Jr.

THE PERSONNEL MAN who made this remark to Mr. Whyte differed from his brothers only in that he had a moment of insight. Actually, "the specific tasks of making things" are now not only regarded by his white-collar fellows as "secondary," but as irrelevant to the vaguer but more "challenging" tasks of the man at the desk. This is true not just of the personnel man, who places workers, replaces them, displaces them—in brief, manipulates them. The union leader also, who represents workers and sometimes manipulates them, seems increasingly to regard what his workers do as merely subsidiary to the job he himself is doing in the larger community. This job may be building the Red Cross or the Community Chest, or it may sometimes be —as the Senate hearings suggest—participating in such communal endeavors as gambling, prostitution, and improving the breed. In any case, the impression is left that the problems of the workers in the background (or underground) have been stabilized, if not permanently solved.

With the personnel man and the union leader, both of whom presumably see the worker from day to day, growing so far away from him, it is hardly to be wondered at that the middle class in general, and articulate middle-class intellectuals in particular, see the worker vaguely, as through a cloud. One gets the impression that when they do consider him, they operate from one of two unspoken assumptions: (1) the worker has died out like the passenger pigeon, or is dying out, or becoming accultured, like the Navajo; (2) if he *is* still around, he is just like the

Reprinted from the *Nation*, CLXXXV, No. 4 (1957), 65-68, by permission of the author and the publisher. (Copyright 1957, by Harvey Swados.)

rest of us—fat, satisfied, smug, a little restless, but hardly distinguishable from his fellow TV-viewers of the middle class.

Lest it be thought that (1) is somewhat exaggerated, I hasten to quote from a recently published article apparently dedicated to the laudable task of urging slothful middle-class intellectuals to wake up and live: "The old-style sweatshop crippled mainly the working people. Now there are no workers left in America; we are almost all middle class as to income and expectations." I do not believe the writer meant to state—although he comes perilously close to it—that nobody works any more. If I understand him correctly, he is referring to the fact that the worker's rise in real income over the last decade, plus the diffusion of middle-class tastes and values throughout a large part of the underlying population, have made it increasingly difficult to tell blue-collar from white-collar worker without a program. In short, if the worker earns like the middle class, votes like the middle class, dresses like the middle class, dreams like the middle class, then he ceases to exist as a worker.

But there is one thing that the worker doesn't do like the middle class: he works like a worker. The steel-mill puddler does not yet sort memos, the coal miner does not yet sit in conferences, the cotton millhand does not yet sip martinis from his lunchbox. The worker's attitude toward his work is generally compounded of hatred, shame, and resignation.

Before I spell out what I think this means, I should like first to examine some of the implications of the widely held belief that "we are almost all middle-class as to income and expectations." I am neither economist, sociologist, nor politician, and I hold in my hand no doctored statistics to be haggled over. I am by profession a writer who has had occasion to work in factories at various times during the thirties, forties, and fifties. The following observations are simply impressions based on my last period of factory servitude, in 1956.

The average automobile worker gets a little better than two dollars an hour. As such he is one of the best-paid factory workers in the country. After twenty years of militant struggle led by the union that I believe to be still the finest and most democratic labor organization in the United States, he is earning less than the starting salaries offered to inexperienced and often semi-literate college graduates without dependents. After compulsory deductions for taxes, social security, old-age insurance, and union dues, and optional deductions for hospitalization and assorted charities, his pay check for forty hours of work is going to be closer to seventy than to eighty dollars a week. Does this make him middle class as to income? Does it rate with the weekly take of a dentist, an accountant, a salesman, a draftsman, a journalist? Surely it would be more to the point to ask how a family man can get by in the fifties on that kind of income. I know how he does it, and I should think the answers would be a little disconcerting to those who wax glib on the satisfactory status of the "formerly" underprivileged.

For one thing, he works a lot longer than forty hours a week—when he can. Since no automobile company is as yet in a position to guarantee its workers anything like fifty weeks of steady forty-hour paychecks, the auto worker knows he has to make it while he can. During peak production periods he therefore puts in nine, ten, eleven, and often twelve hours a day on the assembly line for weeks on end. And that's not all. If he has dependents, as like as not he also holds down a "spare-time" job. I have worked on the line with men who doubled as mechanics, repairmen, salesmen, contractors, builders, farmers, cab-drivers, lumberyard workers, countermen. I would guess that there are many more of these than show up in the official statistics: often a man will work for less if he can be paid under the counter with tax-free dollars.

Nor is that all. The factory worker with dependents cannot carry the debt load he now shoulders—the middle-class debt load, if you like, of nagging payments, on car, washer, dryer, TV, clothing, house itself—without family help. Even if he puts in fifty, sixty, or seventy hours a week at one or two jobs, he has to count on his wife's paycheck, or his son's, his daughter's, his brother-in-law's; or on his mother's social security, or his father's veteran's pension. The working-class family today is not typically held together by the male wage earner, but by multiple wage earners often of several generations who club together to get the things they want and need—or are pressured into believing they must have. It is at best a precarious arrangement; as for its toll on the physical organism and the psyche, that is a question perhaps worthy of further investigation by those who currently pronounce themselves bored with Utopia Unlimited in the Fat Fifties.

But what of the worker's middle-class expectations? I had been under the impression that this was the rock on which Socialist agitation had foundered for generations: it proved useless to tell the proletarian that he had a world to win when he was reasonably certain that with a few breaks he could have his own gas station. If these expectations have changed at all in recent years, they would seem to have narrowed rather than expanded, leaving a psychological increment of resignation rather than of unbounded optimism (except among the very young—and even among them the optimism focuses more often on better-paying opportunities elsewhere in the labor market than on illusory hopes of swift status advancement). The worker's expectations are for better pay, more humane working conditions, more job security. As long as he feels that he is going to achieve them through an extension of existing conditions, for that long he is going to continue to be a middle-class conservative in temper. But only for that long.

I suspect that what middle-class writers mean by the worker's middle-class expectations are his cravings for commodities—his determination to have not only fin-tailed cars and single-unit washer-dryers, but butterfly chairs in the rumpus room, African masks on the wall, and power boats in the garage. Before the middle-class intellectuals condemn these expectations too harshly, let them consider, first, who has been utilizing every known technique of suasion and propaganda to convert luxuries into necessities, and second, at what cost these new necessities are acquired by the American working-class family.

Now I should like to return to the second image of the American worker: satisfied, doped by TV, essentially middle class in outlook. This is an image bred not of communication with workers (except as mediated by hired interviewers sent "into the field" like anthropologists or entomologists), but of contempt for people, based perhaps on self-contempt and on a feeling among intellectuals that the worker has let them down. In order to see this clearly, we have to place it against the intellectual's changing attitudes toward the worker since the thirties.

At the time of the organization of the C.I.O., the middle-class intellectual saw the proletarian as society's figure of virtue—heroic, magnanimous, bearing in his loins the seeds of a better future; he would have found ludicrous the suggestion that a sit-down striker might harbor anti-Semitic feelings. After Pearl Harbor, the glamorization of the worker was taken over as a function of government. Then, however, he was no longer the builder of the future good society; instead he was second only to the fighting man as the vital winner of the war. Many intellectuals, as government employees, found themselves helping to create this new portrait of the worker as patriot.

But in the decade following the war, intellectuals have discovered that workers are no longer either building socialism or forging the tools of victory. All they are doing is making the things that other people buy. That, and participating in the great commodity scramble. The disillusionment, it would seem, is almost too terrible to bear. Word has gotten around among the highbrows that the worker is not heroic or idealistic; public-opinion polls prove that he wants barbecue pits more than foreign aid and air-conditioning more than desegregation, that he doesn't particularly want to go on strike, that he is reluctant to form a Labor Party, that he votes for Stevenson and often even for Eisenhower and Nixon—that he is, in short, animated by the same aspirations as drive the middle class onward and upward in suburbia.

There is of course a certain admixture of self-delusion in the middle-class attitude that workers are now the same as everybody else. For me it was expressed most precisely last year in the dismay and sympathy with which middle-class friends greeted the news that I had gone back to work in a factory. If workers are now full-fledged members of the middle class, why the dismay? What difference whether one sits in an office or stands in a shop? The answer is so obvious that one feels shame at laboring the point. But I have news for my friends among the intellectuals. The answer is obvious to workers, too.

They know that there is a difference between working with your back and working with your behind. (I do not make the distinction between hand-work and brain-work, since we are all learning that white-collar work is becoming less and less brain-work.) They know that they work harder than the middle class for less money. Nor is it simply a question of status, that magic word so dear to the hearts of the sociologues, the new anatomizers of the American corpus. It is not simply status-hunger that makes a man hate work which pays *less* than other work he knows about, if *more* than any other work he has been trained for (the only reason my fellow-workers stayed on the assembly line, they told me again and again). It is not simply status-hunger that makes a man hate work that is mindless, endless, stupefying, sweaty, filthy, noisy, exhausting, insecure in its prospects, and practically without hope of advancement.

The plain truth is that factory work is degrading. It is degrading to any man who ever dreams of doing something worthwhile with his life; and it is about time we faced the fact. The more a man is exposed to middle-class values, the more sophisticated he becomes and the more production-line work is degrading to him. The immigrant who slaved in the poorly lighted, foul, vermin-ridden sweatshop found his work less degrading than the native-born high school graduate who reads "Judge Parker," "Rex Morgan, M.D.," and "Judd Saxon, Business Executive," in the funnies, and works in a fluorescent factory with ticker-tape production-control machines. For the immigrant laborer, even the one who did not dream of socialism, his long hours were going to buy him freedom. For the factory worker of the fifties, his long hours are going to buy him commodities . . . and maybe reduce a few of his debts.

Almost without exception, the men with whom I worked on the assembly line last year felt like trapped animals. Depending on their age and personal circumstances, they were either resigned to their fate, furiously angry at *themselves* for what they were doing, or desperately hunting other work that would pay as well and in addition offer some variety, some prospect of change and betterment. They were sick of being pushed around by harried foremen (themselves more pitied than hated), sick of working like blinkered donkeys, sick of being dependent for their livelihood on a maniacal production-merchandising setup, sick of working in a place where there was no spot to relax during the twelve-minute rest period. (Some day—let us hope—we will marvel that production was still so worshiped in the fifties that new factories could be built with every splendid facility for the storage and movement of essential parts, but with no place for a resting worker to sit down for a moment but on a fire plug, the edge of a packing case, or the sputum- and oil-stained stairway of a toilet.)

The older men stay put and wait for their vacations. But since the assembly line demands young blood (you will have a hard time getting hired if you are over thirty-five), the factory in which I worked was aswarm with new faces every day; labor turnover was so fantastic and absenteeism so rampant, with the young men knocking off a day or two every week to hunt up other jobs, that the company was forced to over-hire in order to have sufficient workers on hand at the starting siren.

To those who will object—fortified by their readings in C. Wright Mills and A. C. Spectorsky—that the white-collar commuter, too, dislikes his work, accepts it only because it buys his family commodities, and is constantly on the prowl for other work, I can only reply that for me at any rate this is proof not of the disappearance of the working-class but of the proletarianization of the middle class. Perhaps it is not taking place quite in the way that Marx envisaged it, but the alienation of the white-collar man (like that of the laborer) from both his tools and whatever he produces, the slavery that chains the exurbanite to the commuting timetable (as the worker is still chained to the time-clock), the anxiety that sends the white-collar man home with his briefcase for an evening's work (as it degrades the workingman into pleading for long hours of overtime), the displacement of the white-collar slum from the wrong side of the tracks to the suburbs (just as the working-class slum is moved from old-law tenements to skyscraper barracks)—all these mean to me that the white-collar man is entering (though his arms may be loaded with commodities) the grey world of the working man.

Three quotations from men with whom I worked may help to bring my view into focus:

Before starting work: "Come on, suckers, they say the Foundation wants to give away *more* than half a billion this year. Let's do and die for the old Foundation."

During rest period: "Ever stop to think how we crawl here bumper to bumper, and crawl home bumper to bumper, and we've got to turn out more every minute to keep our jobs, when there isn't even any room for them on the highways?"

At quitting time (this from older foremen, whose job is not only to keep things moving, but by extension to serve as company spokesmen): "You're smart to get out of here. . . . I curse the day I ever started, now

I'm stuck: any man with brains that stays here ought to have his head examined. This is no place for an intelligent human being."

Such is the attitude towards the work. And towards the product? On the one hand it is admired and desired as a symbol of freedom, almost a substitute for freedom, not because the worker participated in making it, but because our whole culture is dedicated to the proposition that the automobile is both necessary and beautiful. On the other hand it is hated and despised—so much that if your new car smells bad it may be due to a banana peel crammed down its gullet and sealed up thereafter, so much so that if your dealer can't locate the rattle in your new car you might ask him to open the welds on one of those tail fins and vacuum out the nuts and bolts thrown in by workers sabotaging their own product.

Sooner or later, if we want a decent society—by which I do not mean a society glutted with commodities or one maintained in precarious equilibrium by over-buying and forced premature obsolescence—we are going to have to come face to face with the problem of work. Apparently the Russians have committed themselves to the replenishment of their labor force through automatic recruitment of those intellectually incapable of keeping up with severe scholastic requirements in the public educational system. Apparently we, too, are heading in the same direction: although our economy is not directed, and although college education is as yet far from free, we seem to be operating in this capitalist economy on the totalitarian assumption that we can funnel the underprivileged, undereducated, or just plain underequipped, into the factory, where we can proceed to forget about them once we have posted the minimum fair labor standards on the factory wall.

If this is what we want, let's be honest enough to say so. If we conclude that there is nothing noble about repetitive work, but that it is nevertheless good enough for the lower orders, let's say that, too, so we will at least know where we stand. But if we cling to the belief that other men are our brothers, not just Egyptians, or Israelis, or Hungarians, but *all* men, including millions of Americans who grind their lives away on an insane treadmill, then we will have to start thinking about how their work and their lives can be made meaningful. That is what I assume the Hungarians, both workers and intellectuals, have been thinking about. Since no one has been ordering us what to think, since no one has been forbidding our intellectuals to fraternize with our workers, shouldn't it be a little easier for us to admit, first, that our problems exist, then to state them, and then to see if we can resolve them?

HOWARD S. BECKER AND ANSELM L. STRAUSS

Careers, Personality, and Adult Socialization[1]

IN CONTRADISTINCTION to other disciplines, the sociological approach to the study of personality and personality change views the person as a member of a social structure. Usually the emphasis is upon some cross-section in his life: on the way he fills his status, on the consequent conflicts in role and his dilemmas. When the focus is more developmental, then concepts like career carry the import of movement through structures. Much writing on career, of course, pertains more to patterned sequences of passage than to the persons. A fairly comprehensive statement about careers as related both to institutions and to persons would be useful in furthering research. We shall restrict our discussion to careers in work organizations and occupations, for purposes of economy.

Career Flow

Organizations built around some particular kind of work or situation at work tend to be characterized by recurring patterns of tension and of problems. Thus, in occupations whose central feature is performance of a service for outside clients, one chronic source of tension is the effort of members to control their work life themselves while in contact with outsiders. In production organizations, somewhat similar tensions arise from the workers' efforts to maintain relative autonomy over job conditions.

Whatever the typical problems of an occupation, the pattern of associated problems will vary with one's position. Some positions will be easier, some more difficult; some will afford more prestige, some less; some will pay better than others. In general, the personnel move from less to more desirable positions, and the flow is usually, but not necessarily, related to

Reprinted from the *American Journal of Sociology*, LXII (1956), 253-63, by permission of the authors and the University of Chicago Press.

age. The pure case is the bureaucracy as described by Mannheim, in which seniority and an age-related increase in skill and responsibility automatically push men in the desired direction and within a single organization.[2]

An ideally simple model of flow up through an organization is something like the following: recruits enter at the bottom in positions of least prestige and move up through the ranks as they gain in age, skill, and experience. Allowing for some attrition due to death, sickness, and dismissal or resignation, all remain in the organization until retirement. Most would advance to top ranks. A few reach the summit of administration. Yet even in bureaucracies, which perhaps come closest to this model, the very highest posts often go not to those who have come up through the ranks but to "irregulars"—people with certain kinds of experiences or qualifications not necessarily acquired by long years of official service. In other ways, too, the model is oversimple: posts at any rank may be filled from the outside; people get "frozen" at various levels and do not rise. Moreover, career movements may be not only up but down or sideways, as in moving from one department to another at approximately the same rank.

The flow of personnel through an organization should be seen, also, as a number of streams; that is, there may be several routes to the posts of high prestige and responsibility. These may be thought of as escalators. An institution invests time, money, and energy in the training of its recruits and members which it cannot afford to let go to waste. Hence just being on the spot often means that one is bound to advance. In some careers, even a small gain of experience gives one a great advantage over the beginner. The mere fact of advancing age or of having been through certain kinds of situations or training saves many an employee from languishing in lower positions. This is what the phrase "seasoning" refers to—the acquiring of requisite knowledge and skills, skills that cannot always be clearly specified even by those who have them. However, the escalator will carry one from opportunities as well as to them. After a certain amount of time and money have been spent upon one's education for the job, it is not always easy to get off one escalator and on another. Immediate superiors will block transfer. Sponsors will reproach one for disloyalty. Sometimes a man's special training and experience will be thought to have spoiled him for a particular post.

Recruitment and Replacement

Recruitment is typically regarded as occurring only at the beginning of a career, where the occupationally uncommitted are bid for, or as something which happens only when there is deliberate effort to get people to commit themselves. But establishments must recruit for all positions; whenever personnel are needed, they must be found and often trained. Many higher positions, as in bureaucracies, appear to recruit automatically from aspirants at next lower levels. This is only appearance: the recruitment mechanisms are standardized and work well. Professors, for example, are drawn regularly from lower ranks, and the system works passably in most academic fields. But in schools of engineering, young instructors are likely to be drained off into industry and not be on hand for promotion. Recruitment is never really automatic but depends upon developing in the recruit certain occupational or organizational commitments which correspond to regularized career routes.

Positions in organizations are being vacated continually through death and retirement, promotion and demotion. Replacements may be drawn from the outside ("an outside man") or from within the organization. Most often positions are filled by someone promoted from below or shifted from another department without gaining in prestige. When career routes are well laid out, higher positions are routinely filled from aspirants at the next lower level. However, in most organizations many career routes are not so rigidly laid out: a man may jump from one career over to another to fill the organization's need. When this happens, the "insider-outsider" may be envied by those who have come up by the more orthodox routes; and his associates on his original route may regard him as a turncoat. This may be true even if he is not the first to have made the change, as in the jump from scholar to dean or doctor to hospital administrator. Even when replacement from outside the organization is routine for certain positions, friction may result if the newcomer has come up by an irregular route—as when a college president is chosen from outside the usual circle of feeding occupations. A candidate whose background is too irregular is likely to be eliminated unless just this irregularity makes him particularly valuable. The advantage of "new blood" versus "inbreeding" may be the justification. A good sponsor can widen the limits within which the new kind of candidate is judged, by asking that certain of his qualities be weighed against others; as Hall says, "the question is not whether the applicant possesses a specific trait . . . but whether these traits can be assimilated by the specific institutions."[3]

Even when fairly regular routes are followed, the speed of advancement may not be rigidly prescribed. Irregularity may be due in part to unexpected needs for replacement because a number of older men retire in quick succession or because an older man leaves and a younger one happens to be conveniently present. On the other hand, in some career lines there may be room for a certain amount of manipulation of "the system." One such method is to remain physically mobile, especially early in the career, thus taking advantage of several institutions' vacancies.

The Limits of Replacement and Recruitment

Not all positions within an organization recruit from an equally wide range. Aside from the fact that different occupations may be represented in one establishment, some positions require training so specific that recruits can be drawn only from particular schools or firms. Certain positions are merely way stations and recruit only from aspirants directly below. Some may draw only from the outside, and the orbit is always relevant to both careers and organization. One important question, then, about any organization is the limits within which positions recruit incumbents. Another is the limits of the recruitment in relation to certain variables —age of the organization, its relations with clients, type of generalized work functions, and the like.

One can also identify crucial contingencies for careers in preoccupational life by noting the general or probable limits within which recruiting is carried on and the forces by which they are maintained. For example, it is clear that a position can be filled, at least at first, only from among those who know of it. Thus physiologists cannot be recruited during high school, for scarcely any youngster then knows what a physiologist is or does. By the same token, however, there are at least generally formulated notions of the "artist," so that recruitment into the world of art often begins in high school.[4] This is paradoxical, since the steps and paths later in the artist's career are less definite than in the physiologist's. The range and diffusion of a public stereotype are crucial in determining the number and variety of young people from whom a particular occupation can recruit, and the unequal distribution of information about careers limits occupations possibilities.

There are problems attending the systematic restriction of recruiting. Some kinds of persons, for occupationally irrelevant reasons (formally, anyway), may not be considered for some positions at all. Medical schools restrict recruiting in this way: openly, on grounds of "personality assessments," and covertly on ethnicity. Italians, Jews, and Negroes who do become doctors face differential recruitment into the formal and informal hierarchies of influence, power, and prestige in the medical world. Similar mechanisms operate at the top and bottom of industrial organizations.[5]

Another problem is that of "waste." Some recruits in institutions which recruit pretty widely do not remain. Public caseworkers in cities are recruited from holders of Bachelor's degrees, but most do not remain caseworkers. From the welfare agency's point of view this is waste. From other perspectives this is not waste, for they may exploit the job and its opportunities for private ends. Many who attend school while supposedly visiting clients may be able to transfer to new escalators because of the acquisition, for instance, of a Master's degree. Others actually build up small businesses during this "free time." The only permanent recruits, those who do not constitute waste, are those who fail at such endeavors.[6] Unless an organization actually finds useful a constant turnover of some sector of its personnel, it is faced with the problem of creating organizational loyalties and—at higher levels anyhow—satisfactory careers or the illusion of them, within the organization.

Training and Schools

Schooling occurs most conspicuously during the early stages of a career and is an essential part of getting people committed to careers and prepared to fill positions. Both processes may, or may not, be going on simultaneously. However, movement from one kind of job or position to another virtually always necessitates some sort of learning—sometimes before and sometimes on the job, sometimes through informal channels and sometimes at school. This means that schools may exist within the framework of an organization. In-service training is not only for jobs on lower levels but also for higher positions. Universities and special schools are attended by students who are not merely preparing for careers but getting degrees or taking special courses in order to move faster and higher. In some routes there is virtual blockage of mobility because the top of the ladder is not very high; in order to rise higher, one must return to school to prepare for ascending by another route. Thus the registered nurse may have to return to school to become a nursing educator, administrator, or even supervisor. Sometimes the aspirant may study on his own, and this may be effective unless he must present a diploma to prove he deserves promotion.

The more subtle connections are between promotion and informal training. Certain positions preclude the acquiring of certain skills or information, but others foster it. It is possible to freeze a man at given levels or to move him faster, unbeknownst to him. Thus a sponsor, anticipating a need for certain requirements in his candidate, may arrange for critical experiences to come his way. Medical students are aware that if they obtain internships in certain kinds of hospitals they will be exposed to certain kinds of learning: the proper internship is crucial to many kinds of medical careers. But learning may depend upon circumstances which the candidate cannot control and of which he may not even be aware. Thus Goldstein has pointed out that nurses learn more from doctors at hospitals not attached to a medical school; elsewhere the medical students become the beneficiaries of the doctors' teaching.[7] Quite often who teaches whom and what is connected with matters of convenience as well as with prestige. It is said, for instance, that registered nurses are jealous of their prerogatives and will not transmit certain skills to practical nurses. Nevertheless, the nurse is often happy to allow her aides to relieve her of certain other jobs and will pass along the necessary skills; and the doctor in his turn may do the same with his nurses.

The connection between informal learning and group allegiance should not be minimized. Until a newcomer has been accepted, he will not be taught crucial trade secrets. Conversely, such learning may block mobility, since to be mobile is to abandon standards, violate friendships, and even injure one's self-regard. Within some training institutions students are exposed to different and sometimes antithetical work ideologies—as with commercial and fine artists—which results in sharp and sometimes lasting internal conflicts of loyalty.

Roy's work on industrial organization furnishes a subtle instance of secrecy and loyalty in training.[8] The workers in Roy's machine shop refused to enlighten him concerning ways of making money on difficult piecework jobs until given evidence that he could be trusted in undercover skirmishes with management. Such systematic withholding of training may mean that an individual can qualify for promotion by performance only by shifting group loyalties, and that disqualifies him in some other sense. Training hinders as well as helps. It may incapacitate one for certain duties as well as train him for them. Roy's discussion of the managerial "logic of efficiency" makes this clear: workers, not trained in this logic, tend to see short cuts to higher production more quickly than managers, who think in terms of sentimental dogmas of efficiency.[9]

Certain transmittible skills, information, and qualities facilitate movement, and it behooves the candidate to discover and distinguish what is genuinely relevant in his training. The student of careers must also be sensitized to discover what training is essential or highly important to the passage from one status to another.

Recruiting for Undesirable Positions

A most difficult kind of recruiting is for positions which no one wants. Ordinary incentives do not work, for these are positions without prestige, without future, without financial reward. Yet they are filled. How, and by whom? Most obviously, they are filled by failures (the crews of gandy dancers who repair railroad tracks are made up of skid-row bums), to whom they are almost the only means of survival. Most positions filled by failures are not openly regarded as such; special rhetorics deal with misfortune and make their ignominious fate more palatable for the failures themselves and those around them.[10]

Of course, failure is a matter of perspective. Many positions represent failure to some but not to others. For the middle-class white, becoming a caseworker in a public welfare agency may mean failure; but for the Negro from the lower-middle class the job may be a real prize. The permanent positions in such agencies tend to be occupied by whites who have failed to reach anything better and, in larger numbers, by Negroes who have succeeded in arriving this far.[11] Likewise, some recruitment into generally undesirable jobs is from the ranks of the disaffected who care little for generally accepted values. The jazz musicians who play in Chicago's Clark Street dives make little money, endure bad working conditions, but desire the freedom to play as they could not in better-paying places.[12]

Recruits to undesirable positions also come from the ranks of the transients, who, because they feel that they are on their way to something different and better, can afford temporarily to do something *infra dig.* Many organizations rely primarily on transients—such are the taxi companies and some of the mail-order houses. Among the permanent incumbents of undesirable positions are those, also, who came in temporarily but whose brighter prospects did not materialize, they thus fall into the "failure" group.

Still another group is typified by the taxi dancer, whose career Cressey has described. The taxi dancer starts at the top, from which the only movement possible is down or out. She enters the profession young and goodlooking and draws the best customers in the house, but, as age and hard work take their toll, she ends with the worst clients or becomes a streetwalker.[13] Here the worst positions are filled by individuals who start high and so are committed to a career that ends badly—a more common pattern of life, probably, than is generally recognized.

Within business and industrial organizations, not everyone who attempts to move upward succeeds. Men are assigned to positions prematurely, sponsors drop protégés, and miscalculations are made about the abilities of promising persons. Problems for the organization arise from those contingencies. Incompetent persons must be moved into positions where they cannot do serious damage, others of limited ability can still be useful if wisely placed. Aside from outright firing, various methods of "cooling out" the failures can be adopted, among them honorific promotion, banishment "to the sticks," shunting to other departments, frank demotion, bribing out of the organization, and down-grading through departmental mergers. The use of particular methods is related to the structure of the organization; and these, in turn, have consequences both for the failure and for the organization.[14]

Attachment and Severance

Leaders of organizations sometimes complain that their personnel will not take responsibility or that some men (the wrong ones) are too ambitious. This complaint reflects a dual problem which confronts every organization. Since all positions must be filled, some men must be properly motivated to take certain positions and stay in them for a period, while others must be motivated to move onward and generally upward. The American emphasis on mobility should not lead us to assume that everyone wants to rise to the highest levels or to rise quickly. Aside from this, both formal mechanisms and informal influences bind incumbents, at least temporarily, to certain positions. Even the ambitious may be willing to remain in a given post, provided that it offers important contacts or the chance to learn certain skills and undergo certain experiences. Part of the bargain in staying in given positions is the promise that they lead somewhere. When career lines are fairly regularly laid out, positions lead definitely somewhere and at a regulated pace. One of the less obvious functions of the sponsor is to alert his favorites to the sequence and its timing, rendering them more ready to accept undesirable assignments and to refrain from champing at the bit when it might be awkward for the organization.

To certain jobs, in the course of time, come such honor and glory that the incumbents will be satisfied to remain there permanently, giving up aspirations to move upward. This is particularly true when allegiance to colleagues, built on informal relations and conflict with other ranks, is intense and runs counter to allegiance to the institution. But individuals are also attached to positions by virtue of having done particularly well at them; they often take great satisfaction in their competence at certain techniques and develop self-conceptions around them.

All this makes the world of organizations go around, but it also poses certain problems, both institutional and personal. The stability of institutions is predicated upon the proper preparation of aspirants for the next steps and upon institutional aid in transmuting motives and allegiances. While it is convenient to have some personnel relatively immobile, others must be induced to cut previous ties, to balance rewards in favor of moving, and even to take risks for long-run gains. If we do not treat mobility as normal, and thus regard attachment to a position as abnormal, we are then free to ask how individuals are induced to move along. It is done by devices such as sponsorship, by planned sequences of positions and skills, sometimes tied to age; by rewards, monetary and otherwise, and, negatively, by ridicule and the denial of responsibility to the lower ranks. There is, of course, many a slip in the inducing of mobility. Chicago public school teachers illustrate this point. They move from schools in the slums to middle-class neighborhoods. The few who prefer to remain in the tougher slum schools have settled in too snugly to feel capable of facing the risks of moving to "better" schools.[15] Their deviant course illuminates the more usual patterns of the Chicago teacher's career.

Timing in Status Passage

Even when paths in a career are regular and smooth, there always arise problems of pacing and timing. While, ideally, successors and predecessors should move in and out of offices at equal speeds, they do not and cannot. Those asked to move on or along or upward may be willing but must make actual and symbolic preparations; meanwhile, the successor waits impatiently. Transition periods are a necessity, for a man often invests heavily of himself in a position, comes to possess it as it possesses him, and suffers in leaving it. If the full ritual of leavetaking is not allowed, the man may not pass fully into his new status. On the other hand, the institution has devices to make him forget, to plunge him into the new office, to woo and win him with the new gratifications, and, at the same time, to force him to abandon the old. When each status is conceived as the logical and temporal extension of the one previous, then severance is not so disturbing. Nevertheless, if a man must face his old associates in unaccustomed roles, problems of loyalty arise. Hence a period of tolerance after formal admission to the new status in phrases like "it takes time" and "we all make mistakes when starting until. . . ."

But, on the other hand, those new to office may be too zealous. They often commit the indelicate error of taking too literally their formal promotion or certification, when actually intervening steps must be traversed before the attainment of full prerogatives. The passage may involve trials and tests of loyalty, as well as the simple accumulation of information and skill. The overeager are kept in line by various controlling devices: a new assistant professor discovers that it will be "just a little while" before the curriculum can be rearranged so that he can teach his favorite courses. Even a new superior has to face the resentment or the cautiousness of established personnel and may, if sensitive, pace his "moving in on them" until he has passed unspoken tests.

When subordinates are raised to the ranks of their superiors, an especially delicate situation is created. Equality is neither created by that official act, nor, even if it were, can it come about without a certain awkwardness. Patterns of response must be rearranged by both parties, and strong self-control must be exerted so that acts are appropriate. Slips are inevitable, for, although the new status may be fully granted, the proper identities may at times be forgotten, to everyone's embarrassment. Eventually, the former subordinate may come to command or take precedence over someone to whom he once looked for advice and guidance. When colleagues who were formerly sponsors and sponsored disagree over some important issue, recrimination may become overt and betrayal explicit. It is understandable why those who have been promoted often prefer, or are advised, to take office in another organization, however much they may wish to remain at home.

Multiple Routes and Switching

Theoretically, a man may leave one escalator and board another, instead of following the regular route. Such switching is most visible during the schooling, or preoccupational, phases of careers. Frequently students change their line of endeavor but remain roughly within the same field; this is one way for less desirable and less well-known specialties to obtain recruits. Certain kinds of training, such as the legal, provide bases for moving early and easily into a wide variety of careers. In all careers, there doubtless are some points at which switching to another career is relatively easy. In general, while commitment to a given career automatically closes paths, the skills and information thereby acquired open up other routes and new goals. One may not, of course, perceive the alternatives or may dismiss them as risky or otherwise undesirable.

When a number of persons have changed escalators at about the same stage in their careers, then there is the beginning of a new career. This is one way by which career lines become instituted. Sometimes the innovation occurs at the top ranks of older careers; when all honors are exhausted, the incumbent himself may look for new worlds to conquer. Or he may seem like a good risk to an organization looking for personnel with interestingly different qualifications. Such new phases of career are much more than honorific and may indeed be an essential inducement to what becomes pioneering.

Excitement and dangers are intimately tied up with switching careers. For example, some careers are fairly specific in goal but diffuse in operational means: the "fine artist" may be committed to artistic ideals but seize upon whatever jobs are at hand to help him toward creative goals. When he takes a job in order to live, he thereby risks committing himself to an alternative occupational career; and artists and writers do, indeed, get weaned away from the exercise of their art in just this way. Some people never set foot on a work escalator but move from low job to low job. Often they seek better conditions of work or a little more money rather than chances to climb institutional or occupational ladders. Many offers of opportunities to rise are spurned by part-time or slightly committed recruits, often because the latter are engaged in pursuing alternative routes while holding the job, perhaps a full-time one providing means of livelihood. This has important and, no doubt, subtle effects upon institutional functioning. When careers are in danger of being brought to an abrupt end—as with airplane pilots—then, before retirement, other kinds of careers may be prepared for or entered. This precaution is very necessary. When generalized mobility is an aim, specific routes may be chosen for convenience' sake. One is careful not to develop the usual motivation and allegiances. This enables one to get off an escalator and to move over to another with a minimum of psychological strain.

Considerable switching takes place within a single institution or a single occupational world and is rationalized in institutional and occupational terms, both by the candidates and by their colleagues. A significant consequence of this, undoubtedly, is subtle psychological strain, since the new positions and those preceding are both somewhat alike and different.

Climactic Periods

Even well-worn routes have stretches of maximum opportunity and danger. The critical passage in some careers lies near the beginning. This is especially so when the occupation or institution strongly controls recruitment; once chosen, prestige and deference automatically accrue. In another kind of career, the critical time comes at the end and sometimes very abruptly. In occupations which depend upon great physical skill, the later phases of a career are especially hazardous. It is also requisite in some careers that one choose the proper successor to carry on, lest one's own work be partly in vain. The symbolic last step of moving out may be quite as important as any that preceded it.

Appropriate or strategic timing is called for, to meet opportunity and danger, but the timing becomes vital at different periods in different kinds of careers. A few, such as the careers of virtuoso musical performers, begin so early in life that the opportunity to engage in music may have passed long before they learn of it. Some of the more subtle judgments of timing are required when a person wishes to shift from one escalator to another. Richard Wohl, of the University of Chicago, in an unpublished paper has suggested that modeling is a step which women may take in preparation for upward mobility through marriage; but models may marry before they know the ropes, and so marry too low; or they may marry too long after their prime, and so marry less well than they might. Doubtless, organizations and occupations profit from mistakes of strategic timing, both to recruit and then to retain their members.

During the most crucial periods of any career, a man suffers greater psychological stress than during other periods. This is perhaps less so if he is not aware of his opportunities and dangers—for then the contingencies are over before they can be grasped or coped with: but probably it is more usual to be aware, or to be made so by colleagues and seniors, of the nature of imminent or current crises. Fortunately, together with such definitions there exist rationales to guide action. The character of the critical junctures and the ways in which they are handled may irrevocably decide a man's fate.

Interdependence of Careers

Institutions, at any given moment, contain people at different stages in their careers. Some have already "arrived," others are still on their way up, still others just entering. Movements and changes at each level are in various ways dependent on those occurring at other levels.

Such interdependence is to be found in the phenomenon of sponsorship, where individuals move up in a work organization through the activities of older and more-well-established men. Hall[16] has given a classic description of sponsorship in medicine. The younger doctor of the proper class and acceptable ethnic origin is absorbed, on the recommendation of a member, into the informal "inner fraternity" which controls hospital appointments and which is influential in the formation and maintenance of a clientele. The perpetuation of this coterie depends on a steady flow of suitable recruits. As the members age, retire, or die off, those who remain face a problem of recruiting younger men to do the less honorific and remunerative work, such as clinical work, that their group performs. Otherwise they themselves must do work inappropriate to their position or give place to others who covet their power and influence.

To the individual in the inner fraternity, a protégé eases the transition into retirement. The younger man gradually assumes the load which the sponsor can no longer comfortably carry, allowing the older man to retire gracefully, without that sudden cutting-down of work which frightens away patients, who leap to the conclusion that he is too old to perform capably.

In general, this is the problem of retiring with honor, of leaving a life's work with a sense that one will be missed. The demand may arise that a great man's work be carried on, although it may no longer be considered important or desirable by his successors. If the old man's prestige is great enough, the men below may have to orient themselves and their work as he suggests, for fear of offending him or of profaning his heritage. The identities of the younger men are thus shaped by the older man's passage from the pinnacle to retirement.

This interdependence of career may cross occupational lines within organizations, as in the case of the young physician who receives a significant part of his training from the older and more experienced nurses in the hospital; and those at the same level in an institution are equally involved in one another's identities. Sometimes budding careers within work worlds are interdependent in quite unsuspected ways. Consider the young painter or craftsman who must make his initial successes in enterprises founded by equally young art dealers, who, because they run their galleries on a shoestring, can afford the frivolity of exhibiting the works of an unknown. The very ability to take such risk provides the dealer a possible opportunity to discover a genius.

One way of uncovering the interdependence of careers is to ask: Who are the important *others* at various stages of the career, the persons significantly involved in the formation of one's own identity? These will vary with stages; at one point one's agemates are crucial, perhaps as competitors, while at another the actions of superiors are the most important. The interlocking of careers results in influential images of similarity and contrariety. In so far as the significant others shift and vary by the phases of a career, identities change in patterned and not altogether unpredictable ways.

The Changing Work World

The occupations and organizations within which careers are made change in structure and direction of activity, expand or contract, transform purposes. Old functions and positions disappear, and new ones arise. These constitute potential locations for a new and sometimes wide range of people, for they are not incrusted with traditions and customs concerning their incumbents. They open up new kinds of careers to persons making their work lives within the institution and thus the possibility of variation in long-established types of careers. An individual once clearly destined for a particular position suddenly finds himself confronted with an option; what was once a settled matter has split into a set of alternatives between which he must now choose. Different identities emerge as people in the organization take cognizance of this novel set of facts. The positions turn into recognized social entities, and some persons begin to reorient their ambitions. The gradual emergence of a new specialty typically creates this kind of situation within occupations.

Such occupational and institutional changes, of course, present opportunity for both success and failure. The enterprising grasp eagerly at new openings, making the most of them or attempting to; while others sit tight as long as they can. During such times the complexities of one's career are further compounded by what is happening to others with whom he is significantly involved. The ordinary lines of sponsorship in institutions are weakened or broken because those in positions to sponsor are occupied with matters more immediately germane to their own careers. Lower ranks feel the consequences of unusual pressures generated in the ranks above. People become peculiarly vulnerable to unaccustomed demands for loyalty and alliance which spring from the unforeseen changes in the organization. Paths to mobility become indistinct and less fixed, which has an effect on personal commitments and identities. Less able to tie themselves tightly to any one career, because such careers do not present themselves as clearly, men become more experimental and open-minded or more worried and apprehensive.

Careers and Personal Identity

A frame of reference for studying careers is, at the same time, a frame for studying personal identities. Freudian and other psychiatric formulations of personality development probably overstress childhood experiences. Their systematic accounts end more or less with adolescence, later events being regarded as the elaboration of, or variations on, earlier occurrences. Yet central to any account of adult identity is the relation of change in identity to change in social position; for it is characteristic of adult life to afford and force frequent and momentous passages from status to status. Hence members of structures that change, riders on escalators that carry them up, along, and down, to unexpected places and to novel experiences even when in some sense foreseen, must gain, maintain, and regain a sense of personal identity. Identity "is never gained nor maintained once and for all."[17] Stabilities in the organization of behavior and of self-regard are inextricably dependent upon stabilities of social structure. Likewise, change ("development") is shaped by those patterned transactions which accompany career movement. The crises and turning points of life are not entirely institutionalized, but their occurrence and the terms which define and help to solve them are illuminated when seen in the context of career lines. In so far as some populations do not have careers in the sense that professional and business people have them, then the focus of attention ought still to be positional passage, but with domestic, age, and other escalators to the forefront. This done, it may turn out that the model sketched here must undergo revision.

MASON GRIFF

The Commercial Artist: A Study in Changing and Consistent Identities

WHAT HAPPENS to art and creativity, freedom and self-expression, in a mass society? Do they become routinized and rationalized like so many other phenomena? And what of the artist? How does he maintain his identity? How does he preserve his independence and continue to be creative? How is he drawn into the field of art in the first place? What are some of the tensions and anxieties accompanying his recruitment? These are questions which will be discussed in this paper.

The material on which this discussion is based comes from two studies. The first studied a group of students attending a large art school in Chicago.[1] One of the objectives of that study was to discover the reasons for students entering the field of art when the possibilities for success in it are so limited. For example, the estimates of the number of those who are able to support themselves exclusively from the sale of their paintings in this country range from five to fifteen persons.[2] The results of this study revealed that these students understood the difficulties an artist faced and that it would be necessary for them to supplement their income from some other source.

These findings led directly to a second study of what the artist does when he finishes his formal training.[3] One alternative, and the one studied, is to work as a commercial artist. However, the role of the commercial artist is contrary in many fundamental respects to the role of the fine artist. Ideally, the fine artist is free from any restrictions on his work. The commercial artist is restricted by his clients. How then, do artists resolve this conflict in roles? This was the major question asked in the second study.

The charge that commercial art has a corrupting influence on the artist is an old one. Michelangelo rebelled against the Pope's attempt to restrict his paintings, and Rembrandt turned his back on the burghers who had given him wealth and recognition to paint as he wished in solitary poverty. Furthermore, the general problem implied here is not confined only to

Published for the first time in this volume. The author wishes to thank Yvonne Guilbert for critical and editorial assistance.

painters; the same problem can be found among most artists in other fields, such as writers, musicians, and dancers.[4] Finally, it may be seen as a general problem extending beyond the artistic occupations. One can see parallels in the comparison of the pure mathematician or the theoretical physicist with those working in the applied fields. On a more abstract level, the problem can be seen as a general dilemma: the wish to carry out an action in its pure form, as opposed to attempts to qualify the action in some way.[5]

Identity, Recruitment, and Self

Identity, and its connection with an occupation, has many dimensions. If a person identifies with an occupation that is socially sanctioned, the members of that society are supportive of him. If the occupation is not socially sanctioned, the members of the society attempt to prevent, persuade, or erect obstacles to keep him from pursuing that occupation. The legitimacy of the pursuit, from the point of view of society, is the key to understanding the present role and status of the artist in contemporary society. In turn, this explains the reasons for tensions arising in the career of the artist, and the reasons these tensions arise when they do.

Tension points may be described as points of decision. Not all decisions, however, have equal tension-producing force. Some, such as the decision of whom and when to marry, or when and where to move, or what career to follow, are usually more crucial than other decisions. These tension points, which are produced and decided in a social context, i.e., in interrelationships to and with significant others and groups, can be called social tension points, as distinguished from individual tension points. With reference to occupations, such tension points are particularly crucial, since the social meaning of work is pervasive in a society based upon achieved, rather than ascribed status. In such a society, it is through a person's work that he belongs to a specific social class and enjoys, or does not enjoy, certain rewards which society has established as goals: material rewards, in the form of money and the symbols of success which money can buy; and immaterial rewards, in the forms of prestige, status, and pride in accomplishment, which are derived from identification with a socially sanctioned occupation.

The attitude of our society toward art and the artist, specifically toward painting and the painter, is ambivalent. The painter and his work are sanctioned, but only when painting is pursued as an avocation rather than as a vocation. Artistic talents in children are encouraged by teachers, parents, and the community. Presidents, prime ministers, doctors, housewives, and friends who paint are respected for their talent. In short, the pursuit of art is sanctioned when it is undertaken by people who have already achieved identification with some other socially sanctioned role. The vocation itself is even sanctioned when it remains at a safe distance. The lives of Van Gogh and Gauguin have been the subjects of popular novels and movies.

However, difficulties reflecting this ambivalence arise when some member of a family wishes to pursue a career in art. Then two very strong objections present themselves. The first is the fact that the painter cannot hope to support himself solely from the sale of his paintings and that this inability will make it impossible for him to attain many of the symbols of success which the family cherishes. The second is the Bohemian stereotype of the artist, with which the family does not want to be identified because it violates the professed mores, morals, and values of our culture.

The Bohemian stereotype of the artist is, of course, closely related to the financial problems that art as a vocation presents. How did this stereotype arise, and how has it affected the public image of the artist, his recruitment, and his identity?

A century and a half ago, the artist became alienated from his society. The French Revolution, with the destruction of the nobility and the subsequent loss of aristocratic patronage, was the precipitating factor. There were people who could have created a market for paintings, but these people, the bourgeois, were products of a way of life and an ideology antithetical to the support of, or sympathy with, art. Their philosophy was essentially utilitarian. The work of the artist and his ideology are nonutilitarian. Outside of their investment potential, paintings have no utility. Some paintings were purchased, but these were, as they frequently are today, paintings produced in the past with a market value certified by time. Hence they represented a rational purchase involving no gamble on an uncertain commodity such as a purchase from a contemporary, and as yet unknown, artist would entail.

Out of this period and these conditions emerged the stereotype image of the artist which has continued down to the present time: the artist as starving and dying; the artist as a deviant and a suicide; the artist as insane and alcoholic; the artist as an undiscovered genius whose greatness is not recognized until after his death. One is reminded of Van Gogh, Modigliani, and Utrillo—the insane, the alcoholic, and the drug addict, respectively.

Emerging with this stereotype was the Bohemian ideology that was to become so closely attached to the artist. It is an ideology which not only expresses antinomianism—moral, aesthetic, and social—which is central to its ethos, but also implies an active conflict, a war with civil society.[6] The function of the ideology was to give the artist an identity and a sanction justifying his alienation. This was done by affirming certain values

—freedom of self-expression, and the realization of self through artistic fulfillment—as transcending and antithetical to the values supported by bourgeois society. As a consequence, although the artist was in this way able to achieve identity and a sense of community with other artists, he was also committed to alienation and opposition to bourgeois values. Thus, an artist who has accepted this identity and commitment, which is really the only one open to the fine artist in bourgeois society, is presented with new conflicts and tensions should he wish to return to the bourgeois community. This is essentially the problem of the fine artist who, unable to support himself by his work, decides to turn to commercial art. His reasons for doing so are usually associated with the wish to support a family and to have some of the symbols of success which money can provide, such as a comfortable home, a car, and the opportunity to travel. The affirmation of these values, however, conflicts with the Bohemian ideology and consequently challenges his identity as a fine artist. How this problem of identification is resolved is the central subject of this paper.

The reader may protest that the stereotype given above is, after all, only a stereotype which may or may not be valid. He may further question whether or not the Bohemian ideology actually functions in the artist's identity. There is no scientific evidence to document the public stereotype of the artist, but we do have indirect evidence. Hardly an issue of any of a number of popular weekly magazines appears without some caricature of the artist. Everyone is familiar with the painter and his nude model and all the associated implications of immorality. There is the starving painter who absurdly refuses to eat the food serving as a model for his canvas, and the starving and irresponsible artist who is deaf to the common sense pleas of his wife and family and is merely laughable from a practical point of view. Furthermore, evidence gathered from interviews with art students and artists confirms the potency of this stereotype; this is what they believe is the public's image of them. More important, this is what their families believe the artist to be.

How has this stereotype affected the recruitment of people into the art profession? The artist occupies an ambivalent position. Supposedly, both the artist and his work are valued; yet the artist is not rewarded. Consequently his recruitment and identity involve conflicts within himself, and between himself and significant others. Both the Bohemian stereotype, posing the problem of identity, and the recruitment phenomena, posing the problem of a socially sanctioned occupation and the particular significance this has in our society, are relevant to the tensions which occupy his career.

Since the image of the artist as a Bohemian is one which respectable bourgeois society rejects, and since the vocation of artist offers negligible hope for financial security or success, one would imagine that there would be consistency in the *discouragement* of children from becoming artists. On the contrary, however, one finds evidence that both parents and other social agents nourish and *encourage* the complete fulfillment of the child's talents. This fact is reflected in the early career of the artist, where there are no tensions in his incipient career, at least none attributable to a discrepancy between encouragement and reward. This is reflected in such statements as, "When I was in kindergarten, I was separated from the rest of my class and left to paint by myself"; or, "I was always being asked to paint pictures for my relatives and friends"; or, "I was considered the artist among the people I hung around with." This encouragement of the young artist was further suggested by many statements referring to the fact that parents had prominently displayed the child's paintings and had shown them with pride to friends and relatives.

It may be seen that when a teacher separates a child in class or encourages him in some similar manner, the teacher is defining art and artists as valuable. By endowing the young artist with social recognition and esteem, the teacher is implicitly saying that the artist is to be rewarded; this serves to convince the child that he and his creations are acceptable to social authority. When the child is separated from his classmates, the fact that he is in some way distinguished is reinforced in front of his peers. The child begins to understand that his ability to paint is an unusual one which not everyone possesses, and which entitles him to prestige, special consideration, and recognition. Thus, in every way, the child is encouraged to exercise freely that which he most basically feels is himself. He learns that he has the freedom to create, and that the volition to do this is an inherent attribute of the artist. He also learns that his contribution is socially meaningful and constructive. The accumulating social experiences of the child, and the picture which emerges of these early years, is one of congruence between aspiration and fulfillment, encouragement and reward. Tensions or anxieties, which one would expect if there were discrepancies between these variables, are absent. Outside of the normal tensions of childhood and adolescence, all the factors favoring the retention and nourishment of an artist's career are present.

Discontinuities in this process begin abruptly at either of two points: at the end of high school or at the end of art school, usually the former. At these points, parents increase pressure on the child to commit himself to an occupation. Whenever the pressures begin, they become oppressive when the parents discover that the child has the intention of pursuing a career in the fine arts, since they are aware of the financial difficulties he will face. The discovery may be made when the child makes a public declaration that he is going to be an artist, when he enrolls in an art school, or, if he is already in art school, when he breaks an informal agreement to pursue commercial art or art education.

When the student's intention to become an artist is discovered, there is a reversal in the attitude of his parents toward him. A crisis is engendered which becomes greatly aggravated during the period beginning with the announcement of his intentions and ending with the termination of his formal education. The entire family turns against him in a determined effort to dissuade him. Parents and brothers and sisters may realize for the first time that he wishes to enter a profession associated with deviancy. Now he, and with him his family, is identified with the objects of innumerable jokes in the newspapers and magazines. In a word, "the world is laughing at them," and the family feels personally attacked and humiliated. The family begins to remove the student's paintings from the walls where they were once prominently displayed. The student's artistic achievements and the large salaries received by artists become topics to be avoided.

The common reaction to, and resolution of, the crisis may be classified into two major forms. The parents may blame the child, and, if so, disown him; or they may assume personal culpability and declare that they have failed him in some way. Those parents who feel personally culpable for the child's "deviancy" or realize that the child cannot be persuaded to alter his career, accept the situation with the mental reservation that somehow they or some unknown intervening force will induce the individual to renounce his pursuit. At this time, the parents and other members of the family reply to inquiries concerning the future of the young artist by telling the truth, by rationalizing, or by lying.

When members of the family tell the truth, they do so by fortifying themselves against the ridicule and censure of their friends and admitting that they have failed. The constant questions concerning the future of the child generate, and add to, the bitterness of the family. These questions are frequent because, until the time of his decision to make art his life's work, this child had been the member of the family with the greatest prestige, precisely because of his unusual gift.

If the parents rationalize the intentions of the student they do so by telling the truth, but at the same time pointing to past masters and to present-day ones who are internationally famous and receive thousands of dollars for a single painting. In time, they may actually believe that this will come true for their child, and thus reduce their antagonism towards him. At the same time, they avoid mentioning the overwhelming number of painters who have been or are unable to support themselves by their work, or who have attained recognition only after death.

The family that lies about the true situation will convey the impression that their child is pursuing commercial art, usually adding "the respectable aspects," meaning, nothing pertaining to sex or pornography. They imply that he is doing work comparable to that of Norman Rockwell for national magazines, with the added implication of a large salary. In time, the parents may come to believe that this is the true intent of the child, despite contrary evidence which they witness every day.

But isn't there an inconsistency here? Hasn't it been stated that the young artist is a success and that he is encouraged and rewarded for his ability? Hasn't it been stated that his success has been a source of gratification for his parents as well as for him? There is an inconsistency, but one which becomes understandable if the great difference between school success and occupational success is considered. School success is confined to the yardstick of the report card: "My son can paint. He has his posters displayed." "My daughter gets all A's in art." There is recognition in the form of prizes, articles in the local newspaper, or acknowledgment on graduation programs. Yet, the totality of prestige and the measures of success attained from these sources are confined to school. When a child graduates from high school, new standards and criteria of judgment are applied, which are associated with symbols of financial success and social prestige. Art, particularly fine art, is not an avenue conducive to the attainment of these success symbols, and parents and families know this. Moreover, these reactions reflect some significant attitudes toward the fine artist and toward art in contemporary culture.

Contemporary culture stresses conformity, respectability, rationality, practicality, and security. These are a few of the essential values which are incorporated in the cultural complex called by Max Weber, rational bourgeois capitalism.[7] Art and the life of the artist are antinomies of this. Fine art is nonutilitarian. The artist is a nonconformist and violates many of the behavioral patterns set down by society. His choice of career also opposes the success theme so strongly stressed and so pervasive. To parents who value success for their children, as an affirmation and confirmation of their worthiness as parents, there is little comfort in the notion that the young artist may achieve recognition after his death; yet, this is very often all the young artist has to offer as justification for the sacrifices he proposes to make. Is it any wonder that, given the tremendous ideological emphasis on success, parents oppose a child's commitment to a career in art?

Not all students enter art school under conditions of parental opposition or personal rebellion.[8] This is especially true of those who enroll with the express intention of becoming commercial artists. Their career is straightforward. They take commercial art courses, graduate from school with this identity, and immediately enter the commercial art world. A second group are those who enter with the intention of teaching art. They enroll in the required courses, graduate, and pursue an academic career.

The group with which we are concerned, however, is composed of those who pursue fine art throughout their formal training, graduate, and are then confronted with the problem of how to earn a living. Some solve the problem by returning to graduate school, many to qualify for teaching certificates. Others move over to schools like the Institute of Design in Chicago, which teaches commercial and industrial art with a fine-arts ideology. There is still another group who take jobs outside of the art field and continue to paint after work, on week-ends, and during vacations. Most of these, however, eventually return to art in some capacity, many as commercial artists. This change in roles confronts the artist with many of the questions asked at the beginning of this paper. What will working as a commercial artist do to his identity as a fine artist, his freedom for self-expression, and his independence? How will his creativity be affected by using his talents to produce commercial art? The misgivings concerning this step are resolved in various ways described below. The artist's identity undergoes changes which range in type from those who still symbolically accept the role of fine artist to those who reject it completely. Between these two extremes lies a third group which identifies with both roles.

Alternate Role Styles

The *traditional-role* artist works as a commercial artist, but subjectively identifies himself as a fine artist. In enacting this role, he withdraws symbolically from the role of commercial artist and states that he is only temporarily engaged in commercial art, as an expedient until he can accumulate enough money to be financially independent. He feels that only if he is financially independent will he have the freedom and time necessary for his work.

His justification for working in the field of commercial art is that the standards of contemporary society preclude any suitable alternative, since there is not a large enough market to support any but a very small number of artists. Underlying this assumption is the belief that society will give lip-service to, but in reality will not support, his primary identity as a fine artist who lives only from, and solely for, his art. The Bohemian ideology supports him in this belief.

To defend his premise, he cites numerous examples, both past and present, of artists who have attempted but failed to live exclusively from the sale of their paintings, *e.g.*, Van Gogh and Albert Ryder, Pissarro and Cezanne. Coupled with this belief is the fact that many of this group actually attempted to live from the sale of their paintings, and finding this impossible, have turned to the commercial art field. Before doing this, some worked in factories, the post office, or within another field unrelated to art. They have specifically avoided working in fields related to art, because they have felt that to do so would channel some of their creative energy into these other artistic activities. Many of them still do feel that art-related jobs can affect their paintings, because of the habits one falls victim to.

This is the group which suffers the most and has the deepest guilt feelings about working in the commercial art field. These are the artists who left school with the intention of remaining dedicated to art but, through a number of discouraging experiences, felt it was useless to pursue this course. The alternative they have chosen is a difficult one, since the switch to commercial art means that they are accepting a role which they formerly actively rejected.

In this respect they are faced with three important identity problems which they must resolve: (1) they must legitimize relinquishing their former identity as fine artists; (2) they must legitimize the meaning of their new self-conceptions, *i.e.*, they must make their new identity bearable, and they must find rewards in their new role; (3) they must legitimize their new identity as commercial artists to their significant others. Let us examine each of these problems in order.

One basic consideration regarding the abandonment of former roles is evident: the career of the artist is precarious and success uncertain. Of greatest importance here is the fact that, in the recapitulation of their achievements, these artists can find no confirmation of their abilities from others, such as normally functions to indicate progress. Indicative of the importance of this are the statements they make in explaining how they arrived at the decision to leave their former roles; *e.g.*, "I always sold a few but never enough to keep me going"; or "I sell a little but I don't know whether or not my level of painting is improving"; or "You say to yourself, what will I be like when I'm fifty?" or "Painting drives you to a certain madness."

These statements not only indicate uncertainty and the absence of confirmation by significant others, but also that the painter does not have the usual marks indicative of progress such as promotions, raises in pay, and awards to rely upon which are institutionally structured in most occupations. These devices function to communicate, confirm, and be supportive of the fact that the individual is making some progress toward the goals of the institution. The fine artist lacks any such stable frame of reference.

Involved in this is a certain incongruity. The artist, as a member of society, incorporates a future goal-orientation and makes this part of his frame of reference, since he has been inculcated with it as part of his socialization process. Yet, his occupation does not have clear-cut goals toward which he may strive. The ones that do exist are precarious and virtually unattainable. After all, how many artists out of the thousands who have pursued art create an immortal painting? Certainly there are a few markers, such as one-man exhibits, acceptance by a gallery, sales, and commissions, but even these are tenuous. In the totality of an artist's career, they have so little remunerative value and are achieved only after such a long, arduous, and often painful struggle that they cannot compensate for the great insecurity which his career involves. Too many great artists have failed to attain them in their lifetimes to go unnoticed by others in the profession. The possibility of being discovered and recognized after death turns out to be of small comfort, especially when the artist and the people with whom he interacts and from whom he seeks confirmation are under the influence of a society oriented toward remunerative occupations and the rewards and recognition which such occupations provide. The precarious future of the fine artist clashes with the institutional challenges of his culture, *e.g.*, family and dependents and the questions stemming from responsibilities to them. How fair is it to ask them to sacrifice the comforts of life so that the artist may pursue a goal so uncertain of attainment? Very often the artist has deep misgivings about his own abilities, and few are self-confident enough to suggest to themselves or to others that they possess the gifts of a Cezanne, a Picasso, or a Rembrandt.

The second problem which the traditional-role artist faces, legitimizing his new identity as a commercial artist, is essentially one of justifying the pursuit of the new role, without damaging his ego too greatly. The justifications are in the form of recriminations against his former role and those who are still pursuing it. In many cases these justifications are the same, but with a contrary twist, as those once used to justify his identity as a fine artist. He talks of pain when he sees the things that others must do in order to continue to live while pursuing the role of fine artist, *e.g.*, "I was tired of being a bastard from society." He contrasts his work as a commercial artist with the occupations of those with whom he formerly identified, and declares that he is much better off as a commercial artist, even with the liabilities the new role involves.

As time passes, as these artists continue in commercial art, and as they move from one status to another, passing milestones and being occupationally mobile, their change in identity becomes more consistent, integrated, and reinforced. This is especially so as they interact with others and form primary relationships with others who, like themselves, have faced the same dilemma and have resolved it in the same manner. With these added experiences, the justifications become more positive and more sophisticated. For example, they state: "Now I know where commercial art fits in"; "Commercial art is used to beautify the industrial world"; "Commercial art is getting better all the time"; "We raise the standard of living of people." As these quotations indicate, the guilt feelings which were first associated with abjuring to the "enemy's camp" have been dissipated.

In connection with the third problem, that of legitimizing the new role to significant others, the traditional-role artist must satisfy two groups: his former colleagues who are still enacting the fine artist role, and his family and relatives.

In justifying himself to his former colleagues, there is the feeling that he is deserting and betraying them. He has two alternatives in overcoming the bitterness and recriminations against him from former colleagues. Either he can remove himself physically from the geographical location, thereby avoiding interacting with them as would be inevitable if he remained in the area, or he can escape symbolically. The latter appears to be the more difficult alternative, since the artist must always be defensive about working in commercial art.

In justifying himself to his family and relatives, the artist must be prepared to answer questions concerning his reasons for having changed his mind about commercial art. Furthermore, if his feelings were intense and opinionated against commercial art before he entered the field, he very probably alienated his family. If this was the case he must be prepared, like the prodigal son returning home, to face such taunts as "I thought you were so sure of yourself!" or "I see you weren't so clever as you thought!" and the vicious innuendos of those whose sensibilities he offended. The usual solution is to accept this in silence.

Since the traditional-role artists identify themselves as fine artists temporarily engaged in commercial art, they admit that a role conflict exists, that they are aware of it, and that they have personally experienced it. They verbalize this experience in terms of guilt and frustration and they symbolize it in terms of (1) a time problem and (2) an ethical problem. The first concerns the fact that their jobs as commercial artists do not allow them sufficient time to paint. The second concerns the concept of their talent as a "gift" and stems from the belief that the ability to paint is of supernatural or divine origin and is a blessing. If one's parents cannot paint, and if there is no evidence that the ability to paint is inherited, how then can the ability to paint be explained? The answer is that it is a gift from the *deity*. The argument then is that, if the artist is a person who has been endowed with a God-given talent, this gift places an obligation on the artist not to use the gift for anything but the greater glory of God and Man. Since, theoretically, religion and the secular world have, as Durkheim has pointed out, antithetical goals and rewards, then the talent is not supposed to be dissipated, especially in the realm of the material or profane world.

The implication is that when the artist becomes introspective he will be confronted with the above considerations and say to himself, "Is this what the *deity* meant for me to do with my gift which was so carefully rationed out to a chosen few both in the past and in the present?" The fact that the artist is not devoting as much time and energy to the development of the gift as he should is sinful enough, but, in addition, he is using it to sell things and is, therefore, perverting it.

To illustrate further the problem of guilt and conflict, one can examine the interaction of the traditional-role artist with his colleague groups. Since he belongs to two social systems, that of the fine artist and that of the commercial artist, one would expect that within each colleague group he would find support for his self-conceptions and identity. However, since the role of commercial artist has no significance for him and he does not identify with his colleagues in that field, he has little interaction with them except for the exchange of normal amenities. Indeed, any attempt on their part to assuage his feelings has no mitigating effect, since their opinions are not significant to him. As a matter of fact, encouragement from them may only aggravate his conflict, since they represent a group from which he has withdrawn and symbolically rejected.

Neither does he find comfort when he turns to the fine-arts group. Normally one would expect that his former colleagues would be the ones to give him the greatest support, but in fact they are the ones who condemn him the most and are his most severe critics. Since these are the artists whom he considers his peers and the people whose criticism he honors most, their condemnation is devastating to his self-conceptions. These artists regard his working in the field of commercial art as reprehensible and define this in terms of *betrayal to the cause of fine art and the prostitution of a God-given talent.*

The reaction of the traditional-role artist to these attacks is to withdraw and to seek membership in other groups which will not condemn him or may actually reinforce and define his actions as logical and justifiable.

A second mechanism, in addition to withdrawal, which he uses to save his original identity is that of compartmentalization. By means of this, he is able to cope with the serious charge levelled against him by fine artists, art educators, dealers, and gallery owners who maintain that commercial art carries over to fine art. This position holds that the two arts are fundamentally different and that therefore any carry-over from commercial art destroys the artist's ability in fine art. Those who hold this view contend that if an artist continually creates commercial art, his perception and mental processes will unavoidably and irreversibly become habituated to seeing and thinking within the framework of commercial art.

Thus, it is essential for the traditional-role artist to institute both compartmentalization and withdrawal; if he did not, his identity as a fine artist would become untenable. If, for example, he did not compartmentalize, but admitted that commercial art carries over and does affect his perception and thinking, then he would be saying that he is painting from the point of view of his clients or prospective buyers, and that he is inevitably using such common commercial art techniques as making art immediately recognizable and creating a desire in the viewer.

The traditional-role artist reinforces his position that there is no carry-over from commercial art to fine art, by pointing out that the work he does in commercial art is closely related to fine art and that he is relatively free from restrictions. For example, if he is a lay-out man, he points to the fact that the lay-out man is considered the thinker of the studio and that it is he who dictates to others rather than others who dictate to him. Thus, he excludes himself from restrictions. He points out that it is he who tells the illustrators how the ad should appear, what it should contain, and what colors should be used. The illustrator, on the other hand, points out that he is doing finished art work and is therefore as close to painting as it is possible to be in commercial art. The letter man points out that lettering cannot possibly affect his work in fine art because lettering has nothing to do with art. This same point is made by the production men, the paste-up men, and the art directors. They point out that they are never responsible for the creation of the ad, except in a superficial way.

At the other extreme of role identification are those whom I have called the *commercial-role* artists. They organize their role on the basis that both fine art and commercial art are utilitarian. As commercial artists they think of themselves as instruments for the transformation of verbal symbols into visual ones, as dictated by a client, such as an advertising studio, a manufacturer, or a merchant. As a result, their ideological orientation is committed to expectations deriving from the commercial field, especially pleasing and satisfying clients. In conceiving of their role in this manner, the commercial-role artists refrain from interjecting or altering in any way the expressed wishes of their clients, unless specifically asked by the clients to do so. As passive agents, they accept the occupational imperative that "the customer is always right." After all, they state, it is the customer who is paying for the ad.

The consequence of this belief is that the commercial-role artist defines his role as having been successfully fulfilled when the requirements of the client have been met as parsimoniously as possible. This means the creation and execution of illustrations or lay-outs as quickly and cheaply as possible. The major reason for this is that time and deadlines dominate the commercial-art world and have the same meaning as they do in such fields as transportation and newspaper work. Meeting deadlines implies meeting advertising campaigns which are aimed and co-ordinated from a number of standpoints. For example, clothing ads must be ready for the right season. Bathing suit ads must appear in late spring and early summer, and fur coat ads in late autumn and early winter. The importance of time and the synchronization of all phases of advertising can be understood, when it is realized that some advertising campaigns have very large budgets. In some campaigns, not only huge sums of money are at stake, but the very survival of the client, the ad agency, the studio, and the artist. Commercial artists state that one can move, from an income of 50,000 dollars a year, to an income of nothing overnight. It is no accident that part of the culture of this group includes talk about stomach troubles, ulcers, and mental breakdowns. What does one tell his wife and children, his neighbors, the private school his child is attending, when such a disaster strikes?

In contrast to the traditional-role artists, the commercial-role artists reject the idea that they are working in commercial art because of extenuating circumstances. On the contrary, they believe that the traditional-role artists are pursuing a nineteenth-century anachronism which should be discarded as the role of the contemporary artist.

Although it is difficult to say that these artists are faced with a role conflict, since they do not perceive it as such, it is nevertheless valuable to consider their reactions to the role conflict as perceived by the traditional-role artists.

For example, when they are confronted with the fact that their clients dictate to them and that this is contrary to the classical concept of the fine artist, they thoroughly agree that this is so. However they transform what, to the traditional-role artist, is distasteful into a *positive attribute actually having functional significance* for them as artists. They state that restrictions are beneficial to an artist because they provide him with discipline. So, for example, when they do paint they can begin immediately because they know where they are going. They also believe that these restrictions are responsible for the fact that the commercial artist is more creative than the fine artist, because restrictions impose greater problems which require greater ingenuity and creativity to solve. They not only have to work with restrictions on color, subject matter, and budgets, but they must also please a client. Furthermore, they point out that the dangers and the consequences of failing are greater for the commercial artist than for the fine artist. If a commercial artist fails he may lose his job, his income, and his reputation, whereas if a fine artist fails his only penalty is a damaged ego.

When asked about the problem of carry-over, the commercial-role artist admits that carry-over does occur and further states that this is beneficial, since there is basically no difference between the two art forms. As with restrictions, the carry-over is considered desirable because it contributes to the artist's progress and to his ability to produce a painting that will sell. Art is regarded as a utilitarian product no matter what objective the artist may have in painting. Since commercial art is a field producing a product to be sold, and since art is a utilitarian product, knowledge and skills acquired in commercial art constitute a desirable carry-over in any direction, because they will help the artist produce paintings that will sell.

Between the traditional role at one end of role identification and the commercial role at the other, is a third one called the *compromise-role*, a mixture of both the traditional and the commercial roles. Like the commercial artists, the compromise artists believe that they are instruments of the client, but, unlike them, they do not conceive of themselves as passive agents completely at the mercy of the client. They regard themselves as active agents and carry out their role conceptions of themselves by obeying the wishes of the clients, but at the same time trying to persuade them at every opportunity to accept innovations of all types, especially the introduction into their ads of fine arts symbols. In this latter respect they also differ from the commercial artists, since, by conceiving of themselves as active agents, they also imply that they view the client as maneuverable and therefore a personal object, rather than an immovable, impersonal object which is the view of the client held by the commercial-role artists.

In order to implement one of their objectives—"putting art into advertising"—it is essential for them to escape the arbitrariness of the client and, if possible, to attain a degree of social control over him. In order to do this, the status of the artist in relationship to the client must change from that of a subordinate to that of a superior.

There are several ways in which this objective may be accomplished. The most practical is for the artist to win the confidence of his clientele, and this is best accomplished by successfully fulfilling their demands. The limitations of this method are that confidence bears fruit only after a long and enduring relationship and that the relationship between artist and client is still one-sided since the power still ultimately remains with the client.

A more satisfactory solution occurs when the artist achieves a reputation in commercial art, fine art, or both. This may be accomplished by: (1) receiving certain honors in the commercial art field, such as winning an exhibition sponsored by a commercial artists' guild; (2) having a fine arts painting exhibited in a museum; or (3) landing a national account, such as the Container Corporation of America or one of the large weekly magazines, such as the cover of *Time* or *Fortune* or certain parts of the *Reader's Digest*.

Once the artist has achieved a reputation, his relationship to the client is either balanced or reversed. If it is reversed, the client becomes the passive agent and the artist the active one. The artist is then in a position to be selective, rejecting those clients whose work is not amenable to the dictates of progressive commercial art. The greatest achievement in this respect would be to work for clients such as the Container Corporation of America (specifically their *Great Ideas of Western Man* series), the John Hancock Life Insurance Company, or the West Virginia Pulp and Paper Company.

A corollary to the above aspect of the role is that many compromise-role artists feel that they are involved in a crusade for better art. They believe that by raising the standards of their client's art they are at the same time raising the level of the public's taste for art. These feelings become transfigured into their future goal-orientation, and they symbolize this in terms of contributions to and improvements of society in the future. One way of realizing this ambition is by staking out a claim for themselves in an area of advertising art which they believe has been backward and could stand considerable improvement. For example, they will point to an area like heavy industry and say that this is an area in which they would like to make their major contribution to society, by innovating new methods of illustrating the industry. They mention that their ambition is to convince a client that he will eventually increase his sales in this way.

These artists are aware that a conflict exists between commercial art and fine art and feel that their development is hampered by their lack of time to paint and by the fact that they have given a higher priority to their commercial art work than to their fine art work. They do not express these feelings in terms of guilt, as the traditional-role artists do, but rather in terms of regret, and express their lack of time for painting in terms of frustration. They also point out that a person who devotes himself exclusively to painting may make a greater contribution to society than one who remains in the commercial art field. However, they make this statement on a comparative and relative basis aimed at answering the question of who contributes the most to society. They feel that by improving the level of commercial art, and by bringing it closer to fine art, they are making a major contribution to such universals as truth and beauty. They qualify this, however, by saying that perhaps the contribution is not as great as that of the fine artist, *if* he can paint *one* masterpiece.

Another interesting reaction of the compromise-role artists, which reveals their awareness of conflict, is the transformation of symbols. In interviews, they strongly rejected the terms "commercial art" and "commercial artist" and substituted for them "advertising art" and "advertising artist." The intensity and consistency with which they did this suggested that the connotations of the term "commercial artist" were incompatible with their role-identification and self-conceptions. My analysis of this is that there is a stereotype of the commercial artist which operates rather powerfully within the profession and that the image conveyed is that of the self-conception of the commercial-role artist. The connotations of the term are those of typing, of the artist as merely an instrument of the client, and of the work produced as completely utilitarian. The commercial artist functions as an instrument of buying and selling in an impersonal market.

By calling themselves "advertising artists," the compromise-role artists are able to assert their identity *as artists* and their function as creative rather than merely utilitarian. Thus, they can conceive of themselves as responsible for improving the public's taste in art and raising the standard of living, by creating new and better desires. It appears that the term "advertising" is easier for them to rationalize than the term "commercial," and that this rationalization is a crucial mechanism in resolving their role conflicts.

The term compromise-role has been used to indicate that this group employs the mechanism of compromise to resolve the conflict situation. In doing this, the members identify themselves as fine artists and as advertising artists, and state that one can work in both fields and contribute to both fields at the same time. They state further that growth and development in one field helps growth and development in the other. Since compromise implies bringing together at least two viewpoints, this mechanism precludes the use of both withdrawal, which would involve withdrawing from one viewpoint, and compartmentalization, which would involve separating the two roles.

The attitude of the compromise-role artist, *i.e.*, that this linkage is desirable, is in contrast to that of the traditional-role artist and very similar to that of the commercial-role artist. The view is that the artist, by meeting many problems in his commercial work, acquires speed and certainty in solving them. This enables him to reduce delays and, consequently, to devote more time to painting. Furthermore, by constantly being faced with problems which not only have to be solved, but must be solved within a short space of time, the artist acquires an ability that is useful in his fine art work. Thus the time spent in commercial art, which appears to be wasted from the point of view of the traditional-role artist, is in reality productive and beneficial. Unlike the commercial-role artist, however, the compromise-role artist is not particularly interested in selling his paintings. He does, of course, sell them if he can. However, in most instances he prefers using them as a method of advertising himself to prospective clients. He is more concerned than the members of the other two groups to exhibit his paintings where there is the possibility that they will attract a new client or an art director of an ad agency.

Another way in which these artists compromise the situation is related directly to their central role-conception and to their attempts to restrict their clientele. If they were able to have only clients who were good clients and who would be willing to accept innovations and grant the artist the mandate he wants—the right to determine how the ad should appear—then there would be very little difference between what they produce in advertising art and what they produce as fine art.

In this connection, they point out that the two fields are progressively coming together and that more art is continually being added to advertising, so that eventually the two fields will be one field, or, in any event, the differences between the two will be slight.

Their strongest argument for refuting the charge that the two fields are divergent and irreconcilable is to cite examples of artists who have done both, or are doing both, and have still managed to be great painters. If working for clients who impose restrictions is harmful, they argue, then how can one account for the fact that great artists of the past, such as Leonardo and Michelangelo, worked under restrictions and had clients and still managed to produce masterpieces. If it is objected that these examples go back too far in the past, they point to more recent examples, such as Remington and Winslow Homer, who worked as magazine illustrators and yet painted at the same time and produced great works of art. They also like to point to contemporary artists like Picasso and Miró.

The resemblance between the compromise-role and the traditional-role lies in the fact that the members of both groups are concerned with fine art. The difference is that those who adopt the compromise-role do not consider their commercial art work onerous or harmful to their fine art work, nor do they feel that their status as artists should be autonomous and independent of the secular world. They believe, as do the commercial-role artists, that their legitimate position in society lies in the commercial field.

Motives for Painting and Painting Styles

Why do artists who are working in commercial art continue to paint in the fine arts tradition? Is there any connection between role-identity and painting styles?

The painting of the *traditional-role* artist is oriented away from the commercial market and his position is antithetical to that of the other two groups with respect to utilitarian art. He views his work not as a means to further his position in the commercial art world, but as a method of perfecting himself as a fine artist. His explanations are couched in terms of improving and perfecting his ability to depict fine-arts symbols. The predominating themes encompassing and organizing his behavior are self-improvement, correcting mistakes, overcoming unresolved problems, creating an original style, and deriving new forms of aesthetic expression. He refers frequently to the fact that he feels an intrinsic need to paint (which resembles catharsis), and that this is a need which he feels must be fulfilled even at the expense of reducing his income. This reinforces his aim to accumulate enough money so that he will be independent and can then devote his time exclusively to painting. One point should be noted here: although all three groups mention that their background in fine arts has been helpful to their careers in commercial art, the traditional-role artist is the only one who never refers to his paintings in relation to commercial art and never speaks of the benefits that commercial art may have for his fine-arts painting.

These artists emphasize that their paintings serve as lessons. They learn by painting, and, by studying their paintings, they discover errors and how to correct them. They never paint with the idea of selling their paintings or try to paint what would be attractive to the public. Many, as a matter of fact, become emotionally attached to their work and will not part with it, even though opportunities may arise to do so. If the paintings are exhibited, they will often place sold signs on them even though they are not sold in order to retain them, or in other cases place prices on them high enough to insure their retention.

The *commercial-role* artist's characteristic motive for painting is to supplement his income. This motive is congruent with his role-definition, the only difference being that the client has now become an unknown purchaser.

The second motive, which is closely related to the first, centers on the manifest function of perfecting new styles in order to keep abreast of the changes in art fashions which occur so frequently in this field. The latent function stems from the nature of much commercial art, which is extremely exacting and repetitious and often imposes an overwhelming number of restrictions on the artist. As some artists complain, "You can almost feel the client guiding your hand as you draw." Clients also have idiosyncrasies. There is the humorous anecdote of the client who told his artist that he approved of his illustration, but "couldn't he just widen, a little more, the ass of the girl sitting on the fence."

If the artist is to divorce himself from this confining work and in that way find new and better-paying clients, and if, in addition, he is not to be behind the times in art fashion, he must during some part of his career develop an original style. To realize this goal he has only one alternative: find time! However, free time can be found only on week-ends and vacations, and infringing on his free time are his obligations to his primary and secondary groups. He cannot arbitrarily ignore his wife, his children, his parents, his friends and neighbors, no matter how much he may want to or how urgent it may be for his career to do so. Certainly he cannot ignore his business associates, upon whom he depends for routine work, and he cannot neglect his regular commercial-art work because it provides him with a steady income. If he is required to meet a deadline he must do so, even if it means infringing on his nonvocational time such as evenings, week-ends, and vacations. Furthermore, there is an occupational imperative which commands the artist to get as much work as he can, because styles and fashions change so frequently that plenty is often followed by prolonged want. An artist who has a distinctive and popular style may be in great demand at one time, only to be completely forgotten and by-passed at a later date.

Another problem which the commercial-role artist faces is that of typing, which stems from the minute specialization which is prevalent in some areas of commercial art. Thus, the individual artist is labeled as a specialist possessing a circumscribed skill and capable of only that skill. Once this has occurred the artist finds it extremely difficult to escape his specialty. The following interview illustrates this problem.

". . . I had a friend who could do beer bottles well. Perspiration on beer bottles was his specialty. You know, of course, how broken down it is? One person does the head, another the arms, another the furniture, etc. Well, his specialty was beer bottles. He tried to get out of it. He would go to a new client and ask for work and they would ask him what kind of work he had done. He would tell them 'perspiration on beer bottles.' They would say, 'We have work for you on that.' He couldn't get out of it."

As a result of all these factors, the artist is faced with a number of paradoxes and dilemmas. The method of resolving them lies in originating a new style. If he succeeds, he can show present and prospective clients the new style and thereby induce them to give him new types of work. Furthermore, the clients begin to change their conception of the artist and the type of work they associate with him. Should these efforts prove fruitful, the artist is on his way toward improving the quality of his work, toward reaching new markets, and toward increasing his income.

One of the most interesting observations is that, in many cases, the paintings of the commercial-role artists are more real than real life. There is a greater exactness of detail than would be true if one took a photograph. This is in keeping with the commercial-art folkways, because one of the common tendencies in commercial art is to over-exaggerate the details of subject matter so that the viewer can recognize immediately the objects of the illustration and the message they are intended to convey.

The *compromise-role* artist paints for a number of reasons, the most important being that he can, in this way, advertise his work and attract desirable clients. A second reason is the desire to improve his advertising-art style. The third reason is that he has a "need disposition" to paint. All of the artists interviewed, regardless of their role-identifications, stated that they felt an intrinsic need to paint and that they experienced a satisfaction from painting, because this was their only opportunity to paint without restrictions imposed by a client or by the technical processes.

As stated above, the major reason for the *compromise-role* artist's fine arts painting is that it enables him to promote his name and produce a specific style. By having his paintings displayed at exhibitions, he is able to attract the attention of significant persons in advertising and to demonstrate his continued interest in painting. They, in turn, by their criticism and conversations, confirm and reinforce his self-conception as an artist.

Furthermore, there is always the possibility that one or more of his paintings may receive honors or citations, not only from peer groups but from the media devoted to both fine and commercial art, such as art magazines and trade journals. Finally, there is always the possibility that one of his paintings may be hung as either a temporary or a permanent part of the collection of a fine-arts museum. This is the highest achievement for the compromise-role artist because it not only confirms his conception of himself as an artist, but also his conception of himself as a crusader for higher artistic standards in the commercial art world.

To understand fully the importance to the compromise-role artist of attracting the attention of significant others in the commercial-art world, it is necessary to understand the highly competitive nature of his occupation. Commercial art places a premium on new ideas and new methods of presenting visual phenomena, especially those having the ability to direct the attention of new customers to a company's product, in such a way that they will buy the product. By exhibiting, the artist is experimenting with new styles, testing these new approaches in competition with other artists, and attracting the attention of art directors of major firms. To do this is essential to the reinforcement of his role-conceptions for several reasons. The first is related to the constant injunction to derive new styles. The only method available is that of constant experimentation. Such experimentation, however, takes time, and since the commercial artist has little spare time, he must use what he has judiciously. He can do this only by making his free-time painting serve several needs simultaneously. It must serve as a device to attract better clients; it must serve as a means to derive new styles; it must satisfy the artist's need to paint; finally, it must serve as a device to support the artist's self-conception as an artist in the advertising field. By painting and exhibiting, the compromise-role artist not only satisfies these needs but demonstrates objectively, to his peers and to himself, that he is still interested in the sacred aspects of art.

Conclusions

On the basis of this study, together with others in the field of occupations and professions, several conclusions may be drawn about the phenomenon of identity. Identity, despite many of its changes, nuances, and adumbrations of contrary roles, has a fairly stable core of persistent characteristics. How and why this small core-area persists is still unclear, although the importance of cultural imperatives and social agents in reinforcing these imperatives is incontrovertible. As illustrated in this paper, many obstacles may present themselves to change an individual once committed to a role; yet the persistency prevails. The most amazing aspect of the group studied is their continued persistency in identification, even though their objective behavior would preclude their continuance in a given role. Such persistency is commonly referred to as deluding oneself or harboring an illusion. Whatever the label, the phenomenon functions to enable the individual to persist in his identity and, as such, constitutes an important aspect of human behavior which must be accounted for in any study of identity and human behavior.

Fulfillment of the role of artist may be only one small aspect of a person's total behavior, but the retention of that role may still be the most important aspect of his behavior. Its most positive function would appear to be that it answers the question of who he is.

This statement, however, is not adequate for an understanding of identity, since there are a number of peripheral and inferential questions proceeding from this basic concept. One important series pertains to the retention of an original identity, in those situations where the individual is conscious that his identity will be questioned by significant others, for example in choosing between remaining a fine artist or changing his role to that of a commercial artist or an art educator. The field for future research would seem to include classifying these questions, and the situations in which they are asked and answered, to see what similarities and differences emerge.

Several conclusions were reached concerning role-conflict, perhaps the most important being that entrance into commercial art alone was *not* significant in creating conflict. The significant factor was the identity the individual held when he made the decision to enter the field. Concurrent with identity is the experience of conflict and the use of various mechanisms, such as withdrawal, compartmentalization, and compromise, to resolve the conflict. Those individuals who identified as fine artists (the traditional-role) were the ones most apt to experience guilt and conflict, whereas those who identified with the commercial-role experienced the least guilt and conflict. Furthermore, styles of painting were directly related to role-identification. Although this correlation was based on a very limited number of examples, there was definite evidence of observable differences. The paintings of the traditional-role artists were least affected by the commercial-art ideology and its accompanying styles and techniques; whereas, the paintings of the commercial-role artists, except for the fact that there was no specific client to satisfy or product to advertise, were almost exactly a commercial-art product.

A final consideration concerns the broad implications of the inconsistencies, and attendant tensions, produced by the discrepancies between our cultural values and the economic facts and demands of our social structure. Artists and members of other professions are inculcated with belief in the value of creative activity and complete role fulfillment. At the same time, the realities of the situations in which they must work and earn a living preclude, in many ways, the realization of these values. The artist must restrict his freedom; the writer must keep the market in mind or subsidize himself in some way; the scholar must teach first and do the basic research for which he has been trained in his "spare" time; and the student must be tempted to pass courses, even if this means cheating. These antinomies constantly threaten the individual's attempt to achieve not only a stable identity, but one in accord with the ideology that motivates him. How constructive or how destructive the tension resulting from the conflict may be, is a subject that merits further study. It is apparent that some persons are more able than others to resolve role-conflict and make substantial contributions to the arts and sciences, by using the mechanisms of withdrawal, compartmentalization, and compromise. Why this should be so, with its resulting cost to both society and the individual, is a subject with broad implications for the future of our civilization.

LAWRENCE S. KUBIE

Some Unsolved Problems of the Scientific Career

Part I: Problems Arising Out of the Universal Neurotic Process

IT IS MY THESIS that the life of a young scientist challenges our educational system from top to bottom with a series of unsolved problems which await investigation. Among these are certain subtle problems, arising out of unrecognized neurotic forces, which are basically important both in the choice and in the pursuit of scientific research as a career. This will constitute Part I of this paper. Part II will consist largely of a discussion of socio-economic dilemmas

Reprinted from the *American Scientist*, Vol. XLI, No. 4 (1956), and Vol. XLII, No. 1, pp. 3-32, by permission of the author and the publisher.

which also influence the scientist's emotional and intellectual career. It will not be the purpose of this paper to argue that every young scientist should be psychoanalyzed; and the reader is asked to keep this disclaimer in mind. Nevertheless, in any multidisciplinary investigation of these complex interrelated problems, I believe that the psychoanalytic study of a random sampling of scientists, both young and old, would be one of the essential instruments.

In this connection it will be argued that Science in the abstract and Scientists as human beings pay a high price for the fact that during the preparation of young people for a life of scientific research their emotional problems are generally overlooked. This discussion will not attempt to outline a full remedy for this neglect, for it would be premature to make such an attempt before more is known about the problem. Here again, however, in exploring possible remedies, a psychoanalytic study of an adequate sample of young scientists would provide information which would help towards an ultimate solution. I hope that this paper will also contribute to a more general recognition of the fact that many young scientists require special help in their struggles for emotional maturation.

My own clinical experiences with this group suggest that the emotional problems which arise early in the careers of young scientists are more taxing than are those which occur in other careers. Yet without instruments with which to measure and compare these imponderables, this cannot be proved. Nor can it be claimed that the problems to be detailed below are peculiar either to science in general or to any special field of science. In fact, since the stresses which arise in different careers have never been systematically compared, it cannot even be determined whether or to what extent emotional problems vary from one career to another, either in degree or kind. Therefore, the reader may well ask why this paper is published before such investigations have been carried out. Its justification lies in the fact that such studies will themselves require a large investment of time, money, and trained personnel, none of which will be made available until responsible educators become convinced that such studies are essential enough to justify careful planning, a co-ordinated multidisciplinary approach, and generous financial support. Before such studies are made, all that we can do is to indicate fragmentary observations, which suggest that it would be enlightening to make socio-economic studies of the lives of young and old scientists, plus psychoanalytic studies of a statistically adequate random sample of them.

These investigations would throw light on such problems as: (*a*) the special stresses, both economic and psychological, which occur in the life of the young scientist; (*b*) the great variety of conscious and unconscious forces whose interplay determines a young man's choice of scientific research as a career; (*c*) the interplay of conscious and unconscious forces in his subsequent emotional and scientific maturation; (*d*) how the special stresses which develop later in life react upon the earlier emotional forces which originally turned him towards science; (*e*) how unconscious stresses influence the young investigator's general approach to scientific research and scientific controversy; (*f*) how the unconscious symbolic significance of particular scientific problems and theories can distort the logic and the judgment even of men of exceptional ability. This article will attempt only to illustrate the wide variety of problems which are relevant to these general headings.

As a personal note, I should add that my observations, both on myself and on colleagues in various fields of science, have been made at random over a period of nearly thirty years. They began in the twenties, when I was working in one of the laboratories of the Rockefeller Institute. It became known that I had had some previous training in psychiatry. Presently I found that if I were to have any time for my own work I had literally to lock my door for a few hours each day. Otherwise, almost every afternoon, young colleagues and sometimes older ones would drift in to talk, not about scientific issues but about their personal problems. At that time, my psychiatric training and experience were limited, and I knew nothing at all about psychoanalysis. Yet these random and unsolicited revelations made it clear not only that, as one would expect, a scientist's ability to endure the prolonged frustration and uncertainties of scientific research depend on neurotic components in his personality (both masked and overt), but also that there are significant relationships between masked neurotic components in the personality of an apparently normal scientist, and such things as (*a*) the field of work which he chooses; (*b*) the problems within that field which he chooses to investigate; (*c*) the clarity with which he habitually uses his native capacity for logical thinking; (*d*) the ways in which he attacks scientific problems; (*e*) the scientific causes which he espouses; (*f*) the controversies in which he becomes entangled and how he fights; and (*g*) the joy or sorrow which is derived from the work itself and also from his ultimate success or failure. Thus over the intervening years I have seen men of imagination and erudition whose scientific lives were nonetheless baffled and unproductive, and also men with lesser gifts who seemed to function freely, creatively, and productively; scientists who were happy in spite of failure, and others who became depressed in spite of acknowledged and recognized success. Although such facts were new to me twenty-five years ago, they had long been an accepted part of human wisdom. This makes it strange that their deeper sources in human nature and their special importance to scientific workers have never been systematically explored. I cannot attempt such an exploration here, but it may be possible to make articulate the challenge to all scientists which lurks in these ancient and unexplored caverns of the human spirit.

I. The Emotional Equipment Which the Young Scientist Brings to His Career.—The young scientist often reaches maturity after a lopsided early development. In this development he resembles many other intellectuals. A typical history is that an intellectually gifted child develops neurotic tendencies which hamper his early aggressive and psychosexual development. If at this point he is intellectually stimulated by one or another of the emotionally significant adults of his life, he is likely to turn away from athletics and the social life which he finds difficult to more bookish activities, thus postponing indefinitely any facing of earthier challenges. If success rewards his consolatory scholarly efforts during adolescence, he may in later years tend to cultivate intellectual activity exclusively. In this way absorption in the intellectual life will frequently be paralleled by an increasing withdrawal from athletic and social and psychosexual activities. As a result, by the time adult life is reached his only triumphs and gratifications will have been won in the intellectual field, his range of skills will have become restricted, and the life of the mind will be almost the only outlet available. Because of the extra drain of the laboratory on the student's time, the young man who sets out to become a scientist spends his adolescence putting every emotional egg in the intellectual basket to a greater extent than is true for most other young intellectuals. By such steps as these, the sense of security and the self-esteem of the young intellectual come to stand on one leg; so that when research is begun he invests in it a lifetime of pent-up cravings. After such a development, it is inevitable that scientific research will be supercharged with many irrelevant and unfulfilled emotional needs; so that the lifework of the young scientist tends to express both the conscious levels of his intellectual aspirations and his unfulfilled instinctual needs and unconscious conflicts.

Even the most brilliant scientific successes cannot solve unconscious personal problems, nor gratify unrecognized instinctual pressures. Whenever anyone works under the whiplash of unsolved unconscious conflicts, whether he is painting a picture, writing a play, pursuing a scientific discovery, or making a million dollars, the individual is prone to work with desperation. If there is failure, he blames unhappiness on his failure. But, to his amazement and dismay, he discovers that depression may follow success no less than failure. Basically, this is because success also leaves his deeper problems unsolved. If we always bear in mind that the pursuit of unconscious and often unattainable needs plays a determining role in the intellectual career, the familiar phenomena of depression attending success would not perplex us. We should wonder rather at the shortsightedness of a process of scientific education in which self-knowledge is the forgotten man, and in which emotional maturation is left to chance.

II. The Choice of a Career.—The aspects of this vexing problem which are peculiar to a career in science require certain general considerations. I suppose that it is not inaccurate to say that, of the many unsolved problems of human life, two which are of major importance are how to enable successive generations to learn from the mistakes of their predecessors without repeating them, and how to make it possible for young people to anticipate the future realistically. Not literature nor the arts or formal education has solved these two problems, which are interdependent in every aspect of life. Both are relevant to the choice of a career. When a youth decides to become a doctor, a lawyer, a businessman, or an artist, the decision is not made on the basis of a realistic foreknowledge of what one of these careers would be like as compared to another, nor out of a deep introspective knowledge of himself and of how he would fit into the lifework he has chosen. Even if his own father is a lawyer or a doctor, he will have had an opportunity to observe only the outer aspects of that life, the dramatization of its activities; he cannot have felt its joys and sorrows directly. What he will have experienced vicariously through identification with his parent will depend less upon what that life was really like than upon how it affected him; and upon the subtle balance of conscious and unconscious, hostile and loving components in his identification with the parental figure. Nor do adults know how to communicate the truth about their own adult lives to their children. Consequently, the adolescent's and even the college student's anticipation of the quality of life in any future career is dominated by fantasies. To a remarkable degree this is true even of more familiar and humdrum careers. The quality of adult living belongs to the remote and mysterious future; it is something the flavor of which the child cannot anticipate. Until this obstacle to communication between the generations is overcome, successive generations will continue in the future, as in the past, to make their choice in the darkness of fantasy and confusion. The child of a wealthy broker who was "on the street" took these words literally, as children do, and looked for his father in every pushcart peddler who passed. Although the visual misconception of the child was corrected as he matured, an emotional hangover remained which had an important influence in determining the choice of his subsequent lifework. Usually the less familiar the career which a young man chooses, the greater will be the importance of fantasies, both conscious and unconscious, among the forces which determine the initial choice of a career, and also the subsequent adjustment, happiness, and effectiveness in the one selected.

One natural conclusion to be drawn from these considerations would seem to constitute an argument for the wider use of aptitude testing in the choice of careers. Actual experience, however, and a hard-headed and realistic skepticism make one cautious about expecting too much help from these devices. The most extensive trials of the value of aptitude testing were the so-called "Stanines," which the USAAF developed during the war for the screening of air cadets and their allocation to training as pilots, bombardiers, and navigators. In terms of its relevance to this problem, I would summarize the results of this experience as follows:

a) The tests of aptitudes were remarkably accurate as far as they went.

b) It was possible to sort out those with the automatic speed and motor skills and/or the mathematical precision needed for various tasks.

c) Men were placed accurately on a point scale as to their relevant psychometric and neuromuscular capacities.

d) In this way, the tests selected accurately a small group at one extreme, most of whom would succeed in training, and another small group at the opposite pole, most of whom would fail. (There were exceptions to the results even at both extremes.)

e) As was to be expected, however, the vast majority of the men tested fell into the central zone of the normal curve of distribution, while only a relatively small percentage of the tested population was placed at the two extremes.

f) With rare exceptions, the individuals who fell into the extremes knew their own aptitudes and ineptitudes before going through any tests. From their experiences at play, in sports, in school, and on various jobs, they knew already that they were specially adept or specially maladroit with respect to certain types of activity. Indeed the representatives of the two extreme ends of the scale were usually able to describe their strong and weak points almost as precisely as these could be measured.

g) Consequently, the tests are of greatest use when jobs are scarce in times of peace, or else in times of war when a lad may want desperately to be accepted by a special branch of the service for some particular position, and may therefore exaggerate his native skill or hide his native ineptitude. But at other times when there is no special incentive to deception (beyond the usual need for self-deception), the men at the end zones need no tests.

h) The next important lesson of the entire experiment with the "Stanines" was that for the majority, who fall in the great middle zone of the normal curve of distribution, although their minor variations in aptitudes can be measured with considerable precision by various "human engineering" devices, these variations do not determine either success or failure, happiness or unhappiness in a career. By exclusion, therefore, we may conclude from the results of the "Stanines," that for most of us (that is, for the Average Man) a subtle balance of conscious and unconscious forces determines how effectively we use our native aptitudes, whether intellectual, emotional, sensory, neuromuscular, or any combination of these aptitudes. For most of us it is not the minor quantitative differences in the machine itself, but the influence of these conscious and unconscious emotional forces on our use of the human machine which determines our effectiveness. For me this was the ultimate lesson from the experience of the Air Force with the "Stanines," and I believe, furthermore, that this result is what might be expected in any similar effort to predict success and failure in civilian careers by the use of precise aptitude tests alone.

This is the stumbling block against which the aptitude testers always stub their toes, and until they learn how to evaluate with equal precision the influence of unconscious emotional forces, they will continue to mislead young people into thinking that scores on aptitude scales will determine successes and failures, happiness and unhappiness in their lifework.[1]

Although these unconscious, irrational, and symbolic forces are subtle and difficult to describe, they determine how most of us use our equipment, and the fate of our lives under conditions of success as well as failure. We shall attempt to discuss a few of these forces in relation to scientific problems and also to the life of science. To youngsters, the dream of a life of scientific research is charged with complicated and usually unnoticed symbolic connotations, which alter steadily during growth from youth to manhood. Therefore, what science "means" consciously to any mature scientist has as many unconscious layers as the stages of his interest in science. No valid generalizations can be made about this condition until many scientists have been studied analytically and the data collated.

Some of those who show scientific interest and capacity in their youth subsequently lose these qualities completely, whereas others pursue them throughout life. In only a few instances has it been possible to study the evolving symbolic connotations of a scientist's interest in scientific matters. In these few cases the "scientific" interests of early childhood frequently turn out to have been in part a window-dressing for quite different concerns. I cannot overemphasize the importance of keeping the fact in mind that human behavior is like a centipede, standing on many legs. Nothing that we do has a single determinant, whether conscious, preconscious, or unconscious. In singling out certain neglected unconscious symbolic determinants it may often sound as though I were overlooking all of the others. This is only because I want to emphasize the importance of the unconscious forces, precisely because they have been neglected so consistently, and because, as a direct consequence of this neglect, they tend to be destructive.

One of these unconscious forces is the child's fearful and guilt-laden curiosity about the human body, both its tabooed external aspects and its mysterious inner workings. A familiar example of this force may be noted in the physician whose interest in medicine has some of its roots in the child's buried envy of the doctor who could gratify the forbidden bodily curiosities and enter the sickroom from which the child was excluded. How universal this drive would be, and how it would vary with the age of the child and the quality of his relationships to others cannot be decided by guessing. Nor can I document this forcefully without presenting a mass of clinical data for which there is neither time nor space. Somewhat scattered data, gathered during the occasional opportunities to make analytical studies of various kinds of scientists, have shown that even widely varying forms of scientific interest can serve as an acceptable cover for some of the forbidden concerns of childhood. Furthermore, this tendency to utilize various facets of the outer world as a symbolic projection of inner conflicts does not cease when the child becomes adult, but may continue throughout life. This fact is of more than academic interest, since the scientific activities of the adult can be distorted by the same unconscious childhood conflicts out of which his original interest in science may have arisen. Indeed this must result whenever adult activities continue to represent earlier conflicts, and projections of unconscious personal conflicts can often be recognized even through their adult scientific disguises in the reasoning and experiments of outstanding scientists.

As an example of the role of unconscious residues of childhood's battles, I would cite the gynecologist whose ancient and infantile curiosities were not to be satisfied by the justified activities of his profession, and who was plagued by an insatiable compulsion to visit burlesque shows. One could hardly ask for a better experimental demonstration of the fact that unconscious needs cannot be gratified by conscious fulfillment. A comparable example is found in the X-ray man whose choice of a career was determined predominantly by his unconscious curiosity about the internal structure of his mother's body. In all innocence both men dedicated their lives to the service of childhood cravings which were buried in guilt and fear. It should be our goal to learn how to guide gifted young men so that they will not build their entire lives on such psychological quicksands.

III. Neurotic Distortions of Scientific Research: General Considerations.—The first step in any program of scientific research is to observe natural phenomena while taking care not to alter these phenomena by the very process of observing them. In spite of the most meticulous care, however, the ever-present unconscious forces of the observer color in some degree the glasses through which he makes even simple observations. Therefore, it is out of such tinted observations that he develops his scientific theories. Initially, these are hypotheses about possible relationships between the observed data. Hypotheses are always more vulnerable to distortion by unconscious processes than are the primary observations themselves. Therefore the next step for the research worker is to test his theories, together with their inevitable distortions, in experiments which either isolate and quantify the original data, or that test the consequences of the derived theories. Without our realizing that this is occurring, the process of investigation tends in this way to balance the distortions introduced by unconscious bias. Once he has set up his initial experiments, however, the scientist again becomes an observer. Now, however, he no longer observes facts in nature, but rather in a milieu which he has created artificially by means of his experiment.

Each successive step in these scientific processes calls forth a greater investment of conscious and unconscious feeling; yet if the experimenter is to be objective about the outcome of his experiments he must somehow manage to climb out of his own psychic skin so as to be able to criticize his own handiwork. This is as essential to objective scientific work as it is to artistic creativeness, but it is never easy, because it is impossible for an investigator to prevent the intrusion of his unconscious biases into such sequences of experiment and observation.

Furthermore, even these steps constitute merely the foundation for another round of observation, theory, and experiment. From experimentally derived observations, come a second order of theories, in which unconscious biases have even greater weight; and these theories in turn must be subjected to new experimental tests, which require still further sequences of observation and of theory. Thus the structure of science adds layer on layer, each burdened by more subtle and complex unconscious emotional investments, demanding of the scientist an ever greater clarity about the role of his own unconscious processes in his conscious theories and experiments, and each requiring an ever more rigorous correction for the influence of unconscious preconceptions.

For none of this self-critique in depth does our educational process prepare us. Yet much of it was implicit in Claude Bernard's *An Introduction to the Study of Experimental Medicine* (1) when he wrote: "The metaphysician, the scholastic, and the experimenter all work with an *a priori* idea. The difference is that the scholastic imposes his idea as an absolute truth which he has found, and from which he then deduces consequences, by logic alone. The more modest experimenter, on the other hand, states an idea as a question, as an interpretative and more or less probable anticipation of nature, from which he logically deduces consequences which, moment by moment, he confronts with reality by means of experiment."[2] Again in another connection, Claude Bernard pointed out that the scientist and the philosopher are subject to the same internal human laws, prey to the same emotions, prejudices, and biases, and that these operate equally in the philosopher and the scientist. The difference is that for the scientist the fact that a theory seems true to him, that it feels true, or even that it is logically or mathematically possible does not make it true. For the scientist, the theory is not true until he has taken it to the laboratory, "leaving his theories in the cloakroom," and subjected it to the ultimate test of the experimental method (6).

Other observers of the world of science have referred to this fact. Every scientist can read with profit and delight Charles Richet's spirited and witty "*Natural History of a Savant*" (7), and Gregg's sage volume of lectures on "*The Furtherance of Medical Research*" (2), both of which touch on these questions. More recently R. C. Tolman (9) referred challengingly to "the criteria for selecting diligent and competent scientists, the effects of personal bias on results, the relation between subjective origins and objective outcomes of scientific experiments."[3]

This is a portrait of the ideal scientist, ideally in action. It implies that the subtle interplay of reason and emotion, and of conscious and unconscious forces, are as important in the lives and activities of scientists as of anyone else. If this is true then nothing could be more important to science than that scientists should know themselves in the neo-Socratic or Freudian sense, that is, in terms of the interplay between their own conscious and unconscious processes. Yet, as we have already stated (4), in the education of the scientist, as of everyone else, self-knowledge in depth is the forgotten man of our entire educational system (*Cf.* Lombard, [5]).

Since the father of modern physiology, a great immunologist, a senior statesman among medical educators, and a great atomic physicist all have recognized the confusing influence of subtle psychological processes in scientific work, then surely it is time for the problem to be made the central focus of a major investigation, in which psychoanalytic techniques will be one of the essential tools.

THE DISTORTION OF THE CREATIVE DRIVE BY NEUROTIC FORCES. It is rarely recognized that research makes demands upon the young investigator which may exploit his neurotic vulnerabilities. For instance, a drive for "originality" may cloak a difficulty in mastering existing facts and techniques, or it may serve to disguise an unconscious hostility to all existing authority. How often is this drive for originality naïvely mistaken by teacher and student for creative scientific imagination? How often, therefore, is the young investigator encouraged to penetrate into new territory before he has mastered the terrain from which the expedition must start? It is no answer to these questions to say that the same misinterpretations occur among young artists, writers, and musicians. Fallacious values and goals are destructive whenever they occur and in many different fields of work. Nor does it lessen the significance of any of the examples which follow to dismiss them as psychopathological. Such pathology is only an exaggeration of what occurs in more subtle and disguised forms in everyone. The wider and more easily recognized deviations of pathology illuminate the "normal" for us, and sensitize us to slighter anomalies which we otherwise would overlook.

For instance, unresolved neurotic anxieties may impel one overanxious young investigator to choose a problem that will take a lifetime or, alternatively, may drive another into easy, get-rich-quick tasks, which yield a yearly paper, a yearly acclaim, the yearly promotion. The former tendency to postpone the day of reckoning indefinitely occurs in the young scientist who deals with his anxieties by pretending that they do not exist. The latter is found in the man who finds it impossible to endure suspense and uncertainty for more than a few months. Neurotic anxiety can take either form; and young scientists frequently walk a tightrope between these two alternatives, that is, between the annual piecework type of productivity and the long-drawn-out tasks which postpone indefinitely any ultimate testing of theories against experimental data and observations of nature.

Then there is the battle with phobic indecision over which task to undertake, or how to undertake it: an indecision which may arise not out of an inadequate mastery of specific facts and techniques, but from a general neurotic tendency to obsessional doubting. I have seen this symptom work identical destruction in the careers of a young playwright who could not decide which of two equally good plots to use, and of a young chemist who could not decide which of two equally promising leads to follow.

There was also the scientist who had proved his case, but who was so driven by his anxieties that he had to bolster an already proven theorem by falsifying some quite unnecessary additional statistical data. This was a compulsive act, comparable to a kleptomania by a wealthy man, or to the action of a successful and famous writer who suffered from a compulsion to insert a few words from someone else into everything he wrote.

Again, there is the scientist who is always pursuing a new scientific father. This occurs more frequently than is realized. One outstandingly able young scientist ran through five careers, abandoning each one after a brilliant start just as he reached the point of launching his own independent work. When he could no longer postpone accepting a professorship, he broke down and disappeared from the world of science.

But the most ubiquitous tragedy of all is the anxiety-driven scientist who lives on a treadmill—the man who has tasted what it means to gain temporary easement from his anxieties by doing a fine piece of scientific work, but who thereafter is driven not by a quest for further truth but by an insatiable need to repeat the same achievement in an effort to assuage anxieties whose origins were unconscious. This investigator uses scientific research precisely as the man with a handwashing compulsion uses soap and water, or as an addict uses drugs.

I cannot leave this phase of the problem without referring to one highly technical and complex issue. In psychiatry we recognize certain rough parallelisms between types of illness and types of personality. These can have comparable influence in research. During the exploratory phase, while crude data are being gathered, an investigator ought to be free from rigidity. He should be ready to abandon preconceived objectives and anticipated goals, so that any hints that come from unexpected findings can be pursued. He must be psychologically free to follow uncharted courses. Therefore, premature systematization of the data must be avoided. This requires that type of free and imaginative flexibility which is sometimes attributed to the so-called "hysterical" personality. Later, a more rigid process is required, one which has some of the features of the obsessional neurosis, or even some of the tendency of a paranoid patient to organize his delusions into logical systems. Scientific research thus seems to require that, as the work progresses, the investigator should be free to operate now with one type of personality and now with another. It would be profitable to compare analytically the personalities of those scientists who can change in this way and of those who cannot, especially in relation to their scientific productivity. This would seem to be a problem of basic importance for the optimal use of scientific personnel.

Dr. Anne Roe has given me permission to quote a letter of September 13, 1952, in which she summarizes some of her unique studies in this field:

"Any brief summary of these data is necessarily inadequate, and the generalizations require qualifications; but certain differences among these groups of scientists show up, both on the test material and in the life patterns. These are most striking in interpersonal relations, in the handling of anxiety and aggression, in the patterns on intelligence tests, and in the use of imagery.

"The typical physicist and biologist grew up with a minimum of group social activity, entered into heterosexual activities rather late and is now not much interested in any social activities. The psychologists and anthropologists for the most part were early conscious of their own and the family's social status, began dating early and enthusiastically, and are still enormously involved with other persons, one way and another. Both physicists and biologists show an unusual independence of parental ties, without guilt; and present attitudes toward the father are characteristically respectful, but lacking in closeness. Attitudes towards the mother are variable. Many of the psychologists and anthropologists, on the other hand, went through periods of great family dissension, and are still angry with or disparaging of their parents. I am sure it is significant also that in the families of these groups, the mother was most often the dominant character. This was rare in the other groups.

"The biologists, as a group, rely strongly and effectively on rational control. This appears in their lives, in their general unaggressiveness and in their unproductiveness and intense concern with form on the Rorschach. The physicists have a good deal of free anxiety, shown in their behavior and on the Rorschach, particularly in the large amounts of K and k. This is better controlled among the theoretical than among the experimental physicists. The *difference* between biologists and physicists is like the difference between compulsive obsessives and anxiety hysterics (I do not imply that all biologists are obsessives and all physicists hysterics). I am quite sure that there are relationships, of a nature still obscure to me, between the preoccupation with space, the type of symbolization that physics uses (which has spatial concomitants) and the choice of physics as a profession; but I suspect that in so far as space symbolizes distance from other persons (as Schilder says) it is more comforting than anxiety-arousing for these men, and I do not believe that their disinterest in persons is always compensatory. The psychologists and anthropologists are enormously productive on the Rorschach, quite unconcerned with rational controls for the most part, and intensely preoccupied with persons. Their handling of anxiety is quite varied; but as a group they are much the most freely aggressive, and this often has strong oral elements.

"The level of intelligence of my group is extremely high, but there are interesting differences in patterning: the theoretical physicists surpass the others on both verbal and spatial tests; experimental physicists tend to be low on verbal and high on spatial; anthropologists are high on verbal and low on non-verbal; psychologists are high on both; biologists show all combinations, but generally the geneticists and biochemists are relatively higher on non-verbal and the others reverse this.

"Differences in use of imagery during thinking are also fairly sharp. It is not easy to get a good report on this, and I am not happy about my data; yet they are remarkably consistent. In their conscious thinking, biologists are chiefly visualizers; among physicists the experimentalists rely most often on visual imagery, and the theorists on symbolization (usually mathematical and closely allied to verbal symbolization) or imageless thought. Psychologists and anthropologists rely predominantly on auditory verbal thinking. It occurred to me that it was possible that whatever process was most relied upon during the day would be the one to show up in hypnagogic revery. For those who are strongly visualizers or verbalizers, hypnagogic imagery is usually but not always in the same mode; for those whose dominant mode of conscious thought is symbolic or imageless it may be visual or auditory or symbolic, but usually with other twists to it. It would be interesting to find out if there are similar differences in the dream process.

"I should add that the one thing which characterizes every one of my groups of eminent scientists is the high degree of ego-involvement in the vocation, both now and earlier. That this is the major factor in their vocational success seems highly probable; but without a comparison group of less successful scientists I can't be certain about this. The ways in which this came about and the situations that made it possible are, of course, extremely varied. In some instances I can demonstrate quite direct relations between professional activities and specific emotional problems. In others I cannot; and I am not convinced that a genuinely neurotic problem is always involved. But I am convinced that it is the matter of personal involvement that is significant for problems of vocational choice and success."

I have included this long excerpt in spite of the fact that the researches of Dr. Roe in this area are still incomplete and inconclusive—as she herself points out—because even her tentative conclusions are unique, exciting and suggestive, and also because her work gives us an indication of how great an investment of time, effort, personnel, and money an adequate study of this problem would entail (8).[4]

THE INFLUENCE OF UNCONSCIOUS SYMBOLIC PROCESSES ON THE PRODUCTION OF LOGICAL THOUGHT AND LOGICAL ERROR IN SCIENTIFIC RESEARCH. It is obvious that conscious emotions which are close to the surface can influence a man's scientific work, especially perhaps those anxious ambitions and pettier jealousies which are bred by certain special economic and professional insecurities which will be discussed in Part II, and which may induce a young scientist to push for quick and showy results. Of far greater importance, however, is the subtler influence of streams of unconscious feelings which may be represented symbolically yet compulsively in the scientific activity of an individual, just as they are represented in neurotic symptoms and in dreams, or in all artistic and literary creativity. At this point, therefore, I must explain what the concept of symbolic representation means in this connection.

The symbols by which we think are multivalent tools, always representing many things simultaneously, some conscious, some preconscious, and some unconscious. In logical thinking, the conscious and preconscious symbolic processes represent external reality without disguises; what we call "logic," therefore, is in essence a coding of relationships which are inherent among such internal and external data as are accessible to our direct perceptual processes. One might almost say that although logic resides in the mind, its roots are in the relations among external facts themselves. It is a neglected consequence of this principle, that it is literally impossible to be "illogical" about accessible data except when one has an unconscious axe to grind. Failures in logic are a measure of man's capacity to deceive himself with unconscious premeditation, by misperceiving observational data and by misusing conceptual data for his own unconscious purposes. Many years ago, William Alanson White warned that when anyone says that two and two are five, he does so because he has to; and that the way to meet this problem is not to teach him to say by rote that two and two are four, but to discover with him why he needs to believe otherwise.

It is an inevitable consequence of these facts that in spite of any degree of intellectual brilliance, individuals whose psychological development has been distorted by unsolved unconscious conflicts will have significant limitations in their capacity to build concepts out of the accessible data of external reality. This, indeed, is the greatest psychological hazard of the young intellectual—the fact that unconscious emotional forces persist in him in the form of unconscious needs and unconscious conflicts over these needs. In some, these forces will be expressed in obvious neurotic symptoms. In others, they cause subtle distortions of patterns of living. Sometimes they are expressed in distortions of artistic or intellectual (in this instance, scientific) activities. Naturally there are varied combinations of these three alternatives; but it is an impressive paradox that among individuals in whom unconscious problems are expressed in obvious neurotic symptoms their scientific work frequently escapes the distortions which occur in other scientists whose unconscious processes have no outlet through overt neurotic symptoms. This is not always the case; but it is frequently true that the masked influence of unconscious psychological forces can warp the thinking of a brilliant investigator even when he shows no overt neurotic quirks.

Let me give a few brief examples of the operation of unconscious conflicts on scientific work and scientific careers.

I have known scientists of great ability whose work nevertheless always tended to be vague and ambiguous. Some of these men unconsciously designed their laborious experiments so as to prove nothing. For unconscious reasons they could not allow themselves to find out the answers to their own scientific questions. Such an unconscious conflict over seeing and/or knowing with a preponderant unconscious need *not* to see and *not* to know, arises in early years. In adult life, it accounts for some tragic failures among scientists of brilliant capabilities. This conflict can also produce nihilistic critics who, however brilliant, may also be essentially destructive. For them it is as though seeing and knowing were transgressions which were endlessly tempting but always forbidden in the end.

It is conceivable that adequate psychoanalytic therapy early in their training might have saved at least some of these gifted yet wasted and unhappy lives.

Experiments under hypnosis have demonstrated that unconscious processes can take over the intellectual equipment of a scientist and misuse that equipment for their own unrecognized purposes. Under post-hypnotic suggestion, for instance, highly skilled and experienced mathematicians have been led to attempt to prove theorems which they knew to be absurd or to solve mathematical problems which were known to be insoluble. This is the same type of process by which unconscious conflicts and purposes can lead a neurosurgeon to misapply his technical skills, or by which the subtle reasoning of a chemist or physicist, or the ingenuity of a clinical psychologist in devising or interpreting psychological tests, can be misapplied. Actually this is no more mysterious than is the way in which unconscious processes regularly exploit the need for food or the conventional impulse towards cleanliness. One will find in the literature of psychoanalysis many studies of the effects of unconscious processes in disturbances of various normal activities such as eating, washing, dressing, painting, writing, sports, play, sleep, sex, and excretion; but to my knowledge there are no similar studies of the power of unconscious processes to disturb the equally symbolic methods of scientific research. Yet the surreptitious influence of these forces on scientific activities may determine the success or failure of an entire life (3).

That ancient tragedy of human nature, the success which brings no joy with it, occurs at least as frequently in the life of the scientific investigator as in art and business. A life of fruitful scientific exploration may end in a feeling of total defeat, precisely because in spite of scientific success the unconscious goals of the search have eluded the searcher. Sometimes at the end of a career this need to reach some still undefined goal has led a successful scientist to turn to a pseudo-scientific investigation of the supernatural. More often it leads to depression and a total arrest of all scientific productivity. Sometimes success breeds panic directly, as was observed in the case of a graduate student in physics, a man of outstanding ability, when the head of the department came up behind him in the laboratory one day, and said, "You handed in the best ——— examination I have ever received." Thereupon the student laid down his apparatus and left the laboratory in a panic, which prevented his returning for several weeks.

When they operate below the level of conscious awareness and therefore are not subject to conscious control and direction, the early patterns of familial loves and hates, of submissions and rebellions, may exercise a profound influence on the later work of a scientific investigator, even to the extent of determining his choice of science as a career, his field of work in science, the problems he chooses, the causes he espouses, and the very experiments which he undertakes. While this fact has long been acknowledged, it has never been appreciated in sufficient detail.

There is, for instance, the force of unconscious imitation, to which all of us are liable, imitation even of those very traits against which we may have rebelled most vigorously in childhood. Manifestations of this, both gross and subtle, occur all around us and in every aspect of life. There is the child of the alcoholic who hated the parent's alcoholism yet becomes an alcoholic. There is the child of a parent with a tyrannical temper, firmly resolved never to raise his voice in anger against his children, yet who hears his father's voice issue from his own mouth, as he yells at his three-year-old son in an automatic imitation of the voice and manner which he had always hated in his own father. A famous professor of biochemistry in one of our leading medical schools was the son of a fundamentalist minister against whose narrow ranting he rebelled. Yet the son spent an entire afternoon ranting, as his father was wont to do, but this time it was against the gentle religiosity of a hapless salesman of scientific apparatus who visited his laboratory. This same professor used every biochemical controversy as a pulpit from which to expound sarcastic diatribes against his colleagues, quite like the paternal sermons which had offended him during his childhood.

Also in rebellion against a fundamentalist background, a famous professor of psychology showed a missionary zeal in defense of a mechanized concept of human behavior, so narrowly partisan, indeed so "fundamentalist," that in essence the concept destroyed the value of his whole theoretical approach, which could otherwise have been of considerable scientific significance. Again, there was an eminent physiologist whose desiccated approach to certain problems bore the destructive imprint of an early conflict over whether or not to join the priesthood.

Such thought-provoking reactions are not rare. Many more examples could be cited, but they would merely serve to illustrate again the fact that the human beings who do research work are the subtle and complex instruments of their unconscious and conscious processes; and that the very content of a scientist's investigations as well as his vulnerability to the emotional stresses of research will reflect in varying manner the influence of those psychological forces which are unconscious residues from the unresolved neurotic problems of his early childhood. This fact indicates that an essential element is left out of the training of Man the Scientist, namely, an opportunity to free himself from bondage to the unconscious residues of his own childhood.

Research is a strange and challenging occupation for any young man to contemplate. We still know far too little about the unconscious components of the forces which lead a man or woman to go into research, or about the influence of the unconscious elements in determining the success or failure of his efforts. All of these problems, with their general as well as their special human significance, should be explored. How to do this is a matter for special consideration, since it presents many difficulties. Perhaps the first step would be to subject to psychoanalytic exploration, and in selected instances to psychoanalytic therapy a random sampling of: (1) promising young men who hope to make scientific research their life work; (2) men who have already devoted many years to research, including (*a*) men who in spite of high native endowments have been unproductive, (*b*) others who have been creative but who have ended up nonetheless in frustration and despair, and (*c*) finally those who have succeeded and who have enjoyed fully the fruits of their achievements.

Just as psychiatry has had to study elations in order to understand depressions, so in such a study it would be important to keep in mind that it is just as important to study successes as failures. In science as in other fields, success or failure cannot be accounted for by differences in intellectual capacity alone. Consequently, an analytical study of those who succeed and of those who fail and of the many gradations between success and failure would be of value not only to science but also to those foundations and universities that wish to use men wisely to advance the frontiers of human knowledge.

To uncover in this way some of the unconscious factors which determine the choice of a career, and to explore the subtler forces which determine whether or not that career will be externally productive and internally fulfilling, would be a major contribution to human wisdom. To the best of my knowledge no such study has ever been made of any occupational or professional group. A start must be made somewhere, and in view of the paramount importance of science in today's world, it might be appropriate to start with scientists. Such an enterprise would merit the support of scientific foundations. The sums which are spent on research are so huge that it would seem to be common sense, business sense, and scientific sense to study the men who expend these investments.

It is probable that among the scientists who read this article, some may have developed articulate insights into unconscious forces which have helped to determine the choice and direction of their careers. If they will share their insight with me, I will be deeply indebtd to them. They can do this by writing to me, either anonymously or preferably over their own signatures. I will regard all such data as professionally confidential communications, with the assurance to such readers that the material will not be used at any time without complete disguise, and not without specific permission and approval of the text itself by each informant.

Part II: Problems Arising from Socio-Economic Forces

I. The Struggle for Maturity.—In a recent article the problems of maturity in psychiatric research have been dissected in detail and at length (4). Much of that discussion is applicable to other fields as well; for it is not in psychiatry alone that men are needed who are mature as human beings, as specialized technicians, and as seasoned tacticians in the practical world. These needs are important for higher education in every scientific discipline, medical and non-medical alike, and indeed throughout the academic world. Let me give an example from one of these other fields.

One of the world's outstanding economists has taught in the academic world, has organized and led his own university department, has done pure research in fundamental economic theory, and has held government posts of great practical and diplomatic importance during times of war and peace, and during economic crisis. At first hand, therefore, he knows the field of economics as a teacher, as a pure scientist, and as an applied scientist. Indeed, his position in economics has closely paralleled that of the scientific medical clinician, in that both are called upon to bridge the gap between pure and applied science by operating effectively in both fields. From his years of varied, successful, and useful experience this economist now views with concern the processes of higher education in his own field. He finds among his purely academic colleagues an almost total lack of something which is equivalent to what in medicine is called clinical maturity. They seem to him neither to derive their problems from the world's needs nor to test their hypotheses against such realities. He points out that this condition is in part due to the fact that all higher education now takes so long that, among those who succeed in attaining the higher ranks, there will automatically be a large proportion of individuals who harbor a secret inclination to retreat from life, and who are relatively deficient in aggressive, outgoing, reality-oriented impulses.

Furthermore, if the young scholar is to remain in academic work he has to teach, and our economist agrees with me that teaching is a dangerous sport for the young. Teaching makes it easy to appear scholarly and to sound profound, and gradually to believe that one really has these qualities. The young teacher usually has too great an edge on his young audience for his own good; students have no way of gauging the adequacy of the experience which lies behind the teacher's words. Anyone who lives in an atmosphere where nobody can answer back, soon begins to feel omniscient, with the result that effective self-criticism is almost as rare among young teachers as it is among dictators and generals. The fall is painful when those hard realities which have no respect for the pedagogue's fantasies of omniscience are encountered.

When I apply these reflections to my own experience, I think of the contrast between what goes on within me when I am working with a patient in my office, and what goes on within me when I am teaching young medical students. The latter is heady wine. Delusions of psychiatric omniscience could be easily acquired were it not for the fact that in my office every day, hour after hour, I face the toughest and keenest skeptics in the world: namely, a patient and his stubborn unconscious struggles. Such experiences keep the clinician humble; they are also the ultimate test of his theoretical and practical wisdom. What the patient is to the psychiatrist, the challenge of politics and the market place is to the economist. This is the clinic that tests his theories, and the impotence of many economic and political scientists is due to the fact that they are so rarely forced to accept the challenge of testing and implementing their theories. Such economists are comparable to a hypothetical professor of medicine who has never served an internship or treated a patient. Finally, in both fields it takes years to reach full maturity of judgment. Only the slow passing of the years can provide an opportunity to observe the ultimate fates of our pet theories, once they have been put out to work.

These considerations have still another implication for higher education. What happens to the economist who never takes his economics into the market place is precisely what happens to the psychiatrist who never confronts the tough opposition of a sick and needful patient. Without this challenge it is possible for him to feel satisfied with formulations which are superficial, partial, and theoretical. His theories seem to him to represent the truth, because he has never had to subject them to any test more critical than the deceptive test of their internal logical consistency. In any field the theoretician need only be logical; yet internal logic, unless it is buttressed by strict mathematical formulation, is no better proof in science than in a system of paranoid ideas, for such ideas can be logically consistent one with another providing one grants the initial premise. This is true throughout the world of pure science. By contrast, the therapist and all applied scientists must always make their knowledge work, which is a necessary, humbling, and maturing challenge.

This is a long detour, but I have allowed myself to explore it because it is important to realize that comparable problems exist throughout all aspects of higher education. As education requires a longer period, the danger of its becoming more and more remote from reality increases steadily, because: (*a*) the student has so limited an opportunity to confront himself with external reality during the process of education; (*b*) the longer the educational process, the more it tends to select men who secretly want to escape external reality; (*c*) finally, it encourages his vanity by giving him premature opportunities to teach theories which have never been tested. These are the three basic threats to maturity throughout our system of higher education. The appointment of brilliant young theoreticians to professorial chairs merely serves to increase these dangers to the maturity of science in general, at the same time that it stunts the development of the individuals themselves.

II. Special Aspects of the Economic Stresses in the Life of the Young Scientist.—Among the special stresses which beset the life of a scientist, there are external as well as internal forces; and no consideration of the problem would be complete if a discussion of these factors were omitted.

I have frequent opportunities to talk to graduate students who are planning a life of scientific research. On such occasions it distresses me to discover how rarely any of them are facing the future realistically, even with respect to such elementary and basic facts as ultimate financial security and independence. I do not remember one who had included in planning for his career a budget of reasonable living costs for a prospective family, compared with existing academic and research salaries. Nor has it lessened my distress to discover that no one of the scientific mentors of these prospective scientists has felt it to be his duty to confront the student with the basic and inescapable facts.

What then are some of the economic realities which the young scientist fails to anticipate? First of all, he rarely seems to realize that a day in the laboratory is the same for a rich scientist or a poor one, while the price of poverty will be paid by his family at home. He does not accept the full import of the fact that his wife and his youngsters are the ones who will have to spend 24 hours a day in quarters so crowded that they will lack space for peaceful family living and the dignity of privacy. Furthermore, because he is young and takes health and longevity for granted, he rarely includes in his calculations the fact that if he has no personal capital he will have to allocate throughout his life a significant share of his small salary for an over-all insurance program; since insurance will be the only way in which his meager earnings can give his family any protection against illness, ensure the future education of his children, or provide a modest independence for his own old age. Nor does he stop to consider the time-lag between inflationary trends and even a minor adjustment of university or laboratory salaries. For instance, in one major university a top professorial salary of $12,000 was established 35 years ago. At that time the entire $12,000 was usable income, but today over one-quarter of it is required for state and federal income taxes, and 48 per cent of the purchasing power of the remainder has been lost through inflation. Consequently, in that university the salary of the full professor now yields the purchasing power which $4,000 had at the time when the university established its salary scale. Only recently has this university been able to offer salary increases; and even the largest of these nets the recipient only about $1,000 in increased purchasing power, leaving him $7,000 behind his colleague of 35 years ago.

About these problems Alan Gregg (2) recently wrote as follows:

> If it be conceded that it is fair to permit a university professor to marry and have two children, to one of whom he may be allowed to give a professional education, then it is clear that with retirement fixed at sixty-five, the professor, in order to contribute to his children's education till one of them is twenty-five years old, must have his children born before he is forty-one. Since few men are professors before that age and fewer will be in the future—the salary in the ranks under that of professor should be such as a family of four can live on. How many are? The prevailing policy is a stupid one, the result can only be a virtually sterile academic society, a professoriate over-concerned with economic security, and therefore secretly rebellious or timidly resigned, or the academic career open only to those who have inherited money or married it. Men with energy and common sense, but no fortunes of their own will refrain from entering or advising entrance into so timid and defenseless a company. This is particularly serious in our medical schools, because the practice of medicine is so ready an alternative to teaching and research. Five years after graduation the ablest of my contemporaries were making $10,000 a year in practice and have continued at that level or above it. The equally able men who went into teaching or research were at $3000 after six years and a few have worked up to $9500 twenty years later. It may be replied that low salaries eliminate the incompetent. They do not. I may as well say straight out that the incompetents stick on. Low salaries may cause the money-minded and the hard-pressed to go elsewhere. The worst and the best stay on. One cannot pass over the incompetents as negligible. They clog the roads. But the plight of the best is truly distressing. Indeed, I could offer no excuses for what I know, but cannot reveal, regarding the struggles of some of the most eminent scientists in this rich country to raise and educate their none too numerous families. If you detect indignation in these remarks, please remember that the best investigators are men of humility and modesty who do not know how to protect themselves in serving our highly competitive society. That seems to me society's loss, and its shame.[5]

Dr. Gregg wrote specifically of medical scientists, but his comments are equally valid for others. He challenges us to ask ourselves whether it is wise or even honorable to educate young men to high scientific ideals for a life of science, unless we also give them fair and repeated warning that they may never be able to earn a dignified independence for their own old age, or an education for their children which will be comparable to their own. A failure to warn the prospective student-scientist about the practical problems which lie ahead is like training soldiers for war with no emphasis on the fact that many will be wounded and killed. Yet our system of education for scientists engages in a silent conspiracy to deceive the student by never confronting him frankly with the basic facts about the economics of his future career.

This conspiracy of silence shrouds in obscurity many other important facts about a life devoted to science. There are statistics which show how many financial failures it takes to make one stock market success: where are the statistics to show how many scientific failures it takes to make one Pasteur? It would seem to be the duty of scientists and educators to gather such vital statistics on the life-struggles of a few generations of scientists and would-be scientists, and to make sure that every graduate student of the sciences will be exposed repeatedly to the implications such data may have for his own future.

Otherwise the young scientist has no way of giving substance to his anticipatory dreams of what his life will be. In the absence of explicit and forceful indoctrination in these matters, it is not strange that we so rarely find a student who has asked himself such disquieting questions, as "What security can I anticipate if I reach the top of my field? What can my family count on if I turn out to be one of the good men who nears the top but never quite attains it? What if I am one of those who simply straggle along in the middle of the crowd? What if I am relatively a failure?" Instead, most young men view their prospects solely by identifying with their most successful chiefs, never stopping to consider how many must fail for each one who reaches this goal. And what student stops to consider the consequences of the crucial fact that not even his job tenure will be secure unless he reaches the upper levels of academic rank?

Certain of these facts concerning the developing of the personality of the young scientist and the strain of his economic situation have critical effects upon his marriage. There is first of all the initial poverty and the crowded living quarters, at least in our larger centers, where space is at a premium; the pressure of anxiety about the future which increases with the passing years as these insecurities slowly come to be appreciated and the consequent tendency to overwork, with the nights burdened by tasks which cannot be completed in the hypothetical working day. There is the inadequate social life; the cramped and hampered sexual life, which may at the same time be a neurotic residue from those early unconscious conflicts which have contributed to shaping the young scientist's life as a whole; the increasing monastic absorption of the man, and the wife's early fading and gradual loss of vitality and of confidence in herself as a woman. These are some of the effects that may occur. Many examples could be given from the lives of prominent scientists and their wives and children which would demonstrate the high price which is paid by these civilian expendables through their sacrifices to that carnivorous god, the scientific career. If such examples were to be described in clinical detail, it would be easy for anyone who knows many scientists to recognize well-known individuals. Many would silently recognize themselves. Therefore a decent respect for the right to privacy precludes detailed descriptions.

III. Special Careeristic Stresses.—In the young scientist's approach to his career, unrealistic and wishful thinking is not confined to financial matters. He tends to dismiss other painful prospects with a bland assumption that through the intervention of some special magic his life will escape the aches and pains that others have experienced. This was the type of self-deception that precipitated many soldiers into emotional illness. Thus, it was found during the war that the man who went into battle squarely facing the fact that he might be mutilated or killed was less likely to break down under the stress of combat than was the soldier who went into battle with a serene but unrealistic fantasy of his personal invulnerability. Among young scientists we find a similar self-deceiving fantasy: that is, that a life of science may be tough for everyone else, but that it will not be for him. Such an attitude prepares the ground for the high incidence of "nervous breakdowns" among scientists in their middle years.

How, then, can the young scientist be prepared effectively for the stresses which face him, if like most young people he shuts his mind to the implications of most of the warnings which do reach him? Thus he usually hears that even after months and years of hard work and uncertainty the scientist must accept disappointment. But merely hearing this will not sustain his self-confidence through long years of obscurity and disappointment, especially if these years are not crowned with success and recognition. Nor is it easy to help the young scientist to attain emotional maturity, since preparation for his life-work necessitates his remaining for many years in the immature role of the student, economically dependent either on a fellowship or on his family's largesse. This dependence delays his emotional maturation, while at the same time putting him under pressure to engage in get-rich-quick researches on problems which will not take too long to finish. Again the student will often have heard of the pressure that will be brought to bear on him to seek rapid advancement by means of publications; but this will not prepare him for the intensity of the actual conflict between such pressure and his own ideal of mature, slow-paced, and thoughtful work. Furthermore, as the number of young scientists increases, the rivalry intensifies so that it becomes always more difficult to resist career pressures. To deal with them realistically requires that the young man should yield just enough to get ahead, neither defeating himself by blind opposition, nor yet selling out to opportunism. How can his training help him to acquire the inner assurance, the humor, and the equanimity which will make it possible to walk this tight-rope as he attempts to achieve a practical compromise? This is no small order, even for mature and well-established scientists. Surely there is something more than the present *nothing*, which might be tried in an effort to prepare young men to deal with such dominant problems as these.

Paradoxically, a quite opposite difficulty is linked to this same conflict. This hazard, which is psychological rather than practical, arises out of the dangers which are inherent in the ambitious dreams of young men whenever a situation exists which encourages them to dream too long. Because of the length of scientific training and of actual research work, the young scientist may dwell for years in secret contemplation of his own unspoken hopes of making great scientific discoveries. As time goes on his silence begins to frighten him; and in the effort to master his fear, he may build up a secret feeling that his very silence is august, and that once he is ready to reveal his theories, they will shake the world. Thus a secret megalomania can hide among the ambitions of the young research worker, secret fantasies which have their roots in the universal dreams of omnipotence and omniscience of early childhood. Out of these dreams have grown the age-old myths with which childhood fends off its sense of helplessness in an adult world: Hercules, Samson, Paul Bunyan, Jack the Giant Killer, David and Goliath, and the modern Superman. With similar dreams of solving the great riddles of the universe, the immature scientist may hold at bay his secret fears of failure. Thus, the long, silent, waiting years are often infused with unhealthy fantasies which exist side by side with healthy ambitions. With so many practical anxieties dogging him (especially where teaching ability as such is of little help towards his advancement), it is not strange that young research scientists dream unattainable dreams, live unrealistic lives, overwork desperately, and develop a monastic absorption which strains every human tie. It is in this setting of complex psychological tensions that tantalizing near-misses and heartbreaking setbacks occur.

Another way in which the young scientist tries to ease his anxiety is by making a silent bargain with himself that he will try himself out in the field of research for a limited time. Yet with the passing years, the feeling grows that there is no alternative mode of life, that there is no turning back, and that gradually and insidiously all of his life's eggs have been committed to this one basket. One day he awakens, therefore, to find that the opportunity to change his occupation has passed; the chips are down for good, and his life is now permanently committed to a career which is almost devoid of security of any kind, whether financial or scientific. This moment occurs in the life of almost every young scientist. It is a turning point of acute danger to the mental health of many.

One further careeristic hazard is probably the most threatening of all. For every successful piece of research which yields positive results and for which the scientist therefore receives recognition, advancement, and an increased measure of security, there are, and always must be, hundreds of negative experiments, experiments which merely prove that something is *not* so. These negative experiments clear the road for the steady advance of science, but at the same time they clear the road for the more glamorous successes of other scientists, who may have used no greater intelligence, skill or devotion, and perhaps even less. Indeed, which scientist must content himself with the oblivion of the negative result, and which one will win acclaim for positive results may be largely a matter of accidental timing. Essential new techniques or new facts derived from some other scientific discipline may have been one year away, or ten, or fifty. As in prospecting for gold, a scientist may dig with skill, courage, energy, and intelligence just a few feet away from a rich vein—but always unsuccessfully. Consequently in scientific research the rewards for industry, perseverance, imagination, and intelligence are highly uncertain. Success or failure, whether in specific investigations or in an entire career, may be almost accidental, with chance a major factor in determining not *what* is discovered, but when and by whom.[6]

Evidently the rewards of a career in science are slow and also uncertain; bad luck can frustrate a lifetime of sacrifice and ability. Every successful scientific career is an unmarked gravestone over the lives of hundreds of equally able and devoted, but obscure and less fortunate, anonymous investigators. Science too has its "expendables"; but these do not earn security or tenure, or veteran's pensions—not even the honors which accrue to the expendable soldiers of war.

This is the ultimate gamble which the scientist takes, when he stakes his all on professional achievement and recognition, sacrificing to his scientific career recreation, family, and sometimes even his instinctual needs, as well as the practical security of money. Yet young students are not warned that their future success may be determined by forces which are outside of their own creative capacity or their willingness to work hard. This situation tends to create a star system in science, not unlike that of the stage; and it is not surprising that the mental illnesses which occur in the two types of careers should have so many points in common.

Furthermore, with the growing complexity of science, the psychological difficulties of the scientist have increased in special ways. In another connection, we have noted that the lengthening of the training period holds young adults in the relatively juvenile and dependent role of student for added years. However, we did not state the fact that this protracted quasi-adolescence also stirs tides of conscious and unconscious rebellion, thus creating internal conflicts in the young scientist's mind as well as external conflicts directed against the "system" and its growing pressures. This lengthening period of subordination, insecurity, and rebellion creates a wholly new group of intense moral conflicts for the young scientist. Scientific research is conducted largely behind closed doors, and the accuracy of any man's observations and the veracity of his reports depend ultimately upon his honesty. This honesty depends in turn upon maturity, upon some degree of security, and upon a sense of identification and fellowship with competitors. Under present conditions it is a tribute to scientists that violations of their code of honor are so rare that when lapses occur they become historic scandals. This issue is especially delicate in such fields of science as psychology, psychiatry, and psychoanalysis, in which it is difficult to repeat another man's observations for purposes of objective clinical or experimental or statistical confirmation. Consequently in these disciplines, reports of observations become themselves sources of controversy and suspicion. For many reasons I suspect (although I cannot prove this) that we may be seeing today the birth of a new psychosocial ailment among scientists, one which may not be wholly unrelated to the gangster tradition of dead-end kids.

Are we witnessing the development of a generation of hardened, cynical, amoral, embittered, disillusioned, young scientists? If so, for the present the fashioning of implements of destruction offers a convenient outlet for their destructive feelings; but the fault will be ours and not theirs if this tendency should increase through the coming years and should find even more disastrous channels of expression.

Certainly the idyllic picture of the innocent, childlike scientist who lives a life of simple, secure, peaceful, dignified contemplation has become an unreal fantasy. Instead, the emotional stresses of his career have increased to a point where only men of exceptional emotional maturity and stability can stand up to them for long, and remain clear-headed and generous-hearted under such psychologically unhygienic conditions. Thoughtful educators are beginning to realize that the socio-economic basis of the life of the scientist must be entirely overhauled; that the psychological setting of his life needs drastic revision; and that at the same time the emotional preparation for a life of research is at least as important as is the intellectual training.

I have offered a partial diagnosis with no ready corrective. For this I make no apologies. Medicine is proud of the fact that it has had the honesty and the humility to diagnose disease, sometimes for generations, before it could offer a cure. Students of educational, sociological, political, and economic problems would do well to emulate the medical sciences in this humility, instead of feeling that they must immediately suggest a cure, as soon as they recognize the fact that something is amiss.

It is also a fact that in this paper I have described the general nature of problems before they have been studied in detail. For this, as well, I offer no apology; because as I have indicated above, until educators awake to the importance of these problems, it will not be possible to finance, staff, or implement an adequate investigation of them. This paper will have served its major purpose, if it contributes to that awakening.

References

1. Bernard, Claude. *An Introduction to the Study of Experimental Medicine.* Translated by H. C. Greene. New York: The Macmillan Co., 1927.

2. Gregg, Alan. *The Furtherance of Medical Research.* New Haven: Yale University Press, 1941.

3. Jones, Ernest. "The Problem of Paul Morphy—A Contribution to the Psychoanalysis of Chess," *International Journal of Psychoanalysis,* XII (January, 1931), 1-23. Reprinted in *Essays in Applied Psychoanalysis* Vol. I, by E. Jones. London: Hogarth Press and the Institute of Psychoanalysis, 1951, pp. 165-96.

4. Kubie, Lawrence S. "The Problem of Maturity in Psychiatric Research," *Journal of Medical Education* XXVIII (October, 1953).

5. Lombard, George F. F. "Self-Awareness and Scientific Method," *Science,* CXII, (September 15, 1950), 289-93.

6. Osler, Sir William. *The Evolution of Modern Medicine.* New Haven: Yale University Press, 1923.

7. Richet, Charles. *Natural History of a Savant.* Translated by Sir Oliver Lodge. London & Toronto: J. M. Dent & Sons, Ltd., 1927.

8. Roe, Anne. (*a*) "Psychological Tests of Research Scientists," *Journal of Consulting Psychologists,* XV (1951), 492-95. (*b*) "A Study of Imagery in Research Scientists," *Journal of Personality,* XIX (1951), 459-70. (*c*) "A Psychological Study of Eminent Biologists," *Psychol. Monograph No. 331* (1951). (*d*) "Group Rorschachs of University Faculties," *Journal of Consulting Psychologists,* XVII (1952), 18-22. (*e*) "Analysis of Group Rorschachs of Psychologists and Anthropologists," *Journal of Projective Techniques,* XVI (1951), 212-24.

9. Tolman, Richard C. "Physical Science and Philosophy," *The Scientific Monthly,* LVII (August, 1943), 166-74.

b.

THE POLITICAL ESTRANGEMENT

FRANZ NEUMANN

Anxiety and Politics*

ON JANUARY 6, 1941, President Franklin D. Roosevelt proclaimed the Four Freedoms: Freedom of Speech, Freedom of Religion, Freedom from Want, and *Freedom from Fear*. But with the end of the second World War anxiety has not disappeared from the world. On the contrary, it has become even greater and more frightful; it has begun to paralyze nations and to make men incapable of free decisions.[1]

Anxiety is, or ought to be, a central problem of the sciences. Anxiety impairs the freedom of decision, indeed it may make such freedom impossible—only a fearless man can decide freely. The discussion of the problem of anxiety should be open to all the disciplines, not reserved to any one of them, for the great concern of science is the analysis and application of the concept of human freedom.

My task today is to discuss the problem of anxiety in politics, a task which is confronted with many obstacles. In contrast to the traditional disciplines, the science of politics has no method of its own—it has, in the last analysis, only a focus, namely, the dialectical relation between domination and freedom. In other words, the science of politics revolves solely around a problem and uses all kinds of methods to attack this problem. However, with this approach the political scientist runs the danger of

---

* Originally delivered as a lecture before the Free University of Berlin and published in the Series "Recht und Staat," Tübingen, 1954. Translated by Professor Peter Gay.

dilettantism, a danger which he can avoid only by being conscious of his limitations and by giving a hearing to authorities from other disciplines. Thus his contribution will often consist merely in a synthesis of the results of research or perhaps in a felicitous hypothesis.

But a second, even greater obstacle consists in the inadequate state of the discussion of anxiety in psychological literature. If I rely extensively on Freud in what follows I do so not because I accept his therapeutic method—of that I understand nothing—but because his theoretical insights seem to me convincing and not refuted up to now.

My lecture will have to take a position on many questions which have not yet been clarified, and it is my hope that it will move other and more competent scholars to analyze the problems I have raised.

Alienation

1) In his Letters "Ueber die aesthetische Erziehung des Menschen," Schiller has magnificently described man in modern society.[2] "Man portrays himself," he writes, "and what a form is presented in the drama of the modern age? Barrenness here, license there; the two extremes of human decay, and both united in a single period."[3] As Rousseau did before him, Schiller indicts civilization itself: "It was culture itself which inflicted this wound on modern humanity."[4] And this wound was inflicted on man by the division of labor: "Gratification is separated from labor, means from ends, effort from reward. Eternally *fettered* only to a single little fragment of the whole, man fashions himself only as a fragment. . . ."[5] His indictment of modern society reaches its climax in the characterization of love: "So jealous is the state for the sole possession of its servants that it would sooner agree (and who could blame it?) to share them with a Venus Cytherea than with a Venus Urania."[6] Schiller has, of course, taken the two forms of the goddess of love from Plato's Symposium and thus identifies Venus Cytherea with venal but Urania with genuine love.

What Schiller describes so impressively is what Hegel and Marx were to characterize as alienation.[7] Schiller contrasts the "polypus nature" of the Greek states, "where each individual enjoyed an independent existence and. if necessary, could become a whole,"[8] with modern society which is one of hierarchical division of labor.[9] Modern society produces a fragmentation not only of social functions but of man himself who, as it were, keeps his different faculties in different pigeonholes—love, labor, leisure, culture—that are somehow held together by an externally operating mechanism that is neither comprehended nor comprehensible. One may—as I do—consider Schiller's (as also Hegel's) analysis of the Greek state as strongly unrealistic and one may, perhaps, even see certain dangers in the glorification of Greece;[10] nevertheless, his analysis of modern man, pointing far beyond his age, remains valid and it is perhaps only today that we have become fully conscious of how true Schiller's Letters are.

2) In his *Theologische Jugendschriften*,[11] Hegel developed for the first time the concept of alienation. In his draft, entitled "Love,"[12] he defined love as the "whole," as "a feeling, but not a single feeling." "In it, life finds itself, as a duplication of its self, and as its unity." But this love is frequently shattered by the resistance of the outside world, the social world of property, a world indeed which man has created through his own labor and knowledge but which has become an alien, a dead world through property. Man is alienated from himself. Since we are here not concerned with the Hegelian concept of alienation, we may pass over the development of his concept.[13]

It is equally unnecessary for us here to develop fully Marx's concept of alienation.[14] For Marx it is the commodity that determines human activity, that is, the objects which are supposed to serve man become the tyrant of man. For according to Marx, who thus fully agrees with Schiller, Hegel, and Feuerbach, man is a universal being. Man is free if he "recognizes himself in a world he has himself made."[15] But that does not happen. Since "alienating labor (1) alienates man from nature, (2) alienates him from himself, his own active function, his life's activity, it alienates man from his species."[16] The separation of labor from the object is thus for him a threefold one: man is alienated from external nature, from himself, and from his fellow-men. The relations of men to one another are reified: personal relations appear as objective relations between things (commodities).

Man, (not only the worker, since the process of alienation affects society as a whole)[17] is thus for Marx as for Schiller, Feuerbach, and Hegel, a mutilated man.

3) But these theories of alienation are not adequate. While the principles developed by Hegel and Marx must not be given up, these theories need supplementation and deepening. Their inadequacy consists in this, that they oppose universal or nearly universal man (of ancient Greece in Schiller and Hegel) to the mutilated man of the modern world.[18] But there is no historical form of society in which men have ever existed as universal beings; for slavery is not compatible with universality. My meaning may, perhaps, become clearer if I distinguish three strata of alienation: the stratum of psychology; that of society; and that of politics.

We can get at the problem of alienation, and thus of anxiety in politics, only if we start with a clean separation of the three strata and concepts, in order later to bring them together again. Neither alienation nor anxiety is to be found only in modern society and only in modern man, although the different structures of society and of the state modify the forms of expression which alienation and anxiety take. The modifications are hard to determine, and I shall not attempt here to undertake a systematic analysis. But I shall try to point up the problem and to make the theory somewhat more concrete by means of (more or less arbitrary) examples.

Alienation and Anxiety

1) Freud's thesis in his *Civilization and its Discontents* is this: "The goal towards which the pleasure-principle impels us—of becoming happy—is not attainable;"[19] because for Freud suffering springs from three sources: external nature, which we can never dominate completely, the susceptibility to illness and the mortality of the body, and social institutions.[20]

However, the statement that society prevents happiness, and consequently that every socio-political institution is repressive, does not lead to hostility toward civilization. For the limitation, which is imposed upon the libidinal as well as the destructive instincts, creates conflicts, inescapable conflicts, which are the very motors of progress in history. But conflicts deepen with the progress of civilization, for Freud states that increasing technical progress, which in itself ought to make possible a greater measure of instinct gratification, fails to do so. There arises here a psychological lag that grows ever wider—a formulation that I should like to borrow from the "cultural lag" of American sociology.

Thus, every society is built upon the renunciation of instinctual gratifications.[21] Freud finds that it is "not easy to understand how it can become possible to withhold satisfaction from an instinct. Nor is it by any means without risk to do so; if the deprivation is not made good economically, one can be certain of producing serious disorders."[22]

To be sure, according to Freud it is conceivable "that a civilized community could consist of pairs of individuals (who love each other) libidinally satisfied in each other, and linked to all the others by work and common interests. If this were so, culture would not need to levy energy from sexuality."[23] But the opposite is true and has always been true. For at bottom Freud does not believe in this "conceivable ideal." The differences between the different forms of society—which are decisive for us—do not play a decisive role for him.[24] The renunciation of instinctual gratification and the cultural tendency toward the limitation of love operate at all levels of society. It is these renunciations and limitations which we characterize as psychological alienation of man, or perhaps even better as alienation of the ego from the dynamics of instinct.

2) Still another preparatory step is necessary: we have to establish the logical connection between alienation and anxiety. This is extremely

difficult because the discussion of the problem of anxiety has by no means reached the clarity which would make it possible for an outsider—like myself—to adopt an unambiguous position toward the various opinions.[25] Nevertheless it seems to me that the differences in the conception of the origin of anxiety do not have a decisive significance for my analysis, although they are, of course, highly relevant in other contexts. Freud himself had originally derived anxiety from the repression of libidinous impulses, and thus had seen it as an automatic transformation of instinctual energy.[26] This view he later modified.[27] Others claim, on the other hand, that there is a single inborn faculty for being afraid.[28] Rank, in his famous work,[29] derives anxiety from the trauma of birth. And a number of analysts have tried, more or less successfully, to combine the various theories in many ways.[30]

The following propositions seem to me more or less acceptable.

One must distinguish between true anxiety (*Realangst*) and neurotic anxiety. The difference is of considerable consequence especially for the understanding of the political importance of anxiety. The first—true anxiety—thus appears as a reaction to concrete danger situations;[31] the second—neurotic anxiety—is produced by the ego, in order to avoid in advance even the remotest threat of danger. True anxiety is thus produced through the threat of an external object; neurotic anxiety, which may have a real basis,[32] on the other hand is produced from within, through the ego.

Since anxiety is produced by the ego, the seat of anxiety is in the ego, not in the id—the structure of instincts. But from the analysis of the problem of psychological alienation it follows necessarily that anxiety, feelings of guilt, and the need for self-punishment are responses to internal threats to basic instinctual demands[33] so that anxiety exists as a permanent condition. The external dangers which threaten a man meet the inner anxiety[34] and are thus frequently experienced as even more dangerous than they really are. At the same time, these same external dangers intensify the inner anxiety. The painful tension which is evoked by the combination of inner anxiety and external danger can express itself in either of two forms:[35] in depressive or in persecutory anxiety. The differentiation is important because it helps us to evaluate the political function of anxiety more correctly.

In the history of the individual there are certain typical dangers which produce anxiety. For the child, the withdrawal of love is of decisive importance. On this point there seems to be no doubt among psychologists.[36] From the numerous phobias we may learn a great deal about the relation between anxiety and the renunciation of instinctual gratification. For inhibitions are a functional restraint of the ego; the ego renounces many activities in order to avoid a conflict with the id and the conscience.

We know that the phobic symptoms are a substitute for gratifications of the instincts that have been denied or are unattainable. In other words, the ego creates anxiety through repression.

3) If I have correctly reproduced the most important results of analytical theory concerning the origin of anxiety, several important consequences for the analysis of political behavior seem to follow immediately. Anxiety can play very different roles in the life of men; that is, the activation of a state of anxiety through a danger can have a beneficial as well as destructive effect. We may perhaps distinguish three different consequences:

a) Anxiety can play a warning role, a kind of mentor role, for man. Affective anxiety may allow a presentiment of external dangers. Thus, anxiety also contains a protective function[37] for it permits man to take precautions in order to ward off the danger.

b) Anxiety can have a destructive effect, especially when the neurotic element is strongly present; that is, it can make man incapable of collecting himself either to escape the danger or to fight against it; it can paralyze man and degenerate into a panicky anxiety.

c) Finally, anxiety can have a cathartic effect;[38] man can be strengthened inwardly when he has successfully avoided a danger or when he has prevailed against it. One may perhaps even say (although I cannot prove this) that the man who has conquered anxiety in coming to terms with a danger, may be more capable of making decisions in freedom than the one who never had to seriously wrestle with a danger. This may be an important qualification of the proposition that anxiety can make free decision impossible.

Anxiety and Identification

Our analysis of the relation of alienation to anxiety does not yet permit us to understand the political significance of these phenomena, because it is still in the realm of individual psychology.[39] How does it happen that masses sell their souls to leaders and follow them blindly? On what does the power of attraction of leaders over masses rest? What are the historical situations in which this identification of leader and masses is successful, and what view of history do the men have who accept leaders?

1) Thus the question concerning the essence of identification of masses and a leader stands in the center of group-psychological analysis. Without it the problem of the integration or collectivization of the individual in a mass cannot be understood. I assume that the history of the theories of group psychology is familiar.[40] The extraordinary difficulty in the comprehension of group-psychological phenomena lies first of all in our own prejudices; for the experiences of the last decades have

instilled in us all more or less strong prejudices against the masses, and we associate with "masses" the epithet "mob," a group of men who are capable of every atrocity. In fact the science of group psychology began with this aristocratic prejudice in the work of the Italian Scipio Sighele,[41] and Le Bon's famous book[42] is completely in this tradition. His theses are familiar. Man in the mass descends; he is, as it were, hypnotized by the leader (*operateur*) and in this condition is capable of committing acts which he would never commit as an individual. As the slave of unconscious—i.e., for Le Bon, regressive—sentiments, man in the mass is degraded into a barbarian: "Isolated, he may be a cultivated individual; in a crowd, he is a barbarian—that is, a creature acting by instinct. He possesses the spontaneity, the violence, the ferocity, and also the enthusiasm and heroism of primitive beings."[43] Critics of Le Bon, among them Freud,[44] have pointed out that his theory, which rests on Sighele and Tarde, is inadequate in two aspects: the answer to the question, What holds the masses together? is inadequate, for the existence of a "racial soul"[45] is unproved. In addition, in Le Bon the decisive problem—the role of the leader-hypnotist—remains unclarified.[46] As is frequently true in social-psychological studies, the descriptions of psychological states are adequate, the theoretical analyses, the answers to "Why?," are inadequate.[47]

2) From the outset, Freud sees the problem in the way in which we have put it, namely, as that of the identification of masses with a leader—an identification which becomes of decisive significance particularly in an anxiety situation. And he sees in the libido the cement which holds leader and masses together, whereby, as is known, the concept of libido is to be taken in a very broad sense, to include the instinctual activities which "in relations between the sexes . . . force their way toward sexual union," as well as those which "in other circumstances . . . are diverted from this aim or are prevented from reaching it, though always preserving enough of their original nature to keep their identity recognizable (as in such features as the longings for proximity, and self-sacrifice)."[48]

The cement which holds the mass together and ties them to the leader is thus a sum of instincts that are inhibited in their aims.[49] In this manner, I believe, the logical connection between alienation and mass behavior has been established.

Since the identification of masses with the leader is an alienation of the individual member, identification always constitutes a regression, and a twofold one. On the one hand, the history of man is the history of his emergence from the primal horde and of his progressive individualization; thus the identification with a leader in a mass is a kind of *historical* regression.[50] This identification is also a "substitute for a libidinal object tie,"[51] thus a *psychological* regression, a damaging of the ego, perhaps even the loss of the ego.

3) But this judgment is valid only for the libido-charged, i.e., affective, identification of an individual in a mass with a leader; and not as a matter of course (and perhaps not at all) for that of lovers and of small groups. Non-affective identification too, cannot be simply considered as regressive. For identification with organizations (church, army) is not always libidinally charged. MacDougall's emphasis on the significance of organization must therefore be taken seriously.

It is thus necessary to make distinctions. There are non-affective identifications, in which coercion or common material interests play an essential role, either in bureaucratic-hierarchic, or in co-operative form. It seems to me to be incorrect, above all for recent history, to see in the identification of the soldier with the army, i.e., in the loyalty to an organization, an actual identification of the soldier with the commander-in-chief. Surely there are examples of this: Alexander, Hannibal, Caesar, Wallenstein, Napoleon. But the commander-in-chief of the twentieth century is much more the technician of war than the leader of men, and the libidinal tie of the soldier is, if I may coin the phrase, essentially co-operative, namely, with the smallest group of comrades with whom he shares dangers.

Thus I would like to establish two fundamental types of identification: a libido-charged (affective) and a libido-free (non-affective); and maintain generally (as it follows from MacDougall's psychology) that the non-affective identification with an organization is less regressive than the affective identification with a leader. Non-affective loyalty is transferable;[52] personal loyalty, on the other hand, is not. The former always contains strong rationalist elements, elements of calculability between organization and individual, and thus prevents the total extinction of the ego.[53]

But I believe that one must also distinguish two types within affective identification. One may call them co-operative and caesaristic. It is conceivable (and it has probably happened in short periods in history) that many equals identify themselves co-operatively with one another in such a manner that their egos are merged in the collective ego.[54] But this co-operative form is rare, limited to short periods or in any case operative only for small groups. The decisive affective identification is that of masses with leaders. It is—as I have said—the most regressive form, for it is built upon a nearly total ego-shrinkage. It is the form which is of decisive significance for us. We call it caesaristic identification.[55]

Caesaristic Identification and False Concreteness: The Conspiracy Theory in History

Caesaristic identifications may play a role in history when the situation of masses is objectively endangered, when the masses are incapable of understanding the historical process, and when the anxiety activated by the danger becomes neurotic persecutory (aggressive) anxiety through manipulation.

From this follows, first of all, that not every situation dangerous to masses must lead to a caesaristic movement; it follows, further, that not every mass movement is based on anxiety, and thus not every mass movement need be caesaristic.

Thus it is a question of determining the historical conditions in which a regressive movement under a Caesar tries to win political power.

1) However, before we describe these historical situations, I may perhaps point to a clue which will frequently permit us an early diagnosis of the regressive character of such a mass movement. This clue is the view of history which the masses and the leaders employ. It may be called the conspiracy theory of history, a theory of history characterized by a false concreteness. The connection between caesarism and this view of history is quite evident. Just as the masses hope for their deliverance from distress through absolute oneness with a person, so they ascribe their distress to certain persons, who have brought this distress into the world through a conspiracy. The historical process is personified in this manner. Hatred, resentment, dread, created by great upheavals, are concentrated on certain persons who are denounced as devilish conspirators. Nothing would be more incorrect than to characterize the enemies as scapegoats (as often happens in the literature), for they appear as genuine enemies whom one must extirpate and not as substitutes whom one only needs to send into the wilderness. It is a false concreteness and therefore an especially dangerous view of history. Indeed, the danger consists in the fact that this view of history is never completely false, but always contains a kernel of truth and, indeed, must contain it, if it is to have a convincing effect. The truer it is, one might say, the less regressive the movement; the falser, the more regressive.

It is my thesis that wherever affective (i.e., caesaristic) leader-identifications occur in politics, masses and leader have this view of history: that the distress which has befallen the masses has been brought about exclusively by a conspiracy of certain persons or groups against the people.

With this view of history, true anxiety, which had been produced by war, want, hunger, anarchy, is to be transformed into neurotic anxiety and is to be overcome by means of identification with the leader-demagogue through total ego-renunciation, to the advantage of the leader and his clique, whose true interests do not necessarily have to correspond to those of the masses.

Of course, I cannot provide conclusive proof, but I believe that by pointing to certain historical events I can make clear the connection between this view of history and caesarism.

2) An interesting affective identification of leader and masses is the relation of Cola di Rienzo to the Roman people.[56] I assume that his story is familiar—the rise of the hack lawyer, son of a Roman innkeeper and a washerwoman, to Tribune of the Roman people and dictator of Rome, his expulsion and return with the aid of the Church, and his assassination by the Colonna family in the year 1354. The view of history of Cola and of the Roman people was quite simple: Rome has been ruined by feudal lords; their destruction will permit Rome to rise again to its ancient greatness. This is how Petrarca formulates it in his famous letter of congratulation to Cola: "These barons in whose defense you (the Romans) have so often shed your blood, whom you have nourished with your own substance . . . these barons have judged you unworthy of liberty. They have gathered the mangled remnants of the state in the caverns and abominable retreats of bandits. . . . They have been restrained neither by pity for their unhappy country, nor by love for it. . . . Do not suffer any of the rapacious wolves whom you have driven from the fold to rush again into your midst. Even now they are prowling restlessly around, endeavoring through fraud and deceit . . . to regain an entrance to the city whence they were violently expelled."[57] It cannot be denied that the feudal lords, above all the Colonna and Orsini, had pursued a criminal policy. Without this element of truth Cola's propaganda and policy would never have been successful. But fundamentally this was a false concreteness—for even if he had succeeded in liquidating the barons, what would have been decisively improved in Rome? The historical facts—the residence of the Papal Court in Avignon; the economic decay of Rome; the regrouping of class relations through the rise of the bourgeois *cavalerotti*—all that Cola could not change. It can hardly be doubted that anxiety, even purely physical fear of the arbitrariness of the barons, drove the people to Cola. Cola succeeded in strengthening this anxiety by extremely skillful propaganda and achieved victory. But the leader himself must feel no anxiety or at least must not show it.[58] He must stand above the masses. But in this Cola was deficient. In all other matters his relation corresponded exactly to that of the libido-charged identification leader-masses, and it is re-

grettable that time does not permit me to describe and analyze his propaganda themes, his ceremonial, and his ritual. It was Cola's fundamental mistake that he was not enough of a Caesar. To be sure, he publicly humiliated the barons, but he did not liquidate them—whether out of cowardice, decency, or tactical considerations. But the masses of Rome expected that he would act in accordance with their view of history. He did not do this. Thus he had to fall.

I have mentioned Cola di Rienzo because it is a marginal case in which it is doubtful whether we are dealing with a regressive or a progressive movement, that is, a movement which really has the realization of the freedom of man as its goal.

3) The eight French religious wars of the sixteenth century furnish excellent material for the illumination of the character of caesaristic as well as organizational identifications. All three parties—Huguenots, Catholics, and *Politiques*—were faced with grave problems: the disintegration of the old society through silver inflation, loss of wealth on the one hand, enrichment on the other, the beginnings of radical changes in class relations and the dissolution of the absolute monarchy after the death of Francis I. It is against this background that the religious wars must be understood. Their course is doubtless familiar to you.

Catholics and Protestants alike saw the problem of France only as a religious problem, and therefore ascribed the distress of France exclusively to their religious opponents, conjectured (partly justifiably) that these opponents represented a great and sinister conspiracy, developed or employed theories of caesaristic identification, and consistently proceeded to extirpate the opponent wherever opportunity offered.

The Huguenot pamphleteer Francois Hotman in his *Tiger*[59] saw in the Cardinal Guise "a detestable monster," whose aim it was to ruin France, to assassinate the King, and to conspire with the aid of the women near the King and the High Constable of France against "the crown of France, the goods of widows and orphans, the blood of the poor and innocent." Calvin's theory of the secular redeemer sent by God to overthrow tyrants,[60]—in the seventeenth century the basis of Cromwell's leadership—became the Protestant theory of Caesarism.[61] The Catholics —with a longer tradition of tyrannicide—developed a pseudo-democratic theory of identification, above all in the writings of the Leaguist preachers and Jesuits.[62] In these inflammatory pamphlets whose demagogy even surpasses that of the Huguenots, the theory of democracy is fitted out with theocratic traits, the masses of the people are integrated through the social contract, in order to be identified with Henry of Guise with the aid of the theocratic element. Whoever takes the trouble to study the eighth religious war (the War of the 3 Henrys) and the Parisian uprising, will find there all the elements which I consider decisive: appeal to anxiety, personification of evils, first with Henry III, then with Henry of Navarre, identification of the masses with Henry of Guise.

Both positions, the Catholic and the Huguenot, are similarly regressive, while that of the *Politiques,* which Henry IV was later to convert into action, is incomparably more progressive. Indeed, the great merit of the chief representative of the party of the *Politiques,* Jean Bodin, consists in this: he saw the economic problems of France clearly;[63] he understood the false concreteness of the view of history of both parties. If he championed absolute monarchy—that is, the identification of the people with the monarch—he did so because the monarch was to place himself above the religions that were fighting each other[64] and to ally himself with the households[65] of the third estate in order to save France. Despite the absolute submission to the prince which is demanded of the people, this identification contains the two rational elements which I mentioned before: loyalty becomes transferable, i.e., the office is separated from the officeholder; and the relation between citizen and state becomes rational. Thus Bodin has a certain justification in calling his theory a theory of the constitutional state (*droit gouvernement*)[66] despite his absolutism. I believe that the French religious wars of the sixteenth century make my thesis a little clearer: that the non-affective identification with an institution (state) is less regressive than identification with a leader.

4) Naturally I cannot here discuss all similar situations. The religious struggles of the sixteenth and seventeenth centuries are full of such historical constructions.

One need only read, for example, the terrible Calvinist fanatic John Knox in his famous *First Blast of the Trumpet against the Monstrous Regiment of Women* and we will find there: "We se our countrie set furthe for a pray to foreine nations, we heare the blood of our brethren, the membres of Christ Iesus most cruelly to be shed, and the monstruous empire of a cruell woman . . . we knowe to be the onlie occasion of all these miseries."[67] The rule of the Catholic Catherine de Medici, of Marie of Lorraine (the predecessor of Mary Stuart), and of Mary Tudor appears here not only as a violation of divine commandment (because God has subjected women to men) but as a genuine conspiracy against the true religion. Unfortunately, John Knox had the ill luck of seeing Protestantism restored in England by a woman, and he apologized to Elizabeth in a *Second Blast*[68] for his first attack.

5) Instead of continuing with this survey, it may perhaps be more useful to discuss five fundamental models of conspiracy theories, all of which show this sequence: intensification of anxiety through manipulation, identification, false concreteness. They are:

a) the Jesuit conspiracy
b) the Freemason conspiracy
c) the Communist conspiracy
d) the Capitalist conspiracy
e) the Jewish conspiracy.

6) The *Jesuit order*[69] is indeed defined by many as a conspiracy, and the Monita Secreta of 1614,[70] composed by a Polish ex-Jesuit, fulfill the need for a secret plan of operations with the help of which one can hold the order responsible for every crime and every misfortune and can stir up the masses. This has always been relatively simple in times of crisis. St. Bartholomew's Night, the assassination of Henry III by Jacques Clément, the attempt on the life of Henry IV by Barrière and Chastel as well as his assassination by Ravaignac, the English Gunpowder plot of 1605, the outbreak of the Thirty Years' War, to say nothing of innumerable less important crimes and misfortunes, were ascribed to the Jesuits. That these tales should have been believed, is naturally connected with the significance of false concreteness in politics. There is some truth in many of these accusations. It is precisely in this element of truth that the danger of these views of history lies.

7) The denunciation of the freemasons is a similar mattter. Thus, the English believed the Jacobite conspiracies to be the work of freemasons; the French Revolution was ascribed to a mysterious group of Bavarian Illuminati,[71] and this view of history again is closely connected with the anti-Jesuit one, since the Bavarian Illuminati had been founded by Adam Weishaupt in 1776, in order to combat the influence of the Jesuits.[72] Again these assertions have some truth in them. Most of the Encyclopedists were freemasons and more than half of the members of the Estates General belonged to freemasonic lodges. But in this audience surely no detailed discussion is needed to show that the conspiracy theory represents a blurring of history.[73]

8) The theory of the *Communist conspiracy* follows the same model and serves the same purposes. Thus the Russian October Revolution is explained solely as a Blanquist conspiracy,[74] embodied in Trotsky's military revolutionary committee; the German Revolution of 1918 is laid to the charge of the devilish Lenin; the seizure of power by the Bolsheviks in the satellite states is traced back to sinister conspiracies in the Kremlin, and generally the relation of Bolshevism to the world is equated with that of a conspiracy of a small group against the welfare of humanity. Again, this is partly true. The October Revolution was a conspiracy—but in a definite historical situation and with an ideology. The Bolsheviks would gladly have manipulated the German Revolution of 1918—but they had neither the means nor the intelligence to do it, nor could they, even if cleverer, have prevailed in the concrete situation. The Communists in

the satellite states naturally conspired—but they could come to power only because the Red Army stood behind them and because the objective situation favored them. No conspiracy, no matter how clever, would have been of any use and was of any use in Western Europe. Nevertheless, the conspiracy theory is believed not only by the masses, but even by serious writers who, strongly under the influence of Pareto's simplistic antithesis between elite and masses, generally tend to see in politics nothing but the manipulation of the masses by elites, and for whom psychology and political science are nothing but techniques of manipulation.

The purpose of the theory is clear: potential anxiety—whose concrete significance still needs to be clarified—is actualized by reference to the devilish conspirators: family, property, morality, religion are threatened by the conspiracy. Anxiety easily becomes neurotic persecutory anxiety, which in turn can, under certain circumstances, lead to a totalitarian mass movement.

9) We could cite a great many more cases in which history was viewed with false concreteness. Especially American history is full of examples of such movements. There is, for instance, the Know-Nothing Party of 1854-55 with its hatred of the Irish Catholics and the German immigrants. It originated in the secret "Order of the Star-Spangled-Banner" which was founded by native-born Protestants; they mistreated Catholics and when asked about the Order they would answer, "I know nothing."

The Ku Klux Klan is better known. Fear of status loss on the part of the whites, especially of the poor whites, vis-à-vis the Negroes and fear of the Pope and the Catholics were the basic factors which made this secret society into a terroristic organization, from its foundation in 1867 to the present day.

The Populist Party (1892), on the other hand, was born out of an agrarian depression, as a protest against the rule of the railway, industrial, and credit monopolies, and against the gold standard. One of its leaders developed a genuine theory of conspiracy: "According to my views of the subject the conspiracy which seems to have been formed here and in Europe to destroy . . . from three-sevenths to one-half of the metallic money of the world, is the most gigantic crime of this or any other age." (Quoted in S. E. Morrison and H. S. Commager, *The Growth of the American Republic*, Vol. II [1940], p. 245.)

10) In similar fashion, Bolshevism operates with the *theory of capitalist encirclement,* in which the capitalists as a rule are personified by Wall Street. Now again there can be no doubt that there was a policy of encirclement against Bolshevist Russia at the beginning of the revolution; but it would be fatal to believe that the terror was the consequence of the policy of intervention and of the cold war. Possibly the policy of encirclement strengthened the terror, just as the wars of intervention

during the French Revolution gave Robespierre's Terror a new impetus.[75] But the terror as a normal method of politics against the class opponent is contained in the Leninist definition of the dictatorship of the proletariat; it was then extended to the party and finally to the supposedly classless society, without a visible connection with the intensity of the capitalist policy of encirclement. But the Bolshevist view of history, steadily activating anxiety, made possible identification with the leader Stalin and thus underpinned his caesarist dictatorship.

11) The most important type—if only because of its immense political influence—is the theory of the *conspiracy of the Jews* according to the *Protocols of the Elders of Zion*.[76] These contain the secret plans of Jewish leaders, supposedly formulated in the year 1897, for achieving Jewish world domination by force, terror, corruption, the disintegrating influence of liberalism, freemasonry, etc. This world domination was to be a mock-democracy, through which the Jewish leaders were to operate. That the *Protocols* are a forgery, prepared by Czarist Russians, was definitely established by the Bern trial of 1934-35.[77] It is equally beyond question that they are essentially a plagiarism of the work by Maurice Joly directed against Napoleon III, *Dialogue aux Enfers entre Machiavel et Montesquieu*.[78]

But if the *Protocols* represent a forgery, and if the plans for a Jewish world conspiracy belong in the realm of mythology, where then does that kernel of truth lie which according to my view is necessary to make possible the influence which anti-Semitism and the *Protocols* have had?[79] I shall confine my analysis to Germany, but the German situation can be understood only when one becomes aware of the fact that in Germany before 1933 spontaneous anti-Semitism was extremely weak. As early as 1942, I wrote, in opposition to an almost unanimous opinion: "The writer's personal conviction, paradoxical as it may seem, is that the German people are the least anti-Semitic of all."[80] I still hold to this view today; for it is precisely the weakness of spontaneous anti-Semitism in Germany which explains the concentration of National Socialism on it as the decisive political weapon.

The element of truth (if one may call it that) is first of all a religious one: the catechistic representation of the crucifixion and with it the blood guilt of the Jews. But this is a thoroughly ambivalent element: for it is precisely the crucifixion of Christ which makes possible the salvation of Christians (and all men); and the spiritually Semitic origin of Christianity is acknowledged by the Church.[81] While thus the historical-religious defamation of the Jews forms the basis without which anti-Semitism could hardly be activated, the catechistic representation of the crucifixion is not sufficient by itself. The existence of a total anti-Semitism can perhaps be better understood if we start from the policy of National Socialism and seek to understand the role of anti-Semitism within the political system. I can sketch the problem only in its broadest outlines.[82] Germany of 1930-33 was the land of alienation and anxiety.[83] The facts are familiar: defeat, a tame, unfinished revolution, inflation, depression, non-identification with the existing political parties, non-functioning of the political system—all these are symptoms of moral, social, and political homelessness. The inability to understand why man should be so hard-pressed stimulated anxiety which was made into nearly neurotic anxiety by the National Socialist policy of terror and its propaganda of anti-Semitism. The goal of National Socialism was clear: the welding together of the people with the charismatic leader, for the purpose of the conquest of Europe and perhaps of the world, and the creation of a racial hegemony of the Germans over all other peoples.

But how was the people to be integrated, despite all cleavages of class, party, religion? Only through hatred of an enemy.[84] But how could one settle on the enemy? It could not be Bolshevism, because it was too strong; the Catholic Church could not be so designated because it was needed politically and loyalties to it were anchored too securely. The Jews remained. They appeared in the public consciousness as powerful, but were in reality weak. They were relative strangers, and at the same time the concrete symbols of a so-called parasitical capitalism, through their position in commerce and finance; they incarnated a supposedly decadent morality through their *avant garde* position in art and literature; they seemed to be the successful competitors sexually and professionally. With all this, the thesis of the Jewish conspiracy had the element of truth necessary to permit this view of history to become a frightful weapon. It would be mistaken to want to construe a connection between the socio-economic status of a person and his anti-Semitism; that is, to claim that the academically educated person is more immune than the uneducated, or the poorly paid more immune than the better paid. What is correct,[85] however, is that there exists a connection between loss of social status and anti-Semitism. The fear of social degradation thus creates for itself "a target for the discharge of the resentments arising from damaged self-esteem."[86]

This leads us to the analysis of the historical situations in which anxiety grips the masses.

Situations of Collective Anxiety, Identification, Guilt

I can treat these matters only in the form of theses because I deal with them in detail elsewhere.[87] We have distinguished three strata of alienation. The psychological stratum remains no matter what social institutions man lives in. It creates potential anxiety which man in the mass attempts to overcome through ego-surrender. This affective identification with a leader is facilitated by the notion of false concreteness, the theory of conspiracy.

But so far we have not yet said when such regressive mass movements are activated; that is, when potential anxiety can be activated in such a manner that it can become a cruel weapon in the hands of irresponsible leaders.

In order to get at this problem we must take into account the two other strata of alienation: the social and political.

1) Alienation of labor: it is the separation of labor from the product of labor through hierarchical division of labor which characterizes modern industrial society. Probably no one doubts that the division of labor as well as the hierarchical organization of labor have shown a steady rise since the industrial revolution of the eighteenth century. German romantic psychology of labor calls this the "de-spiritualization of labor" (*Entseelung der Arbeit*). This concept as well as the various remedies are dangerous—for they cover up the inevitability of this process of alienation which must be admitted, understood, and accepted. If this does not happen, if one refuses to take account of the inevitability of the division of labor and of the hierarchical ordering of the process of labor, and attempts to "spiritualize" labor instead of restricting it to a minimum, then social anxiety is deepened. The attitude of the so-called "new middle class" (salaried employees) can be understood from this process.[88]

While the so-called new middle class does labor which—to remain with the language of German psychology of labor—is "more de-spiritualized" than that of the industrial worker, and although his average income probably lies below that of the industrial worker, he yet holds fast to his middle class ideology and customs. Thus he refuses to take account of the inevitability of the process and—as in Germany before 1933—becomes the social stratum most susceptible to Caesarism.

2) In a society which is constituted by competition, the competitor is supposed to be rewarded for his effort when he is competent; that is, when he exerts himself, is intelligent, and accepts risks. There is little doubt that the principle of competition dominates not only the economy but all social relations. Karen Horney, a representative of Freudian revisionism,[89] claims that the destructive character of competition creates great anxiety in neurotic persons. Now this is not convincing when genuine competition really prevails, that is, competition in which relatively equally strong persons fight with fair methods; that is, the kind of competition which Adam Smith defines in his *Theory of Moral Sentiments* as follows: "One individual must never prefer himself so much even to any other individual as to hurt or injure that other in

order to benefit himself, though the benefit of the one should be much greater than the hurt or injury to the other."[90] And again, "In the race for wealth and honours and preferments, each may run as hard as he can and strain every nerve and every muscle in order to outstrip all his competitors. But if he jostle or throw down any of them, the indulgence of the spectator is entirely at an end. It is in violation of fair play, which they cannot admit of."[91] I cannot here undertake a social analysis to show that this ethically circumscribed competition does not exist and perhaps never has existed, that in reality a monopolist struggle hides behind it, that, in other words, the efforts of the individual, his intelligence, his vision, his readiness to take risks, are easily shattered by the constellations of power.[92]

Behind the mask of competition, which must not necessarily have destructive effects if it rationally organizes a society, there hide in fact relations of dependence. To be successful in present-day society, it is much more important to stand in well with the powerful than to preserve oneself through one's own strength. Modern man knows this. It is precisely the impotence of the individual who has to accommodate himself to the technological apparatus which is destructive and anxiety-creating.[93]

But even where genuine competition is effective, no effort will help if crises ruin the merchant. The inability to understand the process of crises, and the frequent need to ascribe blame for them to sinister powers, is an additional factor in the destruction of ego. This psychological process operated in the so-called "old middle class" of Germany before 1933. But—to repeat—it is hard to see why fair competition must have destructive functions.[94]

3) In every society that is composed of antagonistic groups there is an ascent and descent of groups. It is my contention that persecutory anxiety—but one that, as we said above, has a real basis—is produced when a group is threatened in its prestige, income, or even its existence; i.e., when it declines and does not understand the historical process or is prevented from understanding it. The examples are too numerous to be possibly mentioned here. German National Socialism and Italian Fascism are classical examples.

But not only social classes resist their degradation by means of such mass movements; religious and racial conflicts, too, frequently produce similar phenomena. The conflict between Negroes and whites in the southern states of the United States, the contemporary struggle of the South African government against the natives, take place in accord with the following scheme: the anxiety of a dominant white minority that it will be degraded through the economic and political rise of Negroes is used in propagandist fashion for the creation of affective mass movements, which frequently take on a fascist character.

4) Social alienation, i.e., the fear of social degradation, is not adequate by itself. The elements of political alienation must be added. Since I devote a separate essay to this phenomenon, I shall only point out briefly what I have in mind. As a rule one is satisfied (above all, in the American literature) with defining abstention from voting at elections as political apathy.[95] But I have pointed out elsewhere that the word "apathy" describes three different political reactions: first, the lack of interest in politics, say, the opinion that politics is not the business of the citizen because it is, after all, only a struggle between small cliques and that therefore fundamentally nothing ever changes; then, the Epicurean attitude toward politics, the view that politics and state only have to supply the element of order within which man devotes himself to his perfection, so that forms of state and of government appear as secondary matters; and finally, as the third reaction, the conscious rejection of the whole political system which expresses itself as apathy because the individual sees no possibility of changing anything in the system through his efforts. Political life can, for example, be exhausted in the competition of political parties which are purely machines without mass participation, but which monopolize politics to such an extent that a new party cannot make its way within the valid rules of the game. This third form of apathy forms the core of what I characterize as political alienation. Usually this apathy, if it operates within social alienation, leads to the partial paralysis of the state and opens the way to a caesarist movement which, scorning the rules of the game, utilizes the inability of the citizen to make individual decisions and compensates for the loss of ego with identification with a Caesar.

5) The caesaristic movement is compelled not only to activate but to institutionalize anxiety. The institutionalization of anxiety is necessary because the caesaristic movement can never endure a long wait for power. This is precisely what follows from its affective basis. While the non-affective mass organization, such as a normal political party, can exist for a long time without disintegrating, the caesarist movement must hurry precisely because of the instability of the cement that holds it together: the libido-charged affectivity. After it has come to power it faces the need of institutionalizing anxiety as a means of preventing the extinction of its affective base by its bureaucratic structure.

The techniques are familiar: propaganda and terror, i.e., the incalculability of sanctions. I do not need to discuss this here. Montesquieu, building on Aristotle and Machiavelli, distinguished between three constitutional and one tyrannical governmental and social system. According to him, monarchy rests on the honor of the monarch; aristocracy, on the moderation of the aristocrats; democracy, on virtue (i.e., with him, patriotism); but tyranny, on fear.[96] It must, however, not be overlooked

—and our introductory remarks about alienation and anxiety had no other meaning—that every political system is based on anxiety. But there is more than a quantitative difference between the anxiety which is institutionalized in a totally repressive system and that which is the basis of a halfway liberal one. These are qualitatively different states of affairs. One may perhaps say that the totally repressive system institutionalizes depressive and persecutory anxiety, the halfway liberal system, true anxiety.[97]

Once the connection between anxiety and guilt is seen, it will at once become obvious that these are different states of affairs.

In his *Peloponnesian War*, Thucydides reports the following about Sparta: "Indeed fear of their [the Helots'] numbers and obstinacy even persuaded the Lacedaemonians to the action which I shall now relate. . . . The Helots were invited by a proclamation to pick out those of their number who claimed to have most distinguished themselves against the enemy, in order that they might receive their freedom; the object being to test them, as it was thought that the first to claim their freedom would be the most high-spirited and the most apt to rebel. As many as two thousand were selected accordingly, who crowned themselves and went round the temples, rejoicing in their new freedom. The Spartans, however, soon afterwards did away with them, and no one ever knew how each of them perished."[98]

With his customary psychological penetration this greatest of all historians saw clearly the connection of anxiety and collective guilt. And then we read Plutarch's description of the terrible Cryptia,[99] the Spartan secret police: "By this ordinance, the magistrates [i.e., the Ephors] despatched privately some of the ablest of the young men into the country, from time to time, armed only with their daggers, and taking a little necessary provision with them; in the daytime, they hid themselves in out-of-the-way places, and there lay close, but in the night issued out into the highways and killed all the helots they could light upon."[100] Here is a striking example of what we have in mind.[101]

Who does not here think of Dostoyevsky's *The Possessed*, when Stavrogin gives the following piece of advice: "All that business of titles and sentimentalism is a very good cement, but there is something better; persuade four members of the circle to do for a fifth on the pretence that he is a traitor, and you'll tie them all together with the blood they've shed as though it were a knot. They'll be your slaves, they won't dare to rebel or call you to account. Ha ha ha!"[102] This famous passage in Dostoyevsky is important not only because it verifies our psychological theory, but also because it shows at the same time that the leader activates anxiety through guilt for his own advantage, not for the sake of the led.

I do not wish here to discuss the psychological theory concerning the relation of anxiety and guilt. According to Freud,[103] man's feeling of guilt stems from the Oedipus complex. It is this aggression that the child represses and thus effects an unconscious feeling of guilt. The feeling of guilt is the superego, man's conscience.[104] But that is precisely why the intensification of the unconscious feeling of guilt permits man to become a criminal.[105]

If one examines the Spartan example, Stavrogin's advice, the Fehme-murders, and the collective crimes of the SS, one may perhaps undertake the following psychological analysis:

There are anxiety and an unconscious feeling of guilt. It is the task of the leader, by creating neurotic anxiety, to tie the led so closely to the leader that they would perish without identification with him. Then the leader orders the commission of crimes; but these are, in accord with the morality that prevails in the group—with the Lacedaemonians, the Nihilists, the SS—no crimes, but fundamentally moral acts. But the conscience—the superego[106]—protests against the morality of the crimes, for the old moral convictions cannot simply be extirpated. The feeling of guilt is thus repressed and makes anxiety a nearly panicky one, which can be overcome only through unconditional surrender to the leader and compels the commission of new crimes.[107]

This is how I see the connection between anxiety and guilt in a totally repressive society. Hence this anxiety is qualitatively different from the anxiety that is the basis of every political system.

Summary

It is time to summarize the results of my analysis:

1) Psychological alienation—the alienation of the ego from the instinctual structure, or the renunciation of instinctual gratifications—is inherent in every historical society. It grows with the growth of modern industrial society, and produces anxiety. Anxiety can be protective, destructive, or cathartic.

2) Neurotic, persecutory anxiety can lead to ego-surrender in the mass through affective identification with a leader. This caesaristic identification is always regressive, historically and psychologically.

3) An important clue for the regressive character is the notion of false concreteness, the conspiracy theory of history. Its peculiar danger lies in the kernel of truth that is contained in this view of history.

4) The intensification of anxiety into persecutory anxiety is successful when a group (class, religion, race) is threatened by loss of status, without understanding the process which leads to its degradation.

5) Generally, this leads to political alienation, i.e., the conscious rejection of the rules of the game of a political system.

6) The regressive mass movement, once it has come to power must, in order to maintain the leader-identification, institutionalize anxiety. The three methods are: terror, propaganda, and, for the followers of the leader, the crime committed in common.

It is my contention that the world has become more susceptible to the growth of regressive mass movements. Perhaps not so much in Germany, because the after-effects of historical experience still work rather strongly, despite all attempts to repress the memory of National Socialism.

You will ask me, "What can be done to prevent anxiety—which cannot be eliminated—from becoming neurotic-destructive? Can the state accomplish this?" Schiller—and with this we return to our point of departure—denies this in his Seventh Letter. He asks and replies: "Should we expect this effect from the state? That is impossible, since the state, as at present constituted, has caused the evil, and the ideal state of reason cannot be the foundation of this improved humanity but must itself be founded thereon."[108]

As educators we may thus perhaps say that education deserves the first rank. But Schiller replies to this in the Ninth Letter with the question, "But are we not proceeding in a circle? Theoretical culture is supposed to induce the practical, and yet the latter is to be the condition of the former? All political improvements should result from education of character—but how can the character ennoble itself under the influence of a barbarous civil polity?"[109]

Surely there are also other individual solutions—such as love. But it is, after all, accidental whether or not one experiences it, and the risk can be enormous with loss of object.[110]

Hence there remains for us as citizens of the university and of the state the dual offensive on anxiety and for liberty: that of education and that of politics.

Politics, again, should be a dual thing for us: the penetration of the subject matter of our academic discipline with the problems of politics —naturally not day-to-day politics—and the taking of positions on political questions. If we are serious about the humanization of politics; if we wish to prevent a demagogue from using anxiety and apathy, then we—as teachers and students—must not be silent. We must suppress our arrogance, inertia, and our revulsion from the alleged dirt of day-to-day politics. We must speak and write. Idealism, as it is expressed so nobly in Schiller's Letters, must not be for us only a beautiful facade, it must not once more become that notorious form of idealism which in the past disguised the most reactionary and anti-libertarian aims.

Only through our own responsible educational and political activity can the words of idealism become history.

E. V. WALTER

The Politics of Decivilization

SINCE THE GENERATION of World War I rediscovered the idea that Western civilization was in a state of decline, and Paul Valéry proclaimed, "a civilization is as fragile as a life,"[1] there has been no end to jeremiads and stock diagnoses, declaring that the crisis of our time is caused by the loss of spiritual convictions, the eclipse of transcendental values, the decline of morality, or the breakdown of traditional belief-systems.[2] With certain exceptions, this genre has offered not sound diagnoses, but truisms and dolorous representations of symptoms; nevertheless, there lurks in them a psychological truth.

Rapid social change, mass society, and, above all, secularization have produced not only a breakdown in morality and traditional beliefs, but have also devitalized the psychological bearer of conscience and morality, the superego. Historically, the cultivation of the superego propagated civilized men and a system of internal controls. Now the deterioration of the superego brings crisis for political power and regression for civilization.

The Deteriorated Superego

The conditions of mass society have destroyed the foundations of political community and have crippled the normal mechanisms of political power. An authentic system of political power blends many forms of social control, rational and irrational. Within the domain of power, however, subordinates are tied to their leaders in a moral and material community—whether the leaders be despots, oligarchs, or democratic representatives—and their obedience to direction is largely voluntary. In contrast, a politicized mass is held together by irrational bonds and manipulated anxiety, supplemented in some states by violence and terror.

Violence is not the same as power; indeed, violence may be considered to be the failure of power. Ultimately, power depends on voluntary obedience which is based on persuasion, and persuasion, in turn, depends on convictions, ideals, and respect. Certainly, force may be used in a domain of power to guarantee prescribed actions and to safeguard the

This essay, originally written for this volume, has appeared in *The American Political Science Review*, Vol. LIII (1959) and is published here with permission.

limits of permitted behavior; nevertheless, sanctions, penalties, and the fear of punishment are merely braces and not foundations. As Rousseau put it, "the severity of penalities is only a vain resource, invented by little minds in order to substitute terror for that respect which they have no means of obtaining."[3] Historically, force has played an important but limited part in the construction of political communities. James Bryce observed:

> As it is the historian who best understands how much Force has done to build up States, so he most fully sees that Force is only one among many factors, and not the most important, in creating, moulding, expanding and knitting together political communities.[4]

A system of political power is an order in which the action of subordinates, directed by leaders, is dependable and predictable, and, in such a system, the use of force is limited to specific cases that are, literally, out of order. Charles Merriam explained:

> In most communities the use of force is relatively uncommon in proportion to the number of regulations, and the success of the organization is not measured by the amount of violence in specific cases, but by the extent to which violence is avoided and other substitutes discovered. The monopoly of force, which is so often declared to be the chief characteristic of the political association, is not meant for daily use, but as a last resort when all other measures of persuasion and conciliation have failed.[5]

What distinguishes political power from crude types of coercion is that it provides a pattern of control more efficient and more desirable than force.

> The functional situation out of which the political arises is not the demand for force as such, but the need for some form of equilibrium, adjustment, *modus vivendi* between the various groups and individuals of the community, as a substitute indeed for force in many cases.[6]

Sometimes political power succeeds in creating a social tie that did not previously exist,[7] but usually its function is to regulate, direct, coordinate, and control existing social relationships. It acts as the control of controls—in the oldest sense of the word, as the "governor" of society. To function properly, political power depends on certain social and psychological conditions. The governing class must, first of all, be able to satisfy material needs of the subordinates.[8] The capacity to satisfy needs, through the control of key institutions, is a major source of power, because it permits governors to manipulate satisfactions and privations and to dispense rewards and penalties. However, as a recent book on political economy has pointed out:

> Not all the rewards and deprivations to which a person responds are external. The source of many rewards and deprivations is internal, in the sense that these rewards and deprivations are inflicted by the self on the self. . . .

> Such internalized rewards and deprivations constitute the individual's conscience (or superego). Because these rewards and deprivations are internalized, once they are built into the individual they are not easily manipulated.[9]

External controls, therefore, are only part of a power system, for unless they are to survey every action, governors must rely on a system of internal controls: the restraints of conscience and morality.

In the literature of the psychoanalytic movement, the hidden motions and dynamics of the superego (the psychological carrier of conscience and morality) are revealed. As a psychoanalytic writer explains,

> Conscience is a *scientific* newcomer. The popular connotation is of course age-old; it refers exclusively to a set of conscious, conventional and necessary precepts of right and wrong, specific for specific societies. *Unconscious* conscience, *the hidden but real master of the personality*, is, on the other hand, almost entirely unknown. The language does not even possess a word for it; Freud supplied the lack with the introduction of the term "superego."[10]

Psychoanalysis is no substitute for social science, but, employed judiciously, it amplifies the perception and comprehension of political events. As Harold Lasswell has pointed out, "the social scientists have received an ultramicroscope from Freud's original work that adds unprecedented depth to the observational tools available for the study of human interactions."[11]

Freud himself declared that "psychoanalysis has never claimed to provide a complete theory of human mentality as a whole, but only expected that what it offered should be applied to supplement and correct the knowledge acquired by other means." The limited but significant perspective of psychoanalytic psychology cannot tell us much about history, economics, or social organization, which are subject to laws of their own, but it can take us inside history and society, so to speak, and, by providing a theory of motivation, show us the psychic forces that move concrete living individuals to action, and explain what that action means to different types of character under varied conditions of stress.

Civil obedience is conditioned and regulated by the superego. It can make men obey when it is against their interest to obey, and it can make men disobey when it is in their interest to remain obedient. Just as obedience has an inner dimension, civil disobedience depends on subjective conditions. To examine a political event such as a revolution, for example, one must be aware of two levels of motivation. On one level, a revolution is the product of abuses imposed by factors of a social and economic nature. But, to understand the intensity of revolutionary violence, one must take into account the other level, and recognize in the subterranean caverns of the soul the Oedipal source of the passion to destroy the father figures who are the representatives and standard-bearers of the institutions under attack.[12]

Thus, there is an inside and an outside to every power relation. The distribution of power in society depends on a number of "external" conditions—the factors of history, economics, military action, status systems, and so on—but there are also important subjective conditions as well; namely, the ways in which people typically respond to domination and subordination. These patterns of response vary with cultural conditions, but a number of elements within them seem to be invariable, for the responses of individuals to domination and subordination are based on prototypes of behavior learned within the family early in life. For this reason, Freud argued that the family is the prototype of social organization and the bridge between individual and social psychology.[13]

In the genesis of the superego, this psychological vehicle of ideals, conscience, and morality becomes the successor and internal representative of the parents and other educators, establishing in the mind a system of controls that were formerly enforced externally. This institution, constructed in the ego by the process of introjection and internalization, opposes the other activities of the mind by observation, criticism, and prohibition.[14] It "may bring fresh needs to the fore, but its chief function remains the *limitation* of satisfactions."[15] Its chief weapon in controlling the personality is the feeling of guilt, an internalized form of the pain or discomfort of punishment.

In the taboos and restrictions established to ward off guilt, Freud and other psychoanalytic writers argued, one finds the beginnings of social organization, moral restriction, and religion. They supposed that the action of the superego was responsible for the whole spiritual aspiration of man and his impressive system of cultural institutions. Identified in the superego they found all forms of inhibition: God, morality, and every idea that restrains men from satisfying their instinctual demands.[16] Although tyrannical superegos produced neuroses, the superego itself made civilization possible, since the latter depended on the renunciation of instinct. The superego was the tragic burden of civilized man.

The forms of imagery and idea through which the superego "speaks" to the personality depend on the cultural matrix, for the superego is also a transmitter of culture. As Freud put it, the superego "represents more than anything the cultural past. . . . In the emergence of the superego we have before us, as it were, an example of the way in which the present is changed into the past. . . ."[17] In some cultures, superego commands come from the powerful and omniscient spirits of departed ancestors, who speak to the individual and come to his aid in time of need.[18] In Western society, I would argue, superego controls tend to take a more abstract form. Though the superego emerges originally from the prohibitions and commands of the parents, it develops according to laws of its own. After introjecting primordial figures from the external world, the normal superego grows by depersonalization and universalization, creating abstract ideals such as justice, obligation, and duty.[19] After creating these internal abstract standards, it projects them into the external world, searching for concrete models to confirm the internal commands.

From the tendency to magnify and universalize, the superego constructs a fantasy of omnipotence from experience with external power and a standard of absolute justice from experience with ethical norms and standards of conduct. The traditional model that incorporates omnipotence and absolute justice is, of course, the idea of God.

The image of God is linked genetically with the child's father, Freud claimed, and authority figures—gods and kings—were "substitutive formations for the father." Clinical evidence suggested:

> that god is in every case modelled after the father and that our personal relation to god is dependent upon our relation to our physical father, fluctuating and changing with him, and that god at bottom is nothing but an exalted father.[20]

The conception of God is a superego model which is not debilitated by the physical and moral weaknesses of the human father. As Freud put it, man, having realized that "his father is a being with strictly limited powers, and by no means endowed with every desirable attribute, therefore looks back to the memory image of the over-rated father of his childhood, exalts it into a deity, and brings it into the present, and into reality."

Though this description of the psychological origins of the idea of God explains something about the genesis of the superego, it tells us little about the direction the superego takes in its development. Certainly, God replaces the parent as the source of moral authority, and the individual's enjoyment of security and ease of conscience does depend on the internal blessing he receives from fulfilling the demands of morality. Nevertheless, the idea of God takes on characteristics of its own, beyond the concrete imagery of primordial authority, and becomes an ideal of ethical perfection, with the characteristics of omnipotence, absolute virtue, and justice. The difficulty of sustaining such an ideal in the modern world is one of the factors leading to the deterioration of the superego and to the crisis in political power.

The processes of secularization have so profoundly weakened traditional religious convictions that the idea of God has become dim—as a result of social and intellectual transformations in the liberal states and of the campaign against religion in the totalitarian states. Consequently, God has become less real as a source to confirm superego commands. The contemporary return to religion is by and large not an authentic movement of the superego but a pragmatic attempt of the ego to make up for the lack of superego controls by engineering piety and by establishing religion as an instrument of comfort, mental health, or morality. Such attempts are superficial and are always swept away.

Also sapping the strength of the superego, the realities of political conflict in the present age have destroyed the moral authority of leadership. In constitutional states, the superego's demand for a balance between power and virtue traditionally has been satisfied by the rule of law. Modern political leaders, especially in the totalitarian states, may satisfy the superego's search for omnipotence, for the leader has, at his disposal, weapons and technological power that make him appear all-powerful. Yet, he is infinitely corruptible, and the spectacle of omnipotence conflicts with the demand for virtue and justice.

There is no point in condemning Machiavellism or in lamenting the contrast between moral man and immoral society, for unwelcome realities in political history are just as immune from maledictions as are earthquakes and pestilences. I am merely pointing to social consequences. To function in the realm of power politics, the state cannot act as a moral entity, but to draw political obedience from its citizens it must depend on trust and moral obligation. The contradiction between its *realpolitischer* role and its moralizing role contributes to the incidence of moral anxiety, restlessness, and political rage. Furthermore, the absence of moral paradigms to confirm internal controls has contributed to the deterioration of the superego.

Clinicians tend to consider the superego primarily as an instrument of torture to the distressed personality, and to treat what Freud called "moral anxiety" exclusively as a neurotic symptom.[21] However, critical social events may evoke moral anxiety in comparatively normal superegos. The spectacle of unrestrained power exercised by political leaders may infuse the personality with more than fear—with malaise, anxiety, and a sense of restlessness, for the superego seeks a model worthy of obedience and respect. For this reason, throughout political history, tyrants have labored to transform control by force and violence into rule by authority. Moreover, there is no want of examples in which the corruption of leaders has destroyed their moral authority. As Harold Laski observed, "It is the record of all history that no class of men can retain over a period sufficient moral integrity to direct the lives of others. Sooner or later they pervert those lives to their own ends."[22]

The dynamics of leadership in mass society tend to take a special form, especially in the totalitarian states and modern dictatorships. The leader controls by fascination rather than by trust and respect. He appears as a savior endowed with magical qualities, binds to himself a corps of disciplined lieutenants, captures the devotion of the masses, and his power to direct their energies according to his command depends on his skill in manipulating free-floating anxiety. This kind of control requires a permanent reservoir of anxiety, strong libidinal ties—between the leader and his lieutenants, and between the leader and the masses—and strong hatreds of scapegoats and alleged enemies. Seeking support for the regime by ideological flattery of the masses and the manipulation of anxiety, this type of leadership has been named caesarism.[23] It is not a new form of control—the very name proclaims its existence in the Roman Republic; the term has been used to describe the leadership of the Bonapartes in France; and Neumann showed that Cola di Rienzo was a caesaristic proto-fascist leader in fourteenth-century Italy.[24]

Caesaristic leaders have eminent stage presence—Napoleon III, for example, was notable for his theatrical talents—but the acting of a modern totalitarian leader, such as Hitler or Mussolini, is more shamanistic than theatrical. He seeks to capture not mere adulation but absolute devotion, for his purpose is not mere persuasion but the possession of souls. Whereas the actor as an artist is content, like the Pied Piper, to draw his audience away from the real world to the world of his illusion, the totalitarian leader directs his masses to an assault on reality, impelling them to remake the real world in the image of his delusion. Institutionalizing and manipulating anxiety to direct the energies of the mass and to strengthen the identifications within it, he substitutes his own authority for the internal authority of the superego.

Freud distinguished a mass from rational and co-operative groups.[25] A mass regresses to what he called a "primary group" dominated by a leader. "A primary group of this kind is a number of individuals who have substituted one and the same object for their ego ideal and have consequently identified with one another in their ego."[26] In the mass, individuals are reduced to a more childlike form of behavior, their normal intellectual functions are lowered, and their emotions made more volatile.[27] The individual gives up his superego, Freud said, "and substitutes for it the group ideal as embodied in the leader." The model of leadership in the mass is hypnosis, and, in the case of hypnosis, "no one can doubt that the hypnotist has stepped into the place of the [superego]."[28]

The mass dominated by a leader, therefore, is a regressive form of organization; its regression is threefold: psychological, political, and cultural. It is a psychological regression, Freud explained, because the members lose ego-function and suffer a loss of superego controls. Secondly, I would add, it is a political regression.

The question of lower and higher forms of political control, distinguishing between domination and political power, is as old as Aristotle, who argued in the first book of the *Politics* that power originates in the household but evolves into higher forms. The political community is a kind of association different from the household and the model of paternal power does not apply to it. Its origin is patriarchal but its end is rational. The question was also debated extensively in seventeenth-century England during the revolutionary period, when the old political structure had collapsed, both in reality and in imagination, and the new forms were not yet clearly perceived. From the literature of this time (the most creative period for Western political theory), emerged the conviction that a rational polity was a higher and more desirable form than the old model of patriarchal authority. Hobbes incurred the suspicion of the royalist party, despite his absolutist ideas and his congenial political sentiments, precisely because he abandoned the patriarchal theory of power and argued for monarchical absolutism from a rational ground. Hobbes also made clear in the *Leviathan* that he understood the distinction between government by "institution," based on rational consent, and "dominion paternall and despoticall." Locke, in the *First Treatise on Civil Government*, demolished the patriarchal theory of authority, as expressed by Filmer. In the *Second Treatise*, he explained that political power was rational and based on consent, not patriarchal and founded on mere domination; although, he suggested, the origins of government may be found in the father's control of the family. Moreover, in the next century, Rousseau distinguished between power by nature and force, which was patriarchal, and power by convention and consent, which was political. In the nineteenth century, under the influence of the idea of evolution, political writers accepted the notion that political forms evolve from family groups dominated by an authoritarian patriarch to higher, more free, rational organizations based on consent. H. S. Maine argued that just as the law evolves from status to contract, political life grows from the patriarchal clan to the modern state with its more rational institutions and more room for individual freedom. And in the second decade of the twentieth century, a psychoanalytic writer, after the abortive 1919 revolution in Germany, declared that the old forms of domination were collapsing in Western society, that a community of "brothers" was emerging, and that we could look forward to a "fatherless society."[29] Thus, in the history of thinking about political power, one finds wide agreement on the idea that social control based on a paternal type of domination is a regressive political form.

Freud also argued that the mass was a cultural regression, since he considered the history of civilization to be the progressive emancipation of mankind from the tyrannical emotional bonds of the horde. By increased rational control of nature through science (a function of the ego), and by the self-discipline of the superego, mankind was becoming more free, progressively emancipating itself from its origins. The work of civilization, to which psychoanalysis was dedicated, was the Faustian wresting of ground from the Zuyder Zee of the unconscious and the liberation of man from all forms of irrational authority.

Freud thought that the religions of mankind must be considered as mass delusions or as wishes and dreams compensating for lack of instinctual gratification, but he also knew that the religious world-view was a hard-won gain for civilization. The main achievement of religion had been the psychic binding of the fear of demons—the conquest of animism. A distinguished orientalist and historian of culture has observed:

> Animism, with its fears, its irrationality, and its imaginative powers, lies in the subconsciousness of every historic faith, because it is part of the inescapable heritage of mankind, the legacy of those 500,000 years which lie behind the 5,000 years of religious development. It is a prime function of religion to discipline and to control these primitive survivals which haunt the background of our conscious existence. Their impulses, which without religious direction remain subjective and anarchical, are governed and directed in and through religion towards less egocentric ends; and the irrational fears which loom so large in animistic attitudes are transformed into ethical and religious reverence.[30]

By defeating animism and magical thinking, religion raised the spiritual condition of mankind. Now, when the religious world-view has lost its grip on men, some elements of the more primitive mentality have sprung back in its place. Demons have reappeared in political form and are used by leaders to their own advantage. Neumann pointed out that the caesaristic leader, who binds men to himself by their anxiety, gives them a view of history that is conspiratorial.[31] I suggest it is the equivalent of a political demonology, attributing social frustrations to concrete malicious wills, increasing the incidence of fear and persecutory anxiety, and it cultivates a mental condition that Freud called animism.

Writers of the ancient world recognized that religion and traditional morality were illusions held for irrational reasons; still, they knew that these institutions made possible a moral climate that was the necessary condition of a rational political order. Philemon Holland's quaint but lively old translation of Plutarch conveys the force of the latter's conviction that religion "constraineth and holdeth together all humane society, this is the foundation, prop, and stay of all Laws. . . ." Contempt for the masses gives their words a cynical ring;[32] still, the writers of classical antiquity perceived that the political necessity of religion was greater than its usefulness to the ruling class. Critias, the oligarch, Plato's uncle, suggested in his play, *Sisyphus*, that since legal punishments could reach only open infractions, and were powerless to restrict actions that escaped detection, social control required the idea of all-knowing gods who perceived every deed, word, and thought.[33] Polybius, a rationalistic, sceptical Greek and an intimate of the Scipionic circle at Rome, lauded the use of religion for disciplinary purposes, claiming that the masses must be restrained by invisible terrors and tragic fears. He wrote: "I think, not that the ancients acted rashly and at haphazard in introducing among the people notions concerning the gods and beliefs in the terrors of hell, but that the moderns are most rash and foolish in banishing such beliefs."[34] Cicero, himself a member of the college of augurs, clearly indicated that divination was a lost art, and suggested that it may really never have existed, yet he asserted that the mystique of divination was not only an invaluable instrument for the ruling class, but also a necessity for the well-ordered state.[35] He expressed most lucidly and dramatically the classical conviction that political power and the order of law must be reinforced by religious superego controls:

> We talk as if all the miseries of man were comprehended in death, pain of body, sorrow of mind or judicial punishments . . . [but] the divine punishment of the impious is double their legal penalties; for it consists in the pang of conscience while they live, and the reported anguish of the dead; so that their chastisement may become manifest, both to the judgment and the satisfaction of the living.[36]

In addition, Cicero believed that religion performed a civilizing function: ". . . to the advantage of human society, there is nothing better than the mysteries by which we are polished and softened into politeness from the rude austerities of barbarism."[37]

Livy, conservative historian of the Augustan age, seeking, like Hegel, to justify established power by a principle of historical development both rational and providential, found the first transformation in the history of Rome to be the movement from a warlike and barbarous society to a sessile, rationally organized, more civilized state. He ascribed this transformation to the work of pious Numa, the legendary second king, who founded anew, on the principles of justice, law, and custom, the kingdom which had been established by arms and violence.[38] The first step in this transformation was to abstain from warfare, for he felt "that a fierce people should be mollified by the disuse of arms" and that they could not be reconciled to principles of justice and morality during time of war. "When he saw that their minds [had] been rendered ferocious by military life," he erected a temple and established religion.[39] Rome was destined, of course, to return to warfare; yet, not as a society of barbarians, but as a state. Livy suggested that religious controls were an alternative to the exclusively military organization that Rome was destined to transcend. Numa established religion because:

> The removal of all danger from without would induce his subjects to luxuriate in idleness, as they would be no longer restrained by the fear of an enemy or by military discipline. To prevent this, he strove to inculcate in

their minds the fear of the gods, regarding this as the most powerful influence which could act upon an uncivilised and, in those ages, a barbarous people.[40]

The Fathers of the Church agreed that an advanced religion was a civilizing force, and Christian writers perennially have conceived one mission of Christianity to be the taming of the barbarians. Christianity helped fashion a coherent order in the Western world: macrocosmically in the social order, microcosmically in the personality of European man. Though it differs in its secular premises, my argument is compatible with that of Christopher Dawson, a distinguished Catholic historian of culture, who writes:

> the importance of these centuries of which I have been writing is not to be found in the external order they created or attempted to create, but in the internal change they brought about in the soul of Western man—a change which can never be entirely undone except by the total negation or destruction of Western man himself.[41]

Ancient and medieval writers knew that religious controls gentled savage behavior and provided a moral climate within which a system of political power could exist. Modern illuminati, optimistic liberals and progressives of various kinds, with certain exceptions, have been on the side of secularization, correctly understanding that the traditional pieties were transmitted and held for irrational reasons and worked as restrictions, limiting the individual autonomy that they conceived to be the goal of civilization. Only Burke, Maistre, and the writers of the counter-Enlightenment sensed that secularization would destroy the political community, leaving behind political wreckage upon which modern dictatorships have built their empires. Likewise, modern liberals, radicals, and other writers on the side of liberation, recognizing that religion was an instrument of the ruling class, supposed that the destruction of that instrument would deprive the governors of an important weapon and would permit the subordinates to upset their oppressors and to establish a rational polity of their own design. These writers were not wise enough to know that religion historically had cultivated a moral order that was a constitutive—not merely regulative—element for political power, and that its destruction would make inevitable certain regressive forms of political domination more harsh than the systems they had condemned.

Yet I will argue that what Dawson calls "the soul of Western man" has been crippled but not negated, that the superego has been debilitated but not destroyed, and, though caesaristic manipulation and totalitarian controls have rendered it inert, that it still survives underground and promises to endure in a state of watchful suspension.

The Atavistic Superego

Even though totalitarian states claim to have constructed a "new order" and to have created a "new man," deteriorated superego controls in those regimes remain as stubborn, irreducible, irrational obstacles that mock their pretensions. Religious movements were not stamped out but went underground. Nationalist movements resisted control and have erupted in the Ukraine, Poland, and Hungary. Both religious convictions and nationalist sentiments are deeply imbedded in the superego, transmitted by parents to children partly by overt teaching and partly by unconscious gesture and the hidden ways concealed in each family's secret world. In the West, except in the cases dramatized for propaganda purposes, the attempt to establish political superego models rival to the parents and to invade the family by enlisting children in youth groups encouraging them to spy on their parents, has fallen short of success.

In portions of the superego dominated by religious elements, there is latent opposition to the regime. German Christians not caught up in the Nazi enthusiasm but still accustomed to passive acquiescence to political authority were not moved to oppose the regime until they conceived of National Socialism as a rival religion. Karl Barth gave a theological explanation of their position:

> National Socialism in the first stage of its power had in fact the character of a political experiment similar to other experiments and . . . the Church in Germany at that time—this is still my conviction today—had the right and the duty to confine herself to giving it, as a political experiment, first of all time and a chance, and therefore to adopting first of all a strictly neutral position.[42]

This kind of neutrality was justified by the conservative Protestant appeal to *Romans* xiii, in which the Apostle Paul enjoins Christians to "be subject unto the higher powers," for "the powers that be are ordained of God." But, Barth continued,

> it must now be said of this political problem so addressed to us that it is definitely not "only" a political problem. . . . National Socialism, according to its own revelation of what it is—a self revelation to which it has devoted all the time and chance till now allowed—is as well without any doubt something quite different from a political experiment. It is, namely, a *religious institution of salvation*. One cannot understand it as a political experiment, if one does not at the same time understand it in this other character, as a religious institution of salvation.[43]

Barth made it clear that a number of German Christians could maintain a position of neutrality in the face of political oppression and moral outrage and that not until National Socialism revealed itself as a rival religion, committing sacrilege and threatening the unity of the Church, did their superegos move them to take a position of intransigent opposition.

In the historical role of early Christianity in the Roman Empire, one may perceive the action of the superego behind the fission and reconstruction of the domain of power. Though the early Christians passively obeyed the Roman government in matters defined as indifferent, their religious convictions opposed the moral authority of the Emperor. In effect, the Christian community established a rival domain of power impervious to Roman control. Their ascetic lives rendered them immune to the manipulation of external rewards and privations. Their religion would not compromise with the Roman pantheon—hence they could not be moved by Roman superego appeals. Nor did fear avail, for they were not intimidated by torture and preferred martyrdom to moral subordination. Only after the Emperor and the ruling class became Christian themselves did the governors move into the Christian domain of power and re-establish themselves on firm superego foundations.

In other cases, when regimes have lost their moral authority, but a rival domain of power has not established itself, the regime may be able to get along entirely with external controls, but they are crude and costly. When subjective controls do not work, constant surveillance is necessary, and a political police is required to organize a system of espionage.

Normally, however, every system has special techniques other than espionage to calculate and control subjective reactions to authority. Each political system, whether it is liberal or authoritarian, has some internal network of alarms designed to reveal subjective disobedience. Ritual actions with little apparent objective meaning function as postural insignia, screening out and isolating intractable superegos. The postures of subordination—the kow-tow, a pinch of incense, salute, form of address, loyalty oath, "attitude," or muscular carriage—far from guarantee *positive* loyalty, but when an individual conforms, he "wears" the insignia and signals the *absence* of strong superego opposition to the symbols of power. If an individual rejects the ascribed posture and does not wear the insignia, refusing, for example, to take an oath, to attend prescribed meetings, to assume a tone of veneration, or to direct his face and muscles in the mask of co-operation, then he sets off an alarm, which draws official attention and marks him as a case of potential insubordination or superego rebellion.

In totalitarian dictatorships, one of the postural insignia is the mask of enthusiasm. Because silent obedience is an uncertain quality, the citizen body is denied the right of silence. "Nobody can hope to be left alone by claiming political ignorance or lack of political interest."[44] Citizens are expected to voice their animated consent to political decisions and to express what the official transcripts of speeches record as "prolonged applause." Moreover, the familiar response of staged enthusiasm reassures leaders who are uncertain of their moral authority, and, when repeated interminably, forces a mechanical reduction of the moral demands in the superegos of subordinates, even when they have serious reservations about a regime.

When intractable superego remnants cannot be absorbed, destroyed, or converted, the only alternative is to keep them in suspension. If individuals find their leaders morally repugnant and if they are free to direct their loyalties, they will seek new leadership and institute a rival domain of power. As Laski put it, "The authority of any group is based, in fact, upon the living and spontaneous trust it can command. If it betrays or stultifies itself it ceases to win the loyalty that is its life."[45] The movement of the superego, impelling men to find leadership with moral authority, has in the past contributed to the formation of faction and the making of sedition, civil war, and revolution. One of the functions of terror in totalitarian regimes is to paralyze potential factions and natural associations that might organize opposition.

Terror paralyzes the impulse to *act* in opposition and inhibits the free movement of the superego. In regimes that are merely authoritarian, terror may produce indignation and may actually harm the regime, destroying its moral authority. But in a totalitarian state, when terror is applied to manipulated masses, increased terror leads to increased conformity.

Used in this way, terror reinforces regressive tendencies, inhibiting the superego, controlling individual aims, reducing moral autonomy, and making the individual ready to co-operate and allow his behavior to be planned according to the aims of the leaders. In concentration camps, the psychological regression of prisoners is striking. In a remarkable article, recording his experiences in such a camp, Bettelheim observed that all the pressures of living seemed to force the prisoners back to childhood attitudes and behavior, molding them into more or less willing tools of the camp administration.[46] The superegos of the prisoners functioned in a curious and stunted way. Many prisoners were anxious to accept and identify with the Gestapo and the SS. They walked and talked like camp guards, imitating their mannerisms, and wore shreds of Nazi uniforms. Some of them took the camp administrators as all-powerful images and even tried to defend their actions. They insisted that they must be secretly just and kind—they were so powerful that they must also be just.[47] All their positive emotions were concentrated on a few officers high up in the hierarchy of camp administrators, and they insisted that these officers were hiding behind their rough surfaces sentiments of justice and kindness. The eagerness of these prisoners to find reasons in fantasy to support their claims was pitiful. In a different context, one may compare the behavior of the intellectuals described in the book by Czeslaw Milosz, *The Captive Mind*, who strove under varying conditions to convince themselves of the rightness of their regime.

Many individuals, especially the new generations reared under totalitarian conditions, apparently have little difficulty in identifying with the regime and making the totalitarian creed the standard of the superego. When commands are consistent with superego ideals, even when they apparently restrict freedom, they are not felt as restrictions. From the stories that have come out of Siberian slave camps, many prisoners who were Communists—members of the Party formerly in good standing—did not have their positive feelings about the regime impaired by their imprisonment. They interpreted their deviations as crimes, were taking their punishment, and would return to function very much as before.[48] In these cases the claims of the superego were identified with the claims of the regime. Waelder explains such behavior by the conclusion that:

> Whenever the ideal which a restriction is intended to serve is *internalized* and forms part and parcel of our superego, the restriction does not seem to interfere with our freedom. But if this purpose or ideal is not part of our superego and the pressure is merely external, it is felt as oppressive and, beyond a certain intensity, as tyrannical.[49]

Religious fundamentalists, whose intransigent superegos were dominated by religious elements, have succeeded in enduring the terrors of totalitarian captivity, and they had no difficulty in opposing the regime since it was obviously an instrument of the devil. Persons who have suffered the most are those who concur partly to values in the totalitarian creed but reject other parts of it, or are internally divided because they are committed to some values opposed to the regime. They tend to become completely demoralized.

With each new generation, the totalitarian regime, through education and indoctrination, attempts to fulfill its boast that it has created a new humanity. The boast would be true if superegos could be shaped entirely by political education, but the superego is obstinate, conservative, and far from being as plastic as leaders would prefer.

It changes very slowly in response to changes in reality. The ideologies of the superego, Freud observed, perpetuate the past—one might call the process "moral lag"—and yield but slowly to the demands of the present. Shaped in silent ways by the family, unconscious traditions, and habits, the superego may be generations behind the new education. It plays a part in life that seems almost independent of external conditions and provokes the patience of officials charged with the construction of a new humanity.

Enduring in hidden ways, the superego finds expression even in institutions that seem to contradict its very principles. Two important instances of its underground working in the totalitarian state are the institution of the public purge and the custom of bribery.

Public purges are opportunities for communal catharsis, not unlike the Greek drama. Moreover secret rage against the corruption of leaders and aggressions caused by frustrations imposed by the regime may be deflected against paradigmatic enemies. The trial makes possible a proclamation of group morality and satisfies the superego's need for retribution and justice. Political violators are declared anathema, and their punishment assuages the guilt felt by citizens for hostile thoughts against the regime. This kind of behavior fits Lasswell's observation that:

> The spectacle of any violation of the accredited order arouses the repressed impulses of the spectator to indulge his own antisocial whims. This produces a crisis of conscience within the personalities of those who see and hear of the violation, and the individual is driven to relieve himself of his own discomfort by externalizing his aggression against those in the environment who threaten the inner equilibrium of his own life. To punish and to have punished the performer of a criminal act is to perform a vicarious act of propitiation of one's own conscience.[50]

Similarly, Fenichel points out that the unconscious basis of this demand for justice is the idea: "What I am not permitted to do, no one else should be permitted either."[51]

Moreover, the widespread custom of bribery in totalitarian states, even extending to the concentration camps, where bribery of guards by prisoners was flagrant, performed a psychological function. Bribery is an act of aggression against the powerful person who is bribed. Lasswell argues:

> The ubiquity of bribery in society is due to the fact that it is learned as a by-product of the experience of being a weak child in a world of strong adults. . . . Bribery is one of the most common of all the techniques by which the weak or the preoccupied can deal with the strong or the obstructive. It has the special lure of damaging the authoritative object even as he is being granted tangible advantages, and as such is particularly designed to throw authority into contempt, and to gratify the antisocial impulses of the personality. Keen pleasure is taken by many bribers in the very act of corrupting those who profess to represent the pomp and circumstance of the conventional order.[52]

Since the subordinates are weak and lack other acceptable means to express aggression, bribery will continue to be an ineradicable part of life in totalitarian regimes.

Superego remnants continue to embarrass militarized mass societies in non-totalitarian states also. The American public was made aware of the problem after the Korean war, when information was released that a large number of soldiers could not bring themselves to fire at the enemy. To cope with this problem, the field of military psychiatry has become the inverse of psychoanalysis, just as the science of bacteriological warfare has developed as the inverse of medical science. Military psychiatry consciously searches for techniques to assist the process of decivilization, to render men pliant under the domination of paternal (in a psychological sense) military leaders, and to loosen their consciences and trigger fingers.

The quality of civil life, of course, is affected directly by the extent to which military organization invades society. Mass societies show a tendency to revert to a military form of social organization and thereby to adopt the social psychology of a specific stage of barbarism—that of the community in arms. In his polemic with Leon Trotsky over the use of terror in the Bolshevik Revolution, Karl Kautsky went so far as to argue that such brutality and savage terrorism would never have been possible, had not extended military experience in the nineteenth century halted the natural progress of social evolution and reversed the civilizing and humanizing effect of the eighteenth century, causing European men to revert to barbaric sentiments and impulses.[53]

Despite the cultural wreckage produced by historical and social changes, remnants of deteriorated superegos and superegos secretly intact survive underground, even though individuals in the manipulated mass are forced into psychological, political, and cultural regression. Freud showed us that man's relation to barbarism is psychological—not solely historical. The mind contains "a survival of all the early stages alongside the final form"; civilized and primitive mental states coexist in every age and in every mind.[54] Freud and the crowd-psychologists before him demonstrated that, in the mass, every civilized man is potentially a savage. Yet, knowing what we do about the obstinate endurance of the superego, it may also be true that mass men are potentially civilized. A restoration or reconstruction will build on foundations that already exist. The future of civilization may depend on whether men will recapitulate their own history and re-enact psychologically what had been accomplished historically.

Men have endured periods similar to the present, although they have not been so formidable. Bishop Stubbs, in his classic political history of England, examined the civil life of the fourteenth century, deplored its decline in moral power and general social disintegration, and concluded: "yet out of it emerges in spite of all, the truer and brighter day, the season of more general conscious life, higher longings, more forbearing, more sympathetic, purer, riper liberty." One never perceives the forces underground until they have accomplished their work—for good or for ill: "the historian has not yet arisen who can account . . . for the tides in the affairs of men."[55] In this same period of decline that Stubbs wrote about, Bryce agreed, "unseen causes were already at work which after no long interval restored the tone and spirit of England. It has often been so in history, though no generation can foretell how long a period of intellectual or moral depression will endure."[56]

Contrived attempts to bring about moral rejuvenation by spiritual tinkering and programs for character building are inauthentic, repugnant, worse than useless, and really fool no one. We shall have to wait. However, Camus has assured: "All of us, among the ruins, are preparing a renaissance beyond the limits of nihilism. But few of us know it."[57]

Restorations and renewals do not respond to invitations, but come silently, unexpectedly, and often in disguise, as if to deceive the powerful forces that would destroy them on recognition. In their secret wisdom, they take devious routes, ignoring our most desperate yearnings for their immediate advent; but once they are on the way, no one can hold them back.

GEORGE ORWELL

Politics and the English Language

MOST PEOPLE who bother with the matter at all would admit that the English language is in a bad way, but it is generally assumed that we cannot by conscious action do anything about it. Our civilization is decadent and our language—so the argument runs—must inevitably share in the general collapse. It follows that any struggle against the abuse of language is a sentimental archaism, like preferring candles to electric light or hansom cabs to aeroplanes. Underneath this lies the half-conscious belief that language is a natural growth and not an instrument which we shape for our own purposes.

Now, it is clear that the decline of a language must ultimately have political and economic causes: it is not due simply to the bad influence of this or that individual writer. But an effect can become a cause, reinforcing the original cause and producing the same effect in an intensified form, and so on indefinitely. A man may take to drink because he feels

From *Shooting an Elephant and Other Essays* by George Orwell (pp. 162-78).

himself to be a failure, and then fail all the more completely because he drinks. It is rather the same thing that is happening to the English language. It becomes ugly and inaccurate because our thoughts are foolish, but the slovenliness of our language makes it easier for us to have foolish thoughts. The point is that the process is reversible. Modern English, especially written English, is full of bad habits which spread by imitation and which can be avoided if one is willing to take the necessary trouble. If one gets rid of these habits one can think more clearly, and to think clearly is a necessary first step towards political regeneration: so that the fight against bad English is not frivolous and is not the exclusive concern of professional writers. I will come back to this presently, and I hope that by that time the meaning of what I have said here will become clearer. Meanwhile, here are five specimens of the English language as it is now habitually written.

These five passages have not been picked out because they are especially bad—I could have quoted far worse if I had chosen—but because they illustrate various of the mental vices from which we now suffer. They are a little below the average, but are fairly representative samples. I number them so that I can refer back to them when necessary:

1) I am not, indeed, sure whether it is not true to say that the Milton who once seemed not unlike a seventeenth-century Shelley had not become, out of an experience ever more bitter in each year, more alien [sic] to the founder of that Jesuit sect which nothing could induce him to tolerate.

Professor Harold Laski
(Essay in *Freedom of Expression*)

2) Above all, we cannot play ducks and drakes with a native battery of idioms which prescribes such egregious collocations of vocables as the Basic *put up with* for *tolerate* or *put at a loss* for *bewilder*.

Professor Lancelot Hogben (*Interglossa*)

3) On the one side we have the free personality: by definition it is not neurotic, for it has neither conflict nor dream. Its desires, such as they are, are transparent, for they are just what institutional approval keeps in the forefront of consciousness; another institutional pattern would alter their number and intensity; there is little in them that is natural, irreducible, or culturally dangerous. But *on the other side,* the social bond itself is nothing but the mutual reflection of these self-secure integrities. Recall the definition of love. Is not this the very picture of a small academic? Where is there a place in this hall of mirrors for either personality or fraternity?

Essay on psychology in *Politics* (New York)

4) All the "best people" from the gentlemen's clubs, and all the frantic fascist captains, united in common hatred of Socialism and bestial horror of the rising tide of the mass revolutionary movement, have turned to acts of provocation, to foul incendiarism, to medieval legends of poisoned wells, to legalize their own destruction of proletarian organizations, and rouse the

agitated petty-bourgeoisie to chauvinistic fervor on behalf of the fight against the revolutionary way out of the crisis.

Communist pamphlet

5) If a new spirit *is* to be infused into this old country, there is one thorny and contentious reform which must be tackled, and that is the humanization and galvanization of the B.B.C. Timidity here will bespeak canker and atrophy of the soul. The heart of Britain may be sound and of strong beat, for instance, but the British lion's roar at present is like that of Bottom in Shakespeare's *Midsummer Night's Dream*—as gentle as any sucking dove. A virile new Britain cannot continue indefinitely to be traduced in the eyes, or rather ears, of the world by the effete languors of Langham Place, brazenly masquerading as "standard English." When the Voice of Britain is heard at nine o'clock, better far and infinitely less ludicrous to hear aitches honestly dropped than the present priggish, inflated, inhibited, school-ma'amish arch braying of blameless bashful mewing maidens!

Letter in *Tribune*

Each of these passages has faults of its own, but, quite apart from avoidable ugliness, two qualities are common to all of them. The first is staleness of imagery; the other is lack of precision. The writer either has a meaning and cannot express it, or he inadvertently says something else, or he is almost indifferent as to whether his words mean anything or not. This mixture of vagueness and sheer incompetence is the most marked characteristic of modern English prose, and especially of any kind of political writing. As soon as certain topics are raised, the concrete melts into the abstract and no one seems able to think of turns of speech that are not hackneyed: prose consists less and less of *words* chosen for the sake of their meaning, and more and more of *phrases* tacked together like the sections of a prefabricated hen-house. I list below, with notes and examples, various of the tricks by means of which the work of prose-construction is habitually dodged:

Dying Metaphors. A newly invented metaphor assists thought by evoking a visual image, while on the other hand a metaphor which is technically "dead" (e.g. *iron resolution*) has in effect reverted to being an ordinary word and can generally be used without loss of vividness. But in between these two classes there is a huge dump of worn-out metaphors which have lost all evocative power and are merely used because they save people the trouble of inventing phrases for themselves. Examples are: *Ring the changes on, take up the cudgels for, toe the line, ride roughshod over, stand shoulder to shoulder with, play into the hands of, no axe to grind, grist to the mill, fishing in troubled waters, on the order of the day, Achilles' heel, swan song, hotbed.* Many of these are used without knowledge of their meaning (what is a "rift," for instance?), and incompatible metaphors are frequently mixed, a sure sign that the writer is not interested in what he is saying. Some metaphors now current have been twisted out of their original meaning without those who use them even being aware of the fact. For example, *toe the line* is sometimes written *tow the line*. Another example is *the hammer and the anvil,* now always used with the implication that the anvil gets the worst of it. In real life it is always the anvil that breaks the hammer, never the other way about: a writer who stopped to think what he was saying would be aware of this, and would avoid perverting the original phrase.

Operators or Verbal False Limbs. These save the trouble of picking out appropriate verbs and nouns, and at the same time pad each sentence with extra syllables which give it an appearance of symmetry. Characteristic phrases are *render inoperative, militate against, make contact with, be subjected to, give rise to, give grounds for, have the effect of, play a leading part (role) in, make itself felt, take effect, exhibit a tendency to, serve the purpose of, etc., etc.* The keynote is the elimination of simple verbs. Instead of being a single word, such as *break, stop, spoil, mend, kill,* a verb becomes a *phrase,* made up of a noun or adjective tacked on to some general-purposes verb such as *prove, serve, form, play, render.* In addition, the passive voice is wherever possible used in preference to the active, and noun constructions are used instead of gerunds (*by examination of* instead of *by examining*). The range of verbs is further cut down by means of the *-ize* and *de-* formations, and the banal statements are given an appearance of profundity by means of the *not un-* formation. Simple conjunctions and prepositions are replaced by such phrases as *with respect to, having regard to, the fact that, by dint of, in view of, in the interests of, on the hypothesis that;* and the ends of sentences are saved from anticlimax by such resounding common-places as *greatly to be desired, cannot be left out of account, a development to be expected in the near future, deserving of serious consideration, brought to a satisfactory conclusion,* and so on and so forth.

Pretentious Diction. Words like *phenomenon, element, individual* (as noun), *objective, categorical, effective, virtual, basic, primary, promote, constitute, exhibit, exploit, utilize, eliminate, liquidate,* are used to dress up simple statement and give an air of scientific impartiality to biased judgments. Adjectives like *epoch-making, epic, historic, unforgettable, triumphant, age-old, inevitable, inexorable, veritable,* are used to dignify the sordid processes of international politics, while writing that aims at glorifying war usually takes on an archaic color, its characteristic words being: *realm, throne, chariot, mailed fist, trident, sword, shield, buckler, banner, jackboot, clarion.* Foreign words and expressions such as *cul de sac, ancien régime, deus ex machina, mutatis mutandis, status quo, gleichschaltung, weltanschauung,* are used to give an air of culture and elegance. Except for the useful abbreviations *i.e., e.g.,* and *etc.,* there is no real need for any of the hundreds of foreign phrases now current in English. Bad writers, and especially scientific, political, and sociological writers, are nearly always haunted by the notion that Latin or Greek words are grander than Saxon ones, and unnecessary words like *expedite*, *ameliorate*, *predict*, *extraneous*, *deracinated*, *clandestine*, *subaqueous* and hundreds of others constantly gain ground from their Anglo-Saxon opposite numbers.* The jargon peculiar to Marxist writing (*hyena*, *hangman*, *cannibal*, *petty bourgeois*, *these gentry*, *lacquey*, *flunkey*, *mad dog*, *White Guard*, etc.) consists largely of words and phrases translated from Russian, German or French; but the normal way of coining a new word is to use a Latin or Greek root with the appropriate affix and, where necessary, the size formation. It is often easier to make up words of this kind (*deregionalize*, *impermissible*, *extramarital*, *nonfragmentary* and so forth) than to think up the English words that will cover one's meaning. The result, in general, is an increase in slovenliness and vagueness.

Meaningless Words. In certain kinds of writing, particularly in art criticism and literary criticism, it is normal to come across long passages which are almost completely lacking in meaning.† Words like *romantic*, *plastic*, *values*, *human*, *dead*, *sentimental*, *natural*, *vitality*, as used in art criticism, are strictly meaningless, in the sense that they not only do not point to any discoverable object, but are hardly ever expected to do so by the reader. When one critic writes, "The outstanding feature of Mr. X's work is its living quality," while another writes, "The immediately striking thing about Mr. X's work is its peculiar deadness," the reader accepts this as a simple difference of opinion. If words like *black* and *white* were involved, instead of the jargon words *dead* and *living*, he would see at once that language was being used in an improper way. Many political words are similarly abused. The word *fascism* has now no meaning except in so far as it signifies "something not desirable." The words *democracy*, *socialism*, *freedom*, *patriotic*, *realistic*, *justice*, have each of them several different meanings which cannot be reconciled with one another. In the case of a word like *democracy*, not only is there no agreed definition, but the attempt to make one is resisted from all sides. It is almost universally felt that when we call a country democratic we

* An interesting illustration of this is the way in which the English flower names which were in use till very recently are being ousted by Greek ones, *snapdragon* becoming *antirrhinum*, *forget-me-not* becoming *myosotis*, etc. It is hard to see any practical reason for this change of fashion: it is probably due to an instinctive turning-away from the more homely word and a vague feeling that the Greek word is scientific.

† Example: "Comfort's catholicity of perception and image, strangely Whitmanesque in range, almost the exact opposite in aesthetic compulsion, continues to evoke that trembling atmospheric accumulative hinting at a cruel, an inexorably serene timelessness. . . . Wrey Gardiner scores by aiming at simple bull's-eyes with precision. Only they are not so simple, and through this contented sadness runs more than the surface bitter-sweet of resignation" (*Poetry Quarterly*).

are praising it: consequently the defenders of every kind of régime claim that it is a democracy, and fear that they might have to stop using the word if it were tied down to any one meaning. Words of this kind are often used in a consciously dishonest way. That is, the person who uses them has his own private definition, but allows his hearer to think he means something quite different. Statements like *Marshal Pétain was a true patriot*, *The Soviet Press is the freest in the world*, *The Catholic Church is opposed to persecution*, are almost always made with intent to deceive. Other words used in variable meanings, in most cases more or less dishonestly, are: *class*, *totalitarian*, *science*, *progressive*, *reactionary*, *bourgeois*, *equality*.

Now that I have made this catalogue of swindles and perversions, let me give another example of the kind of writing that they lead to. This time it must of its nature be an imaginary one. I am going to translate a passage of good English into modern English of the worst sort. Here is a well-known verse from *Ecclesiastes:*

"I returned and saw under the sun, that the race is not to the swift, nor the battle to the strong, neither yet bread to the wise, nor yet riches to men of understanding, nor yet favour to men of skill; but time and chance happeneth to them all."

Here it is in modern English:

"Objective consideration of contemporary phenomena compels the conclusion that success or failure in competitive activities exhibits no tendency to be commensurate with innate capacity, but that a considerable element of the unpredictable must invariably be taken into account."

This is a parody, but not a very gross one. Exhibit (3), above, for instance, contains several patches of the same kind of English. It will be seen that I have not made a full translation. The beginning and ending of the sentence follow the original meaning fairly closely, but in the middle the concrete illustrations—race, battle, bread—dissolve into the vague phrase "success or failure in competitive activities." This had to be so, because no modern writer of the kind I am discussing—no one capable of using phrases like "objective consideration of contemporary phenomena"—would ever tabulate his thoughts in that precise and detailed way. The whole tendency of modern prose is away from concreteness. Now analyze these two sentences a little more closely. The first contains forty-nine words but only sixty syllables, and all its words are those of everyday life. The second contains thirty-eight words of ninety syllables: eighteen of its words are from Latin roots, and one from Greek. The first sentence contains six vivid images, and only one phrase ("time and chance") that could be called vague. The second contains not a single fresh, arresting phrase, and in spite of its ninety syllables it gives only a shortened version of the meaning contained in the first. Yet without a doubt it is the second kind of sentence that is gaining ground in modern English. I do not want to exaggerate. This kind of writing is not yet universal, and outcrops of simplicity will occur here and there in the worst-written page. Still, if you or I were told to write a few lines on the uncertainty of human fortunes, we should probably come much nearer to my imaginary sentence than to the one from *Ecclesiastes.*

As I have tried to show, modern writing at its worst does not consist in picking out words for the sake of their meaning and inventing images in order to make the meaning clearer. It consists in gumming together long strips of words which have already been set in order by someone else, and making the results presentable by sheer humbug. The attraction of this way of writing is that it is easy. It is easier—even quicker, once you have the habit—to say *In my opinion it is not an unjustifiable assumption that* than to say *I think.* If you use ready-made phrases, you not only don't have to hunt about for words; you also don't have to bother with the rhythms of your sentences, since these phrases are generally so arranged as to be more or less euphonious. When you are composing in a hurry—when you are dictating to a stenographer, for instance, or making a public speech—it is natural to fall into a pretentious, Latinized style. Tags like *a consideration which we should do well to bear in mind* or *a conclusion to which all of us would readily assent* will save many a sentence from coming down with a bump. By using stale metaphors, similes and idioms, you save much mental effort, at the cost of leaving your meaning vague, not only for your reader but for yourself. This is the significance of mixed metaphors. The sole aim of a metaphor is to call up a visual image. When these images clash—as in *The Fascist octopus has sung its swan song, the jackboot is thrown into the melting pot*—it can be taken as certain that the writer is not seeing a mental image of the objects he is naming; in other words he is not really thinking. Look again at the examples I gave at the beginning of this essay. Professor Laski (1) uses five negatives in fifty-three words. One of these is superfluous, making nonsense of the whole passage, and in addition there is the slip *alien* for akin, making further nonsense, and several avoidable pieces of clumsiness which increase the general vagueness. Professor Hogben (2) plays ducks and drakes with a battery which is able to write prescriptions, and, while disapproving of the everyday phrase *put up with,* is unwilling to look *egregious* up in the dictionary and see what it means; (3), if one takes an uncharitable attiude towards it, is simply meaningless: probably one could work out its intended meaning by reading the whole of the article in which it occurs. In (4), the writer knows more or less what he wants to say, but an accumulation of stale phrases chokes him like tea leaves blocking a sink. In (5), words and meaning have almost parted company. People who write in this manner usually have a general emotional meaning—they dislike one thing and want to express solidarity with another—but they are not interested in the detail of what they are saying. A scrupulous writer, in every sentence that he writes, will ask himself at least four questions, thus: What am I trying to say? What words will express it? What image or idiom will make it clearer? Is this image fresh enough to have an effect? And he will probably ask himself two more: Could I put it more shortly? Have I said anything that is avoidably ugly? But you are not obliged to go to all this trouble. You can shirk it by simply throwing your mind open and letting the ready-made phrases come crowding in. They will construct your sentences for you—even think your thoughts for you, to a certain extent —and at need they will perform the important service of partially concealing your meaning even from yourself. It is at this point that the special connection between politics and the debasement of language becomes clear.

In our time it is broadly true that political writing is bad writing. Where it is not true, it will generally be found that the writer is some kind of rebel, expressing his private opinions and not a "party line." Orthodoxy, of whatever color, seems to demand a lifeless, imitative style. The political dialects to be found in pamphlets, leading articles, manifestos, White Papers and the speeches of under-secretaries do, of course, vary from party to party, but they are all alike in that one almost never finds in them a fresh, vivid, home-made turn of speech. When one watches some tired hack on the platform mechanically repeating the familiar phrases— *bestial atrocities, iron heel, bloodstained tyranny, free peoples of the world, stand shoulder to shoulder*—one often has a curious feeling that one is not watching a live human being but some kind of dummy: a feeling which suddenly becomes stronger at moments when the light catches the speaker's spectacles and turns them into blank discs which seem to have no eyes behind them. And this is not altogether fanciful. A speaker who uses that kind of phraseology has gone some distance towards turning himself into a machine. The appropriate noises are coming out of his larynx, but his brain is not involved as it would be if he were choosing his words for himself. If the speech he is making is one that he is accustomed to make over and over again, he may be almost unconscious of what he is saying, as one is when one utters the responses in church. And this reduced state of consciousness, if not indispensable, is at any rate favorable to political conformity.

In our time, political speech and writing are largely the defense of the indefensible. Things like the continuance of British rule in India, the Russian purges and deportations, the dropping of the atom bombs on Japan, can indeed be defended, but only by arguments which are too brutal for most people to face, and which do not square with the professed aims of political parties. Thus political language has to consist largely of euphemism, question-begging, and sheer cloudy vagueness. Defenseless villages are bombarded from the air, the inhabitants driven out into the countryside, the cattle machine-gunned, the huts set on fire with incendiary bullets: this is called *pacification*. Millions of peasants are robbed of their farms and sent trudging along the roads with no more than they can carry: this is called *transfer of population* or *rectification of frontiers*. People are imprisoned for years without trial, or shot in the back of the neck, or sent to die of scurvy in Arctic lumber camps: this is called *elimination of unreliable elements*. Such phraseology is needed if one wants to name things without calling up mental pictures of them. Consider for instance some comfortable English professor defending Russian totalitarianism. He cannot say outright, "I believe in killing off your opponents when you can get good results by doing so." Probably, therefore, he will say something like this:

"While freely conceding that the Soviet régime exhibits certain features which the humanitarian may be inclined to deplore, we must, I think, agree that a certain curtailment of the right to political opposition is an unavoidable concomitant of transitional periods, and that the rigors which the Russian people have been called upon to undergo have been amply justified in the sphere of concrete achievement."

The inflated style is itself a kind of euphemism. A mass of Latin words falls upon the facts like soft snow, blurring the outlines and covering up all the details. The great enemy of clear language is insincerity. When there is a gap between one's real and one's declared aims, one turns as it were instinctively to long words and exhausted idioms, like a cuttlefish squirting out ink. In our age there is no such thing as "keeping out of politics." All issues are political issues, and politics itself is a mass of lies, evasions, folly, hatred and schizophrenia. When the general atmosphere is bad, language must suffer. I should expect to find—this is a guess which I have not sufficient knowledge to verify—that the German, Russian, and Italian languages have all deteriorated in the last ten or fifteen years, as a result of dictatorship.

But if thought corrupts language, language can also corrupt thought. A bad usage can spread by tradition and imitation, even among people who should and do know better. The debased language that I have been discussing is in some ways very convenient. Phrases like *a not unjustifiable assumption*, *leaves much to be desired*, *would serve no good purpose*, *a consideration which we should do well to bear in mind*, are a continuous temptation, a packet of aspirins always at one's elbow. Look back through this essay, and for certain you will find that I have again and again committed the very faults I am protesting against. By this morning's post I have received a pamphlet dealing with conditions in Germany. The author tells me that he "felt impelled" to write it. I open it at random, and here is almost the first sentence that I see: "[The Allies] have an opportunity not only of achieving a radical transformation of Germany's social and political structure in such a way as to avoid a nationalistic reaction in Germany itself, but at the same time of laying the foundations of a co-operative and unified Europe." You see, he "feels impelled" to write—feels, presumably, that he has something new to say—and yet his words, like cavalry horses answering the bugle, group themselves automatically into the familiar dreary pattern. This invasion of one's mind by ready-made phrases (*lay the foundations, achieve a radical transformation*) can only be prevented if one is constantly on guard against them, and every such phrase anaesthetizes a portion of one's brain.

I said earlier that the decadence of our language is probably curable. Those who deny this would argue, if they produced an argument at all, that language merely reflects existing social conditions, and that we cannot influence its development by any direct tinkering with words and constructions. So far as the general tone or spirit of a language goes, this may be true, but it is not true in detail. Silly words and expressions have often disappeared, not through any evolutionary process but owing to the conscious action of a minority. Two recent examples were *explore every avenue* and *leave no stone unturned*, which were killed by the jeers of a few journalists. There is a long list of flyblown metaphors which could similarly be got rid of if enough people would interest themselves in the job; and it should also be possible to laugh the *not un-* formation out of existence,* to reduce the amount of Latin and Greek in the average sentence, to drive out foreign phrases and strayed scientific words, and, in general, to make pretentiousness unfashionable. But all these are minor points. The defense of the English language implies more than this, and perhaps it is best to start by saying what it does *not* imply.

To begin with it has nothing to do with archaism, with the salvaging of obsolete words and turns of speech, or with the setting up of a "standard English" which must never be departed from. On the contrary, it is especially concerned with the scrapping of every word or idiom which has outworn its usefulness. It has nothing to do with correct grammar and syntax, which are of no importance so long as one makes one's meaning clear, or with the avoidance of Americanisms, or with having what is called a "good prose style." On the other hand it is not concerned with fake simplicity and the attempt to make written English colloquial. Nor does it even imply in every case preferring the Saxon word to the Latin one, though it does imply using the fewest and shortest words that will cover one's meaning. What is above all needed is to let the meaning choose

* One can cure oneself of the *not un-* formation by memorizing this sentence: *A not unblack dog was chasing a not unsmall rabbit across a not ungreen field.*

the word, and not the other way about. In prose, the worst thing one can do with words is to surrender to them. When you think of a concrete object, you think wordlessly, and then, if you want to describe the thing you have been visualizing you probably hunt about till you find the exact words that seem to fit it. When you think of something abstract you are more inclined to use words from the start, and unless you make a conscious effort to prevent it, the existing dialect will come rushing in and do the job for you, at the expense of blurring or even changing your meaning. Probably it is better to put off using words as long as possible and get one's meaning as clear as one can through pictures or sensations. Afterwards one can choose—not simply *accept*—the phrases that will best cover the meaning, and then switch round and decide what impression one's words are likely to make on another person. This last effort of the mind cuts out all stale or mixed images, all prefabricated phrases, needless repetitions, and humbug and vagueness generally. But one can often be in doubt about the effect of a word or a phrase, and one needs rules that one can rely on when instinct fails. I think the following rules will cover most cases:

i) Never use a metaphor, simile or other figure of speech which you are used to seeing in print.

ii) Never use a long word where a short one will do.

iii) If it is possible to cut a word out, always cut it out.

iv) Never use the passive where you can use the active.

v) Never use a foreign phrase, a scientific word, or a jargon word if you can think of an everyday English equivalent.

vi) Break any of these rules sooner than say anything outright barbarous.

These rules sound elementary, and so they are, but they demand a deep change of attitude in anyone who has grown used to writing in the style now fashionable. One could keep all of them and still write bad English, but one could not write the kind of stuff that I quoted in those five specimens at the beginning of this article.

I have not here been considering the literary use of language, but merely language as an instrument for expressing and not for concealing or preventing thought. Stuart Chase and others have come near to claiming that all abstract words are meaningless, and have used this as a pretext for advocating a kind of political quietism. Since you don't know what fascism is, how can you struggle against fascism? One need not swallow such absurdities as this, but one ought to recognize that the present political chaos is connected with the decay of language, and that one can probably bring about some improvement by starting at the verbal end. If you simplify your English, you are freed from the worst follies of orthodoxy. You cannot speak any of the necessary dialects, and when you make a stupid remark its stupidity will be obvious, even to yourself. Political language—and with variations this is true of all political parties, from Conservatives to Anarchists—is designed to make lies sound truthful and murder respectable, and to give an appearance of solidity to pure wind. One cannot change this all in a moment, but one can at least change one's own habits, and from time to time one can even, if one jeers loudly enough, send some worn-out and useless phrase—some *jackboot, Achilles' heel, hotbed, melting pot, acid test, veritable inferno* or other lump of verbal refuse—into the dustbin where it belongs.

HAROLD ROSENBERG

The Orgamerican Phantasy

AMERICA masks its terrors behind patterns of fact. Here the intolerable discloses its presence not in the grimaces of comedy or tragedy but in the bland citations of the scientific report. Since the War, no novel or play has given body to the larger disturbances of the American consciousness. Literature, one hears, is dead, or too enfeebled to risk arduous adventures. Nevertheless, documents keep appearing that touch upon apprehensions equal to any in the history of men: computations of the daily incidence of outlawed sex in America's bedrooms; records of scientific sadism practiced by governments and their programs to transform the will of individuals; estimates by atomic technicians of the flimsiness of the earth and of the natural shape of the human body. When phenomena of this order are explored in a work of the imagination, its author tends to be exiled to the colony of "morbid intellectuals." Given the form of the report or survey, and authorized by the rhetoric of the professions, the most alarming topics overcome the handicap of their profundity and enter into the conversation of solid men of affairs.

Among the grand metaphysical themes of this decade, the one that has proved perhaps most fascinating and persistent has been that of "alienation"

Reprinted from *The Tradition of the New* (1959), pp. 269-85, by permission of the author and of the publisher, Horizon Press Inc.

—the loss by the individual of personal identity through the operation of social processes. The tone of the post-war imagination was set by Orwell's *1984;* since the appearance of that work, "the dehumanized collective that so haunts our thoughts" (as Mr. William H. Whyte, Jr. calls it in *The Organization Man*) has been a topic for the best-seller lists.

Orwell's melodrama of the pulverized ego was a work of fiction. But Orwell was a Briton; besides, *1984* could be read as a description of life in Stalin's Russia or in a future Labor Party England, rather than of the destiny of America. Of U.S. storytellers who essayed to raise the same spectre, none achieved large public impact. Americans awoke to the menace of robotization when the possibility of it passed from the fiction-writer's yarn to the testimony of the sociologist and cultural anthropologist. Riesman's *The Lonely Crowd*, with its "other-directed" hero-victims of automobile showrooms and P.T.A. meetings, left no doubt that the familiar feeling of being someone else was not a mere after-effect of seeing the wrong movie. Spectorsky's *The Exurbanite*, Whyte's *The Organization Man*, Mills' *White Collar*, Packard's *The Hidden Persuaders* filled in important details of personnel, locale, and method. Like The Man with the Bomb That Can Blow Up the World, The Creature That Lost Himself ceased to be a reflection of the dream-maker's art, or a literary construction of the philosophical moralist, and emerged as a statistical probability from the file-cards of the social scientist.

It goes without saying that the Other-Directed Man, the Exurbanite, the Organization Man, is a *type*, that is to say, the personification of a behavior system, on the order of, say, Sinclair Lewis' Babbitt. In this respect the difference between the sociologist and the novelist reduces itself to the fact that Riesman explains that he is writing about "social characters" and devotes his book to analyzing what they do, while Lewis trots Babbitt out on the stage and has him do it.

The type or character is deficient in individuality *by definition.* Said Strindberg: "The word 'character' . . . became the middle-class expression for the automaton. An individual who had once for all become fixed in his natural disposition, or had adapted himself to some definite role in life—who, in fact, had ceased to grow—was called a character. . . . This middle-class conception of the immobility of the soul was transferred to the stage, where the middle class has always ruled."

Since the immobility or eternal fixedness of the present-day American social type—let us nickname him the Orgman—is presented as something new, in contrast to the dynamism and inwardness of the Inner-Directed Man (Riesman) or the Protestant Ethic Person (Whyte) of the nineteenth century, let us keep in mind Strindberg's point that the image of the person who is identical with his social role has been with us for centuries.

Automata of manners are a feature of traditional literature, as the true automaton, the Golem, Homunculus, Frankenstein, is a familiar figure of mythology and folklore. Most interesting with regard to the type presented by the new American sociology is his relation to the "mechanical man" image conceived by nineteenth-century writers as associated with the effects upon human beings of the new machine culture. Poe, in "The Man Who Was Made Up," imagined a person put together from fabricated parts; while Marx built his political philosophy upon the misery and triumph of that human "product of modern industry," the proletariat.

In the current writings, the type that displaces the human person also originates in the productive and distributive machinery of society. The Orgman is further identified with the older literature of industrial alienation by the part of science in his drama. In Marx, the key force in historical progress is, of course, science; and it is the scientist of revolution who releases the proletariat upon the world; in *1984* the scientist reappears as the personality-crushing interrogator. Says *The Organization Man:* "The first denominator is scientism"; and goes on to demonstrate the presence in all American institutions of the traditional creator of the mannikin, the "mad scientist," now wearing the guise of the personnel expert, the motivational researcher, or some other "soul engineer."

Blood brother to the inhuman "double," the Mr. Hyde, of romantic literature, on the one hand, and to the proletarian of revolutionary socialism, on the other, the Orgman belongs to the latest episode in the saga of the conquest of society by hordes of faceless *directed* men.

Yet the new literature is neither romantic nor revolutionary, and in this lie its most striking characteristics. One no longer hears the metallic lockstep coming closer, like the rising of swarms of beetles or crabs. The enemy of this decade does not come from below. His is neither the face of the ogre over the edge, nor of the ghost behind the window pane. In the muted melodrama of the current sociology, the inhuman does not *invade*. It sits in the living room twisting the TV dial or takes the family for a ride in the two-tone hardtop. It is you.

Recoiling from the outerworld of society's monsters, outcasts, and victims, the analysts of contemporary America center their interest on the majority that benefits from the existing social process. With this shift of attention the spectre has shifted too. The alienated man has left the company town for the suburb; the factory for the office, the drafting room, the lecture hall. The presence within him of the socially constructed Other is, by the testimony of each of our authors, the mark of "the new middle class" man. It is to the absorption of this alter-ego that all his education and training are directed. Says Riesman: "The mass media ask the child to see the world as 'the' child—that is, the other child—sees it."

To be inhabited by the abstract social person is what is currently meant by the terms "normal" and "socially adjusted."

The charge that all our social behavior stands as a power over and against us *is a more extreme accusation of existing American society than that of the preceding radicalism.* Implicating *everyone,* without distinction as to social class or function, in a single deepening process of dehumanization, such works as *The Lonely Crowd, The Organization Man, The Hidden Persuaders,* communicate in atmosphere, if not in stated concept, the sinister overtones of a developing totalitarianism from which there is no escape. In this literature with its subdued manners of scientific analysis, Orwell keeps springing up like a red devil. *The Hidden Persuaders* features Big Brother on the jacket and promises the reader "a slightly chilly feeling along the spine"; an effect which the blurb for Whyte's volume has already delivered through billing its hero as the man who "not only works for the Organization: he belongs to it." The smiling credit manager you spoke to this morning is a piece of company apparatus like the filing case from which he extracts the card that is you; his human appearance is a disguise, and his real name isn't Brown but Agent F-362.

With Marx, the conversion of the individual's "living time" into lifeless commodities was restricted to the routine of the wage worker. In the current studies, no one who participates in any capacity in the system of production and distribution can escape the vampire that drains him of himself. Differences in class functions have ceased to matter. Even the division between labor and leisure has lost its meaning; for the psychic mortification of the individual takes place not only in and through his work but by means of his participation in any form, public or private, of social life, from church going, to cocktail parties, to his relations with his wife and children. Whyte and Mills put the major emphasis on the job as the ground of estrangement; Spectorsky gives mode of employment and style of leisure about equal play, seeing one as the extension (laboratory?) of the other; Riesman regards the externally controlled psyche as a phenomenon of "the consumer age"—and is supported by the evidence of *The Hidden Persuaders* concerning supermarket penetration-assaults and the cold war against the customer by means of the new psycho-sales weapons. All our authors are at one in conceiving the flattening of personality in America as a universal effect of our interrelated economic and social practices.

What the Orgman-critics expose is not a flaw in society but the injurious realities of its normal everyday life. These, however, are presented in a perspective that denudes them of radical implications. Here "scientific objectivity" has become the disguise of a philosophy of fatalism. The emergence of the Orgman is conceived in terms far more deterministic than those of the "historical materialists." Neither Riesman's "age of consumption" nor Whyte's "Organization" was brought into being by the choice, nor even the need, of anyone, whether individual, class, or nation. The "other-directed society" of the first is a manifestation of the population-curve; the new corporate "collectivism" of the second, of an immanent process of expansion and stratification. The vocabularies chosen by Riesman and Whyte of themselves exclude human intervention, in the future as in the past: you cannot redirect an other-directed period, any more than you can refill an Orgman with "Protestant Ethic." Even if you could, there would be no point in doing so, since other-direction and the ubiquity of the Organization are necessities of our time.

In any case, the histrionic effect of the new criticism is unmistakable: the bland deadpan of the Objective Observer has definitely replaced the scowl of the radical accuser. For him such words as "capitalist," "class conflict," "profits," "depression" are at once too bulky and needlessly exciting. Since they draw from the same storehouse of material and cultural consumers' goods, all Americans have become "capitalists"; since they are changed into directed beings by their work and social consumption, all have become "proletarianized." On both counts, there is no cause for conflict and a unanimity of interest prevails. All of us, Whyte thinks, will have to revolt. But whatever basis there was for Marx's conception of a metaphysico-political uprising of human machine parts against a minority of opulent personalities has vanished in the universal estrangement.

In the new Organization America there are no fundamental issues, though some old-fashioned people may not yet have gotten rid of the habit of taking sides. To "moralize the flow of words," says Riesman, through which events are apprehended today, is a tendency of "the inner-directed person who remains still extant in this period"—which is a marvellously ironical way of saying that you know what is happening only through what you're told about it in the mass media, and that if you care one way or another you merely define yourself as a relic. The deadpan, apparently, is a requisite not only of the analyst of society but of all of us. If Riesman's irony goes unnoticed, as Whyte complains his has, it is because his language is too consistently detached from his subject matter to admit any sense of contrast: Orgprose, too, is deadpan.

Evoking the sinister concept of man as a tool and as an object, the new sociology does so in an oddly disembodied and unpainful way. Its tone is one of injury but of injury unsuffered. It would seem that among the "groups," particularly the better-paid ones, that have replaced the classes in Orgamerica, the substitution of a corporate identity for one's own is not the unmixed deprivation it might have been for the twelve-hour-a-day factory hand or for the citizen of the slave state. Before the Orgman can feel put upon, it is only fair that he consider the advantages gained. "It is not," explains Whyte, "the evils of the organization that puzzle him, but its very beneficence." Strange literature which, assembling the proof of society's subversion of both the will and the intelligence of its members, cries out, like the man in the joke, "But good. But good."

When the fear of the unreal becomes mixed with an idyllic dependence on it, a kind of mythic euphoria ensues which is related to the essence of the comic. Chinese folklore is full of the pranks of demons who have shed their awfulness and sit on window sills and above doorways minding one's business like so many other-directed neighbors. These every-day fiends may be as spiteful on occasion as one of Whyte's integration-specialists, but their troublemaking only adds gaiety to the way the "system" to which they belong achieves its generous aims. The tale of the Orgman has as much in common with dream farce as with the Orwellian torture phantasy. If its hero suffers it is in the drugged world of *A Midsummer Night's Dream* laden with bodily pleasures and tremors, where, in the words of *The Organization Man*, "the demands for his surrender are constant and powerful, and the more he has come to like the organization the more difficult does he find it to resist these demands, or even to recognize them."

For both radicalism and conservatism, history is a struggle of winners and losers. In the new American scene, everyone has won a fairy-tale luxury and lost himself. The drama of history has been replaced by a pantomime in which, freed of individual or mass conflicts, bewildered, adjusted beings respond as in a narcosis to mysterious signs, whispers, hints, and shocks, which each receives on his Riesman "radar mechanism." The scientific wand-wielder responsible for these psychological pinches and tweaks which inject dream anxieties into their physical serenity is a kind of affable Puck; for even the scientist, since he is necessary, is no longer a real villain; the evil lies rather in his abstract double "scientism." Riesman and Whyte construct their shadowplay in such a way as to leave no point of resistance. As in Whyte's description quoted above, any struggle against surrender on the part of the individual constitutes a wrestle in a dream. Neither Whyte nor Riesman indicates any direction in which the American person can realize himself in the actual world.

Yet disregarding the nature of the type or "character" as automaton, each holds out the hope that the alter-ego he is describing may some day develop into a human individual. This empty happy-ending is excellent as finale in a farce like *The Three Penny Opera;* as a substitute for protest or for tragic pathos in a portrayal of actual life, such sudden optimism arouses the suspicion of an attempt at ingratiation. Whyte looks forward to a time when "men partially liberated might be tantalized into demanding more"—no doubt by means of mass-persuasion techniques. As for Riesman, he can lift his consumer type out of the trap of "belongingness" only by attaching to him the time-fuse of a self-transforming process:

"these developments (the mass distribution of art and literature) suggest to me that the process of taste-exchanging holds the promise of transcending itself and becoming something quite different, and of signally contributing to the development of autonomy in other-directed men." As if one could go from the abstract to the concrete, the automaton to the organism. Our sociologists' remedy for alienation is not "scientism"—it is sorcery.

Extremist but neither radical nor conservative, the Organization criticism is inspired not by a passion for social correction but by nostalgia. A sigh over the lost person mars the phantasy of American unanimity which has supplanted the ideological Passion Plays of Marxian condemnation and conflict. Whyte's memoir on his training in the Vicks Vaporub rugged individualist sales force of "the old days" (the late thirties) is the most eloquent and touching passage in this entire literature. The Age of the Giants—alas, gone forever. With Vicks's Richardson extinct, every human degradation may be logically anticipated. Today, the Orgman, the "dominant member of society," still lives among the relics of older types. Tomorrow he will tread the stage alone, in conflict only with himself.

It is the business type of yesterday whom the new social criticism has generalized into its "inner-directed" and "Protestant Ethic" abstraction, and in the name of which it fires its barrages against present-day tendencies. If it takes some daring to bury the boss, it takes less if one also bewails him in public. Especially in a situation where he has much to gain by playing dead. In Whyte's indictment of the human exactions of the Corporation, one hears the voice of the Founder deploring "the drift toward socialization."

Loosed from action, for which it can see no aim, the post-radical criticism often exaggerates its complaints, producing a worse impression of conditions than is warranted by the facts, at the same time that it seeks remedies in the wrong direction. For example, Mills, the most emotionally authentic of these writers, undervalues the personal and social expression of the white-collar worker on the job, with an effect of melancholy that seems unreal when one looks at actual men and women coming out of an office building. On the other hand, the salvation through improvement of taste proposed by Riesman, or through a psychic resistance based on private life (far more impoverished for the clerk than his job) suggested by Whyte, are, as we have seen, equally unreal.

But there is more to the conception of the Orgman than regret for an older social type. As the representative of the new post-war employed intelligentsia, the post-radical critic suffers also a nostalgia for himself as an independent individual. For his former abstract sympathy with a nominal working class, the intellectual of this decade has substituted an examination in the mirror of his own social double as insider of the Organization and the Community. It is what he sees there that has caused him to project a morbid image of society compared with which the old "class struggle" America seems not only naif but as relatively healthy as a war with rifles and cannons.

For in regard to the misery of alienation who is a greater victim of what Whyte calls the split "between the individual as he is and the role he is called upon to play" than the member of the intellectual caste newly enlisted *en masse* in carrying out society's functions? As writer, artist, social scientist, he is one with his talents and his education for creative work; in playing his part in the service of the organization he must eliminate any thought of functioning for himself. Through his personal inventiveness he has in the past fifteen years achieved prosperity and social prestige; yet he is the most dependent of wage earners and the most anxiously conscious of his dependence—*The Exurbanites* chronicles this dependence and anxiety to the last installment dollar. (Applying itself to the narrower spectrum of the commercialized intellectuals, *The Exurbanites* is the most realistic of the works we have been considering.)

The intellectual employee also accepts a more total identification with his role than other workers, in that the editorial director, the designer, the copy writer, etc., sells himself more completely in terms of both psychic energy expended and in number of hours worked. With him the division between work and leisure, discipline and freedom, has truly been erased. If the free artist or the founder of a great enterprise builds his life exclusively out of the substance of his work, today's intellectual unbuilds his life in order to live his job.*

Besides being the prime victim and exemplar of self-loss in contemporary society, the "organized" professional cannot escape a conviction of guilt for his part in depriving others of their individuality. He has consented to use his capacities as a tool and to approve in practice the proposition recorded by Whyte that "all the great ideas have already been discovered." His skills tend to relate to human management, e.g., writing, image-making, program-forming; even if his specialty is in engineering or the physical sciences, the results of his work directly augment the force by which society is controlled. The intellectual cannot function as Organization Man without also functioning as Organization-Man moulder; as human object he must also affect others as objects; as manipulated act as manipulator. Thus he cannot help but feel himself to be a betrayer of humanity

* The rule quoted by Whyte for corporation executives generally, "You promote the guy who takes his problem home with him," becomes for the intellectual, "You hire the guy who takes his problem to bed with him." His job has a creative side in which his preconscious must also collaborate. Take this into account in computing his average salary, and the difference between the wage-earner of the suburb and of the company town becomes largely a matter of overtime pay. At $2.50 an hour the totally employed intellectual would earn more than $20,000 a year.

as of his own mind. Helpless to change anything, he is yet the chief culprit of the alienation drama, the driven "scientist," who directs the undermining of the raw individual, whether as motivational expert, inventor of personnel tests, or as preacher of despairing acceptance.

Self-displacement through one's acts is the innermost problem of life in America as of that in all civilized countries. The Social Type has always been among us, of course, despite Riesman's effort to distinguish today's other-directed man from his nineteenth-century counterpart. Tolstoy's Ivan Ilych, who decorated his house entirely according to his own original ideas only to have it turn out exactly like all other houses of his class, is as good an example of automatic "radared" taste-exchanging (Riesman) as can be found in Fairfield County. Tolstoy explicitly insisted that Ilych was a socially made-up man, an "object" guided by public opinion, an example of "dead" living.

In the United States, nineteenth-century literature, whether in the popular stage comedies of manners or in the symbolism of the romantics, centers on society's human abstractions. We mentioned above Poe's hero who owed to industry his moveable parts. A contemporary of this invention was the ubiquitous Salesman-Preacher, whom Melville, writing in a less unctuous age than ours, named the Confidence Man. Like Whyte, Spectorsky, and Packard, Melville saw in this professional who supplied his countrymen with things, ideas, and feeling, the outstanding specimen of man as social artifice. As his complement, he set up the brooding inner-directed Indian Fighter, paranoiac Ahab of the prairies; while from the silent recesses of the office files, he drew forth the white-collared tomb deity, Bartleby.

What is new in America is not the socially reflexive person but the presence of a self-conscious intellectual caste whose disillusionment has induced its members to volunteer for the part. The predicament in which these individuals find themselves is what casts a bar sinister over their image of America. The fear-augury that the Orgman will become everyone in a quiet, unopposable totalitarianism is not a conclusion based on social analysis but a projection of the fate they have chosen for themselves. The American landscape has by no means been remade by the "Social Ethic" compression machine into an electrified Eden set out on porcelain grass. Except in the new suburbs, the physical condition of America's cities, towns, and villages is of itself proof enough that decay, shiftlessness, egotism, and other forms of popular expressionism are more than holding their own against other-direction. Granted that the growth of the supercorporation and the absorption and standardization of small business has changed the independent operator into an agent, at the same time that mechanization has been turning the workman into a technician; granted that Whyte's notation that "the collectivization so visible in the corporation has affected almost every field of work" is indisputable; and that today Orgmen reproduce themselves like fruit flies in whatever is organized, whether it be a political party or a museum of advanced art; given this groundwork for the conquest of America by this "type," still the contention that the nation is, or even might be, subordinated to such a master is at least as ludicrous as it is alarming. The increasing concentration of control and the standardization of work present well-known alternatives which we need not discuss here; but for the individual, the last voice in the issue of being or not being himself is still his own.

The inhabitant of the sacred groves has, however, surrendered all choices. Having accepted self-alienation in trade for social place, the post-radical intellectual can see nothing ahead but other-direction and a corporately styled personality. For him the Orgworld has closed for good. Within these limits the deploring of "conformity" is simply an expression of self-pity. The strategy of fighting the organization through secret resistance behind the outer-shaped mask (Whyte) is, by the measure of the ancient intellectual tradition of denunciation or self-exile, only a dreary professional's ruse for holding on to the best of both worlds. That such a proposal should seem relevant is another proof that the Orgman is, with necessary disguises, none other than the new intellectual talking about himself. Certainly the deft management of the corporate Look which solves things for Whyte would be of no help to the farmer or to the workingman, nor would the boss need to make use of it. The "what to do about it" part of the studies of Whyte and Riesman are clearly sermons for their milieu rather than challenges to history in the name of mankind.

The critics of the new America are disheartened by a revolution won—their revolution, which can go no farther than ending the underground life of the American intellectual mass through economic recognition of the services it has to offer. With his own success achieved, the only issue the intellectual can see as remaining for society is "personality." Somehow, this seems unattainable in "the dehumanized collective" that he is taking a leading part in building. The result is depression—and it is by the power of the depression it generates, in contrast to the smugness of the old-time boosting, that the present sociology is a force against a more radical and realistic understanding of American life.

C.

THE ENCIRCLED MIND

WILLARD WALLER

What Teaching Does to Teachers

TEACHING makes the teacher. Teaching is a boomerang that never fails to come back to the hand that threw it. Of teaching, too, it is true, perhaps, that it is more blessed to give than to receive, and it also has more effect. Between good teaching and bad there is a great difference where students are concerned, but none in this, that its most pronounced effect is upon the teacher. Teaching does something to those who teach. Introspective teachers know of changes that have taken place in themselves. Objectively minded persons have observed the relentless march of growing teacherishness in others. This is our problem.

It is necessary to see this inquiry in its true perspective. The question: What does teaching do to teachers? is only a part of the greater problem: What does any occupation do to the human being who follows it? Now that differences of caste and rank have become inconspicuous, and differences that go with the locale are fading, it is the occupation that most marks the man. The understanding of the effects upon the inner man of the impact of the occupation is thus an important task of social science. It is a problem almost untouched. We know that some occupations markedly distort the personalities of those who practice them, that there are occupational patterns to which one conforms his personality as to a Procrustean bed by lopping off superfluous members. Teaching is by no means the only occupation which whittles its followers to convenient

Reprinted from *The Sociology of Teaching* (1932), pp. 375-409, by permission of the publisher.

size and seasons them to suit its taste. The lawyer and the chorus girl soon come to be recognizable social types. One can tell a politician when one meets him on the street. Henry Adams has expanded upon the unfitness of senators for being anything but senators; occupational molding, then, affects the statesman as much as lesser men. The doctor is always the doctor, and never quite can quit his role. The salesman lives in a world of selling configurations. And what preaching most accomplishes is upon the preacher himself. Perhaps no occupation that is followed long fails to leave its stamp upon the person. Certainly teaching leaves no plainer mark than some other vocations, though it is, perhaps, a mark which a larger number of people can recognize. It is our present task to determine, as objectively as may be and as completely as possible, the effect of teaching upon the person.

The selective pattern which teaching presents to prospective teachers has never been adequately described, and the present writer does not presume to be able to deal with it any better than have his predecessors. It is a known fact that the financial rewards of teaching are not great; the pay low, the opportunity for advancement, for most teachers, slight; and economic security little. Most writers have concluded that this is in itself an explanation of the known failure of the profession to attract as large a number of capables as it should. Yet one may wonder whether merely raising salaries all around would cause the mediocre to be crowded out by the influx of the talented. The social standing of the profession is unfortunately low, and this excludes more capable than incapable persons. Particularly damaging, probably, is the belief that is abroad in the community that only persons incapable of success in other lines become teachers, that teaching is a failure belt, the refuge of "unsalable men and unmarriagable women." This belief is the more damaging for the truth that is in it. The nature of the work of teaching, with its overwhelming mass of routine and its few opportunities for free self-expression, may both deter and attract to the ultimate damage of the profession. On the one hand, the drudgery of teaching, combined with the many restrictions which the community places upon the personal conduct of teachers, may eliminate from teaching many of those virile and inspiring persons of whom the profession has such need, for it is a known fact that such pronouncedly individual persons often have little respect for purely negative morality, and react vehemently against living within the community stereotype of the teacher. On the other hand, teaching, along with the ministry, is known as one of the sheltered occupations, as an occupation where those persons who shrink from the daily battle of life, often very estimable persons, by the way, may find refuge. This quality of not wishing to do battle in the front rank, which would perhaps show a high correlation with introversion, by no means detracts from the teaching ability of every person who has it, but on the whole it probably operates to the detriment of the profession.

Perhaps all those who have treated the topic of the selective factors determining the composition of the teaching population have erred by handling the subject too rationalistically. Rarely does an occupational choice result from a process of rigorous reasoning. More often it is the social experience of the individual which gives him a push into teaching that he cannot resist, and the advantages and disadvantages of teaching remain unconsidered. Perhaps it is an inherent need of the personality for being in some sort of managerial position which prompts one to take up teaching as an occupational goal. Perhaps it is a training which has interested one in the things of the mind so that the attractiveness of other occupations has been dulled and that only teaching is left as a compromise (creative art being left out of consideration for lack of talent). Perhaps it is a training which has made one almost able to enter some other profession, such as law or medicine, but has left him at the door. (Students of one midwestern institution refer to the customary fifteen hours of education as an "insurance policy.") Perhaps it is a desire for ready money which prompts the young graduate to take up teaching, where he can command a slightly higher salary as a beginner than he can in business.

When the mills have ground which supply to each profession its accustomed human material, the teaching profession receives each year a large number of plastic and unformed minds. These new recruits have whatever qualities they may have, and upon the basis of their present personalities their life in the teaching profession will build a different structure. They do not know how to teach, although they may know everything that is in innumerable books telling them how to teach. They will not know how to teach until they have got the knack of certain personal adjustments which adapt them to their profession, and the period of learning may be either long or short. These recruits who face teaching as a life work are ready to learn to teach, and they are ready, though they know it not, to be formed by teaching. When teaching has formed them, what shape will it give them? Their daily work will write upon them; what will it write?

What teaching does to teachers it does partly by furnishing them those roles which habit ties to the inner frame of personality and use makes one with the self. Our method in this discussion will be to describe those social situations which the teacher most often encounters, and to analyze them to discover how the qualities considered to be characteristic of the teacher are produced in them. We must admit that this is a method of empirical analysis, and that it has its first and most important basis in what the writer has seen and thought and done. The only test of such analysis and of the generalizations which come from it is the judgment of other writers who have had equal opportunity to observe. Although this method is vague and is little subject to control, it is the only method available at the present time for pursuing an inquiry of this sort, and we shall endeavor to apply it in as fair-minded a way as possible. Where there seem to be two sides, we shall state both and leave the reader to choose for himself.

Aside from a scattering company of panegyrists, most of those who have presumed to comment on the teacher as an occupational type have done so in an unfriendly manner. This is perhaps regrettable, but certainly significant, for most of those who have passed unfavorable judgments upon teachers have been teachers themselves; from pondering this, one gets a little insight into the conditions of stress and strain in the teacher mind. Unfriendly commentators upon the manners of teachers are able to compile a long list of unpleasant qualities which, they say, are engendered in the teacher's personality by teaching experience. There is first that certain inflexibility or unbendingness of personality which is thought to mark the person who has taught. That stiff and formal manner into which the young teacher compresses himself every morning when he puts on his collar becomes, they say, a plaster cast which at length he cannot loosen. One has noticed, too, that in his personal relationships the teacher is marked by reserve, an incomplete personal participation in the dynamic social situation and a lack of spontaneity, in psychological terms, by an inhibition of his total responses in favor of a restricted segment of them. As if this reserve were not in itself enough to discourage ill-considered advances, it is supplemented, when one has become very much the teacher, by certain outward barriers which prevent all and sundry from coming into contact with the man behind the mask and discovering those inhibited and hidden possibilities of reaction. Along with this goes dignity, the dignity of the teacher which is not natural dignity like that of the American Indian, but another kind of dignity that consists of an abnormal concern over a restricted role and the restricted but well-defined status that goes with it. One who has taught long enough may wax unenthusiastic on any subject under the sun; this, too, is part of the picture painted by unfriendly critics. The didactic manner, the authoritative manner, the flat, assured tones of voice that go with them, are bred in the teacher by his dealings in the school room where he rules over the petty concerns of children as a Jehovah none too sure of himself, and it is said that these traits are carried over by the teacher into his personal relations. It is said, and it would be difficult to deny it, that the teacher mind is not creative. Even the teacher's dress is affected by his occupational attitudes; the rule is that the teacher must be conservative, if not prim, in manner, speech, and dress. There are other traits which some observers have mentioned: a set of the lips, a look of strain, a certain kind of smile, a studied mediocrity, a glib mastery of platitude. Some observers have remarked that a certain way of standing about, the way of a person who has had to spend much of his time waiting for something to happen and has had to be very dignified about it, is characteristic of the teacher. Sometimes only small and uncertain indications betray the profession. Sometimes, as a cynical novelist has remarked of one of his characters, one cannot see the man for the school master. If these traits, or those essential ones which make up the major outlines of the picture, are found among the generality of teachers, it is because these traits have survival value in the schools of today. If one does not have them when he joins the faculty, he must develop them or die the academic death. Opinions might differ as to how widely these characteristic traits are found among the members of the profession and as to how deeply they are ingrained, as to whether the ordinary man might see them, or only one with the curse of satire. But Henry Adams has said that no man can be a school master for ten years and remain fit for anything else, and his statement has given many a teacher something to worry about.

There is enough plausibility in the above description to make us teachers ponder about the future, if not the present, of ourselves and our friends. But there is another side, and we may well pause to look at it before going on with our analysis. Teaching brings out pleasant qualities in some persons, and for them it is the most gratifying vocation in the world. The teacher enjoys the most pleasant associations in his work; he lives surrounded by the respect of the community and the homage of his students. Teaching affords a splendid opportunity for a self-sacrificing person (how many of these are there?) to realize his destiny vicariously; in any case the teacher is less soiled by life than those who follow more vigorous professions. It may well be questioned, too, whether there is any occupational conscience more strict than that of the teacher. Teaching breeds patience in some teachers, patience and fairness and a reserve that is only gentlemanly and never frosty. There are some persons whom teaching liberates, and these sense during their first few months of teaching a rapid growth and expansion of personality. While we are stating this side of the case, we must record the pointed observation of one person on the constructive side of the argument that those very teachers who are bitterest in the denunciation of teaching would not for a moment consider doing anything else, and that even the most discontented teachers can rarely bring themselves to leave the profession. These considerations should be enough to convince us that there are two sides to everything that can be said about the teacher, perhaps that teaching produces radically different effects upon different types of persons. But whatever the classification of the qualities which are produced in the teacher by teaching, they all mark the occupational type. Our theoretical problem should now be clear; it is to account for the genesis of the character traits belonging to the teacher by showing how they flow out of the action of his life situation upon his personality, if possible, to show how different effects are produced upon different basic personality types.

The weightiest social relationship of the teacher is his relationship to his students; it is this relationship which is teaching. It is around this relationship that the teacher's personality tends to be organized, and it is in adaptation to the needs of this relationship that the qualities of character which mark the teacher are produced. The teacher-pupil relationship is a special form of dominance and subordination, a very unstable relationship and in quivering equilibrium, not much supported by sanction and the strong arm of authority, but depending largely upon purely personal ascendency. Every teacher is a taskmaster and every taskmaster is a hard man; if he is naturally kindly, he is hard from duty, but if he is naturally unkind, he is hard because he loves it. It is an unfortunate role, that of Simon Legree, and has corrupted the best of men. Conflict is in the role, for the wishes of the teacher and the student are necessarily divergent, and more conflict because the teacher must protect himself from the possible destruction of his authority that might arise from this divergence of motives. Subordination is possible only because the subordinated one is a subordinate with a mere fragment of his personality, while the dominant one participates completely. The subject is a subject only part of the time and with a part of himself, but the king is all king. In schools, too, subordinated ones attempt to protect themselves by withdrawing from the relationship, to suck the juice from the orange of conformity before rendering it to the teacher. But the teacher is doomed to strive against the mechanization of his rule and of obedience to it. It is the part of the teacher to enforce a real obedience. The teacher must be aggressive in his domination, and this is very unfortunate, because domination is tolerable only when it stays within set bounds. From this necessary and indispensable aggressiveness of the teacher arises an answering hostility on the part of the student which imperils the very existence of any intercourse between them. The teacher takes upon himself most of the burden of the far-reaching psychic adjustments which make the continuance of the relationship possible.

That inflexibility or unbendingness of personality which we have mentioned as characterizing the school teacher flows naturally out of his relations with his students. The teacher must maintain a consistent pose in the presence of students. He must not adapt to the demands of the childish group in which he lives, but must force the group to adapt to him, wherefore the teacher often feels that he must take leave of graciousness and charm and the art of being a good fellow at the classroom door. The teacher must not accept the definitions of situations which students work out, but must impose his own definition upon students. His position as an agent of social control, as the paid representative of the adult group among the group of children, requires that when he has found a pose he must hold it; to compromise upon matters where adult morality runs would be thought treason to the group that pays his salary. There is added a necessity of his professional career which, since men and careers are always mingled and never appear separately, is also of the greatest personal importance: he must maintain discipline, and it is easier to maintain discipline by making continual demands of the same sort and by keeping one's social role constant in conformity with those constant demands than by changing roles frequently and making demands consistent with those changing roles but inconsistent with each other. It is, furthermore, very wearing to change roles when one is responsible for a group, for one must make the fact of the change and all its implications clear to the entire group. It usually requires a certain effort to constellate all the members of the group in the new set of attitudes which take their key from the teacher's changed role; there are laggards who never quite catch the point, and some lacking in social comprehension who cannot know that the teacher is joking or do not observe that he has stopped; there are risks to the teacher-dominated order in the straggling march to a new mental alignment. Therefore the teacher cannot change his role as often as the fulfillment of his personal impulses might dictate. When he does change it, he must label the transition in such a manner as to destroy its point, erect sign-posts, take the salt from his humor by broad hints that he is joking now. But the ability of a person to hold our interest as a person depends in large part upon a shifting of social roles so rapid that the eye must look closely to see it and so subtle that no ready-made labels can fit it.

If there are few roles which classroom life permits the teacher to play, he must put on each of them many times a day. The teacher must alternate his roles because he is trying to do inconsistent things with his students, and he can bring them about only by rapid changes from one established pose to another. He is trying to maintain a definite dominance over young persons whose lives he presumes to regulate very completely. This requires of the teacher aggressiveness, unyieldingness, and determination. If persisted in, this attitude would exterminate in students all interest in subject matter and would crush out every faint inclination to participate in the social life of the classroom, which presents no very alluring vistas at the best. And the teacher who went very long upon this tack would be known for a knave and a fool, and justly hated for a martinet. Sometimes an unimaginative teacher runs into just this situation. The solution is found in alternating this authority role with some other which is not altogether inconsistent with it but which veils the authority so that hostility is no longer aroused. But the authority impression must be continually renewed, and there ensues a long series of rapid but not subtle changes of role. As a result, the limitations and implications of the teacher-pupil relationship are made clear to the pupil group.

A clever friend has perhaps summed up the matter by saying, "The successful teacher is one who knows how to get on and off his high-horse rapidly." (As it happened, the author of this remark did not himself possess this skill, and failed in teaching, as so many other clever men have done, for want of dignity.) Thus one says, "I am your teacher," in a certain unemotional tone of voice. This begets discipline, perhaps some sullenness, certainly emotional and personal frustration on the part of both student and teacher. Before this reaction has been carried through to completion, one says, "But I am a human being and I try to be a good fellow. And you are all fine people and we have some good times together, don't we?" This is role number two, and if taken at its face value it begets a desirable cheerfulness and a dangerous friendliness. If he tarries too long upon this grace note, the teacher loses his authority by becoming a member of the group. He must revert to role number one, and say, with just a hint of warning and an implication of adult dignity in his voice, "But I am the teacher." All this occurs a hundred times a day in every school room, and it marks the rhythm of the teacher's movements of advancement and retreat with reference to his students, the alternate expansion and contraction of his personality. It does not occur, of course, in so obvious a form as this; it is perhaps only the very unskillful teacher who needs to put such things into words. This pulsation of the teacher's personality, with its answering change of posture on the part of students, is usually reduced to a mere conversation of gestures. This conversation, for all that habit has stripped it so bare of identifying characteristics and drained it so dry of emotion, is the most significant social process of the classroom. It is also a very important determinant of the teacher's personality, and one of the points on which transfer is said to be made most easily. After all, it need cause us no amazement if one who has learned to get his way in the school by alternate applications of hot and cold water should fall into that technique of control in his more intimate relationships. In the life of every teacher there is a significant long-term change in the psychic weight of these roles, a not unusual result being that role number one, the authority role, eats up the friendly role, or absorbs so much of the personality that nothing is left for friendliness to fatten upon.

The authority role becomes very much formalized, both because of the psychological law that performances lose their meaningfulness by frequent repetition and because there is an advantage in having it so. Army men speak of a voice of command, a flat, impersonal, unquestionable, noncontroversial tone of voice in which commands are best given. It is a tone of voice without overtones, representing only a segment of the officer's personality and demanding obedience from only a segment of the subordinate. School teachers learn by trial and error, by imitation and practice, to formalize their commands. They develop, too, the voice of exposition, which is a voice perfectly dry and as mechanical as a dictaphone, a voice adapted to the expounding of matter that has long since lost what interest it may have had for the expounder. Lack of enthusiasm has survival value. Hence the paradox that sometimes the best teachers are those least interested in their work, and that others do their best work when least concerned. But all these things contribute to the final flatness and dullness of the teacher who falls a prey to them.

It has often been remarked that a certain kind of dignity is characteristic of teachers. It seems that teachers develop a certain way of carrying themselves which sets them out from the rest of the world. This we may call school-teacher dignity. There seem to be two major roots of school-teacher dignity. One is in the community and in the attitude which the community takes toward the teacher; the other is in the nature of the teacher's work. (These are not unconnected, for the community attitude is determined by the school experience of the adult members of the community.) What happens when a new and unformed teacher first goes about in the community in which he is to teach? Let us say that a person who has never before known deference takes up teaching. Suddenly he finds himself the object of flattering attention from students, catered to by them and addressed respectfully and ceremoniously by fellow teachers. In the community he is called "Professor." Tradesmen approach him obsequiously; plain citizens kow-tow. People profess to show him special consideration on the grounds that he is a teacher. He is supposed to be more trustworthy than other mortals, more moral, more learned. A place of honor is prepared for him. It is a dignity that is unearned, and it is empty because it is unearned. In any other occupation, with the same training and experience, he would still be a menial of low degree, but if he ever fought through the ranks in another profession and attained to his top hat at last, he would merit the distinction, and it would fit him well. Not so teacher dignity, for it is too cheap; only the finest man can give it a high value, and then it is not the profession, but the man, that counts. Some young teachers, knowing that they merit no deference, endeavor to fend it off as gracefully as they can. Others realize vaguely that this external respect of the community is a part of the school-teacher stereotype, that it is the obverse side of a latent hostility and is more than balanced by an inclination to ridicule; sometimes they know that this respect is part of the iron framework that shuts the teacher, as a sacred object,[1] out of society and keeps him from acting as a human being—

these rebel against teacher dignity. Perhaps their rebellion brings them personal disaster, and they are forced to compromise at last with dignity. Perhaps they merely suffer a myriad of tiny hurts from the satire of the dignity, and that gives them dignity by a process of scar tissue. But dignity they must get, rebels or no—somehow. Others accept teacher dignity, and make the most of it. It is a flattering role. They live it. They live it the more determinedly if they ever become aware of the irony that comes with it to the lips of the average man.

The second root of teacher dignity is in the nature of the teacher's work in the classroom. The teacher lives much by the authority role; his livelihood depends upon it. Those who live much by one role must learn to defend its ultimate implications. Dignity is a means of defending the authority role. The necessity of maintaining dignity is increased by the fact that the role which gives rise to it is peculiarly liable to attack. On the objective side this dignity which arises in the classroom is an exaggerated concern over all the ramifications of respect and all the formal amenities due to one who occupies a narrow but well-defined social status. On the subjective side, dignity is first an inhibition of all action tendencies inconsistent with the major role of the school teacher. What is inhibited is usually the teacher's responsiveness to the more minute and subtler stimuli; what the teacher must crush out in himself is his alertness for human participation in unimportant by-play. But since it is this little responsiveness that makes us human, or makes us seem to be human, we say that the teacher, when his dignity has become habitual, has lost the human touch. Since, furthermore, the teacher must demand and obtain respect in all the ramifications of his authoritative role, he must develop certain mechanisms in himself which will defeat any attacks made by others upon that role. Among these mechanisms, perhaps chief among them, is the hair-trigger temper so often observed in the man with the pointer. The person learning to teach must recondition his anger response. The teacher must learn when to get angry and how to get angry quickly. He must learn every by-path of the social interaction of the classroom so that he may know what does and does not constitute an attack upon his dignity. To keep little misdeeds from growing into great ones, he must learn to magnify them to the larger size originally; this is easy because the more his habits are concerned with the established order the more heinous breaches of it will appear. What is even more important, he must learn that breaches of order committed in his presence or when he is responsible constitute direct attacks upon his authority. Teachers are cranky because crankiness helps them to hold their jobs.

If by virtue of unusual personal force or some psychological sleight of hand the teacher is able to dispense with dignity, or if there is in him no need for playing an authoritative role, but rather a revulsion against it, so that he pays the price and goes all undignified, he still stands to have dignity forced upon him by others. Though he avoids the open disrespect which most teachers without dignity encounter, or thinks *camaraderie* a compensation for it, he may still be wounded when he learns that his students compare him unfavorably with their other teachers on account of his lack of dignity or his lack of concern for the respect due him. Or he may find that he loses the friendship of the few students who matter to him because of his tolerance for the affronts of those who do not matter. But most of all is dignity enforced by one's fellow teachers. The significant people for a school teacher are other teachers, and by comparison with good standing in that fraternity the good opinion of students is a small thing and of little price. A landmark in one's assimilation to the profession is that moment when he decides that only teachers are important. According to the teacher code there is no worse offense than failure to deport one's self with dignity, and the penalties exacted for the infraction of the code are severe. A more subtle influence of the teacher group arises from the fact that it passes on its tradition to the new member of the profession and furnishes him with his models of imitation.

One has become a school teacher when he has learned to fear the loss of his dignity. Not that a greenhorn can resolve to be very dignified on the morrow, and become a full-fledged teacher by virtue of his resolution. He must learn to be dignified without the slightest effort, and without being conscious of the fact that he is being dignified; it must be so natural for him to ride upon the high horse that he fears alighting as he would fear falling from a balloon. Usually the psychological process by which one comes to fear the loss of dignity and to be bound by iron habit to the dignified pattern is not at all understood by the person who is going through it. He rarely knows that he is acquiring dignity, and when he has acquired it he does not know that he has it. The process by which dignity is built up in the teacher is apparently about as follows. A few unpleasant experiences build up a feeling of insecurity or a fear of what will happen if one lets the situation get out of hand. This fear produces a limitation of intercourse with students to the starkest essentials and an inhibition of other tendencies to respond to the persons about him. One does not love children when they are likely to become dangerous; one does not even trust them. This paralysis of part of the personality and limitation of action is school-teacher poise and school-teacher dignity; it enables one to cut through all extraneous matter to that core of behavior which involves discipline. The teacher who has it is "all business." When it has become habitual and one has built up a new conception of his role around his delimited activities, one has acquired dignity and one has become a school teacher. Though confidence returns, as it usually does, and though that confidence grows to great proportions, as it sometimes does, the limitation of behavior remains. It should also be noted that the necessity of treating all students alike contributes to the school teacher's dignity, in so far as that is a matter of the social distance between student and teacher.

The wonted seeking-avoiding balance of the teacher, connected with dignity, is not maintained without some inner conflict. Teachers tend to withdraw from non-institutional contacts the while they yearn for the opportunity and the strength to live a life of dust and danger. Their customary routine of duties, their well-known ceremonial of personal relations, come to be their world, a world which they think of as in some sense a shelter. Thus in one mood the teacher reflects that the school year draws to a close and he shudders slightly at the thought of the new contacts which the summer may bring him. Some budding orators have found their powers deserting them as they developed into school teachers; their growing shell made the self-revelation and expression of emotion which are the soul of successful speech-making increasingly difficult; perhaps they even came to take pride in the fact that "gush" was no longer in their line and to look back with shame to their spectacular behavior in the days when their habits of social expression were less restricted. "Don't be an ass," is a rule of conduct which has a special appeal to teachers and to all others who live much in a dominant role. Yet it is a principle that paralyzes, too, and one that cuts the person off from communion with his naive fellows, and the teacher often feels the isolation which his personality traits impose upon him.

Some of the gradual deadening of the intellect which the observer remarks in the teacher as he grows into his profession may no doubt be explained as an effect of age. Perhaps age does dull some persons, and certainly experience disciplines the creative impulse out of many. But if all the deterioration in the teacher is due to age, there must be a special type of short-blooming mind that is attracted to teaching; if this is so, we are thrown back upon the unanswered question of occupational selection. Another type of explanation could be based upon the tendency inculcated upon one practicing any profession to respond to recurring social situations in stereotyped ways. The deepening of some grooves of social expression is apparently inevitable in any occupation, and this emphasis of the part must involve deterioration of the whole. The mental structure of the unspecialized person is necessarily plastic; by specializing and developing particular proficiency along some one line, one nearly always loses some of his general adaptability. Perhaps that was why the elder James regarded so many of the established pursuits as "narrowing." The extent to which a profession stereotypes and narrows the social expression of the individual depends upon the range of variation in the social situations which the practice of the profession presents. The situations which the teacher faces are somewhat more stereotyped than those which the lawyer and the doctor must confront. Perhaps teaching is only a little more rigid in the social patterning which it imposes upon its devotees, but it is a very important little. The over-attention of teachers to tool subjects must certainly be called in to help explain the smallness and unimportance of the contributions which teachers have made ot the arts and sciences. The teacher, from the very nature of his work, must spend most of his time in the classroom in drilling his students upon those subjects which may later open to them the doors that lead to wisdom. Other men, when they have reached maturity, may themselves use those tools to unlock the doors of the palace and enter within. But the teacher, unfortunately, must always sit upon the front steps and talk about the means of opening the door; he must instruct others in the technique of door-opening, and usually he finds when he has finished his task that he has no energy left for explorations of his own. All this is incidental to the fact that the teacher must deal with persons living in a world of childish attitudes and values, and comes himself to live in it part way. This is what one teacher called "the drag of the immature mind."

The creative powers of teachers disappear because the teacher tends to lose the learner's attitude. As Burnham has put it, "Again, one's own opinion based upon personal experience and strengthened by daily repetition[2] is apt to develop a didactic attitude that makes learning impossible. With this mental set, teachers cannot learn because so eager to teach; and nothing perhaps wearies them so much as to hear again what they think they already know. This inhibition of learning by the attitude of the teacher as such, combined with the common critical attitude, made it impossible for a large part of the teachers to profit greatly by the teachings of genetic pedagogy and genetic psychology."[3] Now G. Stanley Hall was one of those rare teachers who keep the learner's attitude to the extent of being anxious to learn from their own students, and this was surely not unconnected with the creativeness of his intelligence.

It is likely that the general adaptability of the teacher suffers also from the over-stable adjustment which the teacher makes to a number of simple, changeless rhythms. Teaching, perhaps, exceeds other professions only in the unvarying quality of these rhythms and the tightness with which they are bound together. There is the rhythm of the class period, which becomes so exact and unvarying that the experienced teacher often has a feeling for the end of the hour which no delayed bell can delude. One teacher has reported that when he had taught for some years in a school where the daily regimen was adhered to strictly, he developed a time mechanism which always told him when two minutes only were left of the hour; at this time, contrary to the rules of pedagogy, he assigned the lesson for the next day. He said that if he forced himself to assign the lesson at the beginning of the hour, as he occasionally did, he might fail to note the nearness of the end, but if the bell were delayed by so much as two or three minutes, he always noticed it. This is no doubt rather an unusual case, but similar mechanisms operate in other teachers with less perfection. Then there is the daily rhythm, with its high points and low, its crises relieving monotony, its automatic transition from one class to another, and its alternation of school duties. There is a weekly rhythm, marked by Monday and Friday, and by special days devoted to special tasks. Where the daily routine differs much from one day to the next, the teacher tends to live by the week; this seems to be true of the college teacher. There is a monthly rhythm; payday, quizzes, grades, and the completion of certain tasks mark off the month. In certain communities, the life of the teacher is from one spring to the next, for at that time it is decided what teachers shall be retained and what ones dismissed, and it is never altogether a foregone conclusion in what class one is going to be. In any case, one reckons time from his years of teaching for the first few years. The myriad smaller habits which cluster about teaching (usually interpretable as the manifestations of central, determining roles) are organized into the pattern of life by being made a part of one of these basic rhythms, and this in part accounts for the meaning which these habits have; a violation of the rhythm in even its smallest detail throws the whole scheme of things out of joint. This extreme routinization amounts almost to stereotypy. Thus a certain man reports that he used to pass a very bad day if he did not have time in the morning to read his paper carefully and smoke his pipe. This external scheme of things, bound together by basic simple rhythms, has a deeper basis in the fundamental motives of the individual, or acquires it by the internal reworking of externals by which time gives values to any life arrangement. Habit, bound together by rhythm, reworked by and in terms of fundamental motives, twisted about until it expresses those motives, accounts for most of the rightness and oughtness of the existent social order. The moss of meaning upon the stone long ago given us for bread can make it bread.

We have touched upon fear in its relation to the non-inventiveness of the teacher mind, and we have elsewhere identified the wish for security with certain mental mechanisms called into action by definite fears. It seems worth while to analyze a little further the results of the dominance of this security motive, based upon fear, in the life of the teacher. That security does receive preferential treatment as contrasted with the other possible values of the teacher's life is obvious enough to one who has known a number of teachers intimately. This preference for security, whether it is a constitutional quality which causes one to choose teaching rather than one of the more risky callings, or whether it is produced by the conditions of teaching, makes for the development of an early and rigid conservatism. When teachers meet and talk freely, one hears talk of positions and the hold that one has upon them; one hears as well of the things that threaten seizin. When it is a group of college teachers, one hears of academic freedom, and though the talk is often bold, one senses the fear it covers up. The established teacher has been playing safe so long that he has lost that necessary minimum of recklessness without which life becomes painful. A realization of the strength of this security motive enables one to understand some of the suspicion with which teachers regard each other; certainly one does not exceed the truth when he asserts that a very large percentage of the numerous quarrels between teachers arise from a belief of one teacher that another is sawing at the strings with which his job is held.

It is odd that this security motive does not usually suffice to make the teacher accumulate extensive savings. For it is generally thought that the savings of teachers do not equal those of business persons in the same income-group. It is quite certain that the savings of teachers are rarely adequate. The high standard of living of the teacher, who has usually travelled a bit further and seen more than the business man of similar income, and the long summer vacation, with its temptation to spend what has been accumulated in the winter, appear to be a basic part of the explanation of the failure of teachers to save. Besides, the check will always be waiting on the first of the month, if only one does not endanger it by unusual doings or unconventional teachings. It is the conduct, then, and not the expenditure, which is controlled. Teachers are crucified between the desire to be safe and the standard of living.

We have spoken of certain situational necessities which mold the teacher, of the roles which these situational imperatives impose upon him, and of the enduring effect of these roles upon personality. It remains to consider in a connected way traumatic learning as a determinant of the occupational type, the effect of shock upon the teacher personality. What we have in mind is that learning which takes place under terrific penalties, and in which the learner is subject to shock if he makes the wrong choices. The pathological effects of shock have been investigated frequently, but these effects have rarely been discussed as learning, nor have they ever been treated in their proper relation to the social organization. Yet, in that learning which involves modification of personality, shock often plays a dominant role, and the giving of shocks is one of the principal means by which the social group tailors persons to its specifications. Traumatic learning is therefore important in both sociology and psychology.

This kind of learning is not easily separable from other sorts of learning, and still it has characteristics which seem to justify a distinction. Traumatic learning is continuous with habit formation, being, perhaps, a special instance of the law of effect; the use of slight penalties is also a common incident of laboratory procedure. Traumatic learning is continuous with the normal molding of personality by social conditioning, and we have already discussed minor shocks which mold the teacher's personality. Traumatic learning is continuous with the modification of personality in crisis situations, but represents the reaction of personality to the most sudden and extreme crises. We are justified in regarding traumatic learning as different from ordinary learning because radical differences appear between reactions to slight shocks and reactions to severe shocks. The psychological and psychopathological effects of shock have indeed been investigated, but their meaning in terms of personality and social organization has perhaps not been sufficiently pointed out.

For the teacher, traumatic experiences usually concern the loss of his position, especially the sudden and unforeseen loss of his position. The loss of control over a class may be traumatic in its effect, and so may a quarrel with a colleague. Various minor shocks arise, and we shall need to reconsider all that we have said concerning the molding of personality by the teaching situation in the light of the new insight furnished by the concept of traumatic learning. Individuals, of course, differ greatly in their ability to assimilate shocks without damage to their personalities.

These shocks which teachers experience may induce light dissociation, more pronounced in persons of hysteric constitution, and associated with a tendency to repeat the traumatic experience in a manner akin to that of the war neuroses. The dissociation very likely prolongs and exacerbates the conflict, since it prevents the individual from facing it and reacting to it, but allows the conflict to produce effects indirectly. Whatever the ultimate adjustment, the mind dwells upon such crises a long time, relives them incessantly for months and even years, elaborates reactions to them without end. Usually, a curiously bifurcated adjustment appears. On the one hand, the individual refuses to accept the responsibility for the shocking event and that part of his behavior which led up to it. He multiplies rationalizations to the same end: "It wasn't my fault," "The circumstances were most unusual," "I was the goat," etc. This is often attended by a conscious or unconscious refusal to evaluate the situation correctly, the face-saving rationalizations demanding that the realization of responsibility be shut from consciousness. On the other hand, the individual behaves as if he accepted responsibility completely, something which he does not find at all inconsistent with his conscious insistence that it was not his fault. He multiplies precautions to prevent the recurrence of the unfortunate event, taking an almost obsessive interest in the protection of that which previously was threatened. This, of course, represents the reaction to the other side of the ambivalence. Likewise, an individual may insist that in a certain collapse of his social world he has lost no status, the while he indulges in no end of behavior which can only be interpreted as compensatory for that loss of status. Much of the ruthlessness of teachers toward students is in the nature of compensation for fears traceable to traumatic discipline experiences.

As a result of shocks, too, there appear effects nearly analogous to the specific conditioning of the behaviorists, behavior mechanisms which are very little dependent upon broader associative contexts and which therefore tend to be set off in quite incongruous circumstances if the specific stimulus is presented. Soldiers acquire certain positive behavior patterns which may be set off whenever the stimulus sound is heard. Teachers come likewise to react violently to specific stimuli. A teacher once found on his desk a note from his principal asking him to call at the office the next morning. He called at the office, and was summarily dismissed. Thereafter he experienced acute fear whenever he received a request to call at the office of a school superior, and this reaction did not rapidly suffer attrition in spite of the fact that his behavior did not again expose him to attack.

Conversion, as a sudden change of the working organization of attitudes in personality, may result from a single shocking experience. Traumatic experiences redefine situations. Where this occurs, it is probably correct to speak of it as a change of the dominant attitude; it is likely to take the form of transposition of opposed sides of an ambivalence. Trauma may result in a complete reversal of moral codes or in radical change of policy; such tergiversation is common among teachers who suffer shocks by reason of being kind to students. Conversion usually involves a change of group allegiance.

Most likely to be subject to the cruder types of traumatic learning are egocentric persons, and other maladjusts of nonconforming type. These persons either fail to observe social necessities, or feel capable of overriding them, and they suffer the consequences. Some persons are completely demoralized by these consequences, and if those consequences are so severe as to entail a collapse of the social world, they usually have most serious results. Undesirable personality traits are in most cases exaggerated rather than remedied by traumatic experiences; these are unusually distressing experiences, and they fall precisely upon the persons least capable of assimilating them. The lunatic fringe of teaching, every year sloughed off and every year renewed, is made up of personalities battered by many trauma.

A minor sort of traumatic learning results from the effect of conflict upon the system of values. Points in one's scheme of life which must be sharply defended come to assume a disproportionate importance. Recurrent crises in the teacher's life, such as interdepartmental squabbles, constellate a temporary organization of personality around the values then to be defended from attack. This temporary organization leaves traces in the nervous system, and as a result of the traces this fighting organization is more easily called into play the next time; the traces may indeed grow so great as to set the tone of the personality. That for which men must often fight is dear to them. This mechanism is very important in the life of the school teacher. The experienced teacher fights harder for discipline than does the novice, and he begins to fight a great deal more readily. The head of the department fights for the privileges of his department much more valiantly than instructors, and has a keener nose for sniffing out conspiracies. In all this the person who has studied the social psychology of conflict groups will find nothing startling or new.

The analysis of dreams is an excellent technique for uncovering the tension points existing within the life-situation of the individual. The dreams of teachers, then, ought to show where the points of stress and strain appear in the school situation as it affects the teacher. Particularly is this true of recurrent dreams, or of similar dreams of different teachers. Any thorough research into this topic would demand that we examine the entire dream life of a number of teachers, but we have chosen to consider here only some highly typical dreams concerning the school situation. Following is the recurrent dream of a male teacher of twenty-six. He has an excellent reputation as a disciplinarian, and has succeeded with some difficult schools.

The record of the dream follows:

> Each year as the horrid conflict of the first month was going on and the feeling against me was considerable and bitter, I would have a dream. It ran as follows:
>
> It is morning. The nine o'clock bell calling the school formally to attention has not rung yet. Part of the pupils are in the school building visiting and playing; others are outside doing likewise. All is going nicely. I bend intently over my work at the desk for several minutes.
>
> Finally a noise in the room draws my attention. Annoyed, I look up quickly. To my surprise a big boy is scuffling with a smaller one. I loudly command them to stop. They do, but reluctantly. About that time some girls start running noisily up and down the aisles. This on top of the scuffling is too much. I tell them to take their seats. They do, but I can see by their faces that they have a notion not to. There is rebellion in the air. By this time the boys in the corner are throwing books at each other. I am amazed. Why, what ails them? Throwing things inside is strictly against the rules. And these boys are usually so docile. But there is Alfred Davis among them, and he is a very mischievous boy and antagonistic towards me. And it was Bernice Keller, ever slow to mind, who led the girls in their racing among the seats. I shout at the boys. They do not heed me. I bawl them out and remark that if they can't find anything better to do they had better wash the blackboards for me. They interpret the remark in the imperative mood, which is correct, and scowling and muttering begin the task.
>
> There is a commotion on the playground. From the window I see the boys fighting over a swing. I go out. They do not stop as I approach. I speak to them. I cuff them. They pay no attention. I am aghast. *Neither look,*

nor speech, nor action, nor presence of the teacher avails. I note some girls running back and forth across the street in front of the passing automobiles. I call to them, but in vain. Wrathfully I start toward the street. The girls run away down the street. I am no child; I will not run after them. Baffled I ring the school bell. It is past nine o'clock anyhow.

Inside pandemonium reigns. The girls whom I left in their seats are dashing about the room upsetting the loose furniture. The boys at the blackboard are pelting each other with chalk and erasers. They pelt me as I appear. I charge upon them. They elude me. This is terrible, *terrible!*

But where are the boys and girls from outdoors? Why do they not come in? Did they not hear the bell? The boys have stopped fighting and are standing looking sullenly at the building. What shall I do? They heed neither teacher nor bell. I attempt to expel them. They will not go home. The girls are standing tantalizingly across the street. I shall take it up with the school board. They laugh at me. They even scorn the board! Then I shall settle this thing by force. I go inside to get a club. They follow me in. The sight of the club quiets them somewhat. They all take their seats.

I preach to them. Smirkingly they listen. We start the lessons, but the conflict reasserts itself everywhere. I leave the desk and the club to help a student whose hand is raised. In the other end of the room a titter arises and increases in volume. Ah! So they're at it again. I seize the club. A few blows restore order. But it is no use. No matter where I turn the club must be used. Nor can I use it fast enough to be effective, to keep order. I shall have to call in the board. I have failed! But no, I will not fail! I redouble my efforts. The students begin breaking up desks and tearing down casements so that they too may have clubs. I seek refuge behind my desk and pound upon it for order. They ignore the act. The whole school gathers itself to rush upon me with clubs. Pale with fear, I square myself for the finish. They start . . . but never reach me because I awake, cold with sweat. Parts of the dream and the faces appear and fade away in the darkness before my eyes. I recall a few pupils—good students, "teacher's pets," friends of mine outside of school, or students with whom my associations in school have been close, who took no part. Vernon Hart, Lucille Ollinger, Harold Childers, and Oscar Olson had nothing to do with it. They stood off in the corners and at the edges staring without expression. They were neutral. They favored neither side. God bless them! I must be better to them in the future. The dream is still real. I begin to plan what I shall do tomorrow to get even with them and to restore order. I excuse myself for letting such a thing get started. I wasn't feeling well, my head ached so, or this would never have happened. Well, if I can't control them, I'll just disappear, I'll skip the country.

Then I become fully conscious. I wonder what I really would do if such a thing should happen. I resolve not to rule with quite such an iron hand. Well, if it ever does happen, they'll never see me again. And thus for an hour or so until I fall asleep again. The dream, however, haunts me for several days.

During my first year of teaching, when this dream came, it frightened me. I thought it must be a bad sign. But nothing of the kind ever happened. Only one little red-haired chap even so much as dared to talk back to me that year. And at the end of the term I was asked to return at an increase in salary; and so in the years of teaching after that I looked upon this dream, when it came, as a good omen, as a portent that the year would be a successful one. (Autobiographical document.)

The discipline dream was found to be exceedingly common. It was frequently stereotyped and recurrent. It was protean in its forms. In several cases, it recurred months or even years after the individual quit teaching.

Supervision dreams ranked next in order of frequency. Typical of these was the following:

> I had this dream while I was doing my practice teaching in Richmond the past summer. I might say that I was teaching Ancient History, a subject I had never studied even in high school. Also that I had a particular horror for the supervisor.
>
> The night I had this dream I had gone to bed early without preparing my lessons and had set the alarm in order to get up early the next morning and do it. I dreamed that the alarm had not gone off and that I awoke just in time to get to school—totally unprepared. I went to my class and decided to give them a study period for fifteen minutes in which I also could prepare the lesson. I had no more than made this decision when in walked the supervisor. I was panic stricken. I opened my book and desperately tried to read a few sentences so that I could ask some questions. I started asking questions that had nothing to do with Ancient History. The supervisor listened for a few minutes and then got up and with a look of scorn started teaching the class herself. I awoke.

Needless to say the affective tone of this dream was most unpleasant.

These supervision dreams were expressions of lightly repressed fears or worries. The situation in which the dreamer was caught in some unethical or tabooed behavior frequently recurred. One man dreamed that his supervisor caught him talking disparagingly about America's entry into the war, and politely reproved him. Another dreamed that two supervisors caught him at a dance with a high school girl. Others dreamed of detection in lateness to class. These dreams show that supervision can be an important source of strain.

Unpunctuality, interpretable in some cases as wish-fulfillment through the avoidance of teaching, and in others as simple fear, recurred as a feature of quite a number of dreams. In several cases it was complicated by the dreamer's losing his way while going to class; this was always associated with some unusual source of unpleasantness in the teaching situation. The fear dreams also reveal the perfection of the social mechanism by which the threat of classroom disorder enforces punctuality upon the teacher.

The phantasy life of school teachers also gives some interesting clues to the nature of the adjustment they have made to their occupation. These phantasies are sometimes purely compensatory, being unrelated in subject matter to the life of the teacher in the school; the classic example of this is the very common case of the teacher of English mooning about breaking into the *Atlantic* as he corrects examination papers. Those plans which so many teachers have of going into some other occupation which will bring them into the heat and dust of the market place, and into the spotlight of publicity, must be regarded as in this class also, for they are rarely more earnest, and almost never any better adjusted to reality. Many of the phantasies of teachers, however, concern the daily problems of the classroom. There is a troublesome boy whom the teacher daydreams of putting in his place, but whom he never does put in his place. Or there is a fellow teacher who presumes too much upon good nature; the teacher may have long phantasies in which he bests this colleague in a battle of words, but the two may never come to words. Sometimes teachers endowed with less than mediocre literary ability start to write, and when they write their hero so closely resembles themselves that the wish-fulfilling character of the writing is more than obvious. There was the sex-starved teacher who had unrealizable dreams of a lovely young thing who would be exceedingly thrilled by himself; he wrote numerous short stories in which this same theme was repeated: a young man of his age and personal characteristics met a girl in her teens; soon there arose between them a perfect understanding. The episodes and the dialogue, in this case, were often identical from story to story. Another man, a failure in teaching because of his inadequate personality and extreme shortness of stature, made his hero an army officer of very small size, and caused this hero to triumph over all kinds of opposition and persecution. Similar to these self-determined phantasies are the books that the teacher reads, for one obtains phantasy gratification in that way, too. It would be very difficult, however, to trace a pattern in these.

Concerning the sex tensions of teachers, especially women, a great deal has been said and some few things have been written. Amateurs in psychiatry have been free with diagnoses. It is true that the choice of teaching as a career condemns many women to remain unmarried, and that the moral order coils so tightly about the woman teacher that even legitimate courtship is often out of the question. But there is not, apparently, a one-to-one correspondence between spinsterhood and that nervous, wracked unhappiness which the amateur psychiatrists say attacks the teacher because she is unmarried. The life history of the unmarried teacher seems to follow a pretty definite pattern. There are a number of years in which the hope of finding a mate is not relinquished. There is a critical period when that hope dies. An informant has suggested that hope has died when a woman buys a diamond for herself. The critical period is an incubation period during which spinsterhood ripens. During this critical period many desperate and pathetic things occur. The woman going through this period falls in love very easily, and may come to make the most open advances upon slight or no provocation. The attentions of a lover being absent, the most perfunctory civility may be magnified to that size, and distorted to fit that configuration. Hence arise deep plots to trick the doctor or the dentist into a declaration. Hence, too, pitiful misinterpretations of the most commonplace remarks. It is a period of the most intense conflicts, and no way of solving the problem is left unthought of; these dignified women sometimes attempt, pathetic to record, to learn the technique of sex lure from the twenty-year-olds of their acquaintance. Perhaps this hope of finding a mate always dies hard and slowly, and requires little stimulant to keep it alive after its time.

The adjustment in which the spinster stabilizes after this critical period tends to be final. Several forms are common. There is the discontented misanthropy of the woman who is bitter because the male sex has passed her by. There is the split-off, phantastic love life of the woman who preserves her susceptibility, perhaps her hope, to an advanced age. There is the sweetly resigned attitude of the woman who accepts celibacy and arranges her life on that basis; this adjustment is easier if the individual is able to live with her own family or with close relatives who have a strong family life which includes her. There is the "bachelor-girl" adjustment, carried off with different degrees of success, and with more or less attendant conflict. There is the adjustment of the teacher who achieves vicarious fulfillment in her students. There is homosexuality, both that which is deeply ingrained and that which is *faute de mieux*, and numerous other adjustments of a pathological nature.

It is true that male values are lacking in the universe in which spinsters live, and that this lack is sometimes sadly obvious. It is a peculiarity of some of these maiden teachers, a peculiarity which has been observed in several widely separated groups, in order to relieve the loneliness of their lives, to give names to inanimate objects. They populate the universe by naming the things about them, especially those articles which are in daily use and may be thought to have something of a character of their own. Thus a car is John, an ashtray Mr. Johnson, a fountain pen Mr. Wright, and so on. It is significant that most of these names are male. The sex starvation, and its attendant isolation from the procession of the generations, are there, and they materially affect the adjustment of maiden teachers to the teaching profession. Yet it is doubtful whether one can advance his explanation very much by following out this line. Spinster teachers sometimes present a sorry picture and one rightly diagnosed as a picture of frustration. But, then, so do the men who teach; and men teachers are free to marry. It is something in the teaching itself, or something in the life of the teacher, which frustrates. No doubt the sex thwarts of spinsters have some effect upon their personalities, but it is an effect which takes the form of an enhancement of a personality distortion produced otherwise. The woman teacher, furthermore, but for the personal thwarting implicit in the necessity of institutionalized domination, is in a very favorable position, associated as she is with many children, to work out a satisfactory sublimation of her sexual life. The major lines of her personality difficulty, therefore, have their causation in the social situations which her profession imposes upon her.

PAUL GOODMAN

The Freedom to Be Academic

A SPECIAL COMMITTEE at Columbia University has worked for three years on the study of academic freedom, and here now are two books by Robert MacIver, and by Richard Hofstadter and Walter Metzger.[1] They are a history of a particular notion of academic freedom in the United States, and a polemical defense of it against current attacks. The particular notion, developed and defended, is "freedom of inquiry." In our times it is mainly in the social sciences that this academic freedom is threatened, and I should like to raise the question, What in this context do these authors mean by "inquiry"? The term is from the pragmatic and instrumental vocabulary. Its implications are more practical and experimental than the Aristotelian questioning in order to know, or than the medieval speculation (*philosophare*); it roughly denotes a search to solve some problem in the on-going process of life: a real, not an "academic," problem, though not necessarily a narrowly utilitarian problem. To what extent do these authors mean this and mean to defend it?

I

Let me start by taking an annoying and apparently unfair tack. In discussing the case of Bertrand Russell, Professor MacIver says, "Actually . . . Russell was dealing, forthrightly and sincerely, with the most prob-

Reprinted from *The Cambridge Review*, No. 5, 1956, pp. 65-82, by permission of the author. (Copyright 1956, by Paul Goodman.)

lematic of all areas of social relationship [sex]." (*Academic Freedom*, p. 156.) This is an innocent passing remark in a relatively minor context in the book, but let us suddenly stop at it short and take the sentence at face-value. If sexual relations is the most problematic of all areas of inquiry, we should expect that most or very many social scientists are inquiring and teaching here, or at least that the chairmen of departments are falling all over themselves to enlist experts for their staffs in this novel field; in the nature of the case much that these people are hypothesizing and affirming must be unconventional and socially unacceptable, for "in no other area of human behavior is there so unbridgeable a gulf between the officially sanctioned ethics and the socially accepted ways" (*Ibid.*, p. 157); and so there must here be lots of cases of infringement of academic freedom. But no such thing. In the 300 pages of MacIver's book, six are somewhat (mostly indirectly) concerned with such cases; in the 500 pages of the history, none. Now this is not, I am convinced, because our authors are prejudiced on the subject or afraid of it; Professor MacIver, by his tone and remarks and the few times I have seen him, seems to me sensible and unusually frank. It is because indeed the most problematic area is not much an area of inquiry in the universities. Consider the following statement:

> We know of no cases where an educator, clearly convicted of flagrantly immoral behavior, defended his position by appealing to the principle of academic freedom. Apart from the fact that such defense would be irrelevant, it is certain that his case would receive no support from his institution or from his colleagues. (*Ibid.*, p. 150.)

If his case would certainly receive no support, the educator would certainly be a fool to press it. But I should like to question the "fact" that such a defense would be irrelevant. The Professor Emeritus knows as well as I that it is not sexual immorality that gets teachers sacked, for this is condoned by his peers, it is among the "socially accepted ways"; but it is the publicity that sometimes accrues; and is this not tantamount to saying that it is not the thing but the proposition that is being penalized? (I know, for instance, of an even closer case, where a teacher in a small progressive college was refused reappointment not because of his delinquent behavior, which was at that place not uncommon and fairly public, but because of his "overt" claim to the right to it.)[2] Could not many such cases quite simply and relevantly be transformed into cases of infringement of academic freedom? But in this problematic area, the theory—in courses in anthropology—is kept far distant from the practice in the on-going process of life.

In my opinion there is, in our times, a still more problematic area of social relationships: how to cope with war and the complex of issues around it, conscription, the expenditure on armaments, international diplomacy. Now in Professor MacIver's book, pacificism is accorded three pages; in the history, more interestingly, the cases of World War I are given a large number of pages, but "academic freedom was relatively little affected during the Second World War." (*Development*, p. 505.) Why was it not? It seems to me that this area and the sexual area have an essential element in common: that in them a strong conviction tends to overt physical, not merely verbal, behavior; that is, the consequences of conviction tend to be dramatic and drastic, e.g., a young man may refuse the draft, a physicist may decline the job. Therefore these areas are sensitive, and therefore they are not much the objects of inquiry. But the suppression is not proximately extramural but intramural, and it is not forced by the president but by the faculty.

I am reasoning somewhat as follows: What is problematic for inquiry is always just beyond the known; in socio-psychological matters this is an area of confusion and anxiety, and of suppression and repression; then its exploration *must* involve interpersonal daring and personal risk, whether or not there is "acting out," and in these matters there is a generic tendency toward acting out. The vital social questions for inquiry are those you are likely to get jailed for messing with. When you are threatened with academic sanctions, it is a good sign that you are on the right track; when you are fired, it is better; but when you are beyond the pale of the academy and "will receive no support from your colleagues," then you are possibly touching the philosopher's stone. My point is not that universities are worthless, nor that they should not or cannot be free, but that one cannot seriously regard them as primarily places of inquiry nor found the case for academic freedom or freedom of inquiry; let me return to this later.

Of course it is unrealistic, and it would be uncharitable, to object to the dropping of a man who by his theory and practice makes his colleagues anxious; after all, they have to live and breathe too and feel themselves part of a team.

> The situations with which we are mainly concerned are those in which an influential or power-holding group endeavors to make or succeeds in making its own predilections the official standards of fitness to teach, even though these predilections are particular to their own coterie or social class. . . . Where such groups exercise control, the freedom of education is seriously infringed, and the more independent and freedom-loving members of the institution are likely to suffer most. It is the teacher who sets the highest value on intellectual freedom who is the most obnoxious to the authoritarians. The higher his standard of responsibility, the lower the respect in which they hold him. (*Academic Freedom*, p. 147.)

Professor MacIver is here precisely not talking about the faculties of universities but about their extramural oppressors; would he not, on reflection, extend the censure to the academic coteries as well?

II

In the main these books seem to me to be written with a generous integrity and *bona fides.* They were occasioned, of course, by the recent investigations of Communists and "Communists"; and in such discussions, where every nuance of rhetoric and the penumbra of connotations is scrutinized by seasoned experts like Dr. Hook, it is impossible to satisfy anybody. But to my ear Professor MacIver's sermons—his book has very many pages of long sermons—all ring solid nickel. There is, however, one major topic in treating which there is evident embarrassment, avoidance, difficulties hinted at but not explored, and letting sleeping dogs lie with one eye open: this topic is the relation of knowledge and action. I do not find it credible that the meetings of so experienced a committee did not evoke more philosophic acumen on this subject than is here revealed.

On the one hand, Professor MacIver (the historians less so) lays great stress on "the intrinsic worthwhileness of the knowledge of things, the moral and spiritual values of the integrity of mind that steadfastly seeks the truth" (*Ibid.*, p. 14), the excitement of the infinite unknown, the grandeur of standing on the brink. He speaks of this with a religious fervor that makes us believe him but that also, I fear, takes it out of the context of a discussion of academic freedom at the University of Illinois or even the colleges of the Ivy League. For a seeker blessed and cursed with thus much of the holy spirit will act accordingly with little help or hindrance from the opinions of presidents or from considerations of his own status and tenure; disciples will seek him out, and if we do not, so much the worse for us. I think, too, the professor is too sanguine about the possibility of inculcating such an ideal by the ordinary processes of education in colleges; those who pick it up there have it in them to pick up.

On the other hand, all our authors are sold on the pragmatic theory of truth (I do not mean an utilitarian theory), namely that truth is successful inquiry, and inquiry is an aggressive handling and coping with problems that claim attention; inquiry is experimental, it intervenes. This implies a close connection of knowledge and action. I am not here speaking of the consequences of inquiry but of the process itself. In the social sciences this must mean very often, must it not, sallying beyond the walls into areas that are troublesome, or even to making trouble where all seemed quiet. Certainly if we consider the masters of the century prior to our generations—whether Comte, Marx, Proudhon, Durkheim, Kropotkin, Sorel, Veblen, Lenin, Freud, Dewey, etc., etc.—we are struck by their activism, their actual or projected experimentation on a civic scale. Some of these men are unthinkable as academics and some had uneasy academic lives. The present-day preoccupation with careful methodology is academically praiseworthy, but it does not lead to intensely interesting propositions. One cannot help but feel that a good part of the current concern with statistics and polling is a way of being active in the "area" without being actively engaged in the subject-matter. There is a good deal of sharpening of tools but not much agriculture.[3]

Professor Metzger eloquently expresses the very point I am trying to make. He is distinguishing the cases of Richard Ely and Edward Bemis who got into trouble on the theory and practice of labor-organization during the 90's:

> A . . . difference lay in the extent to which Ely and Bemis put their theories into action. For all his talk of the need for concrete reform, Ely's criticisms of the social order tended to be general, not specific; hortatory, not programmatic. For all his warm humanitarianism, he made no intimate contact with the multitude. "Only twice in my life," he wrote, "have I ever spoken to audiences of working men, and I had always held myself aloof from agitations as something not in my province–something for which I am not adapted." Replying to the charge by Regent Wells that he *had* acted on his sympathies for labor, he issued a categorical denial. This author of a friendly history of the labor movement denied, at his trial, that he had ever entertained a walking delegate in his home, that he had ever counseled workers to strike, that he had ever threatened an anti-union firm with a boycott, or that he had ever favored the principle of a closed shop. Were these changes true, Ely wrote, they would "unquestionably unfit me to occupy a responsible position as an instructor of youth in a great University." These were the words of a very academic reformer. (*Development*, p. 433.)

When Ely was academically vindicated, Bemis wrote to him:

> "That was a glorious victory for you. . . . I was only sorry that you seemed to show a vigor of denial as to entertaining a walking delegate or counselling strikers as if either were wrong, instead of under certain circumstances a *duty*." This was the difference between them: Bemis was not only a partisan . . . but an active party. . . . The subsequent careers of Ely and Bemis bear out the importance of this point. Ely survived (and in good part renounced) his spoken and written heresies. He remained in a state of academic grace for the rest of his life, taking a post at Northwestern in 1925 and one at Columbia in 1937. Bemis became an academic Ishmael with a reputation as a partisan and a malcontent that he was never able to live down. Except for his brief and ill-starred tenure at Kansas State, he received no further academic appointments. The trustees of the republic of learning could inflict on this kind of miscreant the terrible retribution of neglect. (*Ibid.*, p. 435.)

All this is excellently and feelingly said. But it was an issue of sixty years ago, and today in this area a teacher has "the right to exercise the same political and civil liberties that are enjoyed by other citizens." (*Academic Freedom*, p. 238.) My bother is that our authors do not extrapolate to present-day areas that must have the same borderline characteristics, and then look a little harder for academic freedom cases which might look precisely not like academic freedom cases as reported to the American Association of University Professors.

On this same topic of knowledge and action, let me raise another difficulty concerning the action of teaching itself and the teacher's responsibility for consequences. Our authors, especially the historians, are frequently scornful of the "assumption . . . that a young man yields to the imprint of ideas as easily and uncritically as wax." (*Development*, p. 411.) They stress, rather, the development of freedom to learn, the opportunity to hear all and pick and choose. I do not think these are, in interesting cases, the real alternatives. The young mind is indeed not passive but intensely active, and its activity is to crystallize around an ideal, a system of ideas, or a non-familial personality, that serves as a parent-substitute. Quite apart from sex, the relation of teacher and student is an erotic one, where for the student the attraction is in the excitement, particularly the rebellious excitement, of the system of propositions. The more excellent the teacher, the stronger the charismatic effect of his voice. In itself this is all to the good and is anyway inevitable; it cannot be prevented by doctrinal neutrality for then the very syntax of neutrality itself becomes adorable. But the attempt to prevent the effect or to disown responsibility for it, discourages the student and thwarts and embitters the teacher. Is not the situation familiar, that a powerful teacher is regarded by his colleagues, partly in envy and partly in anxiety, as a seducer of his students and indeed in a conspiracy with them to cast ridicule on themselves? On the other hand, if the strong teacher maintains his reserve, the student, whose needs are more frank, has indeed been rejected and will be either humiliated, disappointed, or angry depending on his character. My guess is that every college term there is more infringement of the freedom to teach by academic timidity along these lines than in the whole history of cases here treated. Worse, is there not a great waste of natural human resources?

Our historians write of the liberation from "doctrinal moralism" (*Ibid.*, p. 353ft), the idea that if, e.g., a man is an atheist he is no doubt a drunkard and unfit to teach: "in scientific criticism the dissociation of the man from his work has become a cardinal principle." This was indeed a great advance, for it heightened the respect for evidence and its accurate presentation and criticism. But I submit that the older theological view had the following merit: that a proposition was fraught with life consequences and had therefore the utmost seriousness; you knew a man by what he professed. I dislike appealing to the romantic and grisly past, but we must bear in mind that the adventure of inquiry has one quality when you are risking disgrace, imprisonment, and even death; and another when you are risking tenure; and quite another when you are risking nothing. Our secular society has great advantages, and even especially for inquiry, but its strong point is not the achievement of vocation or manliness. In his rhetoric of dedication to the Truth with a big T, Professor MacIver is harking back to Spinoza; I wonder if, by and large, he could comfortably use this rhetoric at the Faculty Club. Maybe I am wrong.

To sum up so far: I have tried in a quick and rude way to indicate that the professors fall short in two ways from a standard of inquiry as a phase of an experimental instrumental empiricism: they avoid problematic areas and they do not experiment their hypotheses. Nothing of what I have said, let me add, applies to more old-fashioned notions of academic freedom of inquiry. For instance, the notion of freedom of dialectic, as exemplified in, say, the *Parmenides*, where precisely the attachment and non-attachment to any proposition is used as a therapy of the soul. Or the Aristotelian freedom of curiosity, aimed at *theoria* as the highest happiness. Or the medieval *libertas philosophandi*, with its emphasis on disputation to let new air into an accepted world. Or finally to the Enlightenment's concept of freedom of criticism in the Kantian sense (*quo warranto?*), where the faculty of philosophy serves, as Kant says, as a kind of loyal opposition from the left. All of these base their claim on the proposition that the university is different from, perhaps better than, perhaps a servant of, the rest of the world.

III

I said I had started on an "apparently unfair" tack. Unfair because I chose an innocent sentence in a minor context, and I have been devoting myself to a matter of logic that Professor MacIver's book is mostly not about. Now, what it is about is the defense of such inquiry as does exist from the current attacks upon it, and specifically and explicitly the Communist-hunting of the cold war by many parties, from government agencies to self-constituted vigilantes. Let us then turn briefly to the overt book itself and see if I can show the relevance of the tack I have been taking.

Professor MacIver's findings on the Party and the investigations are the familiar ones of many liberals, and they warrant little fresh discussion here. Summarily: 1. The Party-Communist teacher is unqualified, as authoritarian, suppressive, conspiratorial; but this disqualification is based on his activities not on his theories. (Frankly, this distinction is idiotic, since what is a party that does not constrain to action?) 2. Past affiliation does not disqualify. 3. A Communist, "whether he carries a Party card or not," may be dismissed "if he injects propaganda into his teaching or relationships with students"; but conversely, if he teaches a non-controversial subject and is otherwise circumspect, it is better to let him be. 4. Investigation should be done by the faculty, not by the administration or outsiders. 5. "Any general investigation to uncover possible Communists is wholly undesirable." 6. Loyalty oaths are "derogatory, injudicious, and futile." 7. Student organizations should be permitted to invite C.P. speakers. 8. Communist ideas do not disqualify the student.

It is useful to distinguish two strata in such a list: judgments that could be called anti-McCarthy and those that are anti-anti-anti-McCarthy. Objections to high-handed and unfair pressures, to informing, to lack of due process, to almost all restraints on freedom of speech: this is simple anti-McCarthyism; and at it are leveled charges of political naiveté, of being duped, of not seeing that this is a unique conspiracy, of locking the stable after the horse is gone, and so forth. The response to *these* charges, in turn, is anti-anti-anti-McCarthyism: granting that there are grounds for the investigations, yet their effect is so productive of fear and withdrawal and inhibition of useful functioning that they weaken the body politic rather than purging it; thus they play into the hands of the enemy, etc.

I think that it is this latter attitude, the prevalence of academic anxiety rather than any righteous indignation, that has prompted the books we are reviewing. For the fact seems to be—at least so it is agreed by all sides in this controversy except the investigators themselves—that the Communist infiltration has been trivial, was never large and has steadily waned for years; that the furor of investigation has been out of all proportion. The question, then, is why anything so groundless and inappropriate has been met by anything but simple manly rejection, either quiet, derisive, or indignant, depending on one's temperament. Why such big books? Let me open MacIver at random and quote a few near-by passages:

> There were evidences that in departments or faculties, here or there, disguised or subtile pressures had been applied to prevent the advancement of such nonconforming members or against the renewal of their appointments if they lacked tenure. It was not that the scholars who protested against the oath requirements were themselves nonconformists—there were very many good conservatives among them—but, whatever their economic viewpoints, alike they apprehended a growing peril to academic freedom. (*Academic Freedom*, p. 178.)
>
> No attack seems to be more disruptive than that which emanates from governing boards. . . . They rock the institution. . . . Governing boards are seldom prescient of the effect such edicts produce. . . . Often the disturbance that ensues comes to the governing boards as a complete surprise. . . . Censorial and inquisitorial action on the part of those who themselves are not devoted to the scholar's search for truth is for the true scholar a vital threat. (*Ibid.*)

What concerns us here is that the Tenney warnings and threats and proposals created the most serious apprehensions among leading educators. (*Ibid.*, p. 179.)

This new exercise of authority by a board over a faculty contained implicit threats against the status of the educator, against the two most vital interests of the profession. The protesting faculty members saw in the new requirement on the one hand a threat to academic freedom, on the other a threat to security of tenure. The pro-oath regents denied that any such threats were involved . . . but this lack of understanding is one of the two frequent consequences of the lack of rapport that exists in this country between faculties and governing boards. (*Ibid.*, p. 177.)

I quote at random from adjacent pages; the book is thickly studded with the like. One is ashamed to copy out the passages. What is one to make of this astonishing anxiety on the part of grown-ups, of professors, of supposedly dedicated scholars! "Disguised," "implicit threats," "rock the institution," "vital threat," "most serious apprehensions," "lack of understanding," "they are not prescient"; and all this syndrome where in many cases admittedly no danger existed, and where altogether at the worst no great danger existed. Is it so hard to clear up misunderstanding by bearding the lion? or to force implicit threats to become explicit and have a bang-up fight? Could these persons really be so concerned about losing their jobs? And if they are really concerned for freedom as a principle and a vital need, is this the tone of such a concern?

I fear it is rather the tone of subordinate bureaucrats ridden by self-doubt and with plenty of projected hostility, unable to withstand the least pressure without anxiety. Then I cannot believe in the devotion to inquiry that gives them so little strength of self as this. And I cannot believe in the aggressive intensity of inquiry that gets them into so weak a feeling for the state of things. The job-clinging itself is not so much base as a pathetic symptom. How easily they are deflated of their status! What shall we say of an elite of competence that has so little pride and self-confidence? Is this our proud academic freedom? If I felt it was only this I would tear up my doctorate.

The fear of actual investigation, the paranoiac suspicion of fancied investigation, the economic panic, need for status, clinging to security: these have been familiar in the American middle classes during the past couple of generations; there is no need to discuss in the context of the academic community the causes that have been operating in the whole community. What is specific, however, is that these *are* doctors, with a proud tradition, sacred symbols, a culture far broader than average, the inspiration of beautiful subject-matters and grand authors: in short, a self-transcending responsibility to history past and future that they (we) cannot finally betray without shame and self-betrayal. They *must* rally, even though the form of the rallying reveals the inner conflict of these books.

IV

It is remarkable how, in reading the vigorous and informative history of Professors Hofstadter and Metzger, one can see forming through the decades the lineaments of modern academic man, and an academic notion of inquiry defining itself. The authors call their book a "Development" and they rightly regard as an achievement the present concept of academic freedom with its bill of rights and its highly ramified national system of professional defenses. At the same time, being scrupulous and fairly philosophical and not at all homiletic, they note down the inevitable losses and sloughings-off that have occurred along the way. (It is the great power of history to keep alive lost causes, and even to revivify them.) Now if instead of merely noting these losses, we accumulate them and form them into a picture: what a picture it is! so to speak, an ideal shadow of western Academic Man that, we hope, haunts the modern American academic man, and sheds on him glory, and gives him a bad conscience. Let me collect half a dozen of these contrasts of development and loss.

1) "At the time of their greatest independence," says Professor Hofstadter,

> the universities lived in the interstices of medieval society, taking advantage of its decentralization and the balance of its conflicting powers to further their own corporate interests. [They were guilds of masters or students.] They appealed to king or council against pope, to pope against king or bishop, and to king and popes alike against truculent town governments. Moreover, they had weapons of their own that put them above the level of mere appellants and gave them independent bargaining power. Among these weapons were the cessation or suspension of lectures, the academic equivalents of the modern strike. A still more powerful device arose, oddly enough, from their very poverty. Unhampered . . . by physical apparatus, great libraries, worldly goods, and substantial college foundations, they could and on occasion did migrate, taking with them their large numbers of students and profitable trade.[4] (*Development*, pp. 7-8.)

I suppose this could be taken as the zenith of academic liberty; just as the nadir would be a faculty of science, saddled with its cyclotron, supported 80 per cent by the War Department of a centralized state that dictates the avenues of research, and with a "personnel" subjected to a clearance arrived at by secret investigation.

2) More than half of this history of universities is occupied with the decline of sectarian control of academic selection, thought, and action; the secularizing of learning. The other side, the loss, is of course that thought and action tend to come to us more lightly; few of us, though some, spend sleepless nights of doubt about a detail of phrasing in theory

leading to an inconsistency in behavior perhaps publicly unnoticed anyway. Professor Hofstadter charmingly recounts a touching story of the resignation of the first president of Harvard, Henry Dunster, who had found in his heart that no infant could properly be baptized and had to proclaim the same. (It seems to me, by the way, that this is an inevitable opinion for a college man who should set great store on learning and inquiry.) But Dunster was

> not dismissed, and he could have kept his job if he had promised to be silent about his unacceptable convictions, for everything in the case indicates that the magistrates and ministers never lost personal confidence in him. Dunster, however, submitted a curious letter of resignation which made no clear reference to religious issues but dwelled at some length on the recent investigation of the college and the expansion of the powers of the Overseers at the expense of the Corporation. The General Court gave Dunster the opportunity to take a month to reconsider. Evidently they still hoped that he could be persuaded to swallow his heresy. . . . But a month later Dunster closed his presidency with the utmost finality when he interrupted a baptismal service at Cambridge with a startling speech against infant baptism and the "corupcions stealing into the Church." (*Ibid.*, p. 89.)

What is touching is not so much the president's earnest and dramatic witnessing, exactly in the style of Hawthorne, but the way in which the others respect their brother's right to wrestle with his god and their subsequent solicitude for him. It is unnecessary to mention contemporary contrasts.

3) Again, in discussing the influence on America of the great German universities of the nineteenth century, the historian, Professor Metzger, beautifully analyzes on the one hand what was carried over, the methodic thoroughness, specific competence (but not the universality of interest), the freedom from utilitarian narrowness, dedication to absolute freedom of truth; and on the other hand what was sloughed off or suffered a sea-change.

> We come to the heart of the difference when we compare the American and German conceptions of inner and outer freedom. . . . The German idea of "convincing" one's students, of winning them over to the personal system and philosophical views of the professor, was not condoned by American academic opinion. Rather, as far as classroom actions were concerned, the proper stance for American professors was thought to be one of neutrality on controversial issues, and silence on substantive issues that lay outside of their competence. Innumerable utterances affirmed these limitations. Eliot, in the very address that so eloquently declared that the university must be free, made neutrality an aspect of that freedom: ". . . It is not the function of the teacher to settle philosophical and political controversies for the pupil, or even to recommend to him any one set of opinions as better than another. . . . The student should be made acquainted . . . with the salient points of each system." (*Ibid.*, p. 400.)

Professor Metzger goes on to argue that this norm of neutrality itself springs from an American bias of thought, its empiricism, resistant to intuition, speculation, fantasy—in the end, a suspicion of deliveries not fairly quickly verifiable.[5] I do not think he sufficiently estimates the disadvantages of the limitations to "neutrality" as against the German freedom to "convince." In the first place, with the American limitation, competence almost automatically becomes specialization, for what quickly verifiable fact is to connect the various parts of study? There is no system of facts, only systems of thought. Again, is Eliot's ideal of neutral presentation something that can possibly exist in a classroom? Have you ever listened to a convinced Whiteheadian trying to present the philosophy of Kant? Then is the teacher to have no conviction of his own? It is plausible for the school to be neutral and present all sides, but how can the teacher be neutral? But most important, Eliot and Professor Metzger do not see realistically the situation of the student in the face of neutrality and competence: his moral nature must have some culture or other, and if no ideal or moral connections are made in the university, his culture—unless he has had an unusually lucky upbringing—will fall to the first extramural propagandist, or intramural but extracurricular propagandist, or even worse, it will continue in an infantile set of prejudices and unconscious conventionalities while his intellectual life will be correspondingly arid and without vital strength and prone to panic before Senatorial committees or rabble-rousers. As I have said above, the teacher is responsible either way, whether he freely exerts his influence or withholds it; and I think he does better not to worry about a standard of scientific certainty and impartiality, but, relying on the sense of his own integrity, to act forthrightly according to probabilities, keeping an open mind and heart. Best of all, no doubt, that he have a wisdom and learning that cuts under controversy and relieves its sharpness, but this is not a "stance" but a fact. It is a fact if the professor's urbane detachment, encyclopedic scope, urgent following-up, insistence on accuracy, or ability to make the controversy fascinating in itself (there are several admirable styles of teaching—none of them "neutral"), if these continually provide a new unsettling challenge to the student's wish to have an answer; but it is only a stance if the student feels he has come up against a limit of "no opinion." I don't think the majority of teachers are in fact this good. Finally, it seems likely that an important reason for the American standard of professorial neutrality has been the youth and sexual immaturity of our college students as contrasted with the German university-students of that time; our students are more impressionable; but it is hard to see the logic of, on the one hand, dropping the older paternalism (or giving it over to administrative deans) and, on the other hand, discouraging discipleship; the students are told they are no longer children but young men, but they are forbidden the love-affairs, both physical and intellectual, of young men. Yet where could such affairs be safer than at a university? Indeed, the contradiction is sometimes worse. There was a case at a famous eastern college where in the aftermath of a sexual escapade the dean gave a student's name to the police; a great foreign teacher, who had once served as Rector of a European school, exclaimed indignantly, "We were not *in loco parentis* and we protected them; you act *in loco parentis* and you do not protect them!" There spoke 800 years.

4) Another grievous loss for academic man occurred with the abandonment of the liberal arts course of classics for an elective system geared more to adjustment to the changing social scene. Professor Metzger handles this as follows:

> As the result of deeper social forces at work, the "conserving" function of the college no longer loomed so large. The unhingeing of moral certainties by urban living, the fading out of the evangelical impulse, the depersonalization of human relations in the process of industrial expansion, were destroying that integral vision, that firm and assertive credulity, required of institutions devoted to conservation. . . . A good part of the pre-Civil War academic's opposition to a more secular university and a more vocationalized curriculum stemmed from the desire to protect very fragile values from the crush of a rough society. He sought the freedom not to acquiesce in the philistinism of his age. (*Ibid.*, p. 317.)

I think this is wrongly put; it sounds like Allen Tate who could say, justifiably enough, "undo it!" At the beginning of *Academic Freedom in Our Times* Professor MacIver analyzes the climate of opinion unfavorable to academic freedom and finds a major factor in the want of a common culture and a deep-going communication. Given Professor Metzger's analysis here, this is more and more inevitable, the University cannot cure it but rather tends to worsen it. What is common, integral, and humane is ipso facto out-of-date and fragile and needing conservation; meanwhile the University hastens on to new inquiry. Against this, the Great Books Movement, associated with the names of Hutchins, Adler, McKeon, and Buchanan, has denied that the common culture is out-of-date; but they have made the contrary mistake, it seems to me, of claiming it is "eternal" and resides in the Great Books as "classics." All this is topsy-turvy and looking in the wrong place. The true classics are the structures, whether propositions or methods or habits, that are in fact operative in the present juncture, urban, industrial, depersonalized, or whatever. There is always a classical curriculum to be found, because what is classical is simply what is central, concrete, causally operative, underlying; and indeed in any new situation, the classics never look like "classics," nor, in the present state of literature, are they likely to be books. The Socratic dialogue is classic, and in our times it is to be found in the psychoanalytic group-session, where very soon one reaches what is integral, humane, and communicative. The experimental method is classic and chastens and unites us, but it must not be taught as a laboratory-exercise nor in a course in logic, but rigorously applied to some real practical behavior. Eurhythmics and sports are classic. Mathematizing experience is classic. It is not classic to teach grammar, but it is classic to define the grammar of your speech. The mistake has been to study monuments of classical ages—the Greeks, the Medievals, the Seventeenth Century—rather than to assume that we are presently creating classics. I propose that this is what Dewey meant by reconstruction, to find-and-make ourselves classical techniques and a common culture by a philosophical handling of just where we are on our way. This is not what the university has been doing, and now nobody can teach classics and we do not know what classics we have.

5) Another loss occurred to Academic Man when he became, and agreed to consider himself as, merely an academic man, without some other conception of his competence in the larger society. The historians relate with too much satisfaction, it seems to me, the development of a specialist "profession" from a group of clergymen who perhaps temporarily accepted calls as teachers. But teaching on the university level[6] though it is surely a vocation and requires a special temperament and knack, is not a profession because it does not have a proper subject-matter; it is a universal art applied to a proper subject-matter; one might as well speak of a "professional orator." To the extent that the teacher inquires into the subject-matter proper, however, he is not a teacher, and then why does he hang around the campus so much? One's suspicion is, alas, that the ancient maxim is true: "If you can't do it, teach it." Teaching is certainly a vocation and a responsibility of every expert; very few things are more beautiful to see than good teaching; perhaps nothing is more recreative and enlarging for the expert himself, for he can teach with an integrity generally impossible in practice, and he gets to look at his habit of art with new eyes; even so, the scene of the same aging grown-ups hanging around while generations of youth pass by, has something in it that stinks in the nostrils. As for colleagues, the company of the like-minded is both stimulating and comforting, but to be immured with the like-minded is like—living at Princeton. A disadvantage of the professional situation, of course, is that the academic is economically tied; necessarily he is fearful of losing his tenure; he cannot, under stress, go off to his proper job where he is indispensable because he produces the goods. (In our society, of course, most of those goods do not fetch a price.) But perhaps a greater loss is that whole areas and provinces of science and scholarship have become merely intramural, they no longer importantly exist as the property of adult academies and learned societies, which in turn have tended to become merely honorary memberships that give prizes and sponsor social gatherings. Extramural science is bound to industry, extramural scholarship does not exist at all; yet it is simply by the accident

that there are university libraries and laboratories and stipends that such activities are immured, with correspondingly irrelevant restrictions and duties that must be alleviated by claims to "academic freedom." It is hard to know what to advise the scholar, hampered or often hampered by the atmosphere of colleges, in a society that does not much patronize the study of history, linguistics, and literature, nevertheless, to our ideal picture of the more heroic and free Academic Man we would do well to add the lineaments of the Humanist and the scientist of the seventeenth and eighteenth centuries, who were not professional academics. (*Ibid.*, pp. 49, 195.)

6) Lastly, we must refer to a loss that has come with the coming of the Big University. Professor Metzger reads off the indictments from Veblen's *The Higher Learning in America*:

> Acutely, he discerned the trend toward bureaucratization was transforming the university's personnel, structure, and behavior. This change was already evidenced in the army of academic functionaries—the deans, directors, registrars, and secretaries—who had come upon the scene to manage the affairs of the university. It was evidenced in the organization of the faculty as a graded hierarchy of ranks within which passage was controlled by a series of official promotions. It was evidenced in the writing of rules that defined the rights and obligations of professors and trustees. It marked, though it did not cause, the end of an academic era in which the college had been a community and the faculty a body of peers. (*Ibid.*, p. 453.)

Dealing with this and the rest of Veblen's jeremiad, Metzger seeks to prove, successfully enough, that Big Business as such was not the guilty agent, that the changes were socially pervasive and inevitable. But otherwise, I am baffled by the equanimity of his acquiescence. I should have thought that the faculty *is* the university, and if this university ceases to exist, what is there to write about as a continuing historical entity? We have come full circle from our first historical quotation, about the guild of scholars choosing the interstices of a plural society and willing to preserve itself by migrating bag and baggage; now we have, apparently, merely one wheel in a machine, that needs, to be sure, its own special oil and rules for successful operation, but we can hardly expect to hear from it any unique delivery of the creator spirit. This is not very interesting. If the brothers do not confront one another face to face and communally decide, nothing follows from their being brothers. Academic Man becomes the same as any other American man; this is just what one surmised from the passages of anxiety in MacIver's book—the professors behaving like all the other sheep; it is uncharitable to level at them any special charges or to subject them to any special scrutiny; but then what is all the talk about a peculiar dedication? But I am sanguine enough to believe that the case is not so desperate as this.

The case is, it seems to me—and it is expressed in the tone and matter of both these stimulating books—that there is a double Academic Man.

Looming ever in the background is this ghostly presence or absence that we have been figuring forth by the accumulation of lost causes that can never be lost. I have tried to cull traits that show him in his extramural and intramural relations, in his personal responsibility and community, in his curriculum and livelihood. He is part of a band "intensely self-conscious and self-important," as Powicke said, and that carries colors and a coat of arms, not bashfully. He feels himself the carrier of western culture and the champion of new invention. He has a deserved reputation as a stickler for antique tradition with excessive scrupulosity, and for stirring up entirely gratuitous innovations, just to make trouble. He is prone to terrible knock-down conflicts with his colleagues on the basis of mutual respect, and to erotic devotions, both lenitive and dangerous, toward his students. He goes abroad on his career in the world and sits on the faculty as an independent man of the world. This ghost, I say, is continually trying to break into reality and take over, but he is restrained—in many ways, let me hasten to add, *fortunately* restrained—by the circumstances of social history (very fully explained by our authors). Restrained and nonexistent, but he exerts an eerie fascination on the living body, rouses in him dreams, makes him touchy and irritable and suddenly ashamed and rebellious; and sometimes he gets hold of the speech and utters things like Professor MacIver's somewhat mesmerized sermons.

In the foreground and with us, is the other academic man, frightened by a noisy politician. Caught in a bureaucracy, ridden by authority from above and bullying others from below, he is afraid of a black mark against him, because if he loses his job here he won't have good references elsewhere; there is only one academic world and it is for him the only world. Weighed down by vast mortmain properties, corporately held and that make the living faculty a trivial force; and dependent for current expenses on alien interests that pay the piper and call the tune. Unerotic and at least publicly antisexual, naturally he is subject to anxiety. He uses lofty ethical terms to shame others, but gets remarkably little strength and animation from the reality pretended. He engages in plenty of intramural bickering and jockeying for position, but never in a bang-up fight. He does a good deal of obsessional counting and methodical busy-work that is not very different from telling beads. He is not distinguishable, and circumspectly avoids becoming so by overt action. He and his fellows huddle together not as a totemic band but because it is cold. This is the academic man that speaks in Professor MacIver's reportage.

WILLIAM EARLE

Notes on the Death of Culture

In General

THE CULTURE of the western world has for some time been under diagnosis as though it were a patient sick with an unknown disease. The doctors are agreed only on this: the illness is acute. They differ on when it began, and how long the patient may be expected to live; they differ on how radical the cure must be. But, for a long time, no one has been very happy with it. Hegel, Marx, Kierkegaard, Nietzsche, Matthew Arnold, Spengler, Eliot, Jaspers, Marcel, to name a few, all find something radically wrong. Some, like Hegel, had the sense of living at the end of a great period, a twilight in which they could reflect on the work of the day. Others, like Marx, thought they could perceive the cause in socio-economic factors which were correctable by revolution. Kierkegaard and Nietzsche saw the sickness in religious terms; Kierkegaard in the progressive loss of individuality, inwardness, and passion; Nietzsche saw it in the "herd-men," the "nay-sayers," and prophesied something beyond man, superman, who could at last affirm himself and life. But all the doctors feel that something is *finished*.

The subject is, of course, vast, and no one can hope to see more than can be seen through a tiny crack. Each must make his own diagnosis from his own peculiar standpoint, and that is what I shall try here. There can be no harm in looking once again at what passes for culture, estimating it, and pronouncing our own death sentence. My purpose, however, is not altogether negative; for although culture may be dead, the human spirit is not. If it is not altogether futile to dream, perhaps something better can be hoped for. At the end, then, I shall express my private dreams.

What, then, is culture ideally, and why is western culture dead? It is clear at the start that we are not talking about culture as a leisure-time activity, as entertainment alone; nor simply as that part of the communal work which never earns its own pay and must therefore be supported by tax-exempt donations. Nor is it an affair of snobs. Nor exclu-

Reprinted from *Noonday 1* (1958), pp. 3-26, by permission of the author and the publisher.

sively of universities. Nor of impresarios. There can be no question of isolating it on one page of the newspaper, or of escaping it altogether. For culture in its deepest sense is the whole life of the human spirit in communities. There is no sense, therefore, in seeing culture as only one part of that total life; or rather, when it appears in that light, something is radically wrong with the culture in that community.

Human culture, of course, is not something which has its own independent existence. It is not a rock-formation which requires little or no attention, which simply *is*. It is a product of the human spirit, and that particular sort of product which is never finally produced; that is, culture is nothing but the *life* of human beings, and for culture to be alive means that actual human beings live in it. Culture, then, is that medium which the human spirit creates for its own life; looked at objectively it is found in the works of the spirit, in language, customs, institutions, as well as buildings, monuments, works of art, and symbols; but subjectively, all of these must be lived in. The accumulation of unread books may be important to a statistician, but those works have not entered into culture until they are read.

The human spirit, then, cannot take itself for granted. It may be found in all men and at all times, but what is then found is nothing but potential spirit. For its *life*, it must act; and its action is its life within culture. And so while the planets need not give themselves the slightest trouble over their movement, the spirit must; it is alive only when it is creating its own life. That life is not automatic, nor instinctual; it must be created by the spirit itself. Hence, since the spirit is alive only when it is creating itself, the very life of the spirit is dependent upon its *concern*. Its concern is precisely for itself, for its life, for that life is only possible as a free effort. Concern is one fundamental feature of the spirit, but it should be noted in addition that the concern in question is conscious though not necessarily self-conscious. The spirit *is* nothing but consciousness, its life is conscious, and let it have what subconscious bases and memories it does have, it invariably must *seek* consciousness. It seeks to become lucid about what it itself is and what other things are. *Lucidity*, then, is a second mark of the spirit.

And finally, since the human spirit is inevitably in individuals, the life of the individual must *manifest* itself to others. In culture, each participates in the whole by encountering the expressions of others, and expressing or manifesting itself. Thus, the individual can emerge out of the limitations of his own privacy. In short, the life of the human spirit has three notable aspects: it lives only through its concern with itself, it lives or seeks to live on the plane of lucidity, and it expresses itself in objective works. Now these three features are nothing but functions; functioning together, they create culture. But when they take on a pseudo-life of their own, and desire to become distinct activities, professionalized, and definable in themselves, we arrive at the contemporary scene: *concern* becomes the special province of "religion"; *lucidity* becomes the special province of "science" and "philosophy"; *expression* becomes the speciality of the "arts." And, in a nutshell, this is our own diagnosis. What now passes for "philosophy" is not and does not aspire to be a lucidity of the spirit. It is "technical," that is, pure knowledge devoid of any interest in the concerns of the spirit. What passes for religion is an "ultimate concern" which is not and cannot be made lucid by philosophy or science. And what passes for art, is something thought to be pure expression, with no content, and above all no "message." The net result is that in aspiring toward absolute purity, toward independence, and toward the technical, these activities which might be the supreme expressions of the human spirit have achieved absolute triviality. They are, in our diagnosis, one and all *dead*. Worse, they are on the verge of becoming ridiculous. But before continuing with these bitter reflections, I should add that while I see little or nothing in the contemporary scene worth imitating or continuing, it would be both fatuous and ungrateful to ignore the genius which has gone into making it. Our criticisms are compatible with honor to the great; the creators of contemporary culture had very good reasons for what they did. But we must question whether those reasons are still valid, and whether we wish to continue in the same direction. And it should also be emphasized that there can be no question of imitating some past. If the present is not worth imitating, the past cannot be imitated. The truth is that no living spirit can imitate at all. We must not dream then of some "neo-," but rather of something genuinely new.

Meanwhile, there may still be a question in some reader's mind whether these noble activities are really dead. Perhaps the corpse still twitches. And so let us take a look at the contemporary philosopher, as he sees himself, and pronounce our judgment. And, sad as the picture is, as a professional philosopher I must include myself in the picture I am drawing; but my intent is neither confession nor accusation, but I hope, diagnosis.

The Technical Philosopher

Here I must beg leave to inform the general reader about technical philosophy, since he could not possibly know what it is unless he engaged in it. He most certainly will know the names of contemporary painters and composers; but will he know the name of a single technical philosopher? But this is more or less as it should be, as I shall presently demonstrate. Now, is the philosophy of the technical philosopher quite dead? Someone who could not read might gather that philosophy had never been more active. The number of articles published in our technical journals is staggering; no one could possibly read them all, or remember a single one. These articles, and not books, are our special product. Professional philosophers are men who belong to professional associations, subscribe to professional journals, write these articles, reprints of which they pay for and send to friends, and who earn their living by teaching young men to do the same: write articles and teach young men to do the same. Altogether then we constitute a new phenomenon, the professionalization of wisdom. Let us take a closer look then at the Technical Philosopher.

First of all, his most characteristic temperamental trait is his extraordinary sensitivity to a certain criticism: that of being "edifying." In our inner professional circles, a more pointed sneer could hardly be found than that a work is edifying and suffused with uplift. Such a comment has almost the force of revoking a philosopher's Ph.D.; the accused winces inwardly and can only clear his name by writing not one but several articles for the *Journal of Symbolic Logic*. These articles, however, need not actually be read by his colleagues; everyone knows in advance that there could be nothing edifying in the pages of the *Journal of Symbolic Logic*.

The criticism of edification or uplift is particularly cutting since it touches upon the intent of the philosopher; no one can be edifying unless he intends to be; and it is this intent which represents a disloyalty to all the values of Technical Philosophy. There is another criticism, not quite so devastating since it does not concern itself with one's intent, but only with the worthlessness of one's accomplishment: and that is "muddleheadedness." In the view of Technical Philosophy, all traditional philosophy was muddleheaded, had no idea of what it was doing, and did even that badly. Muddleheadedness is almost a style of thinking, the old style, and is exactly what might be expected of a philosopher who intended to be edifying. For the most part, one need only read the titles of the classics in philosophy to perceive the muddleheadedness from which they sprang. Sometimes the very face of the philosopher is enough; a muddleheaded philosopher will have a softer face, there will be less aggressiveness in it, and sometimes a trace of serenity.

What, positively, does the new Technical Philosopher desire to be? Well, of course, technical, that is, scientific above all. He wishes to regard himself as a philosophical worker, or even "researcher"; his work is thought of as a "research project," and if he can concoct a "co-operative research project," he will have no difficulty whatsoever in getting a grant from a foundation. Can not many think better than one? Has not co-operation proved beneficial in the sciences? If the Technical Philosopher did not retain some faded memory of his tradition, he would be delighted to teach his classes in a white laboratory coat; instead he carries a briefcase.

His inquiries, investigations, and research will be embodied in a "monograph," a short paper with the "problem" clearly stated at the beginning, and at the end a summary of the "results." The monograph must also refer to the other "literature" on the subject. The Technical Philosopher thus is shortwinded; he has an instinctive distaste for the sprawling works of the nineteenth century, when philosophers sometimes sought a larger view of things. One of the most influential of the new philosophers was Ludwig Wittgenstein, whose books were composed of separated pithy sentences and paragraphs, each of which is numbered for easy reference. This unfortunate man did not live to see his work undone; for now each sentence is being reinflated back into an article for the journal, *Mind*. Close to the fear of being edifying is that of being a windbag. The Technical Philosopher feels that everything can be said quickly and to the point. At the meetings of his professional associations, papers are limited to twenty minutes. The president alone can speak at greater length, but since he speaks after dinner, he is obliged to devote a third of his time to telling jokes. And here I must add my own note of approval; when we have nothing to say, surely twenty minutes is not too short a time in which to say it.

The new style of Technical Philosophy is remarkable since it expresses something about the philosophy itself. The style tends toward the telegraphic code. One reason for this is that the paper must be capable of being read during office hours, and make no demands upon the week ends. Technical Philosophy, the reader must understand, is simply one sort of work for which one is paid. It should have no resonance beyond those hours. When carried to ideal perfection, it is expressed in some form of artificial symbolism, which takes years of training to read with any ease. The Technical Philosopher has always envied the mathematician, with his proofs and symbols. And he has always had a fear of natural or ordinary language. Ordinary language is so obscure; words come dripping out of a sea of feelings and related meanings, and are logically unmanageable. Therefore we have devised a new language, symbolic logic, which begins with marks having no meaning at all; whatever meaning they acquire is given to them by other marks, which serve as their definitions. Now everything should be clear, and to some extent it is; but unfortunately the language is so impoverished that nothing of any importance can be said in it, and so artificial in form that error is perhaps more frequent in it than in our mother tongue.

One of the most desirable features of symbolic logic in the eyes of Technical Philosophers is its impersonality. It states the pure core of the argument with no emotional nonsense. The writer is invisible behind his symbols, although some who wish to be extraordinarily sensitive profess to be able still to detect personality now in terms of the "elegance" of the proof. But I do not know if this contention has ever been thoroughly tested. The Technical Philosopher detests "style," for he sees it as expressing personal attitudes, and what difference can they make? Style in an argument is as disturbing and inappropriate as perfume or sweat on the eyepiece of a telescope. The Technical Philosopher desires to *be* impersonal, to write impersonally, and to disappear entirely into his analyses. And to a surprising degree he succeeds, for, to be frank, there isn't much to disappear.

Now these various stylistic features of Technical Philosophy are not accidental peculiarities. They all flow, as I see it, from the substance of the philosophy itself. And so perhaps it is time to look at it. Professor Morton White characterizes our age as the age of "analysis"; and this is exact, unfortunately. The general reader may be tempted to confuse "analysis" with "psycho-analysis"; and that would be a mistake. What the philosopher "analyzes" today is not the psyche, but rather words, phrases, sentences, arguments, which purport to say something meaningful or true. The Technical Philosopher finds everything said more or less confused and unclear. And if you are not initially confused, there is no one like a good analyst to demonstrate the confusion which lurks in the most innocent phrase; and there is no question whatsoever the Technical Philosopher can exhibit confusions which would have confused no one.

Technical Philosophy then is "analysis." But what is analysis? There is no problem here, to analyze anything is to break it down, to dissolve it into its components, to reduce it from its initial totality into its ingredient parts. Then the parts are reassembled back into the whole, and lo! now, for the first time, we "understand" what that whole was. But in all of this, two aspects hit the eye. The first is the assumption that language is not clear in its first usage. It must be *made clear* by the analysis. The second is the fervent assumption that the philosopher himself is entitled only to analyze; that is, his work consists of tearing apart intellectually phrases others have put together. He analyzes syntheses but he makes no synthesis himself. Let us examine more closely both of these assumptions.

The first assumption that language is not clear in its direct employment has the consequence that only the analytical philosopher knows the clear meaning of what others are saying. But, then, if their initial language was unclear in the first place, how could the analytical philosopher know whether his analysis was right or wrong? And so we find in *Mind*, a leading magazine for such discussions, articles written about articles written themselves about articles, all agitating the question whether an analysis really gives us the original meaning. Now if the original meaning was clear itself, what *need* for the analysis; and if it was not clear how could one *verify* the analysis? But the New Philosophers somehow succeed in *making* original utterances unclear in order to clear them up. This activity itself breaks down into two schools; one finds that all ordinary language is obscure, and can only be made clear by translating it into some artificial symbolism. These philosophers are called "ideal language men." A second school is anti-philosophical, and finds that all *philosophic* problems are generated by misunderstanding ordinary language. The "clarify" traditional philosophic problems by showing that there was no genuine problem, only a misuse or misunderstanding of ordinary language. These philosophers are called "ordinary language men." Now the result of both schools is that the new philosopher need know in his professional capacity *absolutely nothing* except how *words* are used. For all Technical Philosophers feel that there are but two matters of concern to knowledge. There are the "facts," and there is the question of how to express these facts clearly. The Technical Philosopher prohibits himself professionally from arguing "facts." All facts are to be drawn from the "sciences," which is another department of the university. And so he has nothing to do but analyze *language,* in a professional indifference to facts. Most of "analysis" then consists of analyzing the language other and more traditional philosophers have used. Here there are no facts.

Now the second aspect of the whole matter is that the Technical Philosopher makes no syntheses himself, i.e., he has nothing to say. This, of course, takes its toll on our mood. For as Technical Philosophers, we can never really say anything new by ourselves. Others have to say it first, and then we *analyze* what they have said. This means we can never speak first, and must wait for somebody else to provide a sentence or phrase which can then be analyzed. And too often it turns out that there is nothing to analyze. The first sentence was perfectly clear to all present except ourselves; and so our analyses have only the function of demonstrating the obvious or explaining the joke. Hence our bad temper. Further, our entire attitude toward sentences is *hostile;* we live in the mood of the hunter stalking the big kill, the phrase which is ambiguous or which contains, in the words of Gilbert Ryle, a "howler." This analytic hostility is, obviously, incompatible with love, with serenity, and with any comprehension of those meanings and subtleties which presuppose sympathy and love for their very sense. No wonder our brows are furrowed, our eyes narrow and glittering, our lips thin and compressed and already twisting into a smile of derision before the sentence is finished; we have detected a howler! The old style of serene sage has definitely disappeared from the scene. The ethic of the New Philosopher was expressed by Morris Cohen in his famous reply to the question why he was always critical: "It is enough to clean the Augean stables." But then the question remains as to the definition of dirt; precisely what is to be cleaned out? The New Philosopher wishes to clean out everything except what the scientists say or what he supposes "common sense" to be. But there is a vast agreement that traditional philosophy is the very ordure which logical, scientific, and clear-headed thinking must flush away as speedily as possible. The British technical philosophers especially trust something they call "common sense"; their American counterparts dote on "science." But in all cases, the content of philosophy is not supplied by philosophy; Technical Philosophy has no content of its own. It is rather a gigantic hose designed to flush the stables of traditional philosophy. Or perhaps a flame thrower, turned not only on filth and confusion, but also stables, horses, and finally the flame-thrower himself. The Technical Philosopher is the point of pure negativity, an eye which would like to see pure light but cannot because of visible things. It is this final phase which is the death of philosophy as well as a darkening of the lucidity possible to the spirit. Philosophy has at last achieved the pure heights of having no content, nothing to say, and nothing to do except analyze the confusions in what others say into an unintelligible jargon of its own.

To ask a Technical Philosopher for his vision of the world is to throw him into the worst of embarrassments. It is hopelessly to misunderstand what philosophy now is. The philosopher's answer will not try to supply that vision, or even recognize its absence; rather it will analyze the meaning of your question in order to show that it really has no meaning at all. It is left for others to supply the vision.

In summary then, the Technical Philosopher analogizes himself to the scientist. He wishes to be brief, technical in style and subject matter, impersonal, unemotional, and unedifying. He does not expect the layman to understand what he says, and would be slightly embarrassed if the layman did. He has nothing positive to offer, no vision of life or the world, no summary attitude or total view. His positive activity is to analyze statements made by others, but never in his professional role to make such original statements himself. He assumes that somehow or other the accumulation of these technical analyses in the library adds up to something of value. The New Philosopher does not wish to speak of matters of human concern. He only wishes to be clear about little things. He does not believe in his heart that one can be clear about big things, or that philosophy should address itself to human concern. One of the classical works most in disrepute today is Boethius' *Consolations of Philosophy*. The Technical Philosopher knows analysis will bring no consolation. He is not the pompous philosopher of the old style; rather he regards himself as a technician who "does philosophy" more or less in his office during school hours. Week ends are another matter, a vacation from philosophy.

Now this was not always so. For the longest stretch of its history, philosophy was, embarrassing as it is to Technical Philosophy, concerned precisely with large visions and the edifying. That is, it was concerned with the human situation and what was to be done about it. For traditional philosophy, as well as for religion, man was regarded as a suffering animal, not merely suffering in life from correctable ills, but suffering from life, from the intrinsic and inevitable ills. Philosophy did not specifically address itself to the particular evils in life, such as sickness, poverty, war, and tyranny. The point of view of philosophy was that even if all these were corrected, we should still be suffering spirits. In short, man seeks some way of saving the meaning of his life in spite of his death, in spite of his guilt, pain, and misery. Philosophy then had its own proper mode of salvation, which was not to live an imaginary life in some beyond, nor systematically to blind oneself to the necessary pain of living, but to comprehend the *meaning* of these things. Philosophy has always been in a more or less gnostic tradition, by which man could save something from the wreck of his life by comprehending it. The mode of salvation offered by philosophy was called *wisdom,* and philosophy is named after its love. By wisdom alone can men rise above dumb and meaningless suffering to a comprehension of its meaning, and that comprehension was the comprehension of something eternal and blessed. Now, all of this is edifying, of course, and moves within the circle of ethical, religious, and esthetic categories. The various "answers" to the question of the "meaning" of life given in philosophy center on the notion of truth; and philosophizing implies as its necessary pre-condition as well as aim, an alteration in *attitude* toward life. And this is the pure edification worked by truth. The formulations of the end or meaning are various: "spectator of all time and existence," "the flight of the alone to the Alone," the "intellectual love of God," "*amor fati,*" "participation in the Absolute Idea," etc. They are not so various, however, but what they do not express is a common meaning, the sense that human life culminates ideally in a lucidity about itself and its highest concerns. Wisdom was never merely a doctrine, although it had its doctrines. It was rather a pursuit of that height of soul from which the last truth could be seen. Now obviously such matters are not fit topics for Ph.D. dissertations, class-room examinations, or "technical analyses." For it is not open to anyone equipped with nothing but the criteria of logic to comprehend the sense of philosophy; in addition, the "analyst" must have a trace of the love of wisdom himself. And so it is not surprising that Technical Philosophers find in traditional philosophy with its flights and soarings, its edification and enthusiasm, nothing but a muddle of banality and mystification. The ambiguities of traditional philosophy are maddening to the new philosophical specialists; but perhaps it was precisely these against whom the ancient doctrine wished to protect itself. How indeed can the same ultimate things be said to young and old alike, to wise and foolish? Better to speak in enigmas which in their very strangeness might suggest a meaning different from that which meets the hasty eye.

Technical Philosophy steers clear of wisdom. Or worse, it is convinced that there isn't any, or if there is, it isn't the philosopher's business. And so the "muddled problems" of traditional philosophy are translated into clear ones, into problems which can be solved by technical means, by objective action rather than any inner transformation. The suffering of life is thus "analyzed" into a series of correctable ills. If it is disease you mean, then medicine will find the answer. If poverty, then social and economic measures are indicated. If ignorance, then more schooling. John Stuart Mill thought that these summed up human misery, and the remarkable thing in such an analysis is that not one requires for its solution an inner philosophic transformation of attitude toward life. One need only remain exactly as one is, see things exactly as they are now, and work out the answer upon which everyone can agree. The fact that no philosopher ever regarded his philosophy as a spurious medicine, economics, or schooling gave him no pause. They must have been muddled about their own real intent. And what is left over after all the medicine, wealth, and education have had their chance to work? A few minor matters such as death, guilt, and the meaninglessness which is always ready to rise up in even the happiest. And suppose disease, poverty, and ignorance could *eventually* be eliminated, as everyone must hope, what is to be done now when they are not?

Technical Philosophers are silent on these matters, or vaguely embarrassed. They have nothing to say. They have no vision, want none, and more or less identify philosophic vision with hallucination. As for "changes of attitudes," if these have any importance at all, there are experts for them too. The psychoanalyst is in best repute, but the flabbier Technical Philosophers feel that this is what the preacher might be for, with his tired old platitudes. In any event, pure knowledge has nothing to do here; it seeks absolute purity, absolute independence, and absolute irrelevance to anything anyone might conceivably be interested in. Thus has a noble discipline committed suicide.

And Art and Religion

Philosophy as wisdom has been dying a long time; but what about art and religion? When we think of the images it once gave of the mystery of human life: Oedipus, Antigone, Medea, Hamlet, Lear, Faust, Ahab; or the gods, heroes and horsemen of the Parthenon; the faces of Rembrandt, the crucifixions of Grünewald, El Greco. . . . And what were these but the human spirit seeking and giving expression to its ultimate clarity about its ultimate concerns? Here there was no question of "pure composition," of "pure expression," or even of the purely "esthetic." They are least of all "sensuous surfaces." The truth of the matter is that while these mysterious images are typically regarded as "art," they are just as much wisdom and religion. Now, the complaint is not that art today is "not as great" as it once was. It is true that it is not; but such judgments remain vacuous unless the question is transposed from the level of accusation to that of principle. There can be no question but that the human spirit potentially has the same eternal depths as always. If its results are incomparably more trivial, it is not due to lack of genius; but it may be due to certain directions taken individually and culturally, to certain *ideals* now dominant, which require examination in art as they do in philosophy. Is it accidental that the most creative painter in our day no longer seeks to give an image of the human reality, but contents himself with images of its distortion; and that when he is moved to express what he sees of life it comes out as the melodramatic slaughterhouse of Guernica? Or is it accidental that this passes for his "human concern," his "insight" into the human reality? But since when has wisdom resided in an intensity of outrage over physical destruction? If we should finally lose our minds over malice, cruelty, and destruction would that be the ultimate achievement of insight and wisdom? The perception of evil some time ago was regarded as the bare *beginning of the problem.*

But then the contemporary arts are not noted for their images of the human reality. In place of such muddles, we find the ideal of "pure expression." The arts must free themselves from foreign emotions, associations, content, "reality," and become what? The purely optical, auditory, verbal? An entertainment for the senses? In literature it used to be Mallarmé, Gertrude Stein, and the puns of Joyce. But we needn't limit ourselves to the passé. The same phenomenon occurs whenever literature aspires toward pure style or whenever we see the emergence of the "professional writer." Professional artists of whatever sort or those whose profession is measured by skill in the manipulation of their respective media. The writer is measured by his ability to use words; but words, unfortunately, are symbols of something which is not words. That of which they are symbols is, of course, their content, but content for the professional is a matter of indifference. As a painter, he can equally well do a wine bottle, a scrap of newspaper or the human face. And so indeed he can so long as the human face is seen as a composition of "lines and planes," since it has this and this alone in common with everything visible. And, so long as we are interested only in compositions of lines and planes, light and shadow, we may as well suppress the human face altogether; it is but a "literary association," or a "photographic" residue; pure creation will create with nothing but color and shape, and all it will create will be color and shape. The writer similarly will be able to write equally well about anything. His prose or poetry will be judged on its own merits; and what are these merits when we have abstracted from their reference to what lies out beyond them? Nothing is left but their "rhythm," "organization," "color," "originality of expression," "style," in short, everything but their truth and content. It is as if one were to judge a dinner exclusively by the plates on which it was served.

And since it is not possible to remove all reference to the human reality, there will be a trace of interest left in the content, that is, in what is exhibited of the human spirit. But since there is now no communal religion or philosophy which might extend the private sensibility of the writer, he must, if he is honest, fall back on his private imagination and feelings; and here we see again and again the impoverishment which the purely private brings. The honest feelings which the artist finally discovers within himself insofar as he rejects what light philosophy and religion might ideally offer, are not higher or more sincere or deeper truths; most frequently they reduce themselves to our old friend, sex.

Without extending the discussion endlessly, the same phenomena can be indicated in the other arts. Music in its turn also desires to be pure music, pure composition, to have nothing to do with "emotion," which is always "extra-musical." When emotion is mentioned, the opponents of it point to the most flagrant examples of Tchaikovsky; is that what is wanted? Or perhaps program music, where the title and accompanying notes *tell* the listener what to feel? And since no one could argue for any such thing, the conclusion is drawn that emotion as such is foreign to music, or music has its own pure emotions. Now the composer is thought of as a species of engineer either tailoring his composition to one record side, to an accompanying film or, if these frankly external limits are abandoned, and he is a pure composer, then the "composition itself" dictates its own form. But, of course, notes and scales do not and can not dictate what is done with them, any more than words can dictate what is said with them. At best they set certain negative limits. The result is that "pure composition" is a radical absurdity, and as meaningless a phrase as "pure expression." The only practical result of such slogans and phrases is to divert the attention of the composer from the significance that emotion *musically expressed* might have, from the possible depths of emotion, to a pursuit of "pure" music, or compositions which are as devoid of feeling as possible; this leaves us on the one hand with paper compositions, supposed to be deep because nothing whatsoever can be felt through what is heard and where the chief delights derive from conceptual patterns emerging from a study of the score, or on the other hand, the delights of purely *aural* contrasts, music which is little but orchestration, a composition of timbres, rhythms, and sudden dynamic shifts, an art of concocting thrills for the ear or tests for high-fidelity phonographs.

In our critical mood, we may as well look at what religion has become.

Some men still take it seriously, bringing themselves to believe it still retains some trace of something or other of concern. But it can hardly be what is contemporary in contemporary religion which could command the slightest allegiance. For now we find the spectacle of a spiritual concern also trying to become a pure activity, and achieving little but absurdity. On the one hand, we find the universalistic tendency where each sect, confession, or denomination has lost confidence in its distinctive creed, and realizing that it is but one *mode* of religion, ashamed of its particularity, desires to become *religion as such*. "True" religion then from this standpoint is simply "having religion," a religion which is indifferently Christianity, Judaism, Islam, Hinduism, as well as Ethical Culture, Unitarianism, Christian Science and, so as to be utterly free of "prejudice," Atheism as well. Or, on the other hand, sensing the absurdity of trying to speak a language which isn't any particular language, religion reverts to its ancient roots and becomes conservative, fundamentalistic, the religion of "our fathers," a religion of absolute faith in a Founder, Book, Church, or Tradition. Within this second tendency, enmeshed as it is with dogmas, beliefs, customs, and words of two or three thousand years ago, or the synthetic concoctions of yesterday, incapable of winnowing the wheat from the chaff for fear of dissolving into an indeterminate religiosity, a peculiar doctrine emerges, that of "two truths." For now the critical examination of "human" reason is feared; there is the *sacred* truth, which must be believed in, assented to, to which one must be "committed," versus a "secular" truth which is but practical, merely scientific, and of course merely human and relative. The former is holy, and touches everything essential; the latter is useful, but subject to suspension by the higher, sacred truth. One *believes* in sacred truth; one *proves and demonstrates* secular truth. Everyone has seen the result of this particular predicament. Fundamentalistic religions pass imperceptibly and without the possibility of self-correction into the blindest of superstitions, the chief pattern of which is to see spiritual truths only as "miracles" in nature. Such a religion, since it cannot employ the demonstrable insights of reason except at its peril, has at its command no instrument whatsoever by which to distinguish the authentically spiritual from the childishly superstitious. Men are thought of as the "children" of God or, worse, of other men denominated "priests." If religion can use reason only to dissolve into a general religiosity, when it dismisses reason it tends to freeze into that impotence of the spirit called "commitment," or "faith." The meaning of symbols is identified with the symbol itself, and the more preposterous the result the more intensely it must be "believed." Religion too in its contemporary forms is as dead as philosophy and art; for just as nothing is so characteristic of the contemporary philosophic mind as its indifference to the spirit, nothing is so characteristic of the contemporary religious mind as its indifference to both art and philosophy, and the resulting engorgement of an indigestible mass of unclarified and unclarifiable "beliefs." What else could result from an attitude where reason is regarded as "merely human" or relative, and inferior to the authentic voice of God himself who must lack reason, and art is regarded as pious decor, at best capable of depicting allegorically stories and commitments fixed in advance and without the contribution of art? When will religion regard the contempt of reason and art as *blasphemous?*

In sum, then, contemporary western culture in its most characteristic manifestations presents us with the spectacle of various functions of the spirit seeking to become autonomous activities, technical, professional, and separated from one another. The whole spirit is to be found in none of these activities, and eventually everyone at last becomes *bored* with them. There is, of course, a superficial activity in all three, and the statistics reveal an "increased interest" in them in the United States; but what figures could be more ambiguous in their meaning? For our part we find nothing significant or particularly valuable in frenetic efforts which express a distracted and bewildered spirit. In fact, it probably is the case that the more the spirit tries to divide itself, the more active it must become, the more frenzied, until it sinks at last into paralysis.

Now, to revert to our first considerations, the death of explicit culture has most important consequences. If the human spirit must live in the medium of culture which it creates for itself, when that medium no longer can command honest allegiance, the spirit reverts into its own dark potential nothingness. If the spirit finds nothing of its genuine concern clarified and articulated in philosophy, what can it do but shun reason as such, look upon it as merely verbal, irrelevant, and logic chopping? When philosophy disappears as an effective clarification of ultimate human concerns, religion becomes anti-philosophical, and sinks into blind commitment; and art reverts to pure expression, which means either an expression of the sensuous or the inexpressive as such. In the absence of philosophy, the individual human spirit sinks back into a reliance upon the senses and the individual sciences for its light. When reason goes out, the senses and technical knowhow are always ready to take over; they at least can operate without the effort at self-creation. When religion becomes preposterous, the honest spirit finds its concern in the instinctual and the appetites. They too need no effort to sustain them, and can provide a facsimile of life. When art no longer presents us with the image of the spirit, the spirit sinks back into the unexpressed; art becomes mere art, and expression or objectification is regarded as trivial. The inner life of the spirit is thought to be higher than its overt expressed life; and that inner life, distrusting expression as falsification, becomes mute and eventually shrinks to nothing. When culture becomes inauthentic the spirit reverts to the irrational, instinctual, dark and mute; this is as close to death as the spirit can come.

Some Dreams

Providing there is any truth in all of this, the next question is what is to be done? But before exploring our dreams, we should be well aware of our limits. A living and authentic culture is not the product of individuals nor can it be planned in advance, particularly on the basis of a dead culture; nor when it emerges, will it take any form necessarily recognizable to us today. There can be no question therefore of dictating where the free and concerned human spirit shall go. Nor of offering concrete suggestions, or attempting to create a new culture tomorrow. But perhaps it is not wholly foolish if we let our dreams wander a bit to explore at least some *directions,* counter to those embodied in our present culture. For while the communal spirit does not operate and should not operate by technical planning, neither is it an instinctual growth like that of coral colonies. It is in the last analysis *consciousness.* And consciousness has the distinctive property of wishing to envisage its end, of taking thought of its goal while it acts. It is precisely the intent of contemporary culture which we find empty; it does admirably what it sets out to do, but is its aim anything of value?

The first remark then is negative. There is nothing viable in the present tendency toward the professionalization and isolation of spiritual functions. They dry up and become meaningless motions. Science in some of its problems can and must be specialized. But philosophy, religion, and art are not activities directed to specific finite aims but rather expressions of what is or should be a whole spirit. They are nothing but various functions of what is itself one. But this negative remark is insufficient.

Is the solution then to be found in an increasingly popular suggestion among educators, that these disciplines must be added to one another? But how can disciplines which are *set up* as separate be fructified by addition? Joint courses or combined curricula are mere shams if what are joined are themselves unjoinable. And, in addition, what profit is contemporary art to derive from contemporary philosophy or religion? None as I see it. And so with the other combinations of these disciplines. The matter lies deeper than this, and life is not generated by the addition of dead ingredients.

Nor is anything to be sought in revivals of the past, as I mentioned earlier. To revive the past is impossible and undesirable; even if it could be "revived," it carries within itself its own dialectic; we should be reverting to a simpler and happier age only to run through the course of history a second time, with minor variants. In short, there was an inner reason for our present predicament; the disease is not to be cured by reverting to an earlier phase. But more importantly, no living spirit can *imitate* anything; its life is precisely its creativity. Hence everything properly called "neo-," "neo-conservatism," "neo-liberalism," "neo-thomism," "neo-realism," "neo-symbolism," "neo-primitivism," or "neo-whateverism" must be excluded from our attention.

But similarly, merely to notice the schizophrenia in the modern spirit is negative and insufficient. Nor will the "interrelation" of functions themselves be any new direction. To relate three functions of the spirit to one another may be a necessary condition for health but the substance is still lacking from our analysis just as it is from contemporary culture itself. If the functions can be defined as *concern*, *clarity*, and *expression*, joining them together still omits any mention of their proper reality: *what* is it that is to be clarified, with which the human spirit is concerned, and which must be expressed? What is the substance of the human spirit? Can the question of culture receive any answer whatsoever which ignores this most difficult of all questions? And while it is true obviously that the spirit *can* take an interest in *anything whatsoever*, still those casual and miscellaneous interests can not define its ultimate intent.

Now it is precisely this living substance which must be *created*. But, certain *general* things might be said in advance. For what could the substance be but the life of the spirit itself? In short, the human spirit is and must be concerned with itself and its life. Now this formula may seem too anthropocentric until it is realized that when the spirit is concerned with its own life it is also concerned with the *absolute context* of that life. There is no such thing as "merely human" life; life is precisely human to the extent that it seeks to relate itself to that which is not merely human but to what it can honestly regard as *ultimate*. And so the human spirit is concerned with its relation to what it sees as ultimate. And what if it sees nothing as ultimate? Then also *that* is its ultimate vision, and constitutes the absolute sense it makes of its life. Thus, with Hegel, it can be said that the human spirit is precisely that effort to clarify and express its ultimate concern, which concern is precisely the sense it can make of itself. And therefore human culture is an attempt to make *sense* out of its concrete historical life, a sense which is lucid, ultimate, and expressed. Now the sense need not be and never is in any great culture a flattering of our desires or a consolation for whining, meanings which are sought only in the decay of culture. But ultimate sense it must be, if philosophy, religion, and art, and with them individual human lives, are not to relapse into the senseless.

My dream then is for a culture which again seeks to make ultimate sense out of the human spirit and its concern with an ultimate context. This would imply a philosophy which gave less attention to symbolic reformulations and would-be "technical problems" such as the problem of induction, the external world, other minds, sense-data, etc., but sought to clarify the concerns of the spirit. It would imply a religious sense which did not despise reason or did not harden itself within a commitment but could see the spirit in what it now regards as the "secular." And finally an art which expressed not expression itself but the image of the human spirit. Each of these functions can make indispensable contributions; but only when each works with its eyes on the others and also on their common substantial aim.

And it is here we must stop; for it is precisely the *content* of this new substance which can not be anticipated. It is exactly this future sense of reality which must be created, and created from deeper dimensions of the spirit than the current professionalized activities now envisage. In a word, the task as it appears now is for culture to create a new sense of reality within which we can live without either pretense or suffocation.

I. A. RICHARDS

The Future of the Humanities in General Education

Even in that certain hour before the fall,
Unless men please they are not heard at all.
—*The Fabulists*

AMONG THE GUESTS at the Conference on the Humanistic Tradition in the Century Ahead, which formed part of the Bicentennial Celebration at Princeton, were men and women with good claim to speak with authority—and still more with responsibility—for their subject. The occasion was felt to be challenging. This conference had been preceded by one on nuclear physics and another on the social sciences; and the skilful planners of our program arranged that we should be aware of this. It was hardly possible throughout the discussion not to wonder where—in the balance of forces that are shaping the future—the humanities did come in. Latish in our deliberations, somebody, perhaps unkindly, said that we had been talking a lot about our traditions. He questioned whether the physicists or the social scientists had said much about their tradition. He thought they were more likely to have discussed their *programs*. The audience looked, it seemed to me, somewhat uncomfortable at that. But indeed all to whom the humanities matter may well feel uncomfortable—extremely uncomfortable, if not indeed distressed and alarmed—about what is happening and *not* happening in the humanities at present. And they matter—by definition as well as in fact—to every man, woman, or child who aspires to become or remain a human being.

The Conference on the Humanistic Tradition in the Century Ahead is one source of the following remarks. Another which should be mentioned is the course on Homer, the Old Testament and Plato as Sources of Our Common Thought which I am giving at the moment as part of the experiments under way at Harvard towards "General Education in a Free Society." The reflections thus prompted sum up to this. The antinomies focused in that title are very far from being resolved, anywhere or by anyone, either in theory or in practice. Certainly reverence and regard for famous books and a backward-looking trust that all will somehow yet be well are, as these very books might teach, an insufficient equipment with which to meet what does seem to be ahead. Conservatism, in a phrase, must continue to be revolutionary in its technique.

In the last hundred years the human race has multiplied threefold. In 1840 there were some 700 millions of us; now we are more than 2,200 millions. In the next fifty years there will be a further and still more critical increase—unless the worst happens meanwhile. Too much reflective attention cannot be given to this fact. It is far more relevant to the problems of our age—and especially to the future of the humanities—than has yet been generally realized. Quantitative factors, unless technique is developed in commensurate degree, can settle qualitative possibilities—disastrously.

Another new fact, even newer and more momentous, is equally relevant, though it is not so easy to state. *Minds have become more exposed than ever before.* (If any point deserves italics, this does.) And this exposure too is undergoing explosive increase. Mental and moral communications, within each culture and between cultures, have suddenly expanded beyond anyone's power to foresee the consequences. The agencies at work—with one exception—hardly need more than mention. They are mass education, with its stress on verbal or nominal literacy, motion pictures, radio, television, modern advertising, and—here is the exception—modern scholarship. These are the new forces which already expose every urbanized mind to a range and variety and promiscuity of contacts unparalleled in history. And this is but beginning. Already some of the effects are showing. It would not perhaps be a culpable exaggeration to suggest that this expansion of our spiritual communications—and the power of minds to influence other minds which goes with it—has already made two wars of a world scale possible. There will at least be no doubt that this new mental exposure makes immense changes necessary in our conceptions of what the humanities have to do and how they can do it. Let us take a brief look at these agencies in action.

Mass education is of course our hope—our one hope, maybe. But in so far as it must use classrooms, how are we to get teachers able to give their pupils any power to select from among the influences to which they become ever more open? Present economic and social conditions repel almost all who might be capable of doing so, and teaching conditions frustrate those whose imagination and devotion still make them enter the profession. And through the decline of the family and for a thousand other well-known reasons there is now incomparably more for the teacher to do. The humanities, being the hardest things to teach, suffer most. They are the hardest to teach because wisdom, which they exist to cultivate, cannot be cut and dried. Much in other subjects can.

Correspondingly, the preparation of a teacher in the humanities is the hardest of all—which brings me to the not, as yet, sufficiently vexed topic of modern specialized scholarship. I have to explain its appearance in my list of disruptive agencies threatening the wholeness of present and future minds.

Modern scholarship is a fearful and wonderful as well as an unprecedented thing. It is unprecedented, I believe, in character as well as in scale, though I would listen eagerly to a modern scholar who was interested in just this historical question. Like so much else which should give us pause, modern scholarship is the product of admirably ingenious innovations in technique, on which Thamus' words to Theuth (*Phaedrus*, 275) are to the point: "Most ingenious Theuth, one man has the ability to beget an art, another to estimate the good or harm it will do to those who are to use it." The words apply equally to the ingenious doings of the nuclear physicists and to all inventions which may threaten us with nuclear fission of our minds. In scholarly technique the innovations are the modern dictionary, the book index, bibliography, the specialized journal, and the museum. Most of them seem to be eighteenth-century inventions. At any rate, as they affect us today they are recent. And it is relevant to note that Chinese scholarship only admitted an index to a book within the memory of those still living: an index being considered a subversive thing which would lead to superficiality and to disrespect for the teacher's authority—grounded on long and deep familiarity with a corpus rather than on quick glances at references.

However this may be, modern scholarship certainly requires ever more intensive and prolonged training of a sort which is of hardly any value to a teacher in general education. It is training in the administration of a vast body, an illimitable proliferation rather, of facts, comments, opinions, and mere phrases, too extensive and diverse to form, in any mind not of a very rare order, any coherent, much less any directing or confirming, view of essential human purpose. Moreover, since this proliferation proceeds geometrically, training in its administration, as we well know, becomes departmentalized, then subdepartmentalized, and scholarship, in so far as it is *that*, becomes less and less useful to a teacher. It may fit him to continue as a specialized researcher—within "areas" or on "points" with no known relevance to any side of the world crisis. It quite certainly does not give him what he needs as a teacher of the humanities—reasonably rich and considered views of a person's human relations to other persons. Worse still, it is intensive distraction from the hard essential task of maturing such views. Worst of all, this training has now become professional qualification offered competitively by rival institutions.

I would not be misunderstood here. This recent achievement of a method by which scholarship becomes accumulative and responsible to a controlled record is one of the glories of our age. It ranks with the partly parallel achievements in mathematics and experimental inquiry. Together with them it holds out infinite promise to man, and must go on. But, for the time being, as with physics, biology, and psychology (on which last I touch later) its present dangers rather than its remote promises should concern us most. It is preventing us from supplying our greatest need—teachers able to help humanity to remain humane.

Literature—a deep enough *and leisurely enough* familiarity with what the best minds have thought and felt about people—used to produce such teachers. Modern scholarship positively gets in the way. The critical apparatus of approach to the great things keeps them from their would-be student. He is daunted incessantly by the thought that somewhere there is something which would, if he only knew it, help him to understand better. He comes to distrust the direct approach, and lives in an unhealthy terror of his ignorance—which will anyhow for all men and to time's end be infinite. He forgets that we do not help ourselves or others by collecting more facts and comments, but by understanding more clearly our problems and theirs. We learn best to do this by reflecting upon such problems and by seeing them through the eyes of the best minds. So we lose our best teachers.

To turn now to mass media. Radio, TV and the screen might provide some remedy for this loss. It is possible to believe, sometimes, that they could become the instruments of our salvation. But we will agree, without difficulty, that they are not that now—for well-known and chiefly technical reasons. Radio, TV and the screen propagate most successfully the most superficial, the most facile, and the least educating elements of a culture. This is partly because, as programs, they have to *go on.* They have to change, every fifteen minutes or twice weekly. There is no time for what they present to be deeply pondered, thought over, returned to and considered afresh. Therefore, it rarely is worth such reconsideration. But in every culture it has been the things which received the most lasting and recurrent attention—the books reread again and again, the stories and sayings known and familiar from infancy to old age, the rites repeated throughout a lifetime, the perennial monuments, the enduring ideas, the constant aesthetic institutions—which have done the most part of the work of the humanities. Mass media, at present, replace such continuous shaping forces by an incessantly shifting play of life and confusing impacts. It is not surprising that they are of little help in seeing life steadily and seeing it whole.

For these and other reasons, just when the humanities are more than ever needed and at a decisive turn of human fate, they are becoming through multifarious distraction—ranging from the movie to the graduate school—inoperative and ineffective. But what is this turn of fate? It is the juncture, at last, of the sciences with the humanities. A juncture is a meeting together, a convergence of different principles into one event; it is also a crisis. What are meeting now head on are two unreconciled ways of conceiving man and his good and how to pursue it. Both wish him well, but they differ radically as to how he can be helped. The physical and social sciences alike—being applications of methods of observation and calculation—conceive men as units subject to forces playing upon them *from without.* A man is a complex unit, no doubt—the psychologist is the last man to overlook this—but differences between men are, for science, to be accounted for in terms of past influences (genes, prenatal supply, early nurture, education, etc.) and present conditions. Any inquiry based upon experimentation and comparison develops such a conception; it abstracts, in its own defence, from other aspects. Thus a man's desires and opinions and beliefs, the springs of his action and sources of his triumphs or sufferings, are likewise, for science, to be studied from without. If they are investigable at all by science, they must be public and they must be manipulatable; that is the methodical crux. It is the modes of such manipulation and the resultant behavior which are really being studied. To the psychologist, education is control of *behavior.* Not unnaturally, therefore, mass influence techniques, by which groups in Germany, Japan, and elsewhere have controlled the behavior of vast masses of population (though the behavior was unfortunate), have come to offer—to better hands, no doubt—alluring prospects of doing man good even against his will.

In contrast, the humanities pin a faith, which is experimentally still ungrounded, on the ideal autonomy of the individual man. He is happiest who is least able to be changed from without, as Socrates averred (*Republic,* 381). Man is not a thing to be pushed about, however kindly or beneficently. He is a spirit who learns—not as a slave learns (*Republic,* 536E), but by exercising the freedom which is his being.

I should illustrate this opposition. I may do so best by an extract from page 18 of *Who Shall Be Educated?*, by Lloyd Warner and R. J. Havighurst, though the authors would, I hope, be horrified by the implications I am about to find in their sentences.

> We will look at our American social system, which largely controls our behaviour, much as we would at a complex maze in which animals learn to behave. In such a system we must be taught to learn our way around as we grow up if we are to live normal lives and to behave normally as adults. This is true for all the Tom Browns, Katherine Greens, and Joe Sienkowitzes of our society. Growing up consists in learning how to behave, and learning how to behave means acquiring the proper responses to the batteries of social stimuli which compose our social order.

It is the last sentence to which I would draw most attention. Should "learning how to behave" mean anything like that? To a humanist (or a Platonist) it should mean learning the *what's* and *why's* of human good—what man's duties and responsibilities and his right relations to his fellows are, and learning how to stick to them under the terrible pressures of pleasure and pain—stronger than any lye or potash (*Republic,* 430)—which forever try to force us from them. We only learn through understanding the differences and connections between things. It is possible, no doubt, to load the phrase "acquiring the proper responses" with all this moral teaching. If we do so, of course, all is well! And I will only have been expounding for my authors their full intention. But is that what the sentence suggests? Does it not much rather suggest some smooth adjustment to and conformity with current fashions in morals, a facile acquiescence in socially acceptable mass-circulated doctrine?

Speaking of fashions, we need be no very deep students of social science to know that the heaviest massed "batteries of social stimuli" directed upon young and old today are the ads. I listed advertisements among the disruptive agencies to which minds are now more exposed than ever before. It seems agreed that Goebbels and his gang learnt much from American advertising techniques. Even though we believe in the virtues of immunization to such attacks, we will do well to consider more seriously than is customary what the ads may be doing today to the humanities. Consider Christmas for a moment.

O never rudely will I blame his faith
In the might of stars and angels

wrote Coleridge. But how about using the might of stars and angels in an attempt to sell one's wares? What's wrong about that? On a page of both stars and angels, under a caption: "*And the Angels bring* . . ." we look to see what they do bring, and read, "*Heavenly gift robes and lingerie along the moon-lit trail leading to our star-studded Christmas collection . . . LUCKY STAR, above left . . . is all dressed up to go lounging in a cherubic rayon crepe . . . Radelle Constellation . . . shining brightly on the angel's arm, dream gown of celestial rayon . . . matching figure-moulding slip for heavenly array . . .* ," not to mention "*panties that lovely women prefer to wear behind the 'seens,'*" and lastly, that no insult should be lacking, "*MOONLIGHT MADONNA GOWN!*" To attend for a second seriously to such exploits will make one wonder if he has lost his sense of humor. But it is more unwise never to reflect upon what an incessant exposure to this sort of thing may be doing to us, if only to the language which channels our inheritance. I have shown this ad to a meeting of teachers of English. My chairman, a superintendent of secondary schools in a great city, took a little umbrage. "Didn't it at least show," he asked, "that the writer had profited by a sound grounding in the classics?" He seemed to think this was a proper outcome of a literary education.

We fail, I think, to realize how omnipresent these degradations are, or how much they may blur and disable the spiritual organs they play with and for what mean purposes. Was so much so skilfully designed to enfeeble and betray human judgment ever directed on a previous generation? We need men inspired by Irving Babbitt's noble and tireless scorn to go on pointing to them. I will add but two examples:

In my first our hero is sitting—drinking his beer—in his overstuffed chair, his dog at his feet, the radio on, his floor strewn with papers whose headlines read, "Cities Bombed," "Famine," "Air Raids." The paper still in his hand says, "Invasion!" Under the picture comes:

IN A WORLD OF STRIFE
THERE'S PEACE IN BEER

In these bewildering times, where can a man turn to replenish the wells of his courage . . . to repair the walls of his faith?

Courage—if you please! Faith—I ask you! Is it surprising that such great words as these have become suspect: so that when people hear or see them they assume they are being got at? Where these words are no longer understood, men no longer understand themselves.

My second: Edison Company placarding the subways in wartime with a bright-windowed villa thus legended: "*In a World of Darkness be thankful for the Light Within*" or some such words. The light within—meaning their products! The strange and dismaying thing about all this is that to those responsible it will be the idea that there is anything objectionable here which will be strange. For this is not blasphemy. Would that it were! It is trivialization, which is truly dangerous. Blasphemy provokes. The trivialized mind is supine, at the mercy of slick manipulators. The outcome can be generations of dehumanized social animals in place of self-controlled, self-judging, self-ruling men and women.

Manipulation and exploitation—for the benefit of the operator, or of the subject—that is the chief danger man incurs through the decline of the humanities. The humanities are his defence against emotional bamboozlement and misdirection of the will. The student of science—without the support of that which has been traditionally carried by literature, the arts and philosophy—is unprotected; the main doctrines and positions which keep man humane are insusceptible, at present, to scientific proof. Present-day science, in fact, like dialectic in Plato's day (*Republic*, 539) or popular philosophizing in pre-Nazi Germany, tends to break them down. Without a vigorous and widespread upkeep of the humanities every country comes to be populated chiefly with "supposititious sons" (*Republic*, 538). And science in the absence of the traditional communal loyalties can only supply their lack by indoctrination in what will probably be (as the samples run so far) nationalistic myths. Dangers due to new weapons will heighten men's susceptibility to such doctrines and also the temptation to teach them. Thus a very gloomy prospect looms up—deriving radically both from the decay of the humanities and from the exuberant vitality of the applied sciences.

It is not, however, the probability of more, and far more destructive, wars which most alarms a humanist. Circumstances are today too easily imaginable in which planetary disintegration would be a welcome release. What is daunting is the possibility that man may be permanently warped through these tensions—that the ideals which made him human may be destroyed—*before* their work can be taken over by science. For that science —or something into which science, given time and education by the humanities, can develop—is the inheritor of their task seems to me a tenet that no true humanist, remembering Book VII of his *Republic*, can yield, any more than he can truly, as a humanist, despair of man.

d.

SECONDARY SOURCES OF IDENTITY IN MASS SOCIETY: RELIGION, RACE, SEX, AND THE FAMILY

BARRINGTON MOORE, JR.

Thoughts on the Future of the Family

Among social scientists today it is almost axiomatic that the family is a universally necessary social institution and will remain such through any foreseeable future. Changes in its structure, to be sure, receive wide recognition. The major theme, however, in the appraisal American sociologists present is that the family is making up for lost economic functions by providing better emotional service. One work announces as its central thesis that "the family in historical times has been, and at present is, in transition from an institution to a companionship." In the past, the authors explain, the forces holding the family together were external, formal, and authoritarian, such as law, public opinion, and the authority of the father. Now, it is claimed, unity inheres in the mutual affection and comradeship of its members. Another recent work by a leading American sociologist makes a similar point. The trend under industrialism, we are told, does not constitute a decline of the family as such, but mainly a decline of its importance in the performance of economic functions. Meanwhile, the author tells us, the family has become a more specialized agency for the performance of other functions, namely, the socialization of children and the stabilization of adult personalities. For this reason, the author continues, social arrangements corresponding rather closely to the modern family may be expected to remain with us indefinitely.

In reading these and similar statements by American sociologists about other aspects of American society, I have the uncomfortable feeling that the authors, despite all their elaborate theories and technical research devices, are doing little more than projecting certain middle-class hopes and ideals onto a refractory reality. If they just looked a little more carefully at what was going on around them, I think they might come to different conclusions. This is, of course, a very difficult point to prove, though C. Wright Mills, in a brilliant essay, has shown how one area of American sociology, the study of crime, is suffused with such preconceptions. While personal observations have some value, one can always argue that a single observer is biased. Here all I propose to do, therefore, is to raise certain questions about the current sociological assessment of the family on the basis of such evidence as has come my way rather casually. In addition, I should like to set this evidence in the framework of an intellectual tradition, represented, so far as the family is concerned, by Bertrand Russell's *Marriage and Morals*, that sees the family in an evolutionary perspective, and raises the possibility that it may be an obsolete institution or become one before long. I would suggest then that conditions have arisen which, in many cases, prevent the family from performing the social and psychological functions ascribed to it by modern sociologists. The same conditions may also make it possible for the advanced industrial societies of the world to do away with the family and substitute other social arrangements that impose fewer unnecessary and painful restrictions on humanity. Whether or not society actually would take advantage of such an opportunity is, of course, another question.

It may be best to begin with one observation that is not in itself conclusive but at least opens the door to considering these possibilities. In discussions of the family, one frequently encounters the argument that Soviet experience demonstrates the necessity of this institution in modern society. The Soviets, so the argument runs, were compelled to adopt the family as a device to carry part of the burden of making Soviet citizens, especially after they perceived the undesirable consequences of savage homeless children, largely the outcome of the Civil War. This explanation is probably an accurate one as far as it goes. But it needs to be filled out by at least two further considerations that greatly reduce its force as a general argument. In the first place, the Soviets, I think, adopted their conservative policy toward the family *faute de mieux*. That is to say, with their very limited resources, and with other more pressing objectives, they had no genuine alternatives. Steel mills had to be built before crèches, or at least before crèches on a large enough scale to make any real difference in regard to child care. In the meantime the services of the family, and especially of grandma (*babushka*), had to be called upon. In the second place, with the consolidation of the regime in the middle thirties, Soviet totalitarianism may have succeeded in capturing the family and subverting this institution to its own uses. At any rate the confidence and vigor with which the regime supported this institution from the early thirties onward suggests such an explanation. Thus the Soviet experience does not constitute by itself very strong evidence in favor of the "functional necessity" of the family.

If the Soviet case does not dispose of the possibility that the family may be obsolete, we may examine other considerations with greater confidence, and begin by widening our historical perspective. By now it is a familiar observation that the stricter Puritan ethics of productive work and productive sex have accomplished their historical purposes in the more advanced sections of the Western world. These developments have rendered other earlier elements of Western culture and society, such as slavery, quite obsolete, and constitute at least prima facie evidence for a similar argument concerning the family. Let us ask them to what extent may we regard the family as a repressive survival under the conditions of an advanced technology? And to what extent does the modern family perform the function of making human beings out of babies and small children either badly or not at all?

One of the most obviously obsolete features of the family is the obligation to give affection as a duty to a particular set of persons on account of the accident of birth. This is a true relic of barbarism. It is a survival from human prehistory, when kinship was the basic form of social organization. In early times it was expedient to organize the division of labor and affection in human society through real or imagined kinship bonds. As civilization became technically more advanced, there has been less and less of a tendency to allocate both labor and affection according to slots in a kinship system, and an increasing tendency to award them on the basis of the actual qualities and capacities that the individual possesses.

Popular consciousness is at least dimly aware of the barbaric nature of the duty of family affection and the pain it produces, as shown by the familiar remark, "You can choose your friends, but you can't choose your relatives." Even if partly concealed by ethical imperatives with the weight of age-old traditions, the strain is nevertheless real and visible. Children are often a burden to their parents. One absolutely un-Bohemian couple I know agreed in the privacy of their own home that if people ever talked to each other openly about the sufferings brought on by raising a family today, the birth rate would drop to zero. It is, of course, legitimate to wonder how widespread such sentiments are. But this couple is in no sense "abnormal." Furthermore, a revealing remark like this made to a friend is worth more as evidence than reams of scientific questionnaires subjected to elaborate statistical analyses. Again, how many young couples, harassed by the problems of getting started in life, have not wished that their parents could be quietly and cheaply taken care of in some institution for the aged? Such facts are readily accessible to anyone who listens to the conversations in his own home or among the neighbors.

The exploitation of socially sanctioned demands for gratitude, when the existing social situation no longer generates any genuine feeling of warmth, is a subtle and heavily tabooed result of this barbaric heritage. It is also one of the most painful. Perhaps no feeling is more excruciating than the feeling that we ought to love a person whom we actually detest. The Greek tragedians knew about the problem, but veiled it under religion and mythology, perhaps because the men and women of that time felt there was no escape. In the nineteenth century the theme again became a dominant one in European literature, but with the clear implication that the situation was unnecessary. Even these authors, Tolstoi, Samuel Butler, Strindberg, and Ibsen, in exposing the horrors and hypocrisies of family life, wove most of their stories around the marital relationship, where there is an element of free choice in the partner selected. Kafka's little gem, *Das Urteil,* is a significant exception. With magnificent insight into the tragedy on both sides, it treats the frustrations of a grown-up son forced to cherish a helpless but domineering father. Henry James's short story, *Europe*, is an effective treatment of the same relationship between a mother and her daughters. Despite some blind spots and limitations, the artists, it appears, have seen vital aspects of the family that have largely escaped the sociologists.

In addition to these obsolete and barbaric features one can point to certain trends in modern society that have sharply reduced rather than increased the effectiveness of the home as an agency for bringing up children. In former times the family was a visibly coherent economic unit, as well as the group that served to produce and raise legitimate children. The father had definite and visible economic tasks, before the household became separated from the place of work. When the children could see what he did, the father had a role to be copied and envied. The source and justification of his authority was clear. Internal conflicts had to be resolved. This is much less the case now.

It is reasonably plain that today's children are much less willing than those of pre-industrial society to take their parents as models for conduct. Today they take them from the mass media and from gangs. Radio and television heroes, with their copies among neighborhood gangs, now play a vital part in the socialization process. Parents have an uphill and none too successful struggle against these sources. Like adult mobs, children's groups readily adopt the sensational, the cruel, and the most easily understood for their models and standards. These influences then corrupt and lower adult standards, as parents become increasingly afraid to assert their own authority for fear of turning out "maladjusted" children.*

The mass media have largely succeeded in battering down the walls of the social cell the family once constituted in the larger structure of society. Privacy has greatly diminished. Newspapers, radios, and television have very largely destroyed the flow of private communications within the family that were once the basis of socialization. Even meals are now much less of a family affair. Small children are frequently plumped down in front of the television set with their supper on a tray before them to keep them quiet. Since the family does less as a unit, genuine emotional ties among its members do not spring up so readily. The advertising campaign for "togetherness" provides rather concrete evidence that family members would rather not be together.

The mother, at least in American society, is generally supposed to be the homemaker and the center of the family. Has she been able to take up the slack produced by the change in the father's role? Is she, perhaps, the happy person whose face smiles at us from every advertisement and whose arts justify the sociologists' case? A more accurate assessment may be that the wife suffers most in the modern middle-class family, because the demands our culture puts upon her are impossible to meet. As indicated by advertisements, fiction, and even the theories of sociologists, the wife is expected to be companion, confidante, and ever youthful mistress of her husband.

If the demands could be met, many wives might feel very happy in this fulfillment of their personality. The actual situation is very different. The father is out of the house all day and therefore can be neither overlord nor companion. With the father absent, radio and television provide the mother with a watery substitute for adult companionship. A young colleague told me recently that his wife leaves the radio on all day merely to hear the sound of a grown-up voice. The continual chatter of little children can be profoundly irritating, even to a naturally affectionate person. The absence of servants from nearly all American middle-class households brings the wife face to face with the brutalizing features of motherhood and housework. If she had the mentality of a peasant, she might be able to cope with them more easily. Then, however, she could not fulfill the decorative functions her husband expects. As it is now, diapers, dishes, and the state of the baby's bowels absorb the day's quota

* It is sometimes claimed that the modern family still represents a bulwark against mass and totalitarian pressures. No doubt this is true in the best cases, those few where parents are still able to combine authority and affection. These are, however, mainly a relic of Victorian times. By and large it seems more likely that the family constitutes the "transmission belt" through which totalitarian pressures toward conformity are transmitted to the parents through the influence of the children.

of energy. There is scarcely any strength left for sharing emotions and experiences with the husband, for which there is often no opportunity until the late hours of the evening. It is hardly a wonder that the psychiatrists' anterooms are crowded, or that both husband and wife seek escapes from psychological and sexual boredom, the cabin fever of the modern family. For the wife, either a job or an affair may serve equally well as a release from domesticity.

A further sign of the modern family's inadequacy in stabilizing the human personality may be seen in the troubled times of adolescence. This stage of growing up has been interpreted as a rejection of adult standards of responsibility and work by youngsters who are about to enter adult life. It seems to me that this period is more significantly one of pseudo-rebellion, when the youngsters copy what they see to be the real values of adult life instead of the professed ones. Even in the more extreme forms of youthful rebellion, relatively rare among respectable middle-class children, such as roaring around in noisy cars to drinking and seduction parties, the adolescents are aping actual adult behavior. Adolescents then do things they know many grown-ups do when the latter think they are escaping the observant eyes of the young. A "hot-rod" is, after all, nothing but an immature Cadillac. Where the Cadillac is the symbol of success, what else could be expected? Adult standards too are made tolerable through commercialized eroticism that lures us on to greater efforts and greater consumption from every billboard and magazine cover. Thus the whole miasma of sexual and psychological boredom in the older generation, pseudo-rebellion and brutality in the younger one, is covered over by a sentimental and suggestive genre art based on commercial sentiment.

No doubt many will think that these lines paint too black a picture. Statistics could perhaps be accumulated to show that families such as the type sketched here are far from a representative cross-section of American middle-class life. Such facts, however, would not be relevant to the argument. As pointed out elsewhere in these essays, the representative character of certain types of social behavior is not necessarily relevant to estimates of current and future trends. This kind of statistical defense of the status quo represents that of a certain maiden's virtue by the claim, "After all, she is only a little bit pregnant."

To refute the appraisal offered in these pages it would be necessary to demonstrate that they misrepresent basic structural trends in the family in advanced industrial countries. The most important argument of this type that I have encountered asserts that the proportion of married people in the population has steadily risen while the proportion of single individuals has steadily dropped. Therefore, people obviously prefer family life to bachelorhood, and the gloomy picture sketched above must be nothing more than vaporings of sour-bellied intellectuals thrown on the dump-heap by the advance of American society.

Before discussing the question further, let us look at some of the relevant facts. The table below shows changes in the proportions of single, married, and divorced persons in the United States from the age of fourteen onward. The source, an authoritative and very recent statistical survey of the American family, has standardized the proportions for age, using the 1940 age distribution as a standard, in order to eliminate changes due merely to shifts in the age composition of our population, which would merely confuse the issue.

Percentage Distribution of Persons 14 Years and Over by Marital Status and Sex in the Civilian Population 1890-1954

	MALE			FEMALE		
Year	Single	Married	Divorced	Single	Married	Divorced
1954	28.4	66.7	1.8	22	65.8	2.2
1950	29.4	65.5	1.5	22.5	64.8	2.1
1940	34.8	59.7	1.2	27.6	59.5	1.6
1930	34.7	59.1	1.1	26.9	59.7	1.3
1890	36.7	57.9	0.2	27.8	57.7	0.4

The figures do show a rise in the proportion of married persons and a decline in the proportion of single ones. They also show that the proportion of married persons is overwhelmingly larger than the number of divorced ones. But the biggest change has been in the proportion of divorced people. For men it has risen ninefold since 1890 and for women more than fivefold. A bigger proportion of people are married now than in 1890, but a *much* bigger proportion have abandoned the marital state. In the long run, the latter change might turn out to be the more important one.

Even the statistical evidence, in other words, does not uphold in a completely unambiguous manner the sociologists' argument for the family. Sometimes an attempt to save the case is made by interpreting the rise in divorce as something that allows greater freedom for the individual to choose marital partners on the basis of congeniality. Thereby divorce allegedly strengthens the family's function as a source of emotional support. By talking about greater freedom for the individual in this fashion one has already taken a long step toward the opponents' view that marriage as such may be superfluous.

The point cannot be considered merely in the light of the facts as they exist now or have existed in the past. To do this in social questions is basically unscientific. Those who dismiss negative appraisals of the family with the crude observation that they reflect personal bias or mere "European decadence" deserve an equally crude reply: "So what if Americans prefer to get married! That simply shows how stupid they are."

Acrimony here unfortunately conceals a genuine issue. It is perfectly possible that conditions exist, perhaps even now, that permit better institutional arrangements than most people would be willing to accept. The word better, of course, implies a definite standard of judgment. One can debate such standards endlessly, and perhaps cannot reach agreement without at some point making arbitrary assumptions. I shall not enter this debate here except to say that any social institution is a bad one that imposes more suffering on people than is necessary when they have sufficient material resources and scientific knowledge to do away with this suffering. This standard, anthropologists tell us, is that not only of Western culture, but of all culture.

What then, are the prospects for the future? We need not take a completely determinist view. Indeed, the perceptions that both plain people and opinion-makers have about the present enter in as a significant component among the forces shaping the future and thereby provide an entering wedge for rational adaptation.

Among those who accept a substantial part of the preceding image of the family as basically correct, one frequently hears the prescription that what American culture really needs is a higher evaluation of the social role of the housewife and of motherhood. The trouble with this prescription, I would suggest, is that it merely increases the element of self-deception already so prevalent in our culture. Under present conditions motherhood *is* frequently a degrading experience. There is nothing to be gained by concealing the facts in the manner of an advertising campaign designed to raise the prestige of a particular occupation. We would not think of trying to eliminate the hazards of coal mining in this way. Why should we try to do it with motherhood? If it is true that under present circumstances the experience of motherhood narrows and cramps the personality rather than promotes the development of its capacities, some other way will have to be found if it is to be a real solution.

The trend towards a continually more efficient technology and greater specialization, which dominates the rest of our culture, may conceivably provide an answer. In regard to the division of labor it is important to recall one widely known but neglected fact. In the past, whenever human beings have acquired sufficient resources and power, as among aristocracies, they have put the burden of child-rearing on other shoulders. Twenty years ago Ralph Linton pointed out that "aristocrats the world over . . . are reluctant to take care of their own children. Anyone who has had to take care of two or three infants simultaneously will understand why. This arduous business is turned over to slaves or servants. . . ."

Since the decline of slavery, a basic trend in European society has been to transfer to machines more and more tasks formerly carried out by slaves. By and large, this change has been accompanied by the growth of large organizations to perform tasks formerly scattered among many small groups. This trend may well affect the family. Specialized human agencies, developing from such contemporary forms as the crèche, play school, and boarding school, might assume a much larger share of the burden of child-rearing, a task that could in any case be greatly lightened by machinery for feeding and the removal of waste products. Can one sensibly argue that the technical ingenuity and resources required to solve this problem are greater than those necessary for nuclear warfare? Are we to regard as permanent and "natural" a civilization that develops its most advanced technology for killing people and leaves their replacement to the methods of the Stone Age?

Against this viewpoint it is usually argued that human infants require some minimum of human affection, even fondling, if they are to survive, and that therefore some form of the family is bound to remain. The premises may be correct, but the conclusion does not follow. A nurse can perform these tasks of giving affection and early socialization just as well as the parents, often better. The argument does not prove anything therefore about the inevitable necessity of the family.

At the same time this point of view does call attention to certain important problems. Industrial society is not likely to produce household nurses, or any form of "servant class" in abundance. On the other hand, as everyone knows who has been in a hospital, nurses in a bureaucratic setting have a strong tendency to treat persons under their care "by the book," without much regard for their individual tasks and requirements. This is a well-known trait of bureaucracy, which tends to treat people and situations alike in order to achieve precision and efficiency. Infants and small children on the contrary require individual attention. For some years they may need to feel that they are the center of the universe. How then can the characteristics of bureaucracy be brought in line with those of maternal affection?

Though this may be the most difficult problem facing any qualitative transformation of the family, it is not necessarily insoluble. In the first place, as Bertrand Russell points out, a good institutional environment may be better for the development of the human personality than a bad family one. In the second place, an increase in the resources allocated to a bureaucratic organization can greatly increase its flexibility and capacity to satisfy variations in individual temperament. Any first-class hotel knows how to cope with this problem. In a few of the best ones in Europe the guest can have privacy and the illusion of being the center of the universe. Finally, one might legitimately expect that the persons who are drawn to serve in any such child-rearing institutions of the future would have more than the average amount of fondness for children, as well as general human warmth and kindliness. Under proper circumstances and management such institutions could give full scope to these benevolent sentiments.

Certain other considerations suggest an alternative that has at least the merit of being much more palatable to the vast majority of people today, since it is more in line with our deep-rooted cultural traditions. These considerations are essentially two. One is the possibility of some innate biological trait roughly resembling the "maternal instinct." The other lies in technological developments that might allow for wider dissemination of machinery to lighten household tasks and to take over the more routine aspects of child rearing. The dish-washing machine, laundromat, and, as a much more extreme device, the "Skinner box" represent prototypes of this technological development that could strengthen decentralized arrangements for rearing children.

I do not know what students of human physiology now believe about the maternal instinct. Common observation is enough to show that it cannot be an instinct like sex or hunger. There are many women who never become fond of children, or who soon cease to be fond of them. For them the institutional outlet just sketched would be the most satisfactory way of providing for their offspring. But for others, possibly the majority, the gestation period with its trials and burdens may be enough to create in the mother a desire to retain the infant under her care, after which she could become reluctant to give it up. If machinery were available to lighten child-rearing and household tasks on a far wider scale than is now the case, mothers might be able to satisfy the more positive desires of motherhood. One that seems to be quite important in the middle class is the desire to mold the child according to some ideal image, though it is now contradicted by fears of damaging the child that derive from superficial popularizations of Freud.

For the home to become again the place where human beings take the first important steps toward realizing their creative potentialities, parents would have to become willing once more to assert their authority. In turn this authority would have to acquire a rational and objective basis, freed of current attempts to revive religious taboos. Thus there would have to be a philosophical as well as a social revolution whose implications we cannot here pursue. One aspect, nevertheless, deserves to be stressed. Rational arguments can be given only to persons competent to understand them. For obvious reasons children are not able to absorb all rational arguments at once, though the present system of education undoubtedly postpones the development of this faculty where it does not destroy it altogether. Therefore parents will have to learn not to be afraid of saying to a child, "You are not old enough yet to understand why you have to do this. But you must do it anyway." The "progressive" family, where every decision turns into an incoherent and rancorous debate, actually contributes to reactionary tendencies in society by failing to equip the next generation with adequate standards of judgment.

There are, however, some grounds for doubting that this conservative solution will eventually prevail as the dominant one. The disappearance of the wider economic functions of the family would make it very difficult, and probably impossible, to restore the emotional atmosphere of a co-operative group in which the father has a respected authority. Furthermore, the bureaucratic division of labor has proved the most effective way of solving recurring and routine problems in other areas of life. Though a considerable part of the task of raising children is not routine, a very great portion is repetitive. For these reasons one may expect that semi-bureaucratic arrangements will continue to encroach on the traditional structure of the family. No doubt many individual variations, combinations, and compromises will remain for some time to come. Yet one fine day human society may realize that the part-time family, already a prominent part of our social landscape, has undergone a qualitative transformation into a system of mechanized and bureaucratized child-rearing, cleansed of the standardized overtones these words now imply. As already pointed out, an institutional environment can be warm and supporting, often warmer than a family torn by obligations its members resent.

Such a state of affairs, if it comes at all, is well over the visible horizon now. Quite possibly it may never come at all. If it does come, there is not the slightest guarantee that it will solve all personal problems and land us in a state of air-conditioned euphoria. Values that many people hold high today may go by the board, such as the affection older couples show for one another who have shared the same pains in life until they have grown but a single scar. It is also possible that a world of reduced family burdens might be one of shallow and fleeting erotic intrigues, based really on commercial interests. Hollywood could conceivably be the ugly prototype of such a future world, especially in its earlier transitional phases. The most that might be claimed by any future apologist for such institutions, if they ever come to pass, is that they gave greater scope to the development of the creative aspects of the human personality than did the family, which had begun to damage rather than develop this personality under advancing industrialism. And the most that can be claimed for the arguments supporting this possibility is that they correspond to some important trends visible in the family itself as well as in the rest of society. Nevertheless, it would appear that the burden of proof falls on those who maintain that the family is a social institution whose fate will differ in its essentials from that which has befallen all the others.

GEOFFREY GORER

The Pornography of Death

"Birth, and copulation, and death.
That's all the facts when you come to brass tacks:
Birth, and copulation, and death."
—T. S. Eliot, *Sweeney Agonistes.*

Pornography is, no doubt, the opposite face, the shadow of prudery, whereas obscenity is an aspect of seemliness. No society has been recorded which has not its rules of seemliness, of words or actions which arouse discomfort and embarrassment in some contexts, though they are essential in others. The people before whom one must maintain a watchful seemliness vary from society to society: all people of the opposite sex, or all juniors, or all elders, or one's parents-in-law, or one's social superiors or inferiors, or one's grandchildren have been selected in different societies as groups in whose presence the employment of certain words or the performance of certain actions would be considered offensive; and then these words or actions become charged with effect. There is a tendency for these words or actions to be related to sex and excretion but this is neither necessary nor universal; according to Malinowski, the Trobrianders surround eating with as much shame as excretion; and in other societies personal names or aspects or ritual come under the same taboos.

Rules of seemliness are apparently universal; and the nonobservance of these rules, or anecdotes which involve the breaking of the rules, provoke that peculiar type of laughter which seems identical the world over; however little one may know about a strange society, however little one may know about the functions of laughter in that society (and these can be very various), one can immediately tell when people are laughing at an obscene joke. The topper of the joke may be "And then he ate the whole meal in front of them!" or "She used her husband's name in the presence of his mother!" but the laughter is the same; the taboos of seemliness have been

Reprinted from *Modern Writing* (1956), pp. 56-62, by permission of the author.

broken and the result is hilarious. Typically, such laughter is confined to one sex group and is more general with the young, just entering into the complexities of adult life.

Obscenity then is a universal, an aspect of man and woman living in society; everywhere and at all times there are words and actions which, when misplaced, can produce shock, social embarrassment, and laughter. Pornography, on the other hand—the description of tabooed activities to produce hallucination or delusion—seems to be a very much rarer phenomenon. It probably can only arise in literate societies, and we certainly have no records of it for nonliterate ones; for whereas the enjoyment of obscenity is predominantly social, the enjoyment of pornography is predominantly private. The fantasies from which pornography derives could, of course, be generated in any society; but it seems doubtful whether they would ever be communicated without the intermediary of literacy.

The one possible exception to this generalization is the use of the plastic arts, without any letterpress. I have never felt quite certain that the three-dimensional *poses plastiques* on so many Hindu temples (notably the "Black Pagoda" at Konarak) have really the highfalutin Worship of the Life Force or Glorification of the Creative Aspect of Sex which their apologists claim for them; many of them seem to me very like feelthy pictures, despite the skill with which they are executed. There are too the erotic woodcuts of Japan; but quite a lot of evidence suggests that these are thought of as laughter-provoking (i.e., obscene) by the Japanese themselves. We have no knowledge of the functions of the Peruvian pottery.

As far as my knowledge goes, the only Asiatic society which has a long-standing tradition of pornographic literature is China; and, it would appear, social life under the Manchus was surrounded by much the same haze of prudery as distinguished the nineteenth century in much of Europe and the Americas, even though the emphases fell rather differently; women's deformed feet seem to have been the greatest focus of peeking and sniggering, rather than their ankles or the cleft between their breasts; but by and large life in Manchu China seems to have been nearly as full of "unmentionables" as life in Victoria's heyday.

Pornography would appear to be a concomitant of prudery, and certainly the periods of the greatest production of pornography have also been the periods of the most rampant prudery. In contrast to obscenity, which is chiefly defined by situation, prudery is defined by subject; some aspect of human experience is treated as inherently shameful or abhorrent, so that it can never be discussed or referred to openly, and experience of it tends to be clandestine and accompanied by feelings of guilt and unworthiness. The unmentionable aspect of experience then becomes a subject for much private fantasy, more or less realistic—fantasy charged with pleasurable guilt or guilty pleasure; and those whose power of fantasy is weak, or whose demand insatiable, constitute a market for the printed fantasies of the pornographer.

Traditionally, and in the lexicographic meaning of the term, pornography has been concerned with sexuality. For the greater part of the last two hundred years copulation and (at least in the mid-Victorian decades) birth were the "unmentionables" of the triad of basic human experiences which "are all the facts when you come to brass tacks," around which so much private fantasy and semiclandestine pornography were erected. During most of this period death was no mystery, except in the sense that death is always a mystery. Children were encouraged to think about death, their own deaths and the edifying or cautionary deathbeds of others. It must have been a rare individual who, in the nineteenth century with its high mortality, had not witnessed at least one actual dying, as well as paid his respects to "beautiful corpses"; funerals were the occasion for the greatest display, for working class, middle class and aristocrat. The cemetery was the center of every old-established village, and they were prominent in most towns. It was fairly late in the nineteenth century before the execution of criminals ceased to be a public holiday as well as a public warning. Mr. Fairchild had no difficulty in finding a suitably garnished gibbet for his moral lesson.

In the twentieth century, however, there seems to have been an unremarked shift in prudery; whereas copulation has become more and more "mentionable," particularly in Anglo-Saxon societies, death has become more and more "unmentionable" *as a natural process*. I cannot recollect a novel or play of the last twenty years or so which has a "deathbed scene" that describes in any detail the death "from natural causes" of a major character; this topic was a set piece for most of the eminent Victorian and Edwardian writers, evoking their finest prose and their most elaborate technical effects to produce the greatest amount of pathos or edification.

One of the reasons, I imagine, for this plethora of deathbed scenes—apart from their intrinsic emotional and religious content—was that it was one of the relatively few experiences that an author could be fairly sure would have been shared by the vast majority of his readers. Questioning my old acquaintances, I cannot find one over the age of sixty who did not witness the last agony of at least one near relative; I do not think I know a single person under the age of thirty who has had a similar experience. Of course, my acquaintance is neither very extensive nor particularly representative; but in this instance I do think it is typical of the change of attitude and "exposure."

The natural process of corruption and decay has become disgusting, as disgusting as the natural processes of copulation and birth were a century ago; preoccupation with such processes is (or was) morbid and unhealthy, to be discouraged in all and punished in the young. Our great-grandparents were told that babies were found under gooseberry bushes or cabbages; our children are likely to be told that those who have passed on (fie! on the gross Anglo-Saxon monosyllable) are changed into flowers or lie at rest in lovely gardens. The ugly facts are relentlessly hidden; the art of the embalmers is an art of complete denial.

It seems possible to trace a connection between the shift of taboos and the shift in religious beliefs. In the nineteenth century most of the inhabitants of Protestant countries seem to have subscribed to the Pauline beliefs in the sinfulness of the body and the certainty of the afterlife. "So also is the resurrection of the dead. It is sown in corruption; it is raised in incorruption: It is sown in dishonour; it is raised in glory. . . ." It was possible to insist on the corruption of the dead body, and the dishonor of its begetting, while there was a living belief in the incorruption and the glory of the immortal part. But in England, at any rate, belief in the future life as taught in Christian doctrine is very uncommon today, even in the minority who make church-going or prayer a consistent part of their lives; and without some such belief, natural death and physical decomposition have become too horrible to contemplate or to discuss. It seems symptomatic that the contemporary sect of Christian Science should deny the fact of physical death, even to the extent (so it is said) of refusing to allow the word to be printed in the *Christian Science Monitor*.

During the last half century public health measures and improved preventive medicine have made natural death among the younger members of the population much more uncommon than it was in earlier periods, so that a death in the family, save in the fullness of time, became a relatively uncommon incident in home life; and simultaneously, violent death increased in a manner unparalleled in human history. Wars and revolutions, concentration camps and gang feuds were the most publicized of the causes for these violent deaths; but the diffusion of the automobile, with its constant and unnoticed toll of fatal accidents, may well have been most influential in bringing the possibility of violent death into the expectations of law-abiding people in time of peace. While natural death became more and more smothered in prudery, violent death has played an ever growing part in the fantasies offered to mass audiences—detective stories, thrillers, Westerns, war stories, spy stories, science fiction and, eventually, horror comics.

There seem to be a number of parallels between the fantasies which titillate our curiosity about the mystery of sex and those which titillate our curiosity about the mystery of death. In both types of fantasy the emotions which are typically concomitant to the acts—love or grief—are paid little or no attention, while the sensations are enhanced as much as a customary poverty of language permits. If marital intercourse be considered the natural expression of sex for most of humanity most of the time, then "natural sex" plays as small a role as "natural death" (the ham-fisted attempts of D. H. Lawrence and Jules Romains to describe "natural sex" realistically but high-mindedly prove the rule). Neither type of fantasy can have any real development, for once the protagonist has done something, he or she must proceed to do something else, with or to somebody else, more refined, more complicated or more sensational. This somebody else is not a person; it is either a set of genitals, with or without secondary sexual characteristics, or a body, perhaps capable of suffering pain as well as death. Since most languages are relatively poor in words or constructs to express intense pleasure or intense pain, the written portions of both types of fantasy abound in onomatopoeic conglomerations of letters meant to evoke the sighs, gasps, groans, screams and rattles concomitant to the described actions. Both types of fantasy rely heavily on adjectives and similes. Both types of fantasy are completely unrealistic, since they ignore all physical, social, or legal limitations; and both types have complete hallucination of the reader or viewer as their object.

There seems little question that the instinct of those censorious busybodies preoccupied with other people's morals was correct when they linked the pornography of death with the pornography of sex. This, however, seems to be their only correct deduction or attempted action. There is no valid evidence to suppose that either type of pornography is an incitement to action; rather are they substitute gratifications. The belief that such hallucinatory works would incite their readers to copy the actions depicted would seem to be indirect homage to the late Oscar Wilde, who described such a process in *The Picture of Dorian Gray;* I know of no authenticated parallels in real life, though investigators and magistrates with bees in their bonnets can usually persuade juvenile delinquents to admit to exposure to whatever medium of mass communication they are choosing to make a scapegoat.

Despite some gifted precursors, such as Andréa de Nerciat or Edgar Allan Poe, most works in both pornographies are aesthetically objectionable; but it is questionable whether, from the purely aesthetic point of view, there is much more to be said for the greater part of the more anodyne fare provided by contemporary mass media of communication. Psychological utopians tend to condemn substitute gratifications as such, at least where copulation is involved; they have so far been chary in dealing with death.

Nevertheless people have to come to terms with the basic facts of birth, copulation, and death, and somehow accept their implications; if social prudery prevents this being done in an open and dignified fashion, then it will be done surreptitiously. If we dislike the modern pornography of death, then we must give back to death—natural death—its parade and publicity, readmit grief and mourning. If we make death unmentionable in polite society—"not before the children"—we almost insure the continuation of the "horror comic." No censorship has ever been really effective.

DAVID MANNING WHITE

The Semi-Adequate Male: A Fable

NOTED SPECIALIST GIVES THE
REAL FACTS ON SEX ADEQUACY

How men can develop their sexual capacity. . . . What men don't know about love. . . . How to satisfy more fully. . . . How to get along with women. . . . What every woman expects from a man. . . . the art of "making love." . . . Overcoming sex frigidity in women. . . . The answer to sex impotence. . . . Understanding the love needs of women. . . . The jealous lover and husband. . . . Steps to overcome sex indifference. . . . What every woman expects in a man. . . . "My wife never wants sex." . . . Rules for sex-after-forty. . . . The prostate gland. . . . Alcohol as stimulant to sex urge . . . and much more.

—Advertisement in *New York Times*
Sunday Book Review, March 15, 1959

OUR FABLE is set in the plush Madison Avenue offices of Grisby, Bolt, Welkins, Wassail, and Donder, enlighteners plenipotentiary. A young copy-writer, Jon Martz, is discussing his latest assignment with Wilson Trantzer, a vice-president of the agency. Trantzer, who regards Martz as a protegé, is concerned about the latter's falling behind on an assignment.

MARTZ: Like you said, Will, I just sat there and let it go from the top of my cranium. But nothing. NOTHING. Everytime I try to squeeze out some copy about those How To Be Virile In Four Lessons books, I feel like I'm going to pot, Daddy-O. That is, if I was still on pot, if you know what I mean.

Published for the first time in this volume.

TRANTZER: I read you loud and clear, Jocko, but let me spell it out for you in 72-point Gothic. The Old Man is going to bench you unless you come up with some zingy copy for the Mandrake Root Press. Helluva big account for us, Jocko, so you've got to come up with a brain baby and quick. No man is an island entire to himself, Jocko, so let the bells toll out loud and sweet for the Old Man, or at least for my sake.

MARTZ: Dammit, Will, why did the Old Man ever put me on this kick! But sweet Why, Daddy-O? I was doing okay on the halitosis beat. Sweet son of the morning star, Daddy-O, the Old Man himself called me into his lair after I thought up the word SMERSEL to describe the odor caused by too strong an underarm antiperspirant.

TRANTZER: I know that, Jocko. I knew you had the stuff the first time I heard you reading your poems down in the Village Vertigo. Your bare feet needed washing and so did some of your verses, but I *knew* you had the flair for sure. Boy, I was plenty proud of you when you came up with SMERSEL, and followed it with a real socko name for that he-mannish magazine. Whatinhell did you call it?

MARTZ: You mean *Viscera: The Magazine with Guts?* Daddy-O, I was battin' 'em out those days, but ever since you pushed this Mandrake account in my lap I've HAD it up to here. Believe me, Will, I've looked over every ad written in the *New York Times Book Review* for six months, and there is *no* new way to sell sex-anxiety.

TRANTZER: Jocko, I never thought a mind that could come up with SMERSEL would crumple up the towel and throw it in. The Old Man is going to retch when he discovers he made a mistake in putting you on the team. Think it through, boy, Mandrake Root has three Nobel Prize winners on its list, not to mention a flock of Pulitzers, but the bread and butter of the house is selling books on how to copulate. And don't stand there in your bare brains and tell me we *can't* sell old *flagrante delicto*. Look here, our research boys came up with some real grinders. (*Shuffles some papers in his hands.*) When a country like ours can spend four- or five-hundred million simoleons a year on feelthy books, pictures, movies, and stag parties, not to mention a damned good business in reprinting *Fanny Hill* and the *Romance of Lust* for guys like the Old Man who can afford $50.00 for a peek through the window of sex, then don't stand there and tell me we haven't got a big, hot commodity.

MARTZ: Why do they want to read about it, Willy? Tell me that, Daddy-O, and I'll bust right out of this pad and write you the coolest copy since Bruce Barton discovered the Lord of Hosts.

TRANTZER: Why? Because sex frightens the hell out of most of us Americans. We'd rather read about it, peek at it over the transom and under the bed, run our mind's tongues over the phantasy, and drool for something that never was, than take it for what it is. And what is it? For most of our slobbering customers, reading "How to Be Virile in Forty-five Minutes" gives them a respectable peek at the old anxiety. Listen, Jocko, old Sigmund had his Geiger counter right on the lode when he told us that the desires we had when we were babes in arms last forever. So we push them down into the furthest pit of our unconscious, but do they die? We grow up and have our own babes in arms, and still the old desire to look, to peep, to hear. Z'ounds, boy, you are writing for all the peepeyed youngsters, deep in the guilt of the night's weird sounds, thrilled and ashamed at the secrets of mamma and papa's bedroom.

MARTZ: By the livin' ghost of Charlie Parker, Will, that's right out of the top drawer. I'm beginning to get it, man. I'm beginning to feel as gone as Johnny Bach sitting at the organ in Dusseldorf Cathedral, making up a hundred new sonatas with Miles Davis from breakfast to lunch.

TRANTZER: Attaboy, you old hidden persuader. Dream it out, boy.

MARTZ: Let's hit 'em with a real slogan. Something like, "Are you a sexual slob?" Wait a minute, Will, a new word! "Do you suffer from Smersex?"

TRANTZER: Too much like SMERSEL, Jocko, but you're on the right beam.

MARTZ: Give them some rules, man, and we've sold fifty thousand books if we've sold one. Americans love rules of any kind that will wrap up all of their problems in one neat little package. "Read Dr. Bertrand Fendrick's great book for fifteen minutes each morning and be a real man, the man your mother wanted you to be." Then we'll follow that with, "Seven Cardinal Mistakes Most Men Make as Lovers."

TRANTZER: Jocko, you're bursting your seams this time. Seven? My wife thinks there are forty-seven. But seven is a magic number. . . .

MARTZ: How's this? "Which is more of a man, you or your prostate gland?" Or this: "Won't you spend ten minutes a day with Dr. Fendrick to prove to yourself you are ADEQUATE?"

TRANTZER: Go, man, go. The Old Man will love this. I can see you getting an engraved silver Miltown box, Jocko.

MARTZ: (*Shouting at the top of his voice, completely entranced with his word magic*): And this: "Even a micro-organism gets his orgasm. Do you?" Or this: "Frigidity is for the birds; not for your wife."

We leave this frenzied scene of creative activity, secure in our knowledge that American know-how and perseverance have won out again. Let us be thankful for men like Dr. Fendrick (not to mention Willy Trantzer or Jocko Martz), who bring out into the open the fears and anxieties that can cripple your life and destroy your happiness. Men who show you how you can free yourself from such fears. Men who break down the anxieties that plague men and women of all ages, even you and me. Men who break down fears about chronic diseases, loneliness, pain, pregnancy, male and female menopause, job failure, deafness, hemorrhoids, impotence, and radiation anxiety.

Of them it may truly be said, *Amor vincit omnia.*

DAN WAKEFIELD

Slick-Paper Christianity

IN THE FORWARD-LOOKING eyes of contemporary religion (fixed more often on the vision ahead than above) the greatest of sins is to be "out of date." The sermons of Norman Vincent Peale speak more of U. S. business men than of Biblical prophets, and one Eastern minister recently devoted his Sunday lesson to the soul-searching topic: "Will Jackie Gleason Get to Heaven?" A report in *Life* on why our ministers are mentally "cracking up" reveals that they are killing themselves in trying to keep up. In an age accelerated by the miracle of the mass media, the most "successful" of the modern religious leaders have adopted the old slogan, "If you can't beat 'em, join 'em." On the *Times* bestseller lists, the books of Peale and Smiley Blanton make Herman Wouk look like a piker, and if Bishop Sheen makes no move to drive the Trendex men from the temple, it is only understandable. His TV rating is the envy of many a comedian.

This current industrialization of Christianity has now reached another milestone with publication of a new Methodist magazine—*Together*. With a prepublication order upped from 600,000 to 700,000 by the clamor of anxious voices who wanted to get *Together*, and the confident expectation of a cool 1,000,000 circulation early this year, the Methodists have the hottest thing in the publishing world since *Playboy* began its rise. While *Collier's*, the *Woman's Home Companion* and the *Town Journal* were

Reprinted from the *Nation*, CLXXXV, No. 18 (1957), 56-59, by permission of the author and the publisher.

folding by the wayside in the waning days of 1956, the Methodist Publishing House was able to report "the biggest year" in its history, with a 6.91 per cent increase in net income, and an all-time high in "church-school literature" circulation of 6,813,956. On this firm foundation was raised the slick and colorful pages of *Together*, which, "If every Methodist Church will put in its annual budget a $2 subscription for each family on its rolls . . . will have approximately three million circulation." The publishing agents of the Methodist Church, two gentlemen whose names (Lovick Pierce and J. Edgar Washabaugh) are as purely Sinclair Lewis as their project, recorded in their first editorial that "It is our hope and prayer that this will be done."

There are other Christians, including Methodists, who do not share these sentiments. Principal Methodist opposition to *Together* came from other Methodist editors, through the Methodist Press Association, which expressed "strong disapproval" of the new magazine and questioned whether the church should publish a periodical so "secular" in nature.

Many outsiders who have been impressed by the good works of the Methodist Church were especially depressed by the creation of *Together*. The *Christian Century*, an outstanding nondenominational religious magazine, praised a new outlay of Methodist funds for higher education announced at the Methodist General Conference last summer, but commented that:

> The special issue of *Together* put out for the General Conference would diseducate a denomination as fast as its colleges and universities could educate it. . . . Methodists, who once had to contend with a caricature of themselves as superficial, hail-fellow-well-met Christians, seem in their new magazine to be bent on inhabiting the caricature. . . . The fact is that a great denomination should have a great magazine, but it takes more than $2.6 million annual budget to create it. It takes a renewed acquaintance with the church's history and a revitalized appreciation of its fathers and their faith.

Together rose from the ashes of the 130-year-old *Christian Advocate* (which was judged by a majority of the Methodist bishops to be too old-fashioned) and is aimed at the popular market, while the more specialized duties of the old *Advocate* are now taken up by a monthly companion magazine of *Together*—a "pastor's journal" known as the *New Christian Advocate*. This new handbook, served up in a format resembling that of the *Reader's Digest*, is a kind of "Agitprop" for the preachers, stocked with handy helps such as "Sermon Suggestions," and articles ranging from theology ("A Protestant Appreciation of Mary") to technique ("Must the Organ Play Second Fiddle?"). Practical matters are taken up which the Gospels could not foresee—e.g., a report on modern church parking facilities, with a quote from a Methodist editor to the effect that "Churches simply cannot expect young couples with three or four children—as most of them seem to have today—to park four blocks away in bad weather."

But professional problems of the pastor make dull fare for the congregation, and the bright pages of *Together* spare the layman from such concerns. Indeed, they are out to assure him that Religion Can Be Fun—it even can be so disguised as to make it almost unrecognizable as religion.

For those who have doubts about a Christian magazine being able to provide good, comfortable fun, certain old-fashioned concepts are cleared up right from the start. In its first (October) issue, *Together* flamed forth with a full-color eight-page feature which essentially expressed the publication's message.

This feature was a series of reproductions of paintings of Jesus Christ as represented by painters from the second century to the present. The moral of the spectacular was that Christ is envisioned by men in the reflected image of their own times. The reader can rejoice: Christ through the ages has grown progressively healthier and happier. A second-century portrait shows the face of a deeply troubled and meditative Christ. His forehead scarred and His lips turned slightly downward. Another of the same century portrays Him with closed eyes in a long, weary face. A dark, stern Christ is shown in an eleventh-century mosaic, and a weeping Christ with blood dripping from the crown of thorns is a sixteenth-century impression. An early twentieth-century Christ is more beautiful, and shows a glow beginning to emerge from the upper regions of His head.

And finally we come to the current Christ—a curly-haired, smiling fellow who is pink of cheek and shorn of scars and sorrows. The caption explains that the painter, an Ohio resident by the name of Ivan Eugene Pusecker, "obviously was influenced by today's theology. . . ."

Pusecker's Christ is the most happy fella imaginable—and more handsome than any man who ever played the role in a Cecil B. De Mille production. It is easy, in fact, to believe in this Christ as the sort of man who would shave his beard, buy a grey flannel suit and join Dr. Norman Vincent Peale in the good doctor's annual (paid) tour of large department stores at the holiday season to instill the employees with "The Christmas Spirit."

When the publishers of the magazine announced in their foreword to the first issue that *Together* would strive for an editorial approach "somewhat comparable to that used by Christ," it was doubtlessly Mr. Pusecker's Christ they had in mind.

Together offers its readers such snappy features as Little Lessons in Spiritual Efficiency and, in order that more Methodists can get together, a What's Your Hobby? directory with names and addresses of Methodists who engage in a variety of soul-building activities. There are Methodists who collect stereopticon slides, tropical fish, key chains, proverbs, model circus wagons and trains, and ivory monkeys—just to name a few.

Recommendations are made for Methodists who want to see the right movies and read the right books, and can be saved, for instance, by *Together*'s warning review of *A Walk on the Wild Side* by Nelson Algren: ". . . It is rough and tough and hardly the book to be recommended to a church-reading circle."

Since *Together* is billed as "The Midmonth Magazine For Methodist Families," there is of course something for all the family—Halloween games for the kiddies and even a trouble column for the teenagers. One "Dick" Richmond Barbour, Ph.D., whose bespectacled face is shown floating in slick white sea above his column, offers advice to the teenagers which, if "Christlike," can be so only in reference to Pusecker's image. It has no connection with the words or ideas of the Christ who preached the brotherhood of men. For instance, an eighteen-year-old girl who wonders whether she is truly in love with her boy friend is advised that, "It's best to have dates with someone in your own church gang. If you can't do that, try to go out with others who are Protestants." Mr. Barbour gives the young girl several key questions to ask herself about this boy friend: "Is he a clean Christian young man? Can he earn a reasonably good living? Does he have a stable personality?"

It is hardly necessary to add the query of whether this boy friend owns a grey flannel suit, and if it has three buttons rather than two. (That specific problem is covered in the December teen column, when Mr. Barbour advises a young man to "Try to wear the same sort of clothes that most boys in your school do.") Blessed are the stable-in-heart, kids, for they shall see good weekly pay checks.

Much in the same way that members of the Sigma Chi fraternity are presented as those who shall inherit the earth in the *Magazine of Sigma Chi*, the Methodists look like the gang to watch from reading the pages of *Together*. Did you know, for instance, that the man who kicked the longest field goal in the world was a Methodist? The first issue carried that gripping and inspiring story, and in the December number, *Together* presented a Methodist All-American team, picked by Fred Russell (Methodist) Sports Editor of the Nashville *Banner*. Methodists everywhere will no doubt take heart from Mr. Russell's report: "Football today is a game of speed, spirit and skill more than ever. To a split T, the first All-American All-Methodist team conforms to these requisites for success."

Perhaps an even more interesting feature will be the announcement of "Miss Methodist Student Nurse," a competition announced in the November issue of *Together*. These promotions indeed open new horizons for the imaginative, "up-to-date" churchmen of all sects. Possibly a candidate from each denomination could be chosen to compete for the title of "Miss Religion," who then could pose for endorsements of the white-leather Bibles, foam-rubber church pews and custom-tailored choir gowns advertised in the pages of *Together*. Perhaps some enterprising sportswriter will match the Methodist All-Americans with an All-Episcopalian squad for a holiday benefit game.

But all this is on the light side, and *Together* is not without its serious moments. Perhaps the most serious and also the most gruesome (though with close competition from the story in the first issue of a little boy with cleft palate whose mother loses her mind) is a piece called "The Hiroshima Maidens Go Home." This tells the story of how twenty-five girls who were badly disfigured in the A-bomb blast at Hiroshima were taken to America by a group including Methodist Church members and given free treatment. The piece is headed with a picture of the girls happily waving as they board the plane back to Japan after treatments; a caption explains that the "Doctor at the right carries the ashes of Tomako Nakabayishi, who died during her third operation."

The Japanese are quoted as deeply grateful for it all. We are told that one of the girls, shortly before entering the operating room, asked an interpreter to give the following message to the doctor who was to perform the operation: "Tell Dr. Barsky not to be worried because he cannot give me a new face. I know my scars are very, very bad and I know Dr. Barsky is worried because he thinks I may expect that I will be as I once was. I know that this is impossible; but it does not matter; something has already healed here inside."

If that is presented to warm the hearts of Methodists or anyone else, then the immorality of our times is so grotesque that we had all better weep for our souls. A small light indeed is the healing of twenty-five girls beside the glare of an atomic bomb that was dropped on a Japanese city. An ordinary human being might imagine that we'd have the morality to hide this pale flicker under a bushel instead of displaying it across the slick pages of a popular magazine to the greater glory of a Protestant sect.

But glory and reward on earth and the message of success are repeated on page after page of *Together* in the most up-to-date magazine style. A brief biography of one *Together* author who is also a minister assures the reader that this clergyman "looks like a successful lawyer and talks like the man next door."

It is a peculiar reassurance that popular Christianity seeks to convey to its followers—that its current disciples are so like the man in the street, and so unlike the Savior of the Bible. In expounding this message, the modern churchmen have sought to transform that Savior into the Christ of *Together*—a face indistinguishable from the rest of the lonely crowd.

In a literature class at Columbia College, Mark Van Doren once noted that the modern image of Christ was that of a man almost unrelated to the Christ who was described in the New Testament as a strong and stern leader, ruthless in following his conception of truth, and iron in his will. "He was not," Van Doren said, "an easy man to follow. He was certainly not like our ministers now who try to be 'one of the crowd' and take a drink at a cocktail party to prove it, or tell an off-color joke. That seems to be their approach today." The professor paused for a moment, and then he said, "Maybe that's why we hate them so much."

Maybe that's why the current religious revival in America is such a hollow pretense, and why it has had so little regenerating effect on the moral temper of the times. Too many religious leaders have sought to be "together" with their era and become shabby followers and imitators rather than leaders. In the desperate effort to be up-to-date, they have dressed Jesus Christ in a grey flannel suit and smothered his spirit in the folds of conformity. The new slick-page Christianity cheerily rises in the midst of a world seeking answers to survival, and offers an All-Methodist football team.

KURT LANG AND GLADYS ENGEL LANG

Decisions for Christ: Billy Graham in New York City

BILLY GRAHAM, the modern mass evangelist, held the first meeting of his Madison Square Garden crusade on May 15, 1957. By the time he departed on September 1, it was reported, some 56,246 persons among two million who heard him had answered his call to come forward right then and there to "make a decision for Christ."

To many, this claim may convey a picture of fallen members of the human race or temporary strays who, by a public declaration of faith, had been won back into the fold. The Graham team, however, insists on

Published for the first time in this volume.

referring to the thousands who responded to the call as *inquirers*—not as *converts*—and quite properly so. This is no idle hair-splitting. The terminological distinction sums up the difference between the more old-fashioned personal form of revivalism and the kind of revivalism practiced in the modern urban crusade.

The "convert" is the product of personal evangelism, in which hell-fire preachers fought for the salvation of men's souls. Every soul so saved was a miracle which resounded to the credit of the Lord; the conversion, since it was abidingly a matter between a man and his Maker, was certain only "in God's book of life" (to borrow a phrase of Weissberger's). It was characteristic of the kind of revivalism in which religion was taken literally and the terrors of Hell loomed very real. Even today, it still flourishes in many store-front churches and in certain rural areas. Converted sinners regain their faith as a result of experiences cultivated in the religious assembly.

The concentrated attack on the irreligiosity of an entire city, by means such as Graham's saturation campaign, is quite a different sort of affair from the earlier phenomenon which fathered it and to which it bears a superficial similarity. The modern "revival" is a massive performance. It is carefully organized and relies quite heavily on gimmickry. The advance preparation, the use of various media of communication, the employment of skilled promoters not only require coordination, but they must be paid for. Jonathan Edwards was able to spark the Great Awakening from his own little acre in Northampton, where he won souls for his own church. The mass evangelist, on the other hand, must be assured of financial and organizational support before he ventures into a strange city. To justify such an effort, the successes must be carefully recorded, and the best over-all measure of accomplishment is the number of cards signed by those who step forward.

From the viewpoint of the churches which supported Graham's crusade, increases in church membership are the only valid criterion. But such statistics are hard to come by. The inquirers fill out cards, on which their preferred denomination and local address are entered. This is their referral slip to a church of their own choosing. On this card, since many inquirers are already practicing church members, there is also room for them to indicate the kind of "decision" they wish to make. The choice presented them ranges from "acceptance of Christ as Saviour and Lord" and "assurance of salvation," to "restoration," "dedication," and "reaffirmation of faith."

The most important social-psychological fact about modern mass evangelism appears to be the following: although a public as well as a highly publicized affair, it does not entail a confession to be made in public. The signing of the decision card is enough to confirm the decision. While this permits statistical validation of the campaign (the primary justification for the effort and expense), it hardly clarifies the psychological nature of the "decision." It is precisely this psychological import that this paper seeks to clarify.

Through the use of mass-observation data on the Billy Graham crusade in New York,[1] we wish, first, to explore the evidence on two points: *who* the persons were whom Graham attracted and *how*, or by which techniques, he appealed to them. Our necessarily cursory description of the audience thus concerns who attended the rallies, what attracted them, and who among those in attendance were the decision-makers. This is followed by observations on the manner in which the audiences were worked up to make the decision and the way the appeals were dramatized. Having presented findings on the "who" among the audience and the "how" of the appeal, we can then consider the question of whether these were conversions in the sense of an abrupt about-face from sin to virtue, or whether the inquiry merely marked the culmination of a gradual religious awakening. Furthermore, we wish to know if the experience so obtained was apt to be a lasting one? Or, in less religious terms, just what was the meaning of the decision for Christ presented to the vast audiences?

The Audience

The audience consisted of two more or less distinct segments: first, the organized *flocks* brought in groups by church organizations and, second, the unorganized flotsam who came to the Garden more or less of their own accord. Even without mass-media promotion, about 60 per cent of the seats would have been filled each night. Ushers, counselors, ministers, a 1,500-voice choir, and others with a vested interest in assuring the success of the Crusade occupied a substantial share of the 19,000 seats. In addition, approximately 7,500 seats had been set aside for the so-called delegation, often out-of-towners brought in by chartered buses.

Our 43 mass-observers (hereafter referred to as observers) clearly differentiated between these organized people, the majority of whom sat "downstairs" in the Garden, and the audience "upstairs" which was largely unorganized in the sense that they found their own unshepherded way to the Crusade.[2] This unorganized flotsam usually made up less than half of the total audience and was far from typical of the Greater New York population.

Here are some observations which constitute the consensus among observers:

1) While men, more than women, were apt to be first nighters, women outnumbered men by a minimum of 5:1 and probably in numbers closer to an 8:1 ratio.

2) About 80 per cent of the "upstairs" crowd came from within the city limits of New York. In light of this, it seems of particular interest that observers uniformly remarked on the small representations from among New York's minority groups—that is, Negroes and Puerto Ricans, many of whom live within easy access of the Garden.

3) While the audience was clearly not "lower class," the majority reported less than high school achievement and, incidentally, were most apologetic and defensive about this lack of formal schooling.

4) The "downstairs" people who came to the meeting through church organizations, and the "upstairs" people were almost without exception Protestants who reported regular church attendance.[3]

5) A clear majority of the "flotsam" were repeaters. This was revealed by the response to Graham's traditional invitation for newcomers to raise their hands—but it was revealed even more sharply by responses to observers' direct inquiries.

6) We need to make one final distinction between the "floaters" who attended for the first time and the "regular" flotsam. The "regulars," who were mostly women wearing hats, seemed to come for the purpose of giving support to the cause and to derive a vicarious pleasure from the decision-making of others. A number of them, by their own declarations to observers, were self-styled former "sinners" who repented years ago. They disclaimed any intent either to step forward or to reaffirm or bolster their own beliefs, nor did they make any effort to proselytize. Rather, they came to watch the salvation of others and to assure themselves that others believed as they did:

> Another elderly lady whom I spoke with told me she lived in Trinidad before coming to New York. She came every night to the Crusade. She said that it was wonderful that Billy Graham came to New York, that she wishes he could always stay here. . . . She had been saved 35 years ago when she had prayed during a serious illness . . . had been in the best of health ever since . . . she had been saved spiritually as well as physically. When she discovered that this was my first visit she said that I should have come sooner to the Garden, but still there was time.

In general, systematic observations confirm the conclusion McLoughlin came to after studying Billy Graham's predecessor, Billy Sunday: though revivalism is popularly conceived of as a lower-class phenomenon, mass evangelism appeals most to the respectable middle-class individual who is already a church member or who has thought about joining a church, but has never had sufficient pressure put upon him to do so.[4]

The Inquirers

One observation about what happened at the Crusade was rather intriguing: the inquirers who stepped forward in response to Graham's appeal were far from a cross-section, demographically speaking, of the total audience.[5] Had the inquirers constituted a group representative of the total audience, one would expect the majority to consist of middle-aged or elderly women who made up so large a segment of both the "organized flocks" and the "regular flotsam." This expectation was not borne out, as a typical description will illustrate:

> His listeners answered his plea by the hundreds. Men, women and teenagers from all parts of the huge arena slowly made their way to the front of the flower-banked platform, where the evangelist stood with a bowed head. . . . Those between 18 and 30 predominate, but there were many older and younger and they apparently come from every economic level. There was a teenage boy in sport shirt and slacks, black motorcycle jacket slung over one arm, walking next to a woman about 30 who wore a black cocktail sheath. A white-haired man in a gray silk suit was followed by a Puerto Rican boy wearing jeans and a T-shirt. . . . At the beginning of the call people responded slowly, but as they concentrated before the platform people just seemed to get up from everywhere in the Garden.

Those going to the platform were men, family groups—including children—teen-agers, and young adults in couples or alone.

It appears, therefore, that the decision-makers were drawn in disproportionate number from the remainder of the audience who did not fall into the category of the typical middle-aged, middle-class woman wearing a hat. Either they were recruited from among the group previously referred to as the floaters, or they came from among those who were but a minority among the "flocks."

This disparity in the composition of the decision-makers and the total audience leads to the suggestion that fewer of the former were "regulars" and that more of them were attending for the first time. If they had come on their own, alone or with a partner, it may have been expressly in order to make a decision. Others, who came as part of a church group along with persons who had already made their decision, may have been brought precisely for that purpose; their decision was eagerly anticipated.

The mass-observation data alone offer no definitive explanation, but it does suggest two possible alternatives: (1) certain persons, found disproportionately among men, young people, etc., were especially susceptible to the appeal made by Graham during the meeting; (2) as implied above, Graham's assured and regular audience was not disposed to make a public decision for Christ, whereas others in the audience came prepared to take such a step or were at least disposed to do so. By the middle of the crusade, perhaps the typical audience-member had already made his inquiry and now wished to see the group of converts further enlarged. It is also possible that some persons considered themselves saved long ago, while others, torn by inner conflict, attended over and over again but deemed themselves unworthy to step forward.

Further insight into the motivations and character of the decision-makers may be gained by turning our attention now to the production of the crusade meeting.

The Build-up

From the outset of the meeting, nothing was left to chance. It began, as one observer put it, "with all the solemnity of a Sunday worship service." The Garden was decorated with a number of flags, flowers, and by a larger banner with the quotation: "Jesus said—I am the Way, the Truth, and the Life." Another observer, a regular and devoted church member, wrote:

> The choir director welcomed the people and acted like a television emcee. He tried to create a casual, friendly atmosphere and had an "everybody happy?" attitude. He asked everyone to join in the singing of the hymn. Then he asked everyone to stand and sing it again. . . .

There was indeed ample borrowing from the pageantry and showmanship of current popular culture.

The preliminary ceremonies were designed to create a congregation fully occupied with rituals to perform and rituals to watch. The choir, made up of volunteers, many of them young people who came night after night, occupied four sections on the first balcony behind the platform. Hymn books, which had earlier been handed out by volunteers, were swiftly collected after the singing. There were calls for contributions, greetings to delegations, announcements of crusade activities, etc. People were asked to stand, and sing the hymn on page 35; together they bowed their heads in prayer. They raised them again, in unison, when told to do so. The applauded on cue and laughed in response to familiar kinds of jokes.

For at least a half-hour before Graham's physical appearance, the audience was actively engaged and kept busy all the time. They became familiar with the setting, and were made to feel relaxed and at home while at the same time they learned to respond on cue. The net effect of all this was to put the audience at ease, to break down any reserve created by the alien surroundings, and to do this around the range of symbols controlled from the platform.

It was after these preliminaries that Billy Graham emerged. "Emerged" seems to be the apt word for he had begun his talk, as if he had been there all along, before some people realized who was speaking. The entrance was without fanfare. He was not introduced, and it took one observer fully five minutes to realize that now the speaker on the platform was Graham.

Once there, Graham dominated the Garden. All that had taken place before his entry was but a prelude to his appearance, and all that the evangelist would do and say after the beginning of the sermon would be but a prelude to the final appeal, the call for decisions for Christ.

By his unobtrusive but compelling entrance into the focus of attention, Graham managed to concentrate all interest on what he was doing and saying. The lights, which had earlier been brightened, were dimmed as Graham took the spotlight. For the first twenty minutes the atmosphere remained "easy." Jokes and quips were rewarded with laughter and held the audience's attention. Graham encouraged his subjects to withdraw attention from the surrounding world and to concentrate it on the experimenter. The staging contributed some kind of hypnotic effect.

Facing his relaxed and pampered audience, Graham was now credible and authentic. His voice, according to observers, was "authoritative but yet calm, soft, inviting, and caressing." Reverentially, he asked his audience to bow their heads and close their eyes as in prayer. All attention was to be centered on Graham's voice. In collaboration with the ushers, the external world was eliminated: persons were calmed and prevented from giving open expression to their feelings. Members of the audience, too, felt impelled to sustain the hushed atmosphere and the common mood. They could suffer no disruptions to break the collective spell:

> A girl (about 25) began crying, stamping her feet, stretching her arms, while those next to her tried to quiet her.
>
> One elderly woman on the main floor was applauding. The usher spoke with her and she stopped.

Some were physically removed from the auditorium. Observer 12 wrote:

> This one man near us seemed particularly carried away and shouted, "Say it again, Billy!" He seemed drunk with emotion and he got up and staggered down the steps. Seems he really was drunk. Two ushers carried him off.

This last observation should leave no mistaken impression that inebriated sinners frequented the Crusade meetings; neither, however, should it be inferred that *all* displays of emotion were summarily broken up by counselors. But affect among the listeners was minimized in favor of a polarization of attention on Graham and a stylization of audience affect. Idiosyncratic emotion simply was not allowed to "catch" or to distract attention from the voice and gestures of the man on the platform.

In this connection we may remark on one other incidental finding of some significance in the comparison with hypnotism. Questionnaires which our own observers had filled out prior to attending the meeting, revealed a rather vivid imagery of Graham though only hazy ideas of the nature of the revival he headed. They saw him as sincere, as a charlatan, as well-meaning, as sinister—but, in any case, they saw him as a human being. However, in reporting what they witnessed at the Crusade, observers say practically nothing about Graham as a person; there is a paucity of description of Graham himself. Observers *listened*, and their reaction to him was mostly to his voice: "I hardly realized he was there or who he was until I heard his voice." Graham himself sets the nature of the experience: "It is not my voice you hear speaking. It is the voice of the Holy Spirit. The Holy Spirit is present in this auditorium."

The comparison with hypnotic influence is suggestive. Attention became riveted not on Graham himself but his *words*, especially the final climactic plea, repeated over and over, "Have you been born again?" Thus the voice of the Holy Spirit, speaking through Graham, was personally inviting every member of the audience to step forward and be born again.

In its net effect, the entire performance serves to make the best of all possible worlds: like a good political spellbinder during campaign oratory, Graham seeks to avoid offending those bound to be "on his side," while so staging the show that some of the yet uncommitted may see the light. Its purpose is to make the act of decision not only plausible, but an obvious climax to all that has gone before.

The Graham meeting, then, follows certain conventions which are, for most of his audience, a familiar part of a Sunday church service. There are the familiar hymns, the choir, meaningful Christian symbolism, a sermon, and the collection. Subjects know how to play their role. The subject relaxes. Then there is Billy Graham who quietly emerges on the scene. Dimming the lights and other effects aim at excluding all noise and emotion which might distract from the exclusive monopolization of attention. His gestures, his voice, and his words exhort people (aided by ushers who *silently* guide them) to go forward and to make their decisions.

The conventional "build up" and the minimization of affect contribute to bringing about a closure around the decision for Christ. First, both the conventionality and the barring of emotion maintain the aura of middle-class respectability which those who come resolved to make a decision have been led to expect; they find nothing too emotional and unusual for their tastes; there is little to threaten them. Second, the minimization of distraction at the same time simulates the stage on which the hypnotist works, encouraging those who, though not explicitly at the meeting for that purpose, are most highly susceptible to the call.

The Meaning of the Decision

In the final plea, the meaning of the decision is left vague. What happens, however, as far as the inquirer is concerned? What motivates his decision?

In terms of theology, the answer is relatively simple. First, one must admit that he is a sinner. Since no one is free from sin, and all are sinners, a person is on the way to a second birth once he realizes this. One should, therefore, rejoice when he knows himself for a sinner, because this means that the Holy Spirit, a voice much higher than Graham's, is calling him to God.

Second, one must confess before man—a confession before man is a confession before Christ. It relieves one of sin which is working within like a disease.

Graham's call, like that of evangelists of all times, serves to arouse and mobilize guilt. Nevertheless, it differs from the more personal methods of promoting conversion in two ways. In the first place, the sins alluded to are rather diffuse and permit any number of subjective interpretations. Second, and perhaps more telling, the decision-maker is not called upon to bare his sin before all those present and to ask publicly for forgiveness. If he confesses, he does so only in brief prayer alone with a counselor after he has left the main auditorium to fill out his decision card.

The inquirer's is a private experience made public only by the act of stepping forward—as one among many. Most who step forward have a clear idea of what is expected of them, that is, through prior talks with friends or acquaintances and through the auspices of the mass-media Crusade publicity; they are already familiar with the mechanics of "coming forward" and what it entails and does not entail.

The making of a decision was represented by Graham as *hard:* "If you say that I'm going to ask you to do a hard thing—the appeal of Communism today is partially because it's a hard thing. They demand great things. Jesus demands no less." But yet the decision was made as *easy* as possible: "I'm not asking you to join a church tonight. . . . All you have to do is come down the escalator. . . . Don't let the distance keep you from God." It was a personal call from Graham who, in turn, merely personified the working of the Holy Spirit: it is Billy Graham who asks you to come forward but "you can come only when the Holy Spirit calls you."

On the one hand there was no reason to be concerned about the attitudes of others: "Soon I will ask you to come forward and you will ask yourselves, 'What will people think?' It does not matter." On the other hand

Graham assured all would-be inquirers that petty arrangements, such as getting home from the meeting, were taken care of: "Your friends will wait for you, and it won't take long."

The typical sermon stressed, according to observers: first, that to make a decision[6] at the meeting was the *only* way to find salvation, i.e., "There may never be another moment like this for you"; second, that it was the *easiest* way; and, third, that to make a decision at the Garden was to join something larger than one's self; Everybody's doing it, why not you? *How many*, Graham asked, will be new people tonight? Come to the platform–*hundreds* are coming. That making a decision was the only way, is implicit in the entire build-up right down to the final plea–Have YOU been born again? All that had gone before pointed to only one logical culmination. The decision might be hard, but to make it at the behest of Graham, meant merely to seize a ready-made opportunity.

While the early phases of the sermon might be expected to arouse a feeling of guilt, i.e., a sense of sin, it is guilt within a respectable aura of sin and salvation characteristic of all church-goers. The sinners are in respectable company, and the public exhibition of private guilt becomes respectable–indeed, the Christian affirmation. That it should occur in the presence of so many others stresses the moral and conforming nature of the act. There is nothing bizarre, unfamiliar, or apt to shame churchgoers in this admission. In the last context, the role of the "regulars" and the flocks who do not step forward must again be noted. Their presence serves above all to validate the collective import of the action.

That the stepping forward was, however, not *always* something in the nature of a ritualistic and middle-class performance can be illustrated in the case of J.,[7] the one genuine "convert," i.e., life-changer, among our observers. Although she went to the meeting to observe, she was so shaken by her experience that no report was forthcoming. Our knowledge of her participation and subsequent experiences came through her companion at the meeting.

> J. went to the Graham meeting feeling that he would have no effect upon her. . . . She kept notes during the proceedings. Her notes were primarily concerned with Graham's sermon. She said she gave him her undivided attention.
>
> Somewhere in the course of the sermon she decided to step forward. She cannot remember exactly when. The next thing she knew was that she had risen and was hurrying to the main floor to declare herself. She felt that this was "right."
>
> Her main reason for stepping forward [as she reconstructed it] was a belief that Graham's preachings could be translated into positive good works by one person towards another. She told me [her companion] that Graham said exactly the same things I always say. It seems that I often lecture her on the way people should act towards each other. . . .
>
> Immediately after her decision, I questioned J. about her feelings while

> making the decision and afterwards. At one point the mention of being a vessel for Christ was made. J. comes from a liberal Jewish background. She said she felt as if she were His vessel. Her primary reaction was one of fright. I received a negative reply when I asked if she felt clean, saved, purged, or ready to lead a good life.
>
> The next morning—Sunday—she called two Unitarian churches, intending to attend services; the services had been called off for the summer months. By the following day she had completely repented. She told me that she did not "love Christ" or believe that he was supernatural. She said that she would not follow through on her decision especially since she felt she did not belong with "these people."

Two weeks later J. felt that she had stepped forward merely out of "curiosity," laughed when she received follow-up literature from the Crusade, and began to view the whole affair as a "lark."

Mass Revivalism and the Susceptibles

The case of J. above supports the overwhelming weight of evidence (from others as well as our own spot checks) indicating that those who made decisions at Madison Square Garden were hardly *converts*. Some, like J., were undoubtedly magnetized by the atmosphere and the voice, and gave way before the slogans. Their loss of self, however, was only temporary; apparently there were no lasting effects.

Nor was a search for real life-changers among the inquirers at Graham meetings very rewarding.[8] Two observers, among our own group, who made their decision during the Crusade had been long-time church-goers. In other instances, where persons professed to having been converted, the decision turned out to be no about-face. It was more like a final initiation into the circle of the righteous, for which the public commitment then served as a psychological legitimation. This is not tantamount to saying that there were no effects, for the inquirers indicated, by their declaration of faith, that they were participating in a larger cause. Through public display, private beliefs acquire a significance they did not have before, even to oneself. The invitation to come forward, made in the full glare of publicity, singled out the "authentically" faithful from the hesitant, thereby giving further authenticity, in their own minds, to their beliefs and their acts.

However, the person so won is hardly the True Believer, in the meaning the term has acquired since Eric Hoffer published his book by that title. The inquirers do not restructure their selves; they are not born again. The conventionality, the demand for only a limited commitment, and the air of organization only strengthen their identifications with an accepted way of life already familiar to them. Nor is Graham's appeal addressed primarily to the outcasts and destitute, for whom the gospel of the conventional church was much too mild. Those susceptible to the call from the platform were hardly ignorant, impoverished, guilt-ridden, lost souls, for whom religion, by promising equality before God, made their present lot bearable. They were not sectarians turning away from a world which had forsaken them.

Rather, the appeal comes from the established churches and is addressed to those normally considered as their proper clientele. Ever since the decline of Puritan ideals in America and the transformation of the religious fellowship of the rural church, the area of contact between religion and this-worldly pursuits has been declining. The churches no longer occupy the central position in the total community. Instead they are microcosms, highly secularized, through which individuals fortify their social positions. To be sure, the Christian saints and martyrs, while they need not be taken as models of behavior, continue to be objects of admiration. But with the coming of industrialism, the vow of poverty and the humble way has had less and less appeal. It has given way to the ostentatious display of material symbols of respectability. To be able to give to charity is an honorific mark of status when giving itself has been institutionalized, but the ability to give requires, first, success in this-worldly enterprises.

The modern revival, then, like any campaign in support of philanthropic causes, is an organized drive to re-establish the importance of religion by dramatizing its urgency. Unlike other campaigns, what is at stake here is not some specific evil to be fought with palliatives, but personal salvation. In this regard, the dramatization evidently plays on certain tendencies, making it effective for some kinds of people. The middle-class person, torn between the simpler, old-fashioned religious prescriptions and the need to accommodate to a mobile society, is unsure of his identity. A strong residue of guilt, which conventional religion is able to assuage only partially, remains fairly close to the surface. The declaration of faith, the decision to take Christ into one's heart, is somewhat akin to a ritual confession and a ritual atonement. For this, neither official Protestantism nor cultural Judaism provide institutionalized opportunities. Parenthetically, it may be remarked that, among our observers, the least "moved" by Graham's appeal were devout Catholics, while a number of young Jewish observers, despite antipathetic predispositions, were emotionally touched; two said they might have gone forward were it a "decision for God" they were asked to make.

One additional point must be made concerning the declining efficacy of simple solutions for the more complicated problems posed by an industrial and mobile civilization. The contrast between the evangelism of Billy Sunday and that of Billy Graham is a case in point. The former may be considered to personify the last desperate stand of religion, in a society which still cherished its individualistic dreams and self-reliant heroes. With the exception of radio and television, every one of Graham's apparent "innovations" in the field organization had already been used by Sunday. Nevertheless, there are differences between the two revivalists' techniques. For Sunday and his audiences, the sins he talked about were not only real enough, but the villains sufficiently vivid to be actively hated. One need only remember the denunciation of "booze" by Sunday to recognize that Billy Graham offers no comparable villain which can be hated with such intensity by all of his followers. The rustic following of Sunday knew what they hated, even while the world in which they had derived their certainty was rapidly disappearing. They keenly felt the changes being wrought, but there were fewer self-doubts. Their conflicts could readily be externalized on the symbols Sunday implored them to destroy. Sunday retained a following long after he had passed the zenith of his power and long after the leadership in the fight against alcoholism, municipal corruption, and "foreign influences" had passed into secular hands.

Graham has not played on hate. He addresses himself to the respectable pillars of the church and to nominal believers who attend his mass rallies in order to be made "authentic." Can you really say, he asks, that you have taken Christ into your heart? The way to *certainty* is presented as easy, and the mass of others who are present makes it even more natural to think of this as the popular and approved and obvious way. Thus, one's beliefs are authenticated without exacting any real price or irrevocable commitment. The sin to be confessed is nominal sin. There is no need to renounce drink, or ambition, or home, or bank account, or smart apparel. Save for generalized sin and vice and juvenile delinquency, there are no real villains, and everyone can be against these. Neither the saloon-keeper, nor the bookie, nor the middle-class climber is to be pilloried; rather, all are called upon to become authentic Christians. And simply by affirming, in public, that they are respectable, believing, upright, moral persons, these decision-makers thus earn the approval of anonymous third persons who, like themselves, wear no crown of thorns but are all for others wearing it. In this acceptable profession of faith, the inquirer sacrifices theology. He continues to hold on to his local church. The work of social improvement, as well as that of "winning souls," is left to the big organization.

The revival thus offers an opportunity to persons who hold on to outmoded ideals for the expression of inauthentic commitments. The slogans, staging, and gimmickry are the marks of organization. Nevertheless, the atmosphere resembles that of a prayer meeting for whose promotion the trappings of popular culture are used. The paradox between personalized religion and the autonomous community church, and the manner of promoting both is brought into sharp relief by the revival.

AARON ANTONOVSKY

Like Everyone Else, Only More So: Identity, Anxiety, and the Jew

"HATH NOT A JEW. . . ." Shakespeare's point is well taken. The Jew, too, is human, and shares all the anxieties of the human condition, as well as those of this time, of this place. Beyond these, he also faces the anxiety of being a Jew.

One type of anxiety is the emotion arising from a gap between label and identity. One learns that he is a Jew—but to whatever extent he has not fully, stably, and acceptingly clarified what this means, he is prone to anxiety. Sartre calls clear identity "authenticity." To be authentic does not mean to be unafraid. The ghetto Jew, under the weight of historical and often of personal experience, knew fear. This emotion may have been, in any given situation, a miscalculation out of proportion to the threat, but it was neither diffuse nor irrational. He was not, however, anxious as a *Jew,* for he knew who he was. The modern, emancipated Jew does not fully know who he is, and much of what he does know he cannot accept. He is the stranger who does not wish to be a stranger. Perforce remaining the stranger, he knows not the why and wherefore. He retains the label of Jew, but has no identity acceptable to himself. It is this lack of acceptable identity which is the core of the problem of anxiety for the Jew *qua* Jew.*

The pain and distress caused by this anxiety are chronic, though they may be tranquillized. One alternative is to be rid of the label Jew. Confronted by the barriers from without, and the tortures of the damned from within, that betrayal would bring, few American Jews have chosen this way. The other alternative is to become authentic.

In groping toward authenticity, most American Jews have postulated

Published for the first time in this volume.

* After this paper was written, it struck me that this problem—in its general terms—was precisely what Kafka was talking about in *The Castle.* The anxiety-laden, nameless K. seeks desperately to fulfill his duties as Land Surveyor to the Castle, i.e.. to develop a working relationship with it. Given Kafka's involvement with his Jewishness, it may well be that one of the meanings of the book is precisely the specific theme developed here.

the absence of conflict between being Jews and Americans.* Retaining the label Jew, they expand their ethnic identity; they seek to define themselves as American Jews. They have said, in essence: Remaining a Jew, I nonetheless wish to be fully part of America, to be accepted as such by other Americans, and to share in the rewards America has to offer.

When things go smoothly—as they have for the American Jew in recent decades, particularly in economic terms—the anxiety is stilled. But has it been resolved? This can be seen only when an experience of traumatic proportions strips away the useful, daily surface defenses and bares the true self, to oneself, if not to others.

It is in this context that the reactions of American Jews to the Rosenberg case are to be understood.

On June 19, 1953, Julius and Ethel Rosenberg were executed. They had been indicted in August, 1950, and found guilty on a charge of conspiring as espionage agents. Their death sentences were carried out after almost three years of legal maneuvering. Their codefendant, Morton Sobell, was sentenced to a prison term of thirty years. The Rosenbergs, Sobell, Irving Kaufmann (the trial judge), Saypol (the prosecutor), Bloch (the defense attorney), Greenglass and Gold (the self-confessed agents turned state's witnesses)—anyone sensitive to ethnic characteristics could not but have been aware that these were all Jews.

The traumatic impact of this case is seen in full when the climate of the period is recalled. At that time (and possibly in all times and places, given its shadowy, self-betraying character), espionage, of all crimes, was considered most execrable by American public opinion. McCarthyism was at its peak. By 1953, there had been seven years of a cold war with Russia and "international communism" (how reminiscent the phrase is of another internationale). The Korean war was not yet over. Hitlerism had been defeated, but Soviet anti-Semitism, culminating in the Prague and Moscow doctors' trials, had come to the fore, almost suggesting that anti-Semitism was universal and omnipresent.

It was during the spring and summer of 1953 that the interviews which provide the basis of this paper were conducted. The problem at hand was not central to the study. One of the fourteen situations to which the respondents were asked to react dealt with the Rosenberg case. But very shortly after the first interviews, it became clear that the material elicited in response to this question was so revealing, so rich in meaning, that it warranted special attention.

The respondents were few—58 in all—and the community was a middle-sized Eastern city whose 22,000 Jews constituted 10 per cent of the

* Small numbers have sought their identity as radicals and/or as intellectuals, not necessarily denying, but most often not confronting, their Jewishness.

strongly Catholic population. These fifty-eight, all married men, made up a small random sample of second generation Jews of eastern European descent living in this community. All but two were over thirty years, the median age being forty-three. In terms of occupation, they represent a cross-section: 18 small businessmen, 13 white collar workers, 7 manual workers, 6 semi-professionals, 5 middle businessmen, 5 professionals, and 4 big businessmen.

It would be misleading to claim that, on all points, the interview data present the views of all American Jews. It is, however, my strong feeling—although I have no data proving this—that stripped of peripheral issues, the responses present the essential, deep-rooted sentiments of a substantial majority of American Jews.

These men were all very much aware of the Rosenberg case, had followed it with a great deal of attention, and had frequently been involved in discussions about it.

They were equally aware of the Jewishness of all the principal characters. Many were also aware—and took the trouble to point out to the interviewer who, as they had almost all previously ascertained, was Jewish—that Hiss, Fuchs, Gouzenko, etc., were not Jewish. This dual awareness indicates some degree of sensitivity to the ethnic identification of alleged Soviet spies.

Furthermore, not a single respondent expressed doubts of the guilt of the accused. Of course, the courts had rendered judgment, and only sixteen interviews were completed before the executions. The interview data, however, strongly indicate that they would have expressed the same certainty even before the trial was over. As far as I can recall public opinion polls, there was a not-microscopic segment of the American public at large which had doubts about the guilt. This difference comes to the fore even more strongly when the question of the death sentence is considered. There were a considerable number of Gentiles—over and above fellow-travellers—who were seriously disturbed by the imposition and carrying out of the death sentence. Yet we find no opposition from the members of our sample, on either moral, legal, or political grounds. In fact, a fair number enthusiastically approved, and others tacitly approved. Frequently it was stressed that the law clearly provided for a death sentence.

No one expressed any doubts about the Rosenbergs having had a fair trial and all the advantages offered by a democratic process of justice. The claim of the Committee to Secure Justice in the Rosenberg Case that the case was sparked by anti-Semitic motives and that it was one manifestation of a general trend toward fascism never occurred to any of them. The suggestion that anyone—from Truman and Eisenhower through Kaufmann and Saypol—was anti-Semitic and hence against the Rosenbergs, or that anyone was using the Rosenbergs to promote anti-Semitism, were thoughts utterly alien to these people. (Interestingly enough, when the question of anti-Semitism arose, which happened not infrequently, only the Rosenbergs themselves were seen as anti-Semitic, that is, "objectively anti-Semitic": their acts were bound to promote anti-Semitism.)

Thus we have unanimity, or near-unanimity, on some attitudes, which contrasts significantly in degree, if not in direction, to the presumed view of the American population as a whole. The greater general liberalism of Jews disappears in this situation.

Other attitudes, although not shared by all in the sample, are even more germane to our problem. First, there is the question of Judge Kaufmann's Jewishness and the death sentence. The respondents were all aware of the former and not opposed to the latter. A substantial majority, discussing Kaufmann's predicament, raised the question of the human elements of sympathetic identification, of empathy, and understanding . . . raised it in order to point out its complete absence. Indeed, Judge Kaufmann, *precisely because he was Jewish,* had no alternative but to impose the death sentence! A Gentile judge might or might not have done so; certainly the law permitted it, and the crime might have warranted it. But a Jew could only have acted in one way. Thus ran the thinking of the respondents.

Two mutually reinforcing factors are seen as the basis for the inevitability of Kaufmann's decision. On the one hand, there was the belief that a sentence short of death, imposed by a Jew, would have aroused a substantial degree of anti-Semitism. No responsible Jew could have avoided imposing the maximum sentence. The second motive ascribed to Kaufmann is even more revealing. As a Jew, it is posited that he could only feel violent hatred for the Jewish Rosenbergs. This phenomenon is, of course, well-known: what greater hatred is there than that of the "loyal" (to whatever cause or group) to the ex-loyal, the "formerly one of us" turned "traitor"? The respondents' sentiments are projected onto Kaufmann.

It is at this point in the interviews that the strongest language emerges. At first, there is a vigorous denial that the Rosenbergs were Jewish: they were atheistic Communists, belonged to no Jewish organizations, etc. However, the very vigor of the denial reveals, and the respondents quickly acknowledge, that this is not the case: in the final summing up they said, in essence, 'once a Jew, always a Jew.' But they go beyond this: whether we see the Rosenbergs as Jewish or not is beside the point; all of America knows that they are Jewish.

Why should there be such wrath directed against the Rosenbergs? To understand this, it is helpful to distinguish between two qualitatively different emotional states. We might call these "cold anger" and "hot anger";

or "condemnation" and "anger." With respect to the Rosenbergs, most Gentiles felt the former, most Jews the latter. The critical distinction between the two is seen when one brings in the ideas of involvement and guilt. I can feel a cold anger at Nazism or Stalinism, injustice or poverty—for, although I may be a victim of these, it is not my fault in any way. I am not guilty! Where I am in some sense guilty, where, in some way, I share responsibility for something reprehensible that has been done, my emotion is that of "hot anger," the intensity of which allows me to displace, and thus to bear, my sense of guilt. For Jews, Rosenberg was "one of us" and hence his guilt is "our" guilt.

There are other factors in the anger, complementary to the above. There is the feeling, frequently expressed in the interviews, that Jews should manifest higher standards than Gentiles. This is not only because "of our own traditions," but because "we are a minority, and hence must be on our best behavior." (There is an interesting parallel here between Jewish attitudes toward crime and toward accidents, expressed in the phrases, "My God, a Jewish boy" and "At least it's not a Jew." Both reveal the identification patterns of a minority.) The Rosenbergs betrayed "us" by violating these standards. Moreover, the Rosenbergs betrayed "a country which has done so much for Jews."

There is one final, highly important, factor in the anger of the respondents: the fear that the crime of the Rosenbergs might—if not mitigated by the death sentence imposed by a Jewish judge, in response to the pleading of a Jewish prosecutor, or even despite this—bring to the fore the latent anti-Semitism existing in America. On the basis of other questions posed during the interviews, the respondents, in the main, felt that, in contemporary America, anti-Semitic attitudes were somewhere between being permitted and preferred. Thus, for example, most felt that at least half of American Gentiles agreed to 11 of 15 statements taken from the anti-Semitism scale of the California Authoritarian Personality studies.

At the extreme—others expressed the same emotion without making such a historical assessment—was the man who said: "If this keeps up, I'm afraid there'll be trouble. They're liable to start revolutions, hatred against the Jews. You never know, they're liable to pass laws against the Jews, to take away the privileges Jews have. . . ." Of the majority expressing this concern, the mildest comment was the laconic, "It couldn't have done us any good." Even with regard to the minority, which argued that the Rosenberg case in no way intensified anti-Semitism (noting that many editorials stressed the irrelevance of the Jewish issue, or that even McCarthy was not anti-Semitic), the important fact is that they considered the question.

A few general comments are in order here, before inferences are drawn with respect to the problems of identity and anxiety. It might simply be said that our respondents spoke as they did as an expression of a more or less rational fear, and that if they were wrong it is because they assessed incorrectly the American situation. After all, these are all mature men. They have memories of the depression and its Father Coughlins and Gerald L. K. Smiths. Most of them had relatives in Europe who were slaughtered by Hitler, while the world stood by indifferently. Almost all of them have had at least some personal experiences of anti-Semitism, particularly in the job world and in the army. Is it not possible that their reactions to the Rosenberg case are primarily fear-reactions to the possibility of a wave of anti-Semitism in America?

This would seem to be indicated by the comments referred to earlier. There, however, we considered attitudes, which are seen as latent predispositions. Here the question is one of concern about action. And, when it comes to this, as responses in the interviews reveal, explicit denial is made of the possibility of an anti-Semitic wave. Anti-Semitic groups today are seen as crackpot fringe groups. Few Americans are seen as willing to participate actively in overt anti-Semitic endeavors. The general attitude of our respondents seems to be: "It* could happen here; America is not immune. But it is very far from happening now." Moreover, the pervasiveness of the involvement with the trial, the intensity of the attitudes toward the Rosenbergs, and the certainty that Kaufmann had no alternative all point to a generalized, diffuse anxiety.

This anxiety can best be summed up by saying, "a goy remains a goy." There is a parallel Southern Negro saying: "White folks is white folks." Both indicate the impossibility, in the last analysis, of trusting "them." But there is a fundamental difference. The Southern Negro has few or no expectations from the Southern white. He structures his life on the premise that at no time will anything be forthcoming from the white; if it does, it is pure gravy. This is, in substance, the attitude of the ghetto Jew. (To the extent that the Negro becomes oriented to acceptance by the white world, his problem shifts to what is posited here as the problem of the American Jew.) The American Jew, by contrast, premises his psychological security, his sense of ethnic identity, upon acceptance by "goyim," but he feels that the "goy" has let him down by not really accepting him. The Rosenberg case, then, does not raise the fear of a wave of anti-Semitism. It does, however, provide the "goy" with ex-

* One of the things that fascinated me in this study was the widespread use of the word "it," in contexts which made it absolutely clear that the referent was anti-Semitism. The parallel to "it" as a sexual referent in a culture beset by sexual anxiety is obvious and conveys in a neat capsule a central theme of this paper.

cellent grounds for expanding his refusal to accept the Jew as an American.

The meaning given by American Jews to the Rosenberg case, as described here, occurs on an unconscious level, and can be fully understood only when associated with another attitude which I call the sense of collective accountability. This is to be distinguished from a sense of mutual responsibility, the notion that "all Jews are brothers." The former is passive, the latter, active. In most of Jewish history, the two attitudes coexist. But in a democratic society, in which integration with the majority is a desired possibility, mutual responsibility declines in intensity. Collective accountability, on the other hand, the attitude that "they"—the majority which can accept or reject "us"—hold all of "us" responsible for what one of "us" does, continues in full force just so long as there is a sense of incomplete integration.

We have seen that the Rosenberg case brought to the surface expressions of a strong sense of anxiety. This anxiety can be stilled under ordinary circumstances and need not prevent reasonably efficient functioning. But, as with anxiety deriving from the unique history of the individual, the defenses that make such functioning possible do not resolve the underlying problem. I have argued that, in the case of American Jews, this problem is ultimately the problem of identity. Implicit here, is the conception of identity that involves the location of the individual in society as a member of a cultural or ethnic entity.* Once the commitment is made—irrespective of the reasons for making it—to seek a given ethnic identity, failure to achieve it produces anxiety. Jews in America, wishing to be American Jews, have not resolved the problem of authenticity and, hence, are beset by anxiety.

* I have made no attempt to deal with the purely individual-family aspect of identity. I would grant that this is basic, that unless this is resolved, there cannot be successful ethnic identification. Very often the latter is sought as a substitute for the former. It doesn't work. But even if the former problem is solved, the latter remains. The fact that the problem of ethnic identity exists has repercussions, through the family, on the problem of personal identity.

HAROLD FINESTONE

Cats, Kicks, and Color

GROWING RECOGNITION that the most recent manifestation of the use of opiates in this country has been predominantly a young peoples' problem has resulted in some speculation as to the nature of this generation of drug users. Is it possible to form an accurate conception as to what "manner of man" is represented by the current species of young drug addict? Intensive interviews between 1951 and 1953 with over fifty male colored users of heroin in their late teens and early twenties selected from several of the areas of highest incidence of drug use in Chicago, served to elicit from them the expression of many common attitudes, values, schemes of behavior, and general social orientation. Moreover, since there was every reason to believe that such similarities had preceded their introduction to heroin, it appeared that it was by virtue of such shared features that they had been unusually receptive to the spread of opiate use. Methodologically, their common patterns of behavior suggested the heuristic value of the construction of a social type. The task of this paper is to depict this social type, and to present a hypothetical formulation to account for the form it has taken.

No special justification appears to be necessary for concentrating in this paper on the social type of the young colored drug user. One of the distinctive properties of the distribution of drug use as a social problem, at least in Chicago, is its high degree of both spatial and racial concentration. In fact, it is a problem which in this city can be pinpointed with great accuracy as having its incidence preponderantly among the young male colored persons in a comparatively few local community areas. The following delineation of the generic characteristics of young colored drug users constitutes in many respects an ideal type. No single drug addict

---

Reprinted from *Social Problems*, V, No. 1 (1957), 3-13, by permission of the author and the publisher.

* This investigation was supported by research grant 3M 9030 from the National Institute of Mental Health, Public Health Service, and was carried on under the direction of Clifford R. Shaw and Solomon Kobrin. The writer acknowledges the generous assistance received in the clarification of the problems dealt with in this paper through discussions with Clifford R. Shaw, Henry D. McKay, and Solomon Kobrin, supervising sociologists at the Illinois Institute for Juvenile Research and the Chicago Area Project.

exemplified all of the traits to be depicted but all of them revealed several of them to a marked degree.

The young drug user was a creature of contrasts. Playing the role of the fugitive and pariah as he was inevitably forced to do, he turned up for interviews in a uniformly ragged and dirty condition. And yet he talked with an air of superiority derived from his identification with an elite group, the society of "cats." He came in wearing a nonfunctional tie clip attached to his sport shirt and an expensive hat as the only indications that he was concerned with his appearance and yet displayed in his conversation a highly developed sense of taste in men's clothing and a high valuation upon dressing well. He came from what were externally the drabbest, most overcrowded, and physically deteriorated sections of the city and yet discussed his pattern of living as though it were a consciously cultivated work of art.

Despite the location of his social world in the "asphalt jungle" of the "Blackbelt" he strictly eschewed the use of force and violence as a technique for achieving his ends or for the settling of problematic situations. He achieved his goals by indirection, relying, rather, on persuasion and on a repertoire of manipulative techniques. To deal with a variety of challenging situations, such as those arising out of his contacts with the police, with his past or potential victims, and with jilted "chicks," etc., he used his wits and his conversational ability. To be able to confront such contingencies with adequacy and without resort to violence was to be "cool." His idea was to get what he wanted through persuasion and ingratiation; to use the other fellow by deliberately outwitting him. Indeed, he regarded himself as immeasurably superior to the "gorilla," a person who resorted to force.

The image of himself as "operator" was projected onto the whole world about him and led to a complete scepticism as to other persons' motives. He could relate to people by outsmarting them, or through openhanded and often ruinous generosity, but his world seemed to preclude any relationship which was not part of a "scheme" or did not lend itself to an "angle." The most difficult puzzle for him to solve was the "square," the honest man. On the one hand the "square" was the hard-working plodder who lived by routine and who took honesty and the other virtues at their face value. As such, he constituted the prize victim for the cat. On the other hand, the cat harbored the sneaking suspicion that some squares were smarter than he, because they could enjoy all the forbidden pleasures which were his stock in trade and maintain a reputation for respectability in the bargain.

The cat had a large, colorful, and discriminating vocabulary which dealt with all phases of his experience with drugs. In addition, he never seemed to content himself with the conventional word for even the most commonplace objects. Thus he used "pad" for house, "pecks" for food, "flicks" for movies, "stick hall" for pool hall, "dig the scene" for observe, "box" for record player, "bread" for money, etc. In each instance the word he used was more concrete or earthier than the conventional word and such as to reveal an attitude of subtle ridicule towards the dignity and conventionality inherent in the common usage.

His soft convincing manner of speaking, the shocking earthiness and fancifulness of his vocabulary, together with the formidable gifts of charm and ingratiation which he deployed, all contributed to the dominant impression which the young drug user made as a person. Such traits would seem to have fitted naturally into a role which some cats had already played or aspired to play, that of the pimp. To be supported in idleness and luxury through the labors of one or more attractive "chicks" who shoplifted or engaged in prostitution or both and dutifully handed over the proceeds was one of his favorite fantasies. In contrast with the milieu of the white underworld, the pimp was not an object of opprobrium but of prestige.

The theme of the exploitation of the woman goes close to the heart of the cat's orientation to life, that is, his attitude towards work. Part of the cat's sense of superiority stems from his aristocratic disdain for work and for the subordination of self to superiors and to the repetitive daily routine entailed by work, which he regards as intolerable. The "square" is a person who toils for regular wages and who takes orders from his superiors without complaint.

In contrast with the "square," the cat gets by without working. Instead he keeps himself in "bread" by a set of ingenious variations on "begging, borrowing, or stealing." Each cat has his "hustle" (4), and a "hustle" is any non-violent means of "making some bread" which does not require work. One of the legendary heroes of the cat is the man who is such a skillful con-man that he can sell "State Street" to his victim. Concretely, the cat is a petty thief, pickpocket, or pool shark, or is engaged in a variety of other illegal activities of the "conning" variety. A very few cats are actually living off the proceeds of their women "on the hustle."

The main purpose of life for the cat is to experience the "kick." Just as every cat takes pride in his "hustle," so every cat cultivates his "kick." A "kick" is any act tabooed by "squares" that heightens and intensifies the present moment of experience and differentiates it as much as possible from the humdrum routine of daily life. Sex in any of its conventional expressions is not a "kick" since this would not serve to distinguish the cat from the "square," but orgies of sex behavior and a dabbling in the various perversions and byways of sex pass muster as "kicks." Some "cats" are on an alcohol "kick," others on a marihuana "kick," and others on a heroin "kick." There is some interchangeability among these various "kicks" but the tendency is to select your "kick" and stay with it. Many of these young drug users, however, had progressed from the alcohol to the marihuana to the heroin "kick." Each "kick" has its own lore of appreciation and connoisseurship into which only its devotees are initiated.

In addition to his "kick" the cat sets great store on the enjoyment of music and on proper dress. To enjoy one's "kick" without a background of popular music is inconceivable. The cat's world of music has a distinctive galaxy of stars, and the brightest luminaries in his firmament are performers such as "Yardbird" (the late Charlie Parker) and disc jockeys such as Al Benson. Almost every cat is a frustrated musician who hopes some day to get his "horn" out of pawn, take lessons, and earn fame and fortune in the field of "progressive music."

The cat places a great deal of emphasis upon clothing and exercises his sartorial talents upon a skeletal base of suit, sport shirt, and hat. The suit itself must be conservative in color. Gaiety is introduced through the selection of the sport shirt and the various accessories, all so chosen and harmonized as to reveal an exquisite sense of taste. When the cat was not talking about getting his clothes out of pawn, he talked about getting them out of the cleaners. With nonchalant pride one drug user insisted that the most expensive sport shirts and hats in the city of Chicago were sold in a certain haberdashery on the South Side. The ideal cat would always appear in public impeccably dressed and be able to sport a complete change of outfit several times a day.

The cat seeks through a harmonious combination of charm, ingratiating speech, dress, music, the proper dedication to his "kick," and unrestrained generosity to make of his day to day life itself a gracious work of art. Everything is to be pleasant, and everything he does and values is to contribute to a cultivated aesthetic approach to living. The "cool cat" exemplifies all of these elements in proper balance. He demonstrates his ability to "play it cool" in his unruffled manner of dealing with outsiders such as the police, and in the self-assurance with which he confronts emergencies in the society of "cats." Moreover, the "cat" feels himself to be any man's equal. He is convinced that he can go anywhere and mingle easily with anyone. For example, he rejects the type of music designated "the blues" because for him it symbolizes attitudes of submission and resignation which are repugnant and alien to his customary frame of mind.

It can be seen now why heroin use should make such a powerful appeal to the cat. It was the ultimate "kick." No substance was more profoundly tabooed by conventional middle-class society. Regular heroin use provides a sense of maximal social differentiation from the "square." The cat was at last engaged, he felt, in an activity completely beyond the comprehension of the "square." No other "kick" offered such an instantaneous intensification of the immediate moment of experience and set it apart from everyday experience in such spectacular fashion. Any words used by the cat to apply to the "kick," the experience of "being high," he applied to heroin in the superlative. It was the "greatest kick of them all."

In the formulation now to be presented, the cat as a social type is viewed as a manifestation of a process of social change in which a new type of self-conception has been emerging among the adolescents of the lower social-economic levels of the colored population in large urban centers. It is a self-conception rooted in the types of accommodation to a subordinate status achieved historically by the colored race in this country, a self-conception which has become increasingly articulated as it responded to and selected various themes from the many available to it in the milieu of the modern metropolis. Blumer's classification of social movements into general, specific, or expressive, appears to provide a useful framework for the analysis of the social type of the cat (2).

In terms of these categories the cat as a social type is the personal counterpart of an expressive social movement. The context for such a movement must include the broader community, which, by its policies of social segregation and discrimination, has withheld from individuals of the colored population the opportunity to achieve or to identify with status positions in the larger society. The social type of the cat is an expression of one possible type of adaptation to such blocking and frustration, in which a segment of the population turns in upon itself and attempts to develop within itself criteria for the achievement of social status and the rudiments of a satisfactory social life. Within his own isolated social world, the cat attempts to give form and purpose to dispositions derived from but denied an outlet within the dominant social order.

What are these dispositions and in what sense may they be said to be derived from the dominant social order? Among the various interrelated facets of the life of the cat, two themes are central, those of the "hustle" and the "kick." It is to be noted that they are in direct antithesis to two of the central values of the dominant culture, the "hustle" versus the paramount importance of the occupation for the male in our society, and the "kick" versus the importance of regulating conduct in terms of its future consequences. Thus, there appears to be a relationship of conflict between the central themes of the social type of the cat and those of the dominant social order. As a form of expressive behavior, however, the social type of the cat represents an indirect rather than a direct attack against central conventional values.

It is interesting to speculate on the reasons why a type such as the cat should emerge rather than a social movement with the objective of changing the social order. The forces coercing the selective process among colored male adolescents in the direction of expressive social movements are probably to be traced to the long tradition of accommodation to a subordinate status on the part of the Negro as well as to the social climate since

World War II, which does not seem to have been favorable to the formation of specific social movements.

The themes of the "hustle" and "kick" in the social orientation of the cat are facts which appear to be overdetermined. For example, to grasp the meaning of the "hustle" to the cat, one must understand it as a rejection of the obligation of the adult male to work. When asked for the reasons underlying his rejection of work the cat did not refer to the uncongenial and relatively unskilled and low paid jobs which, in large part, were the sole types of employment available to him. He emphasized rather that the routine of a job and the demand that he should apply himself continuously to his work task were the features that made work intolerable for him. The self-constraint required by work was construed as an unwarranted damper upon his love of spontaneity. The other undesirable element from his point of view was the authoritarian setting of most types of work with which he was familiar.

There are undoubtedly many reasons for the cat's rejection of work, but the reasons he actually verbalized are particularly significant when interpreted as devices for sustaining his self-conception. The cat's feeling of superiority would be openly challenged were he to confront certain of the social realities of his situation, such as the discrimination exercised against colored persons looking for work and the fact that only the lowest status jobs are available to him. He avoided any mention of these factors which would have forced him to confront his true position in society and thus posed a threat to his carefully cherished sense of superiority.

In emphasizing as he does the importance of the "kick" the cat is attacking the value our society places upon planning for the future and the responsibility of the individual for such planning. Planning always requires some subordination and disciplining of present behavior in the interest of future rewards. The individual plans to go to college, plans for his career, plans for his family and children, etc. Such an orientation on the part of the individual is merely the personal and subjective counterpart of a stable social order and of stable social institutions, which not only permit but sanction an orderly progression of expectations with reference to others and to one's self. Where such stable institutions are absent or in the inchoate stages of development, there is little social sanction for such planning in the experience of the individual. Whatever studies are available strongly suggest that such are the conditions which tend to prevail in the lower socio-economic levels of the Negro urban community (3). Stable family and community organization is lacking in those areas of the city where drug use is concentrated. A social milieu which does not encourage the subordination and disciplining of present conduct in the interests of future rewards tends by default to enhance the present. The "kick" appears to be a logical culmination of this emphasis.

Accepting the emergence of the self-conception of the cat as evidence of a developing depressive social movement, we may phrase the central theoretical problem as follows: What are the distinctive and generic features of the cat's social orientation? Taking a cue from the work of Huizinga as developed in *Homo Ludens* (7), we propose that the generic characteristics of the social type of the cat are those of play. In what follows, Huizinga's conception of play as a distinctive type of human activity will be presented and then applied as a tool of analysis for rendering intelligible the various facets of the social orientation of the cat. It is believed that the concept of play indicates accurately the type of expressive social movement which receives its embodiment in the cat.

According to Huizinga the concept of play is a primary element of human experience and as such is not susceptible to exact definition.

"The *fun* of playing resists all analysis, all logical interpretation. . . . Nevertheless it is precisely this fun-element that characterizes the essence of play" (7, p. 3). The common image of the young colored drug addict pictures him as a pitiful figure, a trapped unfortunate. There is a certain amount of truth in this image but it does not correspond to the conception which the young colored addict has of himself or to the impression that he tries to communicate to others. If it were entirely true it would be difficult to square with the fact that substantial numbers of young colored persons continue to become drug users. The cat experiences and manifests a certain zest in his mode of life which is far from self-pity. This fun element seemed to come particularly to the fore as the cat recounted his search for "kicks," the adventure of his life on the streets, and the intensity of his contest against the whole world to maintain his supply of drugs. Early in the cycle of heroin use itself there was invariably a "honeymoon" stage when the cat abandoned himself most completely to the experience of the drug. For some cats this "honeymoon" stage, in terms of their ecstatic preoccupation with the drug, was perpetual. For others it passed, but the exigencies of an insatiable habit never seemed to destroy completely the cat's sense of excitement in his way of life.

While Huizinga declines to define play, he does enumerate three characteristics which he considers to be proper to play. Each one of them when applied to the cat serves to indicate a generic feature of his social orientation.

a) "First and foremost . . . all play is a voluntary activity." (7, p. 7.)

"Here we have the first main characteristic of play: that it is free, is in fact freedom" (7, p. 8). The concept of an expressive social movement assumes a social situation where existing social arrangements are frustrating and are no longer accepted as legitimate and yet where collective activity directed towards the modification of these limitations is not possible. The cat is "free" in the sense that he is a pre-eminent candidate for new forms of social organization and novel social practices. He is attempting to escape from certain features of the historical traditions of the Negro which he regards as humiliating. As an adolescent or young adult, he is not fully assimilated into such social institutions as the family, school, church, or industry which may be available to him. Moreover, the social institutions which the Negroes brought with them when they migrated to the city have not as yet achieved stability or an adequate functioning relationship to the urban environment. As a Negro, and particularly as a Negro of low socio-economic status, he is excluded from many socializing experiences which adolescents in more advantaged sectors of the society take for granted. He lives in communities where the capacity of the population for effective collective action is extremely limited, and consequently there are few effective controls on his conduct besides that exercised by his peer group itself. He is fascinated by the varied "scenes" which the big city spreads out before him. Granted this setting, the cat adopts an adventurous attitude to life and is free to give his allegiance to new forms of activity.

> b) . . . A second characteristic is closely connected with this (that is, the first characteristic of freedom), namely, that play is not "ordinary" or "real" life. It is rather a stepping out of "real" life into a temporary sphere of activity with a disposition all of its own. Every child knows perfectly well that he is "only pretending," or that it was "only for fun." . . . This "only pretending" quality of play betrays a consciousness of the inferiority of play compared with "seriousness," a feeling that seems to be something as primary as play itself. Nevertheless . . . the consciousness of play being "only a pretend" does not by any means prevent it from proceeding with the utmost seriousness, with an absorption, a devotion that passes into rapture and, temporarily at least, completely abolishes that troublesome "only" feeling. (7, p. 8.)

It is implicit in the notion of an expressive social movement that, since direct collective action to modify the sources of dissatisfaction and restlessness is not possible, all such movements should appear under one guise, as forms of "escape." Persons viewing the problem of addiction from the perspective of the established social structure have been prone to make this interpretation. It is a gross oversimplification, however, as considered from the perspective of the young drug addict himself. The emergence of the self-conception of the cat is an attempt to deal with the problems of status and identity in a situation where participation in the life of the broader community is denied, but where the colored adolescent is becoming increasingly sensitive to the values, the goals, and the notions of success which obtain in the dominant social order.

The caste pressures thus make it exceedingly difficult for an American Negro to preserve a true perspective of himself and his own group in relation to the larger white society. The increasing abstract knowledge of the world outside—of its opportunities, its rewards, its different norms of competition and cooperation—which results from the proceeding acculturation at the same time as there is increasing group isolation, only increases the tensions. (8.)

Such conditions of group isolation would appear to be fairly uniform throughout the Negro group. Although this isolation may be experienced differently at different social levels of the Negro community, certain features of the adaptations arrived at in response to this problem will tend to reveal similarities. Since the struggle for status takes place on a stage where there is acute sensitivity to the values and status criteria of the dominant white group, but where access to the means through which such values may be achieved is prohibited, the status struggle turning in on itself will assume a variety of distorted forms. Exclusion from the "serious" concerns of the broader community will result in such adaptations manifesting a strong element of "play."

Frazier in *Black Bourgeoisie* discusses the social adaptation of the Negro middle class as "The World of Make-Believe." (5.)

> The emphasis upon "social" life or "society" is one of the main props of the world of make-believe into which the black bourgeoisie has sought an escape from its inferiority and frustrations in American society. This world of make-believe, to be sure, is a reflection of the values of American society, but it lacks the economic basis that would give it roots in the world of reality. (5, p. 237.)

In the Negro lower classes the effects of frustrations deriving from subordination to the whites may not be experienced as personally or as directly as it is by the Negro middle class, but the massive effects of residential segregation and the lack of stable social institutions and community organization are such as to reinforce strong feelings of group isolation even at the lowest levels of the society.

It is here suggested that the function performed by the emergence of the social type of the cat among Negro lower class adolescents is analogous to that performed by "The World of Make-Believe" in the Negro middle class. The development of a social type such as that of the cat is only possible in a situation where there is isolation from the broader community but great sensitivity to its goals, where the peer group pressures are extremely powerful, where institutional structures are weak, where models of success in the illegitimate world have strong appeals, where specific social movements are not possible, and where novel forms of behavior have great prestige. To give significance to his experience, the young male addict has developed the conception of a heroic figure, the "ideal cat," a person who is completely adequate to all situations, who controls his "kick" rather than letting it control him, who has a lucrative "hustle," who has no illusions as to what makes the world "tick," who is any man's equal, who basks in the admiration of his brother cats and associated "chicks," who hob-nobs with "celebs" of the musical world, and who in time himself may become a celebrity.

The cat throws himself into his way of life with a great deal of intensity, but he cannot escape completely from the perspective, the judgments, and the sanctions of the dominant social order. He has to make place in his scheme of life for police, lockups, jails, and penitentiaries, to say nothing of the agonies of withdrawal distress. He is forced eventually to confront the fact that his role as a cat with its associated attitudes is largely a pose, a form of fantasy with little basis in fact. With the realization that he is addicted he comes only too well to know that he is a "junky," and he is fully aware of the conventional attitudes towards addicts as well as of the counter-rationalizations provided by his peer group. It is possible that the cat's vacillation with regard to seeking a cure for his addiction is due to a conflict of perspectives, whether to view his habit from the cat's or the dominant social order's point of view.

> c) Play is distinct from "ordinary" life both as to locality and duration. This is the third main characteristic of play: its secludedness, its limitedness. It is "played out" within certain limits of time and place. It contains its own course and meaning. (7, p. 9.)

It is this limited, esoteric character of heroin use which gives to the cat the feeling of belonging to an elite. It is the restricted extent of the distribution of drug use, the scheming and intrigue associated with underground "connections" through which drugs are obtained, the secret lore of the appreciation of the drug's effects, which give the cat the exhilaration of participating in a conspiracy. Contrary to popular conception, most drug users were not anxious to proselyte new users. Of course, spreading the habit would have the function of increasing the possible sources of supply. But an equally strong disposition was to keep the knowledge of drug use secret, to impress and dazzle the audience with one's knowledge of being "in the know." When proselyting did occur, as in jails or lockups, it was proselyting on the part of a devotee who condescended to share with the uninitiated a highly prized practice and set of attitudes.

As he elaborates his analysis of play, Huizinga brings to the fore additional aspects of the concept which also have their apt counterpart in the way of life of the cat. For instance, as was discussed earlier, the cat's appreciation of "progressive music" is an essential part of his social orientation. About this topic Huizinga remarks, "Music, as we have hinted before, is the highest and purest expression of the *facultas ludendi*" (7, p. 187). The cat's attitude toward music has a sacred, almost mystical quality. "Progressive music" opens doors to a type of highly valued experience which for him can be had in no other way. It is more important to him than eating and is second only to the "kick." He may have to give up his hope of dressing according to his standards but he never gives up music.

Huizinga also observes, "Many and close are the links that connect play with beauty" (7, p. 7). He refers to the "profoundly aesthetic quality of play" (7, p. 2). The aesthetic emphasis which seems so central to the style of living of the cat is a subtle elusive accent permeating his whole outlook but coming to clearest expression in a constellation of interests, the "kick," clothing, and music. And it certainly reaches a level of awareness in their language. Language is utilized by the cat with a conscious relish, with many variations and individual turns of phrase indicating the value placed upon creative expression in this medium.

It is to be noted that much of the description of the cat's attributes did not deal exclusively with elements unique to him. Many of the features mentioned are prevalent among adolescents in all reaches of the status scale. Dress, music, language, and the search for pleasure are all familiar themes of the adolescent world. For instance, in his description of the adolescent "youth culture" Talcott Parsons would appear to be presenting the generic traits of a "play-form" with particular reference to its expression in the middle class.

> It is at the point of emergence into adolescence that there first begins to develop a set of patterns and behavior phenomena which involve a highly complex combination of age grading and sex role elements. These may be referred to together as the phenomena of the "youth culture." . . .
>
> Perhaps the best single point of reference for characterizing the youth culture lies in its contrast with the dominant pattern of the adult male role. By contrast with the emphasis on responsibility in this role, the orientation of the youth culture is more or less irresponsible. One of its dominant roles is "having a good time." . . . It is very definitely a rounded humanistic pattern rather than one of competence in the performance of specified functions. (9.)

Such significant similarities between this description and the themes of the social type of the cat only tend to reinforce the notion that the recent spread of heroin use was a problem of adolescence. The cat is an adolescent sharing many of the interests of his age-mates everywhere but confronted by a special set of problems of color, tradition, and identity.

The social orientation of the cat, with its emphasis on nonviolence, was quite in contrast to the orientation of the smaller group of young white drug users who were interviewed in the course of this study. The latter's type of adjustment placed a heavy stress upon violence. Their crimes tended to represent direct attacks against persons and property. The general disposition they manifested was one of "nerve" and brashness rather than one of "playing it cool." They did not cultivate the amenities of language, music, or dress to nearly the same extent as the cat. Their social orientation was expressed as a direct rather than an indirect attack on the dominant values of our society. This indicates that the "youth culture" despite its generic features may vary significantly in different social settings.

In his paper, "Some Jewish Types of Personality," Louis Wirth made the following suggestive comments about the relationship between the social type and its setting.

> A detailed analysis of the crucial personality types in any given area or cultural group shows that they depend upon a set of habits and attitudes in the group for their existence and are the direct expressions of the values of the group. As the life of the group changes there appears a host of new social types, mainly outgrowths and transformations of previous patterns which have become fixed through experience. (11.)

What are some of the sources of the various elements going to make up the social type of the cat which may be sought in his traditions? The following suggestions are offered as little more than speculation at the present time. The emphasis upon nonviolence on the part of the cat, upon manipulative techniques rather than overt attack, is a stress upon the indirect rather than the direct way towards one's goal. May not the cat in this emphasis be betraying his debt to the "Uncle Tom" type of adjustment, despite his wish to dissociate himself from earlier patterns of accommodation to the dominant white society? May not the "kick" itself be a cultural lineal descendant of the ecstatic moment of religious possession so dear to revivalist and store-front religion? Similarly, may not the emphasis upon the exploitation of the woman have its origin in the traditionally greater economic stability of the colored woman?

W. I. Thomas, in one of his references to the problems raised by the city environment, stated, "Evidently the chief problem is the young American person" (10, p. 46). In discussing the type of inquiry that would be desirable in this area he states that it should

> . . . lead to a more critical discrimination between that type of disorganization in the youth which is a real but frustrated tendency to organize on a higher plane, or one more correspondent with the moving environment, and that type of disorganization which is simply the abandonment of standards. It is also along this line . . . that we shall gain light on the relation of fantastic phantasying to realistic phantasying. . . . (10, p. 47.)

Posed in this way the problem becomes one of evaluating the social type of the cat in relation to the processes of social change. This social type is difficult to judge according to the criterion suggested by Thomas. Since many of the cat's interests are merely an extreme form of the adolescent "youth culture," in part the problem becomes one of determining how functional the period of adolescence is as preparation for subsequent adult status. However, the central phases of the social orientation of the cat, the "hustle" and the "kick," do represent a kind of disorganization which indicates the abandonment of conventional standards. The young addicted cat is "going nowhere." With advancing age he cannot shed his addiction the way he can many of the other trappings of adolescence. He faces only the bleak prospect, as time goes on, of increasing demoralization. Although the plight of the young colored addict is intimately tied to the conditions and fate of his racial group, his social orientation seems to represent a dead-end type of adjustment. Just as Handlin in *The Uprooted* suggests that the first generation of immigrant peoples to our society tends to be a sacrificed generation (6), it may be that the unique problems of Negro migrants to our metropolitan areas will lead to a few or several sacrificed generations in the course of the tortuous process of urbanization.

The discussion of the social type of the cat leads inevitably to the issue of social control. Any attempt to intervene or modify the social processes producing the "cat" as a social type must have the objective of reducing his group isolation. For instance, because of such isolation and because of the cat's sensitivity to the gestures of his peers, the most significant role models of a given generation of cats tend to be the cats of the preceding age group. Where, in a period of rapid change, the schemes of behavior of the role models no longer correspond to the possibilities in the actual situation, it is possible for attitudes to be transmitted to a younger generation which evidence a kind of "cultural lag." Thus the condition of the labor market in Chicago is such as to suggest the existence of plentiful employment opportunities for the Negro in a variety of fields. But because such openings are not mediated to him through role models it is possible that the cat is unable to take advantage of these opportunities or of the facilities available for training for such positions.

The social type of the cat is a product of social change. The type of social orientation which it has elaborated indicates an all too acute awareness of the values of the broader social order. In an open class society where upward mobility is positively sanctioned, an awareness and sensitivity to the dominant values is the first stage in their eventual assimilation. Insofar as the social type of the cat represents a reaction to a feeling of exclusion from access to the means towards the goals of our society, all measures such as improved educational opportunities which put these means within his grasp will hasten the extinction of this social type. Just as the "hoodlum" and "gangster" types tend to disappear as the various more recently arrived white ethnic groups tend to move up in the status scale of the community (1), so it can confidently be expected that the cat as a social type will tend to disappear as such opportunities become more prevalent among the colored population.

References

1. Bell, Daniel. "Crime as an American Way of Life," *Antioch Review*, XIII (June, 1953), 131-54.

2. Blumer, Herbert. "Social Movements," in Robert E. Park (ed.), *An Outline of the Principles of Sociology*. New York: Barnes & Noble, 1939. Pp. 255-78.

3. Drake, St. Clair, and Horace R. Cayton. "Lower Class: Sex and Family," *Black Metropolis*. New York: Harcourt, Brace & Co., 1945. Pp. 564-99.

4. Finestone, Harold. "Narcotics and Criminality," *Law and Contemporary Problems*, XXII (Winter, 1957), 60-85.

5. Frazier, E. Franklin. *Black Bourgeoisie*. Glencoe, Ill.: The Free Press, 1957.

6. Handlin, Oscar. *The Uprooted*. New York: Grosset and Dunlap, 1951. P. 243.

7. Huizinga, Johan. *Homo Ludens, A Study of the Play Element in Culture*. Boston: Beacon Press, 1955.

8. Myrdal, Gunnar. *An American Dilemma*. New York: Harper & Brothers, 1944. P. 760.

9. Parsons, Talcott. "Age and Sex in the Social Structure," *Essays in Sociological Theory Pure and Applied*. Glencoe, Ill.: The Free Press, 1949. Pp. 220-21.

10. Thomas, William I. "The Problem of Personality in the Urban Environment," in Ernest W. Burgess (ed.), *The Urban Community*. Chicago: University of Chicago Press, 1926. Pp. 38-47.

11. Wirth, Louis. "Some Jewish Types of Personality," in Ernest W. Burgess (ed.), *The Urban Community*. Chicago: University of Chicago Press, 1926. P. 112.

e.

THE DISSOLUTION OF IDENTITIES

ERVING GOFFMAN

Characteristics of Total Institutions

SOCIAL ESTABLISHMENTS—institutions in the everyday sense of that term—are buildings or plants in which activity of a particular kind regularly goes on. In sociology we do not have an apt way of classifying them. Some, like Grand Central Station, are open to anyone who is decently behaved. Others, like the Union League Club of New York or the laboratories at Los Alamos, are felt to be somewhat "snippy" about the matter of whom they let in. Some institutions, like shops and post offices, are the locus of a continuous flow of service relationships. Others, like homes and factories, provide a less changing set of persons with whom the member can relate. Some institutions provide the place for what is felt to be the kind of pursuits from which the individual draws his social status, however enjoyable or lax these pursuits may be. Other institutions, in contrast, provide a home for associations in which membership is felt to be elective and unserious, calling for a contribution of time that is fitted in to more serious demands.

In this paper another category of institutions is recommended and claimed as a natural and fruitful one because its members appear to have so much in common—so much, in fact, that if you would learn about one of these institutions you would be well advised to look at the others. My own special purpose in examining these institutions is to find a natural frame of reference for studying the social experience of patients in mental hospitals. Whatever else psychiatry and medicine tell us, their happy way

Reprinted from *Symposium on Preventive and Social Psychiatry* (1957), pp. 43-84, by permission of the author and Walter Reed Army Institute of Research.

of sometimes viewing an insane asylum as if it were a treatment hospital does not help us very much in determining just what these places are and just what goes on in them.

Every institution captures something of the time and interest of its members and provides something of a world for them; in brief, every institution has encompassing tendencies. When we review the different institutions in our Western society we find a class of them which seems to be encompassing to a degree discontinuously greater than the ones next in line. Their encompassing or total character is symbolized by the barrier to social intercourse with the outside that is often built right into the physical plant: locked doors, high walls, barbed wire, cliffs and water, open terrain, and so forth. These I am calling total institutions, and it is their general characteristics I want to explore.[1] This exploration will be phrased as if securely based on findings, but will in fact be speculative.

The total institutions of our society can be listed for convenience in five rough groupings. *First*, there are institutions established to care for persons thought to be both incapable and harmless; these are the homes for the blind, the aged, the orphaned, and the indigent. *Second*, there are places established to care for persons thought to be at once incapable of looking after themselves and a threat to the community, albeit an unintended one: TB sanitoriums, mental hospitals, and leprosoriums. *Third*, another type of total institution is organized to protect the community against what are thought to be intentional dangers to it; here the welfare of the persons thus sequestered is not the immediate issue. Examples are: Jails, penitentiaries, POW camps, and concentration camps. *Fourth*, we find institutions purportedly established the better to pursue some technical task and justifying themselves only on these instrumental grounds: Army barracks, shops, boarding schools, work camps, colonial compounds, large mansions from the point of view of those who live in the servants' quarters, and so forth. *Finally*, there are those establishments designed as retreats from the world or as training stations for the religious: Abbeys, monasteries, convents, and other cloisters. This sublisting of total institutions is neither neat nor exhaustive, but the listing itself provides an empirical starting point for a purely denotative definition of the category. By anchoring the initial definition of total institutions in this way, I hope to be able to discuss the general characteristics of the type without becoming tautological.

Before attempting to extract a general profile from this list of establishments, one conceptual peculiarity must be mentioned. None of the elements I will extract seems entirely exclusive to total institutions, and none seems shared by every one of them. What is shared and unique about total institutions is that each exhibits many items in this family of attributes to an intense degree. In speaking of "common characteristics," then, I will be using this phrase in a weakened, but I think logically defensible, way.

A basic social arrangement in modern society is that we tend to sleep, play, and work in different places, in each case with a different set of coparticipants, under a different authority, and without an over-all rational plan. The central feature of total institutions can be described as a breakdown of the kinds of barriers ordinarily separating these three spheres of life. *First*, all aspects of life are conducted in the same place and under the same single authority. *Second*, each phase of the member's daily activity will be carried out in the immediate company of a large batch of others, all of whom are treated alike and required to do the same thing together. *Third*, all phases of the day's activities are tightly scheduled, with one activity leading at a prearranged time into the next, the whole circle of activities being imposed from above through a system of explicit formal rulings and a body of officials. *Finally*, the contents of the various enforced activities are brought together as parts of a single over-all rational plan purportedly designed to fulfill the official aims of the institution.

Individually, these totalistic features are found, of course, in places other than total institutions. Increasingly, for example, our large commercial, industrial, and educational establishments provide cafeterias, minor services, and off-hour recreation for their members. But while this is a tendency in the direction of total institutions, these extended facilities remain voluntary in many particulars of their use, and special care is taken to see that the ordinary line of authority does not extend to these situations. Similarly, housewives or farm families can find all their major spheres of life within the same fenced-in area, but these persons are not collectively regimented and do not march through the day's steps in the immediate company of a batch of similar others.

The handling of many human needs by the bureaucratic organization of whole blocks of people—whether or not this is a necessary or effective means of social organization in the circumstances—can be taken, then, as the key fact of total institutions. From this, certain important implications can be drawn.

Given the fact that blocks of people are caused to move in time, it becomes possible to use a relatively small number of supervisory personnel where the central relationship is not guidance or periodic checking, as in many employer-employee relations, but rather surveillance—a seeing to it that everyone does what he has been clearly told is required of him, and this under conditions where one person's infraction is likely to stand out in relief against the visible, constantly examined, compliance of the others. Which comes first, the large block of managed people or the small supervisory staff, is not here at issue; the point is that each is made for the other.

In total institutions, as we would then suspect, there is a basic split between a large class of individuals who live in and who have restricted contact with the world outside the walls, conveniently called *inmates*, and the small class that supervises them, conveniently called *staff*, who often operate on an eight-hour day and are socially integrated into the outside world.[2] Each grouping tends to conceive of members of the other in terms of narrow hostile stereotypes, staff often seeing inmates as bitter, secretive, and untrustworthy, while inmates often see staff as condescending, highhanded, and mean. Staff tends to feel superior and righteous; inmates tend, in some ways at least, to feel inferior, weak, blameworthy, and guilty.[3] Social mobility between the two strata is grossly restricted; social distance is typically great and often formally prescribed; even talk across the boundaries may be conducted in a special tone of voice.[4] These restrictions on contact presumably help to maintain the antagonistic stereotypes.[5] In any case, two different social and cultural worlds develop, tending to jog along beside each other, with points of official contact but little mutual penetration. It is important to add that the institutional plant and name comes to be identified by both staff and inmates as somehow belonging to staff, so that when either grouping refers to the views or interests of "the institution," by implication they are referring (as I shall also) to the views and concerns of the staff.

The staff-inmate split is one major implication of the central features of total institutions; a second one pertains to work. In the ordinary arrangements of living in our society, the authority of the workplace stops with the worker's receipt of a money payment; the spending of this in a domestic and recreational setting is at the discretion of the worker and is the mechanism through which the authority of the workplace is kept within strict bounds. However, to say that inmates in total institutions have their full day scheduled for them is to say that some version of all basic needs will have to be planned for, too. In other words, total institutions take over "responsibility" for the inmate and must guarantee to have everything that is defined as essential "layed on." It follows, then, that whatever incentive is given for work, this will not have the structural significance it has on the outside. Different attitudes and incentives regarding this central feature of our life will have to prevail.

Here, then, is one basic adjustment required of those who work in total institutions and of those who must induce these people to work. In some cases, no work or little is required, and inmates, untrained often in leisurely ways of life, suffer extremes of boredom. In other cases, some work is required but is carried on at an extremely slow pace, being geared into a system of minor, often ceremonial payments, as in the case of weekly tobacco ration and annual Christmas presents, which cause some mental patients to stay on their job. In some total institutions, such as logging camps and merchant ships, something of the usual relation to the world that money can buy is obtained through the practice of "forced saving"; all needs are organized by the institution, and payment is given only after a work season is over and the men leave the premises. And in some total institutions, of course, more than a full day's work is required and is induced not by reward, but by threat of dire punishment. In all such cases, the work-oriented individual may tend to become somewhat demoralized by the system.[6]

In addition to the fact that total institutions are incompatible with the basic work-payment structure of our society, it must be seen that these establishments are also incompatible with another crucial element of our society, the family. The family is sometimes contrasted to solitary living, but in fact the more pertinent contrast to family life might be with batch living. For it seems that those who eat and sleep at work, with a group of fellow workers, can hardly sustain a meaningful domestic existence.[7] Correspondingly, the extent to which a staff retains its integration in the outside community and escapes the encompassing tendencies of total institutions is often linked up with the maintenance of a family off the grounds.

Whether a particular total institution acts as a good or bad force in civil society, force it may well have, and this will depend on the suppression of a whole circle of actual or potential households. Conversely, the formation of households provides a structural guarantee that total institutions will not arise. The incompatibility between these two forms of social organization should tell us, then, something about the wider social functions of them both.

Total institutions, then, are social hybrids, part residential community, part formal organization, and therein lies their special sociological interest. There are other reasons, alas, for being interested in them, too. These establishments are the forcing houses for changing persons in our society. Each is a natural experiment, typically harsh, on what can be done to the self.

Having suggested some of the key features of total institutions, we can move on now to consider them from the special perspectives that seem natural to take. I will consider the inmate world, then the staff world, and then something about contacts between the two.

The Inmate World

It is characteristic of inmates that they come to the institution as members, already full-fledged, of a *home world*, that is, a way of life and a round of activities taken for granted up to the point of admission to the institution.[8] It is useful to look at this culture that the recruit brings with him to the institution's door—his *presenting culture,* to modify a psychiatric phrase—in terms especially designed to highlight what it is the total institution will do to him. Whatever the stability of his personal organization, we can assume it was part of a wider supporting framework lodged in his current social environment, a round of experience that somewhat confirms a conception of self that is somewhat acceptable to him and a set of defensive maneuvers exercisable at his own discretion as a means of coping with conflicts, discreditings and failures.

Now it appears that total institutions do not substitute their own unique culture for something already formed. We do not deal with acculturation or assimilation but with something more restricted than these. In a sense, total institutions do not look for cultural victory. They effectively create and sustain a particular kind of tension between the home world and the institutional world and use this persistent tension as strategic leverage in the management of men. The full meaning for the inmate of being "in" or "on the inside" does not exist apart from the special meaning to him of "getting out" or "getting on the outside."

The recruit comes into the institution with a self and with attachments to supports which had allowed this self to survive. Upon entrance, he is immediately stripped of his wonted supports, and his self is systematically, if often unintentionally, mortified. In the accurate language of some of our oldest total institutions, he is led into a series of abasements, degradations, humiliations, and profanations of self. He begins, in other words, some radical shifts in his *moral career,* a career laying out the progressive changes that occur in the beliefs that he has concerning himself and significant others.

The *stripping processes* through which *mortification of the self* occurs are fairly standard in our total institutions. Personal identity equipment is removed, as well as other possessions with which the inmate may have identified himself, there typically being a system of nonaccessible storage from which the inmate can only reobtain his effects should he leave the institution.[9] As a substitute for what has been taken away, institutional issue is provided, but this will be the same for large categories of inmates and will be regularly repossessed by the institution. In brief, standardized defacement will occur. In addition, ego-invested separateness from fellow inmates is significantly diminished in many areas of activity, and tasks are prescribed that are *infra dignitatem.* Family, occupational, and educational career lines are chopped off, and a stigmatized status is submitted. Sources of fantasy materials which had meant momentary releases from stress in the home world are denied. Areas of autonomous decision are eliminated through the process of collective scheduling of daily activity. Many channels of communication with the outside are restricted or closed off completely. Verbal discreditings occur in many forms as a matter of course. Expressive signs of respect for the staff are coercively and continuously demanded.[10] And the effect of each of these conditions is multiplied by having to witness the mortification of one's fellow inmates.[11]

We must expect to find different official reasons given for these assaults upon the self. In mental hospitals there is the matter of protecting the patient from himself and from other patients. In jails there is the issue of "security" and frank punishment. In religious institutions we may find sociologically sophisticated theories about the soul's need for purification and penance through disciplining of the flesh. What all of these rationales share is the extent to which they are merely rationalizations, for the underlying force in many cases is unwittingly generated by efforts to manage the daily activity of a large number of persons in a small space with a small expenditure of resources.

In the background of the sociological stripping process, we find a characteristic authority system with three distinctive elements, each basic to total institutions.

First, to a degree, authority is of the *echelon* kind. Any member of the staff class has certain rights to discipline any member of the inmate class. This arrangement, it may be noted, is similar to the one which gives any adult in some small American towns certain rights to correct and demand small services from any child not in the immediate presence of his parents. In our society, the adult himself, however, is typically under the authority of a *single* immediate superior in connection with his work or under authority of one spouse in connection with domestic duties. The only echelon authority he must face—the police—typically are neither constantly nor relevantly present, except perhaps in the case of traffic-law enforcement.

Second, the authority of corrective sanctions is directed to a great multitude of items of conduct of the kind that are constantly occurring and constantly coming up for judgment;[12] in brief, authority is directed to matters of dress, deportment, social intercourse, manners, and the like. In prisons these regulations regarding situational proprieties may even extend to a point where silence during mealtime is enforced, while in some convents explicit demands may be made concerning the custody of the eyes during prayer.

The third feature of authority in total institutions is that misbehaviors in one sphere of life are held against one's standing in other spheres. Thus, an individual who fails to participate with proper enthusiasm in sports may be brought to the attention of the person who determines where he will sleep and what kind of work task will be accorded to him.

When we combine these three aspects of authority in total institutions, we see that the inmate cannot easily escape from the press of judgmental officials and from the enveloping tissue of constraint. The system of authority undermines the basis for control that adults in our society expect to exert over their interpersonal environment and may produce the terror of feeling that one is being radically demoted in the age-grading system. On the outside, rules are sufficiently lax and the individual sufficiently agreeable to required self-discipline to insure that others will rarely have cause for pouncing on him. He need not constantly look over his shoulder to see if criticism and other sanctions are coming. On the inside, however, rulings are abundant, novel, and closely enforced so that, quite characteristically, inmates live with chronic anxiety about breaking the rules and chronic worry about the consequences of breaking them. The desire to "stay out of trouble" in a total institution is likely to require persistent conscious effort and may lead the inmate to abjure certain levels of sociability with his fellows in order to avoid the incidents that may occur in these circumstances.[13]

It should be noted finally that the mortifications to be suffered by the inmate may be purposely brought home to him in an exaggerated way during the first few days after entrance, in a form of initiation that has been called *the welcome*. Both staff and fellow inmates may go out of their way to give the neophyte a clear notion of where he stands.[14] As part of this *rite de passage*, he may find himself called by a term such as "fish," "swab," etc., through which older inmates tell him that he is not only merely an inmate but that even within this lowly group he has a low status.

While the process of mortification is in progress, the inmate begins to receive formal and informal instruction in what will here be called the *privilege system*. Insofar as the inmate's self has been unsettled a little by the stripping action of the institution, it is largely around this framework that pressures are exerted, making for a reorganization of self. Three basic elements of the system may be mentioned.

First, there are the *house rules*, a relatively explicit and formal set of prescriptions and proscriptions which lay out the main requirements of inmate conduct. These regulations spell out the austere round of life in which the inmate will operate. Thus, the admission procedures through which the recruit is initially stripped of his self-supporting context can be seen as the institution's way of getting him in the position to start living by the house rules.

Second, against the stark background, a small number of clearly defined *rewards or privileges* are held out in exchange for obedience to staff in action and spirit. It is important to see that these potential gratifications are not unique to the institution but rather are ones carved out of the flow of support that the inmate previously had quite taken for granted. On the outside, for example, the inmate was likely to be able to unthinkingly exercise autonomy by deciding how much sugar and milk he wanted in his coffee, if any, or when to light up a cigarette; on the inside, this right may become quite problematic and a matter of a great deal of conscious concern. Held up to the inmate as possibilities, these few recapturings seem to have a reintegrative effect, re-establishing relationships with the whole lost world and assuaging withdrawal symptoms from it and from one's lost self.

The inmate's run of attention, then, especially at first, comes to be fixated on these supplies and obsessed with them. In the most fanatic way, he can spend the day in devoted thoughts concerning the possibility of acquiring these gratifications or the approach of the hour at which they are scheduled to be granted.[15] The building of a world around these minor privileges is perhaps the most important feature of inmate culture and yet is something that cannot easily be appreciated by an outsider, even one who has lived through the experience himself. This situation sometimes leads to generous sharing and almost always to a willingness to beg for things such as cigarettes, candy, and newspapers. It will be understandable, then, that a constant feature of inmate discussion is the *release binge fantasy*, namely, recitals of what one will do during leave or upon release from the institution.

House rules and privileges provide the functional requirements of the third element in the privilege system: *punishments*. These are designated as the consequence of breaking the rules. One set of these punishments consists of the temporary or permanent withdrawal of privileges or abrogation of the right to try to earn them. In general, the punishments meted out in total institutions are of an order more severe than anything encountered by the inmate in his home world. An institutional arrangement which causes a small number of easily controlled privileges to have a massive significance is the same arrangement which lends a terrible significance to their withdrawal.

There are some special features of the privilege system which should be noted.

First, punishments and privileges are themselves modes of organization peculiar to total institutions. Whatever their severity, punishments are largely known in the inmate's home world as something applied to animals and children. For adults this conditioning, behavioristic model is actually not widely applied, since failure to maintain required standards typically leads to indirect disadvantageous consequences and not to specific immediate punishment at all.[16] And privileges, it should be emphasized, are not the same as prerequisites, indulgences, or values, but merely the absence of deprivations one ordinarily expects one would not have to sustain. The very notions, then, of punishments and privileges are not ones that are cut from civilian cloth.

Second, it is important to see that the question of release from the total institution is elaborated into the privilege system. Some acts will become known as ones that mean an increase or no decrease in length of stay, while others become known as means for lessening the sentence.

Third, we should also note that punishments and privileges come to be geared into a residential work system. Places to work and places to sleep become clearly defined as places where certain kinds and levels of privilege obtain, and inmates are shifted very rapidly and visibly from one place to another as the mechanisms for giving them the punishment or privilege their co-operativeness has warranted. The inmates are moved, the system is not.

This, then, is the privilege system: a relatively few components put together with some rational intent and clearly proclaimed to the participants. The over-all consequence is that co-operativeness is obtained from persons who often have cause to be unco-operative. A typical illustration of this model universe may be taken from a recent study[17] of a State mental hospital:

> The authority of the attendant in the person of his control system is backed up by both positive and negative power. This power is an essential element in his control of the ward. He can give the patient privileges, and he can punish the patient. The privileges consist of having the best job, better rooms and beds, minor luxuries like coffee on the ward, a little more privacy than the average patient, going outside the ward without supervision, having more access than the average patient to the attendant's companionship or to professional personnel like the physicians, and enjoying such intangible but vital things as being treated with personal kindness and respect.
>
> The punishments which can be applied by the ward attendant are suspension of all privileges, psychological mistreatment, locking up the patient in an isolated room, denial or distortion of access to the professional personnel, theatening to put or putting the patient on the list for electroshock therapy, transfer of the patient to undesirable wards, and regular assignment of the patient to unpleasant tasks such as cleaning up after the soilers.

Immediately associated with the privilege system we find some standard social processes important in the life of total institutions.

We find that an *institutional lingo* develops through which inmates express the events that are crucial in their particular world. Staff too, especially its lower levels, will know this language, using it when talking to inmates, while reverting to more standardized speech when talking to superiors and outsiders. Related to this special argot, inmates will possess knowledge of the various ranks and officials, an accumulation of lore about the establishment, and some comparative information about life in other similar total institutions.

Also found among staff and inmates will be a clear awareness of the phenomenon of *messing up,* so called in mental hospitals, prisons, and barracks. This involves a complex process of engaging in forbidden activity, getting caught doing so, and receiving something like the full punishment accorded this. An alteration in privilege status is usually implied and is categorized by a phrase such as "getting busted." Typical infractions which can eventuate in messing up are: fights, drunkenness, attempted suicide, failure at examinations, gambling, insubordination, homosexuality, improper taking of leave, and participation in collective riots. While these punished infractions are typically ascribed to the offender's cussedness, villainy, or "sickness," they do in fact constitute a vocabulary of institutionalized actions, limited in such a way that the same messing up may occur for quite different reasons. Informally, inmates and staff may understand, for example, that a given messing up is a way for inmates to show resentment against a current situation felt to be unjust in terms of the informal agreements between staff and inmates,[18] or a way of postponing release without having to admit to one's fellow inmates that one really does not want to go.[19]

In total institutions there will also be a system of what might be called *secondary adjustments*, namely, techniques which do not directly challenge staff management but which allow inmates to obtain disallowed satisfactions or allowed ones by disallowed means. These practices are variously referred to as: the angles, knowing the ropes, conniving, gimmicks, deals, ins, etc. Such adaptations apparently reach their finest flower in prisons, but of course other total institutions are overrun with them too.[20] It seems apparent that an important aspect of secondary adjustments is that they provide the inmate with some evidence that he is still, as it were, his own man and still has some protective distance, under his own control, between himself and the institution. In some cases, then, a secondary adjustment becomes almost a kind of lodgment for the self, a churinga in which the soul is felt to reside.[21]

The occurrence of secondary adjustments correctly allows us to assume that the inmate group will have some kind of a *code* and some means of informal social control evolved to prevent one inmate from informing staff about the secondary adjustments of another. On the same grounds we can expect that one dimension of social typing among inmates will turn upon this question of security, leading to persons defined as "squealers," "finks," or "stoolies" on one hand, and persons defined as "right guys" on the other.[22] It should be added that where new inmates can play a role in the system of secondary adjustments, as in providing new faction members or new sexual objects, then their "welcome" may indeed be a sequence of initial indulgences and enticements, instead of exaggerated deprivations.[23] Because of secondary adjustments we also find *kitchen strata*, namely, a kind of rudimentary, largely informal, stratification of inmates on the basis of each one's differential access to disposable illicit commodities; so also we find social typing to designate the powerful persons in the informal market system.[24]

While the privilege system provides the chief framework within which reassembly of the self takes place, other factors characteristically lead by different routes in the same general direction. Relief from economic and social responsibilities—much touted as part of the therapy in mental hospitals—is one, although in many cases it would seem that the disorganizing effect of this moratorium is more significant than its organizing effect. More important as a reorganizing influence is the *fraternalization process*, namely, the process through which socially distant persons find themselves developing mutual support and common *counter-mores* in opposition to a system that has forced them into intimacy and into a single, equalitarian community of fate.[25] It seems that the new recruit frequently starts out with something like the staff's popular misconceptions of the character of the inmates and then comes to find that most of his fellows have all the properties of ordinary decent human beings and that the stereotypes associated with their condition or offense are not a reasonable ground for judgment of inmates.[26]

If the inmates are persons who are accused by staff and society of having committed some kind of a crime against society, then the new inmate, even though sometimes in fact quite guiltless, may come to share the guilty feelings of his fellows and, thereafter, their well-elaborated defenses against these feelings. A sense of common injustice and a sense of bitterness against the outside world tends to develop, marking an important movement in the inmate's moral career. This response to felt guilt and massive deprivation is most clearly illustrated perhaps in prison life:[27]

> By their reasoning, after an offender has been subjected to unfair or excessive punishment and treatment more degrading than that prescribed by law, he comes to justify his act which he could not have justified when he committed it. He decides to "get even" for his unjust treatment in prison and takes reprisals through further crime at the first opportunity. *With that decision he becomes a criminal.*

A more general statement[28] may be taken from two other students of the same kind of total institution:

> In many ways, the inmate social system may be viewed as providing a way of life which enables the inmates to avoid the devastating psychological effects of internalizing and converting social rejection into self rejection. In effect, it permits the inmate to reject his rejectors rather than himself.

The mortifying processes that have been discussed and the privilege system represent the conditions that the inmate must adapt to in some way, but however pressing, these conditions allow for different ways of meeting them. We find, in fact, that the same inmate will employ different lines of adaptation or tacks at different phases in his moral career and may even fluctuate between different tacks at the same time.

First, there is the process of *situational withdrawal*. The inmate withdraws apparent attention from everything except events immediately around his body and sees these in a perspective not employed by others present. This drastic curtailment of involvement in interactional events is best known, of course, in mental hospitals, under the title of "regression." Aspects of "prison psychosis" or "stir simpleness" represent the same adjustment, as do some forms of "acute depersonalization" described in concentration camps. I do not think it is known whether this line of adaptation forms a single continuum of varying degrees of withdrawal or whether there are standard discontinuous plateaus of disinvolvement. It does seem to be the case, however, that, given the pressures apparently required to dislodge an inmate from this status, as well as the currently limited facilities for doing so, we frequently find here, effectively speaking, an irreversible line of adaptation.

Second, there is the *rebellious line*. The inmate intentionally challenges the institution by flagrantly refusing to co-operate with staff in almost any way.[29] The result is a constantly communicated intransigency and sometimes high rebel-morale. Most large mental hospitals, for example, seem to have wards where this spirit strongly prevails. Interestingly enough, there are many circumstances in which sustained rejection of a total institution requires sustained orientation to its formal organization and hence, paradoxically, a deep kind of commitment to the establishment. Similarly, when total institutions take the line (as they sometimes do in the case of mental hospitals prescribing lobotomy[30] or army barracks prescribing the stockade) that the recalcitrant inmate must be broken, then, in their way, they must show as much special devotion to the rebel as he has shown to them. It should be added, finally, that while prisoners of war have been known staunchly to take a rebellious stance throughout their incarceration, this stance is typically a temporary and initial phase of reaction, emerging from this to situational withdrawal or some other line of adaptation.

Third, another standard alignment in the institutional world takes the form of a kind of *colonization*. The sampling of the outside world provided by the establishment is taken by the inmate as the whole, and a stable, relatively contented existence is built up out of the maximum satisfactions procurable within the institution.[31] Experience of the outside world is used as a point of reference to demonstrate the desirability of life on the inside; and the usual tension between the two worlds collapses, thwarting the social arrangements based upon this felt discrepancy. Characteristically, the individual who too obviously takes this line may be accused by his fellow inmates of "having found a home" or of "never having had it so good." Staff itself may become vaguely embarrassed by this use that is being made of the institution, sensing that the benign possibilities in the situation are somehow being misused. Colonizers themselves may feel obliged to deny their satisfaction with the institution, if only in the interest of sustaining the counter-mores supporting inmate solidarity. They may find it necessary to mess up just prior to their slated discharge, thereby allowing themselves to present involuntary reasons for continued incarceration. It should be incidentally noted that any humanistic effort to make life in total institutions more bearable must face the possibility that doing so may increase the attractiveness and likelihood of colonization.

Fourth, one mode of adaptation to the setting of a total institution is that of *conversion.* The inmate appears to take over completely the official or staff view of himself and tries to act out the role of the perfect inmate. While the colonized inmate builds as much of a free community as possible for himself by using the limited facilities available, the convert takes a more disciplined, moralistic, monochromatic line, presenting himself as someone whose institutional enthusiasm is always at the disposal of the staff. In Chinese POW camps, we find Americans who became "pros" and fully espoused the Communist view of the world.[32] In army barracks there are enlisted men who give the impression that they are always "sucking around" and always "bucking for promotion." In prison there are "square johns." In German concentration camps, longtime prisoners sometimes came to adapt the vocabulary, recreation, posture, expressions of aggression, and clothing style of the Gestapo, executing their role of straw-boss with military strictness.[33] Some mental hospitals have the distinction of providing two quite different conversion possibilities—one for the new admission who can see the light after an appropriate struggle and adapt the psychiatric view of himself, and another for the chronic ward patient who adopts the manner and dress of attendants while helping them to manage the other ward patients with a stringency excelling that of the attendants themselves.

Here, it should be noted, is a significant way in which total institutions differ. Many, like progressive mental hospitals, merchant ships, TB sanitariums and brainwashing camps, offer the inmate an opportunity to live up to a model of conduct that is at once ideal and staff-sponsored—a model felt by its advocates to be in the supreme interests of the very persons to whom it is applied. Other total institutions, like some concentration camps and some prisons, do not officially sponsor an ideal that the inmate is expected to incorporate as a means of judging himself.

While the alignments that have been mentioned represent coherent courses to pursue, few inmates, it seems, carry these pursuits very far. In most total institutions, what we seem to find is that most inmates take the tack of what they call *playing it cool.* This involves a somewhat opportunistic combination of secondary adjustments, conversion, colonization, and loyalty to the inmate group, so that in the particular circumstances the inmate will have a maximum chance of eventually getting out physically and psychically undamaged.[34] Typically, the inmate will support the counter-mores when with fellow inmates and be silent to them on how tractably he acts when alone in the presence of staff.[35] Inmates taking this line tend to subordinate contacts with their fellows to the higher claim of "keeping out of trouble." They tend to volunteer for nothing, and they may even learn to cut their ties to the outside world sufficiently to give cultural reality to the world inside but not enough to lead to colonization.

I have suggested some of the lines of adaptation that inmates can take to the pressures that play in total institutions. Each represents a way of managing the tension between the home world and the institutional world. However, there are circumstances in which the home world of the inmate was such, in fact, as to *immunize* him against the bleak world on the inside, and for such persons no particular scheme of adaptation need be carried very far. Thus, some lower-class mental hospital patients who have lived all their previous life in orphanages, reformatories and jails, tend to see the hospital as just another total institution to which it is possible to apply the adaptive techniques learned and perfected in other total institutions. "Playing it cool" represents for such persons, not a shift in their moral career, but an alignment that is already second nature.

The professional criminal element in the early periods of German concentration camps displayed something of the same immunity to their surroundings or even found new satisfactions through fraternization with middle-class political prisoners.[36] Similarly, Shetland youths recruited into the British merchant marine are not apparently threatened much by the cramped arduous life on board, because island life is even more stunted; they make uncomplaining sailors because from their point of view they have nothing much to complain about. Strong religious and political convictions may also serve perhaps to immunize the true believer against the assaults of a total institution, and even a failure to speak the language of the staff may cause the staff to give up its efforts at reformation, allowing the nonspeaker immunity to certain pressures.[37]

A note should be added here concerning some of the more dominant themes of inmate culture.

First, in the inmate group of many total institutions there is a strong feeling that time spent in the establishment is time wasted or destroyed or taken from one's life; it is time that must be written off. It is something that must be "done" or "marked" or "put in" or "built" or "pulled." (Thus, in prisons and mental hospitals a general statement of how well one is adapting to the institution may be phrased in terms of how one is doing time, whether easily or hard.[38]) As such, this time is something that its doers have bracketed off for constant conscious consideration in a way not quite found on the outside. And as a result, the inmate tends to feel that for the duration of his required stay—his sentence—he has been totally exiled from living.[39] It is in this context that we can appreciate something of the demoralizing influence of an indefinite sentence or a very long one. We should also note that however hard the conditions of life may become in total institutions, harshness alone cannot account for this quality of life wasted. Rather we must look to the social disconnections caused by entrance and to the usual failure to acquire within the institution gains that can be transferred to outside life—gains such as money earned, or marital relations formed, or certified training received.[40]

Second, it seems that in many total institutions a peculiar kind and level of self-concern is engendered. The low position of inmates relative to their station on the outside, as established initially through the mortifying processes, seems to make for a milieu of personal failure and a round of life in which one's fall from grace is continuously pressed home. In response, the inmate tends to develop a story, a line, a sad tale—a kind of lamentation and apologia—which he constantly tells to his fellows as a means of creditably accounting for his present low estate. While staff constantly discredit these lines, inmate audiences tend to employ tact,[41] suppressing at least some of the disbelief and boredom engendered by these recitations. In consequence, the inmate's own self may become even more of a focus for his conversation that it does on the outside.

Perhaps the high level of ruminative self-concern found among inmates in total institutions is a way of handling the sense of wasted time that prevails in these places. If so, then perhaps another interesting aspect of inmate culture can be related to the same factor. I refer here to the fact that in total institutions we characteristically find a premium placed on what might be called *removal activities*, namely, voluntary unserious pursuits which are sufficiently engrossing and exciting to lift the participant out of himself, making him oblivious for the time to his actual situation. If the ordinary activities in total institutions can be said to torture time, these activities mercifully kill it.

Some removal activities are collective, such as ball games, woodwork, lectures, choral singing, and card playing; some are individual but rely on public materials, as in the case of reading, solitary TV watching, etc.[42] No doubt, private fantasy ought to be included too. Some of these activities may be officially sponsored by staff; and some, not officially sponsored, may constitute secondary adjustments. In any case, there seems to be no total institution which cannot be seen as a kind of Dead Sea in which appear little islands of vivid, enrapturing activity.

In this discussion of the inmate world, I have commented on the mortification processes, the reorganizing influences, the lines of response taken by inmates under these circumstances, and the cultural milieu that develops. A concluding word must be added about the long-range consequences of membership.

Total institutions frequently claim to be concerned with rehabilitation, that is, with resetting the inmate's self-regulatory mechanisms so that he will maintain the standards of the establishment of his own accord after he leaves the setting.[43] In fact, it seems this claim is seldom realized and even when permanent alteration occurs, these changes are often not of the kind intended by the staff. With the possible exception presented by the great resocialization efficiency of religious institutions, neither the stripping processes nor the reorganizing ones seem to have a lasting effect.[44] No doubt the availability of secondary adjustments helps to account for this, as do the presence of counter-mores and the tendency for inmates to combine all strategies and "play it cool." In any case, it seems that shortly after release, the ex-inmate will have forgotten a great deal of what life was like on the inside and will have once again begun to take for granted the privileges around which life in the institution was organized. The sense of injustice, bitterness, and alienation, so typically engendered by the inmate's experience and so definitely marking a stage in his moral career, seems to weaken upon graduation, even in those cases where a permanent stigma has resulted.

But what the ex-inmate does retain of his institutional experience tells us important things about total institutions. Often entrance will mean for the recruit that he has taken on what might be called a *proactive status*. Not only is his relative social position within the walls radically different from what it was on the outside, but, as he comes to learn, if and when he gets out, his social position on the outside will never again be quite what it was prior to entrance. Where the proactive status is a relatively favorable one, as it is for those who graduate from officers' training schools, elite boarding schools, ranking monastaries, etc., then the permanent alteration will be favorable, and jubilant official reunions announcing pride in one's "school" can be expected. When, as seems usually the case, the proactive status is unfavorable, as it is for those in prisons or mental hospitals, we popularly employ the term "stigmatization" and expect that the ex-inmate may make an effort to conceal his past and try to "pass."[45]

The Staff World

Most total institutions, most of the time, seem to function merely as storage dumps for inmates, but as previously suggested, they usually present themselves to the public as rational organizations designed consciously, through and through, as effective machines for producing a few officially avowed and officially approved ends. It was also suggested that one frequent official objective is the reformation of inmates in the direction of some ideal standard. This contradiction, then, between what the institution does and what its officials must say that it does, forms the central context of the staff's daily activity.

Within this context, perhaps the first thing to say about staff is that their work, and hence their world, has uniquely to do with people. This people-work is not quite like personnel work nor the work of those involved in service relationships. Staffs, after all, have objects and products to work upon, not relationships, but these objects and products are people.

As material upon which to work, people involve some of the considerations characteristic of inanimate objects. Just as an article being processed through an industrial plant must be followed by a paper shadow showing what has been done by whom, what is to be done, and who last had responsibility for it, so human objects moving, say, through a mental hospital system must be followed by a chain of informative receipts detailing what has been done to and by the patient and who has most recent responsibility for him. In his career from admission suite to burial plot, many different kinds of staff will add their official note to his case file as he temporarily passes under their jurisdiction, and long after he has died physically his marked remains will survive as an actionable entity in the hospital's bureaucratic system. Even the presence or absence of a particular patient at a given meal or for a given night may have to be recorded so that cost-accounting can be maintained and appropriate adjustments rendered in billing.

Other similarities between people-work and object-work are obvious. Just as tin mines or paint factories or chemical plants may involve special work hazards for employees, so (staffs believe at least) there are special dangers to some kinds of people-work. In mental hospitals, staffs believe that patients may strike out "for no reason" and injure an official. In army prisons, staff "is ever haunted by the spectre of riot, revolt or mutiny. . . ."[46] In TB sanitariums and in leprosoriums, staff feel they are being specially exposed to dangerous diseases.

While these similarities between people- and object-work exist, it is, I think, the unique aspects of people as material to work upon that we must look to for the crucial determinants of the work-world of staff.

Given the physiological characteristics of the human organism, it is obvious that certain requirements must be met if any continued use is to be made of people. But this, of course, is the case with inanimate objects, too; the temperature of any storehouse must be regulated, regardless of whether people or things are stored. However, persons are almost always considered to be ends in themselves, as reflected in the broad moral principles of a total institution's environing society. Almost always, then, we find that some technically unnecessary standards of handling must be maintained with human materials. This maintenance of what we can call humane standards comes to be defined as one part of the "responsibility" of the institution and presumably is one of the things the institution guarantees the inmate in exchange for his liberty. Thus, prison officials are obliged to thwart suicidal efforts of the prisoner and to give him full medical attention even though in some cases this may require postponement of his date of execution. Something similar has been reported in German concentration camps, where inmates were sometimes given medical attention to tidy them up into a healthier shape for the gas chamber.

A second special contingency in the work-world of staff is the fact that inmates typically have statuses and relationships in the outside world that must be taken into consideration. (This consideration, of course, is related to the previously mentioned fact that the institution must respect some of the rights of inmates *qua* persons.) Even in the case of the committed mental patient whose civil rights are largely taken from him, a tremendous amount of mere paper work will be involved. Of course, the rights that are denied a mental patient are usually transferred to a relation, to a committee, or to the superintendent of the hospital itself, who then becomes the legal person whose authorization must be obtained for many matters. Many issues originating outside the institution will arise: Social Security benefits, income taxes, upkeep of properties, insurance payments, old age pension, stock dividends, dental bills, legal obligations incurred prior to commitment, permission to release psychiatric case records to insurance companies or attorneys, permission for special visits from persons other than next of kin, etc. All of these issues have to be dealt with by the institution, even if only to pass the decisions on to those legally empowered to make them.

It should be noted that staff is reminded of its obligations in these matters of standards and rights, not only by its own internal superordinates, by various watchdog agencies in the wider society, and by the material itself,[47] but also by persons on the outside who have kin ties to inmates. The latter group presents a special problem because, while inmates can be educated about the price they will pay for making demands on their own behalf, relations receive less tutoring in this regard and rush in with requests for inmates that inmates would blush to make for themselves.[48]

The multiplicity of ways in which inmates must be considered ends in themselves and the multiplicity of inmates themselves forces upon staff some of the classic dilemmas that must be faced by those who govern men. Since a total institution functions somewhat as a State, its staff must suffer somewhat from the tribulations that beset governors.

In the case of any single inmate, the assurance that certain standards will be maintained in his own interests may require sacrifice of other standards, and implied in this is a difficult weighing of ends. For example, if a suicidal inmate is to be kept alive, staff may feel it necessary to keep him under constant deprivatizing surveillance or even tied to a chair in a small locked room. If a mental patient is to be kept from tearing at grossly irritated sores and repeating time and again a cycle of curing and disorder, staff may feel it necessary to curtail the freedom of his hands. Another patient who refuses to eat may have to be humiliated by forced feeding. If inmates of TB sanitariums are to be given an opportunity to recover, it will be necessary to curtail freedom of recreation.[49]

The standards of treatment that one inmate has a right to expect may conflict, of course, with the standards desired by another, giving rise to another set of governmental problems. Thus, in mental hospitals, if the grounds gate is to be kept open out of respect for those with town parole, then some other patients who otherwise could have been trusted on the grounds may have to be kept on locked wards. And if a canteen and mailbox are to be freely available to those on the grounds, then patients on a strict diet or those who write threatening and obscene letters will have to be denied liberty on the grounds.

The obligation of staff to maintain certain humane standards of treatment for inmates represents problems in itself, as suggested above, but a further set of characteristic problems is found in the constant conflict between humane standards on one hand and institutional efficiency on the other. I will cite only one main example. The personal possessions of an individual are an important part of the materials out of which he builds a self, but as an inmate, the ease with which he can be managed by staff is likely to increase with the degree to which he is dispossessed. Thus, the remarkable efficiency with which a mental hospital ward can adjust to a daily shift in number of resident patients is related to the fact that the comers and leavers do not come or leave with any properties but themselves and do not have any right to choose where they will be located. Further, the efficiency with which the clothes of these patients can be kept clean and fresh is related to the fact that everyone's soiled clothing can be indiscriminately placed in one bundle, and laundered clothing can be redistributed not according to ownership but according to rough size. Similarly, the quickest assurance that patients going on the grounds will be warmly dressed is to march them in file past a pile of the ward's allotment of coats, requiring them for the same purposes of health to throw off these collectivized garments on returning to the ward.

Just as personal possessions may interfere with the smooth running of an institutional operation and be removed for this reason, so parts of the body itself may conflict with efficient management and the conflict resolved in favor of efficiency. If the heads of inmates are to be kept clean and the possessor easily identified, then a complete head shave is efficacious, regardless of the damage this does to appearance. On similar grounds, some mental hospitals have found it useful to extract the teeth of "biters," give hysterectomies to promiscuous female patients, and perform lobotomies on chronic fighters. Flogging on men-of-war as a form of punishment expressed the same conflict between organizational and humane interests:[50]

> One of the arguments advanced by officers of the Navy in favor of corporal punishment is this: it can be inflicted in a moment; it consumes no valuable time; and when the prisoner's shirt is put on, *that* is the last of it. Whereas, if another punishment were substituted, it would probably occasion a great waste of time and trouble, besides thereby begetting in the sailor an undue idea of his importance.

I have suggested that people-work differs from other kinds because of the tangle of statuses and relationships which each inmate brings with him to the institution and because of the humane standards that must be maintained with respect to him. Another difference occurs in cases where inmates have some rights to visit off the grounds, for then the mischief they may do in civil society becomes something for which the institution has some responsibility. Given this responsibility, it is understandable that total institutions tend not to view off-grounds leave favorably. Still another type of difference between people-work and other kinds, and perhaps the most important difference of all, is that by the exercise of threat, reward or persuasion human objects can be given instructions and relied upon to carry them out on their own. The span of time during which these objects can be trusted to carry out planned actions without supervision will vary of course a great deal, but, as the social organization of back wards in mental hospitals teaches us, even in the limiting case of catatonic schizophrenics, a considerable amount of such reliance is possible. Only the most complicated electronic equipment shares this capacity.

While human materials can never be as refractory as inanimate ones, their very capacity to perceive and to follow out the plans of staff insures that they can hinder the staff more effectively than inanimate objects can.

Inanimate objects cannot purposely and intelligently thwart our plans, regardless of the fact that we may momentarily react to them as if they had this capacity. Hence, in prison and on "better" wards of mental hospitals, guards have to be ready for organized efforts at escape and must constantly deal with attempts to bait them, "frame" them, and otherwise get them into trouble. This leads to a state of anxiety in the guard that is not alleviated by knowledge that the inmate may be acting thusly merely as a means of gaining self-respect or relieving boredom.[51] Even an old, weak, mental patient has tremendous power in this regard; for example, by the simple expedient of locking his thumbs in his trouser pockets he can remarkably frustrate the efforts of an attendant to undress him.

A third general way in which human materials are different from other kinds and hence present unique problems is that, however distant staff manages to stay from them, they can become objects of fellow-feeling and even affection. Always there is the danger that an inmate will appear human. If what are felt to be hardships must be inflicted on the inmate, then sympathetic staff will suffer. And on the other hand, if an inmate breaks a rule, staff's conceiving of him as a human being may increase their sense that injury has been done to their moral world. Expecting a "reasonable" response from a reasonable creature, staff may feel incensed, affronted, and challenged when this does not occur. Staff thus finds it must maintain face not only before those who examine the product of work but before these very products themselves.

The capacity of inmates to become objects of staff's sympathetic concern is linked to what might be called an involvement cycle sometimes recorded in total institutions. Starting at a point of social distance from inmates, a point from which massive deprivation and institutional trouble cannot easily be seen, the staff person finds he has no reason not to build up a warm involvement in some inmates. The involvement, however, brings the staff members into a position to be hurt by what inmates do and by what they suffer, and also brings him to a position from which he is likely to threaten the distant stand from inmates taken by his fellow members of the staff. In response, the sympathizing staff member may feel he has been "burnt" and retreat into paper-work, committee work or other staff-enclosed routine. Once removed from the dangers of inmate contact, he may gradually cease to feel he has reason to remain so, and thus the cycle of contact and withdrawal may be repeated again and again.

When we combine together the fact that staff is obliged to maintain certain standards of humane treatment for inmates and may come to view inmates as reasonable, responsible creatures who are fitting objects for emotional involvement, we have the background for some of the quite special difficulties of people-work. In mental hospitals, for example, there always seem to be some patients who dramatically act against their own obvious self-interest. They drink water they have themselves first polluted; they rush against the wall with their heads; they tear out their own sutures after a minor operation; they flush false teeth down the toilet, without which they cannot eat and which take months to obtain; or smash glasses, without which they cannot see. In an effort to frustrate these visibly self-destructive acts, staff may find itself forced to manhandle these patients. Staff then is forced to create an image of itself as harsh and coercive, just at the moment that it is attempting to prevent someone from doing to himself what no human being is expected to do to anyone. At such times it is extremely difficult for staff members to keep their own emotions in control, and understandably so.

The special requirements of people-work establish the day's job for staff, but this job must be carried out in a special moral climate. For the staff is charged with meeting the hostility and demands of the inmates, and what it has to meet the inmate with, in general, is the rational perspective espoused by the institution. It is the role of the staff to defend the institution in the name of its avowed rational aims—to the inmate as well as to outsiders of various kinds. Thus, when inmates are allowed to have incidental face-to-face contact with staff, the contact will often take the form of "gripes" or requests on the part of the inmate and of justification for prevailing restrictive treatment on the part of the staff. Such, for example, is the general structure of staff-patient interaction in mental hospitals. Further, the privileges and punishments meted out by staff will often be couched in a language that reflects the legitimated objectives of the institution, even though this may require that inmates or low-level members of staff translate these responses into the verbal language of the privilege system.[52]

Given the inmates over whom it has charge and the processing that must be done to these objects, staff tends to evolve what may be thought of as a *theory of human nature*. This verbalized perspective rationalizes the scene, provides a subtle means of maintaining social distance from inmates and a stereotyped view of them, and gives sanction to the treatment accorded them.[53] Typically, the theory covers the "good" and "bad" possibilities of inmate conduct, the forms that messing up take, and the instructional value of privileges and punishments. In army barracks, officers will have a theory about the relation between discipline and obedience under fire, about the qualities proper to men, about the "breaking point" of men, and about the difference between mental sickness and malingering. In prisons, we find currently an interesting conflict between the psychiatric and the moral-weakness theory of crime. In convents, we find theories about the way in which the spirit can be weak and strong, and the ways its defects can be combatted. Mental hospitals, it should be noted, are especially interesting in this connection because staff members pointedly establish themselves as specialists in the knowledge of human nature who must diagnose and prescribe on the basis of this philosophy. Hence, in the standard psychiatric textbooks there are chapters on "psychodynamics" and "psychopathology" which provide charmingly explicit formulations of the "nature" of human nature.[54]

Given the fact that the management of inmates is typically rationalized in terms of the ideal aims or functions of the establishment and that certain humane standards will form part of this ideal, we can expect that professionals ostensibly hired to service these functions will likely become dissatisfied, feeling that they are being used as "captives" to add professional sanction to the privilege system and that they cannot here properly practice their calling. And this seems to be a classic cry.[55] At the same time, the category of staff that must keep the institution going through continuous contact with inmates may feel that they too are being set a contradictory task, having to coerce inmates into obedience while at the same time giving the impression that humane standards are being maintained and that the rational goals of the institution are being realized.

Institutional Ceremonies

I have described total institutions from the point of view of inmates and from the point of view of the staff. Each of these two perspectives contains as one crucial element a role-image of the other grouping; but while this role-image of the other is held, it is seldom sympathetically taken, except perhaps on the part of those inmates, previously described, who take a trusty role and seriously "identify with the aggressor." When unusual intimacies and relationships do occur across the staff-inmate line, we know that involvement cycles may follow, and all kinds of awkward reverberations are likely to occur.[56]. Every total institution, however, seems to develop—whether spontaneously or by imitation—a set of institutionalized practices through which staff and inmates come together closely enough so that each may have an image of the other that is somewhat favorable and also be able to take the role sympathetically that this image suggests. Instead of differences between the two levels, we will then find that unity, solidarity and joint commitment to the institution are expressed.

In form, these institutionalized get-togethers are characterized by a release from the formalities and task orientation that govern inmate-staff contacts and by a softening of the usual chain of command. Often participation is relatively voluntary. Given the usual roles, then, these activities represent "role releases";[57] of course, given the pervasive effect of inmate-staff distance, any alteration in this breach in the direction of solidarity expressions would automatically represent a role-release. It is possible to speculate on the many functions of these comings-together, but the explanations so far suggested seem much less impressive than the singular way in which these practices keep cropping up in every kind of total institution and in what would seem to be the poorest possible soil. One is led to feel that there must be a very good reason for these practices even though none has yet been found.

One of the most universal forms of institutional ceremony occurs through the medium of what is sometimes called the *house organ*—typically a weekly newspaper or a monthly magazine. Usually all the contributors are recruited from within the inmate ranks, resulting in a kind of mock hierarchy of those so engaged, while supervision and censorship are provided by a member of the staff who is relatively congenial to inmates yet reliably loyal to his fellow officials.

Two kinds of material that appear in the house organ may be mentioned. *First,* there is "local news." This includes reports on all recent institutional ceremonies, as well as reference to "personal" events such as birthdays, promotions, trips, deaths, etc., occuring to members of the institution, especially high-placed or well-known members of staff. This content is of a congratulatory or condolence-offering character, presumably expressing for the whole institution its sympathetic concern for the lives of the members. Here, it may be noted, is an interesting aspect of role segregation. Since the institutionally relevant roles of a member tend to set him off against whole categories of other members, it is not these roles that can be used as a vehicle for the expression of institutional solidarity. Instead, use must be made of nonrelevant roles, especially roles such as parent and spouse that are imaginable, if not possible, in all camps.

Second, there is material that can reflect an editorial view. This includes news from the outside world bearing on the social and legal status of inmates and ex-inmates, accompanied by appropriate comment; original essays, short stories and poetry; and editorials. This material is written by inmates but expresses the official view of the functions of the institution, the staff's theory of human nature, an idealized version of inmate-staff relationships, and the stance an ideal convert ought to take. In short, this material presents the institutional line.

The house organ, however, survives in the delicacy of a nice balance. Staff allows itself to be interviewed, written about and read about by inmates, thus coming under some slight control of the writers and readers; and at the same time inmates are given an opportunity to show that they are high enough on the human scale to handle the official language and the official line with educated competence.[58] Contributors, on the other hand, guarantee to follow the official ideology, presenting it for inmates by inmates. Interestingly enough, inmates who make this compact with staff often do not cease to affirm the counter-mores. They introduce whatever open criticism of the institution that the censors will permit; they add to this by means of oblique or veiled writing; they employ pointed cartoons; and among their cronies, they may take a cynical view of their contribution, claiming that they write because this provides a "soft" setting and job or a good route for release recommendations.

While house organs have been known for some time, it is only recently that a somewhat similar medium for role release has appeared in total institutions. I refer here to the several forms of "self-government" and "group therapy." Typically, the inmates speak the lines, and a congenial member of staff performs the supervision. Again, a kind of compact between inmate and staff is found. The inmates get the privilege of spending some time in a relatively "unstructured" or equalitarian milieu and even the right to voice complaints.[59] In return they are expected to become less loyal to the counter-mores and more receptive to the ideal-for-self that the staff defines for them.[60]

A somewhat different type of institutional ceremony is found in the *annual party* (sometimes held more than once a year) at which staff and inmates "mix" through standard forms of sociability, such as commensalism, party games or dancing. At such times, staff and inmates will have the license to "take liberties" across the caste line, and social reaching may be expressed through sexual ones.[61]

Often linked with the annual party in total institutions, we find the *Christmas celebration.* Once or twice a year inmates will decorate the establishment with easily removable decorations partly supplied by staff, in this way banishing from the living quarters what an extra-special meal will then banish from the table. Small gifts and indulgences will be distributed among the inmates; some work-duties will be canceled; visitor time may be increased and restrictions on leave-taking decreased. In general, the rigors of institutional life for the inmates will be relaxed for a day.[62]

An interesting institutional ceremony, often connected with the annual party and the Christmas celebration, is the *institutional theatrical.* Typically the players are inmates and the directors of the production are staff, but sometimes "mixed" casts are found. The writers are usually members of the institution, whether staff or inmate, and hence the production can be full of local references, imparting through the private use of this public form a special sense of the reality of events internal to the institution. Frequently the offering will consist of satirical skits which lampoon well-known members of the institution, especially high-placed staff members. If the inmate-community is one-sexed, as it frequently will be, then some of the players are likely to perform in the costume and burlesqued role of members of the other sex. Limits of license are often tested, the humor being a little more broad than some members of the staff would like to see tolerated.[63] In addition to satirical sketches, there may be dramatic presentations recounting the bad historical past of like total institutions, as a contrast to the presumably better present.[64] The audience for the production will pointedly contain both inmate and staff, although often ecologically segregated, and in some cases even outsiders may be permitted to come.

The fact that the institutional theatrical is sometimes presented before an outside audience no doubt provides inmate and staff with a contrasting background against which to sense their unity. Other kinds of institutional ceremony fulfill this function too, often more directly. Increasingly there is the practice of the annual *open house* during which the kinfolk of members or even the public at large may be invited to inspect the premises. They can then see for themselves that high humane standards are being maintained. At such times, staff and inmates tend to be on visibly good terms with one another, and the price for this usually is that some reduction of ordinary stringencies will be allowed to occur. In the guise of being shown all, of course, visitors are likely to be shown only the more prepossessing parts of the establishment and only the more prepossessing, co-operative inmates. In large mental hospitals, in fact, modern treatment such as psycho-drama or dance therapy may come to play a special role in this regard, the practitioners and patients developing the kind of capacity to perform before strangers that comes from constant experience.

If open house allows outsiders to see that everything is all right on the inside, other institutional practices offer the same opportunity. Thus, for example, there is an interesting arrangement between total institutions and stage performers who were amateurs or ex-professionals. The institution provides a stage and guarantees an appreciative audience; the performers contribute a free show. There can be such a compelling need of each for the services of the other that the relationship may pass beyond the matter of personal taste and become almost symbiotic.[65] In any case, while the members of the institution are watching the performers, the performers are present to see that staff-inmate relations are sufficiently harmonious to allow for what looks like a voluntary assembly of both bent on an evening of unregimented recreation.

Institutional ceremonies that occur through media such as the house organ, group meetings, open house, and charitable performances presumably fulfill latent social functions, and some of these seem surprisingly clear-cut in the case of another kind of institutional ceremony, *intermural* sports. The inside team tends to be a group of all-stars chosen by intramural contest among all the inmates. By competing well with outsiders, the all-stars take roles that palpably fall outside the stereotype of what an inmate is—since team sport requires such qualities as intelligence, skill, perseverance, co-operativeness, and even honor. And these roles are taken right in the teeth of outsiders and staff observers. In addition, the outsider team and any supporters it has managed to bring into the grounds are forced to see that there are natural places on the inside where natural things go on.

In exchange for being allowed to demonstrate these things about themselves, inmates through their intermural team convey some things about the institution. In pursuing what is defined as an uncoercible endeavor, the inmate team demonstrates to outsiders and observing inmates that the staff, in this setting at least, is not tyrannical and that a team of inmates is ready to take on the role of representing the whole institution and is allowed to do so. And by supporting the home team, both staff and inmates quite vocally show a mutual and similar involvement in the institutional entity.

Sunday services and Sunday amusements are sometimes set in opposition to each other; in total institutions this can partly be understood in terms of an unnecessary duplication of function. Like sports and charity performances, a service is a time when the unity of staff and inmates can be demonstrated to each by showing that in certain nonrelevant roles they are members of the same audience *vis-à-vis* the same outside performer.

In all instances of unified ceremonial life that I have mentioned, staff is likely to play more than a supervisory role. Often a high-ranking officer attends as a symbol of management and (it is hoped) of the whole establishment. He dresses well, is moved by the occasion, and gives smiles, speeches, and handshakes. He dedicates new buildings on the grounds, gives his blessing to new equipment, judges contests, and hands out awards. When acting in this capacity, his interaction with inmates will take a special benign form; inmates are likely to show embarrassment and respect, and he is likely to display an avuncular interest in them.[66] In the case of our very large and benevolently oriented mental hospitals, executive officers may be required to spend a goodly portion of their time putting in an appearance at these ceremonial occasions, providing us with some of the last places in modern society in which to observe a lord-of-the-manor feudal role.

A final note should be added about these institutional ceremonies. They tend to occur with well-spaced periodicity and to give rise to some social excitement. All the groupings in the establishment join in and have a place regardless of rank or position, but a place that expresses this position. These ceremonial practices then ought to bear strong witness to the value of a Durkheimian analysis. A society dangerously split into inmates and staff can through these ceremonies hold itself together. Staff and inmates are the two ends of the arch, and these ceremonies are needed for the keystone.

But, except for the claims sometimes made for the effectiveness of group therapy, in many cases it is a nice question whether these role releases hold up anything at all. Staff, to other members of the staff, typically complain of their boredom with these ceremonies and that they have to participate because of their own *noblesse oblige* or, worse still, because of that of their superiors. And inmates often participate because, wherever the ceremony is held, they will be more comfortable and less restricted there than where they otherwise would be. A total institution perhaps needs collective ceremonies because it is something more than a formal organization, but its ceremonies are often pious and flat, perhaps because it is something less than a community.

Institutional Differences

In this paper, total institutions have been considered from the point of view of a single basic articulation: inmates and staff. I think this is the first thing to do, partly because once this has been done we are in a good position to consider some of the limitations of this view. An important and interesting question in a closer study of total institutions would be to ask about the typical differentiation of role that occurs *within* each of the two main groups and to ask about the institutional function of these more specialized positions. Some of these special roles have been mentioned in passing, but in a closer treatment they should be given systematic attention.

Another limitation in the present discussion should be mentioned. When total institutions are brought together and examined by means of a conceptual framework derived from their striking similarities, differences among these institutions are brought to light, too. One difference has to do with the degree (and kind) of role and status differentiation within each of the two groupings, inmate and staff. Other differences have been incidentally mentioned. I would here like to note a few more.

One important difference among total institutions is found in the spirit in which recruits enter the establishment. At one extreme we find the quite involuntary entrance of those who are sentenced to prison, committed to a mental hospital, or impressed into the crew of a ship. It is perhaps in such cases that staff's version of the ideal inmate has least chance of taking hold among the inmates. At the other extreme, we find religious institutions which deal only with those who feel they have gotten the call and, of these volunteers, take only those who seem to be the most suitable and the most serious in their intentions. In such cases, conversion seems already to have taken place, and it only remains to show the neophyte along what lines he can best discipline himself. Midway between these two extremes we find institutions like the army barracks whose inmates are required to serve, but who are given much opportunity to feel that this service is a justifiable one required in their own ultimate interests. Obviously, significant differences in tone will appear in total institutions, depending on whether recruitment is voluntary, semivoluntary or involuntary.

Another dimension of variation among total institutions is found in what might be called their *permeability*, that is, the degree to which the social standards maintained within the institution and the social standards maintained in the environing society have influenced each other sufficiently to minimize differences.[67] This issue, incidentally, gives us an opportunity to consider some of the dynamic relations between a total institution and the wider society that supports it or tolerates it.

When we examine the admission procedures of total institutions, we tend to be struck with the impermeable aspects of the establishment, since the stripping and leveling processes which occur at this time directly cut across the various social distinctions with which the recruit entered. St. Benedict's advice[68] to the abbot tends to be followed:

> Let him make no distinction of persons in the monastery. Let not one be loved more than another, unless he be found to excel in good works or in obedience. Let not one of noble birth be raised above him who was formerly a slave, unless some other reasonable cause intervene.

Thus, the new cadet in a military school finds that discussions "of wealth and family background are taboo," and that, "Although the pay of the cadet is very low, he is not permitted to receive money from home."[69]

Even the age-grading system of the wider society may be stopped at the gates, as nicely suggested in a recent memoir[70] of an ex-nun:

> Gabrielle moved to the place that would ever be hers, third in line of forty postulants. She was third oldest in the group because she had been third to register on that day less than a week ago when the Order had opened its doors to new entrants. From that moment, her chronological age had ceased and the only age she would henceforth have, her age in the religious life, had started.

It is, of course, by suppressing outside distinction that a total institution can build up an orientation to its own system of honor. There is a sense then in which the harshest total institution is the most democratic, and in fact the inmate's assurance of being treated no worse than any other of his fellows can be a source of support as well as a deprivation.

But regardless of how radical a total institution appears to be, there will always be some limits to its reshuffling tendencies and some use made of social distinctions already established in the environing society, if only so it can conduct necessary affairs with this society and be tolerated by it. Thus, there does not seem to be a total institution in Western society which provides batch living completely independent of sex; and ones like convents that appear to be impervious to socioeconomic gradings, in fact tend to apportion domestic roles to converts of rural peasant background, just as the patient garbage crews in our prize integrated mental hospitals tend to be wholly Negro.[71] More important, perhaps, than the fact that total institutions differ in over-all permeability to outside standards, we find that each is permeable with respect to different social standards.

One of the most interesting differences among total institutions is to be found in the social fate of their graduates. Typically, these become geographically dispersed; the difference is found in the degree to which structural ties are maintained in spite of this distance. At one end of the scale we find the year's graduates of a particular Benedictine abbey, who not only keep in touch informally but find that for the rest of their life their occupation and location have been determined by their original membership. At the same end of the scale, we find ex-convicts whose stay in prison orients them to the calling and to the nationwide underworld community that will comprise their life thereafter. At the other end of the scale, we find enlisted men from the same barracks who melt into private life immediately upon demobilization and even refrain from congregating for regimental reunions. Here, too, are ex-mental patients who studiously avoid all persons and events that might connect them with the hospital. Midway between these extremes, we find "old-boy" systems in private schools and graduate universities, which function as optional communities for the distribution of life-chances among sets of fellow graduates.

Conclusion

I have defined total institutions denotatively by listing them and then have tried to suggest some of their common characteristics. We now have a quite sizable literature on these establishments and should be in a position to supplant mere suggestions with a solid framework bearing on the anatomy and functioning of this kind of social animal. Certainly the similarities obtrude so glaringly and persistently that we have a right to suspect that these features have good functional reasons for being present and that it will be possible to tie them together and grasp them by means of a functional explanation. When we have done so, I feel we will then give less praise and blame to particular superintendents, commandants, wardens, and abbots, and tend more to understand the social problems and issues in total institutions by appealing to the underlying structural design common to all of them.

ROBERT J. LIFTON

Methods of Forceful Indoctrination: Psychiatric Aspects of Chinese Communist Thought Reform

I THINK it is very significant that among all the people I interviewed in Korea and in Hong Kong, no one who had been through the experience ever used the term "brainwashing," unless he had first heard it from a Western source. But in searching for a term, or trying to label this process, one runs into a little difficulty.

I remember one suggestion that came to me which may for some people shed some light on the subject. A friend of ours in Hong Kong, a member of the British Diplomatic Service, felt there was too much concern on the part of Americans about "brainwashing," and he particularly deplored the name. He suggested, "Why not simply call the whole thing a 'mental douche'?" But I am not too sure that this would serve as a very scientific name.

But despite much confusion in terminology, the process of *szuhsiang kai-tsao*—translated as "ideological remolding," "ideological reform," or "thought reform"—is very much a reality. Where applied to Westerners, to either prisoners of war or to incarcerated civilians, many of its methods have been written about popularly, and have to a certain extent, been subjected to psychiatric and psychological investigation. But the process applied to the Chinese themselves, and particularly to Chinese intellectuals, has been very little studied.

For this reason, and also in keeping with GAP's policy of trying to present a certain amount of unpublished research,[1] I am going to talk about the most intensive of the "thought reform" programs for Chinese intellectuals as conducted in special institutions known as "revolutionary colleges." These were set up all over China immediately after the Communist takeover.

I wish first to emphasize that thought reform has been applied, in varying degrees of intensity, not only in the special centers I will describe,

---

Reprinted from *Symposium No. 4* (*Methods of Forceful Indoctrination*) (1957), pp. 234-49, by permission of the author and the publisher.

but also in universities, labor, business, and government groups, even among peasants—and in fact throughout the immense population of China. This is in itself a rather amazing accomplishment.

I had the opportunity to study this process in Hong Kong over a period of seventeen months, working with twenty-five Westerners who had been in Chinese prisons,[2] and with fifteen Chinese intellectuals who had undergone the type of process I am going to describe.

Although I could occasionally conduct interviews in English, where the subjects had been exposed to a Westernized education (generally in mission-endowed institutions), I usually worked through interpreters. That set up a very complicated three-way communication system, which I won't discuss now. I found that it was very important to work with a subject over a long period of time, and the most meaningful data that I was able to obtain came through working with people for over a year. There is a very simple reason for this. It is a Chinese—and East Asian—cultural trait to say what one thinks the listener wants to hear, as a form of politeness and propriety. So I would first encounter many cliché anti-Communist statements; one could only get into the real areas of conflict when there developed a meaningful and trusting relationship, and when the subject could realize that I wanted to know about his true feelings.

Who attends a revolutionary college? Students are drawn from many divergent sources: former Nationalist officials and affiliates, teachers who had been associated with the old regime, Communist cadres who had demonstrated significant "errors" in their work or thoughts, party members who had spent long periods of time in Nationalist areas, students returning from the West, and finally, arbitrarily selected groups of university instructors or recent graduates. Many in these groups came in response to thinly veiled coercion—the strong "suggestion" that they attend; but others actively sought admission on a voluntary basis, in order to try to fit in with the requirements of the new regime, or at least to find out what was expected of them.

The college itself is tightly organized along Communist principles of "democratic centralism." One center may contain as many as 4,000 students, subdivided into sections of about 1,000 each, then into classes of 100 to 200 each, and finally into six- to ten-man groups. The president of the institution may be a well-known scholar serving as a figurehead; technically below him in rank are a vice-president and the section heads, who are likely to be Communist party members, and exert the real authority at the center. Under their supervision are the class-heads, each of whom works with three special cadres.

These cadres, usually long-standing and dedicated party workers, play a central role in the thought reform process: they are the connecting link between the faculty and the students, and it is they who perform the day-to-day leg work of the reform process. The three cadres of each class may be designated according to function: the executive cadre, concerned essentially with courses of study; the organizing cadre, most intimately involved with the structure and function of the small group and the attitudes of the individual students who make them up; and the advisory cadre—the only one of the three who may be a woman—offering counsel on personal and ideological "problems" which come up during this arduous experience.

I have divided the "thought reform" process into three stages, referring to the successive psychological climates which are created. These are my subdivisions, but I believe that they are very much in keeping with the Communist view of their own process: first, the Great Togetherness—the stage of Group Identification; second, the Closing in of the Milieu—the stage of Emotional Conflict; and third, Submission and Rebirth—the Final Confession.

The Great Togetherness—Group Identification

New students approach the course with a varying mixture of curiosity, enthusiasm, and apprehension. When a group of them arrives, their first impression is likely to be a favorable one. They encounter an atmosphere which is austere, but friendly—an open area of low-slung wooden buildings (frequently converted from military barracks) which serve as living quarters and class rooms—old students and cadres greeting them warmly, showing them around, speaking glowingly of the virtues of the revolutionary college, of the Communist movement, of the new hope for the future. Then, after a warm welcoming speech by the president of the college, they are organized into ten-man study groups. And for a period of from a few days to two weeks they are told to "just get to know each other."

Students are surprised by this free and enthusiastic atmosphere: some among the older ones may remain wary, but most are caught up in a feeling of camaraderie. Within the small groups they vent their widely shared hostility towards the old regime—an important stimulus to the thought reform process. There is a frank exchange of feeling and ideas, past and present, as they discuss their background experiences, and hopes and fears for the future. There is an air of optimism, a feeling of being in the same boat, a high *esprit de corps*.

Let me illustrate this with a few sentences quoted directly from one of my subjects:

> Everyone felt a bit strange at first, but we soon realized that we were all in the same position. We all began to talk freely and spontaneously; we introduced ourselves to each other, and talked about our past life and family background. . . . The Revolutionary College seemed to be a place

which brought together young people from all over with a great deal in common. We ate, slept, and talked together, all of us eager to make new friends. I had very warm feelings towards the group, and towards the school. . . . I felt that I was being treated well in a very free atmosphere. I was happy and thought that I was on my way to a new life.

Next, through a series of "thought mobilization" lectures and discussions, the philosophy and rationale of the program are impressed upon the individual student: the "old society" was evil and corrupt; this was so because it was dominated by the "exploiting classes"—the landowners and the bourgeoisie; most intellectuals come from these "exploiting classes" (or from the closely related *petite bourgeoisie*) and therefore retain "evil remnants" of their origins and of the old regime; each must now rid himself of these "ideological poisons" in order to become a "new man" in the "new society." In this way, he is told, the "ideology of all classes" can be brought into harmony with the changing "objective material conditions."[3]

Also quoted invariably is a highly significant speech of Mao Tse-tung, the chairman of the Communist party in China:

. . . our object in exposing errors and criticizing shortcomings is like that of a doctor in curing a disease. The entire purpose is to save the person, not to cure him to death. If a man has appendicitis, the doctor performs an operation and the man is saved. If a person who commits an error, no matter how great, does not bring his disease to an incurable state by concealing it and persisting in his error, and in addition if he is genuinely and honestly willing to be cured, willing to make corrections, we will welcome him so that his disease may be cured and he can become a good comrade. It is certainly not possible to solve the problem by one flurry of blows for the sake of a moment's satisfaction. We cannot adopt a brash attitude towards diseases of thought and politics, but must have an attitude of saving men by curing their diseases. This is the correct and effective method.[4]

This illustrates the tone with which thought reform is presented to the student. What we see as a coercive set of manipulations, they put forth as a *morally uplifting, harmonizing, and therapeutic experience.*

Then the formal courses begin—the first usually entitled the History of the Development of Society (to be later followed by Lenin—the State, Materialistic Dialectics, History of the Chinese Revolution, Theory of the New Democracy, and Field Study—visits to old Communist workshops and industrial centers). The subject matter is introduced by a two- to six-hour lecture delivered by a leading Communist theorist. This is followed by the interminable *hsueh hsi* or study sessions within the six- to ten-man group, where the real work of thought reform takes place. Discussion of the lecture material is led by the group leader who has been elected by its members—usually because of his superior knowledge of Marxism. At this point he encourages a spirited exchange of all views, and takes no side when there is a disagreement. The other students realize that the group leader is making daily reports to a cadre or to the class head, but the full significance of these is not yet appreciated; they may be viewed as simply a necessary organizational procedure. Most students retain a feeling of pulling together towards a common goal in a group crusading spirit.

The Closing in of the Milieu—The Period of Emotional Conflict

About four to six weeks from the beginning of thought reform—at about the time of the completion of the first course—a change begins to develop in the atmosphere. With the submission of the first "thought summary" (these must be prepared after each course) there is a shift in emphasis from the intellectual and ideological to the personal and the emotional. The student begins to find that he, rather than the Communist doctrine, is the object of study. A pattern of criticism, self-criticism, and confession develops—pursued with increasing intensity throughout the remainder of the course.

Now the group leader is no longer "neutral"; acting upon instructions from above, he begins to "lean to one side," to support the "progressive elements"; to apply stronger pressures in the direction of reform. He and the "activists" who begin to emerge, take the lead in setting the tone for the group. The descriptions of the past and present attitudes which the student so freely gave during the first few weeks of the course now come back to haunt him. Not only his ideas, but his underlying motivations are carefully scrutinized. Failure to achieve the correct "materialistic viewpoint," "proletarian standpoint," and "dialectical methodology," is pointed out, and the causes for this deficiency are carefully analyzed.

Criticisms cover every phase of past and present thought and behavior; they not only "nip in the bud" the slightest show of unorthodoxy or nonconformity, but they also point up "false progressives"—students who outwardly express the "correct" views without true depth of feeling. Group members are constantly on the lookout for indications in others of lack of real emotional involvement in the process. Each must demonstrate the genuineness of his reform through continuous personal enthusiasm, and active participation in the criticism of fellow students. In this way he can avoid being rebuked for "failure to combine theory with practice."

Standard criticisms repeatedly driven home include: "individualism"—placing personal interests above those of "the people"—probably the most emphasized of all; "subjectivism"—applying a personal viewpoint to a problem rather than a "scientific" Marxist approach; "objectivism"—undue detachment, viewing oneself "above class distinction," or "posing as a spectator of the new China"; "sentimentalism"—allowing one's attachment to family or friends to interfere with reform needs, therefore "carrying about an ideological burden" (usually associated with reluctance to denounce family members or friends allegedly associated with the "exploiting classes"). And in addition: "deviationism," "opportunism," "dogmatism," "reflecting exploiting class ideology," "overly technical viewpoints," "bureaucratism," "individual heroism," "revisionism," "departmentalism," "sectarianism," "idealism,' and "pro-American outlook."

The student is required to accept these criticisms gratefully when they are offered. But more than this, he is expected to both anticipate and expand upon them through the even more important device of *self-criticism.* He must correctly analyze his own thoughts and actions, and review his past life—family, educational, and social—in order to uncover the source of his difficulties. And the resulting "insights" are always expressed within the Communist jargon—corrupt "ruling class" and "bourgeois" influences, derived from his specific class origin.

The criticism and self-criticism process is also extended into every aspect of daily life, always with a highly moralistic tone. Under attack here are the "bourgeois" or "ruling class" characteristics of pride, conceit, greed, competitiveness, dishonesty, boastfulness, and rudeness. Relationships with the opposite sex are discussed and evaluated, solely in terms of their effects upon the individual's progress in reform. Where a "backward" girl friend is thought to be impeding his progress, a student may be advised to break off a liaison; but if both are "progressive," or if one is thought to be aiding the other's progress, the relationship will be condoned. Sexual contacts are, on the whole, discouraged, as it is felt that they drain energies from the thought-reform process.

The student must, within the small group, *confess* all of the "evils" of his past life. Political and moral considerations here become inextricably merged; especially emphasized are any "reactionary" affiliations with the old regime or with its student organizations. Each student develops a "running confession," supplemented by material from his self-criticisms and "thought summaries"; its content becomes widely known to students, cadres, and class heads, and it serves as a continuous indicator of his progress in reform.

Most are caught up in the universal confession compulsion which sweeps the environment: students vie to outdo each other in the frankness, completeness, and luridness of their individual confessions; one group challenges another to match its collective confessions; personal confession is the major topic of discussion at small group meetings, large student gatherings, informal talks with cadres, and in articles in wall newspapers. Everywhere one encounters the question: "Have you made your full confession?"

Confession tensions are brought to a head through a mass, pre-arranged. revival-like gathering where a student with a particularly evil past is given the opportunity to redeem himself. Before hundreds or even thousands, of fellow students, he presents a lurid description of his past sins: political work with the Nationalists, anti-Communist activities, stealing money from his company, violating his neighbor's daughter. He expresses relief at "washing away all of my sins," and gratitude towards the Government for allowing him to "become a new man."

As the months pass, "progressives" and "activists" take increasing leadership, aided by group manipulations by cadres and class heads. Where a group leader is not sufficiently effective, if his reports to the class head are not considered satisfactory, or where there is a general "lagging behind" in a particular group, a reshuffling of groups is engineered from above. The weak group becomes reinforced by the addition of one or two "activists," and the former group leader, in his new group, is reduced to the level of an ordinary student. Although group leaders may still be elected by students, these shifts can insure that this position is always held by one considered "progressive" and "reliable."

At the same time, "backward elements"—students with suspicious backgrounds, whose confessions are not considered thorough enough, who do not demonstrate adequate enthusiasm in reforming themselves and criticizing others, whose attitudes are found wanting—are singled out for further attention. Such a student becomes the target for relentless criticism in his group; and during odd hours he is approached by other students and cadres in attempts to persuade him to mend his ways. Should he fail to respond, friendliness gives way to veiled threats, and he may be called in to receive an official admonition from a class head. As a last resort, he may be subjected to the ultimate humility of a mass "struggle" meeting: in ritualistic form, he is publicly denounced by faculty members, cadres, and fellow students, his deficiencies reiterated and laid bare. It becomes quite clear that his future in Communist China is indeed precarious, and the ceremony serves as a grim warning for other students of questionable standing.

In response to all of these pressures, no student can avoid experiencing some degree of fear, anxiety, and conflict. Each is disturbed over what he may be hiding, worried about how he may come out of this ordeal. Some, recalling either stories they have heard or personal experiences, find revived in their minds images of the extreme measures used by the Communists in dealing with their enemies. All are extremely fearful of the consequences of being considered a "reactionary."

I can again illustrate this through the feelings expressed by another one of my subjects:

> Towards the middle of the semester the intensity of my anti-Communist thoughts greatly increased. I developed a terrible fear that these thoughts would come out and be known to all, but I was determined to prevent this. I tried to appear calm but I was in great inner turmoil. I knew that if I kept quiet no one would know the secret which I had not confessed. But people were always talking about secrets. In small group meetings or large confession meetings, everyone would say that it was wrong to keep secrets, that one had to confess everything. Sometimes a cadre or a student would mention secrets during a casual talk, and I would feel very disturbed. Or at large meetings someone would get up and say: "There are still some students in the University who remain 'anti-organization.'" I knew that no one else was thinking specifically of me, but I couldn't help feeling very upset. The secret was always something that was trying to escape from me.

Students who show signs of emotional disturbance are encouraged to seek help by talking over their "thought problem" with the advisory cadre, in order to resolve whatever conflicts exist. Many experience psychosomatic expressions of their problems—fatigue, insomnia, loss of appetite, vague aches and pains, or gastrointestinal symptoms. Should they take their complaints to the college doctor, they are apt to encounter a reform-oriented and psychosomatically sophisticated reply: "There is nothing wrong with your body. It must be your thoughts that are sick. You will feel better when you have solved your problems and completed your reform." And indeed, most students are in a state of painful inner tension; relief is badly needed.

Submission and "Rebirth"—the Final Confession

The last stage—that of the over-all thought summary or final confession—supplies each student with a means of resolving his conflicts. It is ushered in by a mass meeting at which high Communist officials and faculty members emphasize the importance of the final thought summary as the crystallization of the entire course. Group sessions over the next two or three days are devoted exclusively to discussions of the form this summary is to take. It is to be a life history, beginning two generations back and extending through the reform experience. It must, with candor and thoroughness, describe the historical development of one's thoughts, and the relationships of these to actions. It is also to include a detailed analysis of the personal effects of thought reform.

The summary may be from five to twenty-five thousand Chinese characters (roughly equivalent numerically to English words) and require about ten days of preparation. Each student then must read his summary to the group, where he is subjected to more prolonged and penetrating criticism. He may be kept under fire for several days of detailed discussion and painful revision, as every group member is considered responsible for the approval of each confession presented, and all may even have to place their signatures upon it.

The confession is the student's final opportunity to bring out anything he has previously held back, as well as to elaborate upon everything he has already said. It always includes a detailed analysis of class origin. And in almost every case, its central feature is the denunciation of the father, both as a symbol of the exploiting classes, and as an individual. The student usually finds the recitation of his father's personal, political, and economic abuses to be the most painful part of his entire thought reform. He may require endless prodding, persuasion, and indirect threats before he is able to take this crucial step. But he has little choice and he almost invariably complies.

The confession ends with an emphasis of personal liabilities which still remain, attitudes in need of further reform, and the solemn resolve to continue attempts at self-improvement and to serve the regime devotedly in the future. When his confession is approved, the student experiences great emotional relief. He has weathered the thought reform ordeal, renounced his past, and established an organic bond between himself and The Government. His confession will accompany him throughout his future career as a permanent part of his personal record. It is his symbolic submission to the regime, and at the same time his expression of individual rebirth into the Chinese Communist community.

Although there is not time for much detail, I would like to say a few words about the types of response to the process and the degree of success it seems to achieve, and then indicate what I believe to be some of the more important psychiatric principles it employs and their possible relevance for psychiatric theory and research.

In commenting on the success or failure of thought reform, I can only make what I believe to be a reasonably well-informed speculation, based upon the experiences and observations of my subjects, as well as opinions of many others who had an opportunity to observe its results first-hand. We may roughly identify three types of responses: first, the resisters who felt suffocated by the process, some of whom fled (and I would emphasize that my subjects were limited to "failures"). Some of them had been much more sympathetic to the regime prior to their thought reform, experiencing a reverse effect. But this group would seem to be a small minority. Second, on the other extreme there are the dramatic "converts"—especially among those in their teens and early twenties—who become zealous adherents of the Communist movement. The third, in-between group would appear to be by far the largest, partially convinced but essentially concerned with adapting themselves to these severe pressures and working out some type of future under the new regime. Their attempts to find a way of life and a form of personal identity become more decisive to them than theoretical ideas and beliefs. Some of the people in the second and third groups seem to feel "purified" by the process, the emotional equivalent of taking "bad medicine" which was unpleasant but "good for me."

Finally, in listing the important psychological areas involved, I wish to stress that the four which I will mention are among the most relevant for us here, but by no means the only ones.

1) *Milieu Control.* This is the term which I have used to describe the attempt at *manipulation of all communication in the environment.* Everything said or done can be observed and reported back to a cadre or faculty member, and the information used to specify further manipulations within the group. This type of closed communication system is very close to Orwell's vision of *Nineteen Eighty-Four;* but Orwell,[5] with the mind of a Westerner, saw milieu control accomplished through mechanical means, the two-way telescreen. The Chinese have here done it through a *human recording and transmitting apparatus,* extending their influence more deeply into the inner life of the individual person. There is a blending of external and internal milieux, as the student internalizes the attitudes, values, and beliefs of his environment.

What is the significance of this for psychiatry? In some of our own approaches we attempt to create what we consider to be a therapeutic milieu: in the past we emphasized the "total push" within the mental hospital and more recently we have begun to study not only the complicated relationships within the hospital structure, but also the wider milieux with which we must deal in preventive and public health psychiatry. My work with "thought reform" convinces me that we would do well to retain a certain degree of humility in our own milieu manipulations, and to keep in mind the dangers of imposing too forcefully our own values and prejudices. I believe that psychiatrists are beginning to deal with this question in the more creative type of milieux which their studious efforts have helped to develop in various treatment centers.

2) *Guilt, Shame, and Confession.* Thought reform pressures strongly stimulate both guilt anxiety and shame anxiety. I am here using the concepts developed in recent studies of guilt and shame:[6] guilt anxiety, consisting of feelings of evil and sinfulness with expectation of punishment, shame anxiety of feelings of humiliation and failure to live up to the standards of one's peers or of one's own internalized ego-ideal, with the expectation of abandonment. The student develops a sense of guilt relating to the evils of his past life and further stimulated through his denunciation of his father; he develops a sense of shame through the manifold group pressures, particularly those related to ostracism and public humiliation. The experience here seems to confirm the view that both the sense of guilt and the sense of shame are likely to play important roles in any culture, and that

we must reexamine some of our concepts of guilt and shame cultures. It may be, however, that the shame pressures which function so prominently in the operation of the process are drawn largely from Chinese culture, and that many of the guilt pressures stem from the Communist ideology and frame of reference which has its origins in the West.

In theorizing concerning the individual sources of this guilt, one thinks first of the traditional view, its restimulation from the store of guilt originating in real or alleged transgressions of parental authority during early life. But there is in addition the creation of what may be termed a *guilty environment*. In this atmosphere of accusation, self-accusation, and confession, *one is expected to feel guilty, and one must learn to feel guilty.* A sense of guilt becomes a form of adaptation as well as a means of communication in this milieu. The same is true of a sense of shame, and we may speak of a *shaming environment*. Similarly, confession becomes not only a means of atoning for guilt and shame, but also a vehicle for making "progress" and bettering one's standing. In the *purging environment*, self-debasement leads to increased prestige.

I believe that many questions concerning the nature of guilt, shame, and confession can be further explored through intensive studies of their occurrence in people of other cultures.

3) *Language, Theory, and Behavior*. In thought reform there is a loading of the language to an extreme degree. Such terms as "liberation," "help," "progress," "the people," "proletarian standpoint," "bourgeois," and "capitalistic" become morally charged—either very good or very bad—and they take on a mystical quality. Catch-phrases and semantic manipulations are so prominently developed that the student must find himself thinking and conceptualizing within their sphere. One of them described this to me as follows:

> Using the same pattern of words for so long, you are so accustomed to them that you feel chained. If you make a mistake, you make a mistake within the pattern. Although you don't admit that you have adopted this kind of ideology, you are actually using it subconsciously, almost automatically. . . . At that time I believed in certain aspects of their principles and theories. But such was the state of confusion in my own mind that I couldn't tell or make out what were the things I did believe in.

Thought reform is based upon an implied psychological theory—not completely spelled out but very much present: that adult behavior, attitudes, values, and psychological reactions are determined by one's class origin. Negative qualities such as greed, lack of consideration for others, and the inability to adequately achieve the proletarian standpoint, are attributed to exploiting class origins. More positive qualities of cooperativeness, consideration, and "progressive thought" are ostensibly derived from working class origins. Most of us in Western psychiatry would feel that this theory has severe limitations in explaining human behavior, but in the thought reform milieu it can be made to "work." It is rendered effective by the total support of the milieu and by the discomfort experienced by those who would, through action or statement, bring it into question. In this way, a limited, or even a poorly conceived, theory can become not only an explanation of behavior but also a fulcrum for action.

In our psychiatric work, we are faced with somewhat analogous problems of language and theory. We too must consider the danger of loading of the language with concepts which become morally charged, and in their routine and unquestioned usage lose their original vitality and narrow the scope of our thinking. In evaluating our theories, we are not free of emotional involvements which influence our beliefs: where we disagree with prevailing points of view, we too may encounter pressures in the direction of guilt and shame anxiety, contrasting with the relief of conflict and reinforcement of a positive identity when we accept opinions held in our particular milieu. But equally irrational factors may also be related to the need to rebel against a particular point of view.

4) *Changes in Identity and Belief*. I feel that the thought reform pressures are primarily aimed at bringing about a shift in identity (applying the concept as developed by Erik H. Erikson[7]) in the participating students, both collectively and individually. Traditionally, in Chinese culture, one has well-delineated social roles which are usually defined within the family constellation: the stress was on duty and reciprocal help, but especially upon filial piety. But under the impact of the industrial age, and of strong Western influence, this structure has been under attack by vanguard intellectual groups for at least fifty years, and in the ferment which developed, the young intellectual found himself torn between such identities as that of the rebellious reformer, the uninvolved cynic, and the more traditional filial son. The Communists seek to resolve all existing confusion through supplying a common identity—that of the zealous participant in the new regime.[8] They can readily make use of that of the rebellious reformer, and without too much difficulty undermine that of the uninvolved cynic; but the identity of the filial son has the deepest emotional roots and is the most difficult to change. Thus, the denunciation of the father becomes the central symbolic act of the reform process. The student casts off the old symbol of family and institutional authority, to become an equally filial and loyal "son" in a greater family, that of the Communist regime. The shifts in identity and belief follow those which occur in any ideological or religious conversion: old identities first must become associated with guilt and shame, they are cast out by means of the confession or "emptying" process, and the "convert" emerges with a new or

modified identity whose basic alterations have been supplied by the prevailing milieu. I would also emphasize that, in addition to coercive pressures, the process is furthered by powerful psychological appeals: the "great togetherness" already described, the rewards of catharsis and self-surrender in sharing the strength of a greater power, the bond of participation in a vast "moral crusade," and the overwhelmingly powerful psychological appeal of nationalism, which embodies all these other elements.

It is quite clear then that thought reform resembles, in many features, an *induced religious conversion*, as well as a *coercive form of psychotherapy*. These comparisons can be made profitably, but should not be put forth loosely. There remain important differences among these various approaches to "changing" the individual person. Psychiatry remains quite distinct from religious and ideological "conversion" experiences through a constant re-examination of its goals and its premises, the continuous and critical evaluation of its methods and of the personal involvements of its practitioners.

I would like to close with an emphasis which is perhaps already clear. The psychological forces we encounter in thought reform are not unique to the process; they represent an exaggerated expression of elements present in varying degrees in all social orders. The extreme character of thought reform offers a unique opportunity to recognize and study them. Every culture makes use of somewhat analogous pressures of milieu control, guilt, shame and confession, group sanctions, and loading of the language, in order to mold common identities and beliefs. The problem of any democratic society, including our own, is that of limiting these pressures and achieving a balance in a manner which permits its people to retain feelings of individual freedom, of dignity, and of creativity.

ARTHUR J. VIDICH AND MAURICE R. STEIN

The Dissolved Identity in Military Life

THE CHIEF CHARACTERISTIC of military life is its bureaucratic structure, typified by a sharply defined hierarchy of authority and privilege and by a highly refined, internal specialization of tasks.* In these respects, military organization stands as the model, in point of historical origin and social efficiency, for the factory, the prison, the office, the department store, the corporation, and increasingly for the "social system" as a whole. These are the "systems" that ask the individual to play a part in a much larger drama, the totality of which he is only dimly aware, but which requires a total commitment of at least his public self. However, because of the underlying phasic rhythm of war and peace in Western society, military communities exhibit their own peculiar organizational problems and properties:

1) They expand and contract very rapidly, and so face the problem of forming disparate groups and individuals into the concensus necessary for efficient institutional participation.

2) A high premium is placed upon the interchangeability of the individual participants at the various grades and levels of organization. Interchangeable troop reservoirs are created, so that performance, within minimum limits, can be predicted on a sufficiently safe basis to permit military operations.

3) A generalized attitude toward authority is inculcated in enlisted men and officers, such that the participant will follow the command of superior authority in principle and not out of personal loyalty. Maintaining the "chain of command" as an iron law rests on the threat to authority which is continuously present through loss of members in combat. Combat aggravates the problem of succession and so enhances the need for discipline and mechanical acceptance of leadership.

Published for the first time in this volume. A related discussion of military communities appears in M. Stein, *The Eclipse of Community* (Princeton: Princeton University Press, 1960).

* Portions of the data for this study were collected by the authors as participants in the U.S. Marine Corps and the U.S. Army. Our study was part of a larger project called "World War II." We wish to thank the directors of this project for allowing us to use their facilities.

4) The participating members must be trained to respond to the values, creeds, symbols, and objectives of the military organization, in such a way that his actions and publicly voiced attitudes will sustain and fulfill the organized military objective. Lack of credence or publicly voiced disloyalty are a threat to the fundamental structure of the community.

The ways in which these organizational characteristics are acted out will vary in different historical periods and in different countries. So, also, will there be variations in the psychological basis of individual participation at different times and in different national traditions. We will examine the psychology of self-involvement of the American soldier in World War II, noting particularly the way in which his civilian self adapted to military requirements and was transformed into a new self-style consistent with the objectives instituted by higher authority.

Institutional Initiation

During the thirties, the Armed Services, in spite of widespread unemployment, had never grown larger than 200,000 men. In terms of then prevailing images, the military way of life was regarded as parasitic and without prestige. The grumbling and lack of enthusiasm accompanying the selective service act of 1940 indicated that no significant portion of the male population saw the army as a means to status-enhancement and career success. Men who entered the service during the selective service years lacked respect for the regulars and particularly disliked army authority, caste, and "chicken." They acted out their parts with one eye, and much thought, on an early discharge.

Although Pearl Harbor politically legitimated the need for an army, it did not necessarily legitimate the individual soldier's participation to himself. The conditions of participation for the individual irked the democratic and equalitarian ideologies that the citizen soldier brought with him into the military setting. One of the major irritants was the inequality of sacrifice, or what has been called the degree of "relative deprivation" imposed on the recruit:

> Becoming a soldier meant to many men a very real deprivation. But the felt sacrifice was greater for some than for others, *depending on their standards of comparison.*
>
> Take one of the clearest examples—marital condition. The drafted married man, and especially the father, was making the same sacrifices as others plus the additional one of leaving his family behind. This was officially recognized by draft boards and eventually by the point system in the Army which gave demobilization credit for fatherhood. Reluctance of married men to leave their families would have been reinforced in many in-

stances by extremely reluctant wives whose pressures on the husband to seek deferment were not always easy to resist. A further element must have been important psychologically to those married men who were drafted. The very fact that draft boards were more liberal with married than with single men provided numerous examples to the drafted man of others in his shoes who got relatively better breaks than he did. Comparing himself with his unmarried associates in the Army, he could feel that induction demanded greater sacrifice from him than from them; and comparing himself with his married civilian friends he could feel that he had been called on for sacrifices which they were escaping altogether. Hence the married man, on the average, was more likely than others to come into the Army with reluctance and, possibly, a sense of injustice.[1]

The recruit entered the service without a deep-seated conviction that would lead to willing acceptance of his sacrifice. Rather, he accepted his service on the secular grounds of necessity or expediency, and for this reason found it all the more difficult to accept the differential distribution of privilege defined by the military caste system:

"The distinction made between officers and men is so great that it spoils any attempt to raise our morale by movies and football. All we ask is to be treated like Americans once again. No 'out of bounds,' no different mess rations, and no treating us like children."

"Why must the enlisted man be confined to camp as though he were in a concentration camp, when the officers can go where they damn please. The officers go to town, the officers get the few available women; there are several social affairs given from time to time for officers but nothing for the enlisted man unless it be an exciting bingo party. My pet peeve—to see a commissioned officer out with a girl flaunt her in front of enlisted men, who cannot go out with nurses."

"The officers are getting American whiskey and we are not. I do not think it's fair."

"Too many officers have that superior feeling toward their men. Treat them as if they were way below them. Many of the men have just as good an education, if not better, than many officers and also have come from just as good families. What's the matter with us enlisted men, are we dogs?"[2]

Civilian predispositions led the men to see in the above-cited caste system unequal privileges with respect to consumer goods and sex; their focus of resentment became the officer class which pre-empted privilege and authority, in a pattern alien to the recruit's previous civilian experience.

In the army of a democracy, the civilian brings with him a habit of individualistic behavior-patterns which must be broken and retrained to caste-structured authority. It would be easy to exaggerate this point since we know that factory work, as well as all other occupational bureaucracies, leave only a small margin for individual discretion. Yet in the civilian pattern, "free choice" remains in areas of leisure and family life. The inculcation of instantaneous obedience is more difficult in civilian settings than in the total institution where all roles are brought under a single net. That this is true is shown by the shock effect which caste-guaranteed authority had on soldiers who were asked to express their gripes:

> "I wish the officers would treat us like intelligent adults. Men inducted into the Army are those who were independent in thought and action, in other words worked for their living. Maybe the old Army had men who signed up because of the easy life and lack of responsibility involved in the shaping of the future. I wish there would be less monotonous repetition. Men take less interest in their work, fool around, and consequently annoy the officers, making it hard on everybody. Treat a man like a nitwit and he'll finally act like one."[3]
>
> "The men are usually kept in the dark as to what they are accomplishing, personally or in units, and questions as to the reasons for orders are barked down immediately."[4]
>
> "Constant inspection of equipment prepared for this or that purpose simply to fill up time. In this connection the practice of encouraging soldiers to keep one set of equipment for inspection and another for use puts a wholly false emphasis and takes it off the necessity for having the equipment clean."[5]
>
> "The army is the biggest breaker of morale. The Army idea of class distinction between officers and men is all wrong. The Army does not take advantage of its man resources. Men do not like to be treated as if they were just toys and dogs for someone to play with. We are entitled to the respect we worked for and earned in civilian life."[6]
>
> "The officers of my regiment take advantage of sheer rank by subjugating the private to their every whim and desire. Why should they (the privates) have to wait on their table, clean their dishes, roll and unroll their beds, and a million other things which every healthy man should be able to do for himself? We who were drafted for one year, and probably more, expected to devote that year in learning to soldier. Or was our conception of soldiering wrong?"[7]

The routine repetitiveness of training, the frequent appearance of senseless authority, the investiture of authority in regular noncoms who were frequently less educated than the recruit, the reduction of all training and participation to a common denominator (all of which were supported by established and unquestioned authority), gave pause to the civilian-minded recruit who brought with him a quite different set of attitudes concerning the legitimate grounds of authority.

The civilian-minded expectation, however, merely constituted the raw material with which the military initiation-process had to cope. The mechanisms of initiation transform the civilian profile and self-image sufficiently to make the recruit a reliable soldier who will respond according to expectation. The institutional techniques for accomplishing this involve a process of self-dissolution and reconstruction in ways which, in the American armed services, were not always deliberate nor recognized by the initiate.

The Formation of Militarily Consistent Self-Images

The Soldier's Lack of Ideological Commitment.—One of the major observations of War Department studies of soldiers, as reported in *The American Soldier*, was the soldier's lack of personal commitment to national war aims and the absence of conviction or belief concerning his participation in the armed services. Speier has summarized this finding:

> The data in *The American Soldier* on the personal commitment and on the orientation of soldiers toward the war present a gloomy picture. While some of the individual parts of the picture almost certainly result from the use of methods which do not permit any delicate probing into motivations and convictions, the composite picture leaves no doubt that the American soldier has neither any strong beliefs about national war aims nor a highly developed sense of personal commitment to the war effort. He did not think much about the meaning of the war as a whole and displayed a tendency to "accept momentarily any plausibly worded interpretation of the war."[8]

This lack of identification with major institutional ends is a measure of the soldier's detachment from publicly pronounced, justifying ideologies. That these pronouncements did not serve as sources of motivation does not mean, however, that other sources of self-commitment, and personal motivation of a more private nature, were not present. Moreover, the failure of public values does not lessen the need to affirm and reiterate these values, by those public agencies concerned with upholding them, even though the public agencies themselves, particularly the War Department, were apparently fully aware of their failure. The awareness of the failure simply became another condition that had to be accounted for by those charged with sustaining the motivation for participation. In terms of policy, this led to organizational calculations to incorporate the more private areas of the soldier's psychic life, with the aim of securing the wholehearted commitment of the self to the war. On a less general level than broad war aims, the soldier was made to feel meaningful participation by the integration of his psyche into the army as a way of life. Thus, in spite of ideological disenchantment, the situation of daily action, totally embraced by military life, was more decisive for motivation than were the higher war aims. The indoctrination of the soldier and the militarily organized activities which enveloped all of his time and attention served as a substitute for ideology, and provided the sources of energy necessary for efficient participation.

Indoctrination and Self-involvement.—Taken as a whole, it is abundantly clear that basic training aroused deep anxieties and resentments in the soldiers exposed to it, and that these anxieties and resentments were aroused by the assault made upon their previous life-patterns and self-images. The recruit was immediately stripped of all his civilian ego-supports—property, clothing, family, friends—and a standard uniform with matching dog-tags was provided impartially to all. The trainees were plunged into an all-male world, very different from the civilian setting left behind.

The Marine Corps, because it is an extreme case, can be used as a particularly apt illustration of the psychic impact of indoctrination. Here, the recruit was symbolically separated from society, by removing him to an offshore island which precluded all contact with conventional social symbols and relationships. Immediately upon arrival, the recruit was propelled through the training center *rite de passage* which forced him into a common mold. His civilian clothing was removed; his hair was shorn to baldness; and he was conducted naked through a delousing chamber, at the opposite end of which he was given "shots" and an issue of clothing. Upon regrouping, the training platoon had already lost its previous quality of disparate individuality.

In the next stage, the second rite in the passage, each man was given a full issue of equipment, including rifle, with which he would live for the duration. Carrying this equipment over their shoulders in a sack, the training platoon was then hazed by the drill instructor who conducted it through a senseless and interminably long and circuitous march to quarters, which turned out finally to be only several hundred yards from the beginning point of the march. The recruits were stunned and confused, but out of this common experience had been formed a group that was psychologically held together by the symbols of common uniform and haircut, by the delousing purification and by the new equality of hazing. The drill instructor had become the focal point of authority and resentment, and immediately began to serve as a substitute for the unpatterned resentments and authoritative centers of the recruits' civilian selves.

From a sociological standpoint, basic training served as a degrouping and regrouping agency, so that the psychic unrest engendered by the experience was partly the result of the immense psychic transitions that basic training accomplished. Americans from widely different class, ethnic, and religious backgrounds had to be stripped of old identities and coerced to accept new military roles, even though these violated many of their basic values and self-conceptions. Since such ideological incentives as patriotism could not be counted upon, the training-period had to create incentives that would fit the established purposes of the military machine, particularly, acceptance by the recruit of the self-image of a combat soldier.

The Marine Corps, which prided itself in its exclusively combat role, can again be used to good illustrative advantage. To be a Marine was to be a man, and to be a Marine-man, it was necessary to have had the combat experience. The combat role was held up as *the* major area of self-fulfillment. In line with this, training included the inculcation of new definitions of masculinity, a feature perhaps more necessary in Marine training, since the recruit tended to bring with him a conventional civilian conception of himself as a strong he-man type; many were athletes and some were top collegiate athletes. The civilian self-conception of he-man and athlete was broken down in training by the techniques of physical hazing and rifle calisthenics, wherein the recruit had to accept the hazing mutely and without self-defense and allow himself to be physically taxed in ways to which he was unaccustomed. Frequently, the heroic athlete was selected as the specific object of hazing to the point of collapse, thereby standing as an example to all others of the inadequacy of civilian forms of manliness.

The valued form of manliness found a focus on adeptness in the use of the rifle. A small man with supple muscles could frequently sustain 500 rifle push-ups better than the muscle-bound athlete. In such instances, he would be held up as an example of physical virtuosity. Dropping a rifle or having a dirty one was cause for punishment and humiliation. Disciplinary action, in cases of breach of respect for, or lack of proper care of, the rifle, took the form of requiring the offender to sleep with his "piece," the other term by which the weapon is known in military terminology. In Marine Corps culture, the "piece" was the pre-eminent symbol of masculinity; having to sleep with it introduced a confusion of symbols and cast aspersion on the masculine identity of the degraded victim.

Through a multiplicity of such processes, the recruit was enjoined to participate in the world of military symbols and to reshape or drop previous identities, while picking up new self-images consistent with the terms and framework of the military community.

Not all recruits, of course, participated on the same terms, but there is no question that all were engulfed in the military conditions defining the limits of possible action. Thus, even the "goldbrick," a figure more characteristic of the Army, who made claims for recognition by a withdrawal of energy, could only carry out his resistance and, hence, gain his identity in the context of the situation presented by Army life.

The role of goldbrick or Schweikism in general, which usually took the form of devoting excessive time to assigned tasks and other minor forms of "sabotage" against efficient operations, was a permitted form of resentment response. In fact, the goldbrick who did not make more work for others was held in high esteem, particularly by other enlisted men, and exceptional talents along these lines usually brought considerable prestige from all but overzealous officers. Such forms of sublimated resentment, given content in assigned tasks from instituted authority, served to define the psychological profile of those who elected the goldbrick style of personality.

The patterning and discharging of resentment innocuously was refined much further in the bureaucratic incorporation of all protest, or, psychologically speaking, what would be called efforts at self-expression. The imaginary T.S. card, assumed to be standard equipment-issue for each soldier, was the device employed to channel disparate forms of resentment. The response to idiosyncratic complaints and protest was, "Get your card punched." Though this response automatically defined a situation as humorous, it also ironically implied that the armed services which issued all other equipment also issued the T.S. card presumed to be worth a given number of chaplain's punches. This is the final bureaucratization and taming of all peculiar forms of self-expression, only slightly less passive than the way enlisted men would request their officers, who had left them standing in the rain, apparently forgotten, to take some action. One cannot forget the picture of the assembled troops softly purring, while getting drenched, "Let's get the troops out of the rain," dutifully maintaining, nevertheless, the assigned stance. The sublimation of impulse and idiosyncratic modes of expression was achieved, in spite of democratic ideology, in ways consistent with caste and authoritatively set goals.

Self-image and Caste.—Acceptance of self-images appropriate to caste position in the military hierarchy was one of the most threatening and potentially devisive problems for the maintenance of the integrity of the military community. Under a democratic ideology, as noted, this problem is particularly aggravated by the demand for equality of privilege and sacrifice. A hundred years ago, Toqueville noted this feature of democratic armies:

> . . . Men living in democratic times seldom choose a military life. Democratic nations are therefore soon led to give up the system of voluntary recruiting for that of compulsory enlistment. . . .
>
> When military service is compulsory, the burden is indiscriminately and equally borne by the whole community. This is another necessary consequence of the social condition of these nations and of their notions. The government may do almost whatever it pleases, provided it appeals to the whole community at once; *it is the unequal distribution of the weight, not the weight itself, that commonly occasions resistance.*[9]

Caste exemplifies this unequal distribution of weight. Of course, the problem of adopting a caste identity was not wholly alien to all recruits. Negroes, Puerto Ricans, the lower class in general, and anyone with previous experience in industrial and governing bureaucracies could make the transition to military caste without added increments of strain, since they were already habituated to the personal tensions caused by the caste experience. Nevertheless, there were problems for these as well as other ethnic and class categories of troops, and these problems are most clearly expressed in the characteristic forms in which officer-enlisted relationships were acted out.

The problem for the officers was not too difficult. Here we may refer to the War Department's study of the socialization of the officer to an acceptance of his caste superiority. We must note first the important roles of social segregation in the early socialization phases of officer training and the ordeal experience to which the candidate was subjected:

> . . . the experiences of a candidate in Officer Candidate School not only did not involve much explicit instruction in handling enlisted men, but actually contributed indirectly to making it harder for the new young officer to see the enlisted viewpoint. The Officer Candidate School could be conceived of as an ordeal, with some functions not dissimilar psychologically —in their emphasis on hazing and attention to minutiae—to those of ordeals involved in a college fraternity initiation.[10]

Would-be officers were subjected to the ordeal of close discipline and the constant threat of failure (washing out), and the "chit" system was used as a day-by-day measure of self-performance and tension maintenance. The hostility engendered by the closeness of supervision and the exacting scrutiny of every act was not permitted public expression.

The problem of caste-acceptance by officers was one of finding a way of identifying with the source of the discipline, as an alternative adjustive response to that of expressed hostility. In the course of training, progressive identification with the officer role was achieved by gradually allowing the candidate to assume upper-class and officer prerogatives; play-acting the role of platoon commander, taking clothing measurements for officer uniforms, buying bars, membership in officer's clubs. The aggression that was repressed earlier began to find an outlet against officer-candidates in earlier stages of training. The upper-class candidate retaliated, for the indignities he suffered earlier, against those who were now what he once was, and he thus experienced a restoration of ego which, however, was now adjusted to caste-acceptance.

Later, as the War Department studies tell us, the officer undergoes the same ego experience in relation to the enlisted man:

> The new officer, somewhat insecure in his role and perhaps a little guilty at his favored status over his previous enlisted confreres, reactively asserts his status, and finds in the OCS ordeal a justification for his new prerogatives; he *earned* them. The means whereby he earned them come to have special value for him. He puts a high value on official "GI" ways of doing things, and rationalizes that what was good for him must be good for those under his command.[11]

As it happened, the enlisted man neither knew nor cared about the "ordeal," so he tended to interpret the "overbearing" behavior of "90-day wonders" outside the framework of caste prerogative and ritual. The enlisted man's acceptance of caste rests on a quite different psychology.

It is known that enlisted men were hostile towards officers and resentful of the caste system. In their case, however, the expression of the resentment was permitted. This is adequately illustrated by army newspapers. The B-Bag column in *Stars and Stripes* was filled with comments on this topic. George Baker's cartoon character, Sad Sack, depended on a Chaplinesque satirizing of caste. Bill Mauldin's brilliant and occasionally savage cartoons capture the mood of the enlisted soldier. Two of them come to mind: The first shows two officers looking at a spectacular sunset while one turns to the other and says: "Beautiful view. Is there one for the enlisted men?" In the other, a battle-weary G.I. is seen lying in a hospital bed surrounded by two Medical Corps captains and a major, one of whom says thoughtfully to the others: "I think he should at least try to lie at attention." The resentment theme, however, is paralleled by themes of the moral, spiritual, and sacrificial superiority of the enlisted man who, as indicated in the cartoons described above, is depicted as carrying the burden of the war and its sacrifices. The enlisted man lived and accepted the realities of caste, but he was not able to accept psychologically his situation. The unofficial appeal to his resentment in the services' mass media, at a symbolic plane, provided a mechanism by which the resentment could be continuously discharged without entering into the social realities and requirements of the G.I.'s caste role. In effect the enlisted man could retain a pseudo-identity as a democratic soldier while not being one. His conception of self rested upon an unconscious acceptance of two levels of consciousness, providing the basis on which the individualized patterns of civilian life could be brought within the mold of military caste.

The Self-image in Caste and Combat.—One feature of combat is that it makes impossible the officer's exercise of his usual caste privileges. Deference patterns become dangerous, special uniforms and insignia are likely to bring concentrated enemy fire. At the front, no one has consumer luxuries, and available scarce goods are generally shared without regard to rank.

Combat officers and enlisted men alike have a certain solidarity with one another which distinguishes them from all soldiers who haven't participated in combat. Mauldin recognizes this in his cartoon showing a bearded, unkempt combat captain and his equally unkempt enlisted driver looking at signs: one on an officer's club restricting it to noncombat officers and the other on a soldier's club specifying that ties must be worn. The caption reads, "The hell with it, sir. Let's go back to the front." On the subject of relaxation of discipline, another cartoon shows a grizzled lieutenant playing cards with Willie and Joe in a front line dugout and is captioned with, "By th' way, what wuz them changes you wuz gonna make when you took over last month, sir?" Moreover, *The American Soldier* shows a significant difference in G.I. attitudes towards officers, varying with closeness to the front lines. Resentment against officers was smallest, and confidence in them the greatest among front line troops.[12] In combat, an informal solidarity that cut across caste lines was permitted, and rested on the common experience of the blood bath and the common purpose of remaining alive through the engagement. In combat, then, primary-group loyalties substitute for ritualistically specified caste relationships.

Thus, one of the main functions of primary combat-groups lies in their ability to incorporate officers and enlisted men and, thereby, eliminate the more unpleasant features of caste. Yet, this is a consequence that a caste system is designed to prevent. This paradox deserves closer examination, since it is at this point that the motivational functions of the caste system become meaningful.

Combat was defined as a valued experience that would enable the soldier to fulfill himself. The trainee and the garrison soldier were exposed to vigorous attacks on their self-esteem. Since it is the officer who wields power, acceptance of a preferred self-image by fellow trainees and troops is not capable of restoring the shattered self-esteem of the enlisted man. In training units, with their limited life expectancies and complete domination by officers and noncoms, the emergence of powerful informal groups among the troops was most unlikely. At the same time, it is in the period of training and garrison when informal support is most desperately needed. But impulses for primary-group satisfactions are actually exacerbated in these situations by caste "chicken": the troops are subjected to seemingly irrational disciplinary measures and are prevented from invoking primary group defenses against the assault on their self-esteem.

With this threatening situation in mind, the considerable amount of resentment and anxiety expressed by the troops was to have been expected. The enlisted man is left almost no channel for the recovery of his lost self-esteem. Some, of course, could become officers and enjoy the caste privileges at the expense of their less fortunate comrades. Others could begin the arduous climb through the ranks to achieve the status security available to noncoms. These outlets provided the aspiring soldier with a mechanism for linking the self of civilian-status aspirations with the military promotional system. However, this avenue was not available to all troops; most had to accept the necessity of serving in permanent units as privates, and for them the only alternative was garrison or combat duty. Although the individual had little choice in electing his duty, there is little doubt that most soldiers would prefer garrison to combat assignments. The effect of the soldier's training, however, was to make him feel it necessary to say that combat units would be more acceptable in spite of risks to life and limb.

The image of combat experience that had been built up emphasized the theme that hated caste etiquette was dropped in favor of front-line comradeship. In combat, moreover, the soldier could affirm a self-respecting masculinity. Combat men were looked up to by all, especially in the training camp itself where they were accorded special deference well beyond their nominal rank. In combat, the restoration of self-esteem could be found and a manly self acted out.

The situation of the combat troops and officers who return to garrison after combat presents a different problem. Since formal caste codes had broken down in combat, primary-group relationships and loyalties carried over to the noncombat situation, but this was precisely the point where formal requirements demanded caste conduct. The reintroduction of caste evoked some of the sharpest tensions in army life, because it conflicted with the loyalties and favored self-images engendered by the baptism of fire. When caste was reinstated it could not be established on the same terms as before. It now had a much more abstract quality and could not be acted out genuinely by either the troops or the officers. Instead, a collusive psychology was introduced, wherein the tacit understanding was reached between officer and enlisted man that one must observe etiquette and accept his station because "that's the way the army is." Caste relationships became conscious role-playing made necessary by institutional demands—"the officer is really a good fellow, but he has to act that way."

On the part of officers, the model for this kind of role-playing is given in innumerable Hollywood films. An apparently hard-hearted company commander (flight commander, ship's captain, first sergeant, but never a corporal), despised by his men as a cruel sadist, is shown during the development of the plot to be deeply devoted to his men. He is revealed as knowing that befriending the men might incline him toward partiality or protection of his outfit at the expense of the army, so he accepts the role of harsh taskmaster, secure in the faith that he is doing his duty towards his men and his country. The points in illustration are the undesirable consequence of too-close contact between officers and enlisted men, and the ever present possibility that the officers may be seduced from the perspective of their superiors by the primary-group loyalties evoked in combat.

The enlisted man, then, accepts caste and chicken because that's the way the "social system" works, and the officer enjoys his caste privileges without pangs of conscience. At this stage, both the officer and the enlisted man resolve caste tension by ignoring social reality, through the technique of conceiving their combat-selves to be their true selves. This dynamic was so compelling that it frequently led the soldier to exaggerate his combat experience, and, in some cases, to falsely claim combat experience.

The capacity to achieve an identity rested on the ability to ignore immediate experience and to construct, each according to his situation, a self-image sufficiently serviceable that it would sustain the motivation to act his part. The civilian-self was dissolved, at least for the duration, and in its place was substituted a highly plastic military identity that in some way enabled the soldiers to think of themselves as soldiers and to fight. The soldier seems to develop a capacity to dissolve himself in a situation and then to find a self consistent with it.

The Role of Future Self-Images

Always in the background of this easy adaptability lay an image of a future civilian self. When the army asked its soldiers why they fought, half of them emphasized ending the war or thoughts of home and loved ones.[13] As we have already observed, the real meaning of the war, for the men who fought it, involved only slight identification with a national crusade or even national defense. Soldiers exhibited a striking capacity to see the war, as they had seen the depression a few years earlier, as another dip or temporary set-back in a march towards future success and happiness. The romanticizing of home, girl friends and the States, coupled with anxieties about a possible postwar depression indicated the future-mindedness of American soldiers. The disorganized scramble to get out of the services at the end of the war revealed the desire to shed the military self (this, it must be remembered, was a desire rather than an easy possibility, as revealed by the shock effect which accompanied the actual transition back to civilian life). The future would resolve the caste imbalance and insure a distribution of privileges, as well as consumption commodities, along lines unhampered by caste restraints. Sometimes the future was seen as providing an opportunity for gaining retribution against officers: "If I see that bastard in civilian clothes, I'll kill him." The mythical future was a source of motivational energy and a further reason that enabled the acceptance of caste roles in the military present. The image of a future-self, then, was an added layer of self-consciousness in the present.

Military participation places a severe burden on the self-styles brought to the military community by its participants. Moreover, the requirements of institutional participation do not make possible an easy assumption of self-images serviceable to all experiences in the soldier's career. Rather, shifts in experience require shifts in identity; different career stages evoke different constellations of self-images. Seen in this light, the social-degrouping and regrouping processes of military life are paralleled by a sequence of dissolutions and redefinitions of self. Self-identity seems to be built upon a multiplicity of disparate and shifting layers of experienced reality.

The major mechanism of self-defense for the soldier is to entertain those preferred self-images that allow him to act, irrespective of the consistency, or lack of it, between reality and the preferred image sustained by illusion. Since there seems to be no one self-image that can consistently integrate immediate experience, the soldier's self exists in shifting and disparate layers of consciousness, which parallel similar dynamics in the community as a whole. The civilian past, the defeated self of the training period, the magnified or falsified self of combat, and above all, the future-civilian self all combine in various ways to produce a workable self-mechanism. The capacity to live with self depends upon a capacity to live in a world of multiple realities and multiple self-consciousnesses. The consciousness that falls victim to each new situation constitutes the dissolution of identity in the military community.

JOOST A. M. MEERLOO

Brainwashing and Menticide: Some Implications of Conscious and Unconscious Thought Control

DURING the last thirty years several political agencies have tried to misuse psychological and psychiatric experience to further their private aims. Active psychological warfare and mental torture are now accepted concepts in totalitarian countries. A prime result of the political pressure, both overt and unobtrusive, has been a cynical re-evaluation of human values. A new profession of specialists has emerged whose task it is not to cure, but to aggravate and manipulate the weaknesses of selected victims so that they might become more easily amenable to influence, and to prescribed political ideologies.

We may define such planned enforcement of ideas and mental coercion

---

Reprinted from *Psychoanalysis and Psychoanalytic Review*, XLV, No. 1 (1958), 83-99, by permission of the publisher.

applied as a political tool as "thought control." The provocation of false confessions in the service of political propaganda can be defined as "brainwashing" or "menticide." The United Nations defined the systematic suppression, starvation, and killing of minorities as the crime of *genocide*, the murder of a species. The new, more subtle crime is *menticide*, the murder of the potentialities of the free creative mind.

I wish to say no more at this time concerning the obviously sensational impact of this problem of brainwashing. It is interesting to know, however, why people reacted so hysterically and dramatically to the first detailed news on brainwashing. Terrible fears were aroused in them: especially the fear of conformity and the fear of the evil eye that can see through the person and magically dig the truth out of him.

The psychiatric problem of thought control can be approached from different angles. One may ask "what is the political technique of mental and spiritual terror?" One may make a survey of the political variations in coercive strategy. Various psychiatric and psychological schools have given different explanations of psychodynamics involved in political thought control and brainwashing.

I am here concerned, above all, with the more general question: "What do we clinicians learn from this extensive political experiment on human guinea pigs?"

Enforced interrogation, inquisition, persuasion, and mental coercion in the service of thought control and thought reform exist in many places. What lessons can be derived from the cynical political experiment with human beings? What are its implications?

There is overwhelming evidence that dictatorial regimes have improved their techniques of mental terror and mental coercion in the last quarter-century. I have followed this problem since 1933 when I along with a number of others suspected that one of the psychopathic patients in the Netherlands was used as a political tool and scapegoat in starting the Reichstag fire—the signal Hitler needed so badly in order to take dictatorial power into his own hands. At that time we had hardly any notion that a man could be changed into a servile robot with a built-in gramophone record, speaking his master's voice. When Marinus Van der Lubbe came before a German court and world forum in order to confess his crime in public, psychiatric observers thought that he had been treated with special narcotics and sedatives. At least they felt that he behaved very strangely—as if he were "punch-drunk." There was, of course, no possibility of further study after his conviction and hanging. It was not until the confession at the Nüremberg trials that we heard how Van der Lubbe had been used as a willing political tool and that the very men who had punished and killed him had been the ones who had urged him to start the fire.

True, we knew of the Pavlovian technique of conditioning animals as a kind of scientific training, but, in those days, it was impossible for us psychiatrists to believe that such a laboratory experiment could be used to transform a human's mind, even temporarily, into an imitative voice speaking only the thoughts of the master.

Yet, we must not forget that enforced persuasion and inquisition by means of subtle or not so subtle intimidation had existed as long as mankind itself. As a matter of fact, every time two people meet in exchange of thought, a subtle dialectic battle starts about who is the stronger one in his capacity to communicate and dominate and who is the weaker; who is the more persuasive one and who the more submissive. When, however, psychic arguments are not sufficient, often a different kind of talk with iron fists may start. Religious wars often occurred in the service of enforced persuasion and conversion. The more subtle techniques of coercive interrogation we learned, for example, from the Inquisition of the Middle Ages. Many witches were finally made to "confess" their sexual union with the devil Beelzebub.

What then is new about this question of coercive persuasion and brainwashing?

Two big developments made these old problems of enforced persuasion of decisive importance in our era:

In the first place, the modern strategy of totalitarian governments developed a systematic political thought control and thought reform as a strategy of absolute control over the minds of people. Without such control of man's mind, no dictatorship can remain in existence.

In the second place, the technical development of the means of communication made mankind much more susceptible and sensitive to the influence and mental manipulations by political ideologies and to strange absurd suggestions from the outside. We all live daily in a web of noises and suggestions.

Let us make a survey of the most prominent points that come to the fore in this new development. I prefer to treat the general implications of the problem because they bring the clinical aspects to the fore more clearly, namely: (1) the technique of individual mental coercion and brainwashing; (2) the technique of mass-coercion and mass-seduction; (3) the problem of unobtrusive and unconscious mental coercion, and (4) ways by which a free society can resist, neutralize, and counteract these strange mental intrusions.

The Techniques of Individual Mental Coercion

The totalitarian brainwashing technique involves a double task. First, the mind of the victim has to be broken down—made empty according to the brainwasher's terminology; then a clean gramophone record has to be filled with new grooves, a new ideology.

The methods used are simple enough. Soldiers and officers who were prisoners of war in Korea and China were submitted to a systematic regime of mental submission followed by political propaganda in which hunger and isolation played the most important part in breaking down the victim's mental resistance. If perceptual isolation and coercive persuasion are applied day in and day out, most people will lose their individual critical distinctions and gradually follow the suggestions of their inquisitors. This happens especially when a clever alternation of hunger and giving food is used as a system of Pavlovian conditioning and training. Then new ideas are hammered in with repetitious ideological catchwords, launched after enforced, long-lasting interrogation and sleeplessness.

Especially, however, when the interrogators are able to arouse a man's deep-seated feelings of guilt can they make him even more abject and dependent, more willing to confess any crime. This subtle manipulation of man's feelings of shame and guilt was also the old coercive tool of the inquisitor but is also one of the prominent modern instruments of brainwashing. The prisoners of war in Korea were invited in a seemingly innocent way to write down their autobiographies and to describe their own mistakes and failures in life. In doing so, they inadvertently surrendered to their inquisitors details concerning personal weakness and confusion, which were investigated and analyzed again and again and finally led to mental submission, confession, and conversion. We may also say it this way: The brainwasher blackmails man's inner need to communicate. The need to talk and to communicate in days of loneliness and great boredom gradually becomes a need to confess. Abject dependency arouses all man's masochistic traits.

In the new military regulations, we have to guide the soldiers to adhere strictly to the rules and to give no information at all, and they must learn that willful silence affords better protection than their infantile need to talk and to communicate.

The official data indicate that nearly 70 per cent of the prisoners of war in Korea, unprepared for such subtle psychic attacks on their integrity, communicated with the enemy in a way not permitted by military rules. This does not mean, however, that they may be regarded as real collaborators or traitors.

For psychiatry and social psychology a few facts came to the fore which were rather surprising:

How weak and submissive is the human mind under such abnormal, stressful circumstances! Hunger can break the mental dignity and integrity of most people. When man is alone, without sufficient food, without his daily work and without his usual human contacts, he easily breaks down. He unconsciously accepts the verdict of the inquisitor and accepts the self-image imposed on him by this new father image. In brainwashing, man's masochism is the victor. Psychiatrists could have gathered some of this from previous studies of prison-psychoses and contagious delusions in isolated communities but they had to learn it anew from this political experiment.

In the laboratory this inner breakdown of man can be provoked in a rather short time by the exclusion of sensory contact with the outside world. In many a student—serving as a human guinea pig—such extreme isolation, sensory deprivation and lack of verification of reality caused fearful dreams and actual hallucinations *within twelve hours.*

When the normal sensory stimulation from the outside world fails to enter the mind and the sense of time and space disappears, the inner world of primary unconscious processes begins to take over. These experiments revealed that most men need a continual verification of and confrontation with reality lest their infantile anxieties and fantasies begin to dominate them. We now have a more exact picture of why the lonely and isolated man breaks down so easily especially in the age of advertised togetherness. Isolation and living on one's own inner resources is a state for which one has to be carefully trained.

The methods of political thought control have also directed our attention to the importance of the process of interrogation of patients. We are more convinced now that the ways and methods of interrogation and interviewing are able to influence patients and to bias the information we obtain.

Experiences with brainwashed soldiers have greatly improved our understanding. We are consequently able now to inform the courts of justice how easy it is to imprint subjective feelings on some of the accused. With the help of third degree and even with the threat of so-called truth serum or lie detector one can coerce people into false confessions.

This poses many questions concerning our own communication with patients, our own ways of interrogation and subsequent treatment. Are we sufficiently aware of the fact that the rhythmic, repeated, intimate talks and therapeutic sessions inadvertently can have a subtle, coercive action on patients? Even our benevolent silent attitude can have this effect. What we ascribe as positive and negative transference towards our patients—and from the patients toward us—has a much greater persuasive and suggestive action than many therapists would want to admit.

Unobtrusively we can transplant our ideas to the patients. Current psychotherapy and psychoanalysis are well aware of these facts and try to prevent them by emphasizing the final analysis of the transference as one of the most basic processes in every therapeutic encounter. This awareness of subjectivity and prejudice cannot be granted, however, to other more physical, medical methods where patients are just as much submitted to psychic persuasion and conditioning with neither doctor nor patient being aware of it. Take, for instance, the habit of taking tranquillizers, sedatives, and sleeping drugs. Not only mental and physical health can be affected by it, but, at the same time, the mild addict can gradually become a more submissive, masochistic personality, dependent on the physician and his chemical magic.

In the initial phases of brainwashing technique, narcotics were used as additional means of breaking down mental resistance. The old device "*in vino veritas*"—the truth is in the wine—was the first aphorism dedicated to such forms of coercive thought control. But the totalitarian inquisitor discovered rather soon that hunger, lack of sleep, cold, dirt, and isolation brought about with greater rapidity the regression and mental breakdown they wanted. This is not completely true for the application of pain and physical torture so often used by the inquisition of the Middle Ages. Experience showed that pain more often aroused rebellion and resistance in the person while the "hunger-isolation" treatment led more easily to a submissive form of dependency.

The Techniques of Mass-Coercion and Mass Seduction

The art of convincing other groups and nations of the subjective truth of the "chosen tribe or country" is as old as human history. Most religions have wanted to convert the nonbelievers, often forcefully and with the sword. Napoleon changed such persuasion into a military science in his "Bureau de l'Opinion Publique." In the meantime the science of advertising and propaganda discovered new methods by which to imprint onto the public favorable suggestions before actual selling of the product. Even when people are skeptical about ads, the repeated clichés and slogans have an impact. A gradual penetration into man's unconsciousness takes place no matter how much he may criticize the cheap suggestion. In the end he buys the commodity he did not first need or want.

As far as our subject of thought control is concerned it is not so important that one soap outsells another. Much day-to-day advertising and public-opinion engineering makes use of the psychological experience that a repeated suggestion, no matter how far-fetched, may gradually creep through the barriers of our critical defenses into the deeper layers of our psyche and leave some "memento" behind. The next time we hear the familiar slogan combined with the same musical jingle, our recognition acts automatically. Inwardly we say "Aha," and without critical awareness we buy the soap we will perhaps never use. The advertiser does not even need the trick of subliminal advertising to make some imprint on the minds, provided his product arouses some basic need.

The unobtrusive penetration and unconscious leakage through man's critical barriers that occurs even in a free democracy becomes, however, a thousandfold stronger persuasion when the suggestions are backed by political terror. Then, man's unconscious urge to surrender and merge with the stronger party easily takes over. The passive defense of identification with the aggressor takes hold of man.

The collective terror in a totalitarian state with the help of secret police and concentration camps makes people much more submissive and obedient to the partisans in power. Under such strain and stress the spirit may seem to be critical but the will yields.

Such are the two sides of our problem. On one side we see the engineers of mass opinion trying to use our best psychoanalytic knowledge in the service of propaganda and advertising. On the other side we discover political systems that not only use this unconscious penetration into the psyche to sell products but also to implant and imprint ideologies and slogans in the public mind.

The current Chinese program of thought reform and thought control is an example of how far this idea of mental mass submission may be executed. Hitler's idea of equalization and merging (*Gleichschaltung*) was based on the same coercive principle. In a totalitarian system the luxury of having an individual ego and an individual opinion is superfluous. All thinking and feeling belongs to the monolithic party.

It is not my task here to describe the ways in which the conductor of enforced pessimism and despair relate to the psychological warfare and actual cold war now in progress. A few illustrations may be given of what happens, however, of special affects worked on the individual psyche by such continual mental attack.

Totalitarian strategy in its tactical description of the techniques of mass intimidation and collective control discovered that the arousing of simple panic, fear and terror do not suffice. Too great a mental pressure exerted over a long period of time loses its frightening impact and often stirs rebellion and critical resistance in the people, militating against the final aim of producing obedient automatic thought machines out of human beings.

In order to better reach its goal, the more scientific strategy makes use of *waves of terror* "with in-between periods of relative calm and freedom"—the so-called "*breathing spell,*" (*peredishka*). These intervals of relative freedom and lack of overt tensions can be used to much better advantage for political persuasion and mass-hypnosis provided some new wave of terror is anticipated. It is completely comparable with the patient in hypnotherapy who becomes easier to hypnotize at every session. The alternation of terror and breathing spell, for example, the alternation of a cold war of hatred with the opposite propaganda for harmonious, peaceful coexistence, can gradually cause confusion and increased anxious anticipation in people.

The Nazis had already been playing that psychological cat-and-mouse game very cleverly in the occupied countries. People ask themselves: "But what will happen tomorrow?" Gradually a silent panic saps their critical potentials and the passive expectation of renewed terror makes them easy marks for ideological slogans. According to totalitarian strategists, well-applied waves of terror are the best recipes for terrorizing people into co-operation and collaboration. It is the latent silent panic in people that makes them into more submissive and suggestible beings. On the other hand, overwhelming fear and acute fright may make rebels of them.

I make a special point of this strategy of *fractionalized panic* because its paralyzing influence is not enough known, and in actual politics we can easily be surprised by it.

Unobtrusive Coercion

The study of individual brainwashing has already taught us how far mental intrusion and mental coercion can influence people even when we may not, strictly speaking, refer to an artificial technique of breaking down a human being and remaking him into a new political automaton. It showed us how human feeling and thinking are and have to be in a constant exchange with influences and stimuli from the environment. There exists a continuous need to communicate and to be communicated with. The web of communicative pressure in our actual world is, however, far beyond people's intellectual apprehension.

When man is conscious of the concept of propaganda and psychological warfare and he lives in a country where he can speak his mind freely, he can build up a critical attitude and inner defenses against mental intrusions. Yet, can he always voluntarily select or ward off what tries to penetrate his mind in spite of certain leakage?

The problem is not so simple! As I have mentioned previously, many suggestions and influences reach our mind without our being aware of them. They mold us and change us without our awareness.

Alas, I have to bypass the intriguing chapter of unconscious communication—a field psychology has just begun to explore. Yet, there exist other forms of unobtrusive coercion and inadvertent mental penetration important enough to be mentioned in this context. For a long time psychiatry has shown, for instance, how the newborn child is molded and conditioned not only by the conscious communication of parents and educators but also by subtle persistent actions and attitudes of older persons. The over-anxious mother, with her threatening eye or warning finger, may use the loveliest words but, nevertheless, her frightening gaze can cause the child to withdraw or become very defensive toward her. Both parents may follow very precisely and obviously the modern patterns and book-rules of a loving education, but when they are nevertheless constantly in battling conflict with each other, the child will be more affected by their mutual hypocrisy of love than by the mask they show to the child.

Unexpected influences can have lasting impact on people without their being aware of these emotional intrusions. During recent months I have studied a group of so-called ambulatory psychotic people. In all these cases I was able to discover some emotional shock or trauma as the provocative factor in their withdrawal from reality. Related to our subject is the fact that the accident and traumatic occurrence—as for instance temporary deafness resulting from an ear operation—forced these people to concentrate more than usual on inner psychic stimuli—such as was also the case in the experiments with students in extreme sensory deprivation.

Are we, for instance, aware of the way modern technology is unobtrusively molding our minds? Technique influences our philosophical attitude toward life. Daily it teaches people that the shortest and easiest way is the best way. It calls for "efficiency" and magic gadgets and is therefore in conflict with the psychological rule that toil, resistance, challenge and difficulty form the personality. Healthy, strong egos are not formed by passivity and facilitation, by luxuries and leisure time; the personality has to grow by accepting challenges.

How technology has unobtrusively intruded into the home and into the parent-child relationship can be illustrated by a form of neurosis one may call *TV-apathy*—the unwillingness to have personal relations other than with the fascinating television screen. I have seen children between four and six years of age who could communicate with the TV screen but not with their parents. True, the parents started the problem by being fixed to the TV screens themselves, hardly speaking to one another because of the hypnotizing effect of the new intruding toy. The mother works in a factory during the day and at noon the children go alone to the Automat to exchange their dimes for food. Between the children and the parents has crept a technical mechanical world which keeps them far apart psychologically. No wonder the children refuse to learn to read in school and only crave the warm verbal communication they lack so greatly at home.

Reading not only creates a greater distance from the spoken word but demands extra energy in learning. We may call the child's inner refusal to expend his verbal communication toward a dialectic relation with the printed word by the sophisticated name "reading block." Yet, this neurosis is only the result of the changed and distorted passive attitude of the child toward reality inflicted on the child by parents addicted to gadgets and automats. In some cases I could urge the father to play scrabble (a word game) with the children instead of watching TV. In several cases the child overcame his reading block as a result of a changed, warmer attitude by the father.

These examples mostly serve to show that the technical intrusion into life goes much further than, for instance, the speedomania of the driver or the magic gadgeteering of toyland. Technology provokes our infantile magic thinking and our dependency need. It makes social insects of us and fits us into the prescribed mosaic of patterns. It carries us inadvertently back to the passive infantile dreams of omnipotence. It teaches people a new, cold ritual of knobs and handles and makes them lacking in faith and communion.

The mutual communication and unobtrusive relation between men and gadgets, between persons and machines, are now so intertwined and related that none of us can escape their influence. The mass media of communication—the headlines, slogans, jingles—touch our personal norms and evaluations every day without our becoming aware of their inadvertent suggestions and coercions.

Another unexpected intrusion into man's feeling and thinking is made by a related ogre of modern development: *bureaucratization*. In our actual world, with its increasing social and technical complications, it is impossible to have a universal insight and view on everything happening around us. Modern man needs several institutions as mediators between him and his environment. Therefore, man has created an overwhelming number of organizations to lead and influence him. It starts with the home and ends with the funeral parlor. An army of nursemaids, employees, and civil servants has unobtrusively crept into personal human relations and this whole bureaucratic phalanx has changed the relations between man and his fellow-man. We all have to wear labels and be members of many organizations, witness our psychological and psychoanalytic institutionalism and our frantic efforts "to be in the swim."

Do not misunderstand me! I am aware that people are in dire need of these institutional and intermediary formations, but at the same time, we must realize the new influence those in-between can exert for good or for bad. In general, the impact of the bureaucratic civilization has, with its emphasis on the letter of the law, loosened man's personal ties and faith in human values. The institution is not a moral responsible entity. The member of the S.S., for instance, who committed the most cruel crimes, always hid his moral responsibility behind the rules of the institution that commanded him to commit the cruel acts.

In many cases institutionalism has become a magic ghost, lacking in both moral responsibility and ethical commitment. The technical era has transformed human relations into relations between men and things, men and machines, men and institutions. The cold institution with its automatic rules, rituals, and by-laws, has crept in between the warm human relations. The party, the business, the factory, the hospital, the state, the service corps, have all become impersonal but omnipotent justifiers for everything that takes place. They have led to a spiritual *equalization* and *horizontalization* of man of which we are only gradually becoming aware. Literature itself speaks of "the man in the grey flannel suit," "the corporate man," "the white-collar worker," and the impersonal role of the production machine; of the "suburbanites" and the "power elite"—about all those generalized, cross-sections of people, socially patterned after the other, automatic mass products without individuality.

Everywhere in our technological world and because of our technical world, with its standardization, the pressure for conformity is increasing. Driving the same kind of car, with the same automatic devices, makes of the people the same accident-prone fiends. However, this equalizing conforming pressure, the suggestion to disappear in the anonymity of the mass, also causes ambivalent feelings in the "organization man." Because he has to merge with and be the same as others on behalf of his profession and his career, inner fear and frustration develop. Mainly because man must surrender to the generalizing institution, he continually searches for his own individuality and the lost possibilities of childhood.

"Who am I, with my ready-made suit and with my well-adjusted pattern?" is the new question of the technical age.

This inner conflict between the urge for distinction and the pressure for conformity often leads either to increased neurotic acting out or to passive surrender and greater submissiveness in continual self-pity and depression. No wonder that in psychotherapy the problem of ego strength and lack of individual ego comes more and more to the fore.

How far this process of technical institutionalism has gone in our actual world can be illustrated with a statistical example. The year 1956 was the first year that the number of people in the United States who were directly active in economic production was smaller than all those mediary people in between (*New York Times*, April 1, 1957). It is clear that the impersonal gears between man and man are constantly prospering.

It is not difficult to find other examples of the unobtrusive streamlining of our feeling and thinking by our technical civilization. We may include here some other aspects of social neuroses such as the sportsman, through which we acquire strength and excitement by proxy, the raving frenzy of the highways, making us more and more accident-prone. Aspirinism or tabletmania sells us a cheap magic and success mania advertises a glamorous pseudo-ego, meanwhile the chameleon-like urge to adjust and change color deflates the ego more and more. All these encroaching influences are exerted by the swift social changes we are now experiencing.

For our general theme of thought control, it is important to emphasize the fact that unobtrusively unconscious coercion actually exists. All these new molding forces, with their impact on emotions and thoughts, have tremendous significance for the future of mankind and the human race.

Free Society and Resistance to Mental Coercion

When a student is in the midst of studying a new phenomenon, in this case a form of social pathology, it is rather difficult to talk immediately about curative or preventive measures. Every form of individual and social therapy must be the *result* of an intensive study of the disease. When five years ago the army authorities became aware of the strange treatment to which their soldiers who had been taken prisoner had been subjected, they asked the so-called experts for whom it was just as new a subject: "What can we do against this devilish intrusion and invasion of the human psyche?" "Can we fortify the psyche against mental coercion?" "Can we, through special training and instruction, fortify man's morale and moral resistance in anticipation of such abnormal circumstances?"

I am very much aware that this is an enormously complicated problem rooted in philosophical, psychological, and political ideas and prejudices. I will mention here very briefly what, as a member of the psychiatric profession, I was able to tentatively advise.

The very fact that one is well-informed and aware of the intention and strategy of the so-called inquiring enemy can, in itself, be a protection against his penetration into one's thinking. That was also one of the experiences proved in the concentration camps. Those victims who were not perplexed and who fully understood the enemy's motivations were better able to stand his "treatment." I would expand my subject too much if I described how different characters reacted differently to these forms of stress.

A free country, a free press, the right to be well-informed, gives to man, however, an inner foundation and strength against wild political suggestions. Beyond this, strong, simple belief and faith in one's own ideas and intentions make people less vulnerable. True conviction acquired from a harmonious environment constitutes the mental backbone of the brainwashee.

The first aim of the military should be an adequate, alert, non-sophisticated, education and training of its soldiers. They need to be informed better than they had been previously that a new war will always be a war of ideas. They have to be taught the intentions of brainwashing and what should be their general attitude in a POW camp. For instance, the writing down of one's life history for the enemy—his first psychological testing—is already giving one's self away. There should be no co-operation with the enemy's tests and no political discussions. Confidential or jovial talking of any kind is dangerous and seduces the man to talk more and too much. Only one's serial number and name should be given, according to International Law.

The concept of the strength of the ego, the strength of the personality is a point of great psychological interest. Although there exists a great body of literature on ego-psychology and man's capacity to tolerate danger (mental tolerance capacity) we do not know enough about active methods of strengthening man's mental defenses. But we are very conscious of the fact that leadership and identification with the leader play an important role. As we saw in the third part of this paper, the new technological age has the tendency to weaken the personality. Religious educators and those who educate their students in scientific discipline have more practical experience with education for personal morale and spiritual strength.

We have to inform the authorities of the existing unobtrusive pressure currents in our actual world, for they are not limited to totalitarian countries alone and they may have a weakening effect on the personality. These new universal circumstances make the human personality more sensitive and vulnerable toward mental contagion from without. Education to conformity does not strengthen individual morale either. With the exception of a few oriental schools and a few religious communities, there exists little systematic education in individual and personal strength. Conformity and discipline are the special aims of technical education. When the emphasis is on facts and more facts without the ethos and moral commitment behind them, the school as a fact-factory unobtrusively prints its conformity on the student. Mere knowledge of facts does not strengthen the soul!

The question of individual morale and mental backbone is a problem of education both in the family and in the schools. Modern psychology and especially psychoanalysis believe in the deeply rooted *vertical* education, starting in the nursery and continuing into the personal relations and identifications with educators and leaders. Our technical age of *horizontalism* makes people feel lost, without relations.

Another problem is how to solve the tendency to passivity and greater easiness which the technical civilization suggests to people. An increased material dependency makes people more unwilling to form and express their own opinions. The great material luxury as found in the U.S.A. is often used wrongly by people to fortify their passivity and dependency needs. Sports and "do it yourself" movements can only partially correct these evils. Increased inner activity could be better accomplished if the people grew away from "sportsmania" to a true, many-sided physical and psychical culture.

One can be sure that in a free, democratic form of government a system of different rules and controls has to develop to check the imprisoned thinking and narrowed psychic development provoked by unilateral political infection and mental contagion. Freedom to think for oneself has to be more highly stimulated than ever. Schools have to promote the student's personal initiative to develop new thoughts. It is not only a question of ego strength but also one of how to protect the principle of freedom and independence in a developing personality. From a psychological point of view, the quintessence of a free democracy is the integration of both freedom and discipline, the integration of individual isolation with communal conformity, the integration of natural rebellion with duty and responsibility.

The riddle of a free democratic society is to find the just man and equilibrium between tolerance and intolerance, between the proud battle for justice and the valuable tolerance to bear injustice, that is, man's tolerance to bear the incompleteness and the faults and foibles of the race.

In our epoch people are not willing to accept an authority just because he is powerful. We want to understand him, understand his need for power, and through means of our analysis of his motives, we want to set limits to his urges and compulsions to dominate us.

But the compulsion to understand everything and to explain the unexplainable can be dangerous too. In our illusion that we understand more than we really have a notion of, we can more easily subject ourselves to so-called universal theories and ideologies. When we are unable to live with unsolved riddles and the awe of mystery, we may unknowingly surrender to an easier theory.

We have learned that the mental pressure of brainwashing and thought control can cause an inner conflagration that can lead to an atrophy of ego and personality. Many people who had returned from concentration camps after brainwashing and torture needed months before they were restored to their previous personalities again.

There exist many ways in which to build up man's inner strength and help him become a free and strong self-confident being. Psychiatrists and psychologists have built up appropriate systems of psychotherapy. Yet, we must be aware of the fact that specific political and also cultural currents are in conflict with these psychotherapeutic ideals. The aim of these currents is adjustment, dependency, and conformity; not freedom and self-realization and self-confidence. Our psychiatric battle for the integrity of the individual mind, however, goes far beyond accusing some enemy of brainwashing soldiers; we must see it as a general social phenomenon.

There exist everywhere subtle influences and powers which are able to creep unseen inside the psyche in order to make man more submissive. Take, for instance, the technological suggestion that inner peace and contentment can be found or bought through chemical sedation and the magic of pacifying tablets or through the mild hypnosis of machine-music or the frenzy of speedy, noisy motors.

Man has to battle inwardly for every new insight. That is not only true in psychoanalysis and psychotherapy but more so to attain his political insights and certainties. His inner strength and mental backbone depend on a free, unlimited knowledge of himself and on man's simple self-confidence that he or his heirs eventually will reach that goal. It depends on his unfrustrated belief in human values and on his awareness of belonging to a group of other people, who like him and have esteem for him. It depends, too, on his education in both freedom and self-discipline.

The simple formulation for the cultivation of man's inner morale and strength is a variation of the old formulation the oracle of Delphi gave to mankind:

Know and Trust Thyself.

References

The following titles are only intended to introduce the reader to the literature and problems of the essay:

Anon. "Document on Terror," *News from behind the Iron Curtain.* Vol. I (1952).

Hunter, E. *Brainwashing in Red China: The Calculated Destruction of Men's Minds.* New York: Vanguard, 1951.

Lea, H. C. *The Inquisition of the Middle Ages.* 3 vols. New York: The Citadel Press, 1954.

Meerloo, J. A. M. "The Crime of Menticide," *American Journal of Psychiatry,* CVII (1951).

Meerloo, J. A. M. *The Rape of the Mind.* New York: World Publishing House, 1956.

Reik, Theodor. *Geständniszwang und Strafbedürfnis.* Zurich: Internationaler Psychoanalytischer Verlag, 1925.

Sargant, W. *Battle for the Mind.* New York: Doubleday, 1957.

III

THE EVOLUTION OF PERSONAL STYLES IN MASS SOCIETY

a.

PERSONAL STYLES AND THE ARTS

C. M. BOWRA

Poetry and Tradition

IT CAN HARDLY be claimed that the advance in material civilization has done much for poetry. The growth of large towns has curtailed that intimate connection of man with nature which has in the past provided countless themes for song; the pressure of crowded populations fosters conventions of behavior which are inimical to the free play of imaginative impulse; the spread of standardized education does not always encourage the originality and independence which are necessary to creative work; the specialization of intellectual life diminishes not merely the desire to write poetry but the ability to enjoy it. A mass of evidence shows that poetry is far less popular in western Europe and the United States than in countries like Persia or China or India, whose material civilization is far less advanced but which have kept a traditional taste for the beauty of words. At an even lower level, in societies where conditions are still primitive and existence is indeed hard, poetry may be the main pastime and consolation of peoples like the Asiatic Tartars or the Armenians or the Ainus, among all of whom it is a truly national art practiced with a high degree of accomplishment and enjoyed by whole populations. Compared with such societies, our own mechanized, urban world is indeed feeble and uncertain in its approach to an art which has in the past enjoyed great glory but seems now in danger of becoming an esoteric pursuit of cliques and coteries.

Reprinted from *Diogenes*, No. 22 (Summer, 1958), pp. 16-26, by permission of the publisher. *Diogenes* is a review of humanistic sciences edited by the International Council for Philosophy and Humanistic Studies, Unesco House, Paris.

The situation may even be worse than this. Some of our gloomier prophets foresee a time when poetry will almost have disappeared because there will be no demand for it or, at the best, will have become a specialists' pastime like chess or an antiquated superstition like astrology. It is assumed that the analytical, scientific spirit which informs so much modern thought will have replaced the old imaginative, poetical spirit which seeks to produce a synthesis of experience and to present any given situation as a concrete whole. To these gloomy presentiments the recent history of poetry gives some support. By becoming more intimate and more difficult, poetry has lost some of its old public and has not yet trained a new public to take its place. In its desire to convey the subtler, more elusive movements of the consciousness, it tends to avoid the broad issues which have often given it strength in the past and to concentrate on aspects of experience which are sometimes so special that they can be fully understood by few but the poets themselves. In abandoning much of its old territory and relinquishing it to science or history or theology, poetry makes itself less approachable even to those who wish to enjoy it.

This contraction of poetry is a matter of grave concern. At the lowest level, we may deplore that an art which has for countless centuries given pleasure to multitudes should lose much of its power and find no adequate successor, for few will claim that the novel or the drama or the cinema can do what poetry does or in any sense take its place. If poetry is really shrinking, we may well lament that a great joy is being taken from us and that the art of living will be correspondingly impoverished. But of course the loss would be far worse than this. Poetry is much more than a source of pleasure, more even than a source of joy in the highest and purest sense. It is certainly that, and for this very reason poetry is an essential element in civilization and does much to preserve and enliven it. Since any civilization worthy of the name is much more than a technical application of scientific discoveries and is of no importance unless it brings enrichment to our inner lives, it is dangerous to dispense with poetry or even to reduce its influence. A world without poetry is perfectly conceivable, but it would not be worth living in. For not only would it be bleak and barren; it would lack many valuable qualities which we do not always associate with poetry but which it discovers and keeps alive and makes essential elements in the richness and variety of life.

Poetry lives by tradition. It derives from the past not merely its consciousness of its own nature and function but much of its technique and outlook. In doing this, it not only keeps alive great discoveries made in the world of spirit but makes new discoveries of a similar character for its own age. The tradition of poetry is alive and adaptable in the same way as a tradition of manners. It faces new problems with well-tried instruments and secures new results from them. Though it can never repeat exactly what has been done before, since in poetry, as in all the arts, mere repetition is bound to be dead and useless, it can do in a new way the same kind of thing that has often been done, and its success lies in the new approach and the new vision which it brings to the individual event in the given, recognized field. Like all true traditions, that of poetry selects something significant from the particular scene, preserves this for posterity, and continues to make a similar selection whenever it has a chance of doing so. But traditions are delicate organisms, and, if they are treated too roughly, they cease to do their right work. So, if poetry breaks too violently with the past and conducts experiments in too reckless a spirit, it may well hurt itself. Indeed, it is difficult not to think that something of this kind has happened in our own time, which has indeed been rich in talent but has not quite produced the poetry demanded or deserved by our circumstances. However this may be, it remains true that poetry lives by tradition and that such a tradition is important not merely for poetry but for anything that may rightly be called "civilization."

One of the chief claims of poetry as a civilizing influence is that it presents in a lasting and persuasive form the discoveries which man has made about himself and his circumstances, about the possibilities and the significance of events seen with clairvoyant vision and passionate intensity. The poets whose work survives the corroding influence of time express something so important that it becomes part of ourselves, even though we may be divided from them by many centuries. In such a process the expenditure is of course enormous. For every poem that endures, thousands and thousands perish, and even in the work of great poets there may be much that is remembered only because of the good company which it keeps. And this process not only reflects the capacity of poets to say something worth saying as it should be said but determines the final worth of their achievement, as time and succeeding generations test and judge it. The business of selection goes on until only what is beyond cavil survives, but this is of inestimable worth and forms an essential part of living history.

How poetry chooses and preserves experience may be seen from a glance at some great works in which the poet gives life to what has most touched or stirred him in fact or legend or belief and arms it with an appeal which moves far beyond his contemporary setting to an almost timeless world. The *Iliad*, for instance, is the last word on the heroic world of ancient Greece. In it the concept of heroism, the idea that a man should devote his life to the display of prowess and the acquisition of glory, provides the central theme and the main setting. Achilles is a hero almost without peer. Sigurth may equal him in prowess but is inferior to him in humanity; Roland may be equally tragic but is certainly not so foursquare. In Achilles, the heroic way of life is presented in all its implications, its taste for action and its sense of personalities, its magnificent manners and its inevitable doom. Once Homer had composed the *Iliad*, no other poems could hope to challenge him on such a theme. It is the climax of Greek heroic society and must have been composed when that society was already beginning to be transformed into something else. But just for that reason it presents what matters most in such a world, and the wonderful paradox is that, though we have passed far from any heroic age, Homer's world is still perfectly real to us, not merely in the sense of being vivid and present, but in the sense of making us feel toward its characters what we might feel toward our own friends and acquaintances. Only our feelings toward them are less confused and less cloudy than in any ordinary existence. The art of poetry has made its selection not merely from story but from the complex mass of human nature and found in this what it thinks to be most exciting and moving. Homer gives us something invaluable just because he operates with a world which we do not know and yet, when he presents it, we see it to be somehow intimate and familiar.

What Homer does for heroic Greece, Dante does in his own remarkable way for the Middle Ages. Into the *Divine Comedy* he put not only the science, philosophy, theology, and literary criticism of his time but his own highly individual judgments on men and things. He surveys all history as he knows it from the Bible, the Roman historians, and his own chroniclers; presents its achievements through his own highly discriminating, highly critical judgment; and makes it live through the power of his poetical vision, with the result that it is difficult for us, with our far greater sources of knowledge, to see some characters except as Dante saw them. He has given the final portraits of such men as Farinata or Pietro delle Vigno, and, more than this, he presents through his art a coherent conception of life which people find relevant even today. Even if we do not accept his main assumptions, we must still feel that his is a point of view of absolute value—that, if we absorb it, we shall understand life better than we do and be aware of much which we habitually neglect. Of course the *Divine Comedy* is the work of an almost unique genius, but it derives part of its strength from the world in which Dante lived and which he examined with so sharp an understanding that what mattered most in it is still alive for us today.

If poetry preserves the continuity of civilization by passing to coming generations what matters most in its discoveries, so also it shapes the future by seeing where tendencies still obscure and generally unmarked may lead and what their fulfillment means. It is not too much to claim that, if in Achilles, Homer created the exemplar of heroic valor, he created in Hector the champion of the city-state which had hardly emerged in his time and was to dominate the Greek scene for centuries. If Dante was much concerned with the characteristics of individual Italian towns, he had also a vision of a united Italy which was to dominate men's imaginations for centuries until at last it was realized in fact. Some poets do more than this. Their vision pierces into the distance and sees forms which even they themselves may not fully understand or appreciate but which, through their presentation of them, in due course come into being. Though Virgil tells of Rome as it was in the beginning, he looks forward to a future of order and peace, which was indeed to exist over the Roman world for some two centuries, and beyond this he describes less firmly but not less sincerely certain doubts and misgivings about man's place in the universe which were later to trouble Marcus Aurelius and to do much for the triumph of the Christian church. In this sense poetry is indeed a kind of prophecy, but what it foretells are not events but movements of the spirit, the emergence of hitherto unrecognized powers of the will and intelligence, stirrings in the heart which will change the texture of human life and open vast new vistas to the imagination and affections.

This power to preserve the past and to foresee the future belongs in a special degree to Shakespeare and accounts for the simple but not disreputable belief that in him all knowledge that is worth having is to be found. From one angle we see that he comes at the end of a great period, which he presents in all its richness and inner life. He is indeed the poet of the English Renaissance, which was itself in many ways the culmination of the English Middle Ages. Just as in his historical plays he presents English history from Richard II to Henry VI, so in his own thought he covers a wide range of speculation which touches at one end the ageless, ancient legends of his people and at the other the daring speculations of his own time. The crowded present which he saw and marked with such vivid discrimination provides much of the matter in Shakespeare's plays, but at the same time he follows many unsuspected clues in himself or his acquaintances until he develops themes which were new to his world and have not yet exhausted their freshness, though they have indeed affected the course of history and created new types of men. Hamlet, for instance, may well contain much that Shakespeare knew in himself, but has enabled many men of later generations to see themselves more clearly and to diagnose their own maladies. Without him we can hardly imagine much French or Russian literature of the nineteenth century, and indeed the very type of Hamlet is established in our technique of understanding our fellows. But, of course, Shakespeare's prophetic insight was far greater than the selection of a single character would indicate. Through him, far more than through anyone or anything else, we have formed, often without knowing it, that humanistic philosophy which is the basis of our thought and holds that the only true assessment of man's worth must be made through his own experience as he finds it for himself in facing his own problems.

What these great figures do on a large scale with a prodigious success is done on a small scale by all poets worthy of the name. Any poem that succeeds in being a truly individual and therefore unique work of art preserves something which is worth preserving and passes it to the common heritage of man. Poetry's concern is with the art of life, with the means by which we can live more fully and more abundantly. Through its achievements in each generation it continually extends our imaginative consciousness and through this our whole outlook. Though it may not deal specifically with right and wrong, it deals with a whole world of values as it discovers them in human experience. A poetical tradition is much more than a habit of writing poetry, more than a written record of what men have thought and felt, more even than a vivid, concentrated awareness of the human scene; it is a living, creative force which enlarges our outlooks, quickens our sensibilities, and, by breaking down our habitual limitations of thought and feeling, acts as a powerful antidote to the specialization and departmentalism which afflict so much of organized life.

Such a tradition usually works through a single language, since a poet learns his craft from those who have preceded him in the use of his own speech. This means that it is usually confined to a single country or geographical area, not merely because such an area is the usual unit for a language, but because each country has through its history a set of common experiences which the poet assumes and exploits when he writes for his fellows. Thus, though the rich poetical tradition of Central and South America certainly owes much to Spain, each country has its special, national tradition which inevitably informs its poetry and gives to it an individual character, while beyond this there is an air of the New World which lies outside the scope of Spain but belongs to her former colonies because they are set in a different landscape with different conditions of life. Conversely, a single political unit, which embraces peoples of several languages, is likely to nurture several traditions of poetry which follow their own linguistic habits and may be quite independent of one another. Thus the old Austro-Hungarian Empire did not succeed in producing any poetry representative of its whole domains but produced instead a variety of schools and traditions in German, Hungarian, Czech, and the different branches of South Slavonic. If there is some resemblance between the romantic poetry of the German Austrians and the Czechs, neither has much in common with the heroic lays of the Serbs or even with the powerful, passionate poetry of the Magyars. What matters most is the individual tradition in which a poet works. This is indeed largely determined by local circumstances but is in the main preserved and continued by the literary qualities of a language and the uses to which earlier generations have put them.

A poetical tradition which moves on such lines throws more illumination on the true nature of a people than any record of its external history.

At the least a study of it will confirm and clarify what we already know superficially but do not understand from the inside. The elegance and order of French life reach a new distinction in French verse; the vast metaphysics of Germany have a counterpart in a poetry which relies much upon *Sehnsucht* and is often in search of a *Jenseits;* the deeply rooted individualism of the Chinese permeates a poetry which has a special delicacy and subtlety in treatment of personal relations; the style and variety of Spanish life sustain a poetry remarkable for its dignity and its passion. In such cases poetry may do no more than confirm what we know already, but it makes us look at it in a different way. Something which we have seen from outside reveals its inner nature and the springs of its behavior. Instead of considering abstractions, we see concrete examples, which by their vivid appeal convey much more than any general ideas can. The best clue to the understanding of a nation's character is in its poetry, since this reflects what it has treasured from experience and thinks worth preserving.

The importance of such a study becomes more manifest when a national poetry presents a marked contrast with preconceived ideas of a national character. Such ideas are by no means to be dismissed as foolish prejudices; they are usually based on a knowledge of facts. But they are not based on all the facts, and poetry provides a salutary corrective to them. It is, for instance, a startling paradox that England, the nation of shopkeepers and of sturdy common sense, well known for its love of sport and its love of business, suspected of an innate Philistinism and condemned for too great attention to solid comfort, has nonetheless maintained an unbroken tradition of poetry since the fourteenth century. Nor is this poetry such as we might expect from a people of merchant adventurers and colonial captains. It is intimate and solitary, tender and delicate. It is not even, as it might well be, insular. It is always ready to learn from abroad and to adapt Continental inventions to the native idiom. Nor does the notorious English love of convention hamper it. It is indeed governed by rules, which are part of its admirable style, but it is nonetheless uncommonly generous in its understanding and its sympathies. A man who had studied English history and then turned to English poetry would certainly be greatly surprised by what he found and have to admit that here was something which altered his whole conception of the English character.

Another paradox can be seen in ancient Athens. Perhaps we see it too much through its literature to estimate the appearance it must have presented to other Greek cities. The Athenians were the most ebullient, reckless, adventurous of peoples, always making experiments or trying to impose their will on others or to win everlasting fame through some prodigious exploit, even if it meant incurring universal hatred. Nonetheless, in their poetry they proclaimed and dramatized the all-importance of moderation and the Mean. With all their insatiable appetite for life they would suddenly say that man is but a shadow in a dream and all his desires are dust. This was no mere insurance against the wrath of incalculable gods, no mere conventional tribute to some dim or guilty respect for order. It was part of the Athenian nature and provided the background against which they played their proud and reckless parts. If Athenian tragedy was born from this quarrel with themselves and reflected it in the presentation of superhuman characters coming to appalling dooms, it is also the best means by which we can understand what these men were when they were alive, what swift currents ran in their blood, and how, even if dimly and halfheartedly, they tried to control them.

Though a poetical tradition is essentially national and derives much of its strength from being so, it may at times become international and perform a task between peoples. Sometimes the art of one country will spread its influence abroad and, through translation and adaptations, touch thousands of people whose way of life is alien to it but who nonetheless assimilate it and change their outlook through it just because it appeals to something in themselves which they have not hitherto recognized or opens up new and attractive fields of sensibility. In Asia, Persia was for some centuries the center of such an influence, which spread not only to the Moslem and Hindu peoples of India but to distant mountaineers and pastoral nomads in Georgia, Armenia, and Bactria. In Europe more than one country has played such a role. The rebirth of lyrical poetry in the twelfth century was largely the work of Provence. A highly specialized poetry born in the courts of Languedoc and Aquitaine spread its power to northern France, Germany, Portugal, Sicily, Italy, and England. The local poets took up the Provençal themes and measures and adapted them to their own tongues. But though there is a real community both of technique and of spirit between the songs of Guillaume of Aquitaine and such poems as the English "Alison," or the Portuguese "Leonoreta," or the dawn songs and spring songs of Heinrich von Morungen and Walther von der Vogelweide, this is no case of imitation or of mere adaptation to the local idiom. In each case the Provençal seed falls on a rich, almost prepared ground, in which an indigenous tradition of song has taught men what poetry is and made them ready to accept new forms. The schools of poetry gain a new strength from abroad but lose little of their local color in doing so.

What Provence did for the Middle Ages, Italy did for the Renaissance, Germany and England for the Romantic Age, and France for the end of the nineteenth century. In the sixteenth century, France, England, Spain, and Portugal looked to Italy both for their verse forms and for their main subjects, but in each country we forget the Italian models when we read this lively and varied poetry of the emotions. In the Romantic Age, first Goethe and then Byron carried their own kinds of poetry across Europe, until there is little in France or Russia or Spain which cannot be connected with one or the other of them. In the binetics the French Symbolists and especially Mallarmé evolved a new vision of pure poetry which passed to young poets everywhere and inspired a generation of sublime achievement. Of course in most of these cases such extensive changes would not have taken place if they had not been initiated by men of remarkable originality, but these men would never have had so great an influence if they had not appealed to something which lay hidden in most European countries and responded vigorously to new methods for its expression. In such situations national and European influences combine to produce a notable result. But this itself suggests that divisions between countries hide great similarities between men and that it is the task of the arts to ignore the divisions and explore the similarities. Though poetry cannot ever be so international as music or painting, it can exert a powerful influence in making men of different countries conscious that they have much to learn from one another because they are after all fashioned from the same clay and inspired by the same breath of life. Any system of politics which denounces internationalism in the arts as a heresy is bound in the end to impoverish its own poetry and to lose much which any wise system of government ought to welcome.

The study of poetry is an important element in the study of civilization, just as the writing of poetry is itself a great civilizing force. In such study we should not underrate the value of two techniques which may not look very important but are indispensable to it. First, there is translation. Though it can never be a wholly adequate substitute for the original words, translation is nevertheless a potent influence in spreading new outlooks and ideas, in showing to one people what kind of poetry is written by another, and in suggesting what may be gained by an exploitation of new techniques. The poetry of ancient Rome may almost be said to have begun its mature life when Livius Andronicus translated the *Odyssey* from Greek into Latin and showed how poetry could tell a complex story on a large scale. To a people accustomed to little else than short lays about the doings of their ancestors, this was indeed a revelation and started the series of epics which is one of the glories of Roman literature. Less obvious but no less powerful is the influence which Shakespeare has had in countries not his own. The translations of his poetry into German and Russian are indeed works of true poetry, and the result has been his acclimatization in Germany and Russia, whereas in France and Italy, where he has been far less fortunate in his translations, his popularity and influence have been correspondingly less. Our own century has realized the use of translations and benefited greatly from them. Much, for instance, of the modern approach to Chinese civilization has been determined by gifted men who have conveyed in their own tongue the charm and grace of Chinese poetry. Its form is indeed almost impossible to reproduce in any polysyllabic language like English or French, but its matter, at once so different from that of our own poetry and yet so friendly and ultimately so familiar, has passed into our experience and touched not only our poetry but our lives.

A second important instrument is the anthology, especially if it is truly representative of some national tradition of poetry. It provides the right means to start the study of such a tradition, since through it we form some idea of the complex and yet somehow homogeneous experience which has gone to the making of a nation. This is equally true of a tradition which is old and rich like English or Italian or relatively modern like American. In either case the unfolding panorama of poetry reveals to us what a nation has seen and felt through the vicissitudes of its history and what characteristics it has developed. Such a picture cannot fail to excite our curiosity and engage our attention as we see a civilization growing in variety and responding to new challenges. As we do this, we can hardly fail to enjoy not merely a historical spectacle but chapters of spiritual experience which have their own special color but are nonetheless related to much that we know in ourselves. Just because it is in some respects different from our own, the unfamiliar culture, by exciting our interest in it, enables us at the same time to shift our familiar point of view and to look at our own tradition with fresh eyes. And that, after all, is what anyone desires who believes that the art of life is to be as alive as possible and that for this task poetry is an indispensable means of refreshment and renewal.

IRVING HOWE

Another Way of Looking at the Blackbird

What inmost allegiance, what ultimate religion, would be proper to a wholly free and disillusioned spirit?

—George Santayana

Gradually, under the pressure of time, the masks of Wallace Stevens are wearing away, and not because they have become obsolete or been proven deceptive but because they now seem to have figured mainly as preparations for a homelier

---

Reprinted from the *New Republic*, CXXXVII, No. 20 (1957), 15-18, by permission of the author and the publisher.

reality. Gaudy mystifier, Crispin's pilot, flaunter of rare chromatic words, explorer of Yucatan, enemy of the day's routine, afficionado of strange hats, even the gamesman of epistemology—these roles yield to Stevens' "basic slate," an American poet reflecting upon solitary lives in a lonely age and searching for that "inmost allegiance" by which men might live out their years in thousands of Hartfords.

Stevens was the kind of poet who wrote methodically and a good deal, apparently without waiting for, though always delighted to receive, the blessings of inspiration. Writing verse seems to have become for him a means of wresting convictions of selfhood: the visible token of that which he insistently wrote about. His work is therefore very much of a piece, both in its success and failures. In *Opus Posthumous*—a collection of fugitive pieces, poems omitted from the *Collected Poems*, a few verse plays, a group of aphorisms on poetry, some critical essays and 30 late poems devoted to preparation for death—one can trace out something of the scheme and direction of Stevens' work, perhaps even a bit more easily than in the *Collected Poems*. For *Opus Posthumous* is a much less imposing book, and one therefore in which Stevens' intention juts out all the more sharply.

After the publication of *Harmonium* in 1923, the main job of his critics was to become familiar with his decor: the exotic places, the tropical language, the cheerful jibing at bourgeois norms, the apparent *fin-de-siècle* estheticism, the flip nose-thumbing of his titles. So luxuriant did the world of his poems seem, so free of traditional moral demands, that his early admirers could hardly avoid thinking of this world as primarily a sensuous landscape. It was a view that lingered into Marianne Moore's description of Stevens as "a delicate apothecary of savors and precipitates"—though in that last word there is a hint that Miss Moore, as usual, saw more than she said.

While this was a way of reading Stevens that could yield genuine pleasures, it hardly went very far toward penetrating his deeper concerns, and even when confined to *Harmonium* it could be maintained only if one focused on the shorter poems and neglected "Sunday Morning" and "The Comedian as Letter C." In an early study of Stevens, R. P. Blackmur quickly saw that the strange cries, hoots, and words that ran through the poems, far from being mere exotica, were oblique and humorous tokens of a profoundly serious effort to grapple with the distinctively "modern" in modern experience.

Later there was a tendency to read Stevens as if he were a versifying philosopher, a misfortune for which he was himself partly to blame, since at his prolific second-best he had a way of sounding like a versifying philosopher. Stevens' poetry, now in the hands of new exegetes, was said to be about the writing of poetry, and was regarded as a series of variations on the philosophical theme of the relation between reality and imagination. Both of these statements, while true and useful, were needlessly limiting as aids toward a fuller apprehension of the poetry: the first was too narrow, the second too academic, and from neither could one gain a sense of what might be urgent or particular in Stevens' work.

Poetry written mainly about the writing of poetry—could that be the ground for any large claim as to the interest Stevens might command from literate readers? Imagination and reality—did that not increase the peril of regarding Stevens as a shuffler of epistemological categories? Neither gambit is enough; another way is needed for looking at the blackbird: not the only or the best, but another.

At the base of Stevens' work, as a force barely acknowledged yet always felt, lies a pressing awareness of human disorder in our time—but an awareness radically different from that of most writers. Only rarely does it emerge in his poems as a dramatized instance or fiction; Stevens seldom tries and almost never manages to evoke the modern disorder through representations of moral conduct or social conflict. When in *Owl's Clover* he did write a poem with a relatively explicit politics, the result, as he later acknowledged, was unfortunate: rhetoric overrunning thought, an assault upon a subject which as a poet Stevens was not prepared to confront.

Lacking that "novelistic" gift for portraiture-in-depth which is so valuable to a good many modern poets, Stevens does not examine society closely or even notice it directly for any length of time; he simply absorbs "the idea" of it. A trained connoisseur in chaos, he sees no need to linger before the evidence: there is enough already. And that is why it seems neither a paradox nor a conceit to say that in Stevens' poetry the social world is but dimly apprehended while a perspective upon history is brilliantly maintained: history as it filters through his consciousness of living and writing at a given time. The disorder that occupies the foreground of so much modern literature is calmly accepted by Stevens, appearing in his work not as a dominant subject but as a pressure upon all subjects.

In a somewhat similar way, Stevens, though sharply responsive to the crisis of belief which has troubled so many sensitive persons in the twentieth century, is not himself directly or deeply involved in it. He knows and feels it, but has begun to move beyond it. When he writes that . . .

> The death of Satan was a tragedy
> For the imagination. A capital
> Negation destroyed him in his tenement
> And, with him, many blue phenomena . . .

the force of these lines is clearly secular, releasing an attitude of comic humaneness. Perhaps they are also a little blasphemous, since it is hard to imagine a religious writer making quite this complaint about the consequences of the death of Satan. Here, as elsewhere in Stevens, a secular imagination measures the loss that it suffers from the exhaustion of religious myths and symbols, and then hopes that emotional equivalents can be found in . . .

> One's self and the mountains of one's land,
>
> Without shadows, without magnificence,
> The flesh, the bones, the dirt, the stone.

At times, it is true, Stevens can resemble the typical intellectual of his day (or the idea of the typical intellectual) and describes himself as "A most inappropriate man/In a most unpropitious place." He can appear to regret that "The epic of disbelief/Blares oftener and soon, will soon be constant." Yet if one compares him to Eliot and the later Auden, it becomes clear that Stevens is relatively free from religious or ideological nostalgia:

> The truth is that there comes a time
> When we can mourn no more over music
> That is so much motionless sound.
>
> There comes a time when the waltz
> Is no longer a mode of desire, a mode
> Of revealing desire and is empty of shadow.

Only occasionally does one find in Stevens that intense yearning for a real or imaginary past which has become so prevalent an attitude in our century. There is instead a recognition, both sensitive and stolid, of where we happen to be. And this, in Stevens' reckoning, imposes a new burden on the poet

> . . . since in the absence of a belief in God, the mind turns to its own creations and examines them, not alone from the esthetic point of view, but for what they reveal, for what they validate and invalidate, for the support they give.

Stevens is not, I think, directly affected by the usual religious or intellectual uncertainties, at least not nearly so much as by the predicament—and possibilities—of the mind experiencing them, the mind that still moves within the orbit of some waning belief yet strives for a direction and momentum of its own. Even in those poems, such as "Sunday Morning" and "The Comedian as Letter C," which do seem to deal explicitly with belief, one finds a recapitulation of a progress Stevens has already taken, not in freeing himself entirely from the crisis of belief or its emotional aftereffects (for to claim that would be impudent), but in learning to write as if in his poetic person he were a forerunner of post-crisis, post-ideological man. In "The Man With the Blue Guitar," where the guitar serves as the instrument of poetry, Stevens relates this role to an estimate, lovely in its comic modesty, of his own work:

. . . Poetry
Exceeding music must take the place
Of empty heaven and its hymns,
Ourselves in poetry must take their place,
Even in the chatter of your guitar.

Yet Stevens is too much of a realist, too aware (as in "The Comedian as Letter C") of the sheer inertia of human existence, to suppose that the crisis of belief can be quickly overcome either by private decision or by public commitment.

Accepting the condition of uncertainty and solitariness as unavoidable to man once he has freed himself from the gods, Stevens poses as his ultimate question not, what shall we do about the crisis of belief, but rather, how shall we live with and perhaps beyond it? And one reason for thinking of Stevens as a comic poet is that he makes this choice of questions.

How shall we live with and then perhaps beyond the crisis of belief? —it is to confront this question that Stevens keeps returning to the theme of reality and imagination. Not merely because he is interested in epistemological forays as such—though he is; nor because he is fascinated with the creative process—though that too; but because his main concern is with discovering and, through his poetry, *enacting* the possibilities for human self-renewal in an impersonal and recalcitrant age.

How recalcitrant that age can be, Stevens knew very well. The fragmentation of personality, the loss of the self in its social roles, the problem of discovering one's identity amid a din of public claims—all this, so obsessively rehearsed in modern literature, is the premise from which Stevens moves to poetry. When Stevens does write directly about such topics, it is often with lightness and humor, taking easily on a tangent what other writers can hardly bear to face. An early little poem, "Disillusionment of Ten O'Clock," is about houses that are haunted by "white night-gowns," for Stevens the uniform of ordinariness and sober nights.

None are green,
Or purple with green rings,
Or green with yellow rings,
None of them are strange,
With socks of lace
And beaded ceintures.

In this flat world "People are not going/To dream of baboons and periwinkles." Only here and there an old sailor, one who by age and trade stands outside the perimeter of busy dullness . . .

Drunk and asleep in his boots,
Catches tigers
In red weather.

I hope it will not seem frivolous if I suggest that this drunken sailor embodies a central intention of Stevens' mind, and that when Stevens in his later poems turns to such formidable matters as inquiries into the nature of reality or the relation between the perceiving eye and the perceived object, he still keeps before him the figure of that old sailor dreaming in red weather.

The elaborate conceptual maneuvers of Stevens' longer poems have as their objective not any conclusion in the realm of thought but a revelation in the realm of experience. They are written to rediscover, and help us rediscover, the human gift for self-creation; they try to enlarge our margin of autonomy; they are incitements to intensifying our sense of what remains possible even today. Each nuance of perspective noted in a Stevens poem matters not merely in its own right, but as a comic prod to animation, a nudge to the man whose eye is almost dead. And in Stevens' poetry the eye is the central organ of consciousness.

When Stevens writes about the writing of poetry, he needs to be read not only on the level of explicit statement, but also as if the idea of poetry were a synecdoche for every creative potential of consciousness, as if poetry were that which can help liberate us from the tyranny of mechanical life and slow dying. In that sense, Stevens is a revolutionist of the imagination, neither exhorting nor needing to exhort but demonstrating through poetry the possibilities of consciousness. And he can do this, among other reasons, because in the background of his work loom the defeats and losses of the century.

Time and again Stevens turns to the clause, "It is as if . . . ," for that clause charts a characteristic turning or soaring of his mind, which then is followed by another opening of perception. And these, in turn, are openings to the drama of the mind as it reaches out toward new modes of awareness and thereby "makes" its own life from moment to moment. There may be thirteen or three hundred and thirteen ways of looking at a blackbird, but what matters is that the eye, and the mind behind the eye, should encompass the life of these possible ways and the excitement of their variety. What also matters, as Mr. Richard Ellman has remarked, is that the mind behind the eye should remember that the blackbird, no matter how it may be seen, is always there in its mysterious tangibility.

Putting it this way I may seem to be making Stevens into a moralist of sorts: which readers awed by his urbanity of style might well take to be implausible. But in his relaxed and unhurried way Stevens is, I think, a moralist—a moralist of seeing.

Like any other convention, Stevens' utilization of the theme of reality and imagination as a means of reaching to his deeper concerns, can slide into formula and habit. His extraordinary gifts as a stylist aggravate rather than lessen this danger, since they allow him to keep spinning radiant phrases long after his mind has stopped moving. The reader accustomed to Stevens' habits and devices may even respond *too* well to the poems, for their characteristic inflections and themes have a way of setting off emotions which are proper to Stevens' work as a whole but have not been earned by the particular poem. At other times Stevens' insistence upon human possibility can itself become mechanical, a ruthlessness in the demand for joy. And perhaps the greatest weakness in his poems is a failure to extend the possibilities of self-renewal beyond solitariness or solitary engagements with the natural world and into the life of men living together. (Yet Stevens, humorous with self-knowledge, wrote some of his most poignant lines about this very limitation: "I cannot bring a world quite round,/Although I patch it as I can./I sing a hero's head, large eye/And bearded bronze, but not a man,/Although I patch him as I can/ And reach through him almost to man.")

At his best, however, Stevens transforms each variant of perception into a validation of the self. Sometimes the self is to achieve renewal by a sympathetic merger with the outer world:

> One must have a mind of winter
> To regard the frost and the boughs
> Of the pine trees crusted with snow . . .

At other times the self gains a kind of assurance from entire withdrawal, as if to grant the outer world its own being. In "Nuance on a Theme by Williams," Stevens quotes William Carlos Williams' lines, "It's a strange courage/you give me, ancient star" and then proceeds to tell the star:

> Lend no part to any humanity that suffuses
> You in its own light.
> Be no chimera of morning,
> Half-man, half-star.

The act of discovery by which sentience is regained can

> Be the finding of a satisfaction, and may
> Be of a man skating, a woman dancing, a woman
> Combing. The poem of the act of the mind.

It may be a sheer pleasure in the freshness of the physical world:

> How should you walk in that space and know
> Nothing of the madness of space,
>
> Nothing of its jocular procreations?
> Throw the lights away. Nothing must stand
>
> Between you and the shapes you take
> When the crust of shape has been destroyed.

In the "Idea of Order at Key West" the self "takes over" the outer world by endowing it with a perceptual form:

> She was the single artificer of the world
> In which she sang. And when she sang, the sea,
> Whatever self it had, became the self
> That was her song, for she was the maker . . .

In "Three Travellers Watch a Sunrise," a play printed in *Opus Posthumous*, one of the voices says:

> Sunrise is multiplied
> Like the earth on which it shines,
> By the eyes that open on it,
> Even dead eyes,
> As red is multiplied by the leaves of trees.

And finally in Stevens' last poems, which form the glory of *Opus Posthumous*, the cleared mind listens for solitary sounds in winter, waiting patiently for death. These astonishing poems, like Chinese paintings in their profound simplicity and rightness, are Stevens' last probings, the last quiet efforts to realize life through connecting with whatever is not human. The idea of the world, now as lucid as its single sounds, becomes the final object of contemplation:

> The palm at the end of the mind,
> Beyond the last thought, rises
> In the bronze distance,
> A gold-feathered bird
> Sings in the palm, without any human meaning,
> Without human feeling, a foreign song.

Reading these last poems one encounters again the theme of discovery, the desire to transform and renew, that has given shape to all of Stevens' work. Here, if anywhere, is the answer to Santayana's question, the "ultimate religion" of our secular comedy:

> The honey of heaven may or may not come,
> But that of earth both comes and goes at once.

b.

PERSONAL STYLES AND HUMAN PSYCHOLOGY

JOHN COHEN

Individuality of Thought

In the psychological study of thought we are not concerned with the logical, moral, or social quality of the final product of thinking, but primarily with its mode of development and operation. It is not the business of the psychologist to classify the "ripe apples" of thought. Nor does historical or causal analysis of the end-product of thought provide any criterion of its value. We may enquire, as Piaget[1] has done, whether there are laws governing the changing structures of thought through different stages from birth to maturity, or we may study particular ideas or systems of ideas and trace their origin and manner of growth. It is this second problem which I wish here to discuss.

Since there can be no thoughts without a thinker, thinking must be taken to mean some *person-thinking*. The form of one's thought, the sort of explanation or suggestion that occurs to a person's mind, the specific hypothesis he entertains or feels moved to explore, and the amount of effort he exerts, must, we may assume, be characteristic of him as an individual with a distinctive life history. For the psychologist, everything a person says or does must be seen as an item in a context, the context of personal history and present situation.[2] In seeking an illustration we are reminded of an incident recorded by Plutarch in his *Life of Alexander*.

Reprinted from the *Bulletin of the John Rylands Library*, XXXVII, No. 1 (1954), 103-19, by permission of the author and the publisher. (Copyright, 1954 by the John Rylands Library.)

King Darius had offered Alexander ten thousand talents and certain territories as ransom for prisoners of war. Parmenio, the friend of Alexander, advised his master: "If I were Alexander I would accept the offer," to which Alexander replied: "So would I if I were Parmenio." Plutarch tells us that Longinus described Alexander's reply as something great and sublime.

It need not be denied that one stage in the development of many theories and inventions is often a collaborative effort. But this is usually during the early phases. It is comparatively rare for a notable discovery to be the joint product of two or more investigators working together. This may be partly due, as W. B. Cannon[3] has suggested, to the strong individualism which often marks the expert investigator. Those instances in which two minds have independently made the same original contribution to science or announced the same theory as, for instance, Darwin and Wallace, illustrate the infrequent situation in which a common climate of thought is at least as important a factor as biographical distinctiveness. It is perhaps possible for productive thinking to occur in groups of people working as a unit,[4] but the final act of discovery is bound to be an individual achievement.

Is Individuality Susceptible to Scientific Study?

It may be said that the personal and individual character of thought, being unique, is of no concern to a scientific psychology the task of which is to establish statistical laws which presuppose repeated events. This view seems to me to be based on a false antithesis. The point at issue has been debated at least since Windelband[5] attempted to distinguish between generalizing (nomothetic) and individualizing (idiographic) sciences. Among the protagonists of the possibility of a true idiographic science of psychology, Lewin[6] and G. W. Allport[7] have been specially prominent. Lewin's solution was designed to bridge the gap between descriptions of individual events and the formulation of general principles. He denied that frequency had anything to do with "lawfulness." Allport, on the other hand, distinguished between actuarial and psychological laws. Psychological causation, he declared, is always personal, never actuarial. Let us take an example of the kind considered by Allport. Suppose that for twenty consecutive years 70 per cent of the children in the top class of a primary class have won scholarships. Provided the conditions remain much the same, we can predict with confidence that in the twenty-first year about 70 per cent will again succeed. As Allport correctly states, it does not follow that each child has a 70 per cent chance of success. If we knew all the relevant influences affecting a given child, we should be able to make a perfect prediction. But we should still presumably arrive at the figure of 70 per cent. There is no incompatibility therefore between personal causation and actuarial prediction.

The antithesis seems to disappear if we accept the view of Reichenbach[8] that statistical laws are simply general forms of causal laws, which are themselves special instances of perfect correlation. "Necessary" must be taken to mean "always." We need not therefore segregate psychology from other disciplines on the alleged ground that it is only concerned with unique events; any one physical event for that matter is unique and in this respect does not differ from personal or historical events. Nor need we say that psychology should be restricted to nomothetic studies. The logic of explanation is the same for individualizing and generalizing sciences alike and consists in showing that the nature of the event is such that general relationships could, in principle, be established.

Personal Elements in Philosophical and Scientific Thought

Common sense tells us that a man's personality is reflected in the kind of philosophy he creates. Fichte[9] accepted the common-sense view when he wrote: "The kind of philosophy a man chooses depends upon the kind of man he is. For a philosophic system is no piece of dead furniture one can acquire and discard at will. It is animated with the spirit of the man who possesses it." Gasset[10] expressed a similar view in speaking of those historians of philosophy who describe systems of thought as though they had emanated from the minds of "Unknown Philosophers," anonymous and abstract creatures outside time and space: "into the phrase 'Kant's philosophy' Kant enters not in the concrete role of the person who did the philosophizing but as an adventitious name connected with a philosophy. Yet the true and real philosophy of Kant is inseparable from the man."

Cassirer,[11] however, takes a different view. He argues that the individuality of a philosopher does not impress its stamp on his ideas, and he supports this statement by referring to the profound mutual understanding that existed between Kant and Rousseau, who seemed to be poles apart in temperament as well as in social rank. Kant, the stern and Spartan thinker, dreading change of any kind contrasts hugely with Rousseau who could write only in the intoxication of passion and wanderlust. But in the case of *scientific* discovery he concedes elsewhere[12] that it "bears the stamp of the individual mind of its author. In it we find not merely a new objective aspect of things but also an individual attitude of mind and even a personal style." But while this is of psychological interest it has no systematic relevance. Furthermore, "in the objective content of science these individual features are *forgotten and effaced*, for one of the principal aims of scientific thought is the elimination of all personal and anthropomorphic ideas" (my italics). The expression "forgotten and effaced" is perhaps misleading. Individual features may be irrelevant when we come to evaluate the content of science, but they constitute in themselves a legitimate subject for scientific study, the results of which will provide a different content. The psychology of thought cannot afford to forget and efface the personal factors which lead to the discovery of impersonal content.

Consider, for example, the discovery of "imaginary quantities" in mathematics. As I have suggested[13] this illustrates in striking fashion the personal distinctiveness of ideas even in the realm of number. For centuries the apparent absurdity of the expression $x = \sqrt{-1}$ prevented its use by Hindu and Arab mathematicians as a root of the equation $x^2 + 1 = 0$. It was not until the year 1545 that someone bold enough appeared who had the intellectual courage to face this situation. This was the Italian mathematician Cardan, who deliberately committed the absurdity. We are indebted to Hadamard[14] for reminding us that Cardan was a man of strange and wild temperament. Far from forgetting and effacing this fact it is of the greatest interest for us if we wish to know why Cardan and not anyone else discovered "imaginary quantities," which, indeed, bear the mark of his personal style and character. The fact that imaginaries now constitute part of the objective content of mathematical science does not debar the study of their psychological origin from qualifying as a legitimate subject of scientific enquiry.

The same relationship between a mans' ideas and his character is illustrated in the life of Jeremy Bentham, and here the relationship is expressed not simply in one idea but in his entire life's work. We are told[15] that Bentham was never interested in real problems of life. What he worried about was rather the "mechanism of living" and "his reforms were a series of political gadgets." This acquires a new meaning when we read what John Stuart Mill[16] had to say about Bentham: "He (Bentham) had neither internal experience nor external. . . . He never knew prosperity and adversity, passion nor satiety: he never had even the experiences which sickness gives; He knew no dejection, no heaviness of heart. He never felt life a sore and weary burden. He was a boy to the last."

It would no doubt be pertinent to consider here the problem of vocational choice in all its vast diversity. Why, for instance, does a man become a gynecologist and spend his life probing the minute parts of female genitalia? Clearly this cannot be "explained" in terms of conscious reasons or motives alone; the causal mechanisms assumed by analytic theory must also be invoked. Let us take one more example from scientific thought. It has been suggested[17] that Ehrlich's early passion for bright colors may have stimulated his absorbing interest in the study of dyes, thus influencing in powerful fashion the entire course of his intellectual activity.

We can illustrate the same effect in drama by reference to Voltaire. "If you render Voltaire less sensitive to criticism," said Diderot,[18] "he will no longer be able to penetrate the soul of Meropé."

Proust[19] showed the same profound insight in the following passage:

> A man who falls into bed like a log, and lies there as though dead until he awakes in the morning when it is time to get up, can never expect to make—I won't say discoveries of major importance—but even a few comments on the nature of sleep. A dose of insomnia is of no little value to those who would appreciate the gift of sleep, who would seek to cast even the feeblest ray into that mysterious darkness.

I suspect that this remark was prompted by the action of a publisher who rejected Proust's great novel because he could not understand why anyone needed to devote thirty pages to a description of the process of falling asleep.

Finally as an illustration of individuality expressed in content rather than form we may take an opera of Wagner. In this instance we appear to have a man who infused his private yearnings into his art without adequate transmutation. "Wagner poured into *Tristan and Isolde* his adultery with Mathilde Wesendonck, and if we want to enjoy this work we must, for a few hours, turn vaguely adulterous ourselves."[20]

Forms of Intellectual Audacity

Individuality is not only expressed in the "personal style" of a particular idea, but also in the daring with which one allows oneself to contemplate it. The absurd must be divested of its uninviting character. In Faraday we see a man who was not, like Cardan, fascinated by the sheer perversity of an idea, but who enjoyed a marvellous intellectual mobility and freedom from barriers to thought. He was quite tireless in permitting himself to ponder on analogies between the known and unknown. Nothing seemed impossible to him before it had been put to the test; the most incredible things seemed credible.[21]

We may compare Cardan's audacity with the courage of Freud which consisted not in advancing crazy ideas but in the dispassionate analysis of material marked by a heavy social taboo. Imagine that eminent Victorian, Dr. Arnold of Rugby anticipating Freud and enunciating a sexual theory of dreams! Freud boldly unravelled the Gordian knot of convention. How different are those timid ones among us ever fearful of the impressions they may make on others and unable to resist irrelevant ideas. These "mental parasites" eventually consume our own original thoughts feebly seeking expression.

There can be no individuality of thought if one entertains only the ideas of other people and shrinks from contemplating one's own. This seems to be the meaning of Proust's parable *L'Étranger*. A gifted young man, Dominique, is always surrounded by a circle of admirers. Once when Dominique is alone a stranger comes to him and reproaches him because he receives everyone except himself. Dominique, intrigued and attracted by the stranger, promises to include him among his friends. The stranger replies: "If you receive me you must send away your usual friends." "This I cannot do," replies the young man, "because I cannot be alone." "Choose quickly," warns the stranger, even as the other guests are arriving. "Who are you?" cries out Dominique to the departing stranger. The sorrowing reply comes: "I am your soul." "I am yourself."[22]

Indiosyncrasies in Habits of Work

Individuality expresses itself in idiosyncrasies of work habits. We can picture Rousseau working bare-headed in the full blaze of the sun so as to increase the flow of blood to the brain. Bossuet preferred a cold room with his head wrapped up. Schiller used to sit with his feet immersed in cold water, and his efforts seem to have been invigorated by the smell of decay—fading autumnal leaves, the sepulchral odor of the churchyard or a store of rotten apples in his desk.[23] Descartes and Leibnitz whilst at work placed themselves in an almost horizontal position. Bishop Lammenais walked about and followed his thoughts "in the midst of the noise of festivals as well as in silence and darkness."[24] Balzac, garbed in a monk's cowl, consumed enormous quantities of fresh fruit and struggled right through the night. This continued for long periods while the inspiration lasted. Many are the famous poets and scientists who worked best at night or while lying in bed late in the morning. Some are inert and immobile or, like Beethoven, shut themselves in a room and shout and rush about like madmen.[25] The mathematician Hadamard writes that he finds pacing up and down the room very helpful during thinking and he quotes, in this connection, Augier's remark that "legs are the wheels of thought." Apart from individual differences in work habits or marked preferences for characteristic postures during work, there are variations in muscular tone. One person may find a tense state more conducive to intellectual effort, another may prefer a relatively relaxed condition. A third may prefer to linger and ruminate. Others are more productive during states of mental fatigue if there is at the same time a feeling of relaxation. "Happy ideas" never come to Hadamard either when he is tired or when sitting at his desk, but an hour after the fatigue of mental work has entirely passed away. Complete mental relaxation is rarely associated with intellectual activity of a high order.

Individuality in Problem-Solving

If we ask a number of people individually to carry out a certain task we usually find that there are characteristic differences in their approach. Let us take an example given by Katz[26] in a rather different connection. A nail has to be knocked into a piece of wood. If no hammer is provided one person may use a pair of pliers which is at hand. If he has no pliers he may use his shoe. In order to perceive the relevance of the shoe he must be able to "restructure" it, i.e., put aside the idea of the shoe as something to wear and see it as having a hard surface useful for hammering. This may not occur to another person who otherwise is equally intelligent. This second person may be too shy to remove his shoe (supposing that this is required), or perhaps he is finicky about handling rather dirty objects, and so the idea of "restructuring" the shoe will not occur to him.

The ability to see a situation in a new light means being free from rigidity in thinking, resourceful in evolving new hypotheses and seeing new possibilities of solving a problem when old methods fail. Some rigidity may be due to "overlearning" which tends to mechanize behavior, reduce educability and blind one to new ways of doing things. If rats are overtrained to run a certain path towards a goal they will continue to prefer that path even when shorter ones are later made possible. Hilgard[27] remarks that overtraining may lead to a common adult preference for artificial methods learnt in infancy. But here we must make a reservation. Increasing mastery of a pattern of behavior does not invariably lead to a standard method of responding. In swimming or ice-skating, for example, it is characteristic of the novice to perform his single "act" and play safe. The expert, with greater self-assurance, varies his movements in ways barred to the beginner. So overlearning does not necessarily lead to rigidity. Whether it will or not probably depends, at least in part, on the degree of versatility achieved in alternative and associated skills.

Some preliminary experimental evidence[28] lends support to the view that rigidity in problem-solving tends to be associated with characteristic features of the personality as indicated by a Rorschach test. In the experiment a child is first asked to solve a simple problem, such as bringing a certain quantity of water in several containers of different size. This is followed by a series of similar problems which require a more complex method of solution. Finally, a third series is presented which can be solved by the simpler method if the child can overcome the "set" established while doing the intermediate problems. The experiment suggests that "rigid" and "flexible" children (i.e., those who continue to use the complex method and those who return to the simpler method) also differ in personal characteristics. "Rigid" children give fewer responses, which have a narrower content and are less well-organized. They are slower to respond and, judged by their reaction to color and form, seem to be emotionally impoverished. There are also signs that they are more likely to act uncertainly in new situations, to avoid crises, and generally to be less well adjusted than "flexible" children.

Personal Factors and Types of Thought

If intellectual activity is an integral part of one's total personal life we should expect individuality to characterize both one's reactions to the theories of others and to leave a mark on one's own theories. We shall confine ourselves here to one or two illustrations from psychology. How can we understand Pavlov's outright rejection of Gestalt theory without assuming some profound personal antipathy to a seemingly elusive abstract concept, and a liking for the specific and concrete? He wrote: "I feel a *strong repugnance* to, and emphatically reject any theory that claims to embrace fully everything comprising our subjective world, but I cannot refrain from analysing it, from obtaining a simple understanding of it, at separate points"[29] (my italics).

The work of E. B. Tichener illustrates the way a preference for imagery of a certain kind enters into an elaborate theory as a universal property of the human mind. The following passage brings out this point:

> I rely in my thinking upon visual imagery in the sense that I like to get the problem into some sort of visual schema, from which I can make my way out and to which I can return. As I read an article or the chapter of a book, I instinctively arrange the facts or arguments in some visual pattern, and I am as likely to think in terms of this pattern as I am likely to think in words. I understand, and to that extent I enjoy, an author whom I can thus visualize.[30]

E. C. Tolman's use of spatial models illustrates the same tendency, for he expresses a preference for kinaesthetic imagery.[31] Tolman himself tacitly accepts the notion of individuality when he sees in Lewin's humanitarianism an explanation of his emphasis on the *situation* in which a person is placed as the source of the causes of behavior.[32]

When a number of individuals exhibit a tendency towards the same pattern of thought, they may be said to constitute a type.[33] Cardan's feat, for example, is of the kind that provokes the question: "how could such a strange idea enter anyone's mind?" This comment, as Hadamard[34] writes, may be contrasted with the typical reaction to a different kind of discovery: "how wonderful, but how obvious! Why did no one think of it before?" Here again we can see the effect of the individual distinctiveness of the innovator. Chesterton, who himself belonged to the second type, advised us to look at familiar objects until they look strange. Up to a point this is within everyone's competence—the former type is perhaps much more rare.

Other specimens have also been distinguished among the flora and fauna of human thinkers. F. Th. Vischer has described "subject-matter specialists" and "interpretive specialists" respectively. "The fact-greedy gullet of the former can be filled only with legal documents, statistical work-sheets and questionnaires, but he is insensitive to the refinement of a new idea. The gourmandise of the latter dulls his taste for facts by ever new intellectual subtleties."[35]

The formation of types, due to occupational habits of thought, sometimes obscures a desirable individuality. Dr. Brock Chisholm, a former Director-General of the World Health Organization, has described some types of delegates to international conferences. Lawyers are often given the responsibility of cultivating official contacts but their training in rules and precedent is likely to prove a handicap. Soldiers skilled in tactical manoeuvring to gain predetermined ends at the expense of the enemy are hardly suited for such a task. Military activity presupposes an opponent whom one has to circumvent and defeat. It does not usually teach us how to co-operate with other people who may be as sure they are right as we are. Nor does the business man's training in profit-making prepare him for situations calling for co-operative rather than competitive effort.[36]

Early Feelings and Later Thought

In the previous paper referred to above[37] an example was given which showed how an idea occurring to a given person at a particular propitious time turned out to be the cognitive expression of deeply felt experiences during the years of childhood. Without the assumption of individuality in thought it would be difficult to account for the fact that this person and not one of the two hundred others who were present at the time had this particular idea. The example brings to mind the remark of Claude Bernard that feeling always takes the initiative in thought. If so, it is a methodological error in the study of thought to disconnect it from feeling. It is an error characteristic of the obsessive mind which, by ignoring the affective sources of thought, renders its study an impossible task.

We arrive at the same conclusion by a study of the way experiences in early life may affect creative writing in later years. Such a study has been made of the poetry of Keats with reference to its countless allusions to food.[38] One readily recalls such phrases as "roots of relish sweet and honey wild and manna dew," "Canary wine," "juicy pears," "dainty pies," "ripening fruits," "honey crammed cells," "oozing cider press." The poet W. B. Yeats compared Keats to a starving child pressing his nose against a bakery window. In his poems, sucking, eating and erotic experience merge into one. All his heroines are associated with food. We cannot digress here to speculate on the origin of these oral preoccupations. It suffices to suggest that we are not dealing here with a mere coincidence, but rather with the working-out in poetic art of deep-lying early experiences specific to Keats alone.

Freud's experience provides an interesting example of early intellectual influences on later thought. When he was 14 years old he was given a present of the works of Ludwig Börne, who had devised a recipe on how to become an original writer in three days. The instructions were to write down for three days everything that comes into the head without falsification or hypocrisy. Ernest Jones,[39] who tells us about this, suggests that the experience may have been the germ of Freud's later discovery of the technique of free association.

The Role of Detachment in Thinking

The capacity to observe in a fresh and original way is likely to depend to some extent on being able to discriminate between a situation as it is perceived by others and as it is perceived by us. This implies becoming aware of our "personal context."[40] Such an awareness is likely to increase our sensitivity to our data in relation to ourselves and to put us on our guard against distortion, over-valuation and projection. If the introduction of technical expressions will not obscure the issue, the point may be put in this way: we have to distinguish a private or perceptual structure from a social structure, if we are dealing with a human problem, and from a reality situation, if we are confronted with a physical problem. The degree of personal involvement may be so slight as not to mar a realistic grasp of a given situation. Or it may be so intense as to lead to a misreading or misrepresentation of the facts. The feeling of anxiety in relation to any topic may lead to selective inattention or banish it from awareness altogether.

The place of detachment in productive thinking has a prominent place in Gestalt theory. According to this theory, the thinker must ignore what he wants to happen, if he wishes to get at the root of a problem. He must forget about himself and allow his thinking to follow the structural requirements of the situation. He has to become an "obstetrician" and extract the solution from the "matrix" in which it is embedded. If his personal needs dominate his thinking, he may attempt a short-cut solution where a detour is objectively required. This view seems to imply that complete impersonal detachment from the possible outcome of one's enquiries is an essential condition of productive thinking. It is hard to accept this if it means that the thinker must be *indifferent* to the results of his investigations. An optimal emotional involvement is not the same as apathy or neutrality. The characteristic feature of the scientific investigator, for example, is not aloofness but a willingness to recognize when a particular result cannot be obtained by one method and a readiness to try out other methods instead.[41] Scientific method does not demand an absence of intention to try and reach a particular result. Many scientists have eagerly sought to confirm their favored hypothesis and any sign to the contrary has brought sharp disappointment. If enthusiasm is unbounded, there is, of course, a danger of blinding oneself to the shortcomings of a theory. In general, the greater the desire to reach a given result, the greater the care that must be taken to avoid overlooking errors.

In problems which require a detour rather than a short-cut method for their solution, it is useless to increase the attractiveness of the goal. This would make the task more difficult. For the more attractive the goal, the harder it is to move away from it and make a detour. Expectation of too great a reward or punishment, by transfixing the attention, may therefore hamper performance. There is then little scope for freedom of choice between alternatives. That is what tends to happen in a crisis. When the valence of the goal deviates from the optimal, conditions do not favor a correct grasp of the entire situation.

Nothing is more likely to endanger intellectual mobility than an undue attachment to one's own settled point of view. The thinker who keeps to his own ideas too long has been compared to a hen sitting on boiled eggs. This is what Claude Bernard probably meant when he said that "those who have excessive faith in their ideas are not fitted to make discoveries," and Souriau's observation that "in order to invent one must think aside," embodies a similar thought.

Because a task which is easy for one person is hard for another, its performance probably requires a degree of motivation which varies from person to person. Many experiments supporting this view have been carried out since the Yerkes-Dodson law was suggested some forty years ago. In their experiments "motivation" is induced at various levels of intensity and the habits to be formed vary in their level of difficulty, the aim being to determine the optimal level of motivation for learning. In one experiment, for example, rats had to distinguish between stimuli varying in brightness, an electric shock being given for incorrect discrimination. The shock could be relatively mild, moderate or severe and the discrimination also varied in difficulty. Experiments with human subjects have studied the effects of weak and strong shock on the speed and accuracy of sorting. The conclusion seems to follow, at any rate for these simple and artificial laboratory situations, that the easier the habit to be acquired (or the task to be carried out) the higher is the level of motivation required. There is an optimal strength of motivation for each level of difficulty.

As Young[42] has suggested, some practical lessons may be drawn from these experiments. If the same task is easy for brighter pupils and hard for duller ones, the motivation to be induced must vary with the difficulty of the task for each pupil. A threat of punishment may severely disturb the dull child instead of evoking his best efforts. Again, the more exacting or delicate a task, the easier it is to disrupt it. An interruption or noise which would have no effect on the operator of a pneumatic drill is liable to drive an intellectual worker to distraction. This helps us to understand why a famous conductor once violently threw his baton at his orchestra when someone played a false note.

Summary

An attempt has been made in this paper to show that thinking has an individual distinctiveness which is characteristic of the thinker. Just as a place for a *perceiver* is needed in a theory of perception, so room must be left for a *thinker* in a theory of thought. The fact that each act of thought is unique does not remove it outside the bounds of scientific study any more than the uniqueness of an earthquake, or for that matter, any physical event, debars it from scientific analysis. In considering psychological factors that may affect preferences for different philosophical systems, a distinction must be made between the impersonal formal content of the final system and the factors that led to the construction or choice of such a system.

In general it may be supposed that a relationship exists between the character of a person and the kind of theory he chooses. Types of intellectual boldness have been described and idiosyncrasies of work-habit illustrated. The way individual differences might be expected to affect the approach to a problem or the invention of a theory has been briefly indicated. Finally, the relation between feeling and thought has been touched upon and an effort made to clarify the problem of optimal detachment in thinking.

HERBERT FINGARETTE

The Ego and Mystic Selflessness

I

THE SPECIFIC OBJECTIVES of this paper are twofold. First, I wish to provide a significantly amplified theoretical psychoanalytic analysis of mysticism. The discussion touches upon the complex but urgent problems in connection with creativity and pathology, sublimation and regressive defense, the role of infantilism and fantasy in normal or creative psychic equilibria, and the processes of transition from some of these states to others. Second, I hope to illuminate aspects of both mysticism and psychoanalysis by showing how the mystic way, when successfully pursued, at times runs parallel to the way of psychoanalytic therapy, how the two eventuate ideally in results which in important respects are congruent.* Crucial psychological processes underlying both "ways" will be shown to be the same.

It would be absurd to suppose that the two "ways" are identical. Until now, however, the genuine and important *differentiating* characteristics have usually been stressed, partly due to the fact that early studies were largely id-oriented. I shall therefore leave brief discussion of the latter aspects of the matter until the end of this paper. Appearing, as they will, after extensive discussion of the similarities and common psychological processes, the important differences between psychoanalysis and mysticism will not disappear but will reappear in a new light. It behooves us, however, to devote our main energies here to developing the picture in terms of the developments in psychoanalytic ego psychology—a viewpoint which tends to reveal similarities rather than differences.

II

By way of setting the stage, let us review at once, although quite briefly, the apparently extreme opposition between the ideal mystic state and the

Reprinted from *Psychoanalysis and Psychoanalytic Review*, XLV, No. 1 (1958), 5-41, by permission of the author and publisher.

* The "answers" given by "the mystic" in the following pages of this essay are, when in single quotes, taken directly from the literature of mysticism, and, of course, used in the spirit of the original context.

ideal therapeutic goal of the psychoanalyst. We often think of the two as contrasting, and I shall try to set the problem in the form of the sharpest possible contrast.

In the great mystical writings of East and West it is said that the mystic insight results ideally in egolessness, selflessness, absence of desire and of striving, passivity instead of control, cessation of logic, thought, and discrimination, a life beyond morality, beyond sensation, and perception. The psychoanalyst, however, aims (ideally) at using insight to strengthen the ego, and to develop a self—a self with a rich variety of goals and with substantial ability to gratify desires, with reasonable self-control and mastery of the environment, and with the ability to perceive realistically, discriminate clearly, and act with a sense of the appropriate values.

The way of psychoanalytic therapy aims at minimal disruption of everyday life. The mystic way notoriously involves unusual practices and symptoms, for example, trances, ecstasies, visions, asceticism, and stigmata.

I wish to present now, in an informal and preliminary way, some data which suggest the hypotheses I shall subsequently develop. Essentially I propose to set side by side some introspective reports of a psychoanalytic patient and some mystic sayings. In this way we can begin to probe the degree of contrast and of similarity in terms of the primary materials rather than in terms of the typical, generalized "summary" of mysticism and of psychoanalytic goals.

Strange to say, in the literature of psychoanalysis, it is difficult to find a sensitive and extensive account, in nontechnical language, of the "feeling" of one's "subjective" experience *after* successful analysis. I present here a few extracts from a nontechnical, informal, and introspective report in which a woman compares her postanalytic with her preanalytic experience.

No detailed account of the interviewee's analysis or life history is given since the interview material is not intended to function as evidence for the thesis of this paper. The interview material, obtained by the writer, is illustrative. It is presumed that, with a slight effort at empathy, the naturalness and appropriateness of Katherine's language will be apparent to those with psychoanalytic experience.

Katherine is a woman in her early thirties who has worked through some important neurotic conflicts in psychoanalytic psychotherapy. It is essential to note that while Katherine, a housewife, is an intelligent college graduate and a woman of culture, she is not a "professional intellectual" nor is she particularly interested in psychoanalytic theory. She has nothing but the most casual acquaintance with mysticism. Insofar as she has any conception of the life and literature of mysticism, she conceives of it as obscurantist, pathological, and alien to her life and her intellectual loyalties.

Katherine is asked, specifically, to consider her relationship with Alice, a friend around whom strong conflicts formerly raged and with respect to whom an important segment of her analysis was concerned. The interviewer requests that technical, psychological terms be avoided. She is not to worry about being systematic, "scientific," or logical. She is to try as best she can to "get across" the "feel" of life by talking about herself, her desires, her feelings, her judgments, and so on. As a starter, she is asked what are her present desires in connection with Alice.

Katherine reflects a moment and then says, "Well, I don't have any desires now. I used to want Alice to be shown up in her true colors, to have people see how wrong she was. Now I just don't think about it. I just act. I get along."

Katherine's spontaneous and informal comments are challenged by her interviewer. Surely she cannot mean *exactly* what she says. Surely if she has social relations with Alice, there must be thinking going on; the existence of at least some ordinary desires is implied in saying that they ate, talked, and generally co-ordinated their activities during social visits? And, finally, does Katherine mean to imply that she gets along now because she lets herself be stepped on at will, ignoring the rights and wrongs of Alice's behavior toward her? The interviewer expresses his assumption that the relationship is not one of total passivity and self-abnegation on Katherine's part.

"Well, of course," replies Katherine, "I still may think that what she's doing is wrong at times, but it doesn't matter much. That is, well, I would defend myself if she did anything wrong to me . . . but, well, I wouldn't *dwell* on its being wrong. I'm just not involved. It doesn't matter *in the same way*."

Katherine was impressed by the peculiar nature of the comments she had made, examining them, as it were, in reflective retrospect. She volunteers: "It's funny, but if anyone ever looked at what I've said, they'd get the impression of a very strange and quiet person without real emotion, someone who didn't care about anything. That's not a good picture of me at all. It's true, it takes a lot more effort to get angry now, and yet I explode all the time. The difference is that I used to get angry all the time and never exploded. Now, when I'm angry, I explode and yell, but somehow I'm not really even worked up about it." (In her observable behavior, Katherine is neither affectless nor meek. She is, if anything, a person who tends to hold strong opinions, can act and speak forcefully, and when she violates the "mean" at all, tends toward the pole of intense participation, warmth, and empathy rather than withdrawal, coldness, or tranquillity.)

At one point in the interview, Katherine is asked about her attitude toward being praised, something which used to mean a great deal in her life. She replies: "I used to get a lot of satisfaction out of it. Now I don't get any." Upon being challenged by the interviewer, she adds that what she has said may be misleading. "I did get satisfaction, for example, out of being praised for making that dress a while ago, but that was because I *had* done it very well. But the praise was just *that*, period! All the competition's sort of left, too. I'm calmer; I don't try so hard."

It is of interest to add here another comment of Katherine's when asked whether she was angry when, as she said, she "exploded." Her answer was: "No! . . . well . . . yes, that is . . . I'm angry at the thing and not in general. It's hard to explain."

Under the conditions set by the interviewer, Katherine spontaneously—and without ever having spoken this way before—finds herself forced to use locutions which she realizes are unusual, contradictory, inadequate, and in constant need of corrections which are in turn bound to be inadequate. It is clear that she is trying to put something into language which the language is not equipped to communicate in any routine, news-reporting fashion.

Nevertheless, she does not feel that language fails her entirely. One senses that *to her* the words communicate in some sense. There is, in fact, a kind of "logic" or "order" in her exposition which I shall eventually make explicit.

I shall, for convenience, introduce here the notion of "the language of self." By "the language of self," I mean our everyday language insofar as it expresses experience in terms of the self as an acting and suffering *person* rather than a physical, physiological, psychological, or social process. "I think, I feel, I want, I believe, I see, I hear, I ought"—these when used in the context of personal action, enjoyment, or commitment rather than that of scientific description or philosophical speculation, are the stuff of the "language of self."

Katherine's comments are paradoxical. She tends to begin her account by denying self-activities such as desiring, thinking, judging, emoting; then she proceeds to acknowledge the existence of these very self-activities; and finally she suggests that everything is meant in a different sense making the whole affair difficult or impossible to express. Nevertheless, she continues in fact to express herself in this language.

In Katherine's remarks—as I shall show next—there is a precise, detailed, and systematic parallelism to the language of the mystic. (When this was pointed out to Katherine subsequently, she was surprised, annoyed, and interested.)

III

I have spoken so far of "mysticism," but it is time now to state more precisely what I have in mind. While I particularly wish to stress that the present analysis is relevant to the main traditions usually labelled "mystical," I shall, as a practical matter, limit myself largely to one such tradition. I select from several thousand years of Asian mysticism a number of reasonably accessible sayings and doctrines. The principal sources are Hindu, Taoist, and Buddhist (especially Zen Buddhist). Occasional references to Western mystics, and in particular to Meister Eckhart, will be found to fit easily into the tradition in question. The strain of mysticism selected from this vast literature is one which is, as mysticisms go, especially congenial to the Western mind. In the form of Zen, it has become relatively known in the West during the past two decades.

It is, as was recalled earlier, well known that the Eastern mystic cultivates "desirelessness." Could we interview a hypothetical "composite" mystic of this type, he would tell us that the enlightened ones are without desire, beyond good and evil, uninvolved, neither thinking nor discriminating, without ego, utterly serene. (Recall Katherine: "I don't have any desires"; "I just don't think about it"; ". . . what she's doing is wrong at times, but it doesn't matter much"; "I'm just not involved"; "Somehow, I'm not really even worked up about it.")

Suppose, however, that we challenge our hypothetical mystic with a series of further questions.

"When you speak of 'enlightenment' in this fashion, you are speaking of some sort of trance state, no doubt?" we ask. The mystic's denial is clear and sharp. In analogy to Katherine who denied that her words betokened pathological behavior, we are warned by our composite mystic against those who seek Buddha by "going off by themselves in solitude." (10.) "All of this is ignorance," we are told. "Those who sit quietly and try to keep their minds blank are 'foolish people,' 'heretics.' " (10.) Zen (that is, mystic enlightenment) is your "ordinary mind." (24.)

We are reminded that even the great Christian mystics, St. Theresa and St. John of the Cross, warn the one who treads the mystic path against being seduced by the raptures and delights of trances and visions (29).

"But in this case," we argue, "in spite of what you said earlier about desirelessness, you must in truth experience desire?"

"Of course," replies the mystic, apparently contradicting his earlier statements. " 'Even a wise man acts according to the tendencies of his own nature.' (2.) 'If you have the wisdom of Prajna, you can practice Zen in the world of desires.' (20.) 'Desire flows into the mind of the seer but he is never disturbed.' " (2.)

We continue trying to catch the mystic in further contradictions: "If you are not speaking of trance states of one kind or another, then you must have not only desires but sensations and perceptions; you must think; you must make judgments of better and worse, and you must have feelings and emotions after all."

"What you say is true," says the mystic. " 'Ignorant ones . . . imagine that Nirvana consists in the future annihilation of the senses and the sense-minds (10). This is not so with the genuinely enlightened,' '(nor does the enlightened one try to) get rid of notions of good and evil.' (10.) And as for thinking—'It is a great mistake to suppress all thinking.' " (10.)

"As for emotions," continues our mystic, "you must recall the famous Zen master who yelled vociferously when dying; (22) recall also the other Zen master whose laugh was heard over several counties." (25.) (The enlightened one) "is found in company with wine-bibbers and butchers." (22.)

At this point we throw up our hands and accuse the mystic of flagrant self-contradiction. All his talk of egolessness, desirelessness, serenity, and such is now completely denied, it seems. To this, he replies: " 'I am trying to describe to you something that intrinsically is ineffable, in order to help you get rid of fallacious views. If you do not interpret my words too literally, you may perhaps know a wee bit of Nirvana.' " (10.)

Should we ask at this point how we can ever be informed of the ineffable, the mystic either remains silent or proceeds to talk in much the same manner as before—or, if he is a Zen master, perhaps he calls us a fool and gives us a blow with his stick.

It is understandable that Leuba, the renowned student of the psychology of mysticism, could say of this kind of talk that it is "obviously nonsense!" (16.) Yet, on the other hand, we are not surprised to find logical nonsense in poetry or "falsehoods" in novels. Careful examination of our own everyday speech convinces us of the remarkable communicative power of non-logical, nonscientific modes of speech. The intellectually fascinating model of scientific language—an esoteric language, after all—blinds us to the ubiquity and efficiency of non-logical modes of speech in everyday life. To interpret the mystic as scientist or theoretician of any sort is a blunder comparable to pointing out the contradictory statements within a poem.

As a first hypothesis, I suggest that the mystic is trying to distinguish between two important but different kinds of experience, both naturally expressed by the same introspective self-language. He wants us to achieve one kind of experience and to guide us away from another mode of experience which, as it happens, is expressed by the same sort of language. Later I shall pursue the question as to the nature of this difference in modes of experience.

With this hypothesis, we can take a step toward making sense of the mystic's paradoxes: since the only language we have for both modes of experience is the one language, the language of self, it inevitably appears that the mystic constantly contradicts himself. Furthermore, the only means he has of hoping to make the distinctions clear is to use the language with a keen sense of context, a careful sensitivity to both his own and the other's experience at the moment. Hence he must sense as quickly as the swordsman the play of the shifting modes of experience within changing contexts, and he must, as quickly, shift his way of talking until the listener is somehow able to perceive the pattern underneath the superficial nonsense of his talk. There is something here partly analogous to and partly identical with Freud's technique. As Freud found that the transference could be the chief instrument of therapy rather than the ultimate obstacle, so the mystic finds that the troublesome paradox inherent in his plight, when its use is carefully selective and timed, is a powerful device for enlightenment.

"My words have an ancestry, my deeds have a lord; and it is precisely because men do not understand this that they are unable to understand me," says the mystic sage, Lao-Tse (27). This is understood to mean that his words are neither "savage" nor "wild"; they are related to a "definite system of thought." But their utter simplicity is not perceived because their "ancestry" is unseen; therefore they are "murky."

We must understand that "system" does not mean "logical system." The Chinese word "lord" with its anthropomorphic connotation of a pattern of *purposes* is closer to the fact than the impersonal English word "system." The mystic's words are "skillful means" to the practical purpose of evoking enlightenment. They are not elements in a theoretical system.

The mystic's words are like an analyst's therapeutic interventions: they are designed to be effective in producing specific change, not to embody universal truths. The "pattern" underlying the mystic's words is, in short, pragmatic, not logical.

The mystic, then, uses the one language of self in paradoxical ways in order to distinguish two overlapping modes of subjective experience and in order to shift the balance in favor of one mode as against the other.

In the following section, I shall propose some psychoanalytic hypotheses as to the conditions under which a person might be expected to communicate the nature of his subjective experience in language identical to or analogous to that of the mystic.

IV

I propose now to inquire whether there is a significant relationship between any psychoanalytic usage of the term "self" and the usage of "self" and related terms in mysticism. Ultimately, however, I am concerned with developing a psychoanalytic understanding of the mystic self regardless of whether the latter includes anything which can be called self in the psychoanalytic sense.

In psychoanalysis, the term "self" has no unambiguous systematic use.

It occurs usually as part of hyphenated compounds used in varying context and with differing connotations. In his early views, Freud (6) used the term "self" in connection with such notions as the "self-preservative instincts." These early notions, later substantially modified, involved no specifically psychoanalytic conceptions of the self. Freud was using the word to connote loosely the total person in his status as an individual rather than as a member of the species.

The term "self" has been used by Freud (6), however, in close connection with the term "ego." In the early days of Freud's inquiries, he often used "ego" interchangeably with "self." Later "ego" came to have a specific and much narrower meaning. It is this shift in the meaning of "ego" that has at times confused discussions of the self. "Ego," in its later and still current use in psychoanalysis, is a theoretical term referring to a hypothesized (metapsychological) structure. This structure consists of a set of dispositions, specifically the dispositions to perceptual, thinking, evaluative, integrative, and executive behavior of the person.

The ego is therefore not only to be distinguished from id, superego, and reality environment, it is to be distinguished from the introspectable "contents of the mind." Like id and superego, it is a theoretical entity, not a datum of perception. The effects of its action, however, *may* be conscious.

It is clear from the previous that the ego is neither the total psychic self nor is it the "self" of introspection. It is therefore not the self of the mystic, according to the hypotheses already proposed. I might add that it is not the self in any of the usual moral senses of the term, either. Hence moral or mystic "egolessness" is not equivalent to "egolessness" in any psychoanalytic sense. The use of "ego" in introspectively oriented discussions about moral or spiritual questions is exceedingly common and leads to frequent confusion when it occurs in close connection with psychoanalytic ideas.

To psychoanalysts, the mystic's stress on loss of self and the "unity of all with all" is likely to suggest that there is a psychotic-like confusion of "inner" and "outer," a loss of the self-object distinction as in hallucination and paranoid delusions (18). The decisive evidence for the inadequacy of this view arises from observation of the behavior of great mystics and of those ordinary persons such as Katherine who speak in a quasi-mystic way. For, far from showing a confusion between self and environment, they act with unusual effectiveness and with a clear sense of the social realities. They often show great practical organizing ability and a particularly keen sensitivity to the real relationships between their own attitudes and desires and those of the persons they deal with.

Let it be recalled here, and with emphasis, that the trance states and visionary states so commonly identified with the culminating mystic enlightenment are in truth only frequent forerunners. Insofar as enlightenment is achieved, visions and trances, if they were present at all, are given up, and active life within the world is resumed or simply continued. As varied a group of the classic commentators on mysticism as Underhill (29), Leuba (16), and Bergson (1) agree on these questions. *Thus the self which is lost in mystic enlightenment is not the self essential to the practical carrying on of one's ordinary daily activities; nor is it the ego in the psychoanalytic sense.*

Another use of self in psychoanalysis is found in the notion of "self-representation" which has been taken up in the recent psychoanalytic literature. "Self-representation" is a term which—"analogous to the term object representations—refers to our mental concept of the self; that is, to the unconscious and preconscious images of our body self and of our own personality." (12). The self-representation is thus not supposed to be the introspectable. This being so, the self-representations are not the self of the mystic. The mystic is concerned with his introspectable, subjective experience, not with hypothesized processes.

I should like to urge an additional and important reason, however, why the self-representations are not the object of our search. It is important to remember that the mystic does not claim that he is *in every sense* unaware of himself. Just as he admits to perceiving, thinking, and desiring in *some* sense of those terms, so he must admit to being aware of himself even when he is "selfless." The mystic, in the advanced stages of his development, lives in the world, among "wine-bibbers and butchers," and acts effectively in his relationships with others. This implies that he takes into account his body, his social situation, his personal qualities, powers, and purposes. It is in just these respects that the self-representations play an essential role, for they are the psychic perceptions of the person and his powers and purposes. Hence they cannot be the self which the enlightened mystic has *lost*, and it is this latter "self" that I am directly concerned with.

Another use of the world "self"—a use which *is* relevant to the mystic's use—is in such combinations as "self-criticism," "self-esteem," "aggression against the self," "self-consciousness." These concepts are used with varying degrees of precision. Some of this family of "self-" terms are at times used to refer to metapsychological non-introspectable processes. Thus "aggression against the self" is used to mean a cathexis of the ego by the superego with aggressive drive energy. Such a process is quite distinct from, although at times causally related to, the subjective experience of "hating oneself," or the overt behavior describable as self-mutilation or suicide.

Insofar as these concepts refer to non-introspected processes, they are not included in the mystic concept of self. But they become much closer in meaning when they are used to describe subjective experiences of the sort expressed by such phrases as: "I could kick myself"; "I guess I'm not much good"; "I'm so embarrassed"; "I guess I showed them I'm pretty good after all." In such situations, the "self" in the mystic sense is very definitely there; "its" presence is in some sense weighty, at the center of experience—too much so.

It is difficult to find plain and more succinct language, other than the quoted typical phrases, to describe this subjective experience. The term which best covers this whole family of experiences is "self-conscious." This, of course, is not at all the same as being conscious of one's total person. Nor is this "self-consciousness" simply a consciousness of specific self-representations. The self-representations function in some degree in all voluntary behavior, but not all voluntary behavior includes "self-conscious" feelings. "Self-consciousness," in this colloquial sense, is very much a part of what the mystic means by the sense of self from which we need liberation. Before proceeding to an examination of the metapsychological conditions associated with "self-consciousness," I wish to discuss another important kind of subjective experience which is also directly associated with that "self" which the mystic is concerned with.

Federn (5) has developed the concept of "ego-feeling" in connection, particularly, with the phenomena of estrangement and depersonalization. This concept has not been readily accepted. Among other things, it confuses concepts appropriate to subjective experience ("feeling") with metapsychological concepts ("ego"). Nevertheless, Federn's data and his concerns are important and illuminating in the context of the present inquiry in spite of the conceptual confusion.

Federn describes estrangement and depersonalization as experiences involving an absence of "ego-feeling." The language confusion is unfortunate here, for what he calls an "absence of ego-feeling" is in truth not an absence of a feeling but a *positive feeling*—the feeling that something is absent. In these experiences, the sufferer clearly experiences his activities and feelings, and he knows in a kind of intellectual or "external" way that they are his—but he feels that something is missing. Somehow he feels that *he* is not really doing and feeling these things, and the feeling is distressing, often acutely so. The patient breaks out in despair to say: "Language has no words to describe my state, but it is as I say." Federn tells us that "(The patients) use similes and symbolic language because they find that the usual expressions are unsatisfactory." (5.)

An ego process (hence a non-introspectable process) is certainly involved in this matter. But the subjective effect (the introspectable phenomenon) produced by that process is not an *absence of feeling* but a peculiar and distressing *feeling of absence*. On the other hand, Federn's language requires us to say that when we are perceiving normally, there is present an appropriate kind of "ego-feeling." This phrasing obscures the point that what, according to Federn, is the presence of "ego-feeling" is, subjectively, not a feeling at all but an *absence* of any noticeable feeling. Federn himself makes this last point very effectively (but without seeing its implications for his terminology) when he says, "Normally, there is no more awareness of the ego than of the air one breathes." (5.) One could hardly put the matter more incisively! Of course we must add that there is never any awareness of the *ego* as such, but one need here only substitute the world "self" for "ego." Then it is evident that Federn has pointed to a fundamental feature of our normal subjective experience.

The introspective "sense of self" occurs in the context of the *disruption* of "normal" ego activity. We do not normally have the *feeling* that our actions and decisions are or are not ours; we simply act or decide. The normal introspective self-"feelings" are like the feeling of the air we breathe. *Normally* we neither feel that the air exists nor that it has ceased to exist. Only when there is trouble do we become aware of the air. At such times we may have a sensation of "absence," of something missing; or it may be that we have a sensation of something present but noxious or troublesome. So, with our introspective sense of self: sometimes, as in self-consciousness, it "weighs" upon us; at other times, as in estrangement, it seems positively absent. Both are "abnormal" situations. Both give rise to a subjective concern with self (26).

The theoretical question which requires immediate consideration is that of the meaning of "abnormal" in this context. Such an inquiry will lead to a formulation of the metapsychological conditions of the concern with self. And this formulation, in turn, will confirm itself by leading to additional important phenomena of mysticism which we have not yet dealt with in this section of the paper.

The relevant ambiguity in the phrase "abnormal functioning of the ego" is avoided, I believe, if we formulate the matter in terms of the concept of anxiety. Of course anxiety itself is, in a very important sense, a perfectly "normal" ego phenomenon. However, the crucial condition for that "normal" subjective unconcern of self which is like our normal unawareness of the air we breathe is the *absence* of significant amounts of anxiety.

In terms of anxiety, the fundamental question implicitly raised by our concept "abnormal functioning of the ego" is as follows: Is the psychological context one of defensive functioning of the ego stimulated by anxiety, the latter, in turn, generated out of intrapsychic conflict? Or is the psychological context one of anxiety-free, autonomous ego functions, that is, functions activated by sublimated (neutralized) instinctual energy operating within a conflict-free portion of the ego? In the latter case we have the sense of "normal ego functioning" which is relevant to the present inquiry. (Where the ego function is anxiety-motivated, the ego may very well be functioning adaptively and in that sense "normally." I am not concerned here to legislate in general about the use of the word "normal.")

The matter may be put briefly and suggestively, if not too precisely, as follows: the introspected, self-conscious "*I*" is not in fact a perception of one's own total person; it is some particular part affect, idea, or action of the person as perceived by the person in a context where the dynamically dominant affect is some form of anxiety. These experiences are often expressed in the language of self: "I feel," "I am so worthless," "I desire," "I believe," "I love," "I am hated by," "I must have," and so on. "Consciousness of self" is not an awareness of some self-identical entity; it is, rather, *any consciousness colored by intra-psychic conflict and anxiety.*

This fundamental relationship between the sense of self and anxiety was clearly stated by Freud. According to him, prototypical anxiety is generated by the earliest separation-situations (8). It is out of these painful (quasi-anxiety filled) separation-situations that he supposed both anxiety proper and the distinction between "self" and "other" to arise. The earliest separation situation was a prototype of intrapsychic conflict, for the mother was included in the primal "self."

Where, on the other hand, the ego-functions are anxiety-free, we have that "self-forgetfulness"[13] so characteristic of autonomous ego functions using neutralized instinctual energy. "Self-forgetfulness," let it be noted again, is not the failure to take oneself and one's functions into account; on the contrary, this latter is most efficiently done in the context of subjective self-forgetfulness, of "*un*-self-consciousness."

What relationship does the "language of self" have to anxiety? The language of self, in its ordinary use, expresses without distinction either of two profoundly different forms of subjective experience, the anxiety-generated *or* the anxiety-free. The subtler aspects of the linguistic manner or style may differ, but the words and the grammar are the same.

We should not be surprised that, partly as a result of the ambiguity of the language of self, many persons fail in one degree or another to distinguish these two different forms of subjective experience. This is true even though the difference, once perceived, is profound. Certain anxiety symptoms (for example, "nervousness," faintness) are easy to distinguish. But most often the anxiety-motivation of behavior is masked, the behavior frequently being rationalized. Thus the man who has always worked compulsively at his job is likely to be unable to distinguish his behavior from that of industrious and enthusiastic but anxiety-free work. The attempts of others to use language to suggest to him the subtle but profound difference in the "feel" of the two experiences will most likely be met by him either with incomprehension or defensive scorn, or both. When he asks them to describe in "plain" language how *they* approach their work, victory is his—for they have to use the very same language-forms he does. If someone says that anxiety-free work has a kind of absorbed and devoted character, the compulsive replies that those are just the words that describe his work! And he is right.

It is for such reasons, among others, that the mystic renounces the attempt to communicate by means of generalized, theoretical discourse. This renunciation is closely related to the psychoanalyst's recognition that general and theoretical discussion of neurotic (anxiety dominated) behavior fails to help the neurotic. If I may be permitted a crude but suggestive analogy: the mystic is always interested in therapy, not theory, and, therefore, to him the attempt to introduce psychological or other rational theory is resistance, defense, an evasion of the heart of the matter. The general statements about the self which have one meaning for the therapist or mystic are easily misinterpreted in quite another meaning by the neurotic and the unenlightened. The language of self is fatally ambiguous.

From the standpoint of his own personal achievement rather than communication with others or helping them, the central task of the mystic is that of achieving an unusually strong ego within an unusually well-integrated personality. This implies maximal ego-autonomy and neutralization of drives, and it implies minimal conflict, anxiety, and defense. If, for the moment, we consider the self to be the same as character in Reich's (19) sense—the relatively enduring defensive "armor"—then the mystic aims at minimal defensive-armor and hence the "death" of such a self. The process of achieving a mature personality with an extreme minimum of defensive character armor ordinarily involves major (and stormy) personality reorganization. The soul-wracking death which leads to blissful "rebirth" is the death of the subjectively experienced, anxiety-generated "self" perception; it is the emergence into the freedom of introspective "self-forgetfulness," of the psychically unified self.

V

It is now appropriate to test the metapsychological hypotheses presented up to this point by developing their implications and determining whether they are consistent with a reasonably broad sample of the language and phenomena of mysticism. Such an examination will show, I believe, the validity of these suggestions. It will also reveal the need for important amplifications of the psychological analysis. These amplifications will, in effect, show how the more traditional psychoanalytic interpretations of mysticism are to be integrated with the present one to form a more comprehensive view in which the interrelations of ego and id are exhibited.

We assume, in general, that both Katherine and the mystic are trying to express that introspected difference in the quality of experience correlated with the metapsychological shift from anxiety and defense to sublimation and ego-syntonic experience. On this basis one can see the naturalness of denying any "striving." The very word "compulsion," used by Freud in connection with characteristic symptoms of defense against anxiety, is of a piece with such words as "bondage," "attachment," "striving." This peculiar subjective sense of pressure, of need, of not-to-be-brooked desire is in sharp contrast to the subjective experience associated with anxiety-free cathexes. The latter we naturally express as "freedom," especially freedom of inner initiative ("free-will"). We have here an experience which, as Knight points out (14), needs to be distinguished carefully from the deceptive subjective sense of "freedom" associated with certain other types of psychological conditions. This deceptive sense of "freedom" occurs in the child during flights of fantasy; it is also reported by the person who, unconsciously driven by intense defiance, carries out criminal, libertinist, or other spurious acts of "independence." I call this a deceptive sense of freedom because freedom includes much more than merely subjective feelings. Furthermore, it is possible, though not easy, to distinguish introspectively the genuine subjective experience from the pseudo-free feeling.

For the child and the neurotically rebellious to be able to introspect the distinction between the "mature" and the "immature" subjective sense of freedom requires, as we know, long and arduous self-exploration and self-transformation. Nevertheless, from the theoretician's and the trained observer's standpoint, the distinction can be made relatively easily with the aid of the appropriate psychological distinctions and techniques. "Absence of anxiety, of irrational doubt, and of those inhibitions and restrictions which paralyze both choice and action" (14) are the negative indicators of the mature sense of freedom. The ability to make effective, ego-syntonic choices is among the positive criteria.

For the relatively mature person, minor decisions are made with an unqualified subjective sense of freedom. In connection with weighty decisions in life, there is the more complex feeling that one is free and yet that, in terms of one's integrity, "one can do no other." (14.)

This latter point of Knight's shows that the subjective experience of one who is psychologically mature could quite naturally be described in terms of the mystic paradox of complete freedom coexisting with utter passivity. As a person of thoroughgoing psychological integrity, it is true that "one can do no other"; but in thus doing, while not consciously concerned with "self," one gives expression to a unified and accepted self, an undivided and effective will. "The truth is that the more ourselves we are, the less self is in us." (4.) This is precisely the way "emotionally mature, well-integrated persons" feel their activity to be (14).

Mature individuals, says Knight, have achieved an harmonious integration of the instinctual drives, the superego standards and restrictions, the ego perceptions and discriminative faculties, and the real possibilities offered by the environment (14). Thus they are at once perceptive and yet, as was noted earlier, "self-forgetful." "Desire flows into the mind of the seer, but he is never disturbed." (2.)

In describing generally those who have failed to achieve such an ideally strong ego and well-integrated personality, Knight's language is sharply reminiscent of the language of the Eastern mystics when they talk about *maya* and *samsara*, the world of birth-and-death in which the unenlightened live. Persons who have failed to achieve such harmonious integration, says Knight, meet with obstacles whose nature they do not understand (ignorance), or they are driven by "intense defiance or greed or hostile impulses." (14.) Ignorance, pride, lust, and hatred—here is the universally acknowledged "syndrome" associated by mystics with the disease of self-ishness. The psychoanalytic explanation of neuroses is analogous. Unsublimated libido and aggression (lust, hatred, and greed) result in distorted, fantasy colored experiences ("ignorance," "illusion"). The general traits of self-ishness and conflictful experience thus being established as parallel, it now is appropriate to consider more specific notions found in mysticism.

"Freedom from striving" and "acceptance," key notions of the mystic, are often misinterpreted to mean systematic refusal to take the initiative, consistent absence of goals of any sort, submissiveness. This the unenlightened read into the words in spite of the evidence before their eyes that those who best exemplify mystic enlightenment are people who obviously do take the initiative, who clearly execute well-organized, purposive behavior, and who have indeed modified the world. The misinterpretation is encouraged by the fact that, not uncommonly, those who are *trying to achieve* enlightenment go through a phase of submissiveness.

In order to obviate this particular misunderstanding the mystic must eventually qualify his remarks. He must confess that he *does* have desires and does not merely "submit." He thus admits that the natural way of expressing the matter is unfortunately ambiguous. His language originally suggests a *loss*, an absence, a "giving up." He now tries to suggest that the aspect of his experience in question involves neither sense of presence nor of loss, neither a sense of striving *nor* of surrender. Hence he says that, in truth, what he speaks of is *beyond* "desire" or "no-desire"; it is *beyond* "freedom" or "bondage." What he really wishes to express is the fact that feelings of these kinds, one way or another, simply do not exist. He tries, tentatively, to speak of Nothingness or *Sunyata* (4). Yet to speak of *Nothingness* suggests mere emptiness or absence—a gap. Yet life, in truth, is *full*. Worst of all: in the moment of speaking of experience "beyond desire," he lies, for in order to make the point he must make reference to the category of desire and thus he is no longer "beyond" desire!

If only the audience would *see*—there is only one way of taking his language consistently with the facts. But, of course, the audience does not, *will not,* see. Like the patient in psychoanalytic therapy, the mystic's disciple, too, must be ready for the insight or else the interpretation will meet not merely with blank ignorance but with positive resistance. The context of anxiety is then substituted, and all the words are taken in a foolish, paradoxical, or positively hurtful sense.

The mystic says:

> When striving and gaining are balanced, nothing remains,
> Aimless striving is quite different. . . . (20)

In the same spirit the psychoanalyst says: defensive equilibria consist of pitting one set of inner demands against another, thus warding off dangerous impulses by an inner stalemate. Such equilibria are basically self-defeating; they produce ever higher levels of tensions. Ego-syntonic activity is "quite different"—it is genuinely gratifying. The "aimlessness" of the mystic thus refers always to the absence of *inner* aims, i.e., the aims of repression. The mystic language is a language of subjective experience—it does not have to do in the first instance with "external" aims, obviously an inevitable part of life. The confusion arises because our "external" aims—jobs, love conquests, cars—are so often the rationalizations of inner defensive aims. It is in the latter sense of "aim" that the enlightened are aimless. Thus the mystic may well acknowledge that he enjoys food, friends, kindred, honor, and comfort provided he is not anxiously dependent upon them, unable to cope with their opposites (4). Thus, in a fundamental sense aimless and open to experience, the enlightened pursue and enjoy whatever concrete aims seem appropriate.

Closely related to the absence of striving, of aimlessness, are the phenomena which the mystic describes as "no discrimination," "no perception," "no sensation," "no thought." If our hypothesis is correct, we should expect that what he is denying is the compulsive, obsessive, acutely self-conscious focusing of attention upon our feelings and our perceptions, our theoretical distinctions and our logical proofs. What the mystic decries is, in terms of the psychological conditions which are associated with it, the neurotic drive to achieve security by fitting all experience into a firm, clear, and neat logical system within which one can then manipulate the elements in an absolutely regularized way.

On the other hand, according to our psychological analysis, we should expect that sensing, perceiving, thinking, discriminating are essential functions within the enlightened life, but that they are used less self-consciously, uncompulsively, and flexibly in accordance with the integrity of the individual and the demands of the real environmental situation. They are *used;* they do not dominate.

(The enlightened) use their sense organs when occasion requires,
But the concept of "using" does not arise (10).

Consistent with our inference is the mystic's statement that enlightened meditation is "(observing) things in the phenomenal world, yet (dwelling) in emptiness." Perception *is* present, but it comes as it will to a mind that is "empty," i.e., without compulsive, stereotyped modes of perceiving and thinking.

One way of putting the matter is in terms of the Buddhist notion of "abiding." It is the (neurotically rigid) abiding with specific thoughts or sensations that is the mark of the unenlightened.

> In action Prajna (the wisdom of enlightenment) is everywhere present, yet it "sticks" nowhere. What we have to do is to so purify the mind that the six aspects of consciousness (sight, sound, smell, taste, touch, mentation) in passing through their six sense-gates will neither be defiled by nor attached to their six sense-objects. . . . *To refrain from thinking of anything, in the sense that all mental activity is suppressed, is to be Dharma-ridden; this is an extremely erroneous view* (10). (Italics added.)

To suppose that Nirvana is the "mere stopping of discrimination" is to commit the error typical of the philosopher (who takes everything in its abstract, theoretical sense) as distinguished from the person with genuine mystic insight (10).

The previous discussion makes it clear—and it is consistent with our psychoanalytic theses—that when we speak of enlightenment, we are not talking of an existence divorced from the "everyday world." On the contrary, it consists of life within this world. Zen, says one of the great Zen masters, "is your everyday mind." (24.) "Birth-and-death (i.e., our everyday world) and Nirvana are not separate from one another." (10.)

This world is the Buddha-world
Within which enlightenment may be sought.
To seek enlightenment by separating from this world
Is as foolish as to search for a rabbit's horn. (10.)

At the same time we confidently infer from the psychological analysis what mystic literature also suggests at times: that so far as the subjective feel of life goes, there is in some sense a "world" of difference between that of enlightenment and that of birth-and-death. How can one distinguish the subtle but profound difference between these "worlds" in terms of a subjective language? This difference may be reported as, for example, action in which one "remains poised in the tranquillity of the Atman." (2.) It is an "inner light" which does not flicker while the everyday life goes on (4). It is that engagement in the world of joys and sorrows which Eckhart compares with the door which swings back and forth while the hinge at the center remains fixed and solid (4). It is the life of the Bodhisattvas who are "joyous in heart but ever grieved over the sight of suffering beings. . . ." (25.) It is the "inner stillness" which is the "joy of Brahman, which words cannot express and the mind cannot reach . . . free from fear." (30.) It is "the inaction which is in action." (2.) It transforms the experienced world with its coming. In the poetic language of Indian mysticism,

> . . . there will be music; not only music made by human lips and played by human hands on various instruments, but there will be music among the grass and shrubs and trees, and in mountains and towns and palaces and hovels; much more will there be music in the hearts of those endowed with sentiency. (10.)

In Knight's more prosaic clinical terminology, the free man is one with "feelings of well-being, of self-esteem, of confidence, of inner satisfaction based on successful use of one's energies for achievement that promotes the best interests of one's fellow men as well as one's own." (14.) This language is a remarkable parallel to another expressive mystic report which I shall now quote. I trust the reader will tolerate my esthetically inexcusable parenthetical interpolations.

> Free from the domination of words you will be able to establish yourselves where there will be a "turning about" in the deepest seat of consciousness by means of which you will attain self-realization of Noble Wisdom and be able to enter into all the Buddhaland and assemblies. There you will be stamped with the stamp of the powers, self-command, the psychic faculties, and will be endowed with wisdom and the power of the ten inexhaustible vows. . . . There you will shine without effort like the moon, the sun, the magic wishing-jewel, and at every stage will view things as being of perfect oneness with yourself, uncontaminated by any self-consciousness. Seeing that all things are like a dream (i.e., seeing that your life has been lived until now in the neurotic fantasy-world), you will be able to enter into the stage of the Tathagatas and be able to deliver discourses on the Dharma to the world of beings in accordance with their needs (i.e., in the manner of therapeutic interventions or the well-timed advice of the wise layman rather than formal lectures or general theories) and be able to free them from all dualistic notions and false discriminations. (10.)

We know that neither Knight nor the writer of the Lankavatara Sutra intend us to understand that the enlightened one is a "self-satisfied," neurotically dedicated "do-gooder." We know that for the one who seeks enlightenment to "hold in his mind any arbitrary conceptions about kindness" (10) would be a gross mistake. "Kindness, after all, is only a word and charity should be spontaneous and selfless." (10.) Put negatively and in psychoanalytic terms, doing well by others is not the outcome of a moralistic program of "altruistic" action rationalizing narcissicism or other neurotic gratifications. Likewise the *thought* that one has attained "Highest Perfect Wisdom" or that one is on the way there is evidence that one is *mistaken*. One who *is* confident does not have a conscious feeling of confidence; one who is wise does not consciously think to himself that he is wise. Those who have such thoughts or feelings reveal that, perturbed by anxiety and doubts, they have had to react with reassurances to themselves.

The enlightened one is, therefore, not only an unassuming and "ordinary" person (as well as an extraordinary one), he is in many ways "more ordinary" than most people. He is not overly proud, not driven by ambition, not prone to keeping up with the Joneses, not given to disingenuous logical or theoretical disquisitions. He tends to shun words. He suffers, enjoys, knows pain and pleasure, but he is not driven and dominated by these. Sensual without being sensualist, he is also aware of his ills without being hypochondriacal. "He does not call attention to himself." (27.)

At the same time there are ways in which he clearly stands apart: "I alone am dark . . . blown adrift . . . intractable and boorish." (27.) Such a person does not always quite fit because, while he may often conform, he is not a conformist. He will even at times appear "ruthless." (27.) For when the ordinary ways conflict with his own integrity, when realism calls for breaking through sentimentality, when life has shattered the old facades, he acts accordingly. His ruthlessness is kindliness in the same way as the parent's realistic discipline may be kinder than a guilt-motivated "permissiveness."

In the last analysis, then, the mystic way is a "simple" and "obvious" way—for those who will open their eyes. For the mystic experience is the achievement of "emptiness," of "nothingness." That is to say, it is not the achievement of any finally fixed state of mind or any universal doctrine at all. It is the liberation from neurotic fixation and dogma of all kinds.

> Right views are called "transcendental,"
> Erroneous views are called "worldly,"
> But when all views, both right and erroneous, are discarded,
> Then the essence of Wisdom manifests itself. (10.)

This is the emptiness of a mind which is thoroughly open to the world. As Hui-Neng says, it is the "voidness" which can be filled (10). It is not mere "vacuity" or idealessness. Bergson has spoken in this connection of the "open soul." (1.)

Dwelling in such a (psychic) "emptiness," our life is full, but not full of our repetitive fantasies. It is pervaded by an elusive but profound sense of joy. How natural then to express this pervasive "peace" as the presence of God. But then God becomes the "atmosphere" of life rather than an object within life. "God," said St. Augustine, "is the Country of the soul: its Home, says Ruysbroeck." (29.) The mystic God is "Nothingness" in the sense that God is not an object of contemplation; He is the realm within which all objects exist. It is Emptiness which, in Christian language, appears as the "poverty of the spirit" which is an ultimate joy. Poverty here is not to be identified with asceticism or moral masochism; it is absence of pretense, absence of anxious dependence or "clinging," "openness" to life. God is perceived as a radical "inner stillness." The psychological condition of this perception is, according to our hypothesis, the growth of personality beyond anxiety and intrapsychic conflict to primarily conflict-free integrity.

> One must achieve this unself-consciousness by means of transformed knowledge. *This* ignorance does not come from lack of knowledge but rather it is from knowledge that one may achieve this ignorance. (4.)

Eckhart here means to distinguish, on the one hand, the naïvete of the unsocialized child or of the neurotic who *will* not learn and, on the other, the humility and spontaneity of the person who uses his learned skills and his knowledge as a means of *meeting* life in its novelty instead of insisting that life conform to his stereotyped nursery fantasies.

To achieve this simplicity is, as we know, the most arduous struggle, the most radical and intricate operation which we need to perform in our lives. "The Great Way is right before your eyes but difficult to see." (25.)

VI

It follows from the thesis we have presented that there are likely to be significant similarities between the ways in which the mystic and the psychoanalytic patient achieve "enlightenment." To review this aspect of the matter briefly will help illuminate and validate our theses. As I have said before, there are, of course, substantial differences between the mystic and psychoanalytic "ways." However, with the exception of the last portions of this paper, I am concerned with stressing the similarities.

Lao-Tse says:

> Yet by seizing on the way that was
> You can ride the things that are new.
> For to know what once there was, in the Beginning,
> This is called the essence of the Way. (27.)

The literal meaning of Lao-Tse's term translated above as "essence" is "main-thread." One could not put Freud's views better than to say that the main-thread by means of which one masters the present is the thread which leads to the past. We cannot do more than note here that the Chinese reference to the past has a double meaning which parallels Freud's treatment of the psychologically significant past. For Lao-Tse refers in his verse both to the archetypal or archaic past and to the past of the individual's personal history.

Freud provides us with detailed classifications of the various typical roots of our present psychic troubles. The mystic, however, usually provides us either with very concrete, personal, and hence idiosyncratic accounts, or else he offers very broad but suggestive generalizations. The mystic's fundamental generalizations are remarkably reminiscent of some of Freud's basic postulates. Hui-Neng tells us that

> When neither hatred nor love disturb the mind,
> Serene and restful is our sleep. (10.)

While this is surely not meant simply in a literal way, we know from Freud that the literal meaning of the image is perfectly apt. Provided one interprets "hatred" and "love" as unsublimated aggressive and libidinal instinctual drives, one hardly needs to change a word to consider the verse as a basic psychological truth. Likewise we could consider the following verse in the Bhagavad-Gita as an almost word for word analysis, according to Freud, of the roots of neurotic self-deception in current unresolved libidinal and aggressive conflicts and the unconscious fantasies connected with them:

> When a man lacks lust and hatred,
> His renunciation does not waver.
> He neither longs for one thing
> Nor loathes its opposite:
> The chains of his delusion
> Are soon cast off. (2.)

The total picture that we get of the state of existence of man prior to entering upon the path of Enlightenment is expressed in the great Eastern image of the wheel of birth-and-death. Lust, anger, and ignorance bind man ever more tightly to the wheel of suffering. This is the very model of the self-harassed and self-driven neurotic.

How can we control such behavior? More important yet, how can we break away from the wheel entirely? The Buddhist formula is threefold. At the most primitive level, the rules of morality, if strictly adhered to, help to prevent *actions* leading to bad Karma. As a second step, mental and moral concentrated effort help to *suppress* the *thoughts* and *feelings* which lie behind such actions. But to get to the root, to eradicate the source of such thoughts, feelings, and actions, what is needed is insight. It is, in practice, the proper concurrent use of all three which can lead, step by step, to broader and deeper insight with eventual liberation from the wheel (28). *Perfect* enlightenment seems to be a mythic ideal in mysticism. The ever present potential in real life for still further deepening insight is expressed in the concept of the stages of enlightenment.

This picture of successive rebirths in Samsara eventuating ideally in release from Karma and the achievement of Nirvana is a wonderful image which parallels in the essential psychological aspects the process of psychoanalytic therapy. We start with neurotic behavior and experience (samsara). The neurotic, motivated by unresolved instinctual conflict (lust and anger), unwittingly ignorant, creates his own half-fantasy experience (the illusory world of Maya). This world provides temporary gratification at the cost of increasing enslavement to the very anxieties and conflicts which are so painful. Thus the neurotic is ever more tightly bound to the wheel. Social codes, repressions, and suppression can, however, keep the actions and thoughts within some control. But the move toward maturity requires insight. Yet psychoanalytic insight takes place not in a vacuum or all at once: it proceeds (ideally) by limited and partial insights in a setting of substantial social conformity (no acting-out) and continuing suppression and repression (no "wild analysis," careful timing and dosage in therapeutic interventions). The "complete" analysis is a theoretical ideal ("Buddhahood").

As for the "medium" within which enlightening communication takes place:

> . . . the way of instruction presented by the Tathagatas is not based on assertions and refutations by means of words and logic. (10.)
>
> If I should tell you that I had a system of Dhyana to transmit to others, I would be deceiving you. What I try to do to my disciples, is to liberate them from their own bondage, by such devices as each case requires. . . . (10.)
>
> As circumstances arise, (the enlightened) take appropriate action; they give suitable answer according to the varying temperaments of their questioner. (10.)

That is to say, liberation is achieved as a way of life and by means of "pragmatic," not theoretical communication, communication oriented to the immediate context and the particular person. It is not a question of proving or disproving theories. Likewise, the psychoanalytic therapist, *as a therapist*, is not primarily concerned with establishing the truth of some general theory; he is concerned to provide specific interventions which enable the patient to *undergo the experience* with concurrent insight.

When Hui-Neng says that "they give suitable answers," he is speaking of responding "therapeutically," not of giving the person directions as to how to live his life. Tai-tz'u Huan-chung, the Zen teacher, said: "I do not know how to make answers; I only know where diseases are." (25.) This is analogous to the analyst's task which, according to Freud, is to "unmask the roots," not "to play the part of prophet, saviour, and redeemer to the patient . . . but to give the patient's ego *freedom* to choose one way or the other." (7.)

The manner of the psychoanalyst is, ideally, that of the Bodhisattva: one "who practice(s) compassion but (is not given up to petty kindnesses . . . practice(s) indifference but never cease(s) benefitting others." (25.) This is a clear description of important aspects of the ideal therapeutic relationship.

The actual occasion of insight (out of which decisions flow spontaneously) involves a peculiar shifting of mental gears, as it were.

Suzuki says (24): "In our religious life, passivity comes as the culmination of strenuous activity; passivity without this preliminary condition is sheer inanity. . . ."

The activity leading up to enlightenment is imbued with a "spirit of inquiry" requiring that we pursue the advice of the master: "ask of your self, inquire into your self, pursue your self, investigate within your self. . . ."

At the moment preceding *satori*, the Zen enlightenment, we are like a man at the "edge of a precipice." (24.) It is a moment of uneasiness, despair, death. At this point, by "letting go," the disciple is as awakened from a stupor.

The characteristic terms for this moment of enlightenment are "one bursting cry," "the bursting of the bag," "a sudden snapping," "a sudden bursting," and so on (24). It is difficult to avoid recalling the comparable phrases used to characterize insight experience in Western terminology, phrases such as the "Aha! experience," or, in the simple formula of Greenson's patient, "Bong!" (11.)

The sense of passive receptiveness in the ultimate phase of mystic enlightenment appears to occur characteristically in all the mystics (24).

From the psychoanalytic side, Kris (15) has discussed the relation between insight and passivity at length, and he concludes one such discussion by asserting that "the maturing of thought, the entry into awareness from preconsciousness to consciousness tend to be experienced as derived from outside, as passively received, not as actively produced. The tendency toward passive reception takes various shapes and forms, appears under the guise of various modalities, but the subjective experience remains one of reception."

Kris holds that in the creative solution of problems as distinguished from mere fantasy gratification, there is a feeling of satisfaction as well as mere relief.

We might amplify slightly as follows. The "letting go" is the cessation of defensive "striving." The joy is associated psychologically with the sudden availability of the energy previously expended in the repressive process, energy which is now freed by the "creative" solution of the problem but would not be by a neurotic "solution." In the neurotic "solution" the diminished anxiety accounts for the sense of relief, but there is no "joy" because the neurotic solution requires the energies of repressive counter-cathexis.

This combination of felt passivity and heightened joy at the moment of insight is a characteristic mark of mystic enlightenment. This, as part of the characteristic behavior and affect patterns of the mystic, is important evidence that the mystic enlightenment of which we speak is, psychologically, a creative solution of a problem rather than merely regressive fantasy gratification.

VII

Kris, in the course of the discussion of insight and passivity cited above, introduces a number of closely connected issues which are appropriately introduced here in our discussion of mysticism. These issues have to do with the specific fantasy and symbolic content of the mystical experiences. They lead to that major amplification of the psychoanalytic theses with which I shall terminate the present discussion.

In spite of the fact that I am not primarily concerned in this paper with what I shall call broadly the symbolism of mysticism but rather with mystic "selflessness," it remains a fact that symbolism in mysticism is so pervasive as to require some comment. I must at least indicate how what I have said up to this point is consistent with the symbolic aspects of mysticism. For this purpose I propose to confine the discussion to the ubiquitous symbols of "oneness" in mystic writings. This will, in turn, lead us back in a new way to the more traditional, id-oriented formulations of the psychological conditions of mystic experience.

The all-engulfing sense of Oneness, the loss of distinction between self and object, is frequently asserted in both Eastern and Western mysticism to be of the essence of the experience of enlightenment. This aspect of mystic experience has been commented upon by a number of psychoanalytic writers including Freud himself.

Freud's suggestion (9) was that this "oceanic feeling" of oneness, of ineffable ecstasy, is a concomitant of regression to the primal unity with the mother, a unity in which there were yet no ego boundaries and in which gratification was direct and complete. As Lewin says, the experience is felt as *known*, as more certain than anything, because it is the closest we come to what is primal, immediate, unquestioned experience as distinguished from experience mediated by concepts and the subject-object distinctions. It represents the primitive narcissistic trust in sensory experience (17).

It is, of course, essential to recall that the frequently quoted erotic and often orgastic language of a number of the Christian mystics is not interpreted as a symptom of "genital" orgasm in the psychological sense. Rather what is meant is that the experience, while intensely *libidinal* and orgastic, is on the earliest infantile oral level, the level of primal unity through incorporation.

There is no doubt that the images and the language of the mystics do suggest strongly feelings of total gratification and of omnipotence ("A snap of the fingers, and eight thousand gates of the teaching are established" [20]). There is no doubt that, at crucial stages along the mystic way, at least momentary trance or ecstasy states occur. This, according to Lewin (17), is to be expected if we associate the subjective experience with regression to infantile narcissistic gratification at the mother's breast—for this is a state culminating in ecstasy-sleep.

Although the mother image pervades religious and mystical literature, Lao-Tse's language is most explicit and sharp:

> . . . The Doorway of the Mysterious Female
> Is the base from which Heaven and Earth sprang.
> It is there within us all the while;
> Draw upon it as you will, it never runs dry.
>
> . . . wherein I most am different from men
> Is that I prize no sustenance that comes not from the Mother's breast. (27.)

The views of Freud and Lewin as to the psychological conditions of the mystic experience are clearly quite different from those which I have developed in the earlier sections of this discussion. I have stressed the fact that the experience of loss of self and loss of the sense of subject-object relations is a loss of a certain kind of anxiety generated self-consciousness; it is a creative rather than a regressive movement. Specifically, it results from ego-syntonic conflict resolution, drive neutralization (sublimation), and consequent absence of anxiety and defense. Furthermore, the sense of joy and power associated with this mode of experience was interpreted, psychologically, as the characteristic result of realistic problem solutions rather than (regressive) fantasy gratifications. The more typical psychoanalytic interpretations just cited, however, imply that this sense of joy and power is, in contrast to what Kris's thesis seems to imply, a result of deeply regressive fantasy gratification. I wish to show now how these two contrasting interpretations are complementary rather than incompatible. *Indeed it is the very fusion of the two processes which constitutes the characteristic psychological condition of the mystic experience.*

The crux of the problem is touched if we follow Kris's well-known development of the psychoanalytic theory of creativity in terms of "regression in the service of the ego." Kris states:

> This relationship between creativity and passivity exemplifies once more one of the leading theses of this presentation: the integrative functions of the ego include self-regulated regression and permits a combination of the most daring intellectual activity with the experience of passive receptiveness. (15.)

The implication of such a view is that, in "regression in the service of the ego," it is the movement toward maturity rather than the concurrent regression which is psychodynamically primary. The appropriateness of this conception as applied to the regressive aspects of mysticism needs now to be shown.

We have already seen that the mystic is one who "returns to the Beginning" in order to "ride the present." We have held that this is analogous to the psychoanalytic exploration of the past as inherent in current self-exploration and re-creation. The return to the Beginning is in essential respects an uncovering of infantile history and a reintegration of the personality on the basis of the insights achieved. We must expect, then, that in the course of following the Way, the mystic would become subjectively aware of, and would more or less frequently act out many of the fantasies and feelings associated with the various infantile stages of development in his own life. This, in turn, means that the mystic's history would be filled with the language—and frequently the symptomatology—of infantile conflicts. We would expect, ideally, that he would eventually uncover the earliest infantile memories, the most archaic fantasies and feelings. Such a thoroughgoing self-exploration and stripping off of the defensive character "armor" is bound to be a dramatic and long-drawn out struggle. We should not be surprised if, frequently, the motivation sufficient to continue such a painful effort is a threatening sense of personal disintegration on a massive scale as the only alternative to success. Such a struggle, while not inevitable, should be relatively common among mystics (30).

Thus regressive symptomatology is of the essence of the movement toward maturity. This is precisely the case with psychoanalytic self-exploration. What makes the process in both cases essentially *pro*gressive when successful rather than *re*gressive is the fact that the fundamental context is established by the ego in its movement toward increasing integrity and strength. This may, perhaps, be more evident in psychoanalytic therapy which is characterized by the systematic attempt to maintain continuously the "splitting of the ego" into the "observing," realistic ego as well as the regressive ego. The mystic (and the creative artist?) may be supposed at times to take the more radical—and risky—step of a more total ego regression, a more total reliving of the old conflicts in the course of creating new, ego-syntonic solutions.

There is a second way in which regression enters the mystic experience: it is inherent not only in the stages leading to enlightenment but in the "enlightenment" experience itself. In the most advanced stage of mystic experience, it is true, the pathological symptomatology, trances and visions are finally superseded by highly ego-syntonic behavior. Such mature gratifications produce, as has been noted earlier, a subjective experience which is without anxious self-consciousness, without compulsive intellectualization or defensive striving. But the strength of ego and the radicalness of the self-exploration implicit in achieving such enlightenment justify certain further assumptions. We may suppose that such persons have retained, far more than most, a significant degree of accessibility to infantile fantasies and a tolerance of partial instinct gratification within a context of essentially mature behavior. Infantile fantasy and partial instinct gratification would therefore not dominate current experience and make it *anti*-realistic, but they would be less rigidly repressed, more ego-syntonic.

Thus the selflessness of anxiety-free experience would be "deepened" and "colored" by the quite different but now complementary selflessness of the primal fantasy. The sense of joy and power generated by conflict-free functioning would have the ecstatic "overtones" of the fantasies of primal gratification and omnipotence. The core of reality perception would be enlivened and enriched by the peripheral but compatible illusions associated with residual partial instinct gratifications. This process is, in effect, no more than a broadening and deepening of processes we know to be characteristic of our "everyday" life (21), whether the latter involves doing arithmetic, eating dinner, or experiencing sexual orgasm.

We are now in a position to suggest in general terms the lines along which we should differentiate mystic experiences, one from another, and also from other related types of experience.

What I have outlined as a psychological schema of the mystic way is an idealized and oversimplified structure. For example, the experience of enlightenment is not a self-identical, permanent, and total experience. Mystic literature often seems to suggest this just as psychoanalytic literature often seems to suggest the goal of being "finally and completely analyzed." In both cases, whenever the issue is at the focus of attention, it is clear that such suggestions do not do justice to the facts: there are, after all, many varieties of enlightenment and "degrees" of enlightenment; the scope of enlightenment is limited, its persistence under stress variable. Such variation is found as well in psychoanalysis, *mutatis mutandis*.

In psychological language, we can express such differences from individual mystic to individual mystic in terms of such matters as the relative balance of regressive fantasy and realism, the specific content of the fantasies which predominate, the strength of the ego, and the scope of the conflict-free area of the latter. The differing linguistic patterns, philosophic-religious trends, and, more broadly, the cultural traditions which contribute to the total experience, provide a basis for differentiating types of mysticism. These differentiating factors are not "frills" on an underlying psychological "reality." Importance depends upon purposes and these are, for many purposes, at least as important or more important than the psychological factors common to the various kinds of mystic experience. Their analysis, involving humanistic, historical, and scientific studies of varied sorts, is, of course, in the highest degree complex.

Similar considerations hold with regard to the relation of mysticism and psychoanalysis. The psychoanalytic patient's experience is patently different in many important respects from the mystic's. This is in many ways obvious, in others not; but such a discussion is beyond the scope of this paper.

A final question which we cannot entirely ignore remains. Are we suggesting that, while the mystical experience is not identical with the psychoanalytic process, it is still, after all, only a "subjective" experience and therefore not a "genuine" revelation of or union with God?

Extended discussion here of such an issue is obviously out of the question. Nevertheless, since this is an issue on the borderline of the psychological, it calls for at least brief comment.

The burden of what I have said is, of course, not that there is no union with God in the mystic's experience; it is rather that I am saying there *is* union with God, "dwelling in" God. To let go of this is to let go of the essence. But to suppose that union with God or dwelling in God is union with a substantial person or existence in a definite place is naïve. For the mystic tells us—and it is essential to listen seriously to him—that he is not concerned with a sensual or substantial being, nor is the "place" in which he dwells a physical or quasi-physical place having measurable dimension.

Let us consider an analogous situation. The experience of "three-dimensional space" in a painting is not an experience of physical three-dimensional space. Nor is it an "illusion," for no one is deceived by it. It is an *obviously* different experience from that of three dimensional physical space. Still, it is sufficiently reminiscent, in certain limited ways, of the physical space experience so that we borrow physical space *language* in talking of it. We call it "esthetic space"—a phrase which perhaps overemphasizes the (limited) similarity. Esthetic space certainly exists, however, and it is no more a mystery than any other perception. To call it an "illusion" or "subjective" is to attack a straw man—as if the artist had ever said or intended us to think that it was *literally* the same as three dimensional physical space! If one takes it to be physical space, one *is* deluded, of course. But taken as it is, it is a genuine and distinct phenomenon in nature having for some persons its own intrinsic and special value. Just so, the mystical experience of God is illusion only if it is taken naïvely to be what the mystic constantly insists that it is not: a logically impossible, quasi-physical or mental union with a quasi-substantial being who has quasi-human traits.

There is no way of *verbally* communicating about the experience of esthetic space except by means of the potentially misleading analogies with physical space. Just as this esthetic language of space misleads, so the mystic language of personification misleads and suggests a kind of mysterious anthropomorphism.

Not everyone perceives the drama inherent in the forms of esthetic space. Those who do not often feel comfortable calling art an illusion. Such persons find in esthetic space only that trivial value which consists in supposing that it is the product of ingenious technique intended to deceive, having no intrinsic interest other than as deception. But for some persons the perception of esthetic space is, in and of itself, of momentous value; it establishes a world of its own. And for some, needless to say, the same is true of the experiences of God.

Summary

Most psychoanalytic studies of mysticism have been "id-oriented." The development of psychoanalytic ego psychology makes appropriate a basic review of mystic language and experience. Such a review not only expands our understanding of various forms of spiritual creativity, it clarifies and extends our knowledge of the processes of regression, sublimation, therapeutic communication, and consciousness.

"Ego-oriented" study of mysticism tends to reveal the significant marks of insight and maturity which have long been associated with the great mystics. The spontaneous and colloquial verbal expression of her subjective experience by a person who has achieved insight in psychoanalysis shows marked similarity in form and content to the language of certain mystics. This is not an isolated parallel but it is one which is often obscured by widespread stereotypes about mystics and by the failure to collect systematically such impressionistic postanalytic statements. This parallel suggests strongly that the traditional "id-oriented" analyses of mysticism with their stress on regressive phenomena have been substantially incomplete, although essentially correct as far as they go.

The language of the classic literature of Eastern mysticism—especially but not exclusively that of Zen Buddhist mysticism—is examined. It is a language expressive of subjective, conscious experience. It centers around an ubiquitous paradox-form: basic mental functions (e.g., self, mind, sensation, desire) are denied, then acknowledged, and finally dismissed as "irrelevant." To account for mystic paradox, the writer postulates that the mystic is concerned with two contrasting modes of psychic functioning for which there is only one form of linguistic expression. Hence the mystic must use paradox to help us distinguish what ordinary use of language leaves ambiguous. The problem now remains to describe psychoanalytically the nature of the distinction in question.

Since "selflessness" is a characteristic mystic concept associated with the "enlightened" state, the language and theories of psychoanalysis are examined in order to find a clue to the psychological conditions of mystic "selflessness." It does not mean the absence of a self in the psychoanalytic sense of that term, nor does it refer to the absence of the ego or of the "self-representations," or to the loss of ability to distinguish "inner" and "outer" as in hallucination or estrangement. It is shown that none of these come anywhere near being correct for the contexts in which "selflessness" is used. "Selflessness," being a term in a "subjective" language, expresses the lack of conscious awareness of self. But this is true in a sense which cannot be made unambiguous in ordinary language. We can point to the unawareness in question by referring to its psychological conditions: it is that "normal" unselfconsciousness characteristic of experience which is primarily non-anxious and motivated by neutralized drives functioning within the non-conflictful portions of the ego. It is an unselfconsciousness akin to the normal unawareness of our breathing.

This thesis is developed in terms of a variety of the key ideas of the mystics and in terms of mystic behavior. The naturalness of the various mystic paradoxes is now revealed when we see that they are used to point to the many types of conscious experience but always with the object of distinguishing what is, in psychological terms, the anxiety-motivated (defensive) form of the experience from the ego-syntonic form. The mystic uses language as a "therapeutic" tool, not as universally valid and meaningful theory.

The theses already presented imply that to achieve such enlightenment should require a long and arduous course of controlled regression with self-observation, the uncovering of infantile material, insight, and sublimation. This, in turn, suggests the probability of phases of infantile and "pathological" symptomatology. Such inferences are shown in detail to be justified by reference to the literature of mysticism. Parallels to and divergences from the general features of psychoanalytic self-exploration are noted.

Finally it is shown that what is distinctive of mystic enlightenment—as distinguished from the "pathology" typical of the struggle to achieve enlightenment—is the simultaneous presence in experience of highly ego-syntonic behavior (and thus unselfconscious in this sense) alongside the now acceptable residue of deeply infantile fantasy. The latter functions now as a regression in the service of the ego; it colors and enriches experience with the "oceanic" feeling, the undifferentiated unselfconsciousness and sense of omnipotence which derives from the fantasy of the primal unity with the mother.

Some possible misinterpretations as to the "theological" implications of the theses of this paper and of the mystic outlook are briefly discussed.

References

1. Bergson, H. *The Two Sources of Morality and Religion.* New York: Doubleday Anchor Books, 1954. Pp. 227-28, 38.

2. Bhagavad-Gita. Translated by Prabhavananda and Christopher Isherwood. New York: New American Library (Mentor), 1954. Pp. 84, 43, 52, 56-57.

3. Boisen, A. T. *Exploration of the Inner World.* New York: Harper & Bros., 1936.

4. Eckhart. "Writings and Sermons," in *Meister Eckhart.* Translated by R. B. Blakney. New York: Harper & Bros. (Torchbook), 1957. Pp. 17, 226, 231, 25, 246-47, 87, 107.

5. Federn, P. *Ego Psychology and the Psychoses.* New York: Basic Books, 1952. Pp. 244, 242.

6. Freud, S. "Instincts and Their Vicissitudes" (1915), in *Collected Papers,* Vol. V. London: Hogarth Press, 1949.

7. Freud, S. *The Ego and the Id* (1923). Translated by J. Riviere. London: Hogarth Press Ltd., 1949. P. 72.

8. Freud, S. *The Problem of Anxiety* (1926). Translated by H. A. Bunker. New York: W. W. Norton & Co., 1936.

9. Freud, S. *Civilization and Its Discontents* (1930). Translated by J. Riviere. London: Hogarth Press Ltd., 1955.

10. Goddard, D. *A Buddhist Bible.* New York: E. P. Dutton & Co., 1938. Pp. 352-54, 515, 352, 324, 547, 546, 519, 352, 324, 521, 38-39, 318-19, 91, 521-22, 514, 521, 284, 549, 550.

11. Greenson, R. R. "On Boredom," *Journal of the American Psychoanalytic Association,* I (1953), 7-21, esp. 12.

12. Jacobson, E. "Contribution to the Metapsychology of Psychotic Identifications," *Journal of American Psychoanalytic Association,* II (1954), 239-62, esp. 241.

13. Jacobson, E. "The Self and the Object World," in *Psychoanalytic Study of the Child,* Vol. IX. New York: International Universities Press, Inc., 1954. P. 94.

14. Knight, R. P. "Determinism, 'Freedom,' and Psychotherapy," in Knight, R. P. and Friedman, C. R. (eds.), *Psychoanalytic Psychiatry and Psychology.* New York: International Universities Press, Inc., 1954. Pp. 372, 376, 378, 372.

15. Kris, E. *Psychoanalytic Explorations in Art.* New York: International Universities Press, Inc., 1952. P. 318.

16. Leuba, J. H. *The Psychology of Religious Mysticism.* New York: Harcourt, Brace & Co., Inc., 1925. Pp. 43, 202.

17. Lewin, B. D. *The Psychoanalysis of Elation.* New York: W. W. Norton & Co., Inc., 1950. Pp. 149, 150.

18. Nunberg, H. *Theory and Practice of Psychoanalysis.* Nervous and Mental Disease Monograph 74. New York, 1948. Pp. 31 ff.

19. Reich, W. *Character-Analysis.* New York: Orgone Institute Press, 1949. Chapter IV.

20. Senzaki, N., and R. McCandless. *Buddhism and Zen.* New York: Philosophical Library (Wisdom Books), 1956. Pp. 69, 55, 61.

21. Sperling, O. E. "Illusions, Naive and Controlled," *Psychoanalytic Quarterly*, XX (1951).

22. Suzuki, D. T. *Essays in Zen Buddhism* (*First Series*). New York: Harper & Brothers, 1949. Pp. 252-53, 34.

23. Suzuki, D. T. *Manual of Zen Buddhism*. London: Rider & Co., 1950.

24. Suzuki, D. T. *Essays in Zen Buddhism* (*Second Series*). Boston: Beacon Press, 1952. Pp. 85, 276, 127, 91, 118, 412, 29.

25. Suzuki, D. T. *Essays in Zen Buddhism* (*Third Series*). London: Rider & Co., 1953. Pp. 57, 116, 46, 55, 116.

26. Szasz, T. S. *Pain and Pleasure*. New York: Basic Books, Inc., 1957. Chapter VII.

27. Tao Te Ching. Translated by A. Waley. In A. Waley, *The Way and Its Power*. New York: The Macmillan Co., 1956. Pp. 230, 143, 168-69, 147, 159, 149, 169.

28. Thittila, M. T. U. "The Fundamental Principles of Theravada Buddhism," in K. W. Morgan (ed.), *The Path of the Buddha*. New York: Ronald Press Co., 1956. Pp. 107-8.

29. Underhill, E. *Mysticism*. New York: Meridian Books, 1957. Pp. 279-81, Chapter X, p. 420.

30. *Upanishads*. Translated by Prabhavananda and F. Manchester. New York: New American Library (Mentor), 1957. P. 58.

C.

PERSONAL STYLES AND THE STUDY OF HISTORY

ERIC DARDEL

History and Our Times

Is HISTORY at present in a position to sustain the dialogue of our times? Is it not rather, like an album of faded pictures, a curiously anachronistic story for a century infatuated with progress, speed, and productivity?

It is true that the pursuit of historical research is always in evidence, and that an interested public still exists for it. More significant perhaps is the historical sensitivity which our epoch attests. This same twentieth century, to which discoveries and innovations of all kinds appeal, likes reconstitutions, encourages prehistorical exhumations, and sees to the accurate restoration and preservation of monuments. Careless restoration would not be countenanced today, nor would the demolitions of the nineteenth century, when, because of a lack of feeling for history, too many precious relics were squandered. This piety does not emanate solely from the aesthetic order. What readily comes to light, emerging from this rubble and its picturesque quality, is the atmosphere of early days, the conditions and even the "states of mind" of men of long ago, as if we still were expecting something from that voice that rises out of the centuries.

This feeling for the past is accompanied by a devaluation of historical science. The nineteenth century was the century of history par excellence because of the high quality of the historians, because of the repercussions

Reprinted from *Diogenes*, No. 21 (Spring, 1958), pp. 11-26, by permission of the publisher. *Diogenes* is a review of humanistic sciences edited by the International Council for Philosophy and Humanistic Studies, Unesco House, Paris.

of archeological "discoveries," and because of the fervor blended with romanticism with which this encounter with "history" was welcomed. Michelet, Quinet, and Renan, Niebuhr, and Ranke were more than mere technicians of history, more than masters of narration or exposition. With them history became the ultimate expression of humanism. For them it was a faith, the revelation of a human order in time. In doing the work of historians, they were working for the improvement of man, for the advent of justice and liberty. The budding twentieth century felt itself borne away by progress toward sunnier climes where peace, abundance, and happiness would mark the end of history.

Since then the event has descended upon us. This euphoria was not proof against two wars of planetary dimensions or against the malevolence, inscribed in flesh, by death camps or scientific massacres. Rather, the entire course of history turns crimson with a sinister glimmer; its realism, suddenly unmasked, presents to our eyes misfortunes, failures, infamies during the course of the centuries, on which greatness or reason sheds but a fugitive light.

In the resentment of a disillusioned era (history is being brought to trial in our times—Spengler or Valéry, Guéhenno, Gide, or Sartre) the forms of the accusation vary, but everywhere history is called into question or depreciated. It appears as a relentless power against man, as an awesome evil genius. Many of our contemporaries have come to doubt that history has a meaning.

Although we reject the optimism of earlier days, we do not do so in order to wallow in a pessimism of principle. With the exception of concrete situations which call for pessimism, a sorry disillusion sterilizes that "pessimism of weaklings" denounced by Nietzsche. A "pessimism of strong men" knows itself to be provisional. It sets aside old values, established truths, and false securities, but only to await the truth of new values. We reject the official optimism of yesterday in favor of the myopia of its messianism of peace and happiness. Philosophies of history, despite the caution of Hegel or Marx, inspire us with distrust, because they falsify the historical perspective by setting up as a definitive truth the "views" of a moment. Yet one cannot dismiss all philosophy in order to fall back upon a ready-made artlessness. Let us merely hope that thought will become critical enough to save us from false absolutes and to preserve all the richness of historical reality. In denying that the course of history paves the way for the advent of the ideal city so dear to Marxist dogma, we do not, however, resign ourselves to the absurd and the chaotic. But, in forsaking those flowered paths where our illusions lay dreaming, we enter a universe where we must fight for justice, agitate for peace, defend liberty. These do not represent indestructible "boons." They must be won over again and again and protected at every moment. In taking cognizance of this internal exigency, history, emancipated from false ideologies, once again discovers something to say to our times. For every existence derives from history guideposts that help it to ascertain its position in the world and experiences that equip it to meet the challenge of future battles.

History and the Past

We are all more ancient than ourselves—history reminds us of this each day. We are surrounded by, and we come across in ourselves, a reality which we have not created but which stems from past centuries and presents obstacles or opens up new ways to us. That which is no more still remains present in one form or another, and we are obliged to take it into account. However, the positivist epoch has falsified the perspectives of this relationship with our past.

The years we have just lived through have freed us from the superstition of objectivity. We ourselves are in history. It is what happens to us and our reaction to events; it is what we do with our life. History is ourselves. Outside of time and history, no one can gain access to a bay window whence he could, without risk or emotion survey the course of events, score the points, and referee the match. To write history is also to realize its existence, to "historicize one's self."

The "presence" of the historian in the history he writes, inevitable as it is, is also the condition and the guaranty of a truthful history. His knowledge and his intellectual qualities are not enough. His moral worth, his probity, his breadth of vision, the intensity of his search, as broad an understanding as possible—all this, by guiding his "subjectivity," insures the validity of his work, his "objectivity." The best way of exorcising subjectivity wherever it might degenerate into arbitrariness or fantasy, the only true opposition to subjectivism, is not to deny its role in a work of science but to be aware of it.

It is said that history is the "science of the past." But the error of this commonplace is precisely that it overlooks the distinctive quality of the historical fact: its singularity and its reality as a living experience. The past constricts the men of whom history speaks into puppets with incomprehensible gesticulations. Knowledge acquired about the past by assembling information and records still does not guarantee the capacity to "understand" it. To do so, one would have to penetrate the potentialities, the concerns, and the beliefs of men and to go back with them over part of the road they traveled in their universe. How can an "object" lend itself to a communication of this order? Only a "presence" has something to say to us; it alone can open up to us, tell its tale.

The past with which the historian is concerned is not that which rusts old weapons or lends a patina to outmoded furniture. For man the "truth" of the past constitutes his present. The invasion of the Huns was the calamity of the day for contemporaries. The historian evokes this present buried beneath the past, imbued with its atmosphere of beings and things —a present like our own, vibrant with purpose, concerns, and hopes. The king who attempts to extend his power or his state does so with his eye on the future. Should he limit himself to defending his crown or his kingdom, it is still with the future in mind. History is realized by the advent of this future.

The present takes on purpose; the dream takes shape in the form of enterprises; institutions spring up from decisions made in a day. This "passage" of the future into the present is the way that history is created. Historical "reality" is not a "thing"; its very inconsistency attests that it is essentially "realization," in other words, movement. Lastingness is perceived in a flash of light, and the event in the traces it leaves and in works. History speaks to us of the present, the living, not of the dead. The Greek temple, the Roman cloister, and the châteaux of the Renaissance still convey in hushed tones the presences, plans, the sweetness of life plucked on the wing and bitter struggles to survive.

The past is usually thought of as a continuity, a chain of events leading from a distant past to a near present. On the contrary, however, history has to do with that which is a split with the past. History's "object" is that which intervenes in the objective continuity that is fixed in its chain of events. Historical reality is, more than anything else, event.

As Paul Thevenaz writes, the event is "the power of eruption" proper to "the catastrophe that descends upon us, to the war that breaks out, to the decisive encounter or the internal conversion."[1] The event foils all calculations; it changes the "aspect of things" and the "course of history": the slaves' revolt, the discovery of new lands, and invention in all its novelty, the boldness of prophets and reformers, the genius in the flush of his creation. It is nonsense and can become outrage, but it also forces us to seek a new meaning, to revive our scale of values. If one did away with this shock and this innovation, what would remain of history? The "natural" course of the world, the stagnation of routine, the comfort of a settled state of torpor, but definitely no "innovation," no institution, no progress.

Innovation jolts the "past" and agitates the present. A political change is deemed subversive, a religious reform seems a sacrilege, a want of understanding stalks the masters of art and philosophy. Freedom must forge its way past the barriers of an established world, acquired situations, intellectual conformities, sacred customs.

When creative liberty governs the event, the notion of the source eclipses the causal explanation. When the event is a Corneille, a Rembrandt, or a Beethoven, history penetrates into the realm of qualities. To accumulate records, to draw up comparative tables, to detect influences and filiations—all this patient "objective" labor would doubtless be adequate for handling the secondary works of those who continue or imitate a trend. In the presence of creations of genius it can, at the very most, show what is not a masterpiece by giving the reader or the audience a better understanding of where the literary or aesthetic "creation" springs from. Rotrou is as "interesting" as Racine, Auguste Barbier as "important" as Victor Hugo, in regard to "objective" method and causal exposition. For genius to assume its full significance in relation to history, the essential solitude by which genius reveals itself must be safeguarded in one way or another.

Virgil is not the "cause" of Dante, nor is Victor Hugo the "consequence" of Shakespeare. A work of genius is a unique event, without precedent and incomparable to other works. Along with genius something exceptional and new enters the world, as if by a leap or a surge. Originality and not derivation, it is not a condition, but it creates instantaneously. Nothing is more disappointing than the biographies of great artists or illustrious writers for those who seek in them a kind of "genial nature" that nutures all actions. Narrowness and flaws mar the grandeur that one would wish to find ever present. Genius evidences itself intermittently, like a grace bestowed as a precarious right.

Genius and the masterpiece are certainly "in history." But just as certainly they are constituents of history, before history, at the origin of history. Through them history advances and makes itself known. The masterpiece achieved in the present is created for the future, revealing a truth that had been hidden until then—a point of departure for subsequent developments. Dramatic art is no longer the same after Molière; Cézanne and Van Gogh opened up fresh dimensions to painting. Bach is not a Vivaldi, a Marc Antoine Charpentier, a Buxtehude, or a combination of these three "influences." Something begins with him: an intensity, a joyfulness, a kind of fresh dimension is proffered to the world.[2]

Great statesmen, inventors, explorers, to the extent that they open up new vistas, triumph over the interplay of deductions and causes that levels all originality. The founders of religion shake the weight of customs and doctrines. Decisions, undertakings, and institutions are historical only to the extent that they terminate the past and embark upon the future: a spirit of adventure is always present in the most succinct calculations. "Historical revivals" are conceived only when they return to prior problems or efforts in an actual and living relationship with the world. Napoleon repeats Caesar but in the atmosphere of his times.

For the notion of a continuous thread that unravels from prehistoric times to our day one must substitute the idea of a discontinuous thread, knots of events, some empty, some full, noteworthy dates and insignificant periods. Certain "events" are central, lighting up entire areas of history—Greek philosophy, the advent of Christ for Christianity, the "enlightenment" in the eighteenth century, the industrial revolution in England. A global point of view, in regrouping isolated and homogeneous "facts," enables one to acquire a more precise interpretation of each one of them: German unity in the nineteenth century is a movement of the whole, a totality which carries with it many particular facts and gives them meaning.

The Underside of History

The reader might be tempted to conclude from the preceding pages that history has a penchant for noise and agitation, for spectacular enterprises, resounding speeches, open revolts, and scandals. But this hubbub cannot make us forget the "historical silences": the heavy silence of oppressed peoples, devotion concealed, quiet loyalty; the daily tasks that form the background canvas of "great history." Greatness is enveloped in silence, but so is crime or betrayal. Poison or the sword of treason are made ready in the shadows, and defection, in keeping silent, awaits its hour.

Silence grows heavy during the "historic" hours when the destiny of a people is decided. Parliamentary assemblies are filled with silence when grave circumstances bring the head of the government to the platform to confront each man with his "historic" responsibilities: war or peace. This silence is history passing.

The historian is in a good position to know that silence, as much as noise or speech, is the raw material of history. It allows him to enter where the plot is being hatched, into the private assemblies where the sovereign makes his decisions, to witness the slow maturation of crises and revolutions. He sees through the vanity and insignificance of the farce played by false great men posturing before history. There are texts that must be "read between the lines," mute witnesses that must be interrogated, hidden grandeurs that must be acknowledged. One has to detect the truth beneath the mask and even on the mask, make silence speak without betraying it. A conspiracy is concocted between the historian's probity and history's "secrets," which allows a suppressed word, an authentic admission, to escape.

For history is, in essence, the word. Nature itself is silence where there is harmony and song. To become history is to speak out and give meaning to this eternal silence. Narration is the mode of communication proper to history. The event already has a meaning in itself; even when it surprises or eludes, it poses a question that demands an answer. In the presence of occurrences history is a "listening post" that waits for the being, for events to reveal something of the world.

It is the historian, because he himself is life and "subject," who alone can understand the secret meaning of the historical reality through his encounter with other lives. Beneath appearances and words which frequently mask the truth, he penetrates to the hidden springs and deeper motives that guide men to the all-powerful impulses which have given rise to the "myths."

These myths are not just error or fantasies. They stem from living experiences or from collective patterns of action. They translate into symbols a certain concrete relationship with the world. They carry with them the heart's profound attachment and are mingled with judgments, "truths" which we profess to such an extent that we declare false whatever contradicts our myth and true whatever confirms it. Nation, class, system of government, cannot be inclosed in geographical, economic, or juridical definitions. The nation rests on national sentiment. Class-consciousness adheres to its own concept and nourishes it. No political regime is capable of subsisting without monarchical or republican loyalty, without a minimum of civic spirit. These realities are based upon collective sentiments, participation, rites, symbols which, although not entirely rational, nonetheless have their own coherence and "logic."

Historical "movements" interpret movements of the soul, communicable emotions, enthusiasms, or fanaticisms. How can one "understand" the revolutionary days, the impetus toward nationalism, the "revolt of the masses," without participating in the affective conditions and in the myths that gave them their strength and their pungency? To do so is not to indulge in pathos but to acknowledge the real in all the vibrations of being. Objective and subjective are not contradictory but complimentary. An objective subjectivity, a receptivity that allows the object to appear just as it is, an understanding that is already, to a certain extent, by itself permeated with affectivity and will—only these attributes adapt themselves to that moving and complex "object" which constitutes historical reality. Better than a so-called impartiality, this total comprehension, capable of accepting the irrational and of respecting surprise, is necessary to the historian. To judge other peoples, he will be wary of prejudices and aversions that stem from his own national loyalty, but his own allegiance will make the foreigner's attachment to his land more understandable, even though he might be an enemy. A Catholic historian studying the Reformatian will find it difficult to avoid a certain almost instinctive distrust of Protestant "heresy"; a Protestant will find it hard to overcome resentment of "intolerance" and "deviations." An atheist will readily yield to the illusion that his own "position" will immediately insure his impartial judgment, forgetting perhaps too readily that his "neutrality" at one stroke closes to him the mental universe of Catholics and Protestants.

There are very different ways of "orienting" history, even with the best of will. It can be written, as was done in earlier days, from a strictly national point of view: "History of France," "History of England," "History of Russia," and so on. But our epoch witnesses the appearance of "histories" that are envisaged within a European or even a universal framework. From the viewpoint of a history of France, Charlemagne's empire is a kind of monster whose dismemberment represents the birth of France; from the standpoint of a history of Europe, this dismemberment comprised the political formation of the Continent and led to ten centuries of "provincial" antagonisms. There exists, therefore, a secret spring that animates the historian's purpose and governs all emphasis.

Inquiries and publications are the consequence of a decision and represent "viewpoints," a selection in which the personality of the historian intervenes. Among great historians like Renan, Taine, and Michelet, Gabriel Monod showed how personality determined the design and the shadings of history.[3] Because of his intellectual honesty, it was toward critical history that Renan directed his attention; Michelet, the great visionary, found the perfect expression of his sensitivity in the tableaux of history as resurrection; Taine wanted to elevate history to the rank of a science, a rigorous exposition based upon laws. Confronted by such different "histories," who, then, would dare to deny their validity, once their point of view has been accepted? Truth does not emanate from "the nature of things"; it requires a decree of the mind, a decision about life that runs a risk in order to partake of the truth.

Such an attitude is doubtless a departure from the concept of history that was in favor during the end of the last century at the very moment when, for example, Langlois and Seignebos defined the general rules of historical discipline: "History is written with documents."[4] The document from which methodical inquiry extracts the fact is master of the truth, a kind of pre-existing truth, that is concealed within the texts. We know today that the very notion of science in modern times depends on a conception of truth that emanates from the fundamental orientation of thought since Descartes. The consequence of "subjectivity," which is the basis of our contemporary behavior, seeking truth from purely internal criteria on man as subject, acknowledges as true only that which we can project before us as images, as "objects." We reduce the entire world to a universal panorama, to what Heidegger calls a "*Weltbild*."[5] When we manipulate "facts" like bits of "truth" and resort to documents as to a supreme judge of the true and the false, we act as though truth came to us from the outside, from objects. We forget that, according to modern thought which considers man the source and the master of truth, it is ourselves, in the last analysis, who decide the truth, having dismissed all authority with the same sovereign liberty which, through its knowledge and technique, nurtures the giant works of the universe.

Threats to History

In the long course of its labor of inquiry, criticism, and exposition, history is a "ghost hunt." The historical represses the legendary and the imaginary and only preserves the real. "To re-establish facts" in the face of fiction, to resist the persistent seduction of the fantastic and the miraculous, but also to pluck from legends and tales the element of historical truth that is hidden in them—all this represents an incessant struggle. The anxiety to wage it has been bequeathed to us by the positivist discipline. No one can challenge this critical attitude. But there are muffled threats more difficult to exorcise either because they stem from the exigencies of the strictest logic or because they are confused with the evolution of history itself in modern times.

Determinism is both history's ally and its enemy. History would have no foundation in a world devoid of natural laws. In the absence of determinism, chance would decree man's fate, subjected as he is to anarchical forces. But if it is an absolute, determinism crushes freedom and, therefore, all history. Confronted with a continuous chain of cause and effect, historical science would be but a simple affirmation.

History is history solely because of its freedom. A history of slavery has meaning only if the conditions of servility run counter to a capacity for freedom. A history of techniques reveals that man is intent upon liberating his freedom from natural necessities. Freedom, it is true, causes an outcry in the world of reason. It is bitterly contested and can always be contested: it cannot be subtracted from nothing. "As an objectively scientific knowledge, it does not exist," writes Karl Jaspers.[6] It can be seen only as concrete and living; it exists in the mute protests of the oppressed, in resistance to the invader, flight from servitude. Freedom cannot be demonstrated; it manifests itself, or it hides, which is still another way of revealing itself. Beneath the cold eye of the observer what remains of this freedom? Immobility or dream—it is that door to the future through which history enters the world.

But here is a more disturbing and more stubborn specter than determinism: springing from the embers of negativeness, nihilism undermines our epoch with its destructive force. The century is made dizzy by noise and sensations; it takes great pride in its giant cities, its bold constructions, its speedy transportation. But, silently, nihilism is on the prowl, debilitating vital forces, lying in wait for a time of fatigue or boredom, for those rare moments of quiet when modern man is accessible.

Wave follows wave, spring follows winter, insensitive to good or evil: nihilism whispers to man that the world is that nature which knows nothing and has no desires. Called "nonsense," "incredulity," "despair," it is the perfidious "Why?" raised by doubt in the face of the technical progress and comfort of our times. Nihilism undermines all moral strength through political cynicism. It says in *Mein Kampf*, "A colossal lie has the power to dissipate doubt." It is wafted on the air of the century with all the nausea of the "scientific death" camps. And it is this giddy power which the "atomic revolution" intermingles with the vision of tomorrow's planetary upheavals.

Nietzsche's philosophy is outside our concern in this essay. But his historical significance is of importance to us to the extent that his bitter and fiery words herald a decisive event in our epoch—the wound that is buried in the heart of modern man and causes him to oscillate between excess and failure, defiance and absurdity.

Nietzsche did not "invent" nihilism. He merely demonstrated it at work in Western metaphysics since Descartes, and he forced it to become aware of itself. One might doubt Nietzsche would have stopped there. Not only did he free us of facile negations, of vulgar atheism, and insipid immorality, but, further, carried away by his corrosive logic to the point of "devouring his own doctrine,"[7] it would seem that, in turning his power of negation against nihilism, he neutralized its poison. Negation does not result in negations. An outcry, whether anguish or hope, reverberates throughout the void, like a freedom restored, like a passionate question seeking the being.[8]

Without doubt, Nietzsche's "nihilism" does not in itself warrant either faith or atheism. It merely opens up a "free area" where man, emancipated from false absolutes and specious doctrines, can ask his fundamental questions. The mind no longer proceeds along the paths of deduction or syllogism but rather in a more direct and simple relationship with the world; life, with its humble tasks, reunited through poetry and creativity, its liberty, and its truth—in short, its historicity. With this vision of the world, history, renewed by astonishment and discovery, freed from the superstition of objectivity and the so-called "laws of history," can in the end but gain in depth and lucidity. It is no longer a harmless game but a decisive battle; throughout other periods and through other men, history is really a matter that concerns man, his relation to the world, his destiny, his life—the concrete, actual living man of the past confronted with the same preoccupations and dangers as our own.

Toward a New Historical Spirit

During the last century the historian's working conditions have profoundly altered.

A. The purely technical plane does not need to be stressed here, since it has already been analyzed many times.[9] The contemporary historian is the beneficiary of an imposing and varied production left to him by his predecessors; of an abundant documentation, of working tools on a scale which other periods never knew: libraries, archives, collections of texts, specialized periodicals.

In our times the historian runs the risk of being buried beneath the very abundance of documents of all kinds. The labor of research often defies the limitations of a human life and of an individual effort. The obstacle is the reverse in regard to ancient periods; because of a lack of sufficiently explicit documents, conjectures are often clumsy and hazardous. And in our day, of course, one can appeal to the human sciences: archaeology, history of religions, ethnology.

Our epoch, demanding in regard to precision, has inherited a precious legacy from the critical method perfected by prior generations. But the spirit in which the critical apparatus must be applied needs to be more flexible, since historical "science" possesses a broader significance than in earlier days.

B. The field of historical knowledge has, indeed, been broadened and its perspective expanded. It is no longer limited to a political and military study of states. In accordance with the thinking of Karl Marx and the socialist theorists, history introduced problems of a social, economic, and cultural order into its sphere. Rural history, the history of cities, history of techniques, history of art and literature, ideas or concepts of the world —thus our vision of the universe branches out into diverse and complementary images. In the fervor of these discoveries we have come to the point of contrasting the "history of civilization" with the "history of events": a profitable distinction on condition that the diversity of the real is respected, but a harmful one should it become exclusive. The very landscape, the shapes of tiles, of fields and barns, which a Lucien Fèbvre utilizes for historical documentation are "events," realities that evolve in time, and in which a human presence manifests itself, with its concerns and interests.

Inversely, even a history of reigns and of battles is inconceivable today without at least a background of the economic, social, and religious circumstances. All history must be placed within its geographical context; it must be "fixed" in its proper place. The forms of geographical space play a part in the fate of the "Greek world" or in the changes in the British Commonwealth. History takes hold of space. Certain places are charged with history, and this historical flavor is blended with the place itself: Athens, Rome, Paris. At Aigues-Mortes, at Pompeii and Paestum, one "inhales" the past like a presence, a nostalgic aroma. History teaches us, through its ruins and its ancient sites, that peoples and cultures die but also that the past is part of ourselves; the past bids us to remember our life, to look deeply into it.

The "march of history" has drawn historical reality away from us. For a century and a half technology has opened up an entirely new period through the conditions of life available to the Western world. A civilization that has at its command railroads, electricity, airplanes, instantaneous communication, virtually unlimited sources of energy, not only differs from other eras by virtue of its equipment and its way of life. It is the mental universe itself that has changed, thanks to man's progress in sovereignty—thanks also on occasion to the dizziness he feels in the face of a power that sweeps him along as often as it obeys him. Comfort is not solely an ensemble of needs and material advantages; it is a "state of mind," a need that contemporary man imposes upon the community.[10] This need, combined with a Westernization of the earth and with the ubiquity conferred today upon man by rapid transportation, tends to mold his sensitivity and orient his thought to such an extent that the worlds of "another age" seem impenetrable: antiquity, the Middle Ages, and even the century of Louis XIV.

C. The problem of "mental universes" should occupy the foreground of the present-day preoccupations of the history of science. It is precisely this problem that Lucien Fèbvre dealt with successfully in his work, *Problème de l'incroyance au XVI^ieme^ siècle*, which appeared in 1942. The many attempts to depict Rabelais as an unbeliever of the same ilk as Voltaire and Renan are anachronisms. The allusion to atheistic rationalism was made blindly, at a time when the sixteenth century was still imbued with a mentality steeped in magic, in occult practices, and in vague philosophies in which Catholic survivals were obscurely intermingled with "Lutheran inspirations." Rabelais moves in a universe where belief and disbelief coexist and intersect, where our rational impossibilities do not as yet obtain, rationality being still three-quarters mythology. In order to apprehend the mental universe of Rabelais, one must rid one's self of the nineteenth century's way of thinking and go back over the sinuous paths, still semimedieval, which the sixteenth century treads in order to uncover its "truth."

In another category of ideas, the domain of art, one cannot immediately assess Greek statuary, Byzantine mosaics, Dutch painters, "fauvism" with identical norms or the same sensitivity. There are sensitivities which are mutually exclusive—irreducible worlds, not games or diversions. A major obstacle to historical knowledge, the boundary of mental universes is also the decisive threshold leading to an authentic understanding of other times and other peoples, of other modes and other ideas.

We can never separate ourselves completely from our mental horizon. History merely opens up vistas into other universes. Even so eminent a thinker as Hegel lived and reflected within the framework of the "truth" which Western metaphysics proffered. He did not doubt the universal validity of this viewpoint. It required the philosophical invectives of a Kierkegaard or a Nietzsche, the rebellion of events against history, the lesson taught us by the human sciences, to reveal to us that the West was "a history" itself, a historical moment and place—that modes of thought, sensitivity, and even reason were changing. History, in turn, is a "moment" of history, a belated and perhaps fragile awareness in the mental universe inherited from Greece, from Judeo-Christian tradition, and from the Renaissance. Entire civilizations, like those of India or China, have ignored this concern. For a long time a mentality imbued with myths excluded the quasi-totality of the earth from its vision. Can one be certain that the historical perspective will prevail in the end?

D. The contemporary world is a problematical one. Intellectual security, moral ease, established truths—everything is once again called into question. Thus, in the midst of uncertainties or self-surrenderings, man's freedom asserts itself; but the fortuitousness of his life asserts itself as well. History should fear most today not a misapplication of determinism but rather the intoxication of a human freedom that comes to naught, or of a fortuitousness in which the individual being is no longer able to attach himself to a meaning, to an order, to a stability—in other words, to a history.

The grandiose idea of a universal history that can be embraced in a single glance, a history that is objectively impartial and definitive, is daily losing its esteem. But, inversely, history has drawn closer to man and to his life. Its proper mission would seem to be that of protecting the concrete integrity of man from the oversimplifications of the scientific mind; to safeguard the singular, the unique, from the general, the abstract, and the essence. In so doing, it also protects man from the modern temptation of disorder, despair, and excess. It is man's concept of himself; it helps him to exorcise his own myths and to choose his way in the world with clarity and realism.

History is neither a "rose-colored story" nor a course in morality. It does not warrant an optimism that covers up with edifying tales the tragedy of reality where failure, misfortune, crime, treachery, and mediocrity are to be found. But, in contrast to those who would readily darken with their pessimism the entire course of events, history protests that it is born from a "Yes" as its response to an appeal from the world. Each morning, plans and hopes spring up to relieve the ennui of the disappointing pasts to make the present arise and face future struggles. People who have lived through the most bitter and bruised period of history still cannot believe that the children who come to take their place will not protect the lost causes better than they have done. Humanity is not a being that time has lined and wrinkled. Each generation offers history a new chance. History attests man's youth: it is youth itself, the ardor for existence, the gift of the being which is renewed at every moment. The present that it experiences is, according to Péguy's expression, "the very brink of the future on the side of the present." The word that resounds in historical narrations communicates, from age to age, that presence, incessantly renewed, which, during its earthly stay and within its human limitations, breathes, struggles, and waits, its gaze turned toward the future and the light.

KARL JASPERS

The Axial Age of Human History

PHILOSOPHY strives to interpret history as a single totality. In the West, the philosophy of history developed on the foundation of the Christian faith. In great works from St. Augustine to Hegel, history is seen as the work of God, and God's acts of revelation define the decisive epochs. So late a thinker as Hegel could write: "All history moves toward Christ and begins with Christ. The coming of the son of God is the axis of world history."

But such a view of universal history can be valid only for Christians; Christianity is but one faith, not *the* faith of mankind. Through a specific historical development beginning in late antiquity, Christianity has become the faith of the Western world; but even in the West, the Christian has not allowed his religion to determine his view of history as human experience: even for him, a statement of faith is not a statement about the actual course of history, and sacred history remains in essence

Reprinted from *Commentary*, VI (1948), pp. 430-35, by permission of the publisher. (Copyright 1948, by the American Jewish Committee.)

different and separate from profane history. The believing Christian can examine the Christian tradition just as he might examine any other object of his experience.

If there does exist such a thing as an axis, or turning point, in history, it must be based on observable or recorded fact; and it must be valid for all men, including Christians. Such an axis would be that point in history where man first discovered the notion of himself that he has realized since, the point in time where there occurred that shaping of man's being which has produced the most important results. And the existence of this turning point would have to be, if not absolutely demonstrable, at least convincing on an empirical basis for Europeans, for Asiatics, and for all men, without the need to appeal to the criterion of a definite religious doctrine. Only thus could it provide a common frame of historical self-understanding.

Such a historical axis, or turning point, seems to be situated in the years around 500 B.C.E., in the intellectual development that took place between 800 and 200 B.C.E. There lies, it appears to me, the most crucial turning point in history; it was then that man as he is today was born. Let us, for the sake of brevity, refer to this period as the "axial age."

Many extraordinary developments were crowded into this epoch. In China lived Confucius and Lao-Tse, and all the characteristic Chinese philosophical tendencies were born; such thinkers as Mo Ti, Chuang-tze, Liadsi, and innumerable others were at work; in India it was the period of the Upanishads, of Buddha, and, just as in China, every philosophical possibility was then developed, including scepticism, materialism, sophistry, and nihilism; in Iran, Zoroaster taught the dramatic cosmology of the struggle between Good and Evil; in Palestine, it was the age of the Prophets, from Elijah to Isaiah, Jeremiah, the Deutero-Isaiah; in Greece it was the age of Homer, of the philosophers Parmenides, Heraclitus, and Plato, of the dramatists, of Thucydides and Archimedes. All the great developments that these names suggest occurred in those few centuries—and almost simultaneously in China, India, and the West, though none of these three worlds was aware of the others.

The new element that appeared in this epoch was that man became aware of existence as a whole, of his self, and of his limitations. He experienced the awesomeness of the world and his own weakness. He raised radical questions and, in his quest for liberation and redemption, came face to face with the abyss. While gaining consciousness of his limitations, he set himself the highest aims; he experienced the absolute in the depth of selfhood and in the clarity of transcendence.

Man became aware of consciousness itself; the fact of thought became itself an object of thought. Spiritual battles arose, in which men strove to convince others by the communication of ideas, reasons, experiences. Contradictory possibilities were explored. Discussion, partisanship, the splitting-up of the intellectual sphere into antithetical tendencies that yet remained closely related by their very opposition—all this produced an unrest bordering on spiritual chaos.

This age produced the basic categories within which we still carry on our thinking, and the beginnings of the world religions by which man has lived until today. In every sense, a step was made towards the universal.

Opinions, customs, conditions that had been unconsciously accepted were now scrutinized, questioned, dissolved. The world became a retort in which the substance of tradition, still living and real, was brought to consciousness and thereby transformed.

The age of myth—age of the static and self-evident—came to an end, and there began the battle of rationality and practical experience against myth (*logos* versus *mythos*); the battle for the transcendence of the one God against the demons who did not exist; the battle of an aroused ethical sense against the false gods. Religion was informed with ethics, and thus the idea of divinity was enhanced. The myth became the vehicle of a language that expressed something entirely different from what the myth had originally meant; the myth became parable. Myths were transformed and given new depth; and during this transition period, new myths were still produced even while the myth as a whole was being destroyed. The mythical world slowly receded, but it remained, in the beliefs of the masses, the background of all life (and therefore it could triumph again in later periods over wide areas).

This whole transformation of man's condition may be called a spiritualization. An impulse surging from the unexplored depths of life loosened the mainstays of existence, transforming stable polarities into antinomies and conflicts. Man was no longer self-sufficient. He had become unsure of himself, and thus open to new and boundless possibilities. He could hear and understand what until then no one had questioned or even noticed. Wonders were made manifest. Along with his world and his ego, Being itself now became perceptible to man, but not finally: the question remained. And his highest upsurge ended in new questions.

For the first time there were philosophers. Men dared to rely on themselves as individuals. Hermits and wandering thinkers in China, ascetics in India, philosophers in Greece, prophets in Israel—they all belong together, however much they may differ in faith, content, and inner orientation. Man was now able to set his inner life in opposition to the whole world; he discovered in himself the principle through which he could rise above both himself and the world.

In speculative thought man soared to the level of Being, which he grasped without duality; subject and object disappeared, and opposites became one. The objective formulations of speculative thought express, ambiguously and in a manner open to misunderstanding, what man in his highest flights experiences as a discovery of himself within the whole of Being, or a *unio mystica*, a merging with the godhead, or else a transformation of the self into an instrument of God's will, or a consciousness of the self as transcending the arbitrary particularity of the *hic et nunc*.

Imprisoned in a body fettered by passions, separated from the light and only dimly aware of himself, man longs for liberation and redemption; and he finds that he can achieve liberation and redemption in the world, whether it is by an ascent to the Idea; or in *ataraxia*—passive resignation; or by immersion in thought; or in the knowledge of himself and the world as Atman, the Universal Self; or in the experience of Nirvana; or in harmony with the Tao—the cosmic order; or in surrender to the will of God. There are, it is true, great differences among the various faiths, but they all alike come to serve as instruments by which man transcends himself, by which he becomes aware of his own being within the whole of Being, and by which he enters upon pathways that he must travel as an individual. It becomes possible for him to renounce the goods of the world and retire to the desert, the woods, the mountains; he can become a hermit and discover the creative power of solitude, and return to the world as philosopher, sage, prophet. What took place in this axial age was the discovery of what later was to be called reason and personality.

The conquests of individuals did not become the property of all; the distance between the heights of human possibility and the crowd was enormous. But what the individual became, changed everything indirectly; humanity as a whole took a leap forward.

Even sociological conditions in China, India, and around the Mediterranean show similarities during this age. There is an abundance of small states and cities, and a battle of all against all, making at first for astonishing prosperity, a development of power and wealth. In China, under the impotent empire of the Chou dynasty, cities and petty states flourished; the over-all political process consisted of the aggrandizement of small states by the subjection of other small states. In Greece and the Near East, there existed an independent life of small social units, even, in part, for those under the dominion of the Persians. In India also were many independent states and cities.

Within the three worlds, travel and trade created intellectual movement. Previously the world had known relatively stable conditions under which, despite catastrophes, everything repeated itself, horizons were restricted, and intellectual movement was gentle and very slow, unconscious and hence not understood. Now out of constant tension came tumultuous and swift movement, leading to revolution; and this was on the conscious plane.

The Chinese philosophers, Confucious and Mo Ti and others, roamed the country, gathering together in famous places favorable to intellectual life. They established schools which the Sinologists call academies, like those of the Sophists and philosophers in Hellas; or else, like Buddha, they spent their lives wandering from town to town.

Men became conscious of history; an extraordinary age was beginning, but men felt and knew that an endless past had gone before. Thus at the very outset of this awakening of the truly human spirit, man was already preoccupied with memories, conscious of lateness, even of decadence.

Now men wished to take the course of events into their hands: to restore conditions that had existed in the past, or to create new conditions. History was conceived as a series of stages: either as a process of steady deterioration, or as a cycle, or as an ascent. Thinkers began to speculate on how men could best live together, how their lives could best be administered and governed. Ideas of reform inspired political activity. Philosophers wandered from state to state, acted as counselors and teachers, were despised or courted, argued with one another. There is a sociological analogy between Confucius' failure at the court of Wei and Plato's failure in Syracuse, and between the school of Confucius and the academy of Plato, in both of which future statesmen were trained.

This long epoch represents no simple ascending development. It was both destructive and creative, and its potentialities were never fully realized. The highest possibilities realized in individuals did not become common property because the mass of men could not follow. What started out as freedom of movement ended as anarchy. When the creative power of the epoch was lost, the same thing happened in all three worlds: a petrifaction of dogmas and a general leveling; out of a disorder that had become intolerable there grew an urge toward a new stability, toward the restoration of static conditions of life.

The process of constant change first came to a stop in the political sphere. Great, all-encompassing empires came into being almost simultaneously in China (Chin Shih-Huang Ti), in India (the Maurya dynasty), and in the West (the Hellenistic empires and Rome). Everywhere collapse brought initial gain in the form of a highly systematized order. But nowhere was the relation to what had gone before completely extinguished; the achievements and figures of the axial age became models and objects of veneration: the Han dynasty in China established Confucianism, Asoka established Buddhism in India, and the Augustan age in Rome set up the conscious Greco-Roman cultural tradition.

The universal empires that developed at the end of the axial age were considered to be established for all eternity. But their stability was illusory; although these empires lasted a long time measured by the political standards of the axial age, all ultimately declined and disintegrated, and the subsequent millennia have brought enormous changes. Since the end of the axial age, political history has been a history of the decline of great empires and the founding of new ones.

In order to establish the truth of a historical conception, it is not enough to glance at a few facts, as I have done. An accumulation of historical analysis must increasingly clarify the thesis, or else it must be abandoned. The observations I have made are intended merely to invite further exploration.

Assuming, however, that this idea of an axial age is true in the main, it seems to illuminate the whole of world history in such a way that something resembling a structure emerges. I shall attempt briefly to indicate this structure:

1) Age-old high civilizations everywhere end with the axial age. The axial age melts them down, takes them over, submerges them, whether by internal revolution or foreign conquest. Much that existed before the axial age was indeed magnificent—for example, the cultures of Babylonia, Egypt, or the Indus, and the primitive culture of China—but all this has something unawakened about it. The old cultures survived only in those elements that were assimilated by the new beginning and became part of the axial age.

Measured by the radiant humanity of the axial age, a strange veil lies over the preceding ancient cultures, as though in them man had not yet truly come to himself; this remains true despite such impressive, isolated impulses—therefore without general or future influence—as can be found, for example, in an Egyptian literary document, the well-known "Dialogue of a Man Weary of Life with His Soul," or in the Babylonian penitential psalms or the epic of Gilgamesh. The axial age continued to venerate the monumental in religion and religious art, and the corresponding monumental phenomena in the political realm—the great authoritarian states and legal systems. These things were even regarded as prototypes—by Confucius and Plato, for example—but if so, it was in a new conception that informed them with the spirit of the new age.

Thus the imperial idea, which at the end of the axial age achieved new force and politically speaking, ended the age, was inherited from the old monolithic civilizations. But whereas the imperial idea had originally been the culture-creating principle, it now served to entomb and stabilize a declining culture. It is as if the principle which had once served to drive humanity upward, and which had been a despotic principle *de facto*, now broke through in the form of a *conscious* despotism that congealed and preserved like frost.

2) Mankind is still living by what happened in the axial age, by what it created and what it thought. In all its later flights mankind returns to that age and gathers new fire. The return to this beginning is the ever-

recurring event in China, India, and the West; the renaissances that have brought new spiritual surges have consisted in the recollection and re-awakening of the possibilities of the axial age.

3) Although the axial age began within a relatively limited area of the globe, its historical effect was universal. Those peoples that did not participate in the developments of that age have remained "primitive peoples," continuing the unhistorical lives they had been leading for tens or hundreds of thousands of years. Men living outside of the three worlds of the axial age either remained apart from the stream of history or were drawn into it by coming into contact with one or the other of the three intellectual centers of radiation, as was the case, for example, with the Germanic and Slavic peoples in the West, and the Japanese, the Malays, and the Siamese in the East. Some primitive peoples died out as a result of this contact. All men living after the axial age were either relegated to the status of primitive peoples or took part in the fundamental new world process. Once history had begun, the life of primitive peoples took on the character of an enduring prehistory, which became increasingly restricted in area and has only recently definitively ended.

4) When the three worlds that experienced the axial age meet with one another, a profound understanding is possible. They recognize when they meet that their concerns are the same. Despite great distances, each deeply affects the others. To be sure, there is no truth common to all three that can be put into objective statement—this exists only in science, with its conscious and compelling methodology, which can be disseminated without change throughout the world and to which all men are called to contribute—but, even so, the authentic and unconditional truth that is lived historically by men of different origins is reciprocally seen and heard.

To summarize: out of the vision of the axial age grow the questions and criteria through which we approach all previous and all subsequent development. The high civilizations that went before lose their distinct contours, and the peoples who were their vehicles become invisible as they merge into the movement of the axial age. Prehistoric peoples remain prehistorical until they are absorbed in the historical movement that spreads out from the axial age—or until they die out. The axial age assimilates everything else. From that age history gains the only structure and unity that survives, or that has survived up to now.

The fact of the threefold axial age is a kind of miracle, in the sense that any really adequate explanation lies beyond our present scientific horizon. And in any case, the hidden meaning of this phenomenon cannot be found empirically, as if it were a meaning that someone had consciously sought to create. Rather, to inquire after this meaning is to ask: what are we to make of this fact, what does it give to us? If, in attempting to answer these questions, expressions may occur that make it appear as if we were thinking of some plan of providence, they are to be understood only as metaphors.

Really to see the axial age, to gain it as a foundation for our universal view of history, means to gain something that is common to all mankind above and beyond all differences of faith. It is one thing to see the unity of history only from the background of one's own faith; it is quite another to conceive the unity of history in communication with every other human background, combining one's own consciousness with that which is foreign to one. In this sense, it may be said of the centuries between 800 and 200 B.C.E. that they constitute the empirically ascertainable axis of history for *all* men.

The transcendental history of Christian revealed faith knows creation, fall, the steps of revelation, prophecies, the coming of God's son, redemption, and last judgment. As the faith of a historical group of men, it remains intact. But it is not on the basis of revelation that men can come together; the basis of solidarity can only be experience. Revelation is the form of a particular historical faith; experience is accessible to man as man. Through our experience of history we—all men—can know in common the reality of the universal transformation of mankind that took place in the axial age. This transformation was, to be sure, limited to China, India, and the West, but, although there was at first no contact among these three worlds, it laid the basis for universal history, it drew the minds of all men into it.

The threefold historical form of the great advance of the axial age is something like a summons to boundless communication. To see and to understand others helps us toward the greatest clarity concerning that narrowness which is the danger in every self-enclosed history, and to make a leap into the distance. This venture in boundless communication is once again the secret of achieving humanity, not in the prehistoric past but in ourselves.

The call to such communication—which arises from the very fact that our historical origins are threefold—is the strongest force opposing the fallacy that any faith enjoys exclusive possession of the truth. For faith must always be conditioned by historical existence; it cannot, like scientific truth, be stated universally for all. The claim to exclusive truth—that weapon of fanaticism, of human pride, of self-deception through will to power, that scourge of the West in particular, with its secularization in dogmatic philosophies and so-called scientific *Weltanschauungen*—can be overcome precisely by the knowledge that God has revealed himself historically in many ways and opened up many paths to himself. It is as if God, speaking the language of universal history, were warning us against exclusive claims.

If the axial age takes on significance according to the depth of our immersion in it, the question arises: is this age and its creations a criterion for all that has happened since? Even if we disregard the quantitative aspect, the geographical scope of political events, the pre-eminence that intellectual manifestations have enjoyed through the centuries, do we not find that the austere greatness, the creative clarity, the depth of meaning, the élan toward new intellectual worlds manifested in the axial age constitute the intellectual summit of all history up until now? For all their greatness and uniqueness, does not Virgil pale before Homer, and Augustus before Solon?

Surely any mechanical answer would be false. What has come later has assuredly its own value, which was not present in that which went before, a maturity of its own, a sublime splendor, a spiritual depth, above all in its "exceptional" manifestations.

We cannot organize history into a hierarchy simply by setting up some universal idea and drawing automatic inferences from it. But the conception of the axial age may lead us to question what came later, perhaps even to form a prejudice against it—and this may lead us to a recognition of that which is truly new and great and which does not belong to the axial age. For example: the student of philosophy who has spent months with the Greeks may find in St. Augustine a liberation from too much coolness and impersonality, since Augustine raises questions of conscience that were unknown to the Greeks but have been with us ever since; but then a period spent in the study of Augustine may impel him to return to the Greeks, in order to cleanse himself from the mounting impurity. Nowhere on earth is there an ultimate truth, a perfect salvation.

The axial age was shattered. History continued.

I hold only this as certain: whether we adopt or reject this thesis, the conception of an axial age affects our contemporary consciousness of our situation and of our history in fundamental ways which I have been able to intimate only partially. What is involved is nothing less than the question of how the unity of mankind can become concrete for each of us.

PAUL RADIN

The Literature of Primitive Peoples

I

To SPEAK of oral narratives or song-poems, particularly those of primitive peoples, as constituting true literature has until recently met with the greatest suspicion not only from the general public but from students of literature and, indeed, from ethnologists as well. Their objections are basically of two kinds. No literature is possible, they contend, without writing, and the languages spoken by primitive peoples are inadequate both in vocabulary and the range of ideas which can be expressed in them to permit the development of what we call true literature. Both of these contentions are, I feel, quite incorrect. One has only to read such studies as those of F. Boas[1] and Edward Sapir[2] to realize on how slight a basis of fact such statements rest. There is no need, consequently, to spend any time refuting the theories of philosophers like Lévy-Bruhl[3] or E. Cassirer[4] concerning the structure of primitive languages. The only thing that can be said in defense of their generalizations is that, given the manner in which many of the recorders of these languages presented their data and the many loose statements they made, it is easy to see how Lévy-Bruhl and Cassirer and those who were influenced by them arrived at their unsound generalizations. The first objection, particularly, that without writing no substantial literature can possibly develop, will, I am certain, be adequately disproved by the examples of prose and poetry which I am presenting in this essay.

The absence of writing does, however, entail a number of consequences for the forms which certain types of compositions assume and upon one of these I would like to comment. I am referring particularly to traditional prose narratives. These can best be understood if we regard them as dramas in which the reciter, the raconteur, impersonates the various characters of the tale or novelette he is narrating. His role as an actor is here more important than his role as transmitter of a specific traditional text, for it is by his skill and excellence as an actor that his audience judges him. His personality, his temperamental make-up, his style, in consequence,

Reprinted from *Diogenes*, No. 12 (Winter, 1955), pp. 1-28, by permission of the publisher. *Diogenes* is a review of humanistic sciences edited by the International Council for Philosophy and Humanistic Studies, Unesco House, Paris.

play a determining role. He may interpolate or omit, amplify or shorten, reorganize or reinterpret to an amazing degree without encountering any serious criticism as long as what is regarded as the basic core of the plot is not affected. These interpolations are rarely creations of his own, but consist of traditionally fixed episodes, themes, motifs, imagery, epithets. Interpolations of one kind or another, let me point out, have always been the privilege of actors. We find them in the classical drama of ancient Greece, in that of the Golden Age in Spain and in that of the Elizabethan Age. They are found even today, especially in comedy. An oral dramatic text is never as fixed as one which is primarily to be read.

We thus come to one of the essential problems of all traditional oral narratives. Does a fixed text in our sense of the term exist? The answer must be in the negative. The reasons for this are many, the two most important being that, first, the community demands of the author-raconteur fixity only for the basic plot and secondly that the actions and behavior of the figures in the plot are always supposed to be intelligible to a contemporary audience. This means that a text is being continually re-edited. Under such circumstances one would expect considerable confusion in the structure of these narratives, which is indeed frequently true. However, accomplished narrators succeed in integrating their material with amazing skill, although rarely is this integration perfect.

Where the raconteur-actor-editor plays so all-dominating a role one might very well ask what is left for the audience. Does it, like the audience at our theatre, simply listen and pass judgment on the skill of the raconteur-actor? It does all this and more. Strange as it may seem to us, an audience in an aboriginal tribe is far better prepared to understand the implications of their literature than we often are of our own. Every person there—parts of Africa and Polynesia-Micronesia perhaps excepted—has an all-embracing knowledge of his culture and participates in every aspect of it; every person has a complete knowledge of his language. There are no "illiterate" nor ignorant individuals. An audience thus comes prepared esthetically, culturally, and critically, to listen to a narrative in a manner that can only be compared to an Athenian audience of the fifth century B.C.—on a different level, of course.

I have so far spoken primarily of the imaginative traditional prose narratives where, strictly speaking, there are no authors but only rearrangers, reinterpreters and editors. But there exist in each tribe, in addition to these traditional narratives which can be said to constitute the classical literature, other narratives constituting the contemporary literature, which have true authors and where the themes are taken from the life of the community and from personal events in the life of an individual. These two types of narrative differ fundamentally in subject-matter, in diction, and, at times, in vocabulary. In many tribes, especially in North America, they have special designations. Unfortunately, ethnologists have neglected the contemporary because they have so largely concentrated their attention upon the classical and sacred literatures. However there is also a marked tendency for native priests, medicinemen, and tribal dignitaries, from whom, after all, most of our material is obtained, to place the contemporary literature in a lower category.

In these contemporary narratives, of course, much depends upon the skill and artistry of the author. Although he generally follows the style or styles laid down by older literary traditions he can also embark on experiments and attempt to create new styles. Such new styles are often due to contacts with other tribes. Here we have some controls. The recent contact with white investigators, for instance, has led to the emergence of a number of new literary categories. I am thinking particularly of autobiographies and the descriptions of the various aspects of culture, especially of religion and ritual. These never existed before the coming of the ethnologists. It is therefore of great significance for the history of primitive literatures to determine the degree to which the new categories and styles resemble the older ones. It is also of unusual interest for the student of comparative literature to realize that within less than two generations American Indians have developed the technique for composing well-rounded autobiographies which compare more than favorably with those of the ancient Greeks and Romans and can, indeed, stand comparison with some of the best in our own cultures. *The Autobiography of a Winnebago Indian*[5] which I collected some years ago can very well take its place by the side of that of so consummate a master as Benvenuto Cellini.

In poetry the text, likewise, is not fixed, except for the larger epics of the Polynesians and some of the Malayan tribes and, generally, for religious chants as a whole. Naturally, poems are composed in traditional forms, but within these forms the composer is permitted absolute freedom to a far greater extent, in fact, than even in the contemporary prose narratives. He can use any image he wishes and he can be as personal in his allusions as he desires to be. One of the difficulties of understanding many short poems, particularly those of the American Indians, is that they are often so personal as to be unintelligible without a commentary.

There are thus both varying texts and unalterably fixed texts among primitive peoples, although unquestionably fixity of text is not regarded as a virtue, as it has come to be in Western European civilizations, particularly during the last two centuries. We cannot emphasize too strongly the fact that the excellence of a literature has nothing to do with the number of fixed texts found in it. If I seem to overstress this point, that is because it has at times been contended that where there is so great a variability for a given narrative no possibility for the development of a significant literature exists.

We come now to the last of the basic questions to be clarified before we can turn to our specific task, the characterization of some of the main aboriginal literatures. How is an author-raconteur trained? How does he learn his art? And how does one compose a poem in the absence of writing, and, what is far more important, in the absence of privacy? Be it remembered that privacy can hardly be said to exist in aboriginal communities.

The first question is easily answered. A raconteur learns his art directly from an elder, generally a relative. Such training may take a long time and it is always expensive. As a result, only those individuals who have real talent and ambition persevere. However, the recital of narratives is not confined to specially trained individuals. Many persons know a few traditional narratives, own them, in fact, and can often tell these few as well as the "professional" raconteur. No training certainly is required for the recital of the contemporary narratives. In the Americas, in fact, and in most areas where no caste systems or markedly developed class organizations exist, there actually are no true special groups or guilds of professional raconteurs, i.e., individuals who spend a considerable part of their time at such a task. This is quite different in many portions of Africa, Polynesia, and certain parts of the Southwest Pacific. There we find well-organized guilds of professional raconteurs who alone know the narratives and have the right to tell them.

The second of our questions is more difficult to answer, not only because of the nature of the subject but because we have little information to fall back upon. Moreover it is complicated by the additional fact that most poems are enclosed in a musical framework. We know enough about the interrelationship of this musical framework to the words to state that sometimes the music is primary, sometimes the words, the exact nature of the relationship often being dependent upon the poet and his inspiration. I see no reason for believing, however, that, by and large, the situation encountered here with regard to the interrelationship between words and music is very much different from what existed in the case of the Greek lyric poets or what held for the choruses of the Greek dramas of antiquity. We are possibly also dealing here with meters, although this is still problematical.

There is often a native theory of inspiration. Among most American Indian tribes, poems are supposed to come to individuals in dreams, dreams here meaning that they have come more or less unsought. An Eskimo named Orpingalik, known for his poetical gifts, gave the great Danish ethnologist, Knud Rasmussen, a well-thought-out theory of inspiration that leaves little unsaid on the subject. "Songs (poems) are thoughts,"[6] he told Rasmussen, "sung out with the breath when people are moved by great forces and ordinary speech no longer suffices. Man is moved just like the ice floe sailing here and there out in the current. His thoughts are driven by a flowing force when he feels joy, when he feels fear, when he feels sorrow. Thoughts can wash over him like a flood, making his breath come in gasps and his heart throb. Something like an abatement in the weather will keep him thawed up. And then it will happen that we, who always think we are small, will feel still smaller. And we will fear to use words. But it will happen that the words we need will come of themselves. When the words we want to use shoot up of themselves—we get a new song."

Similar in strain is the explanation of how songs are composed which was given Rasmussen by the Greenland Eskimo Kilimé. "All songs come to man when he is alone in the great solitude. They come to him in the wake of tears, of tears that spring from the deep recesses of the heart or they come to him suddenly accompanied by joy and laughter which wells up within us, we know not how, as we ponder upon life and look out upon the wonders of the world around us.

"Then, without our volition, without our knowledge, words come to us in song that do not belong to everyday speech. They come to us with every breath we take and become the property of those who possess the skill to weave them together for others."[7]

This is, of course, pure theory and tells only half of the story. The other part consists of the arduous labor required for fitting the words into their proper frame, and knowledge of the traditional rules, of the stereotyped images, and formulae. All this our Eskimos Orpingalik and Kilimé must have known, for their poems conform strictly to the rules, but this they forgot to tell us. Other less philosophically inclined poets fortunately give us a better clue as to how they go about the task of composing a poem. On the island of Buin in the Solomon Islands, for instance, there are professional poets who, according to Thurnwald,[8] all compose in the same way. A man goes into the forest to be undisturbed, selects a melody and then attempts to fit words to it. He will test these words repeatedly until he is satisfied that they conform to the rhythms of the melody. But to judge from the numerous song-poems Thurnwald has published this again is only half of the explanation and represents the portion that our Eskimo poets omitted. Poetic inspiration plays as great a role here as everywhere else. The professional poets of Buin are, after all, selected for their special gifts. That they often are commissioned to compose a poem for a particular occasion and are even told to include certain details, is of secondary importance. So was Pindar commissioned. As poets they wish to appeal to the listener's emotions and this they will do by striking imagery, by mythical allusions, by a special language, and a special phrasing. The rhythmical units of the melody which Thurnwald emphasizes so strongly are pushed into the background. In short, our Buin poet's description of how he composes possesses no more validity than did that of the Eskimos Orpingalik and Kilimé.

In parts of Africa we find a description of the technique for composing song-poems strictly analogous to that given by the Buin. For example, among the Ila and Thonga of southeastern Africa there exists a class of song called *Impango,* sung only by women on any occasion when people gather together, at work, at a so-called beer-drink, in preparation for a journey, etc. There are in each village a number of women who are well-reputed composers of the music for such songs. Should a woman want such a song composed she first selects a subject for it and then the words. The words may be in praise of her husband, of her lover, or of herself and will be connected with certain specific events such, for instance, as her husband's prowess in killing some fierce animal. She will then have some provisional melody accompany her words. With these she goes to the music-composer and sings the first half dozen words. The music expert, having ascertained whether, for instance, she wishes her song to start on a low or a high tone, then composes a few phrases of music which will conform to the first phrase as sung to her by the composer of the words. Then the music expert sets to work and composes the music for the whole song.

Yet here again the poems belie the theory. No fitting of words simply for the purpose of having them conform to the rhythm of a melody could possibly produce poems like the two following from the *Fan of the Congo.*

DIRGE ON THE DEATH OF A FATHER[9]

Father, my father, why have you left your hearth?
O father, did someone strike you down?
Someone whom vengeance demand that you slay?
And now your ghost has wandered to the other shore.

Father, my father, why have you left your hearth?
Though the skies have cleared, our vision is obscured.
From the trees the water falls in measured drops;
The rat has left his hole.

Behold our father's home!
Gather the grass for his grave
And spread it now here, now there.
Things once invisible he now can see.

SONG TO THE FIRE-GOBLIN[10]

I Fire seen only at night,
The deep night;
Fire which burns without heat
And shines without burning;

Friendless, knowing no home and no hearth,
Bodiless, yet you fly.
Transparent fire of the palms,
Fearless, I ask for your aid.

II Sorcerer's fire! Tell me
Who was your father, who was your mother?
Where do they dwell?
But, indeed, you are your father, you your mother!
You go your way and we see no mark.
Dry woods have not given you birth,
No ashes did you give to mankind.
Though you die yet you know not death!
Tell me, are you some wandering soul
That has taken your form unaware?

III Sorcerer's fire!
O spirit of waters below, of the air overhead!
Light that shines from afar
Fly that illumines the marsh
Bird without wings, form without body,
Essence of fire, hear!
Fearless I ask for your aid.

Despite the fact that professional poets functioning very much as described for the Buin are to be found in many portions of the aboriginal world, the composing of poems is definitely not an art confined to them alone. In all primitive civilizations there are occasions when every person will attempt to compose a poem. We find accordingly, many individuals in every tribe who have composed at least one or two. To do so, some special skill and certainly special knowledge were required. Naturally when thousands of poems are composed in one generation few will have great merit, either from our point of view or from that of primitive peoples. Yet it is quite surprising how good some of these are from any point of view. Let me give a few examples from North America, composed by individuals who were not professional poets, to show the nature of their subject-matter, the technical knowledge which was required of the composer, and what a listener had to know in order to understand the allusions contained in them and to appreciate the meaning of the imagery, free and stereotyped.

I. ESKIMO[11]

The white hounds of dawn I see approaching.
Away, away, or I will yoke you to my sleigh!

This is a poem composed by an Eskimo woman as she lay dying and fighting death. Both these lines are well known stereotyped images, one for death, the other for life.

II. TLINGIT[12]

Drifting along toward the shore runs the nation's canoe,
With it my uncle. He is destroyed.
Never again can I expect to see him here.
To him it has happened just as to Kashkatkl and his brothers.
They waded out across the Stikine.
Their sister, disobeying, looked at them
And they became stone.

To understand this poem one has to know an episode in a well known myth. *Nation's canoe* means an important chief; *to become stone* signifies being drowned.

III. TLINGIT[13]

Would that I were like her who was helped by Taxgwas!
If I were like the one he helped, that woman,
Indeed I could build my brother's house anew!
But he, my brother, I fear, has gone into the trail of the sun.
And that never again I will see him.

This song was composed by a woman about her drowned brother, Taxgwas. The first two lines refer to some incident in his life; the last three are stereotyped poetical formulae.

IV. WINNEBAGO[14]

I, even I, shall die some day.
Of what value is it then to be alive?

This is a poem composed by an Indian after a day of drinking and debauchery. It subsequently became a favorite drinking song.

V. OJIBWA[15]

1. A loon I thought it was,
Yet it was my love's splashing oar.

2. To Saulte Ste Marie he has departed.
My love, he has gone before me
And never again will I see him.

VI. OJIBWA[16]

As my eyes search the prairie
I feel the summer in the spring.

VII. OJIBWA[17]

The odor of death, the odor of death,
I smell the odor of death
In front of my body.

VIII. TLINGIT[18]

If one had control of death,
Very easy it would be
To die with a Wolf Woman.
It would be very pleasant.

Let me compare a poem by an extremely gifted Eskimo with these poems by amateurs.

1. A wonderful occupation[19]
Making songs!
But all too often they
Are failures.

2. A wonderful fate
Getting wishes fulfilled!
But all too often they
Slip past.

3. A wonderful occupation
Hunting caribou!
But all too rarely we
Excel at it
So that we stand
Like a bright flame
Over the plain.

From this brief discussion one fact assuredly emerges clearly: that the conditions for the development of true literatures among primitive peoples exist in abundance. There are creative artists; there exist highly developed literary forms for both prose and poetry, and there exists a mature and educated audience. How varied these literatures can be, how in each area special literary styles and literary forms have arisen so that we can legitimately speak of an African literature, for instance, as set off against a Polynesian, Melanesian, North American Indian, or Eskimo literature, how within each area, indeed, within each tribe, multiple styles exist, I shall now attempt to demonstrate, although I shall limit myself primarily to the African and Eskimo literatures.

II

Most of the older students of primitive cultures and, unfortunately, not a few of the more recent ones, have always tacitly assumed that aboriginal societies had no history or at least that they possessed no significant historical sequences. As these cultures were a thousand or more years ago, so, essentially, they are today, or were until the appearance of the white man. Nothing could be more erroneous. The civilizations of few sections of the aboriginal world can be understood unless we realize that contacts with other tribes and other cultures took place long before the influence of the great European and African-Asiatic civilizations was ever felt. With these contacts must have come about numerous changes. In fact, indications of such cultural transformations, sometimes slight, sometimes profound, are clearly discernible. With the recognition of this fact—that all aboriginal civilizations have had a long history with periods of stability alternating with periods of crisis and change, and with periods of isolation followed by periods of contact—we must begin. Otherwise it will be impossible to understand why one area or one tribe has developed one type of literature, and another a second type, and what has brought about the special physiognomies of the various literatures. I do not, of course, mean that the specific traits of a given culture are to be regarded simply as a function of such changes. Other factors of equal and, at times, far greater importance must also be taken into consideration, such as the physical environment, the degree of culture integration achieved, and specific events occurring within each tribe. Bearing this in mind, let us now attempt our characterization of primitive literatures. I shall confine myself to just two such literatures, referring to the others only incidentally. I am selecting for comment those of Negro Africa and of the Eskimo because of the contrast they offer.

By Negro Africa I mean, roughly speaking, Africa south of the Sahara, always excepting the Bushmen. Its traditional imaginative prose literature is set off sharply in form and content from that of all other areas. Nowhere else, for example, do we find anything remotely approaching the sophistication which we encounter here. Nowhere else do we find man and human relations depicted with such stark realism. How are we to account for it? Explanations in terms of race or climate are out of the question. It must be the reflection of a particular social milieu, and here an understanding of the history of Negro Africa is vital. Rarely, in any area, have there been such frequent impingements of cultures upon one another, cultures often differing fundamentally in type and complexity. Moreover, nowhere in the aboriginal world were there so many crises, so much shifting of population, so much chaos and confusion. It is during the breakdown of a culture, in periods of transition, that man tends to be sophisticated, realistic, cynical, and sceptical, and that certain aspects of the creative imagination find no expression. In Africa, for instance, it would seem that the mythopoeic imagination, using this term here in its broadest sense, is apparently no longer permitted to function freely, at least in the traditional narratives, and that where it does persist it has been given a new, essentially rationalistic, dress. To indicate what I mean by this statement let me compare the following short narratives, one from the Ojibwa of Ontario,[20] Canada, and the other from the West African Ekoi:[21]

1) Once an old man said to his children, "In two days he is going to pass, the white animal." The children were very glad that they were going to see this animal and one of them asked his father, "Father, is this the animal who brings the morning?" And the father answered, "Yes. After a while you will hear him coming along and singing."

So within two days' time he told his children, "Remember, today you will hear him just before dawn. Look! Look! He is coming now."

"*Awihihi, awihihi.*" Thus he passed along toward the west singing and it was morning.

2) Mouse goes everywhere. Through rich men's houses she creeps and she visits even the poorest. At night, with her bright little eyes, she watches the doing of secret things, and no treasure chamber is so safe but she can tunnel through and see what is hidden.

In olden days she wove a story child from all that she saw and to each of these she gave a gown of different color—white, red, blue, or black. The stories became her children and lived in her house and served her because she had no children of her own.

Comment here is just as unnecessary as it is when we contrast the conventional opening of many Ojibwa narratives, "Once my story lived," with the conventional beginning of those of the Ashanti, "We really do not mean, we really do not mean that what we are going to say is true." Two utterly distinct and different cultural and literary traditions are involved here. To say that in the first case we are dealing with a simple, undifferentiated culture where man is still completely under the sway of his dream life and his fantasies, as quite a number of scholars, notably psychoanalysts, would contend, is belied by the facts. No such people exist. Be it also remembered that in civilizations far more complex than the Ojibwa, in most of North and South America and Polynesia, for instance, the mythopoeic imagination is still functioning in full vigor. Nor should we forget that it is found in Aeschylus and in all the great sophisticated oriental civilizations.

What has happened in Negro African cultures then, and finds its expression in their traditional prose literature, is thus only to be explained by their history and the influence of historical conditions upon their attitude toward animals, man, society, nature, and God. In my *African Folktales*, narrative upon narrative brings this out clearly. Animals, nature, God, they have all been thoroughly humanized and, having been humanized, can then be assessed as man is assessed. Perhaps that is why there is no special genre devoted to satire in African literature, neither in prose nor in poetry. Man is depicted as he is. That is a sufficient satire. So likewise are animals, God, and nature depicted. They cast no shadows; they have no protecting *personae*. However only destruction and tragedy can result when man meets his fellowman, nature, and God in such fashion.

Let us examine the plots of four narratives given in *African Folktales*,[22] The Bantu Bena Mukuni tale entitled *Let the Big Drum Roll*,[23] the Bena Mukuni *How an Unborn Child Avenged his Mother's Death*,[24] the Bantu Baronga *The Wonder Worker of the Plains*,[25] and the Bantu Baila tale of *The Woman Who Went in Search of God*.[26] Basically there is no reason why, in the first, the king should be murdered, that in the second the husband should murder his pregnant wife, that in the third the whole tribe should be destroyed, and that in the fourth the old woman should not die. But if man insists upon approaching his fellowman, nature, and God naked, without protecting illusions or fictions, only violence can be the outcome and he is consumed and destroyed. Nor is it without significance that nowhere in any of these tales are the actors represented as penitent or aware of their crimes. Indeed it is wrong to call their actions crimes. Given the viewpoint that is reflected in these narratives, the actors are simply morally unaware.

Although themes reflecting this attitude toward man and the world are the dominant ones today, this does not mean that they always have been so. It is best, in fact, to regard the prevalence of these themes as part of a style, originally reflecting certain social conditions developed many generations ago, which has persisted in the traditional prose narratives and driven out other styles. Yet other themes and styles are still found today although they are not common. Take, for example, the Bantu Ambundu tale of *The Son of Kimanaueze* and *The Daughter of the Sun and Moon*.[27] That themes of this type were at one time much commoner we may safely assume. We can, in fact, still find them in many tales that have been today completely revised and reorganized in terms of the newer realistic style. This older viewpoint is also evident in many of the animal tales, particularly among the Southern Bantu.

The only respect in which the nontraditional narratives differ from those of other areas is in the development of formal semi-religious, semi-philosophical discourses such as those found in West Africa among the Ewe.[28] In the latter we find the same realistic appraisal of the world so characteristic of the traditional narratives. One example will have to suffice:

> God made everything in the world. He alone has been great from the beginning of time. God made all men. . . . God is wise for he has created everything on the earth and accompanies men and animals everywhere. . . . No person can understand his wisdom. . . . He himself made the good and the bad people. He is compassionate. But he does not always know how to act justly for he gave us death.

God acts unjustly for he made some people good and others bad. I and my companions work together in the fields; the crops of one prosper and those of others fail. This proves that God is unjust and treats men unequally. God treats us, our children and our wives who perish, unkindly. If men behave like that we say nothing, but when God acts thus it hurts us. From this we are right in inferring that God is unjust.

In the other main branches of prose literature which have attained significant development, in aboriginal Africa, the riddles and the proverbs, sophistication and realism are also dominant. The realism of the proverbs is accompanied by a profound and detached philosophic insight and understanding in which love and compassion are given their due place, something which is strikingly absent from the traditional prose narratives. Perhaps nowhere in the world has the proverb attained a more artistic expression than here in Africa. Rarely has so much been said in so concise, pithy, and artistic a form. We have today a tendency to dismiss such a literary genre with a shrug of the shoulders. That, of course, is a Western European prejudice. The proverb is still a legitimate literary form in the Orient and it was not despised in ancient Greece.

In contrast to the prose, no generalizations can be made for the poetry that would hold for the whole continent. There exist a few stylistic forms that are found everywhere, such as the poems consisting of solo and chorus or those that serve as a text for a prose expansion, or the dirges for the dead. But apart from these, each area and tribe has developed its own forms and stresses themes referring to its own interests and connected with its own special history. Where monarchies exist or where societies are complexly organized the poets often constitute a professional and privileged order. They play the role of poet-laureates whose duty it is to glorify the rulers and the particular interests and ideals of their nation. Let me select the Bantu Ruanda to illustrate what these poets take as their subject matter.

Among the Ruanda there are three main genres of poetry, all of them taking the form of odes or small epics, those in praise of the king, those in praise of the warrior and his deeds, and those in praise of their most prized possession, the cow. These odes are one of the distinctive achievements of Africa. Those in praise of the king consist of a long series of stereotyped compliments, stereotyped images and allusions which only a member of the tribe could possibly understand and appreciate. As an example, let me quote part of an ode composed to celebrate the accession to the throne of the king Mutara in 1810.[29]

You are a vessel forged without defect,
Fashioned by hammers, chosen and select;
Born of Ruaniko's most sacred trees,

Your brethren, scions of Cyillima.
Indolence never touched you nor did sloth.
Your arms, unfailing, brought us victory
Just as it did your kin, Ruganda's ancient kings.

You are the happy searcher after game.
You nourish us and grant us your protection.
O king of great renown and without blame,
Have we not seen the deeds where you excelled?
A king of many virtues, hero you.
A jewel precious are you and so large
That from Buriza down to Buremera you stretch.

Ruler of Tanda, you, all-powerful,
From days of old your fief it was Rutanga,
Your ancient home Gasabo,
There where the heifers play.
Hero without fault and without blame,
Giver of laws, unalterable words,
Owner of lands that overflow with wealth,
Master and king, your subjects here we stand
And in Ruanda may you always rule. . . .

Equal you are to those that I have praised,
In no way second,
O clothed in joy and happiness!
These drums attest your gentleness and worth.
Young though you be, in valor you are clothed.

Your horns already stand erect and straight
Despite your youth, most precious calf!
Mighty will you become I know,
When you have come to man's estate,
Mighty and strong and proud, a bull.
Great conqueror of hungers.
Where will the nations flee,
Those who were slow to serve you?
Protector of our flock, lengthen this day,
Give me your ear that I may pay respect. . . .
I am not one who falters, whom slander finds;
Others may hesitate, this well I know, not I.

Pleasure and happiness reside within my breast
Since that rare day when to your home I came.
Giver of joy, our refuge,
Turn upon us the fulness of your power.
And now a happy message do I bring,
I who did find the chambers of our lord,
That gracious home, radiant and full of smiles,
Immaculate and clean as kaoline.
There did I see and come upon the king,
In semblance like a newly risen moon,
His features like a diamond without flaw.

Resplendent did his beauty flash on me
And there came a new afflatus added to the old.
Upon my head a garland there was placed.
And thus I danced crowned with the sacred badge,
Nor can the best of bards find me at fault.

Here we are in a world comparable to that of Pindar, a world in which heroic lays and odes are born, as the well-known French scholar, Père Laydevant, has justly pointed out.[30] The poetic inspiration found in these odes is not generally of the highest kind. Negro African poetry at its best is to be found elsewhere, in the elegies for the dead, in the religious "hymns," and in the short philosophic lyrics. Take, for example, the following "hymns" from the upper Guinea coast.[31]

I.

1. The sun shines brightly, it burns down upon us.
In glory rises the moon, rises into the skies.
Rain falls on earth and, changing, the sun shines upon us.
Sun, moon and rain may change, but over them all there towers
God, from whose eye nothing escapes and is hidden.
Though you may stay at home, or though you may live on the waters,
Though under darkest shade of the trees you recline
Over it all dwells God.

2. Did you think in your pride or believe an orphan was ever below you,
You could covet his wealth and secretly then betray him,
There would be none to behold and none to detect you?
Call but to mind the fact that God is there, ever above you
And in the days to come he will find and he will repay you,
Though not today, today, though not today it may be.
Yes, in the days to come God will find and he will repay you.
Was in your mind the thought, was in your heart the feeling
It is a slave I have robbed, only, indeed, an orphan?
But in the days to come God will find and he will repay you,
Though not today, today, though not today it may be.

II.

O Sango, you, you are the master.
You punish in wrath, evil and guilty alike,
And you take in your hands the stones, the fiery weapons,
To crush those below; all these are broken.
Fires break out, the woods burn and all is consumed.
Trees fall, are destroyed, death threatens the living.

Or take again the following from the Ewe of West Africa.[32]

I. Death has been with us from all time;
The heavy burden long ago began.
Not I can loose the bonds.
Water does not refuse to dissolve
Even a large crystal of salt.
And so to the world of the dead
The good too must descend.

II. Large is the city of the nether world
Whither kings too must go
Nevermore to return.
Cease then your plaint, O mother of an only child!
Your plaint O cease, mother of an only child!
For when did an only child
Receive the gift of immortality?
So be it, mother of an only child,
And cease your wail, and cease your wail!

III. (The singers approach)
A great thing we desire to do,
A *kposu* song, an *adzoli* song,
To sing we shall begin:
Awute here lies dead,
He now lies on his bier.
Death did announce himself to him.
O dead friend lying on your bier
Return once more, your bonds to loose!

(The deceased appears and speaks)
You all now know
Within my body the word has perished,
Within Awute speech has died.

Who was it destroyed my body?
'Twas death dragged it away;
A warrior snatched it from my body.

(Death appears and speaks)
Now my turn it is to sing!
I came and thundered,
I had my lightning flash upon the tree
And threw him down!
Come let us go!
Footsteps I hear, people are approaching.
An evil brother does announce himself;
Inopportune he comes.

With these poems I shall leave African literature and turn to one which could not possibly be more different, that of the Eskimo. Here too a stark realism pervades both prose and poetry, but there is no oversophistication and, above all, no cynicism. Nowhere is death and starvation so omnipresent, nowhere is nature so cruel and nowhere is man, possibly, so violent. What then has made for the amazing contrast between the two types of realism? The answer, I feel, is simple. Cruelty, bloodshed, destruction among the Eskimo are not palpably man-made as in Africa. No conquests, with all their attendant horrors and with the demoralization which comes in their wake, have swept over this land. No aboriginal civilization is more completely integrated. It is this integration which has protected the Eskimo against inherently false emphases and evaluations and which has permitted him to retain one virtue which is seemingly absent in the civilizations of Negro Africa and many parts of Indonesia, Malaysia and Melanesia: humility. This humility brings with it a philosophic detachment which can critically evaluate man, yet still sympathize with him even in misfortunes he has brought upon himself. The Eskimos can do this because they see man in his proper proportions as a mote in an enormous universe and as a being forced by nature and life itself to do violence to other living creatures which have as much right to life as has man.

In no area in the world, civilized or aboriginal, is there more respect for life, for all life, human and nonhuman, and so much unadulterated enjoyment of life. The will to live under the conditions existing in Arctic North America is an achievement and as such the Eskimos celebrate it. Only because it is something that has to be achieved can they face life, acquiesce in what it offers of good and evil, of misfortune and happiness, and only because it has to be achieved does it mean so much to them. An informant of Rasmussen tells how she came upon a woman who, when she and her family were isolated during a terrible winter, saved herself from death by consuming the dead body of her husband. When discovered, half crazed, she shrieked at her rescuers not to approach her, that she was defiled and unfit for human companionship. The answer of the rescuers was simple and direct: "You had the will to live."

But life to the Eskimo means life at its best moments: youth and maturity, not old age. Old age is a time for recalling the past when one was happy and active. Such reminiscences form the theme of innumerable poems. Some of them have a touch of the sentimental which a delightful sense of humor generally corrects, for on truthfulness in such matters the Eskimo lays great stress. "Our narratives," an old Eskimo told Rasmussen, "deal with the experiences of man and these experiences are not always pleasant or pretty. But it is not proper to change our stories to make them more acceptable to our ears, that is if we wish to tell the truth. Words must be the echo of what has happened and cannot be made to conform to the mood and the taste of the listener."

Let me quote one of the best of such poems:[33]

1. Often I return
To my little song.
And patiently I hum it
Above the fishing hole
In the ice.
This simple little song
I can keep on humming,
I, who else too quickly
Tire when fishing—
Up the stream.

2. Cold blows the wind
Where I stand on the ice,
I am not long in giving up!
When I get home
With a catch that does not suffice,
I usually say
It was the fish
That failed—
Up the stream.

3. And yet, glorious is it
To roam
The river's snow-soft ice
As long as my legs care.
Alas! My life has now glided
Far from the wide views of the peaks
Deep down into the vale of age—
Up the stream.

4. If I go hunting the land beasts,
Or if I try to fish,
Quickly I fall to my knees,
Stricken with faintness.
Never again shall I feel
The wildness of strength,
When on an errand I go over the land
From my house and those I provide for—
Up the stream.

5. A worn-out man, that's all,
A fisher, who ever without luck
Makes holes in river or lake ice
Where no trout will bite.

6. But life itself is still
So full of goading excitement!
I alone,
I have only my song,
Though it too is slipping from me.

7. For I am merely
Quite an ordinary hunter,
Who never inherited song
From the twittering birds of the sky.

In the traditional prose narratives purely human themes greatly predominate. These are really novelettes and are probably not very old. But the Eskimo places them in the category of narratives referring to events of the ancient past, to which also the comparatively few animal tales belong. They are often difficult to distinguish from narratives that belong to the second category, that of contemporary literature. However, the most characteristic compositions in their contemporary literature belong to the domain of their shamanistic experiences. They are really snatches of autobiography.

Yet, excellent as is their prose, the real achievement of the Eskimo lies in the realm of poetry. Here they have not been equalled by any other aboriginal people, with the possible exception of the Polynesians. That they should have as their subject matter the joy of living and the beauties of the world is not strange considering the nature of Eskimo philosophy.

All primitive peoples celebrate the happenings of their life, important or unimportant, in song, but such technical perfection as that of the Eskimo has been achieved by few others. This is manifest in every composition. Take, for example, the following poems:

I.[34]

I arise from rest with movements swift
As the beat of a raven's wings,
Thus I arise
To meet the day.
My face is turned from the dark of night
To gaze at the dawn of day
Now whitening in the sky.

II.[35]

The lands around my dwelling
Are more beautiful
From the day
When it is given to me to see
Faces I have never seen before.
All is more beautiful,
All is more beautiful,
And life is thankfulness.
These guests of mine
Make my house grand.

III.[36]

Ajaha, ajaha!
I journeyed in my kayak
To search for some land.
Ajaha, ajaha!
And I came upon a snowdrift
As it began to melt,
Ajaha, ajaha!
Spring now I knew was near,
Winter was past.
Ajahaija, ajaihaija!
And I was afraid
That my eyes would become
Weak, far too weak
To behold all that glory.
Ajahaija,

Ajahaija,
Ajaha.

IV.[37]

1. Fear seizes me
When I think of being alone.
What a wish, to be far from men
As happy one sits among friends!

2. What a joy it is to sense,
To witness summer's approach
As it comes to this world of ours;
To behold the sun,
The day-sun, the night-sun,
Going its ancient way!

3. Fear seizes me
When I mark the winter's approach
As it comes to this world of ours;
To behold the moon,
The half moon, the full moon,
Going its ancient way!

4. Whither does all this tend?
Would that my steps went eastward!
Yes, never again, well I know,
Will I see him, my father's kin.

The Eskimos have a large number of special genres of poetry, the most famous being the versified lampoon. On specified occasions men and women assemble to hear individuals, generally gifted poets, hurl insults at one another. These versified lampoons are highly stylized and very difficult to understand because they deal with incidents in the personal lives of the combatants. Such poetic duels can be quite long, lasting at times an hour. They consist of attacks and answers. In many of these poems it is regarded as artistic to compose in riddles, or only to give hints without stating clearly what is meant. The audience is thus kept in a continuous state of tension, although rarely for long, since among the Eskimo everyone's affairs are matters of community knowledge.

Let me quote snatches from one such poetic duel[38] where the meaning is clear. The contest is between a man named Marratse and one named Equerqo, who had stolen Marratse's wife.

MARRATSE'S ATTACK

Words let me split,
Small words, sharp words,
Like the splinters
Which, with my axe, I cut up.
A song I shall sing of old days,
A breath from the distant past,

A sad and a plaintive song,
Forgetfulness to bring to my wife,
She who was snatched from me
By a prattler, a liar.
Bitterly has she suffered from him,
That lover of human flesh,
Cannibal, miscreant,

EQUERQO'S ANSWER

Only amazement I feel
At your preposterous words.
Only anger they cause
And the urge to laugh,
You with your mocking song,
Placing on me that guilt.
Did you think you could frighten me,
I who many a time challenged death?
Hei, hei! So you sing to my wife
Who once was yours in the days
When kindness you forgot.
Alone she was in those days.
Yet never in combats of song
Did you challenge your foes for her.
Ah, but now she is mine.
Never again shall false lovers like you,
Deceivers, come singing into our tent.
Spewed up from starvation days!

Eskimo poetry is exclusively lyrical, but within that genre what has been achieved is amazing. Equally amazing is the Eskimos' awareness of their technique. As one of them once said, "The most festive of all things is joy in beautiful, smooth words and one's ability to express them."[39] It is not by chance, then, but because they have occupied themselves with the problem, that they attempt to explain what poetic inspiration is. I have already given one such explanation; let me now add another. "All songs," so an old Eskimo claimed, "come to us in the great solitary open places. Sometimes they come to us in the form of tears, at other times from the depths of our hearts or, again, they may come in the form of joyous laughter springing from the happiness which wells up within us as we behold the grandeur of the world and ponder over the meaning of life. Without our knowing how, words and melodies come into being, words we do not use in common speech."[40]

How are we to account for this amazing literary achievement? It is an important question to answer. A highly developed literary tradition must lie behind it, and we have difficulty, at first, in believing it was achieved in the inhospitable and frightful environment in which the Eskimo now lives. Is it conceivable, as they themselves claim, that song and laughter was the answer they gave to the challenge of nature? Possibly. But this is only part of the answer. To explain the Eskimo literary achievement, to completely explain the literary achievement of any aboriginal civilization, we must assume that all peoples, at all times, carry within them the possibilities of developing significant and mature literatures if social and economic conditions are not too destructive. Only on such an assumption can we explain the song cycles of the Australian aborigines of Northeastern Arnhem Land, cycles that are true epics—this song, for instance, that a "lowly" Australian poet sings:[41]

Tidal waters flowing,
White foam on the waves,
Fresh water flowing,
From rains into the stream.
Into the waters falling,
Soft bark of the papertrees,
Rain from the clouds falling,
The stream's waters swirling—
Thus she emerged
And walked upon the land.

d.
PRODUCTIVITY AND EXISTENCE

MARTIN BUBER

Productivity and Existence

"A REMARKABLE and charming man, your friend," said the professor; "but what does he really do? I mean . . . in the intellectual sphere?"

"In the intellectual sphere. . . ." I answered, "H'mm . . . in the intellectual sphere . . . he is simply there."

"How do you mean?"

"Well, his occupation is not, in fact, of a very intellectual nature, and one cannot really assert that he makes anything out of his leisure time."

"But his thoughts?"

"He contents himself for the most part with images. When they want to combine and condense into a thought, he gladly helps them and is pleased if something real comes out of them. At times, in conversation, as just now, he also shares some of these clear and fulfilled images."

"Then he does not write?"

"Oh, he once confessed to me, almost against his will, that occasionally, now and then, when his thoughts congeal, he enters a few lines in a secret book, in order, as he put it, to distinguish from then on what is actually won from what is merely *possible*."

"Then will he perhaps eventually publish something comprehensive?"

"I do not believe that he has that in mind. He has no need to enter into relation with men other than the friends life has brought him in contact with. He trusts life like a child. He said once that intensity is the only dimension that unceasingly rewards traveling."

"But why do not you, his friends, persuade him to collect his thoughts and share them with the general public? I have heard enough of them to say with certainty that they are worth while."

"We feel that his real unity lies in his personality and that only there can it exist. And we feel that we would injure his vitality, which means more to us than any book, if we induced him to store it between covers instead of pouring it into our souls, repaying living with living. He does not give away any part of himself; he only lends it, to receive it back transformed, so that all being then blooms in his presence as young faces, young gestures. That alone makes the blessing of his sharing; that calls up and enlivens ever new levels in him and renews him, indeed, time after time. In the sureness of our glance, in the buoyancy of our plan, in the sacrificial power of our undertaking, he reads the fiery writing of his transformed words. When one of our circle died, I marked that our friend went on reading him in an immortal sphere."

"But the world—you forget the world! You speak as if a book were an end in itself, whereas it is only a transmitter that bears our voices to unknown ears and hearts. I write what I am inspired to; I fling it out beyond all that is personal, into the whirl of the market, and the whirl carries it into reading-rooms and lamp-lit parlours where men whom I have never seen and never will see hear my words—and perhaps really understand. Is a book not a significant mixture of the personal and the impersonal? The book works and woos out there, and yet it is also myself. Thus separated from myself, I flow into all the world—into distant houses and perhaps into distant generations also—elevating, pleasing, angering who knows, but always in some way educating the human spirit. This thousandfold journey, this victory over all limits of individual existence, this bond with the unknown—for ever misused by vanity and yet never wholly desecrated—this is the predestined way of the thinker."

"I am familiar with this way, for at times I, too, publish a book. I know the joy of it and its terror—yes, its terror; for it is something dreadful to know that the ghost of my thought hovers in the dreams of confused and impure men, confused and impure as they. But I also know its joy—I remember how it moved me when an old beekeeper wrote me that he had read my book every day for a week on a bench in his garden in the bright hours of the afternoon, from the coming of the apple-blossoms till their withering. And, in order to be entirely fair, I shall also recall the great and creative gifts which I myself owe to books. Now I feel wholly what they are. And yet—more powerful and more holy than all writing is the presence of a man who is simply and immediately present. He need not cry through the loud-speaker of a book to that special circle of contemporary and future readers the writer calls the world. He has spoken without a medium, from mouth to ear, silently and overpoweringly, from his countenance to an eye and to an entranced soul: he has spoken in the magic fullness of togetherness to those men he calls his friends—and who are now full of the spirit because it has laid its hands upon them. Such a man will rarely produce a book. And if he does anything of this sort, the original source of the book is the life of a man who is present only in a direct way."

"Then all those who are not among the friends of such a man must remain excluded from his teaching?"

"Not all, for those who are transformed through his teaching are forthwith, one and all, apostles—even though they do not repeat anything of it, nor even proclaim the name of the teacher; as transformed men, they are apostles through their existence, and whatever they do is done in apostleship, through the essence of his teaching which they express therein. In the life of his friends, in the life of all who meet him, and thus to distant generations, immediacy is transmitted."

"You wish, then, if I understand you rightly, to regard productivity as a lower rung of existence?"

"Rather, I regard productivity, in general, as existence only when it is rooted in the immediacy of lived life. If the man whom you call productive, the one who expresses himself in a creative work, is inferior in power, in holiness, to him who only expresses himself in his life, he is still, in so far as he is grounded in immediacy, superior to him in the noble faculty of creating form. But if you consider an individual who has shrunk to mere form the streaming, living potency, there stands before us a masquerading hobgoblin who cannot form himself but can only disguise himself in forms. No, what I said of the immediate man was not said against the productive one: I was attacking the dominant delusion of our time, that creativity is the criterion of human worth. But illegitimate creativity, creation without immediacy, is no criterion, for it is no reality. It is an illusion—and I believe in the absolute eye before which it cannot stand for a moment. Only that can be a criterion from which genuine creativity arises: that is, the immediate."

"Certainly, man can be judged only by what he is. But does not his creating, along with his acting, belong to his being?"

"Yes, when it functions as a valid organ of the living body; no, when it indicates a mere excrescence. Artifice has so much got the upper hand that the fictitious dares to usurp the place of the real. The overvaluation of productivity that is afflicting our age has so thrived and its par-technical glance has set up a senseless exclusiveness of its own that even genuinely creative men allow their organic skills to degenerate into an autonomous growth to satisfy the demand of the day. What the born deceivers never had, they give up: the ground where the roots of a genuinely lived life alone can grow. They mean, they strive for, and at last they contain nothing but creativity. Instead of bringing forth a natural creation, in a gradual selective progression from experiences to thoughts, from thoughts to words, from words to writing, and from writing to public communication, they wear themselves out turning all experience to account as public communication; they renounce true necessity and give themselves over to the arbitrary. They poison experience, for already while it is taking place they are dominated by the will to produce. Thus they prostitute their lives and are cheated of the reward for their ignominy; for how can they expect to create anything save the artificial and the transitory? They forfeit both life and art, and all that they gain is the applause of their production-mad contemporaries."

"But it appears to me that the will to create is a legitimate part of the experience of every productive man. Thus the painter is the man who paints with all his senses. His seeing is already a painting, for what he sees is not merely what his physical sight receives: it is something, two-dimensionally intensified, that vision produces. And this producing does not come later, but is present in his seeing. Even his hearing, his smelling, are already painting, for they enrich for him the graphic character of the thing; they give him not only sensations but also stimulations. In the same way the poet creates poetry with all his senses; in each of his experiences the form in which it will be phrased is immediately announced. His perceiving is already a transformation of the thing perceived into the stuff of poetry, and in its becoming each impression presents itself to him as an expression of rhythmic validity."

"That is indeed so. But this dynamic element that you find in the experience of the creative is no will to create but an ability to create. This potentiality of form also accompanies every experience that befalls the non-artistic man and is given an issue as often as he lifts an image out of the stream of perception and inserts it into his memory as something single, definite, and meaningful in itself. For the creative man this potentiality of form is a specific one, directed into the language of his particular art. If an intention is expressed in this direction, it is that of his genius, not that of a self-conscious resolution. The dynamic element of his experience does not affect its wholeness and purity. It is otherwise when in perceiving he already cherishes the deliberate intention of utilizing what he perceives. Then he disturbs the experience, stunts its growth, and taints the process of its becoming. Only the unarbitrary can grow properly and bear mature and healthy fruit. That man is legitimately creative who experiences so strongly and formatively that his experiences unite into an image that demands to be set forth, and who then works at his task with full consciousness of his art. But he who interferes with the spontaneity of perceiving, who does not allow the inner selection and formation to prevail, but instead inserts an aim from the beginning, has forfeited the meaning of this perception, the meaning that lies above all aims. And he who meets men with a double glance, an open one that invites his fellows to sincerity and the concealed one of the observer stemming from a conscious aim; he who in friendship and in love is cleft into two men, one who surrenders himself to his feelings and another who is already standing by to exploit them—this man cannot be delivered by any creative talent from the blight that he has brought upon himself and his work, for he has poisoned the springs of his life."

"You wish, then, to reintroduce into aesthetics the ethical principle that we have finally succeeded in banishing from it?"

"What was banished from aesthetics was an ideology that had degenerated into rhetoric and had thereby become false. It certainly signified a conquest of sure ground when the perspective was established that evaluated a work of art—approving or rejecting it—not by its relation to the aspirations of the artist but by its intrinsic qualities. Now for the first time we can, without promoting misunderstanding, strive towards the deeper insight: that this approval affords entrance into the outer circle only, but in the inner circle those works alone count that have given form to the meaning of being. Similarly, a gain in clarity and solidity was achieved when it was recognized that the significance of an artist does not depend upon his morals: now for the first time we can attain the deeper clarity that in inner development mastery and power accrue only to that artist who is worthy of his art."

Notes

The Problem of Ego Identity

ERIK HOMBURGER ERIKSON

1. Austen Riggs Center, Stockbridge, Massachusetts, and University of Pittsburgh School of Medicine, Pittsburgh, Pennsylvania. The research on which this paper is based is supported by a grant of the Field Foundation to the Riggs Center.

2. At the 35th Anniversary Institute of the Judge Baker Guidance Center in Boston, May, 1953, and at the Midwinter Meetings of the American Psychoanalytic Association, New York, 1953.

3. ". . . die klare Bewusstheit der inneren Identität" (17).

4. My italics.

5. Child Guidance Study, Institute of Child Welfare, University of California.

6. William James speaks of an abandonment of "the old alternative ego," and even of "the murdered self" (26).

7. For a new approach see Anna Freud's and Sophie Dann's report on displaced children (16).

8. See Chapters VIII (Status and Role) and XI (Social Class) in (31). For a recent psychoanalytic approach to Role and Status see (1).

9. I owe new insights in this field to Robert Knight (28) and to Margaret Brenman (6).

10. David Rapaport's ego-psychological approach to "Activity and Passivity" sheds new light on the ego's role in such crises (36).

11. This example illustrates well the balance which must be found in the interpretation given to such patients between *sexual symbolism* (here castration) which, if overemphasized by the therapist, can only increase the patient's sense of being endangered; and the *representation of dangers to the ego* (here the danger of having the thread of one's autonomy cut off) the communication of which is more urgent, more immediately beneficial, and a condition for the safe discussion of sexual meanings.

12. See, however, (34).

13. Here, as in previous publications, I refrain from referring to more comprehensive modifications of psychoanalytic theory (Dollard, Fromm and Kardiner) because I am as yet unable to establish the convergencies and divergencies between that which they have stated systematically, and that which I am trying to formulate.

14. My italics.

15. My italics.

16. See the concern over personal children, patients, and germinating ideas in Freud's "Irma Dream" (12).

17. In this paper, I cannot more than approach the possible relation of the problem of identity to ideological processes; and I can only parenthetically list possible analagous correspondences between stages of psychosocial development in the individual and major trends of social organization. The problem of Basic Trust (and Basic Mistrust) seems to have such a correspondence with the institutionalization of a faith and an evil in organized religion or other forms of moral world imagery; the problem of Autonomy (versus Shame and Doubt) with the delineation of individual rights and limitations in the basic principles of law and justice; the problem of Initiative (versus Guilt) with the encouragements and limitations emanating from the dominant ethos of production; and the problem of workmanship with the predominant techniques of production and their characteristic division of labor.

18. Organized by Professors E. Eisenstadt and C. Frankenstein of the Hebrew University. The initial impressions presented here are mine.

19. We may state tentatively that the elites which emerge from historical change

are groups which out of the deepest common identity crisis manage to create a new style of coping with the outstanding danger situations of their society.

20. I.e., relative communism within the individual community, which, however, in its relation to the national economy, rather represents a capitalist co-operative.

Culture Change and Character Structure

MARGARET MEAD

1. I say "many societies" advisedly, because in giving an account of Arapesh socio-economic life ("The Mountain Arapesh, III." "Socio-Economic Life, IV." "Diary of Events in Alitoa," *Anthropological Papers of the American Museum of Natural History* [XI (1947), 159-220]), I found it impossible to give an adequate sociological statement which did not include the specification of each actor in terms both of his social position and of his personality. The specification in terms of social position alone could, of course, be made without invoking individual psychology, and I am not prepared to say that another investigator, with a more purely sociological frame of reference, might not have devised a way of presenting the peculiarities of Arapesh social organization without this extra degree of specification.

2. E.g., the fields of neural codification, perception, *Gestalt,* developmental psychology, motivation, learning, constitutional type, formal analysis of social interaction, etc.

3. Bateson, *Naven* (Cambridge: Cambridge University Press, 1936). *Idem,* "Morale and National Character," in Goodwin Watson (ed.), *Civilian Morale,* 2nd Yearbook of the Society for the Psychological Study of Social Issues (New York: Houghton Mifflin Co., 1942), pp. 71, 91. *Idem* and Margaret Mead, *Balinese Character, A Photographic Analysis* (New York Academy of Sciences, 1942). Ruth F. Benedict, *The Chrysanthemum and the Sword* (New York: Houghton Mifflin Co., 1947). E. H. Erikson, "Childhood and Tradition in Two American Indian Tribes," in *The Psychoanalytic Study of the Child* (New York: The International Universities Press, 1945), pp. 319-50. G. Gorer, "Themes in Japanese Culture," *Transactions of the New York Academy of Sciences,* Ser. II, Vol. V (March, 1943), 106-24. Margaret Mead, *And Keep Your Powder Dry (The American Character),* (New York: Penguin, 1944).

4. This use of the word "homogeneous" does not exclude caste societies or societies with many different subgroups, so long as the relationships among such groups are part of the common shared culture and change slowly. Thus gypsies, foreign migratory workers, dissident religious sects, etc., may come to be so included in the recognition of the other members of a culture as not actually to interfere with its homogeneity.

5. For a more detailed discussion see M. Mead, "The Implications of Culture Change for Personality Development," *American Journal of Orthopsychiatry,* XVI (October, 1947).

6. The development of the boys' gang in large American cities is a typical example. Born of European parents who are no longer able to serve as models, and reared in a world which demands that parents accord applause to their children (which the European parents are unable to give), the adolescents segregate themselves into a world of their own, in which the values of the gang leader and of the gang members are paramount over the values of the larger society. The boarding school which, on a small scale, attempts to substitute a new standard culture for the diversities of the homes from which individuals come, also tends to develop the same sort of overriding emphasis upon the immediate judgment of the group of contemporaries.

7. Margaret Mead, "Trends in Personal Life," *New Republic,* CXV (September 23, 1946), 346-48.

8. E. H. Erikson, "Ego Development and Historical Change," *The Psychoanalytic Study of the Child,* II (New York: The International Universities Press).

9. Such an atomization of external reality is, of course, not in itself incompatible with an integrated culture, provided the character formation of the individuals is such that there is a genuine relationship between the series of temporary patterns imposed upon the aggregation of bits. Balinese culture is filled with instances in which some material or event sequence is first atomized and then rearranged in a new form, and of instances in which the violent disruption of some ceremonial event sequence by an irrelevant interruption is ignored because of the persistent pattern into which the Balinese themselves reassemble what appears to the Western observer to be shattered, discontinuous bits. Extreme atomization of alien cultural elements is a characteristic cultural phenomenon by which culture contact is rendered relatively ineffective in Bali. The conspicuously small amount of routine fatigue and the capacity of the Balinese to shift easily from one activity to another are probably also systematically related to the way in which the individual responds only partially to external stimuli or imposed tasks. When Balinese ceremonial is analyzed regionally, the jig-saw puzzle figure becomes more meaningful, because many details in a *rite de passage* are unintelligible unless referred to some equally meaningless detail in the *same rite de passage* in another village or district. Without a historical record it is impossible to interpret this curious distribution further. There may be a premium upon reducing the meaningfulness so as to reduce its coercive effect upon the attention of the individual. Such a reduction would, in fact, be made possible by a random dissection of ritual wholes into disconnected items which could no longer reinstate the whole. Another possible—and undemonstrable—explanation would attribute the random distribution of various apparently related bits to some process of assimilation af alien elements, in which one community had selected one set of bits, another community another. It has been suggested by Dr. Theodora Abel, after an analysis of the responses of Balinese subjects to her "limited free design test" ("Free Designs of Limited Scope as a Personality Index," *Character and Personality* [1938], 50-62) that this reduction in the meaningfulness of external detail is related to a very great rigidity of personality at a deeper level—a rigidity which may be partly preserved by this cultivated lack of attention to the external world.

10. M. Mead, "How Religion Has Fared in the Melting Pot," in B. Willard Sperry (ed.), *Religion in the Post-War World Series* (*Religion and Our Racial Tensions*, III), pp. 61-82.

11. The European, to whom differences in material objects are related to a more incommensurable set of values, of course *experiences* American culture as a manifold of bewildering and unordered complexity.

12. Granville Hicks, in his recent study of a small, up-state New York community (*Small Town* [New York: The Macmillan Co., 1946]), comments extensively on the prevalence of such judgments as, "I can put up with drunkards, but I can't stomach them in church."

13. Else Frenkel-Brunswik, and R. Nevitt Sanford, "Some Personality Factors in Anti-Semitism," *Journal of Psychology*, XX (1945), 271-91. Also unpublished materials on this research.

The Stranger: An Essay in Social Psychology

ALFRED SCHUETZ

1. Instead of mentioning individual outstanding contributions by American writers, such as W. G. Sumner, W. I. Thomas, Florian Znaniecki, R. E. Park, H. A. Miller, E. V. Stonequist, E. S. Bogardus, and Kimball Young, and by German authors, especially Georg Simmel and Robert Michels, we refer to the valuable monograph by Margaret Mary Wood, *The Stranger: A Study in Social Relationship* (New

York, 1934), and the bibliography quoted therein.

2. This insight seems to be the most important contribution of Max Weber's methodological writings to the problems of social science. Cf. the present writer's *Der sinnhafte Aufbau der socialen Welt* (Vienna, 1932).

3. John Dewey, *Logic, the Theory of Inquiry* (New York, 1938), Chapter IV.

4. For the distinction of these two kinds of knowledge cf. William James, *Psychology,* I (New York, 1890), pp. 221-22.

5. Max Scheler, "Probleme einer Soziologie des Wissens," *Die Wissensformen und die Gesellschaft* (Leipzig, 1926), pp. 58 ff.; cf. Howard Becker and Hellmuth Otto Dahlke, "Max Scheler's Sociology of Knowledge," *Philosophy and Phenomenological Research,* II (1942), 310-22, esp. p. 315.

6. Robert S. Lynd, *Middletown in Transition* (New York, 1937), Chapter XII, and *Knowledge for What?* (Princeton, 1939), pp. 58-63.

7. As one account showing how the American cultural pattern depicts itself as an unquestionable element within the scheme of interpretation of European intellectuals we refer to Martin Gumpert's humorous description in his book, *First Papers* (New York, 1941), pp. 8-9. Cf. also books like Jules Romains, *Visite chez les Américains* (Paris, 1930), and Jean Prévost Usonie, *Esquisse de la civilisation américaine* (Paris, 1939), pp. 245-66.

8. In using this term, we allude to Cooley's well-known theory of the reflected or looking-glass self (Charles H. Cooley, *Human Nature and the Social Order,* rev. ed.; New York, 1922, p. 184).

9. Therefore, the learning of a foreign language reveals to the student frequently for the first time the grammar rules of his mother-tongue which he has followed so far as "the most natural thing in the world," namely, as recipes.

10. Karl Vossler, *Geist und Kultur in der Sprache* (Heidelberg, 1925), pp. 117 ff.

11. It could be referred to a general principle of the theory of relevance, but this would surpass the frame of the present paper. The only point for which there is space to contend is that all the obstacles which the stranger meets in his attempt at interpreting the approached group arise from the incongruence of the contour lines of the mutual relevance systems and, consequently, from the distortion the stranger's system undergoes within the new surrounding. But any social relationship, and especially any establishment of new social contacts, even between individuals, involves analogous phenomena, although they do not necessarily lead to a crisis.

Centrality of the Problem of Anxiety in Our Day

ROLLO MAY

1. See especially *Look Homeward Angel* (New York, 1929) and *You Can't Go Home Again* (New York, 1934), and the later *Of Time and the River* (New York, 1935). It is exceedingly interesting that the central psychological theme of Wolfe's writings, the relation of the individual to his mother and the conflicts stemming from that relationship, is one of the central problems in any discussion of the origins of anxiety. In cases demonstrating anxiety it is observed that anxiety frequently, and in many cases basically, hinged on the issue symbolically expressed in Wolfe's title, *You Can't Go Home Again.* In these cases neurotic anxiety occurred because the patients were unable to accept the psychological meaning of not going home again, namely psychological autonomy. One could wonder (realizing that literary artists symbolically express, often with remarkable fidelity, the unconscious assumptions and conflicts of their culture) whether these symbols in Wolfe's writing could be taken to mean that many people in the late 1920's and early 1930's were beginning to realize that one cannot go home again, e.g., that it was impossible to depend for security on past economic, social, and ethical criteria, and that the upshot of this realization would be the increasing emergence of overt anxiety as a conscious prob-

lem, along with a feeling of "homelessness." This conjecture is, to be sure, an oversimplification, but if we take it as speculation about the central symbols of the home and the mother, it may usefully raise a problem that we shall be confronting, in much more specific form, time and again in this study of anxiety.

2. W. H. Auden, *The Age of Anxiety* (New York, 1947).

3. *Ibid.*, p. 3.

4. *Ibid.*, p. 45.

5. *Ibid.*, p. 44.

6. *Ibid.*, p. 42.

7. The present writer was excited to discover, during the preparation of this manuscript, that Leonard Bernstein has composed a symphony, which had its premiere in 1949, entitled *Age of Anxiety*. On the basis of his conviction that Auden's poem truly presents the "state of our age" in general, as well as speaking for the particular individual members of that age like himself, Bernstein has translated the poem into the symbols of instrumental music.

8. Quoted in the *New York Times*, December 21, 1947, Sec. 7, p. 2.

9. Franz Kafka, *The Castle* (New York, 1930).

10. Max Brod, in Appendix to Kafka's *The Castle*, p. 329.

11. Herman Hesse, *Steppenwolf*, trans. Basil Creighton (New York, 1947); originally published in German in 1927. The awareness of traumatic social change in the twentieth century occurred in Europe before it did in America; thus what Hesse wrote is much more relevant to conscious problems in this country in the 1940's than in 1927. Belatedly, Hesse received the Nobel prize for literature in 1946.

12. *Ibid.*, p. 28.

13. R. S. Lynd and H. M. Lynd, *Middletown* (New York, 1929), and *Middletown in Transition* (New York, 1937).

14. *Middletown*, p. 87.

15. On a Sunday afternoon the regular practice of many people was to get in their cars, drive fifty miles, and then drive back again. One is reminded of Pascal's description of some symptoms of covert anxiety: the constant endeavor of people to divert themselves, to escape ennui, to avoid being alone, until "agitation" becomes an end in itself.

16. *Op. cit.*, p. 493.

17. *Middletown in Transition*, p. 315.

18. *Ibid.*, p. 177.

19. *Op. cit.*, p. 315.

20. Paul Tillich, *The Protestant Era* (Chicago, 1947), p. 245.

21. Cf. Goldstein, p. 57, below. Also, Herbert L. Matthews, observer of Italian and Spanish fascism, writes: "Fascism was like a jail where the individual had a certain amount of security, shelter, and daily food."—*The Education of a Correspondent* (New York, 1946).

22. Arthur M. Schlesinger, Jr.: "[Communism] has filled the 'vacuum of faith' caused by the waning of established religion; it provides a sense of purpose which heals internal agonies of anxiety and doubt."—*New York Times*, February 1, 1948.

23. See also Erich Fromm, *Escape from Freedom* (New York, 1941).

24. *World Communism Today* (New York, 1948).

25. A task which awaits doing on the part of students of anxiety is the detailed study of dictatorship as an anxiety phenomenon. To some extent, it might be said, dictatorships are born and come to power in periods of cultural anxiety; once in power they live in anxiety—e.g., many of the acts of the dictating group are motivated by its own anxiety; and the dictatorship perpetuates its power by capitalizing upon and engendering anxiety in its own people as well as in its rival nations. Just how completely, however, such statements can be made awaits a good deal of investigation; the present writer, for one, believes such a study would be very fruitful.

26. *Modern Man Is Obsolete* (New York, 1945), p. 1. First printed as an editorial in *The Saturday Review of Literature* and then published in book form.

27. Arnold Toynbee, "How to Turn the Tables on Russia," *Woman's Home Companion*, August, 1949, 30 ff. Toynbee gives an analogy which is such a vivid parable of the constructive uses of anxiety that we summarize it here. The fishermen bringing in their herring from the North Sea were faced with the problem of the fish becoming sluggish in their tanks and thus losing some of their market value for freshness. Then one fisherman conceived the idea of placing a couple of catfish in the herring

tanks. Because of the threat of death in the presence of these catfish, the herring not only did not grow sluggish but became even more active and flourishing. Of course, whether the reaction of the Western world to the catfish (Russia) will be constructive or not is another question; in other words, whether we *shall* use the anxiety in our world situation predominantly for constructive purposes remains largely to be seen. There are some momentously constructive signs. e.g., the Marshall Plan; psychologically, this experiment has, in the present writer's opinion, the expansive, cooperative, courageous characteristics of a typically constructive approach to anxiety. But on the other hand there are the ominous tendencies in the ("spy scares," "witch hunts," etc., which, again speaking in psychological analogy, look very much like the retrenchments and phobic withdrawals which classically characterize the neurotic approach to anxiety.

28. In the light of Nietszche's idea that the philosopher is a "physician of culture," the thought of these writers is to be regarded not as the product of ivory-tower speculation, but is a diagnosis and articulation of one phase of the condition of our culture.

29. This concept of Tillich's was of course formulated before the emergence of the atom bomb, but the bomb is undoubtedly a symbol by which many more people are able to comprehend the immediate threat of nonbeing.

30. Cf. Kierkegaard's description of anxiety as the "fear of nothingness."

31. References to Tillich's explanation of the causes of the prevalence of meaninglessness in our culture will be made in later Sections.

32. Reinhold Niebuhr, *The Nature and Destiny of Man* (New York, 1941), p. 182.

33. *Ibid.*

34. R. R. Willoughby, *Magic and Cognate Phenomena: An Hypothesis,* in Carl Murchinson (ed.), *Handbook of Social Psychology* (Worcester, Mass., 1935), p. 498.

35. *Ibid.*, p. 500.

36. An important fact in America is that divorces for "cruelty" are "solely responsible for the increase, all other causes steadily declining." Willoughby interprets "cruelty" as a matter of increase of anxiety—"if the conduct of the spouse is such as to exacerbate anxiety, it is 'cruel.' "—(*Op. cit.*)

37. P. M. Symonds, *The Dynamics of Human Adjustment* (New York, 1946), p. 138.

38. Sigmund Freud, *General Introduction to Psychoanalysis* (American ed.; New York, 1920), p. 341.

Psychiatric Aspects of Anxiety

FRIEDA FROMM-REICHMANN

1. Rollo May's book is most stimulating as a monograph in its own right, but also as an excellent survey of the theories of anxiety. The proceedings of the 39th Annual Meeting of the American Psychopathological Association, 1949 (Grune & Stratton, 1950), edited by Hoch & Zubin ought to be quoted as another useful compendium on the subject.

2. I will elaborate on this topic in my forthcoming publication "Philosophy of Psychotherapy."

The Social Psychology of Fear

KURT RIEZLER

1. These remarks refer to experiments made in the Institute for Psychiatry at the University of Chicago and to earlier experiments by Pavlov.

2. K. Goldstein, *Human Nature in the Light of Psychopathology* ("William James Lectures," Cambridge University Press, 1940). Based upon various studies by K. Goldstein and A. Gelb.

Repression, Anxiety, and the Self

LEO SCHNEIDERMAN

1. H. B. Reed, "Factors Influencing the Learning and Retention of Concepts: I. The Influence of Set," *Journal of Experimental Psychology*, XXXVI (1946), 71-87.

2. V. Hazlitt, "Children's Thinking," *British Journal of Psychology*, XX (1930), 354-61.

3. J. Piaget, *The Child's Conception of the World* (New York: Harcourt, Brace, 1929).

Careers, Personality, and Adult Socialization

HOWARD S. BECKER and ANSELM L. STRAUSS

1. Everett C. Hughes, of the University of Chicago, has undoubtedly done more than any other sociologist in this country to focus attention and research on occupational careers. Several of our illustrations will be drawn from work done under his direction, and our own thinking owes much to his writing and conversation.

2. Karl Mannheim, *Essays on the Sociology of Knowledge*, ed. Paul Kecskemeti (New York: Oxford University Press, 1953), pp. 247-49.

3. Oswald Hall, "The Stages in a Medical Career," *American Journal of Sociology*, LIII (March, 1948), 332.

4. Cf. Strauss's unpublished studies of careers in art and Howard S. Becker and James Carper, "The Development of Identification with an Occupation," *American Journal of Sociology*, LXI (January, 1956), 289-98.

5. Cf. Hall, *op. cit.*; David Solomon, "Career Contingencies of Chicago Physicians" (unpublished Ph.D. thesis, University of Chicago, 1952); Everett C. Hughes, *French Canada in Transition* (Chicago: University of Chicago Press, 1943), pp. 52-53; Melville Dalton, "Informal Factors in Career Achievement," *American Journal of Sociology*, LVI (March, 1951), 407-15; and Orvis Collins, "Ethnic Behavior in Industry: Sponsorship and Rejection in a New England Factory," *American Journal of Sociology*, LI (January, 1946), 293-98.

6. Cf. unpublished M.A. report of Earl Bogdanoff and Arnold Glass, "The Sociology of the Public Case Worker in an Urban Area" (University of Chicago, 1954).

7. Rhoda Goldstein, "The Professional Nurse in the Hospital Bureaucracy" (unpublished Ph.D. thesis, University of Chicago, 1954).

8. Donald Roy, "Quota Restriction and Goldbricking in a Machine Shop," *American Journal of Sociology*, LVII (March, 1952), 427-42.

9. Donald Roy, "Efficiency and the 'Fix': Informal Intergroup Relations in a Piecework Machine Shop," *American Journal of Sociology*, LX (November, 1954), 255-66.

10. Cf. Erving Goffman, "On Cooling the Mark Out: Some Aspects of Adaptation to Failure," *Psychiatry*, XV (November, 1952), 451-63.

11. Bogdanoff and Glass, *op. cit.*

12. Howard S. Becker, "The Professional Dance Musician and His Audience," *American Journal of Sociology*, LVII (September, 1951), 136-44.

13. Paul G. Cressey, *The Taxi-Dance Hall* (Chicago: University of Chicago Press, 1932), pp. 84-106.

14. Norman Martin and Anselm Strauss, "Patterns of Mobility within Industrial

Organizations," *Journal of Business,* XXIX (April, 1956), 101-10.

15. Howard S. Becker, "The Career of the Chicago Public Schoolteacher," *American Journal of Sociology,* LVII (March, 1952), 470-77.

16. Hall, *op. cit.*

17. Erik H. Erikson, *Childhood and Society* (New York: W. W. Norton & Co., 1950), p. 57.

The Commercial Artist: A Study in Changing and Consistent Identities

MASON GRIFF

1. Mason Griff, "The Recruitment of the Artist" (unpublished manuscript, 1955). Also see Anselm Strauss, "The Art School and Its Students: A Study and Interpretation" (unpublished manuscript.)

2. The number is not large in any country.

3. Mason Griff, "The Commercial Artist: A Study in Role Conflict and Career Development (Unpublished Ph.D. dissertation, University of Chicago, 1958).

4. See, for example, Howard S. Becker, "The Jazz Musician and His Audience" (Unpublished Master's thesis, University of Chicago, 1949).

5. In this connection, see Talcott Parsons and Edward Shils (eds.), *Toward a General Theory of Action* (Cambridge: Harvard University Press, 1951). See especially the discussion of the pattern variable called universalistic-particularistic.

6. Edward Shils, "Ideology and Civility," *The Sewanee Review,* LXVI (Summer, 1958), 467-68.

7. Talcott Parsons, *The Structure of Social Action.* (Glencoe, Ill.: The Free Press, 1949), pp. 503-16.

8. For an extended discussion of the Art School, its importance in defining roles, and its implication for the art world, see Anselm Strauss, *op. cit.*

Some Unsolved Problems of the Scientific Career

LAWRENCE S. KUBIE

1. As a sharp contrast to the engineering approach of the aptitude testers, I would cite the studies which Anne Roe has been making since 1946. She has used various projective techniques, certain aptitude and psychometric devices, personal documents, life histories, and personal interviews to study the personalities of various kinds of scientists, scholars, and artists (8). Her results are necessarily still fragmentary but already they offer many suggestive leads, and her bibliographies are essential guides to the scanty literature in this field. The results also indicate how enormous is the amount of work which remains to be done.

2. Bernard, *op. cit.,* pp. 27-28.

3. In the same paper (p. 4) Dr. Tolman makes a further series of comments which are directly relevant to our problem. ". . . he (the scientist) selects this program . . . not to obtain results . . . but to satisfy his own subjective needs. . . ." "The origin of problems is a subjective one. . . ." "On the basis of many such nightly reflections, that which has objective validity is finally abstracted out from the welter of subjective experience in which scientists as well as other human beings are immersed. . . ."

4. Dr. Anne Roe, *The Making of a Scientist* (New York: Dodd, Mead & Company, 1953).

5. Alan Gregg, *The Furtherance of*

Medical Research, pp. 106-7.

6. There are many examples of scientists who missed making basic discoveries by a hair because of accidental external circumstances: for example, the story of Minkowski's place in the discovery of insulin by Banting, and of Freud's role in the application of cocaine in local anesthesia, which was completed by Koller. The opposite is also true: "Eight simultaneous discoveries of the cellular basis of plant and animal life. At least three independent demonstrations of artificial immunity following inoculation with attenuated cultures of anthrax bacillus. Five officially recorded demonstrations of the clinical value of cowpox vaccinations. Five independent discoveries of the phenomenon of heartblock. Three simultaneous demonstrations of vaso-constrictor nerves. Five independent introductions of ether as a surgical anesthetic." (W. H. Manwaring, *Science*, p. 361, April 1940; referring to B. J. Stern, *Social Factors in Medical Progress*, quoted by Gregg [2] in *op. cit.*, p. 88.)

Anxiety and Politics

FRANZ NEUMANN

1. A few lines referring to a German pamphlet on child psychology omitted—ed.

2. C. G. Jung has forcefully pointed to the significance of Schiller's Letters for our problem. *Psychologische Typen* (Zurich, 1921), pp. 97-192. For the quotations from Schiller's Letters, I have used as a basis J. Weiss's translation of 1845, and modified where necessary. (*The Aesthetic Letters, Essays, and the Philosophical Letters of Schiller* [Boston, 1845].)

3. *Fifth Letter* (cf. Weiss, p. 16).

4. *Sixth Letter* (cf. Weiss, p. 21).

5. *Op. cit.* (cf. Weiss, p. 22).

6. *Op. cit.* (cf. Weiss, p. 23).

7. The connection between Schiller and Hegel-Marx is clearly seen by Heinrich Popitz, *Der entfremdete Mensch. Zeitkritik und Geschichtsphilosophie des jungen Marx* (Basel, 1953) esp. pp. 28-35.

8. *Sixth Letter* (cf. Weiss, p. 22).

9. That is expressed in the sentence, "But even the scanty fragmentary portion, which still binds single members to the whole, depends not upon forms that present themselves spontaneously . . . but is prescribed to them with scrupulous strictness by a formula to which the free discernment of each one is restricted." *Ibid.*

10. E. M. Butler, *The Tyranny of Greece over Germany* (New York and Cambridge, 1935). Chapter V is on Schiller.

11. Ed. by Hermann Nohl, Tübingen, 1907.

12. *Ibid.*, pp. 378-82. Cf. esp. Herbert Marcuse, *Reason and Revolution. Hegel and the Rise of Social Theory* (New York, 1941) pp. 34-35.

13. Cf. Marcuse, *ibid.*

14. Marcuse, *op. cit.*, pp. 274-87, and Popitz, *op. cit.*, who adds little to Marcuse's analysis, but is interesting in that he constantly confronts Hegel and Marx.

15. "Oekonomisch-philosophische Manuskripte" in Marx-Engels *Gesamtausgabe*, First Div., Vol. III, p. 89.

16. *Op. cit.*, p. 87.

17. *Ibid.*, p. 118.

18. Cf. esp. the two articles by Erich Fromm, "Die Psychoanalytische Charakterologie und ihre Bedeutung für die Sozialpsychologie," and "Die sozialpsychologische Bedeutung der Mutterrechtstheorie," in *Zeitschrift für Sozialforschung* (1932), pp. 253-77, and 1934, pp. 196-227. Both articles were written prior to Fromm's revisionist period, but the former already points toward it.

19. (London, 1930), p. 39. This sentence is in itself valid only for patriarchal society. Whether it holds true for matriarchal society may be left open here. According to J. J. Bachofen, matriarchal right is "natura verum, the father only jure civile," (*Das Mutterrecht*, ed. by K. Meuli, Vol. I, p. 102); the stage of matriarchal right is that of poetry (pp. 124-25). Cf.

also Fromm's article cited above.

20. Freud, *Civilization and its Discontents,* p. 43.

21. *Ibid.,* p. 63.

22. *Ibid.,* pp. 63-64.

23. *Ibid.,* p. 80.

24. For the systematic connection between sexuality and society in Freud (and in other theories) cf. Roger Bastide, *Sociologie et Psychoanalyse* (Paris, 1950) pp. 211 ff.

25. The most important recent works are probably the following: K. Abraham, "A short study of the development of the libido, viewed in the light of mental disorders," in *Selected Papers on Psycho-Analysis* (London: Hogarth Press); Ernest Jones, "Fear, Guilt, Hate," in *Papers on Psycho-Analysis* (5th ed.; London, 1929); Ernest Jones, "The Pathology of Morbid Anxiety," (1911) in *Papers on Psycho-Analysis* (4th ed.); Melanie Klein, "On the Theory of Anxiety and Guilt," in *Developments in Psycho-Analysis* (The International Psycho-Analytic Library, No. 43, London, 1952), pp. 271-91; Paula Heimann, "Notes on the Theory of Life and Death Instincts," in *Developments in Psycho-Analysis,* pp. 321-37. The following works of Freud: *Civilization and its Discontents* (London, 1930); *Beyond the Pleasure Principle* (London, 1922); *The Ego and the Id* (London, 1927); *The Problem of Anxiety* (New York, 1936).

26. *The Ego and the Id,* pp. 84-85.

27. In *The Problem of Anxiety.*

28. Ernest Jones, "The Pathology of Morbid Anxiety."

29. Cf. Freud's critique in Chapter X of *The Problem of Anxiety.*

30. Cf. Paula Heimann's survey, "Notes on the Theory of Life and Death Instincts."

31. For Freud—who follows Rank in this respect—when a danger situation appears which resembles birth. Cf. *The Problem of Anxiety,* Chapter XI.

32. Sören Kierkegaard, *The Concept of Dread* (tr. Walter Lowrie, Princeton, 1944), p. 38, distinguishes fear and anxiety. Fear is the reaction against a concrete, external danger, while anxiety (the "dread" of the title) is a condition of being anxious.

33. Cf. also Melanie Klein, "On the Theory of Anxiety and Guilt," *loc. cit.,* p. 275.

34. Cf. Freud in *The Ego and the Id.* The best formulation is in Franz Alexander, *The Psychoanalysis of the Total Personality* (New York, 1949), p. 101.

K. Abraham, "A short study of the development of the libido," *op. cit.,* was probably the first to point out the connection between cannibalism on the one hand and anxiety and guilt on the other.

35. Melanie Klein, *op. cit.,* p. 282. See also R. E. Money-Kyrle, *Psychoanalysis and Politics* (New York, n.d.).

36. But cf. Franz Alexander, *Psychoanalysis of the Total Personality,* concerning the two main types of pathogenic educational methods: the excessively soft and indulgent and the excessively severe, loveless. Cf. Freud, *Civilization and its Discontents,* pp. 115, 117.

37. There is agreement on this point. Cf. Freud, *The Problem of Anxiety,* Chapters IX and XI, B.; Melanie Klein, *op. cit.,* p. 279, and many others.

38. This is evidently what Freud has in mind in *The Ego and the Id,* pp. 71-72; and Melanie Klein, *op. cit.,* p. 279.

39. However, this is not completely correct, as Freud has pointed out: *Group Psychology and the Analysis of the Ego* (London, 1922) p. 1. After all, individual psychology can never do without relations to others (or at least one other person). The only exception is narcissism. But it does seem useful to retain the prevalent distinction of individual and social (or group) psychology.

40. A useful compilation is in Paul Reiwald, *Vom Geist der Massen. Handbuch der Massenpsychologie* (Zurich, 1946).

41. The most important book: *La Foule Criminelle* (2d ed.; Paris, 1898). Cf. Walter Moede, "Die Massen und Sozialpsychologie im kritischen Ueberblick," in *Zeitschrift für paedogogische Psychologie und experimentelle Paedogogik,* 1915, Vol. XVI.

42. Gustave Le Bon, *The Crowd* (London, 1896). A concrete application of his theory is in *La Révolution Française et la Psychologie des Révolutions* (Paris, 1912).

43. *The Crowd,* p. 36. However, Le Bon admits (*ibid.,* p. 37) that the masses can have a moralizing effect on the individual.

44. *Group Psychology and the Analysis of the Ego.*

45. Against this also Walter Lippmann, *Public Opinion* (New York, 1922), p. 197.

46. Thus Freud, *op. cit.,* pp. 21-22.

47. This also holds true for William MacDougall, *The Group Mind* (Cambridge, 1920) and for his theory of "primary induction of affects," for this too is at bottom nothing but imitation or suggestion. The positive element in MacDougall's theory will be worked out later.

48. *Group Psychology and the Analysis of the Ego*, p. 38.

49. *Ibid.*, p. 120.

50. *Ibid.*, p. 91.

51. *Ibid.*, p. 65.

52. Ranyard West, *Conscience and Society. A Study of the Psychological Prerequisites of Law and Order* (New York, 1945) p. 227.

53. In the postscript (XII) to *Group Psychology and the Analysis of the Ego*, Freud formulates it a little differently. In the relation soldier-superior he assumes ego-idealization, in the relation of comrade to comrade he assumes ego-identification. The former may or may not be true. It may well be that the soldier does not identify himself in any way with the army or with his superior, or he may undertake ego-idealization with the superior or identify himself rationally with the army as such. The "ego-community" (co-operative identification, as I have called it) is in my opinion correctly described.

As far as the identification with a church is concerned, one must again make distinctions. Frequently, especially in Latin countries, the identification is strongly rationalist; in Germanic countries, above all under the influence of Catholic Romanticism, it is strongly libidinal. General statements may, perhaps, be made, but this does not seem to me possible at this time.

54. In political theory, Rousseau's *volonté générale* would correspond to this.

55. Therefore R. Osborn's thesis is completely mistaken. In his attempt to integrate Marxism and Psychoanalysis (*Freud and Marx* [London, 1937]), he demands that leadership be crystallized in the form of a leader, and that we must idealize some individual for the masses on whom they can lean, whom they can love and obey.

56. I use here, in place of many sources, Paul Piur, *Cola di Rienzo* (Vienna, 1931); Mario Emilio Cosenzo, *Francesco Petrarca and the Revolution of Cola di Rienzo* (Chicago, 1913); Max Horkheimer, "Egoismus und Freiheitsbewegung," in *Zeitschrift für Sozialforschung*, V (1936), pp. 161-231, is the most important analysis.

My essay on *The Theory of Dictatorship*, which is now in preparation, contains a detailed discussion; also an analysis of other caesarist movements.

There were many such movements at the end of the Middle Ages. An excellent survey is contained in G. Franz, *Die agrarischen Unruhen des ausgehenden Mittelalters* (Marburg, 1930).

57. Var. XVVIII, Hortatoria, cited after Cosenzo, *op. cit.*, pp. 16-44.

58. Freud, *Group Psychology and the Analysis of the Ego*, p. 89.

59. *Le Tigre de 1560*. Facsimile edition by Charles Read (Paris, 1875).

60. *Institutio Christianae Religionis*, IV, cap. XX, 30 and summarized in the last of the 100 aphorisms.

61. In addition to the well-known theory of resistance of Calvin, which is developed by Hotman in his *Francogallia* and Junis Brutus in his *Vindiciae*.

62. The most important ones for France are those of the Parisian preacher Jean Boucher: *De Justa Henrici Tertii Abdicatione*, etc. (Paris, 1589), and *Sermons de la simulée conversion et nullité de la prétendue absolution de Henry de Bourbon* (Paris, 1594).

The pseudo-democratic character of these and similar Leaguist theories is discussed by M. Ch. Labitte, *De la démocratie chez les prédicateurs de la Ligue* (Paris, 1841); on Boucher, pp. 193 seq.

63. In his *La response de Jean Bodin à M. de Malestroit* (1568). New edition by Henri Hauser (Paris, 1932) in the series: "La vie chère au XVIème siècle."

64. Cf. his *Das Heptaplomeres des Jean Bodin* (tr. by Guhrauer, Berlin, 1841).

65. *Les six livres de la République*, Book I, Chapters II and IV; Book VI, Chapter IV.

66. *Op. cit.*, Book I, Chapter 1.

67. Edited by E. Arbor (Westminster, 1895), pp. 3-4.

68. In the Appendix of the Arbor edition.

69. The literature is immense. Bernhard Duhr, S. J., *Hundert Jesuitenfabeln* (Freiburg i. B.) compiles the "fables"—but proves too much. *The Secret Policy of the English Society of Jesus* (London, 1715) is a good English example; Kaspar Schoppe,

Arcana Societatis Iesu publico bono vulgata cum appendicibus utillissimus (Geneva (?), 1635), a German one; *A Startling Disclosure of the Secret Workings of the Jesuits,* by a former French Roman Catholic, published by the author 1854, a French one. Rene Fueloep-Miller, *Macht und Geheimnis der Jesuiten* (Leipzig, 1929) is the best-known German general survey.

70. On this cf. G. Monod in Academie des Sciences, Morales et Politiques, *Séances et travaux,* Vol. 1910, pp. 211-29.

71. Gaston Martin, *La Franco-maçonnerie française et la préparation de la révolution* (Paris, 1926, 2d ed.).

L. R. Gottschalk, "French Revolution—Conspiracy or Circumstance," in *Persecution and Liberty, Essays in Honor of G. L. Burr* (New York, 1921), pp. 445-72.

72. Details in Eugen Lennhoff, *Politische Geheimbünde* (Zurich, 1931) pp. 17 ff.

73. Friedrich Wichtel's well-known book, *Weltfreimaurerei, Weltrevolution, Weltrepublik* (1919) traces all distress after 1917-18 back to the freemasons. Cf. Eugen Lennhoff, *Die Freimaurer* (Zurich, 1929), p. 412.

74. Curzio Malaparte, *Die Technik des Staatsstreichs* (Berlin, 1932) is the best-known example.

75. On this point cf. the cautious analysis by Donald Greer, *The Incidence of the Terror during the French Revolution* (Cambridge, U.S., 1935).

76. The following editions: German: Z. Gottfried Beck (Pseud. Ludwig Mueller von Hausen), "Die Geheimnisse der Weisen von Zion," (Charlottenburg, 1919). This edition was acquired by the NSDAP in 1929. French: Mgr. E. Jouin, *Le péril judéo-maçonnique,* Vol. IV (Paris, 1920). English: V. E. Marsden (trans.), *The Protocols of the Learned Elders of Zion* (London, 1921).

American: *The Protocols and World Revolution* (Boston, 1920) and many others. The excellent book by John S. Curtiss, *An Appraisal of the Protocols of Zion* (New York, 1942) contains the best account of the history of this famous forgery. The work of Curtiss was written under the auspices of thirteen of the most notable American historians.

77. Cf. E. Raas and F. Brunschvig, *Vernichtung einer Fälschung: der Prozess um die erfundenen Weisen von Zion* (Zurich, 1938).

78. First ed., 1864. New ed. (Paris, 1948).

79. The reasons which made National Socialism adopt the *Protocols* are detailed by Hitler himself. *Mein Kampf,* pp. 423 ff.

80. In my *Behemoth: The Structure and Practice of National Socialism* (New York, 1942; 2d ed., 1944), p. 121.

81. Cf. Jacques Maritain, *Anti-Semitism* (London, 1939), p. 27.

82. For details cf. my book, *op. cit.,* pp. 120-29, and the appendix to this chapter in the second edition (New York, 1944).

83. The connection between anxiety and anti-Semitism has been empirically verified by Bruno Bettelheim and Morris Janowitz, *Dynamics of Prejudice. A Psychological and Sociological Study of Veterans* (New York, 1950), Chapter VI.

84. Carl Schmitt saw this correctly, *Der Begriff des Politischen,* but made a general theory of it instead of limiting it to regressive mass movements.

85. This point is also illuminated by the Bettelheim-Janowitz study.

86. Harold D. Lasswell, "The Psychology of Hitlerism," in *The Political Quarterly* (1933), pp. 373-84; also in *The Analysis of Political Behavior* (New York, 1949), pp. 235-45. Quotation on p. 236.

87. In my essay, "The Theory of Dictatorship."

88. Cf. my essay, "Social Structure and National Socialism" (unpublished).

89. *The Neurotic Personality of Our Time* (New York, 1937), Chapters XI and XII.

90. *Theory of Moral Sentiments* (2 vols., 1790) Vol. I, Part III, Chapter III, p. 339.

91. *Ibid.,* Vol. I, Part II, Sect. II, Chapter II, p. 206; on the juristic problem, see Franz Boehm, *Wettberwerb und Monopolkampf* (Berlin, 1933).

92. Erich Fromm who, in *Man for Himself* (New York, 1947), pp. 67-81, regards the market operation (i.e., exchange) as depersonalizing and empty, and claims that it leads to rising discontent, seems to overlook this. Fromm's more correct thesis (in *Escape from Freedom,* New York, 1941) that the loss of the ego results from the discrepancy between the ideology of free competition and the actual monopolization of power can also not be fully accepted. Against this, correctly: Theodor

W. Adorno, "Zum Verhältnis von Psychoanalyse und Gesellschaftstheorie," in *Psyche,* VI, 1952-53, p. 10.

93. In a study now in the process of completion, on "Concept of Virtue in Politics," I attempt to bring this proof. (This study was not completed—ed.)

94. To this claim corresponds in the social sphere the petty bourgeois socialism, say of a Proudhon, to whom the distress of society seems to stem from exchange, not from the process of production.

95. Now in France, too: Charles Henri Sévène, *L'abstentionisme politique en France* (Paris, n.d., 1953?).

96. On this cf. my introduction to Montesquieu, *The Spirit of the Laws* (New York, 1949).

97. One has to be clear about the fact that a totally repressive system is held together not by neurotic anxiety alone—it depends on keeping this anxiety alive in significant groups—but that material advantages and prestige are equally important.

98. Book IV, Chapter LXXX (tr. Crawley, New York, 1934).

99. Modern research, synthesized by H. Michell, *Sparta* (Cambridge, England, 1952), pp. 162-66, accepts the reports of Thucydides and Plutarch.

100. *Lycurgus* (tr. Dryden, revised by A. H. Clough).

101. Preston H. Epps, "Fear in Spartan Character," in *Classical Philology*, January 1933, pp. 12-30, proves, successfully in my view, that anxiety was the constitutive element of the Spartan character. Cf. Plutarch, *Cleomenes,* 9, and *Lysander*, 30.5; Herodotus, VI, 79-80.

102. Part II, Chapter VI, p. 393 (tr. Constance Garnett, New York, 1936).

103. *Civilization and its Discontents*, p. 118.

104. *The Ego and the Id*, p. 77.

105. In Kierkegaard (*op. cit.*, pp. 65, 67), we find the following formulations—naturally from different theoretical presuppositions:

1. The individual produces sin in his dread of sin.
2. The individual in dread (not of becoming guilty but) of being thought guilty becomes guilty.

106. The significance of the superego for Freud's theory is not quite clear to me. If it means the "social conscience," that is, the sum of moral convictions that prevail in a society, one gets into difficulties when antagonistic convictions confront each other. But if it is the individual, unconscious feeling of guilt, then social norms could play no part.

In our example it is indifferent which interpretation of the superego should be accepted. According to the former: the prevalent moral convictions of Germany, even under National Socialism, proscribed murder. The orders of superiors to gas Jews because that would be useful to Germany collided with the prevailing morality. This is shown by the fact that these murders had to be committed in secret.

According to the latter interpretation: since the SS murderers had their childhood experiences under the old morality, they must have had at least an unconscious feeling of guilt.

107. In his article "The Covenant of the Gangsters" in *The Journal of Criminal Psychopathology*, Vol. IV, No. 3 (1943), pp. 445-58, Ernst Kris develops a similar thesis which he, however, does not limit to the immediate participants in the crime but extends to the whole German people. That the National Socialists made the attempt to make the whole people into accomplices is, of course, beyond doubt. It can hardly be claimed that they succeeded.

108. Ed. Weiss, p. 29.

109. *Ibid.*, p. 35.

110. Freud, *Civilization and its Discontents*, p. 38.

The Politics of Decivilization

E. V. WALTER

1. Paul Valéry, "Le crise de l'esprit," *The Athenaeum* (London, 1919), p. 182-84.

2. The most cogent sociological analysis is the now classic work by Karl Mannheim, *Diagnosis of Our Time* (London: Kegan Paul, Trench, Trubner, 1943).

3. "A Discourse on Political Economy," *The Social Contract and Discourses,* trans. G. D. H. Cole ("Everyman's Library"; New York: Dutton, 1950), p. 295.

4. *Studies in History and Jurisprudence* (New York: Oxford, 1901), p. 471.

5. Charles E. Merriam, *Political Power* (Glencoe, Ill.: The Free Press, 1950), p. 21.

6. *Ibid.*

7. *The Sociology of Georg Simmel,* trans. Kurt Wolff (Glencoe, Ill.: The Free Press, 1950), p. 192.

8. In a comprehensive work that is little known today, a conservative writer of last century claimed that all political forms may be derived from the collective patterns in which minorities manage to satisfy mass needs. See Karl Ludwig von Haller, *Restauration der Staats-Wissenschaft,* 6 Bde (2te Aufl.; Winterthur: Steinerischen Buchhandlung, 1820-34). Haller's perspective is important, but he was reluctant to recognize the other side—that political superiors also *need* the services of their subordinates.

9. R. A. Dahl and C. E. Lindblom, *Politics, Economics and Welfare* (New York: Harper, 1953), p. 113-14.

10. Edmund Bergler, *The Superego: Unconscious Conscience* (New York: Grune and Stratton, 1952), p. vii; italics in the original.

11. Harold D. Lasswell, "Impact of Psychoanalytic Thinking on the Social Sciences," in L. D. White (ed.), *The State of the Social Sciences* (Chicago: University of Chicago Press, 1956), p. 89.

12. Cf. Marie Coleman, "Integrative Approach to Individual and Group Psychology," *Psychoanalytic Review,* XXXVI (1949), 389-402.

13. Sigmund Freud, *Totem and Taboo* (first published in 1913), trans. A. A. Brill, in *The Basic Writings of Sigmund Freud* (New York: The Modern Library, 1938); *Group Psychology and the Analysis of the Ego,* trans. James Strachey (London: Hogarth, 1949).

14. Ernest Jones, "The Genesis of the Superego," *Papers on Psychoanalysis* (5th ed.; London: Buillière, Tindall and Cox, 1948), pp. 145-52.

15. Freud, *An Outline of Psychoanalysis,* trans. James Strachey (New York: Norton, 1949), p. 19.

16. Freud, *Totem and Taboo; The Future of an Illusion,* trans. W. D. Robson-Scott (New York: Doubleday, 1957); *Civilization and its Discontents,* trans. Joan Riviere (London: Hogarth, 1930); *Moses and Monotheism,* trans. Katherine Jones (New York: Knopf, 1939).

17. *An Outline of Psychoanalysis,* pp. 123, 124.

18. Cf. Wulf Sachs, *Black Anger* (Boston: Little, Brown, 1947).

19. Cf. Freud, *The Problem of Lay-Analyses,* trans. A. P. Maerker-Branden (New York: Brentano, 1927), p. 125.

20. *Totem and Taboo,* pp. 919, 922.

21. Cf. Edmund Bergler, *The Battle of the Conscience* (Washington, D.C.: Washington Institute of Medicine, 1948); *The Superego: Unconscious Conscience.*

22. *A Grammar of Politics* (5th ed.; London: Allen and Unwin, 1948), p. 290.

23. Franz Neumann, "Anxiety and Politics," in Herbert Marcuse (ed.), *The Democratic and the Authoritarian State* (Glencoe, Illinois: The Free Press, 1957), pp. 278 ff.; reprinted in this volume.

24. Walter Bagehot, "Caesarism after Thirteen Years," *The Economist* (London), 1865, in Forrest Morgan (ed.), *The Works of Walter Bagehot* (Hartford, Connecticut: Traveler's Insurance Company, 1891), II, 440 ff. Neumann, "Anxiety and Politics," *loc. cit.; Behemoth: The Structure and Practice of National Socialism* (New York: Oxford, 1942), pp. 465-67.

25. *Group Psychology and the Analysis of the Ego.* The original German title uses the word *Massenpsychologie,* and perhaps "mass psychology" would be a more appropriate translation.

26. *Ibid.,* p. 80. Freud later substituted the term "superego" for "ego ideal." Today, in the vocabulary of psychoanalysis, "ego ideal" refers to only a part of the superego.

27. Cf. Heinz Hartmann, "On Rational and Irrational Action," *Psychoanalysis and the Social Sciences* (New York: International Universities Press), Vol. 1 (1947), pp. 359-92.

28. *Group Psychology and the Analysis of the Ego,* pp. 102, 77.

29. Paul Federn, *Zur Psychologie der Revolution: Die Vaterlose Gesellschaft* (Wien: Anzengruber-Verlag Brüder Suschitzky, 1919), expanded from an article in *Der Österreichische Volkswirt,* 1919.

30. H. A. R. Gibb, "The Structure of Religious Thought in Islam," *The Muslim World,* XXXVIII (1948), 27.

31. "Anxiety and Politics," *loc. cit.*

32. Altheim contends that in Rome the nobles purged *superstitio* from *religio,* but that the other classes did not. See Franz Altheim, *A History of Roman Religion,* trans. Harold Mattingly (London: Methuen, 1938), p. 333 ff.

33. Cf. Benjamin Farrington, *Head and Hand in Ancient Greece* (London: Watts, 1947). The classical view of religion as a form of thought control has been restated often. In Elizabethan times, Richard Hooker observed that laws "have no farther power than over our outward actions only, whereas unto men's inward cogitations, unto the privy intents and motions of their hearts, religion serveth for a bridle." *Laws of Ecclesiastical Polity,* V, ii, 3.

34. Polybius vi. 56. Cf. F. W. Walbank, *A Historical Commentary on Polybius* (London: Oxford University Press, 1957), Vol. I, p. 741.

35. Cicero *De Div.; De Leg.* ii.

36. "The Treatise on the Laws," in *The Political Works of Marcus Tullius Cicero,* Vol. II, trans. Francis Barham (London: Spettigue, 1842), p. 111.

37. *De Leg.* ii, 14; trans. Francis Barham, in C. D. Yonge (ed.), *The Treatises of Cicero* (London: Bell, 1887), pp. 444-45.

28. Livy i, 19.

39. *Ibid.*; trans. D. Spillan (New York: Harper, 1896), Vol. I, p. 39.

40. *Ibid.*, trans. W. M. Roberts ("Everyman's Library"; London: Dent, 1926), Vol. I, p. 23.

41. *Religion and the Rise of Western Culture* (New York: Sheed and Ward, 1950), p. 274.

42. Karl Barth, *The Church and the Political Problem of Our Day* (New York: Scribner, 1939), p. 31.

43. *Ibid.*, pp. 37, 41; italics in the original.

44. Robert Waelder, "Authoritarianism and Totalitarianism: Psychological Comments on a Problem of Power," *Psychoanalysis and Culture* (New York: International Universities Press, 1951), p. 185.

45. H. J. Laski, *op. cit.*, p. 259.

46. Bruno Bettelheim, "Individual and Mass Behavior in Extreme Situations," *Journal of Abnormal Psychology,* XXXVIII (1943), 417-52.

47. Likewise, Jones discusses cases of individuals who insisted that since Hitler was irresistible, he must also be right. Ernest Jones, "The Psychology of Quislingism," *Essays in Applied Psychoanalysis,* Vol. 1 (London: Hogarth, 1951), p. 280.

48. See Joseph Scholmer, *Vorkuta,* trans. Robert Kee (New York: Holt, 1955).

49. Robert Waelder, *op. cit.*, p. 195.

50. Harold D. Lasswell, "The Triple-Appeal Principle," *American Journal of Sociology,* XXXVII (1932), 537.

51. Otto Fenichel, *The Psychoanalytic Theory of Neurosis* (New York: Norton, 1945), p. 294; cf. Freud, *Group Psychology and the Analysis of the Ego*; Franz Alexander and Hugo Staub, *The Criminal, the Judge, and the Public* (London: Allen and Unwin, 1931).

52. "The Triple-Appeal Principle," *loc. cit.*, 537-38.

53. Karl Kautsky, *Terrorismus und Kommunismus; ein Beitrag zur Naturgeschichte der Revolution* (Berlin: Verlag Neves Vaterland, 1919).

54. *Civilization and its Discontents,* p. 20; "Thoughts for the Times on War and Death," *Collected Papers,* Vol. IV (London: Hogarth, 1953), p. 301.

55. William Stubbs, *The Constitutional History of England,* Vol. II (2nd ed.; London: Macmillan, 1878), p. 626.

56. Bryce, *op. cit.*, p. 498.

57. Albert Camus, *The Rebel,* trans. Anthony Bower (New York: Knopf, 1956), p. 305.

What Teaching Does to Teachers

WILLARD WALLER

1. Cf. Durkheim, Emile, *Elementary Forms of Religious Life.*

2. Strengthened by repetition, we should say, under circumstances which do not

admit of challenge. The preacher and the teacher are infallible because it is not permitted to argue with them.

3. Wm. H. Burnham, *Great Teachers and Mental Health* (New York: D. Appleton & Company, 1926), p. 211.

The Freedom to Be Academic

PAUL GOODMAN

1. Robert M. MacIver, *Academic Freedom in Our Times* (New York: Columbia University Press, 1955). Pp. 304.

Richard Hofstadter and Walter P. Metzger, *The Development of Academic Freedom in the United States* (New York: Columbia University Press, 1955). Pp. 506.

2. One major, and surprising, defect in these books is their omission of any discussion of the small radical colleges like Antioch, Black Mountain, Goddard, etc., founded on more liberal principles than the authors', and therefore with both a more intransigeant standard of freedom and more embarrassment in being consistent. I should have thought their careers would be valuably relevant for comparison and contrast.

3. But consider the dilemma: Such massive research and experiment must be financed, if not administered, by Foundations; and those chosen by or for Foundations tend to be at least "sound" if not "safe."

4. So Black Mt. College was founded by a migration in the early 1930's, and the migrant faculty was thenceforth the owner of the college, without a governing board of trustees.

5. This "neutrality" certainly has also a simpler and more traditional spring: the detachment of the wise and experienced, and the tradition of the academy as the home of the wise and experienced, with the motto *nil admirari*. Such an attitude is, of course, not neutral at all, but the provision of a background of security predifferent to controversial opinions, and relying on which, youth can risk having definite opinions.

6. Teaching at the primary level is different, for there the emphasis is on teaching the pupil, not the subject-matter; and there is then a profession of pedagogy analogous to medicine, and of which the remedial branch is psychotherapy.

Decisions for Christ: Billy Graham in New York City

KURT and GLADYS E. LANG

1. The authors of this paper directed 43 mass-observers, volunteers from among students enrolled in sociology courses in the Summer session of Queens College. Systematic reports, covering objective observations and subjective experiences, were handed in on 46 meetings—several observers attending more than once. Content analysis of three Graham sermons was used to supplement these data. Also, two group discussions with "converts" among the observers were recorded.

This paper draws primarily on systematic interpretation of nine reports of the same evening, the night of July 9. By collating observations in these nine reports, it was possible to get a check on the reliability of reports and to develop interpretations concerning the significance of the Crusade.

2. Of 109 organized groups present on July 9, 39 per cent came from within city limits, 55 per cent within commuting distance, and some 6 per cent from farther away, some as far as Delaware and North Carolina. Observer spot checks "upstairs" obtained the following over-all counts: New York City limits 80 per cent; commuting areas 17 per cent; and only 3 per cent were out-of-town visitors beyond the normal commuting zone.

3. In view of the importance of this

point and the claims that a high proportion among the inquirers were without prior church affiliation, it seems worthwhile to point out that there is some support for our observation. For example, the correspondent of the Christian Century in his queries of 40 people at the Garden discovered only two who were not church members. It is of course recognized that in such spot checks the figure on church membership may be somewhat exaggerated.

4. W. G. McLoughlin, Jr., *Billy Sunday Was His Real Name* (Chicago: The University of Chicago Press, 1955), Chapter VI. His description of the Sunday campaign bears some striking parallels to our own observations summarized above.

5. They made up roughly 3 per cent of the audience.

6. This is confirmed by the content analysis of these sermons.

7. A twenty-three-year-old, part-time graduate student.

8. The Graham organization has never seen fit to release figures on the characteristics of inquirers, and efforts to obtain any kind of breakdowns directly from them were rebuffed. Surveys by the Protestant Council of the City of New York during the Crusade indicated that about 40 per cent were not church members. But a *New York Times* survey of ministers in the city four months after the meetings left the impression that most churches gained very few new members. In a similar survey taken in London after a very dramatic campaign, less than 15 per cent of the inquirers referred to a church (i.e., who had not been churchgoers but were still attending) could be counted as a gain to the churches eight months after. A long-term statistical study of church membership in New England by S. W. Dike (cf. *American Journal of Sociology*, XV [1909], 361-68) reported increases in church membership immediately following the revival but a subsequent falling off to balance the increase.

Characteristics of Total Institutions

ERVING GOFFMAN

1. The category of total institutions has been pointed out from time to time in the sociological literature under a variety of names, and some of the characteristics of the class have been suggested, most notably perhaps in Howard Roland's neglected paper, "Segregated Communities and Mental Health," in F. R. Moulton (ed.), *Mental Health Publication of the American Association for the Advancement of Science*, No. 9 (1939). A preliminary statement of the present paper is reported in Bertram Schaffner (ed.), *Third Group Processes Proceedings* (Josiah Macy Foundation, 1957).

2. The binary character of total institutions was pointed out to me by Gregory Bateson, and proves to be noted in the literature. See, for example, Lloyd E. Ohlin, *Sociology and the Feld of Corrections* (New York: Russell Sage Foundation, 1956), pp. 14, 20. In those special situations where staff too is required to live in, we may expect staff members to feel they are suffering from special hardships and to have brought home to them a status-dependency on life on the inside which they did not expect. See, Jane Cassels Record, "The Marine Radioman's Struggle for Status," *American Journal of Sociology*, LXII (1957), 359.

3. For the prison version, see, S. Kirson Weinburg, "Aspects of the Prison's Social Structure," *American Journal of Sociology*, XLVII (1942), 717-26.

4. An illustration may be found in Mary Jane Ward's fictionalized record of her sojourn in a mental hospital. *The Snake Pit* (New York: Signet Books, 1955), p. 72.

> "I tell you what," said Miss Hart when they were crossing the dayroom. "You do everything Miss Davis says. Don't think about it, just do it. You'll get along all right."
>
> As soon as she heard the name, Virginia knew what was terrible about Ward One. Miss Davis. "Is she head nurse?"

"And how," muttered Miss Hart. And then she raised her voice. The nurses had a way of acting as if the patients were unable to hear anything that was not shouted. Frequently they said things in normal voices that the ladies were not supposed to hear; if they had not been nurses, you would have said they frequently talked to themselves. "A most competent and efficient person, Miss Davis," announced Miss Hart.

5. Suggested in Ohlin, *op. cit.*, p. 20.

6. An interesting reflection of the no-payment world of total institutions is found in the culture of State mental hospitals in the practice of "bumming" or "working someone for" a nickel or dime to spend in the canteen. This practice is indulged in, often with some defiance, by persons who would consider such actions beneath their self-respect were they on the outside. Staff persons, interpreting this begging pattern in terms of their own outsider's orientation to earning, tend to see it as a symptom of psychological sickness and one further bit of evidence that inmates really are unwell persons.

7. An interesting marginal case here is the Israeli kibbutz. See, Melford E. Spiro, *Kibbutz: Venture in Utopia* (Cambridge: Harvard University Press, 1956).

8. There is reason then to exclude orphanages and foundling homes from the list of total institutions, except insofar as the orphan comes to be socialized into the outside world by some process of cultural osmosis, even while this world is being systematically denied him.

9. This is certainly not a new practice, and can be clearly illustrated from such documents as Saint Benedict's Holy Rule (Chapter LVIII):

Then forthwith he shall, there in the oratory, be divested of his own garments with which he is clothed and be clad in those of the monastery. Those garments of which he is divested shall be placed in the wardrobe, there to be kept, so that if, perchance, he should ever be persuaded by the devil to leave the monastery (which God forbid), he may be stripped of the monastic habit and cast forth.

10. A further statement of these mortifications is given in Schaffner, *op. cit.*, and they are considered in detail in a forthcoming paper, "The Moral Career of Mental Patients."

11. Wider communities in Western society, of course, have employed this technique too, in the form of public floggings and public hangings, the pillory and stocks. Functionally correlated with the public emphasis on mortifications in total institutions is the commonly found strict ruling that staff is not to be humiliated by staff in the presence of inmates.

12. The span of time over which an employee works at his own discretion without supervision can in fact be taken as a measure of his pay and status in an organization. See, Elliot Jacques, *The Measurement of Responsibility: A Study of Work, Payment, and Individual Capacity* (Cambridge: Harvard University Press, 1956). And just as "time-span of responsibility" is an index of position, so a long span of freedom from inspection is a reward of position.

13. Staff sometimes encourages this tendency for inmates to stand clear of one another, perhaps in order to limit the dangers of organized inmate resistance to institutional rule. Through an interesting phrase, inmates may be officially encouraged to "do their own time."

14. For the version of this process in concentration camps, see, Elie A. Cohen, *Human Behaviour in the Concentration Camp*, Jonathan Cape, n. p., 1954, p. 120. For a fictionalized treatment of the welcome in a girls' reformatory, see, Sara Norris, *The Wayward Ones* (New York: Signet Pocket Books, 1952), pp. 31-34.

15. Melville's report of life on a man-of-war in the mid-nineteenth century (*White Jacket* [New York: Grove Press, n. d.], pp. 62-63, 140) contains a typical illustration:

In the American Navy the law allows one gill of spirits per day to every seaman. In two portions, it is served out just previous to breakfast and dinner. At the roll of the drum, the sailors assemble around a large tub, or cask, filled with the liquid; and, as their names are called off by a midshipman, they step up and regale themselves from a little tin measure called a "tot." No high-liver helping himself to Tokay off a well-polished sideboard smacks his lips with more mighty satisfaction than the sailor does over his tot. To many of them, indeed, the thought of their daily tot forms a perpetual perspective of ravishing landscapes, indefinitely receding in the distance. It is their greatest "prospect in life." Take away their grog, and life possesses no further charms for them.

* * *

It is one of the most common punishments for very trivial offenses in the Navy, to "stop" a seaman's grog for a day or a week. And as most seamen so cling to their grog, the loss of it is generally deemed by them a very serious penalty. You will sometimes hear them say, "I would rather have my wind *stopped* than my grog!"

For examples of the same process in POW camps, see Edgar H. Schein, "The Chinese Indoctrination Program for Prisoners of War," *Psychiatry*, XIX (1956), 160-61.

16. See S. F. Nadel, "Social Control and Self-Regulation," *Social Forces*, XXXI (1953), 265-73.

17. Ivan Belknap, *Human Problems of a State Mental Hospital* (New York: McGraw-Hill, 1956), p. 164.

18. For example, see, Morris G. Caldwell, "Group Dynamics in the Prison Community," *Journal of Criminal Law, Criminology and Police Science*, XLVI (1956), p. 656.

19. There are some interesting incidental social functions of messings up. First, they tend to limit rigidities which might occur were seniority the only means of mobility in the privilege system. Secondly, demotion through messing up brings old-time inmates in contact with new inmates in unprivileged positions, assuring a flow of information about the system and the people in it.

20. See, for example, Norma S. Hayner and Ellis Ash, "The Prisoner Community as a Social Group," *American Sociological Review*, IV (1939), 364 ff., under "Conniving Processes"; also, Caldwell, *op. cit.*, pp. 650-51.

21. See, for example, Melville's extended description of the fight his fellow seamen put up to prevent the clipping of their beards in full accordance with Navy regulations. Melville, *op. cit.*, pp. 333-47.

22. See, for example, Donald Clemmer, "Leadership Phenomenon in a Prison Community," *Journal of Criminal Law, Criminology and Police Science*, XXVIII (1938), 868.

23. See, for example, Ida Ann Harper, "The Role of the 'Fringer' in a State Prison for Women," *Social Forces*, XXXI (1952), 53-60.

24. For concentration camps, see the discussion of "Prominents" throughout Cohen, *op. cit.*; for mental hospitals, see Belknap, *op. cit.*, p. 189. For prisons, see the discussion of "Politicos" in Donald Clemmer, *The Prison Community* (Boston: Christopher Publishing House, 1940), pp. 277-79, 298-309; also Hayner, *op. cit.*, p. 367; and Caldwell, *op. cit.*, pp. 651-53.

25. For the version of this inmate solidarity to be found in military academies, see, Sanford M. Dornbush, "The Military Academy as an Assimilating Institution," *Social Forces*, XXXIII (1955), 318.

26. An interesting example of this re-evaluation may be found in a conscientious objector's experience with nonpolitical prisoners, see Alfred Hassler, *Diary of a Self-Made Convict* (Chicago: Henry Regnery, 1954), pp. 74, 117. In mental hospitals, of course, the patient's antagonism to staff obtains one of its supports from the discovery that, like himself, many other patients are more like ordinary persons than like anything else.

27. Richard McCleery, "The Strange Journey," *University of North Carolina Extension Bulletin*, XXXII (1953), 24. Italics are McCleery's.

28. Lloyd W. McCorkle and Richard Korn, "Resocialization Within Walls," *The Annals*, May 1954, p. 88. See also p. 95.

29. See, for example, the discussion of "The Resisters," in Schein, *op. cit.*, pp. 166-67.

30. See, for example, Belknap, *op. cit.*, p. 192.

31. In the case of mental hospitals, those who take this line are sometimes called "institutional cures" or are said to suffer from "hospitalitis."

32. Schein, *op. cit.*, pp. 167-69.

33. See Bruno Bettelheim, "Individual and Mass Behavior in Extreme Situations," *Journal of Abnormal and Social Psychology*, XXXVIII (1943), 447-51. It should be added that in concentration camps, colonization and conversion often seemed to go together. See, Cohen, *op. cit.*, pp. 200-3, where the role of the "Kapo" is discussed.

34. See the discussion in Schein, *op. cit.*, pp. 165-66 of the "Get-Alongers," and Robert J. Lifton, "Home by Ship: Reaction Patterns of American Prisoners of War Repatriated From North Korea," *American Journal of Psychiatry*, CX (1954), 734.

35. This two-facedness, of course, is very commonly found in total institutions. In the state-type mental hospital studied by the writer, even the few elite patients selected for individual psychotherapy, and hence in the best position for espousal of the psychiatric approach to self, tended to present their favorable view of psychotherapy only to the members of their intimate cliques. For a report on the way in which Army prisoners concealed from fellow offenders their interests in "restoration" to the Army, see the comments by Richard Cloward in Session 4 of *New Perspectives for Research on Juvenile Delinquency*, ed. by Helen L. Witmer and Ruth Kotinsky, U. S. Department of Health, Education and Welfare, Children's Bureau Bulletin, 1955, especially p. 90.

36. Bettelheim, *op. cit.*, p. 425.

37. Thus, Schein, *op. cit.*, p. 165 fn., suggests that Puerto Ricans and other non-English-speaking prisoners of war in China were given up on and allowed to work out a viable routine of menial chores.

38. Much material on the conception of time in total institutions may be found in Maurice L. Farber, "Suffering the Time Perspective of the Prisoner," part IV, pp. 155-227 of *Authority and Frustration*, by Kurt Lewin *et al.*, Studies in Topological and Vector Psychology III, University of Iowa Studies in Child Welfare, Vol. 20, 1944.

39. The best description that I know of this feeling of not-living is Freud's paper, "Mourning and Melancholia," where the state is said to come about as a consequence of losing a loved object. See, *Collected Papers of Sigmund Freud*, Vol. IV (London: Hogarth Press, 1953), pp. 152-70.

40. Thus, one of the virtues of the doctrine that insane asylums are treatment hospitals for sick people is that inmates who have given up 3 or 4 years of their life to this kind of exile can try to convince themselves that they have been busily working on their cure, and that once cured the time spent getting cured will have been a reasonable and profitable investment.

41. See, for example, Hassler, *op. cit.*, p. 116: "Even more impressive is the almost universal delicacy when it comes to inquiring into another man's misdeeds, and the refusal to determine one's relations with another convict on the basis of his record." Similarly, in our State mental hospitals inmate etiquette allows one patient to ask another what ward and service he is on and how long he has been in the hospital, but questions about why one is "in" are not quickly asked and are rarely answered openly.

42. Such activity is, of course, not restricted to total institutions. Thus, we find the classic case of the bored and weary housewife who "takes a few minutes for herself" to "put her feet up" and removes herself from home by reading the morning paper over a cup of coffee and a cigarette.

43. Interestingly enough, staff is expected to be properly self-regulating upon first coming to the total institution, sharing with members of other kinds of establishments the ideal of needing merely to learn procedure.

44. The strongest evidence for this, perhaps, comes from our knowledge of the readjustment of repatriated brain-washed prisoners of war. See, for example, Lawrence E. Hinkle, Jr., and Harold G. Wolff, "Communist Interrogation and Indoctrination of 'Enemies of the State,'" *Archives of Neurology and Psychiatry*, LXXVI (1956), 174.

45. As Cloward, *op. cit.*, pp. 80-83, implies, one important kind of leverage staff has in regard to inmates and one factor leading inmates to act convertible in presence of staff is that staff can give the kind of discharge that may appear to reduce stigmatization. Prison barracks officials can hold up the possibility of the inmate's "restoration" to active duty and, potentially, an honorable discharge; mental hospital administrators can hold up the possibility of a "clean bill of health" (discharged as cured) and personal recommendations.

46. Cloward, *op. cit.*, p. 82.

47. Thus, some attendants in mental hospitals prefer to work on regressed wards because patients there tend to make fewer

time-consuming requests than do patients on better wards who are in good contact.

48. The visiting rooms in some total institutions represent a nice attempt to resolve this problem. Decor and conduct in these places are typically much closer to outside standards than what prevails in the actual living quarters. The view that outsiders get of inmates functions then to decrease the pressure these outsiders might otherwise bring against the institution. It is perhaps a melancholy human fact that after some time all three parties to the fiction—inmate, visitor, staff—realize that the visiting room presents a dressed-up view and realize that the other parties realize this too, and yet all tacitly agree to continue with the fiction.

49. Extremely useful material on TB sanitariums as total institutions will be available in the forthcoming work by Julius A. Roth, Committee on Human Development, University of Chicago. Preliminary statements may be found in his articles "What is an Activity?" *Etc.*, XIV (Autumn 1956), 54-56, and "Ritual and Magic in the Control of Contagion," *American Sociological Review*, XXII (June, 1957), 310-14.

50. Melville, *op. cit.*, p. 139.

51. For comments on the very difficult role of guard, see, McCorkle and Korn, *op. cit.*, pp. 93-94, and Gresham M. Sykes, "The Corruption of Authority and Rehabilitation," *Social Forces*, XXXIV (1956), 257-62.

52. A clear example of this is provided by Belknap, *op. cit.*, p. 170, in describing what happens when a patient breaks a rule and is punished:

> In the usual case of this kind, such things as impudence, insubordination, and excessive familiarity are translated into more or less professional terms, such as "disturbed" or "excited," and presented by the attendant to the physician as a medical report. The doctor must then officially revoke or modify the patient's privileges on the ward or work out a transfer to another ward where the patient has to begin all over to work up from the lowest group. A "good" doctor in the attendants' culture is one who does not raise too many questions about these translated medical terms.

53. I derive this from Everett C. Hughes' review of Leopold von Wiese's *Spätlese*, in *American Journal of Sociology*, LXI (1955), 182. A similar area is covered under the current anthropological term "ethnopsychology," except that the unit to which it applies is a culture, not an institution.

54. The engulfing character of an institution's theory of human nature is nicely expressed currently in progressive psychiatric establishments. The theories originally developed to deal with inmates are being applied more and more in these places to the staff as well, so that low-level staff must do its penance in group psychotherapy, and high-level staff in individual psychoanalysis. There is even some movement to bring in consulting sociological therapists for the institution as a whole.

55. For example, Harvey Powelson and Reinhard Bendix, "Psychiatry in Prison," *Psychiatry*, XIV (1951), 73-86, and Waldo W. Burchard, "Role Conflicts of Military Chaplains," *American Sociological Review*, XIX (1954), 528-35.

56. See Erving Goffman, *Presentation of Self in Everyday Life*, Monograph 2, Social Sciences Research Centre (Edinburgh: University of Edinburgh, 1956), pp. 127-29; McCorkle, *op. cit.*, pp. 93-94.

57. This term was suggested by Everett C. Hughes and is employed in an unpublished paper on institutional catharsis by Joseph Gusfield.

58 The scholarly legal petitions which circulate in many prisons and mental hospitals, and which are written by inmates, seem to serve the same function.

59. As with contributors to the house organ, inmate use of the official staff language and staff philosophy in discussing gripes is a mixed blessing for staff. Staff becomes open to manipulation by inmates of staff's own rationalization of the institution, and in general, social distance between the groupings is threatened. Hence, in psychotherapy at mental hospitals we find the engaging phenomenon of staff using stereotyped psychiatric terminology in talking to each other, but chiding patients for being "intellectualistic" and for avoiding the issues when patients use this language too.

60 Perhaps the distinctive thing about

this form of institutional role release is that a group of academically oriented professionals are interested in it, and so there is already more literature on this aspect of total institutions than on most other aspects combined.

61. Of course, the "office party" found in establishments not of the total kind has similar dynamics, and was the first no doubt to give rise to comment. See, for example, Gusfield, *op. cit.* The best reports on these events are still to be found in fiction. See, for example, Nigel Balchin's description of a factory party in *Private Interests* (Boston: Houghton-Mifflin, 1953), pp. 47-71; Angus Wilson's description of a hotel staff-guest party in his short story "Saturnalia" in *The Wrong Set* (New York: William Morrow, 1950), pp. 68-69; and J. Kerkhoff's version of the annual party in a mental hospital in *How Thin the Veil: A Newspaperman's Story of his Own Mental Crack-up and Recovery* (New York: Greenberg, 1952), p. 224.

62. A prison version is reported in Anthony Heckstall-Smith, *Eighteen Months* (London: Allan Wingate, 1954), p. 199:

> The authorities did their best to cheer us. On Christmas morning we sat down to a breakfast of cornflakes, sausages, bacon, beans, fried bread, margarine and bread and marmalade. At Midday we were given roast pork, Christmas pudding and coffee, and at supper, mince pies and coffee, instead of the nightly mug of cocoa.
>
> The halls were decorated with paper streamers, balloons and bells, and each had its Christmas tree. There were extra cinema shows in the gymnasium. Two of the officers each presented me with a cigar. I was allowed to send and receive some greeting telegrams, and for the first time since I had been in prison, I had enough cigarettes to smoke.

See also Hassler, *op. cit.*, p. 157. For Christmas license in a mental hospital, see Kerkhoff, *op. cit.*, pp. 183-85, 256. The same on a man-of-war is presented by Melville, *op. cit.*, pp. 95-96.

63. See Kerkhoff, *op. cit.*, p. 229, and Heckstall-Smith, *op. cit.*, pp. 195-99. Melville, *op. cit.*, p. 101, in commenting on the relaxation of discipline during and immediately after a theatrical on board ship, has the following to say:

> And here White Jacket must moralize a bit. The unwonted spectacle of the role of gun-room officers mingling with *the people* in applauding a mere seaman like Jack Chase filled me at the time with the most pleasurable emotions. It is a sweet thing, thought I, to see these officers confess a human brotherhood with us, after all; a sweet thing to mark their cordial appreciation of the manly merits of my matchless Jack. Ah! they are noble fellows all around, and I do not know but I have wronged them sometimes in my thoughts.

Melville proceeds then to comment bitterly that soon after this role release, the officers seemed to have a capacity to revert fully to their usual strictness.

64. Neither the "before" nor "after" need have much relation to the facts, since each version is meant to clarify a situation, not to measure it, and in any case the "past" may be slyly presented because of its similarity to the present. I have seen mental patients from good wards give a well-advertised public stage performance of conditions which presumably used to prevail in backward mental hospitals. Victorian costumes were used. The audience consisted of psychiatrically enlightened well-wishers from the environing city. A few buildings away from where the audience sat, equally bad conditions could be observed in the flesh.

65. We appreciate how needful total institutions are of entertainment charity, but we tend to be less aware of how desperately nonprofessional entertainers need audiences for whom to be charitable. For example, the mental hospital I studied apparently had the only stage in the vicinity large enough for all the members of a particular dancing school to perform on at once. Some of the parents of the students did not particularly like coming onto the hospital grounds, but if the school was to have any ensemble numbers, the hospital stage had to be used. In addition, fee-paying parents expected their child to appear in the annual school show, regardless of how much training the child had had, or even in fact whether she was old enough to absorb training. Some numbers in the show, then, required an extremely indulgent audience. Patients can supply

this since most patients in the audience are marched to the auditorium under the discipline of an attendant; once there, they will watch anything under the same discipline, since infraction of rules may lead to cancellation of the privilege of leaving the ward on such occasions. The same kind of desperate bond ties the hospital audience to a group of mild office workers who belong to a bell-ringing choir.

66. He can do this, of course, because, like all uncles, he does not have direct responsibility for disciplining inmates, this job being left to lesser members of staff. Interestingly enough, one of the functions of well-known inmates is to provide ranking members of staff with subjects whom they know enough about to use as reciprocals for the avuncular role.

67. If the analogy were to be carried out strictly, we would have to say of course that every total institution had a semipermeable membrane about it, since there will always be some standard equally maintained on the inside and outside, the impermeable effects being restricted to certain specific values and practices.

68. St. Benedict, *op. cit.*, Chapter 2.

69. Dornbusch, *op. cit.*, p. 317. The classic case of this kind of echelon leveling is found perhaps in the fagging system in British public schools.

70. Kathryn C. Hulme, *The Nun's Story* (Boston: Little, Brown & Co., 1956), pp. 22-23.

71. It seems to be true that within any given establishment the topmost and bottommost roles tend to be relatively permeable to wider community standards, while the impermeable tendencies seem to be focused in the middle ranges of the institution's hierarchy.

Methods of Forceful Indoctrination

ROBERT J. LIFTON

1. Some of this material has since been published. R. J. Lifton, "Thought Reform of Chinese Intellectuals, a Psychiatric Evaluation," *Journal of Asian Studies*, XVI (November, 1956).

2. R. J. Lifton, "Thought Reform of Western Civilians in Chinese Communist Prisons," *Psychiatry*, XIX (1956), 173-95.

R. J. Lifton, "Chinese Communist Thought Reform: The Assault upon Identity and Belief." Presented before the Annual Meeting of the American Psychiatric Association, May, 1956. *To be published.*

3. Ssu-Ch'i Ai, "On Problems of Ideological Reform," *Hsueh Hsi*, III (January 1, 1951).

4. C. Brandt, B. Schwartz, and J. K. Fairbank, "Correcting Unorthodox Tendencies in Learning, the Party and Literature and Art," *A Documentary History of Chinese Communism* (1952), p. 392.

5. George Orwell, *Nineteen Eighty-Four* (New York: Harcourt, Brace and Co., 1949).

6. G. Piers and M. B. Singer, *Shame and Guilt*. (Springfield, Ill.: C. C. Thomas, 1953.)

H. Baskowitz, H. Persky, S. J. Korchin, and R. R. Grinker, *Anxiety and Stress*. (New York: McGraw Hill, 1955.)

7. Erik H. Erikson, "The Problem of Ego Identity," *Journal of the American Psychoanalytic Association*, IV (1956), 56.

Erik H. Erikson, "On the Sense of Inner Identity," *Health and Human Relations* (New York, 1953).

8. R. Bunzel, and J. H. Weakland, "An Anthropological Approach to Chinese Communism," *Columbia University Research in Contemporary Cultures.*

W. La Barre, "Some Observations on Character Structure of the Orient: II. The Chinese," *Psychiatry*, IX (1946), 215-37.

The Dissolved Identity in Military Life

ARTHUR J. VIDICH AND MAURICE R. STEIN

1. Samuel A. Stouffer, *et al., The American Soldier*, Vol. I (Princeton: Princeton University Press, 1949), pp. 125-26.
2. Samuel A. Stouffer, *et al.*, Vol. I, *ibid.*, pp. 371-72.
3. Samuel A. Stouffer, *et al.*, Vol. I, *ibid.*, p. 71.
4. Samuel A. Stouffer, *et al.*, Vol. I, *ibid.*, p. 70.
5. Samuel A. Stouffer, *et al.*, Vol. I, *ibid.*, p. 78.
6. Samuel A. Stouffer, *et al.*, Vol. I, *ibid.*, p. 74.
7. Samuel A. Stouffer, *et al.*, Vol. I, *ibid.*, pp. 74-75.
8. Hans Speier in Robert K. Merton and Paul F. Lazarsfeld (eds.), *Continuities in Social Research* (Glencoe, Ill.: The Free Press, 1956), p. 116.
9. Alexis de Tocqueville, *Democracy in America*, Vol. II (New York: Vintage Books, 1954), p. 286.
10. Samuel A. Stouffer, *et al.*, Vol. I, *ibid.*, p. 389.
11. Samuel A. Stouffer, *et al.*, Vol. I, *ibid.*, p. 390.
12. *Ibid.*, Vol. I, p. 366.
13. *Ibid.*, drawn from Table I, Vol. II, p. 109.

Individuality of Thought

JOHN COHEN

1. J. Piaget, *The Psychology of Intelligence* (London, 1950).
2. E. Mayo, *The Psychology of Pierre Janet* (London, 1951), p. 21.
3. W. B. Cannon, *The Way of an Investigator* (New York, 1945), p. 14.
4. J. Cohen, "Social Thinking," *Acta Psychol.*, Vol. IX (Hague, 1953), pp. 146-58.
5. W. Windelband, *Geschichte und Naturwissenschaft* (Strasbourg, 1904) (republished in Praludien, Tubingen, 1907).
6. K. Lewin, "Field Theory and Learning," *Forty-first Year Book, National Society for the Study of Education* (Chicago, 1942), pp. 215-42.
7. G. W. Allport, "The Use of Personal Documents in Psychological Science," *Bulletin of the Social Science Research Council*, No. 49 (New York, 1942).
8. H. Reichenbach, "Probability Methods in Social Science," in D. Lerner and H. D. Lasswell (eds.), *The Policy Sciences* (Stanford, 1951).
9. J. G. Fichte, *Sämtliche Werke*, Vol. I, p. 434 (quoted by E. Cassirer in *The Problem of Knowledge* [New Haven, 1950]).
10. J. Ortega y Gasset, *Concord and Liberty* (New York, 1946), pp. 97-98.
11. E. Cassirer, *Rousseau, Kant, Goethe* (Princeton, 1945), p. 55.
12. E. Cassirer, *Essay on Man* (Yale, 1945), p. 228.
13. J. Cohen, "Ontogenesis of Thought," *Psychiatry*, XV (1952), 27-31.
14. J. Hadamard, *The Psychology of Invention in the Mathematical Field* (Princeton, 1949), p. 135.
15. E. L. Woodward, *The Age of Reform, 1815-1870* (London, 1938).
16. J. S. Mill, *Dissertations and Discussions: Political, Philosophical and Historical*, Vol. I (New York, 1873), pp. 379-80 (quoted by H. Morgenthau, *Scientific Man versus Power Politics* [1947], p. 199).
17. W. I. B. Beveridge, *The Art of Scientific Investigation* (London, 1951), p. 138.
18. J. Stewart and J. Kemp, *Diderot: Selected Writings* (London, 1937), p. 244 (the quotation is taken from "Rameau's Nephew").
19. A. Maurois, *Proust: Portrait of a Genius* (New York, 1950), pp. 18, 182.

20. J. Ortega y Gasset, *The Dehumanization of Art* (Princeton, 1948), p. 26.
21. P. Lenard, *Great Men of Science*, trans. H. Stafford Hatfield (London), pp. 252-62.
22. D. Leon, *Proust: His Life, His Circle and His Work* (London, 1940).
23. K. Birnbaum, *Psychopathologische Documente* (Berlin, 1920).
24. R. E. M. Harding, *An Anatomy of Inspiration* (Cambridge, 1942).
25. G. Humphrey, *Directed Thinking* (New York, 1948).
26. D. Katz, *Gestalt Psychology* (New York, 1950), p. 86.
27. E. R. Hilgard, *Theories of Learning* (New York, 1948), p. 340.
28. E. L. Cowen and C. G. Thompson, "Problem-solving, Rigidity and Personality Structure," *Journal of Abnormal Social Psychology*, XLVI (1951), 165-76.
29. Y. P. Frolov, *Pavlov and His School* (London, 1937).
30. J. Downey, *Creative Imagination* (London, 1929), p. 38.
31. E. C. Tolman, "The Psychology of Social Learning," *Journal of Social Issues*, Suppl. Ser. No. 3 (1949).
32. E. C. Tolman, "Kurt Lewin: 1890-1947," *Psychological Review*, IV (1948), 1-4.
33. J. Cohen, "Physical Types and Their Relations to Psychotic Types," *Journal of Mental Science*, LXXXVI (1940), 602-23.
34. J. Hadamard, *The Psychology of Inventions in the Mathematical Field* (Princeton, 1948), p. 135.
35. M. Weber, *The Methodology of Social Sciences* (Illinois, 1949), p. 112.
36. G. B. Chisholm, "Social Responsibility," *Journal of Social Issues*, Suppl. Ser. no. 1.
37. J. Cohen, "Ontogenesis of Thought," *Psychiatry*, XV (1952), 27-31.
38. H. G. McCurdy, "La Belle Dame Sans Merci," *Character and Personality*, XIII (1944), 166-77.
39. E. Jones, *Sigmund Freud: Life and Work* (London, 1953).
40. F. F. Lombard, "Self-Awareness and Scientific Method," *Science*, CXII (1950), 289-93.
41. L. Hogben, *The Retreat from Reason* (London, 1936), p. 9.
42. P. T. Young, *Motivation of Behaviour* (New York, 1943), pp. 280-87.

History and Our Times

ERIC DARDEL

1. "Événement et historicité," *L'Homme et l'histoire, Actes du VIe Congrès des Sociétés de Philosophie de Langue Français* (Paris, 1952), p. 219.
2. On the subject of aesthetic creation see Gaëtan Pican, "L'Esthétique et l'histoire," *Diogenes*, No. 4, pp. 31-51.
3. *Les Maîtres de l'histoire: Renan, Taine, Michelet* (Paris, 1895).
4. *Introduction aux études historiques* (Paris: Hachette, 1897).
5. Cf. *Holzwege* (Frankfort, 1950), study entitled "Das Weltbild."
6. *Origine et sens de l'histoire*, trans. H. Naef (Paris, 1954), p. 195.
7. M. Dufrenne and P. Ricoeur, *Karl Jaspers et la philosophie de l'existence*, p. 257.
8. On this problem see the fine article by Heidegger, "Nietzsches Wort Gott ist tot," in *Holzwege*.
9. Particularly in H. I. Marrou's book, *De la connaissance historique* (Paris: Éditions du Seuil, 1954).
10. Cf. A. C. Pigou, "Some Aspects of the Welfare State," *Diogenes*, No. 7, pp. 1-11.

The Literature of Primitive Peoples

PAUL RADIN

1. *Handbook of American Indian Languages*, Bulletin 40 (Wash., D.C.: Bureau of American Ethnology, 1911-1935).
2. *Language: An Introduction to the*

Study of Speech (New York: Harcourt Brace, 1921).

3. *Les fonctions mentales dans les sociétés inférieures* (5th ed.; Paris, 1922), pp. 151-257. Eng. ed.: *How Natives Think* (London: Allen & Unwin, 1926).

4. *Philosophie der symbolischen Formen.* Vol. I, *Die Sprache* (Berlin, 1923). Eng. ed.: *The Philosophy of Symbolic Forms* (New Haven: Yale University Press, 1953).

5. P. Radin (Berkeley: University of California Publications in American Archeology & Ethnology, 1920), Vol. 16, pp. 381-473.

6. *The Netsilik Eskimos,* Report on Fifth Thule Expedition (Copenhagen, 1931), Vol. VIII, p. 321.

7. *Grönlandsagen* (Berlin, 1922), p. 229. Translated from the German. Cf. his *The Eagle's Gift* (New York, 1932), pp. 8 ff.

8. R. C. Thurnwald, *Profane Literature of Buin* (New Haven: Yale University Publications in Anthropology, 1936), pp. 3-15.

9. Translated from the French. Cf. Blaise Cendrars, *Anthologie Nègre* (Paris, 1947), p. 24.

10. P. H. Trilles, "Les légendes des Bena Kanioka et le Folklore Bantou," *Anthropos,* Vol. IV (Vienna, 1909), p. 965. Translated from the French.

11. Unpublished.

12. J. R. Swanton, *Tlingit Myths and Texts* (Wash., D.C.: Bureau of American Ethnology, Bull. 39, 1909), p. 410.

13. *Ibid.,* p. 411.

14. P. Radin, *op. cit.,* p. 423.

15. F. Densmore, *Chippewa Music II* (Wash., D.C.: Bureau of American Ethnology, Bull. 53), p. 129.

16. *Ibid.,* p. 254.

17. *Ibid.,* p. 83.

18. J. R. Swanton, *op. cit.,* p. 415.

19. K. Rasmussen, *op. cit.* in n. 6, p. 511.

20. P. Radin, manuscript.

21. P. A. Talbot, *In the Shadow of the Bush* (London, 1912).

22. *African Folk Tales* (New York, 1953).

23. J. Torrend, *Specimens of Bantu Folklore from Northern Rhodesia* (London, 1921), pp. 24-26.

24. *African Folktales and Sculpture,* pp. 186 ff.

25. *Ibid.,* pp. 229 ff.

26. *Ibid.,* p. 305.

27. *Ibid.,* pp. 73 ff.

28. J. Spieth, *Die Ewe-Staemme* (Leipzig, 1906), pp. 834-36.

29. Translated from the French of the unpublished essay by A. Kagame, "La Poésie au Raunda," kindly placed at my disposal.

30. "La Poésie chez les Basuto," *Africa,* Vol. III (London, 1930), pp. 523-35.

31. D. Westermann, "Gottesvorstellungen in Oberguinea," *Africa,* Vol. I, pp. 195, 204. Translated from the German.

32. J. Spieth, *Die Religion der Eweer* (Göttingen, Vanderhoeck & Rupprecht, 1911), pp. 236 ff. Translated from the German.

33. K. Rasmussen, *op. cit.,* n. 6, p. 509.

34. K. Rasmussen, *Intellectual Culture of the Iglulik Eskimos,* Report on Fifth Thule Expedition, Vol. VII (Copenhagen, 1929), p. 27.

35. *Ibid.,* p. 47.

36. K. Rasmussen, *Grönlandsagen,* text-translated into German by J. Koppel (Berlin, 1922), p. 238. Translated from the German.

37. K. Rasmussen, *Rasmussen's Thulefahrt,* translated into German by F. Sieburg (Copenhagen, 1926), p. 430. Translated from the German.

38. *Ibid.,* pp. 235-36. Translated from the German.

39. K. Rasmussen, *The Eagle's Gift.*

40. K. Rasmussen, *Grönlandsagen,* p. 230. Translated from the German.

41. R. M. Berndt, *Kunapipi* (Melbourne, Cheshire, 1951), p. vii.

HM271 .S84
c.1
Stein, Maurice Rober
100106 000
Identity and anxiety; survival
3 9310 00013199 3
GOSHEN COLLEGE-GOOD LIBRARY